Garry Kasparov's Greatest Chess Games

Volume 1

Igor Stohl

First published in the UK by Gambit Publications Ltd 2005
Reprinted 2007, 2022
Copyright © Igor Stohl 2005

The right of Igor Stohl to be identified as the author of this work has been asserted in accordance with the Copyright, Designs and Patents Act 1988.

All rights reserved. No part of this publication may be reproduced, stored in or introduced into a retrieval system, or transmitted, in any form or by any means (electronic, mechanical, photocopying, recording or otherwise), without prior permission of the publisher. In particular, no part of this publication may be scanned, transmitted via the Internet or uploaded to a website without the publisher's permission. Any person who does any unauthorized act in relation to this publication may be liable to criminal prosecution and civil claims for damage.

ISBN: 978-1-915328-08-3

DISTRIBUTION:
Worldwide (except USA): Central Books Ltd, 50 Freshwater Road, Chadwell Heath, London RM8 1RX, England.
Tel +44 (0)20 8986 4854 Fax +44 (0)20 8533 5821. E-mail: orders@Centralbooks.com

Gambit Publications Ltd, 27 Queens Pine, Bracknell, Berks, RG12 0TL, England.
E-mail: info@gambitbooks.com
Website (regularly updated): www.gambitbooks.com

Edited by Graham Burgess
Typeset by John Nunn
Cover photographs by Cathy Rogers

10 9 8 7 6 5 4 3

Gambit Publications Ltd
Directors: Dr John Nunn GM, Murray Chandler GM, and Graham Burgess FM
German Editor: Petra Nunn WFM
Bookkeeper: Andrea Burgess

Contents

Symbols
Bibliography
Preface
Introduction

	Players (White first) and event	*Opening*	*Page*
1	**Kasparov – Muratkuliev**, *Baku jr tt 1973*	Ruy Lopez (Spanish) [C84]	17
2	**Lputian – Kasparov**, *Tbilisi 1976*	King's Indian Defence [E80]	20
3	**Magerramov – Kasparov**, *Baku 1977*	Queen's Gambit Declined [D58]	24
4	**Kasparov – Roizman**, *Minsk 1978*	Ruy Lopez (Spanish) [C61]	28
5	**Yuferov – Kasparov**, *Minsk 1978*	King's Indian Defence [E99]	32
6	**Kasparov – Palatnik**, *Daugavpils 1978*	Alekhine Defence [B04]	37
7	**Kasparov – Polugaevsky**, *USSR Ch 1978*	Sicilian Defence [B43]	41
8	**Kasparov – Přibyl**, *Skara Echt 1980*	Grünfeld Defence [D85]	46
9	**Kasparov – Chiburdanidze**, *Baku 1980*	King's Indian Defence [E92]	50
10	**Kasparov – Åkesson**, *Dortmund jr Wch 1980*	Queen's Indian Defence [E12]	53
11	**Kasparov – Romanishin**, *Moscow tt 1981*	Grünfeld Defence [D85]	57
12	**Beliavsky – Kasparov**, *Moscow 1981*	King's Indian Defence [E83]	61
13	**Vaiser – Kasparov**, *USSR Cht 1981*	King's Indian Defence [E77]	65
14	**Kasparov – Fedorowicz**, *Graz tt 1981*	Queen's Indian Defence [E12]	69
15	**Kasparov – Andersson**, *Tilburg 1981*	Queen's Indian Defence [E12]	73
16	**Kasparov – Yusupov**, *USSR Ch 1981*	Bogo-Indian Defence [E11]	76
17	**Tukmakov – Kasparov**, *USSR Ch 1981*	King's Indian Defence [E74]	80
18	**Kasparov – Petrosian**, *Bugojno 1982*	Bogo-Indian Defence [E11]	84
19	**Kavalek – Kasparov**, *Bugojno 1982*	King's Indian Defence [E90]	87
20	**Kasparov – Gheorghiu**, *Moscow IZ 1982*	Queen's Indian Defence [E12]	90
21	**Korchnoi – Kasparov**, *Lucerne OL 1982*	Modern Benoni [A64]	93
22	**Kasparov – Beliavsky**, *Moscow Ct (5) 1983*	Queen's Gambit Declined [D58]	98
23	**Kasparov – Tal**, *USSR Cht 1983*	Queen's Gambit Declined [D44]	102
24	**Kasparov – Portisch**, *Nikšić 1983*	Queen's Indian Defence [E12]	107
25	**Kasparov – Smyslov**, *Vilnius Ct (3) 1984*	Queen's Gambit Declined [D52]	111
26	**Kasparov – Karpov**, *Moscow Wch (32) 1984/5*	Queen's Indian Defence [E12]	115
27	**Behrhorst – Kasparov**, *Hamburg simul 1985*	Grünfeld Defence [D93]	119
28	**Hübner – Kasparov**, *Hamburg (1) 1985*	English Opening [A21]	123
29	**Kasparov – Andersson**, *Belgrade (5) 1985*	Catalan Opening [E06]	126
30	**Kasparov – Karpov**, *Moscow Wch (1) 1985*	Nimzo-Indian Defence [E20]	130
31	**Karpov – Kasparov**, *Moscow Wch (16) 1985*	Sicilian Defence [B44]	134
32	**Karpov – Kasparov**, *Moscow Wch (24) 1985*	Sicilian Defence [B85]	139
33	**Kasparov – Timman**, *Hilversum (4) 1985*	Queen's/Nimzo-Indian [E13]	144
34	**Kasparov – Karpov**, *London/Leningrad Wch (4) 1986*	Nimzo-Indian Defence [E20]	149
35	**Kasparov – Karpov**, *London/Leningrad Wch (16) 1986*	Ruy Lopez (Spanish) [C92]	153
36	**Kasparov – Karpov**, *London/Leningrad Wch (22) 1986*	Queen's Gambit Declined [D55]	160
37	**Kasparov – Smejkal**, *Dubai OL 1986*	Ruy Lopez (Spanish) [C92]	165
38	**Hübner – Kasparov**, *Brussels 1986*	Grünfeld Defence [D90]	169

39	**Kasparov – Tal**, *Brussels 1987*	Nimzo-Indian Defence [E48]	173
40	**Züger – Kasparov**, *Zurich simul 1987*	Queen's Gambit Declined [D34]	176
41	**Kasparov – Karpov**, *Seville Wch (8) 1987*	English Opening [A36]	180
42	**Kasparov – Karpov**, *Seville Wch (24) 1987*	Réti Opening [A14]	184
43	**Kasparov – Karpov**, *Amsterdam 1988*	Caro-Kann Defence [B17]	189
44	**Ljubojević – Kasparov**, *Belfort 1988*	Sicilian Defence [B81]	194
45	**Kasparov – Andersson**, *Belfort 1988*	Queen's Gambit Declined [D36]	198
46	**Kasparov – A. Sokolov**, *Belfort 1988*	English Opening [A19]	202
47	**Kasparov – Ivanchuk**, *USSR Ch 1988*	English Opening [A29]	206
48	**Kasparov – Smirin**, *USSR Ch 1988*	King's Indian Defence [E97]	209
49	**Timman – Kasparov**, *Reykjavik 1988*	King's Indian Defence [E88]	213
50	**Ehlvest – Kasparov**, *Reykjavik 1988*	English Opening [A28]	217
51	**Kasparov – Campora**, *Thessaloniki OL 1988*	Queen's Gambit Declined [D35]	220
52	**Speelman – Kasparov**, *Madrid rpd 1988*	King's Indian Defence [E92]	223
53	**Yusupov – Kasparov**, *Barcelona 1989*	King's Indian Defence [E92]	226
54	**Korchnoi – Kasparov**, *Barcelona 1989*	King's Indian Defence [E97]	230
55	**Kasparov – Salov**, *Barcelona 1989*	English Opening [A34]	235
56	**Piket – Kasparov**, *Tilburg 1989*	King's Indian Defence [E99]	239
57	**Ljubojević – Kasparov**, *Belgrade 1989*	Sicilian Defence [B96]	244
58	**Ivanchuk – Kasparov**, *Linares 1990*	Sicilian Defence [B97]	248
59	**Psakhis – Kasparov**, *La Manga (5) 1990*	English Opening [A26]	253
60	**Kasparov – Karpov**, *New York/Lyons Wch (2) 1990*	Ruy Lopez (Spanish) [C92]	257
61	**Kasparov – Karpov**, *New York/Lyons Wch (20) 1990*	Ruy Lopez (Spanish) [C92]	261
62	**Kasparov – Gelfand**, *Linares 1991*	Queen's Gambit Declined [D46]	266
63	**Kasparov – Anand**, *Tilburg 1991*	Sicilian Defence [B48]	270
64	**Kasparov – Wahls**, *Baden-Baden simul 1992*	Pirc Defence [B07]	274
65	**Kasparov – Karpov**, *Linares 1992*	Caro-Kann Defence [B17]	278
66	**Kasparov – Anand**, *Linares 1992*	French Defence [C18]	283
67	**Shirov – Kasparov**, *Dortmund 1992*	King's Indian Defence [E86]	287
68	**Kasparov – Loginov**, *Manila OL 1992*	King's Indian Defence [E84]	291
69	**Kasparov – Nikolić**, *Manila OL 1992*	Slav Defence [D10]	294
70	**Short – Kasparov**, *Debrecen Echt 1992*	Sicilian Defence [B82]	298
71	**Karpov – Kasparov**, *Linares 1993*	King's Indian Defence [E86]	302
72	**Kasparov – Kamsky**, *Linares 1993*	Sicilian Defence [B80]	306
73	**Kasparov – Short**, *London Wch (7) 1993*	Ruy Lopez (Spanish) [C88]	310
74	**Short – Kasparov**, *London Wch (8) 1993*	Sicilian Defence [B86]	314

Index of Opponents 319
Index of Openings 320

Symbols

+	check
++	double check
#	checkmate
!!	brilliant move
!	good move
!?	interesting move
?!	dubious move
?	bad move
??	blunder
Ch	championship
Cht	team championship
Wch	world championship
Wcht	world team championship
Ech	European championship
Echt	European team championship
ECC	European Clubs Cup
Ct	candidates event
IZ	interzonal event
OL	olympiad
jr	junior event
rpd	rapidplay game
tt	team tournament
simul	game from simultaneous display
corr.	correspondence game
1-0	the game ends in a win for White
½-½	the game ends in a draw
0-1	the game ends in a win for Black
(n)	nth match game
(D)	see next diagram

Bibliography

Books

Ispytanie vremenem (The Test of Time), G.Kasparov; Azerbaidzhanskoe gosudarstvennoe izdatelstvo, 1985
Match na pervenstvo mira Karpov-Kasparov (World Championship match Karpov-Kasparov) Y.Averbakh, M.Taimanov; Fizkultura i Sport, 1986
Dva matcha (Two matches), G.Kasparov; Fizkultura i Sport, 1987
Bezlimitny poedinok (Unlimited Duel; Russian edition of *Child of Change*), G.Kasparov; Fizkultura i Sport, 1989
Stol dolgoe edinoborstvo (The long struggle), A.Suetin; Moskovsky rabochy, 1989
The Mammoth Book of the World's Greatest Chess Games, G.Burgess, J.Nunn, J.Emms; Robinson, 1998
Understanding Chess Move by Move, J.Nunn; Gambit, 2001
Moi velikie predshestvenniki 2 (Garry Kasparov on my Great Predecessors, Volume 2), G.Kasparov; Ripol klassik, 2003

Periodicals

Informator
New in Chess [Magazines & Yearbooks]
Shakhmaty v SSSR
Schachmagazin 64

Preface

In 1986 I was covering the World Championship rematch between Kasparov and Karpov for one of the few Slovak national dailies, *Praca*. On that September evening I recall I was together with my friend Ivan Novak in the editorial office, waiting for the moves of game 16 to come by telex. (This was long before the days of Internet and on-line commentaries.) The moves were coming in batches and as the deadline was nearing, we both tried to analyse the proceedings on a chessboard, as well as write a coherent article at the same time. As the tension grew, this proved to be absolutely impossible and the violent denouement took us completely by surprise. (The readers can follow the full and exciting story in Game 35.) While hastily revising our former notes and impressions about White's imminent demise, I didn't have any time for more general thoughts. However, on the way home I felt distinctly: this guy will change chess as we know it...

Nearly two decades later we can see the past events from a broader perspective. From the early 1980s and his meteoric rise towards the world title, Garry Kasparov's approach and style differed significantly from the chess played by the elite during Karpov's reign. Even before he became World Champion in 1985, he had topped the world rankings, as indeed he still does to this day. Most of the recent important changes in our royal game were either pioneered directly by Kasparov himself, or at the very least, he contributed to them and adapted them effectively and with ease. To name just a few: very deep and thorough preparation with a psychological insight; calculated risk together with an even closer intertwining of strategy and tactics; and the use of computers, initially as electronic databases, later as effective analytical tools. This list could well continue and become more specific and concrete, but readers will find more details in the Introduction and naturally Kasparov's games themselves provide the best evidence of these trends. Here just let it suffice to say we are justified to speak about the Kasparov era. Its beginning can be placed somewhere in the mid-1980s, and in spite of Kasparov's unexpected decision to retire from professional chess after his victory in Linares 2005, we'll still have to let some time elapse before we can say it is over. After all, Garry Kasparov is still only 42 ...

As Kasparov continued to play chess at the highest level, surprisingly enough for a long time there have been no attempts to map his creative path. Kasparov himself has chronicled his career up to the moment when he became Karpov's challenger (1984) in the *Test of Time*; subsequently he wrote about how he gained and defended the world title in 1985/6. The Russian edition of the latter book was called *Two Matches* and the depth of his analysis as far as publications about World Championship matches are concerned still remains unsurpassed. After that, no comprehensive collection of Kasparov's games has been published, the only exception being books about his matches. In this sense *Garry Kasparov's Greatest Chess Games* is a logical undertaking, which is clearly somewhat overdue.

Writing about one of the very few chess-players (and perhaps the only one!) who is a world-wide household name is certainly not easy. The wealth of the accessible material is enormous. I went through not only literally thousands of games, but also Kasparov's interviews touching upon chess subjects, as well as checking what others wrote about him. This has enabled me to get a fuller picture of a fascinating personality and to see many annotated games in a broader context. After all, these are the crux of the book and present modern chess at its best. Although the selection of games inevitably reflects the author's personal taste, I trust the readers will not be disappointed and will find a lot of instruction, excitement and beautiful fighting chess, for which Kasparov is justifiably renowned. The first part of his career up to 1986 is understandably represented with relatively fewer examples; we have already mentioned above that Kasparov himself did a very good job in this respect. The theoretical phase of the games usually contains only brief coverage and quite often refers mostly to Kasparov's past and present treatment of the opening in question. The notes draw from various sources, which are included in the Bibliography. In the text I tried to give credit to all the annotators who came up with interesting ideas, not only to Kasparov himself. I also strove to weed out any mistakes, which inevitably occurred especially in pre-computer notes to games with a rich tactical content. In the *Test of Time* Kasparov himself stressed the necessity to revise game annotations with the passage of time and this trend is even clearer in his current series *My Great Predecessors*. Although I have tried to come up with ideas and recommendations of my own as much as possible, the resulting notes have no pretensions to be exhaustive and this is very often quite impossible, given the complex nature of Kasparov's play. Despite this, the text proceeded to grow at an alarming rate, something that I experienced to a lesser degree with my earlier book *Instructive Modern Chess Masterpieces*. As the current work was intended to contain more than twice as many games, a split of the book into two separate volumes became necessary. Volume 1 covers Kasparov's career up to his match with Short in 1993, and Volume 2 takes up the story from 1994 onwards. A small technical note: "Game" with a capital G refers to the numbering in this book, while "game xy" denotes its number in a match.

Just as I started, I'll conclude this short preface on a personal note. Although I was not quite convinced I was the right person to write about someone like Kasparov, Gambit and especially Graham Burgess did a good job in overcoming my initial reservations. I would like to thank them for more than one reason. Quite recently Kasparov's indirect influence inspired me make an intuitive sacrifice of two pawns and win a nice attacking game; believe me or not, this is something rather rare in my practice. Perhaps even more important and pleasant is that annotating Kasparov's games brings back something from those happy days when I was a carefree student, enthusiastically writing for the daily press about the K-K match-games and staunchly rooting for the greatest player of our times.

Igor Stohl
Bratislava, April 2005

Introduction

Garry Kasparov was born in Baku on 13th April 1963. He learned the rules of chess around the age of five and started playing and training seriously two years later, showing considerable promise from the very beginning. His early games show a penchant for attacking chess and lively piece-play, as well as good calculating abilities, something that many strong players possess from a tender age. However, an unmistakable sign of talent is usually an ability to curb the flights of fantasy when necessary and play in accordance with the needs of the position. Game 1 provides some evidence of this: Kasparov's 23 ♕g5! is a very practical and surprisingly mature decision.

An important year for Kasparov's future career was 1973, when he met up with two people who significantly influenced his chess development in his early teens. He began to attend the famous Botvinnik Chess School and the patriarch of Soviet chess recommended him an experienced regular trainer between the sessions – Vladimir Makogonov. Makogonov was from Kasparov's hometown and after his own career peaked in the period 1935-1947, he gradually withdrew from practical chess and turned to coaching; for instance, he assisted Smyslov during all his matches for the world title in the 1950s. He was renowned for his classical positional chess and helped Kasparov to develop a more universal style. His influence is also clear on his pupil's early opening repertoire: the young Kasparov played the Caro-Kann and the solid Tartakower Defence of the Queen's Gambit Declined (Game 3), which in Russian chess literature bears Makogonov's name, and still occasionally appears in his games. However, as Kasparov himself emphasized more than once, the five years of Botvinnik's lessons were decisive in his formative period. Even after 1978, the former World Champion gave him useful advice and they continued to meet regularly for the next nine years. Mikhail Botvinnik certainly needs no introduction. His aforementioned recommendation of Makogonov indicates what his own style was – a paragon of active positional play. His approach to chess was always highly scientific and from him Kasparov imbibed the importance of independent analysis and thorough opening preparation, connected with a profound understanding of the resulting middlegame positions. He also understood that scaling the chess heights requires not only talent, but also hard work – Botvinnik, Fischer and Kasparov are undoubtedly the most diligent of the post-war champions. Botvinnik was in more than one sense the first modern world champion; he made a giant step forward from the pure positional play of Capablanca and Rubinstein in the direction of modern chess. His method of creating strategic imbalances from the very start and thus increasing the tension (the Winawer French and especially the Botvinnik System in the Semi-Slav are the two best examples) has become both widespread and universally accepted, with lines such as the Sveshnikov Sicilian being currently extremely popular. However, Botvinnik was not intent on bringing up carbon copies of himself and he developed Kasparov's creativity in the right direction, channelling his early admiration for Alekhine's dynamic style with its numerous positional sacrifices into a more modern context. A good illustration is Kasparov's effort against Lputian (Game 2), in which his growing understanding of the King's Indian enabled him to find complex tactical resources over the board. It was his first game to appear in *Informator* and the harmony between the opening strategy, the combinative phase and the confident realization of the achieved advantage makes it a real masterpiece. By the way, most of Kasparov's early King's Indians show his willingness to invest material to keep Black's counterplay alive (Game 5, 12 and 17).

Under Botvinnik's tutelage Kasparov won the USSR Junior Championship in both 1976 and 1977. This was a considerable achievement when we realize most of his opponents were older than him and sometimes the gap was even 6 years – a lot of time in the development of a young player (at their age Kasparov was already a World Championship Candidate). The following year, 1978, brought Kasparov a whole string of successes. He convincingly gained the master title and at the age of 15 became the youngest player ever to qualify for the final of the USSR Championship, where he performed very creditably and retained his place in the next year's event.

His style also started taking more definite forms. Kasparov further developed his obvious combinative talent (Game 6) and strove to play complex active chess. In his first encounters with the world elite he showed considerable courage; a notable example is his game against the highly experienced Polugaevsky (Game 7). Facing an unknown position, he decided to change its character abruptly with 10 e5?!, followed by a bishop sacrifice three moves later. Although objectively dubious, this proved to be a psychologically sound decision, reminiscent of the young Tal. The sacrifices greatly increased the value of every move and Polugaevsky, known for his excitability, threw away first his advantage and finally even equality. A comparison of Kasparov's approach with his future great rival springs to mind. When faced with a novelty, the pragmatic Karpov only rarely opted for the most principled reaction and satisfied himself with neutralizing instead of refuting his opponent's idea. This will become even clearer from the notes to the excellent Game 31.

Although Kasparov had outgrown the ranks of Botvinnik's school, his mentor still continued to help him and arranged his debut on the international scene in 1979 in Banja Luka. Contemporary prodigies at the age of 16 are usually already GMs with high-level experience, but in those days the convincing victory of an unrated and untitled teenager ahead of Smejkal, Petrosian, Adorjan, etc., caused a sensation. However, Kasparov was a very exceptional talent even by today's standards and by the time he completed the requirements for his GM title a year later, he was fast closing in on the world elite.

Around this time Kasparov began to work very seriously on his opening repertoire. Following Botvinnik's example he started to build his 'own theory' and presumably with this in mind he became an almost exclusively 1 d4 player, something that was to change only during and especially after his matches with Karpov. By narrowing down his repertoire he could concentrate on deeper analysis of systems that were to become his trademark later on. Apart from the aforementioned King's Indian, the best example is the Petrosian Variation of the Queen's Indian. The whole 4 a3 line had been under a slight cloud ever since the 1969 World Championship match, when Petrosian won a nice game with Spassky, playing against his own invention. However, Kasparov with White developed it into an extremely dangerous weapon, which brought him many attractive wins. In this book it's represented no fewer than five times, starting with Game 10. The opening systems that Kasparov analysed and used with success soon became generally popular thanks to his efforts, which in turn guaranteed their further rapid development. However, Kasparov himself remained very flexible and once he considered his pet systems exhausted, he was quick to turn his attention elsewhere. Thus in the mid-1980s he started allowing the Nimzo-Indian.

Meanwhile Kasparov's dynamic and concrete play was quickly taking the established chess hierarchy by storm. In 1980 he played for the mighty Soviet national team for the first time, significantly contributing to the gold medals in both the Olympiad and the European Team Championship. The following year featured further milestones in his career – in February he played Karpov for the first time and in both games the reigning World Champion was on the verge of losing. Kasparov participated in a super-tournament for the first time in Moscow two months later; here Karpov was in top form and won the event clearly. However, the young GM performed creditably and his shared 2nd place was certainly a success. Later that year he won the coveted gold medal in the Soviet Championship and in 1982 scored his first super-tournament victory in Bugojno. A typical example of Kasparov's creativity from this period is his encounter with Kavalek (Game 19). Good understanding of the strategic nuances allows him to get a promising position from the opening and the unexpected tactical stab 13...♘b4! only underlines this. Kavalek loses his way only to be temporarily reprieved by the inaccurate 16...fxg3?!, but he returns the favour and Kasparov winds up the game convincingly. Even his mistake is in itself characteristic: handling the tension he creates is not easy and often requires utmost precision, something that is very hard to achieve. In 1981 in Moscow and Tilburg he had paid a price for this against Petrosian, but their game in Bugojno showed Kasparov had added growing positional technique to his typical youthful aggression (Game 18). After all, winning super-tournaments requires a more balanced style and Kasparov understood that on the top level he must often curb his maximalist attitude. Against stronger opposition such a decision as 27 ♗xf6?! in Game 10 might well backfire. This doesn't mean Kasparov started to avoid all-out risk; Game 17 indicates just the opposite and also shows his powers of psychological insight and ability to 'understand' the opponent and not only his chess intentions, but also his ambitions or attitude, were growing. Another example of strategic risk (15 ♕a4!? and especially 17 ♖ac1?!) to create an unbalanced situation is Game 14.

The situation at the top of the chess pyramid at the end of the 1970s was rather exceptional. The World Champion Karpov was not only clearly the strongest player, but also much younger than most of the world elite. His fine positional understanding, excellent manoeuvring technique, endgame prowess and especially his highly refined intuitive sense for piece coordination brought him a long string of tournament victories. Karpov's sense of danger and defensive technique could be compared only with Petrosian's, but he was a more direct and active player. His style was both admired and considered ideal, which made him seemingly invincible. This was to change with Kasparov's quick progress. By the time he played his first (and only) Interzonal in 1982, the GM from Baku was not only the main favourite of the new Candidates cycle, but many saw him as Karpov's worthy successor. Another interesting fact, more or less clear from the lines above, is that in terms of chess style Karpov and Kasparov were the antithesis of one another. While it's difficult to measure talent, and Karpov was also immensely gifted, Kasparov was certainly the more industrious of the two. Karpov usually successfully interpreted the opening ideas of others; from an early age Kasparov preferred the more difficult but ultimately more rewarding method of independent theoretical research. However, the main contrast between them lies in their respective attitude towards risk. While Karpov rarely attempted to unbalance a position on his own accord, Kasparov revelled in complex and double-edged positions and often strove to achieve them, confident of his own strength.

Returning to the year 1982, Kasparov was the No. 2 player in the world and the gap between him and Karpov was closing fast. However, to challenge the World Champion he still had to overcome a host of obstacles. Kasparov acquitted himself well and although his path to the title match was not without difficulties, from a purely sporting point of view it was very straightforward. Qualifying from the Interzonal in Moscow was the first task and he achieved this convincingly with a powerful finish (4 out of 4; see also Game 20) after overcoming some shaky moments in the earlier rounds against Andersson and Beliavsky. Kasparov was the only participant who remained unbeaten and his cautious play in some games showed that he rationally followed his main goal throughout the event. In the first serious match in his life against Beliavsky, superior opening preparation played a decisive role. Kasparov practically refuted the line of the Queen's Gambit Declined that Beliavsky obstinately used in nearly all his games as Black (see Game 22). With Black himself, Kasparov managed to surprise his opponent in nearly every game. The first shock was a new addition to his repertoire, the Tarrasch Defence, which brought him the important initial victory in game 2. However, this was flexibly discarded in favour of a sharp sacrificial line of the King's Indian in game 8, when Beliavsky direly needed a win. The GM from Lvov reacted feebly and the match was over.

The uncertainty over the date and place of the semi-final matches had at least one positive effect – it allowed Kasparov to get some extra practice. Unburdened by qualification considerations or match tactics, he played his typical principled chess. Game 23 shows a characteristic trait – Kasparov even nowadays rarely avoids a theoretical duel and trusts his home analysis. He convincingly won the strong event in Nikšić; Game 24 is a typical example of his forceful attacking style. The duel against Korchnoi started in November 1983 in London and turned out to be the toughest test Kasparov had faced until then. Korchnoi, the challenger from the previous two cycles, had extensive match experience; moreover, he was excellently theoretically prepared and their exciting encounter from the previous year (Game 21) gave him important extra information how to blunt Kasparov's attempts to complicate matters. In the first half of the match Korchnoi was in full control. He immediately scored a full point with a less-known line against the Petrosian Variation of the Queen's Indian and also as White put Kasparov under pressure in the following games. However, his unwillingness to allow complications enabled Kasparov to escape and game 6 became the turning point. Korchnoi relied greatly on his endgame technique and when he achieved an advantageous queenless middlegame, he threw caution to the winds and decided it was time to increase his lead. The game was adjourned in a complex but drawish position and White finally threw away the half-point in a relatively simple rook endgame. Korchnoi firmly believed in his endgame supremacy and couldn't overcome this blow; when in the following game Kasparov outplayed him in a quiet simplified position, the match was practically over. The final against Smyslov was plain sailing: Kasparov was only once in serious danger and scored most of his points in endgames (see Game 25). His increasing confidence in this phase of the game was a promising sign.

Thus the stage was set for the start of the greatest rivalry of all chess history. Glancing forward a little, let's have some statistics: Kasparov and Karpov contested five World Championship matches and have so far played 167 serious games against each other. The current situation in world chess guarantees this record will remain unbeaten for the foreseeable future and the only two pairs able to get close were Karpov-Korchnoi and Botvinnik-Smyslov; they both played three matches on the highest level. Although Botvinnik fought Smyslov for the chess crown 30 years earlier (1954-58), the parallels between these duels are interesting. Both Botvinnik and Kasparov, as his pupil, always inclined to an analytical and concrete approach to chess, while Smyslov and Karpov were renowned for their intuition and natural feeling of harmony on the chessboard. Here the similarities end; the K-K matches with large teams of seconds concentrating especially on opening preparation belong to a different era.

At the time their first duel began in September 1984, Karpov was still the more complete and mature player with a lot of previous match experience. This showed clearly at the start, when Kasparov sacrificed material with abandon a couple of times, only to find himself trailing by four points. After misplaying and even losing a promising position in game 6, the trusted Tarrasch Defence, which brought him superb results against Beliavsky, Korchnoi, and Smyslov and in Nikšić 1983, failed him twice; especially Karpov's subtle technical play in game 9 was impressive. The desperate situation called for drastic measures and indeed Kasparov abandoned any ambitions and concentrated foremost on surviving and outliving the pressure. He was sorely criticized for his passive approach, which resulted in 17(!) draws in a row, but playing his aggressive and demanding type of chess without the necessary self-confidence against an on-form Karpov would have been suicidal. In game 27 the World Champion increased his lead to 5-0 with another technical masterpiece, but his energy was waning and he didn't manage to deal the final blow (the winner had to score six wins in an unlimited number of games). Karpov had an extra pawn in game 31, but squandered his chances and immediately in the following game the challenger managed to break an important psychological barrier by scoring his first win (Game 26). In the following long series of draws the initiative was more often on Kasparov's side and by the time he scored two further wins in a row (games 47 and 48), Karpov's play showed visible signs of exhaustion. At this point the match was terminated without declaring a winner. A new match with changed rules was scheduled to start in September 1985; this time the number of games was limited to 24.

For Kasparov, this gave him time to process the valuable information from the unfinished encounter and prepare thoroughly for a new attempt. Given his capacity for hard work, it was clear that this time Karpov would have to face a stronger and even more determined opponent. In the training matches he played during the interim period, he showed he had lost none of his readiness for surprising tactical solutions (12...♘e4!! in Game 28), as well as an increased willingness and ability to play technical positions (Game 29). The second K-K match started without any warmups: Kasparov prepared a modern line in the Nimzo-Indian, quickly gained a strong grip on the position and convincingly converted his advantage (Game 30). His opening choice had not only objective, but also psychological merits. The resulting unorthodox positions with strategic imbalances (traces of Botvinnik's approach!) were not to Karpov's taste and even later he suffered in this line despite managing to solve the opening problems satisfactorily (see Game 34). Kasparov could even have increased his lead with Black in the following game and as the missed chance preyed on his mind, Karpov struck back. With two wins in a row he bounced back into the lead; especially instructive was the way he outmanoeuvred Black in game 4. However, Kasparov, after trailing badly in the unlimited match, was accustomed to and prepared for such a situation. Contrary to their first encounter, Kasparov remained true to his active style and didn't shy away from sacrifices, but didn't take excessive risks. He was rewarded for his persistence by Karpov's gross blunder in game 11. In a higher sense the match was decided in game 16. The depth of Kasparov's preparation, followed by a great blend of prophylaxis and attacking chess, must have shaken Karpov; the notes to Game 31 give a fuller picture. The World Champion was forced to take risks, something he was never accustomed to do. Although he still had a chance to defend his title, he chose an uncharacteristically violent method to achieve his goal and Kasparov deservedly won the match (Game 32).

At the age of 22 Kasparov became the youngest World Champion in history and his relief showed clearly in his short matches against Timman later that year and Miles in 1986; Game 33 is typical for the attractive unencumbered chess the players produced. However, the K-K duel was far from over, as the new rules guaranteed Karpov a rematch in one year. Thus in July 1986 Kasparov had to face a much better prepared Karpov once again. The challenger abandoned 1 e4 for good and was well armed against Kasparov's usual repertoire, but despite this the new World Champion's superiority was obvious. The close result was mainly due to the teething problems with the newly adopted Grünfeld Defence, where most of Karpov's novel ideas caused him problems and resulted in three of his four losses. The Grünfeld takes getting used to and although in his subsequent practice Kasparov developed a good feel for this dynamic opening (see Game 38), against Karpov he always had to struggle. The London half of the match was rather sedate, the notable exceptions being game 8, which Kasparov won after creating confusion in a risky Tal-like manner, and the exciting draw in game 11, where for a change Karpov was the instigator of complications. In the Leningrad half Kasparov himself took up 1 e4 and twice outplayed his opponent in a sharp Ruy Lopez. Especially thrilling was the climax of Game 35, possibly the most complex K-K game ever. Kasparov's turn to falter came after he increased his lead to three points. He became extremely vulnerable with Black and after he misplayed a won position in game 18, the score was suddenly equal again! The Grünfeld was scrapped for the rest of the match, as patience and circumspection were indicated. We can see this spirit in the decisive encounter (Game 36), in which Kasparov gradually outplayed his opponent in a manoeuvring struggle.

After this, both protagonists had more than a year to take a rest from each other (in 1987 Karpov won a match against A.Sokolov, again gaining the right to play for the world title) and play in other events. Kasparov won the OHRA tournament in 1986 and in Brussels 1987 he shared 1st place with Ljubojević thanks to a last-round win against Tal (game 39). His quick and impressive rout of the wizard of attack was the result of well-aimed opening preparation. This in itself is certainly not unusual in Kasparov's practice; see Games 38, 46, 47, 56, etc. However, against Tal he aimed not so much for a concrete line, as for the typical and seemingly innocuous symmetrical structure after 10 exd4!?, which had brought him success in an earlier game. His understanding of the position quickly proved superior and after 10...♗xc3? White rapidly launched an irresistible attack.

Despite getting some serious tournament practice before the new match, in Seville 1987 Kasparov was not in his best form. He often got into time-trouble and this cost him dearly more than once (games 2 and 5). An interesting fact was that the length of the K-K fight sometimes caused a reversal of the players' typical roles. In Seville this tendency was the most noticeable – Karpov didn't avoid sharp play with Black and was successful with the Reversed Sicilian. He also reintroduced the older idea 12 ♗xf7+!? in the Exchange Grünfeld, connecting it with new strategic plans and motifs. On the other hand, Kasparov, especially with White, played very solid and technical chess (see Game 41 and 42; one can spot this tendency also in Game 43, played in their first tournament after the match). The match was slightly marred by two heavy blunders (Karpov in game 11, Kasparov in game 23), but this was compensated by the dramatic finish. After losing the penultimate game Kasparov found himself in a must-win situation, identical to the one Karpov had been in two years earlier. Game 42 shows the World Champion again proved his worth on the field of chess psychology; restrained and patient play allowed him to create the necessary tension and finally retain the title due to excellent analysis of the adjourned endgame.

So why did Kasparov supersede Karpov on the chess throne? The question is simple enough, but the answer inevitably has to be more complex. In my opinion, Kasparov's main advantage over his rival was his capacity to learn, to process the information from their encounters and use it in his favour. He went a great way from the inexperienced challenger, who suffered greatly in the first half of the unlimited match, to a mature and highly versatile player. Kasparov found a way to remain true to his dynamic and resourceful attacking chess even in the face of Karpov's formidable defensive abilities. To simplify his own words, throughout chess history we can follow this clash of attack and defence. When the quality of defence improved, the further development of the game required the emergence of great attacking players. Thus Alekhine was able to beat Capablanca, and Tal was successful, albeit only temporarily, against Botvinnik. Kasparov himself brought the attack to a higher level and deposed Karpov. To bring this train of thought up to date, currently he in turn is finding Kramnik an extremely tough nut to crack. Kasparov was also able to understand Karpov better than the other way round. His superior psychological insight enabled him not only to attain a higher level of opening preparation (we have already mentioned Game 31 as an outstanding example), but also to weigh correctly the important decisions in the further course of their games (e.g. 24 ♕e3! in Game 36).

In the late 1980s Kasparov clearly dominated the chess world and his preponderance over Karpov only increased with the onset of the electronic era. When the World Champion used the database software ChessBase in 1987 to prepare for his second clock simul against HSK Hamburg (see Game 27 from the first event in 1986), he immediately recognized its potential. The accessibility, as well as the amount of available information literally at one's fingertips, increased many-fold – this, combined with Kasparov's creativity and his extensive chess knowledge, allowed him and his team quickly to find a weak spot in the opponent's repertoire and develop tailor-made new ideas. (An excellent example of this approach is Game 56.) The computer can also be used to dig up hitherto unnoticed ideas of other players that deserve further scrutiny (see Game 46). After Seville 1987, Kasparov had time to concentrate on developing his trademark openings and often his analysis stretched beyond the boundaries of 'official' theory well into the middlegame. Especially the King's Indian profited from this; in Games 49, 52 and 53 he shows that although he had come a long way since his junior years, he had not lost his touch for dynamic counterplay in his beloved opening. Kasparov enriched the strategic understanding of typical positions arising from the Exchange Variation of the Queen's Gambit Declined (see Games 45 and 51), and a significant new addition to his repertoire was the Nimzo-Indian with 4 ♕c2. In his games from this period we often find early pawn sacrifices for various forms of compensation such as play on the dark squares (Game 46), an active bishop-pair (Game 47), or simply to liberate a cramped position, as in Game 58. In the aforementioned King's Indian games the sacrifices were usually made in the interests of piece-play, the key motif being activation of the g7-bishop (against Yusupov it was even worth an exchange!). Needless to say, Kasparov lost none of his combinative or attacking skills (Game 55). An especially effective attacking method in his hands was the gradual concentration of forces on the part of the board where the decision will fall; often he invests material just to achieve ideal piece coordination. A good example is Game 59, and an even better one Game 61, and to a somewhat lesser extent this goes for Game 51 as well.

Kasparov's superiority also showed in his results. He won most of the tournaments he participated in outright and by large margins, and only a few times did he have to share victory with Karpov. In 1990 he broke Fischer's long-time record and his rating reached the 2800 mark. The gap between him and Karpov grew to a full 70 points, but despite the emergence of promising younger players (Ivanchuk, Short, and Salov) his perennial rival still remained his main competitor and proved this by winning the Candidates cycle. The last K-K match was also no easy affair for Kasparov. This time, with the exception of the last game, the World Champion played solely 1 e4 and started impressively; the surprising novelty 19 f3! in game 2 enabled him to deal Karpov's favourite line in the Ruy Lopez a heavy blow (Game 60). With the black pieces Kasparov had no problems and even came close to winning game 3 after an enterprising queen sacrifice (see the notes to Game 9). Although he didn't manage to increase his lead, Kasparov probably became overconfident. As early as game 4 he nearly paid the price for his hazardous play and in game 7 overambitious treatment of the opening together with a tactical oversight allowed Karpov to equalize the score and get back into the match. From now on the initiative passed to the challenger; with Black Karpov was doing well in the Ruy Lopez, while Kasparov managed to survive in the Grünfeld mainly thanks to his opponent. Finally he achieved a turnaround with the help of the Scotch, winning the long game 16 after two adjournments. This must have exhausted Karpov and although he struck back in the following game, Kasparov refuted a dubious novelty in the Ruy Lopez to restore his lead immediately. The fate of the title was decided in style with a splendid attacking effort in the following even-numbered game (Game 61).

At this point of his career Kasparov must have felt an understandable lack of motivation and this showed soon enough. The beginning of the 1990s saw more bright talent appear on the scene; in addition to the players mentioned in the previous paragraph, Gelfand, Anand, Shirov and Kamsky made their way into the world elite, and by 1993 the teenage Kramnik was already on their heels. In 1991 the World Champion won only one of the four super-tournaments he took part in (Tilburg); he was runner-up in Linares (won by Ivanchuk), Amsterdam (Short and Salov) and Reggio Emilia (Anand). However, there was also an objective reason for this temporary slump – Kasparov concentrated on introducing 1 e4, which he earlier used almost exclusively only against Karpov, into his general repertoire. This naturally took some time and energy and in 1992 his results went up again. After winning Linares, sharing victory in Dortmund and excellent performances in team events (Olympiad and European Championship) Kasparov regained the rating points he had lost in 1991 with interest. His last tournament in 1993 before defending the world title was Linares, which he again won convincingly.

By the early 1990s most professionals generally used computers and databases and as a result modern high-level chess became even more opening-oriented. From this point of view, a gradual shift to the most aggressive opening move 1 e4 was only logical and Kasparov's practice has shown it suits his style no less than 1 d4. Game 66 is vintage Kasparov with a positional pawn sacrifice to expose Black's weakened dark squares (11 ♘f3!). In Game 65 we see very original piece-play, when White creates pressure against the queenside by rook manoeuvres on the opposite flank (17 ♖h5!, 23 ♖h4!, 31 ♖h5!). Even playing against his own pet Sicilian Defence, he was successful; in the combinative assault against Anand (Game 63), the final slalom of White's queen, starting with 20 ♕h5, creates a strong impression. When facing the Scheveningen, the notes to Game 72 show how Kasparov's clever opening strategy renders Black's usual reactions inadequate. However, his creativity was not limited solely to 1 e4. In Game 69, 6 ♗d2! opened new vistas for White in the Slav and the original 12 fxe3! created the preconditions for a piece attack against Black's king, which persisted even into the endgame. With Black Kasparov's play was no less dynamic, the King's Indian (Game 67 and 71) still remaining his favourite.

Most experts predicted another K-K match was on the cards, but Karpov was no longer the powerhouse he had been and he lost a tough semi-final match against Nigel Short. The English GM is only two years younger than Kasparov and even as a junior he possessed fine strategic understanding and good technique. After considerably sharpening his repertoire and increasing his aggressiveness, he entered the world elite in the late 1980s. In the Candidates cycle Short eliminated Speelman, Gelfand, Karpov and Timman, showing good nerves and stamina, as he was trailing at some point in all(!) of the matches. Nevertheless in the title match, played under the auspices of PCA, Kasparov was a clear favourite. Although the games themselves were full of exciting fighting chess, this better suited the more experienced champion and he convincingly confirmed his role with a one-sided final result 12½-7½. With White Short held his own against the Sicilian and even put his opponent under a lot of pressure (Game 74), but with Black it was altogether a different story. Against the Ruy Lopez Kasparov introduced a new strategic concept in the Anti-Marshall (see Game 73) and this practically decided the duel, as it brought him 3 full points. Also in the Nimzo-Indian pointed home preparation brought him a win in game 9, extending his lead to 5 points, which was to be the final margin of victory.

How did Kasparov fare in the age of computer analysis, the Internet and numerous teenage prodigies? We'll follow his chess path in Volume 2; now let his games do the talking.

Game 1
Garry Kasparov – Shohrat Muratkuliev
Under-18 teams, Baku 1973
Ruy Lopez (Spanish) [C84]

At the tender age of 10 Kasparov had only been playing chess for about four years, but the following game shows considerable talent and surprising maturity.

1	e4	e5
2	♘f3	♘c6
3	♗b5	a6
4	♗a4	♘f6
5	d4	

Kasparov chooses a less played line, which experienced an increase of popularity in the early 1970s. Later in his career he played exclusively the main move 5 0-0.

5	...	exd4
6	e5	

The alternative 6 0-0 ♗e7 7 ♖e1 is harmless as well: 7...b5! 8 e5 (8 ♗b3 d6 9 ♗d5 ♗b7 10 ♘xd4 ♘xd5 11 ♘xc6 ♗xc6 12 exd5 ♗b7 is also only equal) 8...♘xe5 9 ♖xe5 d6 10 ♖e1 bxa4 11 ♘xd4 ♗d7 12 ♕f3 0-0 13 ♘c6 ♗xc6 14 ♕xc6 ♘d7!? 15 ♘c3 ♘b6 leads to a rather sterile position.

6	...	♘e4
7	0-0	

7 ♘xd4?! runs into 7...♘xf2! 8 ♔xf2 ♕h4+ 9 ♔e3 b5 10 ♗b3 ♘xd4 (harassing the exposed king with 10...♗c5!? also deserves attention) 11 ♕xd4 ♕xd4+ 12 ♔xd4 c5+, regaining the piece advantageously.

7	...	♗e7

The most usual move, but 7...♘c5 leads to similar positions.

8	♖e1	

This move promises White nothing, but even after the stronger continuation 8 ♘xd4 Black has little to fear. Playable is the simple 8...♘xd4 9 ♕xd4 ♘c5 10 ♘c3 0-0 or the more complicated 8...0-0!? 9 ♘f5 d5 with equality in both cases.

8	...	♘c5
9	♗xc6	dxc6
10	♘xd4	0-0
11	♘c3 *(D)*	

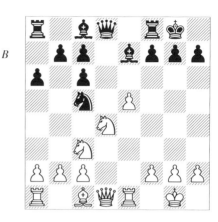

Structurally the position resembles the currently popular Berlin Defence of the Ruy Lopez. Also here White has a better pawn-structure, but the advance of the e-pawn to e5 increases Black's light-square control and greatly hampers the possibility of White converting his kingside pawn-majority. Black's potent weapon is his bishop-pair; furthermore, compared with the Berlin here he has no problems with his development and can look forward to a promising middlegame. However, Black's first task is to prevent White's possible kingside expansion.

11	...	♘e6?!

In the light of the above note this move is not ideal. Earlier Black tried 11...♖e8, but the most consistent move is Pachman's 11...f5! (11...f6!? is possible as well). Although it gives White a passed pawn, the blockade on e6 is practically unbreakable, while Black gets active possibilities on both flanks. Opening the position with 12 exf6 (12 ♘ce2 ♘e6 13 ♘xe6 ♕xd1 14 ♖xd1 ♗xe6 15 ♘d4 ♗c8! and after ...c5 the bishop can return to e6) 12...♗xf6 13 ♗e3 ♘e6 activates Black's forces and it's now White who has to tread carefully.

12	♘f5	♗g5 *(D)*

Strategically the exchange of dark-squared bishops favours White. But Black must fight for equality even after 12...f6!? 13 ♘xe7+ ♕xe7 14 exf6 ♕xf6 15 ♘e4.

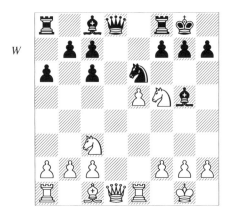

13 ♕g4

After 13 ♕xd8 Black can avoid further simplification with 13...♗xd8!.

13 ... ♘d4

Black wants to solve his problems tactically. Simplifying into an endgame with 13...♗xc1 14 ♖axc1 ♕g5 15 ♕xg5 ♘xg5 16 ♘e7+ ♔h8 17 h4 ♘e6 18 ♖cd1! ♖e8 19 ♘xc8 ♖axc8 20 ♘e4 gives White a permanent advantage, Prins-Stalda, Venice 1949.

14 ♗xg5

14 ♕xd4 ♗xf5 15 ♕b4 ♖b8 is only about equal. Kasparov chooses a stronger continuation.

14 ... ♗xf5 (D)

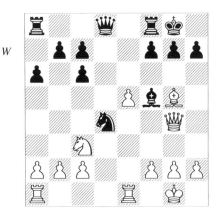

15 ♕g3?!

This slip could have cost White his advantage. Better is 15 ♕h4!, keeping an eye on the d4-knight. Black has two options:

1) 15...♕d7 16 ♖ad1 c5 17 ♗e7 ♗xc2 and now White has a choice:

1a) 18 ♗xc5 ♗xd1 19 ♖xd1 ♘e2+ 20 ♔h1 ♕f5! (20...♕e6? loses immediately: 21 ♗xf8 ♘xc3 22 ♖d8) 21 ♘xe2 ♕xe5 22 ♕c4!. White has a slight material advantage and is somewhat better.

1b) 18 ♗xf8!? seems to be more promising: 18...♗xd1 (18...♖xf8 19 ♖c1 and Black doesn't have enough for the exchange) 19 ♗xg7! (19 ♗xc5 ♘e2+! 20 ♘xe2 ♗xe2 21 ♕e4 ♕b5 enables Black to extricate himself). Now Black's kingside is seriously weakened, so he should strive for an endgame with 19...♕g4 20 ♕xg4 ♗xg4, though White remains firmly on top after 21 ♗f6.

2) The seemingly more committal 15...f6 16 exf6 gxf6 17 ♗h6 ♖f7 is somewhat better, although even here Black's vulnerable king gives White the initiative.

15 ... ♕c8?!

Black also falters. After the unprejudiced 15...♕d7! 16 ♖ad1 c5 he could have supported his centralized knight and it's difficult to prove any advantage for White; for example, 17 b4 b6!? (17...cxb4 is weaker: 18 ♗f6 ♗g6 19 e6!) 18 bxc5 bxc5, followed by ....♗xc2.

16 ♖ad1 ♘xc2

16...c5?! 17 ♗e7 or even 17 ♘d5 immediately costs Black material. 16...♘e6 is more solid, but after 17 ♘e4 White is better, so Muratkuliev decided to give the text-move a go.

17 ♖e2 ♕e6

Now White gets a solid positional advantage. After 17...♘b4, 18 ♗e7 costs Black an exchange. Seemingly the most logical defence was 17...♔h8, but after the central break 18 e6! (18 ♖dd2 h6 is less clear) 18...fxe6 19 ♖dd2 h6 (19...♘b4 20 ♗e7 or 19...♘a1 20 f3 and Black pays for his sidelined knight) 20 ♗h4 g5 (20...♘a1 21 f3 is similar to 19...♘a1, since 21...g5 fails to 22 ♕e5+ and 23 ♗f2) 21 ♗xg5! hxg5 22 ♘e4 White regains the sacrificed piece with a continuing attack: 22...♘b4 23 ♕c3+ or 22...♘a1 23 ♖d1.

18 ♗f6 ♗g6 (D)

Forced, because 18...g6? 19 ♕f4 leads to mate.

19 ♗xg7!

19 ♖xc2? gxf6 gets White nowhere.

19 ... ♔xg7

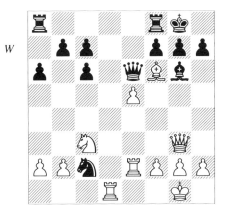
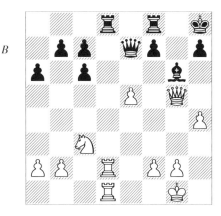

20 ♖xc2

Black's king is permanently weak. Not only does White have attacking chances, but also his kingside majority has grown to 4-2. Kasparov elegantly exploits the latter fact.

20	...	♖ad8
21	♖cd2	♕e7?!

Black understandably doesn't want to hand over the d-file, but stronger was 21...♖xd2 22 ♖xd2 f6 with a defensible position.

22 h4!

White creates some *luft* while threatening h5. A third idea behind White's move will become apparent soon enough.

22	...	♔h8?

More or less necessary was 22...♖xd2 23 ♖xd2 ♔h8 with the idea 24 ♕g5 f6!? and Black can still fight on.

23 ♕g5! *(D)*

This is the point. The young Kasparov rationally abandons any attacking ambitions and forces his opponent to simplify into a hopeless endgame.

23	...	♕xg5
24	hxg5	♖xd2

24...♖de8 25 f4 (25 g4!? is possibly even more incisive) 25...♗h5 26 ♖f1 ♖d8 27 ♖ff2 doesn't change the evaluation of the position.

25	♖xd2	♗f5

Black can't allow ♖d7.

26	f4	♔g7
27	♔f2	h5

Otherwise White will improve his position with ♔f3 followed by g4, f5, ♘e4, ♔f4, etc.

28	gxh6+	♔xh6
29	♔f3	♖g8

Black must prevent g4; 29...♔h5 30 ♘e4 is similar.

30	♘e4	♗g4+
31	♔e3	♔g6? *(D)*

This blunder shortens Black's suffering. However, 31...♗f5 (31...♗e6 32 ♘f6 ♖g3+ 33 ♔f2 followed by ♖d8 is even worse for Black) only prolongs his resistance. After 32 ♘f6 ♖g3+ 33 ♔f2 ♖d3 34 ♖xd3 ♗xd3 35 g4 there is no good defence against ♘e8, followed by a gradual advance of White's kingside pawns.

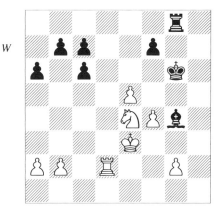

32 ♘f6 1-0

Black loses a piece.

Game 2
Smbat Lputian – Garry Kasparov
Caucasus Youth Games, Tbilisi 1976
King's Indian Defence, Sämisch Variation [E80]

1	d4	♘f6
2	c4	g6
3	♘c3	♗g7
4	e4	d6
5	f3	♘c6!?

An unorthodox and provocative move-order. Until the early 1980s Kasparov usually countered the Sämisch variation with the ...♘c6 system. Later, he gradually shifted to the classical 5...0-0 6 ♗e3 e5; see also Timman-Kasparov, Reykjavik 1988 and Shirov-Kasparov, Dortmund 1992 (Games 49 and 67 respectively).

6 ♗e3

White resists the temptation and calmly continues his development. Chasing the knight with 6 d5 ♘e5 7 f4 exposes White's centre and gave Black sufficient counterplay after 7...♘ed7 8 ♘f3 0-0 9 ♗d3 c6 10 0-0 ♘c5 11 ♗c2 ♕b6 12 ♔h1 ♗g4 13 ♖b1 cxd5 14 cxd5 ♖ac8 15 ♗e3 ♕b4! in Yusupov-Spassky, Linares 1983.

6 ... a6 *(D)*

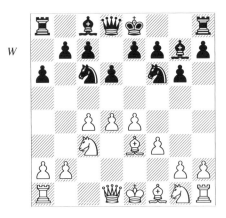

7 ♕d2

After 7 ♘ge2 Black can still postpone castling with 7...♖b8. An attempt to exploit this with 8 ♘c1?! e5 9 d5 ♘d4! 10 ♗xd4 exd4 11 ♕xd4 0-0 12 ♕d2 c5 13 a4 ♘h5 gave Black excellent compensation with his unopposed dark-squared bishop in Korchnoi-Kasparov, Leningrad (simul) 1975. Our game is further proof that early on Kasparov knew and could creatively apply typical King's Indian motifs.

7 ... ♖b8 *(D)*

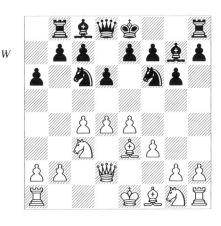

8 ♖b1

White also puts off his kingside development. He reasons he can make a few useful moves before resorting to the rather cumbersome manoeuvre ♘ge2-c1, when often a further move (♘1e2 or ♘b3) is required to get rid of Black's d4-knight. Lputian also clearly indicates he is not interested in a tactical slugfest with opposite-side castling, although this is a dangerous test of Black's set-up. Kasparov has later given up the whole system, presumably due to 8 ♘ge2 0-0 (8...b5 9 cxb5 axb5 10 d5 ♘e5 11 ♘d4 b4 12 ♘cb5 costs Black a pawn, and it's hard to see any adequate compensation) 9 h4 (see also Kasparov-Loginov, Manila OL 1992, Game 68). However, current theory still rates 9...h5!? as unclear.

8	...	0-0
9	b4	

White continues the strategy outlined in the previous note. This, however, allows Kasparov to lash out. The main move, 9 ♘ge2, is more circumspect and objectively better. Recent practice after the logical follow-up 9...b5 10 cxb5 axb5 11 b4 e5 12 d5 ♘e7 13 ♘g3 has favoured White, so Black should probably look for earlier improvements.

9 ... e5!?

Although this is a standard King's Indian move, Kasparov played it only after 25 minutes of thought. However, he invested his precious time well, and calculated most of the following tactical sequence. Although objectively Black can't claim an advantage after the text-move, psychologically it proves too difficult for White to adapt to the sharp increase in tension.

10 d5

Consistent, but even now White could have played it safe. 10 ♘ge2!? exd4 11 ♘xd4 is approximately equal.

10 ... ♘d4
11 ♘ge2 (D)

White sensibly doesn't even consider giving up his important bishop with 11 ♗xd4? exd4 12 ♘ce2 ♘h5 – here Black's initiative is even stronger than in the similar position in the note to move 7.

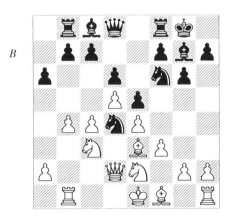

But how does Black justify his concept now?

11 ... c5!

11...♘xe2?! 12 ♗xe2 gives White a clear-cut queenside initiative, so the pawn sacrifice is not only consistent, but also more or less forced.

12 dxc6 bxc6!

White is better after 12...♘xc6 13 ♗g5.

13 ♘xd4

White obviously can't allow the knight to remain on d4. Although 13 ♗xd4 exd4 14 ♘xd4 wins a tempo by attacking c6, Black's tactical chances after 14...♕b6 give him excellent compensation to say the least.

13 ... exd4
14 ♗xd4 (D)

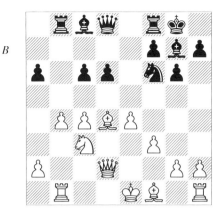

14 ... ♖e8!

A clever preparatory move, which maintains the tension. Now White has to reckon with both ...c5 and ...d5. The immediate 14...c5?! 15 bxc5 ♘xe4 16 fxe4 ♕h4+ is premature:

1) The safe move is 17 ♔d1 ♖xb1+ 18 ♘xb1 ♕xe4 19 ♗xg7 ♕xb1+ 20 ♕c1 ♗g4+ 21 ♔d2 ♕xc1+ (21...♕xa2+? 22 ♕b2) 22 ♔xc1 ♔xg7 23 cxd6 ♖d8 24 c5 ♖c8 25 ♗xa6 ♖xc5+ 26 ♔b2 ♖c6 27 ♗b5 ♖xd6 28 ♔c3. After a series of forced moves White has an outside passed pawn and a better endgame.

2) Inspiration for more adventurous types is 17 ♔e2!? ♖xb1 (17...♗g4+ 18 ♔d3 ♗xd4 19 ♖xb8 ♖xb8 20 ♔xd4 and with the knight coming to d5 there is nothing decisive in sight) 18 ♗xg7 ♔xg7 (after 18...♗g4+ 19 ♔d3 ♖xf1 20 ♖xf1 ♔xg7 21 cxd6 ♕xh2 22 ♔c2 White's king is safe) 19 ♕d4+ (19 ♘xb1 ♕xe4+ 20 ♔f2 ♕xb1 21 ♕d4+ ♔g8 22 cxd6 ♖e8 is dangerous) 19...♔g8 20 ♘xb1 dxc5 21 ♕e3 ♖d8 22 ♘d2 and again White should be able to untangle gradually with his extra piece.

15 ♗e2

With his lag in development White must tread extremely carefully. Although the text-move is not an outright blunder, it nevertheless plays into Black's hands. Other moves were:

1) A computer-like idea is 15 b5, when Black should play 15...axb5 (15...d5?! 16 cxd5 cxd5 17 ♗xf6 ♕xf6 18 ♘xd5 ♖xc4+ is best refuted by 19 ♗e2!) 16 cxb5 d5. White's king is in danger; e.g., 17 ♗e2 dxe4 18 ♗a7 ♕a5! 19 ♗xb8 e3 with a raging attack.

2) The prudent 15 ♗d3!? d5 16 e5 ♘d7 17 f4 f6 allows Black to regain his pawn with an unclear position.

15 ... c5!
16 bxc5

White is consistent. 16 ♗e3?! cxb4 17 ♘d5 ♘xd5 18 ♕xd5 ♗e6 gives Black the initiative. He also has a pleasant position after 16 ♗xf6 ♗xf6 17 0-0 (17 ♘d5 ♗d4 is dangerous for White) 17...cxb4 18 ♘d5 a5.

16 ... ♘xe4!! *(D)*

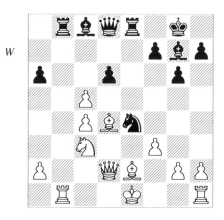

With this sacrifice Kasparov's major pieces explode into action.

17 fxe4 ♕h4+
18 g3?

A shocked Lputian immediately goes wrong. After this move the game is beyond saving. Let us look at the alternatives:

1) 18 ♔d1? ♖xb1+ 19 ♘xb1 ♕xe4 20 ♗xg7 (20 ♕d3 ♕xg2! 21 ♖g1 ♕xh2 and White can't meet all the threats such as ...♗xd4, ...dxc5 and ...♗f5) 20...♕xb1+ 21 ♕c1 ♕xc1+ 22 ♔xc1 ♔xg7 followed by ...dxc5. Converting Black's healthy extra pawn into victory is a straightforward technical task.

2) 18 ♗f2 is stronger. Now 18...♗xc3 19 ♗xh4 ♖xb1+ 20 ♔f2 ♗xd2 21 ♖xb1 dxc5 22 ♖b8 (or 22 ♗d3) leads to an approximately equal position.

3) Eleven years later, this position again arose in practice and White chose the circumspect 18 ♔f1 ♖xb1+ 19 ♘xb1 ♕xe4 20 ♗xg7 ♕xb1+ 21 ♕d1 (21 ♗d1?! ♔xg7 22 cxd6 ♖e6 23 ♕d4+ ♖f6+ 24 ♔g1 ♕b4 regains the pawn advantageously) 21...♕f5+ 22 ♗f3 ♔xg7 23 cxd6. The resulting position is drawish; e.g.,

23...♕e5 (23...♗e6 24 ♕d4+ ♔g8 25 ♔f2! ♕c2+ 26 ♔g3 can only favour White, Quigley-Henry, Chicago open 1987) 24 ♔f2 (24 g4 is weaker: 24...♖d8! 25 ♕d5 ♕f4) 24...♕e3+ 25 ♔g3 h5 26 h4 and Black seems to have nothing more than a perpetual.

18 ... ♖xb1+
19 ♔f2

19 ♘xb1? ♕xe4 is now out of the question for White.

19 ... ♖b2! *(D)*

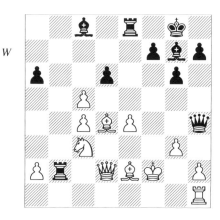

Black moves one of the two attacked pieces with decisive effect, leaving White an exchange down. It's quite probable Kasparov foresaw this resource as far back as when he made his 9th move, as White's reactions are all very natural. An impressive feat, at the age of 13 probably comparable only with the brilliancy D.Byrne-Fischer, New York 1956.

20 gxh4

Forced, since 20 ♕xb2? loses on the spot to 20...♗xd4+.

20 ... ♖xd2
21 ♗xg7 ♔xg7
22 ♔e3 ♖c2
23 ♔d3 ♖xc3+!

Just as in Game 1 Kasparov prefers a clear technical solution to the messy complications that might arise if he were to allow White to play cxd6.

24 ♔xc3 dxc5 *(D)*

White's passive pieces and shattered pawns make the endgame untenable despite temporary material equality.

25 ♗d3 ♗b7
26 ♖e1

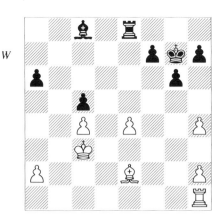

White's activity quickly peters out after 26 ♖b1 ♗xe4 27 ♖b6 ♗xd3 28 ♔xd3 ♖e6.

26 ... ♖e5!

Blockade and then destroy. Black doesn't trouble himself with lines such as 26...f5?! 27 e5 ♗e4 28 ♗xe4 ♖xe5 29 ♔d3 and first stops the e-pawn in its tracks. Now ...f5 is a real threat.

27 a4

Passive defence with 27 ♖e2 ♖h5 (27...f5?! is premature: 28 exf5 ♖xe2 29 f6+!) 28 e5 (28 ♖b2 ♗c8) 28...♗c8! is just as hopeless: White will lose at least a pawn and won't even get rid of all his weaknesses.

27 ... f5
28 ♖b1 ♗xe4
29 ♖b6 f4!

Kasparov's passed pawn simply marches on and any counterplay on the queenside is far too slow.

30 ♖xa6 f3

30...♗xd3 31 ♔xd3 f3 is less convincing due to 32 ♖a7+ ♔f6 33 ♖a8.

31 ♗f1

31 ♖a7+ ♔f6 (31...♔h6? 32 ♗xe4 ♖xe4 33 ♖f7) 32 ♗xe4 (32 ♗f1 ♗f5 is similar to the game) 32...♖xe4 33 ♖a8 ♔e7 34 ♖a7+ ♔e6 35 ♖a8 ♖xh4 36 ♖f8 ♖h3 is also more or less winning by force. After 37 a5 Black has, among others, 37...f2+ 38 ♔d2 ♖xh2 39 ♔e2 f1♕+! 40 ♔xf1 ♖a2.

31 ... ♗f5! *(D)*

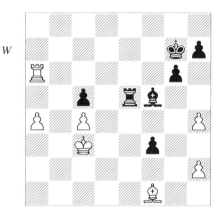

Black threatens ...♖e1. The f-pawn is unstoppable and will cost White at least a piece.

32 ♖a7+ ♔h6
33 ♔d2 f2
34 ♗e2 ♗g4
35 ♗d3 ♖e1
36 ♖f7 ♗f5!
37 a5 ♗xd3
38 ♖xf2 ♖f1!

Black forces an exchange of rooks, after which the bishop stops the a-pawn from g2.

0-1

Game 3
Elmar Magerramov – Garry Kasparov
Training match, Baku 1977
Queen's Gambit Declined, Tartakower Defence [D58]

1	♘f3	♘f6
2	d4	e6

Magerramov, who was 19 at that time, is Kasparov's compatriot from Baku and this game was part of a short training match. Striving to develop a more universal style, Kasparov decides to test some different openings apart from his then usual King's Indian.

3	c4	d5
4	♘c3	♗e7
5	♗g5	0-0
6	e3	h6
7	♗h4	b6

The solid Tartakower Defence became Kasparov's 'emergency' weapon in his first unfinished match against Karpov after he suffered heavily in the Tarrasch. Even nowadays it remains a part of Kasparov's repertoire.

8	♕b3	♗b7
9	♗xf6	♗xf6
10	cxd5	exd5
11	♖d1 (D)	

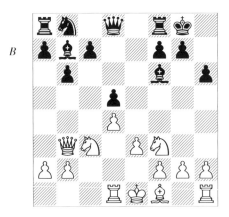

The idea behind White's set-up is to limit Black's central ambitions: his latent pressure against d5 aims to stop the advance ...c5. To develop his knight to d7 Black must often play ...c6, boxing in his b7-bishop, and then White's central break with e4 becomes more effective. Kasparov will have none of this and reacts actively.

11	...	c5?!

Although this break is tactically sound, it doesn't solve Black's strategic problems. The following facts also support this view: Kasparov himself played this line with White a year later against Beliavsky in his first USSR Championship. His opponent, just as a mature Kasparov in later encounters (e.g. in the Candidates match with Korchnoi 1983, etc.) played the more usual move 11...♖e8. One recent example is 12 a3 (after 12 ♗d3, the break 12...c5 13 dxc5 ♘d7 gains in strength) 12...c6 (12...♖e7!? is less tested, but interesting: 13 ♗d3 allows 13...c5, while 13 ♗e2 c6 enables Black's knight to use a different route with ...♘a6-c7-e8-d6) 13 ♗d3 ♘d7 14 0-0 g6 15 ♗b1 (15 e4 deserves a try; e.g., 15...c5 16 ♗b5 dxe4?! runs into 17 ♘e5!) 15...♗g7 16 e4?! ♗a6! 17 ♖fe1 ♗c4 18 ♕c2 dxe4 19 ♖xe4 ♖xe4 20 ♕xe4 ♗b3 21 ♗c2 ♘f6 and in this equal position a draw was agreed in Kramnik-Kasparov, Moscow (3) 2001.

12	dxc5	

Anything else would justify Black's previous move.

12	...	♘d7
13	c6!?	

White sensibly returns the pawn immediately. He had several ways to keep his material advantage:

1) 13 ♘a4?! ♕e7 practically forces 14 cxb6 axb6. Now White is too far behind in development and catching up is not easy, as after 15 ♗e2 ♘c5 16 ♘xc5 bxc5 Black regains the pawn and keeps the initiative.

2) 13 ♘xd5 ♘xc5 14 ♘xf6+ ♕xf6 15 ♕c3 ♕xc3+ 16 bxc3 ♘a4 also gives Black good compensation, although he can hardly claim an advantage yet.

3) Consistent, but risky, is 13 cxb6 ♘c5 14 ♕c2 (14 ♕b4 ♕d6! 15 a3 a5 16 ♕c4 ♖fd8 17 ♕a2 ♕xb6 18 ♗e2 ♘e6 19 0-0 d4 20 exd4

♘xd4 21 ♘xd4 ♗xd4 gives Black enough play to hold the game, Relange-Goldgewicht, Montpellier 1997) 14...d4! (14...axb6 15 ♗e2 and 14...♕xb6 15 ♘xd5!? ♗xd5 16 ♖xd5 ♖ac8 17 ♗c4 are less testing: in both cases White retains an advantage) 15 ♘xd4 (15 exd4 ♗xf3 16 gxf3 ♘e6!? is even more dangerous for White) 15...♕xb6. Although objectively the position is far from clear, one feels Kasparov would enjoy playing it with Black – the active bishop-pair and lead in development force White to tread with great care.

13 ... ♗xc6 *(D)*

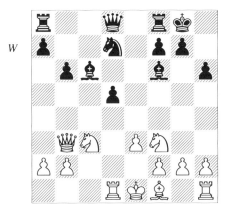

14 ♘d4?

However, this natural move is a serious mistake. 14 ♘xd5 ♘c5 15 ♘xf6+ ♕xf6 16 ♕c3 ♕xc3+ 17 bxc3 leads to the position from line '2' in the above note, the only difference being Black's bishop is on c6 instead of b7. Although this favours White, Black has little to complain about after 17...♗xf3 18 gxf3 ♘a4 19 ♖d3 ♖ac8. Instead of positional considerations White should have concerned himself with his uncastled king and played the cautious 14 ♗e2 ♘c5 15 ♕a3 with a slight but more or less permanent edge.

14 ... ♗xd4!

Played without prejudice. In principle Black usually strives to keep his dark-squared bishop, but in this concrete position time is the more important factor and the blockade of the isolated d5-pawn is only illusory.

15 ♖xd4?!

Although unpleasant, 15 exd4 ♕g5! 16 g3 ♖fe8+ 17 ♗e2 was still the lesser evil. After, e.g., 17...♕g4 18 ♕c2 ♕h3 19 ♔d2 White can castle by hand and retain defensive chances. On the other hand in an open position his problems will grow rapidly.

15 ... ♘c5
16 ♕d1

16 ♕c2 ♘e6 17 ♖d2 d4 18 ♘e2 ♖c8 is similar to the game and no less dangerous.

16 ... ♘e6
17 ♖d2 d4! *(D)*

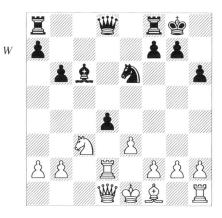

It's difficult to consider this typical break a sacrifice; White's king stuck on e1 literally asks for it.

18 exd4?!

Just as on move 15 Magerramov opens the position, when he should have tried to keep it closed. A better chance was 18 ♘e2 ♕d5 19 b4 (19 exd4 ♖fe8! and White is practically stalemated), but even here Black is clearly better. After the text-move the attack will prove very strong.

18 ... ♖e8
19 f3!

This is best. Nothing else can be recommended. 19 ♕g4, with the idea of escaping to the queenside, fails to 19...h5! 20 ♕g3 h4 21 ♕g4 f5, when the queen has to return ignominiously. After the natural 19 d5 ♘f4+ 20 ♗e2 (20 ♘e2 loses to 20...♗xd5 21 ♖d4 ♘xe2 22 ♗xe2 ♕g5!) 20...♘xg2+ 21 ♔f1 ♗d7! the knight is taboo due to 22 ♔xg2? ♕g5+ 23 ♔f1 ♗h3+ 24 ♔e1 ♕g2 and White's forces remain sadly uncoordinated.

19 ... ♗xf3! *(D)*

Very energetic. This is, surprisingly, also the only way to a clear-cut advantage. 19...♕h4+? 20 g3 gets Black nowhere, and 19...♘xd4+? 20

♔f2 would force Black to take a perpetual after 20...♕g5 21 ♖xd4 ♖ad8 22 ♖xd8 ♕e3+.

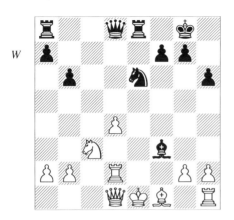

20 gxf3

20 ♕xf3 ♘g5+ 21 ♕e2 ♕d6! is hopeless for White.

20 ... ♕h4+
21 ♖f2 ♘xd4+

21...♘g5+ 22 ♗e2 ♘h3 23 ♖hf1 is unclear.

22 ♗e2

22 ♘e4? loses immediately to 22...♖xe4+.

22 ... ♘xf3+
23 ♔f1 ♕h3+
24 ♖g2 *(D)*

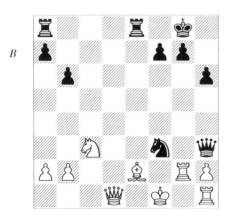

24 ... ♘h4?!

As only Magerramov's error on move 26 allows Kasparov to wrap the game up, one can also question Black's moves. Here 24...♖d8! is more convincing. After the forced 25 ♗xf3 ♖xd1+ 26 ♗xd1 ♖e1+ 27 ♔xe1 ♕xg2 White's uncoordinated forces are no match for Black's mobile queen and pawns.

25 ♖g1 ♖ad8
26 ♕e1?

After a series of forced moves White instinctively keeps his queen close to his king, thus squandering his last slight chance. 26 ♕b3? loses to 26...♖xe2 (26...♖e6 and 26...♖d3!? are alternative solutions) 27 ♘xe2 ♕f5+ 28 ♔e1 ♘f3+. However, 26 ♕a4! *(D)* is far more resilient.

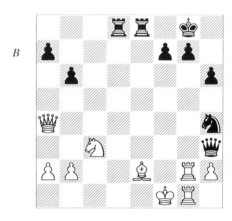

The queen wants to join the defence via g4, at the same time eyeing the e8-rook. Now the most practical solution is 26...♘xg2 (Nikitin recommends 26...♘f5, but after 27 ♔e1!? ♕e3 28 ♕c2 the defences still hold; 26...♖e6 27 ♕g4 ♖f6+ 28 ♔e1 ♘xg2+ 29 ♖xg2 somewhat prematurely forces the queens off) 27 ♖xg2 ♕e3. Black has a slight material advantage and good attacking chances as well, but to haul in the point would still require patience and technique.

26 ... ♖d3!
27 ♕f2

The threat was ...♖f3+, and 27 ♘d1 ♘f3 28 ♕b4 ♖xe2 29 ♔xe2 ♘xg1+ leads to mate.

27 ... ♘f3! *(D)*

White is in zugzwang!

28 ♖h1

Moving the knight allows a pretty mate by 28...♖d1+! 29 ♗xd1 ♘xh2#. The only other move with a piece is 28 ♕g3, but it loses to 28...♘d2+ 29 ♔e1 ♖xg3 30 ♖xg3 ♘f3+! 31 ♔f2 ♘xg1.

28 ... ♖de3
29 ♖hg1

29 ♕g3 ♘d2+ 30 ♔e1 ♖xg3 31 ♖xg3 ♕d7 is hopeless for White.

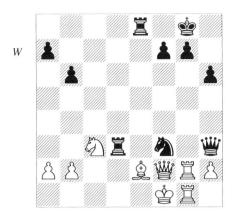 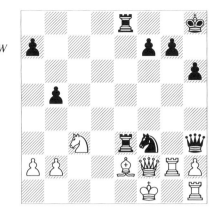

29 ... ♔h8

Kasparov emphasizes White's helplessness, but 29...♖xc3! 30 bxc3 ♘xh2+ 31 ♔e1 ♕xc3+ is a more direct path to victory.

30 ♖h1 b5! *(D)*

This modest pawn move finally overloads White's defences.

0-1

After 31 a3 a5 the threat of ...b4 followed by ...♖xe2 decides the game.

Game 4
Garry Kasparov – Abram Roizman
Sokolsky Memorial, Minsk 1978
Ruy Lopez (Spanish), Bird Defence [C61]

The Sokolsky memorial in Minsk was a significant landmark in Kasparov's career – by winning the event he overstepped the master norm by an unbelievable 3½-point margin. Here he also played his first one-on-one game against a GM.

1	e4	e5
2	♘f3	♘c6
3	♗b5	♘d4
4	♘xd4	exd4

The Bird Defence doesn't have a very good reputation and is rare in current tournament practice. Although the d4-pawn takes away the knight's most natural square, this comes at a cost – Black's pawn-structure is less flexible and he is behind in development. After a game with Kupreichik later in 1978 it was another 24 years before Kasparov faced this position again.

5	0-0	♗c5 *(D)*

The brave man who recently ventured the Bird against Kasparov was Khalifman in a short rapid match, but he had prepared a different option. After an initial draw he made the mistake of repeating his opening choice and was crushed instructively: 5...c6 6 ♗c4 d5 7 exd5 cxd5 8 ♗b5+ ♗d7 9 ♖e1+ ♘e7 10 c4! a6 11 ♗xd7+ ♕xd7 12 d3 0-0-0 13 ♘d2 ♔b8 14 b4! dxc4 15 dxc4! ♘c6 16 b5 axb5 17 cxb5 ♘b4 18 ♘c4 ♕f5? 19 ♖e5 ♕c2 20 ♗f4 with a decisive attack, Kasparov-Khalifman, Moscow rpd 2002.

6	d3

A natural developing move, but 6 ♗c4!? is more accurate. The threat of ♗xf7+ enables White to win a tempo and his light-squared bishop can exert strong pressure on Black's position. After 6...d6 7 d3 ♘e7 (7...c6 transposes into the game) 8 ♗g5 0-0 9 ♕h5 ♗e6 10 ♕h4 ♖e8 11 ♗xe6 fxe6 12 f4! ♕d7 13 ♖f3! ♘g6 14 ♕h5 ♘f8 15 ♘d2 a6 16 ♖af1 d5 17 ♖g3 White had a dangerous attack in Brenke-Binder, corr. 1994.

6	...	c6

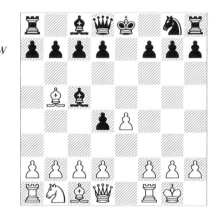

7	♗c4	d6?!

Theory and practice have shown Black has good chances for full equality after the direct 7...d5!, a move played by Henry Bird himself as long ago as 1876!

8	f4

Botvinnik, who was sufficiently impressed by the young Kasparov to annotate this game, remarks that this active move is characteristic for his enterprising style. However, despite its aggressiveness the text-move isn't ideal. Kasparov had played 8 c3 against Gorelov in 1975 and won after a dramatic fight, but stronger is 8 ♕h5!? ♕e7 (8...g6 seriously weakens the kingside, and White is better after 9 ♕f3 ♗e6 10 ♗xe6 fxe6 11 ♕h3 ♕d7 12 f4) 9 ♗g5 ♘f6 10 ♕h4 h6 11 ♘d2 (or 11 f4!?). The endgame after the inevitable ♗xf6 gives White a pleasant and permanent edge due to Black's shattered pawn-structure.

8	...	♘f6
9	e5?! *(D)*	

Still in the same optimistic spirit. Later games featured the more sedate 9 ♘d2, although this can hardly promise White an opening advantage.

9	...	dxe5?

Opening the position is premature and wrong in principle. Botvinnik mentions 9...♘d5 as a

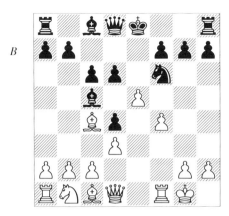

safer choice; after 10 ♗xd5 cxd5 Black has no problems. 9...♘g4!? is also food for thought; then following 10 h3 (10 ♗xf7+? ♔xf7 11 e6+ ♗xe6 12 f5 ♕h4! 13 fxe6+ ♔e7 14 h3 ♘e3 and Black's attack decided quickly in Bashkov-Meister, Tåby open 1991) both 10...♘h6 and 10...d5!? seem promising for Black.

10   ♗xf7+

Now Black loses his castling rights and will have to cope with his shaky king until the very end. However, it seems that this tempting idea is in fact inferior to the simple 10 fxe5!? ♘d5 (10...♗g4? 11 ♗xf7+!) 11 ♕h5 (11 ♘d2!?), followed by ♘d2 with a promising attacking position.

10   ...   ♔xf7
11   fxe5   ♕d5! *(D)*

Black first of all stops ♕h5+. He couldn't have avoided the isolation of his kingside pawns anyway; considerably worse is 11...♗e7?! 12 exf6 ♗xf6 13 ♗g5, when White is clearly better.

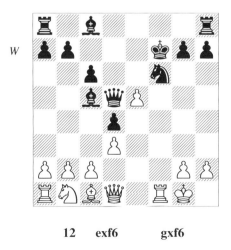

12   exf6   gxf6

13   ♘d2 *(D)*

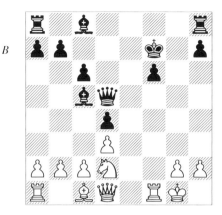

The tactical phase of the opening is over. Now both sides have to finish their development.

13   ...   ♖g8

Apart from the aforementioned drawbacks, Black's position also has its pluses – an active bishop-pair and play on the semi-open g-file.

14   ♘e4   ♗e7
15   ♗f4

White closes the f-file for the time being, but retains the possibility of defending his own king with ♗g3. The seemingly more active 15 ♕f3 doesn't radically change the evaluation of the position after 15...♗e6 (15...♗g4?! is inferior due to 16 ♕f4 with the threat of ♘g5+ – once White manages to exchange a pair of minor pieces he can claim an advantage; however, 15...♖g6 deserves attention) 16 ♗d2 ♖g6 – it remains sharp and approximately balanced.

15   ...   ♖g6
16   ♕e2   ♗g4 *(D)*

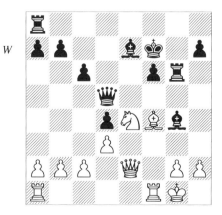

17 ♕f2 ♖ag8

This move indicates Black is optimistic about his chances. As we'll see it's not so bad in itself, but 17...♔g7 18 ♖ae1 ♔h8 is certainly more circumspect, first safeguarding his own king, with an unclear position.

18 ♖ae1 h5?!

After 18...♔g7 Black must reckon with the unpleasant 19 c4 or 19 c3!?. However, 18...♗e6! is more in keeping with the previous move; then 19 ♗g3 h5 20 ♕f4 f5 gives chances for both sides.

19 ♗g5! (D)

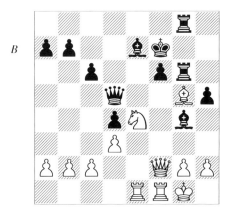

The first tactical blow, which is still quite easily parried by Black.

19 ... ♕d8?!

19...♖xg5? loses quickly to 20 ♘xf6, as after 20...♗f3 21 ♘xg8 the pin on the f-file nets White a decisive material advantage. However, the immediate retreat was not necessary, and even now Black could have first forced a concession with 19...♗e6!? and played ...♕d8 only after 20 ♔h1 or 20 g3.

20 ♕f4

The less committal 20 ♗h4!? keeps the f6-pawn under pressure without cutting off the bishop, and gives White an edge.

20 ... ♗e6 (D)

20...♔g7 21 ♗h4 is only a better version of 20 ♗h4!? from the previous note, so Black wants to increase his pressure on the g-file by transferring the bishop to d5.

21 h4!

Kasparov continues to increase the tension by creating threats involving ♗xf6 followed by ♘g5+.

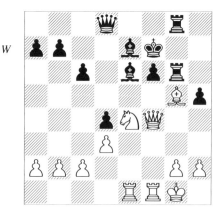

21 ... ♗d5

A natural reaction; it's too late for 21...♔g7? 22 ♘xf6. However, Botvinnik's recommendation 21...♗g4!?, which he in fact considered to be the only move, certainly deserves attention. After 22 ♗h6 ♖e8! (Black can't play 22...♖h8? 23 ♘g5+ ♔e8 24 ♖xe7+! ♔xe7 25 ♗g7!; also 22...♗c8 23 ♘g5+ ♔e8 24 ♘h7! ♔f7 25 ♗g5! ♗e6 26 ♕e5 gives White a strong attack) Black calmly frees g8 for his king and White still has to prove he can aspire for more than a repetition after 23 ♗g5.

22 g4!! (D)

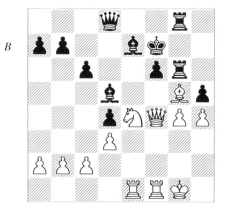

All for the attack! Kasparov isn't afraid to advance a pawn that only a short time ago was an object of Black's pressure. The weakening of his own king is only of secondary concern, as Black has problems keeping his defences from falling apart.

22 ... ♔g7?

A shocked Roizman quickly goes under without a fight. Black had better moves:

1) 22...♗xe4 (22...hxg4? fails to 23 h5) is not ideal either, since 23 gxh5 ♖h6 (23...♖6g7 is worse, since after 24 ♖xe4 Black can't effectively unpin his f-pawn) 24 ♖xe4 ♖xh5 25 ♕g4 ♖h7 26 ♕e6+ ♔f8 27 ♖g4 ♖gg7 (White's threat was ♗h6+, and 27...♖g6 is even worse due to 28 h5! with the idea 28...♖xh5? 29 ♗xf6! ♖xg4+ 30 ♕xg4) 28 ♔h2 gives White a large advantage. The seemingly plausible 28...♕d5 runs into 29 ♖xf6+! ♗xf6 30 ♕xf6+ ♖f7 (or 30...♔g8 31 ♗h6!) 31 ♗h6+, regaining the exchange with a won endgame.

2) However, the seemingly passive 22...♖h8! is considerably more resilient:

2a) The tactical operation 23 ♗xf6 ♗xf6 (23...♖xg4+? loses on the spot: 24 ♕xg4 hxg4 25 ♗xe7+ ♔xe7 26 ♘c5+!) 24 g5 ♗xe4 25 ♖xe4 is insufficient for an advantage: 25...♖f8! (after 25...♔g7? 26 ♖e6! ♖f8 27 ♔h2 White regains the piece with a huge advantage) 26 ♖xd4 (26 ♔h2? ♔g8! is now even losing for White, while 26 ♕f5 ♔g7 27 ♖e6 allows 27...♕d5 28 ♕xd5 cxd5 and the resulting endgame is a draw) 26...♕e8 (26...♕c7? 27 ♖d6 ♔g8 28 ♕e4! and White regains the piece) 27 ♔h2 (27 ♖d6?! ♔g7 now doesn't work, as the bishop will retreat to e7; 27 ♖e4 ♕d8 only repeats) 27...♔g7!? (27...♔g8 28 gxf6 ♖fxf6 is also sufficient for a draw) 28 gxf6+ ♖fxf6 29 ♕c7+ ♔h6 30 ♖e4 ♕xe4 31 dxe4 ♖xf1 32 ♕e5 and either White or Black will force a perpetual.

2b) The fighting try is 23 gxh5! ♖xh5 24 ♘g3 ♖h7 (24...♗d6 forces the dangerous queen sacrifice 25 ♕xf6+! ♖xf6 26 ♘xh5 ♗h2+! 27 ♔xh2 ♕b8+ 28 ♘f4 and here White has good attacking chances against Black's more vulnerable king) 25 h5 ♖g8 26 ♔h2!. Now White threatens ♖xe7+ and as the trick 26...♖xh5+? 27 ♘xh5 ♗d6 28 ♖e5 doesn't work, he can claim an advantage.

23	gxh5	fxg5
24	♕e5+	♔h6 (D)

Both 24...♗f6 25 ♘xf6 ♖xf6 26 hxg5 and 24...♖f6 25 h6+ ♔h7 26 ♘xf6+ ♗xf6 27 ♕xf6 gxh4+ 28 ♔h2 are hopeless for Black. In the latter case he has only a few checks.

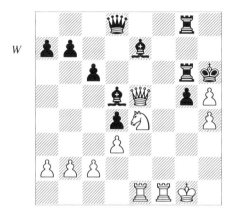

25	hxg6	gxh4
26	♖f5	♔xg6

This move loses immediately, but the same goes for 26...♖xg6+ 27 ♔h2 ♖g5 28 ♖xg5 ♗xg5 29 ♘xg5 ♕xg5 30 ♕h8+. Black's king can't survive out in the open for long even after 26...♗xe4 27 ♖h5+!? (27 ♖xe4 ♖xg6+ 28 ♔h1 is sufficient as well) 27...♔xg6 28 ♖xe4.

| 27 | ♔h2 | 1-0 |

Game 5
Sergei Yuferov – Garry Kasparov
Sokolsky Memorial, Minsk 1978
King's Indian Defence, Classical Main Line [E99]

1	d4	♘f6
2	c4	g6
3	♘c3	♗g7
4	e4	d6
5	♗e2	0-0
6	♘f3	e5
7	0-0	♘c6
8	d5	♘e7 (D)

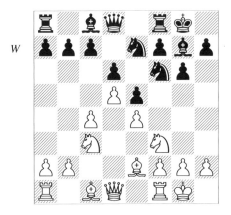

The King's Indian has been a trademark of Kasparov throughout his career and especially in the Classical Variation he can boast numerous significant contributions to the development of opening theory. (See also Piket-Kasparov, Tilburg 1989 and Korchnoi-Kasparov, Barcelona 1989: Games 54 and 56 respectively.)

9 ♘e1

At the time this game was played, this was White's main try, but the forcing character of the fight, together with the fact that White's king often has to endure all sorts of discomfort to have chances for final success have led to a shift of trends. Later 9 ♘d2 became the most popular option, while now 9 b4 is the height of fashion. In both lines Black can't concentrate solely on a kingside offensive, as he would be overrun on the opposite flank, and must seek more complex means of counterplay. The last time Kasparov himself faced 9 b4 in a tournament game was in Novgorod 1997 against Kramnik. He went astray in a sharp position, lost the game and hasn't played the King's Indian since. It's possible to speculate about his reasons, but the one he presented himself in a later interview is very plausible: keeping analytically up-to-date in both the Najdorf Sicilian and the King's Indian is extremely demanding in terms of time and energy, so currently he concentrates only on the Najdorf.

9	...	♘d7
10	♘d3	f5
11	♗d2	♘f6
12	f3	f4
13	c5	g5 (D)

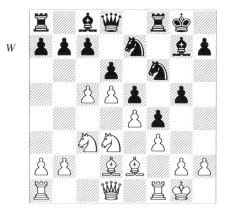

The plans of both sides are clearly defined by the respective pawn-structures. To put it simply, White's arena of activity will be the queenside, while Black's basic aim is to mate his opponent. The battle tends to become very sharp and as the line has been around since the 1950s, numerous strategic manoeuvres and tactical motifs have been tested.

14 cxd6

The c-file is White's main avenue of attack and this release of tension is an integral part of his plan. He could have postponed it by playing 14 ♖c1, but Yuferov reserves this square for his other rook. By playing ♖fc1 White also frees a possible escape-route for his king.

14 ... cxd6 *(D)*

15 ♘f2

A flexible continuation. White will sooner or later need his knight on f2 to keep an eye on the ...g4 break. The main line in the 1980s was 15 ♖c1 ♘g6 16 ♘b5 ♖f7 17 ♕c2 ♘e8 18 a4 h5 19 ♘f2 ♗f8 (Black can also choose another set-up, aiming to activate his dark-squared bishop with 19...♗d7 20 ♕b3 ♗f6!? 21 ♖c2 ♕b8 22 ♖fc1 ♗d8) 20 h3 ♖g7. The current theoretical opinion is Black has enough counterplay: 21 ♕b3 ♘h4 22 ♖c2 a6 23 ♘a3 ♘f6 24 ♗e1 g4 25 hxg4 hxg4 26 ♘xg4 ♘h5! 27 ♘c4 ♘g3 28 ♗xg3 fxg3 29 ♕b6 ♕e7 30 ♘ce3 ♖h7 31 ♖fc1 ♗xg4!? 32 ♘xg4 ♘g6 33 ♖c7 ♕g5 34 ♖xh7 ♕xc1+ 35 ♗f1 ♔xh7 36 ♕xb7+ ♘e7! 37 ♕xa8 ♗h6 38 ♕a7 ♔g6 and White couldn't disentangle his forces effectively to realize his material advantage in Bang-Hertel, corr. 1988.

15 ... ♘g6

A more accurate move-order is 15...h5!?. Then if White wants to move his queen from d1, he'll have to play h3 first. Compare also with the following note.

16 a4

Nowadays White usually moves his a-pawn only after Black plays ...a6, with the possibility of a5 and ♘a4-b6 in mind. A recent example shows this line still has its unexplored nuances: 16 ♕c2 ♖f7 17 ♖fc1 a6 (here after 17...h5 White can play 18 ♘b5 and do without h3) 18 a4 h5 19 h3 ♘h4 20 a5 g4 21 fxg4 f3!? 22 ♗xf3? (according to Baklan White can claim an advantage after 22 ♗g5! ♘xg2 23 ♗xf3 ♘f4 24 gxh5) 22...♘xg4! 23 hxg4 ♘xf3+ 24 gxf3 ♕h4 25 ♘cd1 ♕g3+ 26 ♔f1 ♗d7 27 ♗e3 ♖xf3 and Black's attack broke through in Kekelidze-Baklan, Batumi Ech 2002. This game also shows one of the possible drawbacks of playing ♖fc1 – the rook might be missed in the defence.

16	...	♖f7
17	♘b5	h5
18	h3	♗f8
19	♕c2 *(D)*	

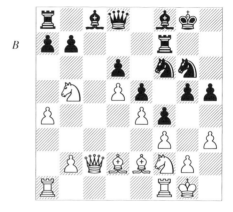

19 ... a6

Black as yet doesn't want to burn his boats with the more forcing 19...g4 20 fxg4 hxg4 21 hxg4 a6 22 ♘a3 ♖g7. Now 23 ♖fc1 ♘h4 24 ♕d1 transposes to a position we will analyse below in the note to Black's 22nd move. However, 23 ♘c4!? is more promising. After 23...♘h4 24 ♕d1 (24 ♗a5!? followed by ♕d1 is similar) White intends to play ♗a5 and ♘b6; the a1-rook may also join the defence via a3. Violent measures are still not impressive enough; for example, 24...♘h5 (after 24...♘xg2? 25 ♔xg2 ♘xg4 26 ♘xg4 ♗xg4 27 ♗xg4 ♕h4 28 ♖g1! ♖xg4+ 29 ♕xg4+ White remains a piece up) 25 ♗a5 ♕g5 26 ♘b6 ♘g3 27 ♘xa8 ♖h7 28 ♘h3.

| 20 | ♘a3 | ♖g7 |
| 21 | ♖fc1 | |

Even here 21 ♘c4!? deserves serious attention. 21...g4 will transpose to the previous note, while the passive 21...b6 22 ♕b3 gives White an advantage, as his queenside attack already has concrete targets.

| 21 | ... | ♘h4 |
| 22 | ♕d1 | ♗d7 |

Kasparov still postpones kingside action, as the consequences of an immediate break are difficult to evaluate clearly. Consistent, but far from clear, is 22...g4!? 23 fxg4 hxg4 24 hxg4 ♗xg4! *(D)* (otherwise the tactics don't work; after 24...♘xg2? 25 ♖xc8! White wins simply enough and for 24...♘xg4? 25 ♘xg4 ♗xg4 26 ♗xg4 see line '2a') and now:

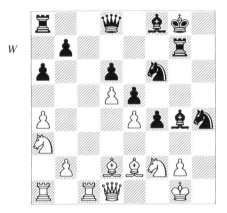

1) 25 ♗xg4 ♘xg4 (25...♘xg2? is no good, since after 26 ♗e6+ ♔h8 27 ♔f1! the black queen can't join the attack) 26 ♘xg4 ♘xg2! (26...♕g5 27 ♗e1! forces an endgame that clearly favours White) 27 ♔xg2 (27 ♘h6+? ♔h7 28 ♕h5 ♕h4! and Black regains the piece) 27...♕h4 and although White currently has two extra pieces, he can't avoid repetition after 28 ♕h1 ♖xg4+ 29 ♔f3 ♖g3+ 30 ♔e2 ♖h3 31 ♕g2+! (weaker is 31 ♕g1+? ♔h8!) 31...♖g3.

2) 25 ♘xg4 is a more fighting move:

2a) 25...♘xg4? 26 ♗xg4 ♘xg2! (26...♕g5? 27 ♗e6+ ♔h8 28 g4! loses for Black, Sosonko-Kavalek, Wijk aan Zee 1977) 27 ♗e6+ ♔h8 28 ♔f1!? and White's king escapes via e2.

2b) Therefore Black must play 25...♘xg2! 26 ♖c3 (26 ♔xg2 ♘xg4 27 ♗xg4 ♕h4 28 ♕h1 ♖xg4+ transposes to line '1', but the untested 26 ♔f1!? is interesting) 26...♘e3 27 ♗xe3 ♘xg4 28 ♗xg4 ♕h4 29 ♔f1! ♖xg4 30 ♗g1 ♖c8!?, Lubrano-Calzolari, corr. 1987. In the resulting position Black has compensation, as it's not easy for White to coordinate his forces and achieve full consolidation.

23 ♘c4

The prophylactic 23 ♗e1!? is interesting, as it prevents the following operation.

23 ... g4!

Good or bad, Black must go for it.

24 hxg4 hxg4
25 fxg4 ♘xg2?! *(D)*

This gives White a chance to fight for an edge. 25...♗xg4? 26 ♘xg4 ♘xg2 27 ♔f1 gets Black nowhere, but stronger is 25...♘xg4! 26 ♘xg4 (26 ♗xg4 ♘xg2 is similar) 26...♘xg2! 27 ♔xg2 ♗xg4 28 ♗xg4 ♕h4 29 ♕h1 (29 ♔f1 ♖xg4 30 ♔e2 ♖g2+ 31 ♔d3 ♕g3+ regains the piece) 29...♖xg4+ with a draw as in note '1' to move 22.

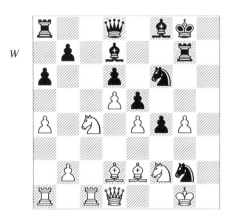

26 ♔xg2

Flicking in 26 ♗a5 ♕e7 doesn't improve White's position.

26 ... ♘xg4
27 ♗xg4 ♗xg4
28 ♕xg4!?

Yuferov wants more than the repetition indicated above after 28 ♘xg4 ♕h4 29 ♕h1. His move gives White a small material advantage, but his king is still not quite safe.

28 ... ♖xg4+

28...♕h4 is worse due to 29 ♕xg7+ and 30 ♖g1.

29 ♘xg4 ♖c8!? *(D)*

A tricky move. White finds it easier to consolidate after the natural 29...♕h4 30 ♖g1! ♕g3+ (30...♖c8 is weaker: 31 ♔f3!) 31 ♔h1 ♕h3+ 32 ♘h2+ with good winning chances. Hitting the c4-knight makes it more difficult for White to activate his rooks.

30 ♘h2?!

This is dubious, as now White's knight loses touch with the important e4-pawn, and Kasparov forcefully exploits this. The alternatives were:

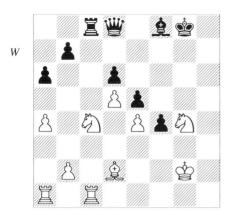
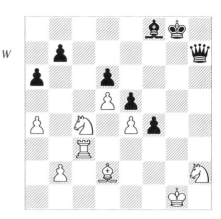

1) 30 b3? protects the c4-knight, but after 30...♕h4 31 ♘f2 ♕g3+ 32 ♔f1 the surprising 32...♖xc4! 33 bxc4 ♗e7 suddenly renders White helpless against ...♗h4 and ...f3.

2) The most natural reply is 30 ♘f2. After 30...♕g5+ 31 ♔f1 ♕g3 32 ♖a3 f3 33 ♘e3 ♖xc1+ 34 ♗xc1 ♗e7 White's position holds together, but unravelling it and realizing the material advantage will be difficult.

3) Thus the most promising is 30 ♔f3. After 30...♕h4 White has the tactical 31 ♖g1! at his disposal, retaining winning chances after 31...♕h3+ 32 ♔e2.

30	...	♕h4
31	♖c3?	

A serious error. After 31 ♗e1 f3+! (weaker is 31...♕h5 32 ♘d2 ♕e2+ 33 ♔h1) 32 ♘xf3 ♕xe4 Black has reasonable compensation and hardly risks losing, but this was definitely the way to go for White. The text-move tips the scales heavily in Black's favour.

31	...	♖c7
32	♖g1	

32 ♔h1 ♖g7 threatens ...♕g5 and transposes into the game after 33 ♖g1, as 33 ♖f3 ♕g5 34 ♖f2 ♕g3 35 ♖af1 ♕d3 is even worse.

32	...	♖g7+
33	♔h1	♖xg1+
34	♔xg1	♕h7! (D)

Suddenly White can't protect his central pawns. After they fall, Black's own connected passed pawns will decide the game. Yuferov resorts to desperate measures.

| 35 | ♗xf4 | |

After 35 ♘f3 ♕xe4 36 ♔f2 (36 ♘b6 ♕e2! and there is no defence against ...e4) 36...♕xd5 the pawns are ready to move on.

35	...	exf4
36	♘d2	

White desperately tries to coordinate his forces, but he has far too many weaknesses to hold the position.

36	...	♕d7

36...♕g7+ 37 ♔f1 ♕d4 also wins a pawn.

| 37 | ♖c4 | |

37 ♖b3 ♕xa4 38 ♖xb7? fails to 38...♕d4+, and 37 a5 ♗g7 followed by ....♗xb2 is hardly much better.

37	...	♗g7?!

The materialistic 37...♕g7+ 38 ♔f1 ♕xb2 39 ♘hf3 b5 wins faster and more convincingly.

38	b3	♗d4+!
39	♔h1	

39 ♖xd4? ♕g7+.

39	...	♗c5 (D)

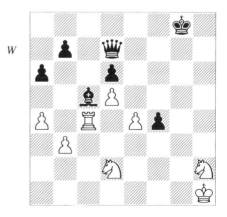

White has managed to safeguard his pawns for the time being, so Black first shuts the c-file and frees his queen for action.

| 40 | ♘df3 | |

40 b4? ♗e3 or 40 e5 ♕f5 only loosens White's position.

40	...	b5
41	♖c2!?	

After 41 axb5 ♕xb5 42 ♘d2 ♗e3 43 ♘hf3 ♗xd2!? 44 ♘xd2 ♕b6 Black's queen penetrates into White's position. White wants to create some counterplay at any cost.

41	...	♕e8

Kasparov probably didn't want to permit 41...bxa4!? 42 ♖g2+ ♔f8 43 ♘g5, although even here after 43...♔e8 Black is practically winning; e.g., 44 ♘e6 ♕h7.

42	♖g2+	♔f8
43	♘g5	♕h5
44	♘e6+	♔e7
45	♖g7+	

45 ♖g4 is insufficient; after 45...f3 46 e5 f2 47 ♖g7+ ♔e8 White doesn't have a perpetual.

45	...	♔f6
46	♖g4	bxa4
47	bxa4	

After 47 ♘xc5 dxc5 48 ♖xf4+ (48 bxa4 ♕e5) 48...♔e7 49 bxa4 c4 the c-pawn quickly decides the game. 47 ♖xf4+ ♔e7 48 bxa4 ♕d1+ (or 48...♗d4!?) also doesn't help White.

47	...	♗e3
48	♘xf4	♗xf4
49	♖xf4+	♔e7 (D)

Dogged defence and a few inaccuracies from Black have enabled White to struggle on. However, even now Yuferov is fighting for a lost cause, as he can't defend his vulnerable a-pawn.

50	♔g2	

50 ♖g4 and 50 ♖f3 both run into 50...♕e5.

50	...	♕d1
51	♘g4	

The only way to keep the a-pawn alive is 51 e5, but after 51...dxe5 52 ♖g4 ♔d6 White's pieces are too badly coordinated to put up any resistance.

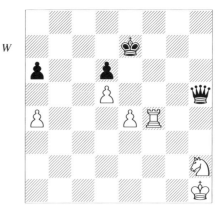

51	...	♕xa4
52	♘e3	a5
53	♘f5+	♔d7
54	♖h4	♕c2+
55	♔f3	a4

55...♕c3+ is even stronger.

56	♖h7+	♔d8
57	♖a7	

Now Black wins quickly, but also after 57 ♘xd6 a3 58 ♘b7+ (58 ♖a7 a2 doesn't help) 58...♔c8 (58...♔e8? throws away the win: 59 d6 ♕d3+ 60 ♔f4) 59 ♘d6+ (59 d6 ♕b3+ 60 ♔f4 ♕xb7!) 59...♔b8 60 ♖h8+ ♔a7 61 ♘b5+ (61 ♖h7+ ♔a6 and the pawn queens) 61...♔a6 62 ♖a8+ ♔xb5 63 ♖xa3 ♔c5 White can't create a fortress and will lose his pawns.

57	...	♕d3+
58	♘e3	

58 ♔f4? ♕f1+ and ...♕g1+ costs White a rook, while after 58 ♔f2 Black can choose between 58...♕xe4 and 58...a3.

58	...	a3
59	♔f4	♕b3
60	♘f5	♕b2

0-1

The main threat is ...♕f2+; moreover the a-pawn is unstoppable.

Game 6
Garry Kasparov – Semion Palatnik
USSR Ch qualification, Daugavpils 1978
Alekhine Defence [B04]

By winning the 13-round qualification Swiss in Daugavpils Kasparov qualified directly for the Top League of the USSR Championship for the first time. With the following game from round 7 he took over the leadership from his opponent, who had started with 5/6.

1	e4	♘f6
2	e5	♘d5
3	d4	

Fighting against a strong and quite often mobile pawn-centre makes the Alekhine a very demanding defence. Kasparov himself has never essayed it with Black.

3	...	d6
4	♘f3	g6
5	♗c4	♘b6
6	♗b3	a5 *(D)*

Then a favourite of the Odessa masters Palatnik and Alburt. Nowadays Black more often opts for 6...♘c6 or 6...♗g7. In the latter case, play can transpose back into the game after 7 a4 a5.

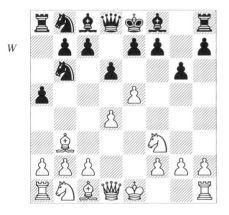

7 a4

7 e6 ♗xe6 8 ♗xe6 fxe6 9 ♘g5 ♘c6 10 ♘xe6 ♕d7 11 ♕e2 ♘d8 12 ♘xf8 ♖xf8 13 0-0 gives White perhaps a slight edge, but this position had occurred earlier in Palatnik's practice and Kasparov decided to prefer a more complicated line. However, the main problem with Black's 6th move is 7 ♘g5!? d5 (7...e6? is weak: 8 ♕f3 ♕e7 9 ♘e4) 8 c3 with a comfortable space advantage.

7	...	♗g7
8	♘g5	e6

At the time our game was played this natural move was a novelty. Black retains pressure against the centre, as 8...d5 9 0-0 (or 9 f4) would make it easier for White to concentrate on a kingside attack in a blockaded position.

9 f4 *(D)*

The time has not yet come for a radical solution like 9 ♕f3 ♕e7 10 ♘e4 dxe5 (10...d5!? 11 ♘f6+ ♗xf6 is also far from clear; even here the insertion of a4 and ...a5 favours Black) 11 ♗g5 ♕b4+ 12 ♘bd2. Now taking yet another pawn is too provocative, but the sensible 12...♘8d7!? 13 ♘f6+ (after 13 dxe5 ♗xe5 or 13 c3 ♕f8 White could well end up with insufficient compensation) 13...♘xf6 14 ♗xf6 ♗xf6 15 ♕xf6 0-0 16 ♕xe5 ♘d7 leads to approximate equality.

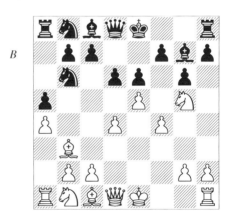

9	...	dxe5
10	fxe5	c5
11	0-0?!	

A slip, which gives Black a good extra option. The stronger 11 c3 cxd4 12 0-0! 0-0 13 cxd4 leads to a position that we'll examine below.

11 ... 0-0

Black could have sought relief in exchanging queens; better was 11...♕xd4+! 12 ♕xd4 cxd4 13 ♘xf7 (13 ♖xf7 ♗xe5 is also OK for Black) 13...0-0 14 ♘d6 ♖xf1+ 15 ♔xf1 ♗d7 16 ♘xb7. White temporarily has an extra pawn, but Black has enough counterplay and the position remains balanced after 16...♘c6 17 ♘c5 ♔f7 or Kasparov's recommendation 16...♘a6!?; e.g., 17 ♗d2 ♖b8 18 ♘xa5 ♘c5.

12 c3

12 dxc5 ♕xd1 13 ♖xd1 ♘6d7 14 ♘e4 is interesting, but inconsistent – White's main goal is to keep his centre intact as long as possible.

12 ... ♘c6?

This mistake is much more serious than the inaccuracy on the previous move, as now White manages to keep his central pawn-chain. Necessary was 12...cxd4 13 cxd4 ♘c6 14 ♘f3 (a forced retreat; weaker is 14 ♗e3?! ♘d5 15 ♗xd5 exd5!, when Black can fight for the initiative) 14...f6 (D).

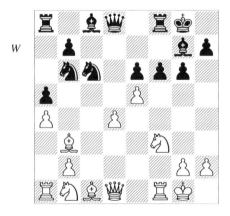

Now White has a choice between the circumspect 15 exf6 ♕xf6 16 ♗e3 ♘d5 17 ♗f2, with a slight advantage, and the more ambitious 15 ♘c3!?. This pawn sacrifice was actually Kasparov's preference, and White gets a dangerous initiative after, e.g., 15...fxe5 16 ♗g5 ♕d7 17 dxe5 ♘xe5 18 ♘xe5 ♖xf1+ 19 ♕xf1 ♕d4+ 20 ♔h1 ♕xe5 21 ♗d8! (this line shows that the insertion of a4 and ...a5 can also sometimes favour White).

After the text-move, however, Black will be subjected to a vicious kingside attack without any material compensation. His suffering is caused mostly by the fact that he will not be able to play ...f6 or ...f5 in time.

13 ♘e4!

This is the point: now White isn't forced to defend d4 passively.

13 ... ♘d7

This ugly reaction is more or less the only move, as Black must protect the c5-pawn, and 13...cxd4 14 ♗g5 ♕c7 (14...♕d7? 15 ♘f6+ ♗xf6 16 ♗xf6 and the attack via the dark squares decides quickly) 15 cxd4, followed by ♘bc3 or ♘f6+, is even worse for Black than the game continuation.

14 ♗e3!

Kasparov calmly strengthens his central bastions. 14 ♗g5? is premature due to 14...♕b6, when with d4 falling the all-out attack has little chances to succeed.

14 ... ♘e7

Left to his own devices White will simply pile up the pressure with, e.g., ♘d6 and ♘d2-e4. Palatnik intends to boost his kingside by transferring his knight to f5, and also toys with the idea ...b6 and ....♗b7. After 14...♕b6 White maintains his centre with 15 ♗f2 or even 15 ♘a3!? with the idea 15...cxd4 16 ♘c4.

15 ♗g5! (D)

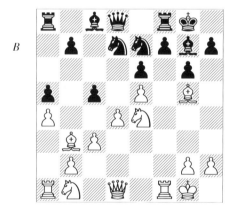

Kasparov is very alert and free of any dogmatic prejudice. In contrast to the situation one move earlier, this is very strong, as the pin it creates will force Black to weaken his kingside, thus making holes for White's attacking forces.

15 ... cxd4

An important tactical point of White's previous move was that 15...h6 16 ♗h4 g5? loses immediately to 17 ♗xg5! hxg5 (17...cxd4 18 ♗xe7) 18 ♕h5 ♘f5 19 ♖xf5! exf5 20 ♘xg5 and avoiding mate costs Black his queen. Palatnik prevents this only by freeing the ideal c3-square for White's knight.

16 cxd4 h6
17 ♗h4 g5
18 ♗f2

Here 18 ♗xg5? hxg5 19 ♕h5 doesn't work because of 19...♘xe5!.

18 ... ♘g6

Black's pieces lack space and coordination, so it's difficult to recommend anything else. White has a large advantage after 18...♘f5 19 ♘bc3 or 18...b6 19 ♘bc3 ♗a6 20 ♘b5.

19 ♘bc3 ♕e7 *(D)*

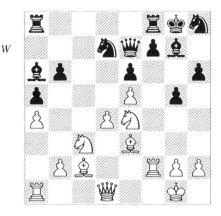

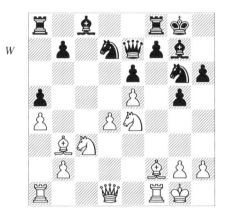

By protecting e6, Black finally prepares a liberating advance of the f-pawn. However, White's fully-developed forces can contain any such activity.

20 ♗c2 b6

After 20...f5 21 exf6 (21 ♘d6!? is also strong) 21...♘xf6 22 ♘xg5 White wins a pawn.

21 ♗e3 ♗a6
22 ♖f2 ♘h8?! *(D)*

Kasparov energetically shows there is no time for such long-winded manoeuvres. However, even after 22...f5 23 ♘d6 (23 exf6 ♘xf6 24 ♘xg5 ♘d5!? is less incisive) White has a clear advantage.

23 ♗xg5!

Some two years afterwards Kasparov indicated that 23 h4!? gxh4 24 ♕g4 f5 (24...♘g6 25 ♕h5 and the kingside crumbles) 25 exf6 ♘xf6 26 ♘xf6+ ♖xf6 27 ♖xf6 ♕xf6 28 ♕e4 ♖d8 29 ♕h7+ ♔f8 30 ♘b5! is a more rational way to score the point without complications. True enough; after 30...h3!? 31 gxh3 ♘f7 32 ♖f1 ♕h4 33 ♕g6 ♖d7 34 ♔h2 White has an overwhelming position, but the text-move is both objectively stronger and aesthetically more pleasing.

23 ... hxg5
24 ♕h5 f5

Closing the b1-h7 diagonal provides only temporary relief. However, other defences are also insufficient:

1) 24...f6 25 ♘xg5 ♖fc8 (25...♖fd8 doesn't help: 26 ♕h7+ ♔f8 27 ♗b3!) and here White has more than one decisive continuation. For instance, 26 ♕h7+ ♔f8 27 d5! wins easily.

2) 24...♖fc8 is not much better. Following 25 ♘xg5 White will break through by increasing his pressure against f7. After 25...♖a7 (25...♘f8 26 ♘ce4 threatens ♘f6+ and forces the knight back) 26 ♗h7+ (26 ♗g6 ♘f8! is less convincing) 26...♔f8 27 ♗g6! ♘b8 (after 27...♘xg6 28 ♕xg6 or 27...f6 28 ♘ce4 Black's defences are overloaded) 28 ♘ce4 ♖ac7 (28...♖c6 fails to 29 ♘xf7 ♘xf7 30 ♘g5!) 29 ♖d1!? (29 ♗xf7 ♖c1+ 30 ♖f1 is also sufficient) apart from other threats such as ♘f6, Black can't stave off ♘xf7 or ♗xf7 at a moment of White's choosing.

25 ♘xg5 ♖f7!

The most resilient defence, which was surprisingly accompanied by a draw offer.

Otherwise, one pretty finish is 25...♖fd8? 26 ♖xf5! exf5 27 ♗b3+ ♔f8 28 ♘h7#, while after 25...♖fc8 White has a wide and pleasant choice between 26 ♘d5, 26 ♗xf5! cxf5 27 ♘d5 and 26 ♕h7+ ♔f8 27 ♘xe6+. Finally, after 25...♗xe5 26 dxe5 ♘xe5 White wins rather mundanely with 27 ♖e1 ♘hg6 28 ♗b3 ♗c8 29 ♘d5!.

26 ♗xf5! *(D)*

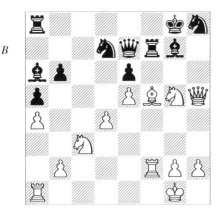

White naturally ignores the offered exchange and by sacrificing the bishop decisively exposes Black's king.

    26   ...   ♖xf5

After 26...exf5 27 ♘d5 ♕e8 both 28 e6 and 28 ♘c7 are winning for White.

    27   ♖xf5   exf5
    28   ♘d5   ♕e8

Black's queen has only one square left.

    29   ♕h7+   ♔f8
    30   ♕xf5+   ♔g8

30...♘f7 loses to 31 ♘e6+ ♔g8 32 ♕g6.

    31   ♕h7+   ♔f8
    32   ♖a3

Kasparov stylishly activates his last passive piece, but 32 ♘f4 ♗c4 33 ♖f1! is equally effective.

    32   ...   ♖c8

The alternative 32...♕g6 is also hopeless: 33 ♖f3+ ♔e8 34 ♕g8+ ♗f8 (34...♘f8 35 ♖xf8+! ♗xf8 36 ♘f6+ and now Black must give up his queen in order to postpone mate) 35 ♘c7+ ♔e7 (35...♔d8 36 ♘ge6+ either mates after 36...♔e7 37 ♘d5+ ♔e8 38 ♖xf8+ or wins loads of material following 36...♔c8 37 ♖xf8+) 36 ♖f7+! (36 ♕xg6 ♘xg6 37 ♖f7+ is also good enough) 36...♕xf7 37 ♘xf7.

    33   ♖f3+   ♘f6 *(D)*

After 33...♘f7 34 ♖xf7+ ♕xf7 35 ♘xf7 ♖c1+ 36 ♔f2 ♖f1+ 37 ♔g3 ♖xf7 the powerful 38 ♕h4! threatens mate and wins more material.

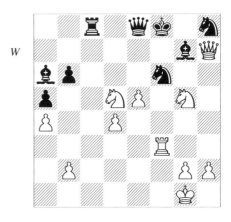

34 h3!

In his quest for beauty Kasparov spurns the simple and sufficient 34 ♖xf6+ ♗xf6 35 ♘xf6 ♖c1+ 36 ♔f2. Now White's king has a safe hideaway on h2 and the attack finally triumphs.

    34   ...   ♕g6
    35   ♖xf6+   ♗xf6
    36   ♘e6+   ♔e8
    37   ♘xf6+   1-0

Game 7
Garry Kasparov – Lev Polugaevsky
USSR Ch, Tbilisi 1978
Sicilian Defence, Paulsen Variation [B43]

1	e4	c5
2	♘f3	e6
3	d4	cxd4
4	♘xd4	a6

This was one of Kasparov's first games against a world-class GM. Throughout his career, Polugaevsky was a great connoisseur of the Sicilian, considerably enriching especially the Najdorf and Scheveningen with his theoretical research. However, against the talented junior he specially prepared the solid Paulsen.

5 ♘c3

Kasparov always used to prefer this move and has only lately started to play 5 c4 ♘f6 6 ♘c3 ♕c7 7 a3.

5	...	♕c7
6	♗e2	

6 ♗d3 is more ambitious, and also recently included by Kasparov in his repertoire.

6	...	b5 *(D)*

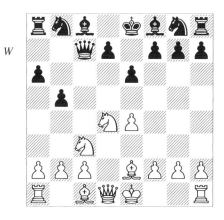

7 ♗f3

An interesting parallel to our game went 7 0-0 ♗b7 8 ♖e1 ♘c6 9 ♘xc6 dxc6 10 e5 ♘e7!? 11 ♗d3 ♘g6 12 ♕h5 c5 13 ♗g5 ♗e7 14 ♘e4 ♗xe4 15 ♗xe4 ♖d8 16 ♗xe7 ♘xe7 17 ♖e3 ♘g6 18 ♗xg6 fxg6 19 ♕g4 ♕e7 and Black equalized in Kasparov-Ye Jiangchuan, Europe-Asia rpd, Batumi 2001. Presumably this encounter prompted Kasparov to look for more challenging ways to fight the Paulsen, mentioned in the above notes.

7	...	♗b7
8	0-0	♘c6

This remains Black's favourite option to this day. Transposing into Scheveningen structures with 8...d6?! 9 a4! b4 10 ♘a2 is suspect due to White's lead in development, so Black retains the option of deploying his f8-bishop more actively.

9 ♘xc6

After 9 ♖e1 the most reliable road to equality is 9...♗d6!? 10 g3 ♘xd4 11 ♕xd4 ♗e5.

9	...	dxc6 *(D)*

After 9...♗xc6?! Black has to reckon with the dangerous 10 ♘d5!.

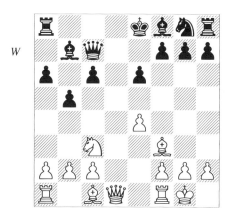

10 e5?!

More restrained continuations such as 10 a4 ♗d6 11 g3 ♘f6 allow Black to catch up with his development and achieve a comfortable position, so White decides to 'go for it'. Kasparov's inclination to strive for activity in an unfamiliar situation was especially notable in his junior years and although objectively the sacrifice is dubious, one has to commend his courage.

10	...	♕xe5

Taking the pawn is consistent and more or less necessary. Interpolating 10...b4 is not ideal, as the loosening of the queenside pawns gives White extra chances after 11 ♘e4 (11 ♘a4!?) 11...♕xe5 12 c3!?.

11 ♖e1 ♕c7

11...♕d6!? definitely deserves attention. Although the queen is exposed on the d-file, Black wins an important tempo for his development. After 12 ♕e2 ♘f6 White still has to prove he has enough play for the pawn.

12 ♗h5 *(D)*

The point of White's 10th move, but Black's reaction refutes Kasparov's idea. Later White at least partly rehabilitated the sacrifice with 12 a4!? ♘f6! (Black wisely returns the pawn; 12...b4 13 ♘c4 gives White a promising position) 13 axb5 axb5 14 ♖xa8+ ♗xa8 15 ♘xb5 cxb5 16 ♗xa8 ♗d6 17 g3 0-0 18 ♗g2 b4 19 ♗g5 ♗e5, although even here Black has a tiny edge, Velimirović-Rublevsky, Yugoslav Cht (Herceg Novi) 1999.

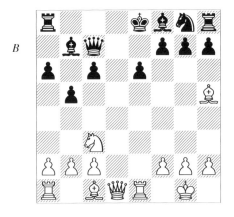

12 ... ♗e7!

The best reaction. One can understand Black didn't want to waste time with passive defensive moves such as 12...♗c8. Other alternatives are:

1) 12...♖d8?! 13 ♖xe6+ ♗e7 14 ♕f3 g6 transposes into the game after 15 ♖e1, but White also has the dangerous extra option 15 ♗f4!.

2) 12...♘f6 13 ♖xe6+ ♗e7 14 ♘e4!? (otherwise Black plays ...0-0 with an excellent position) 14...♘xh5 15 ♕xh5 0-0 16 ♗f4 ♕d7 17 ♖e5 (17 ♘g5 ♗xg5 18 ♖d6 ♕f5 is also equal) 17...f6!? 18 ♖d1 ♕e8 and White should bail out with 19 ♘d6, as 19 ♘xf6+?! gxf6 20 ♕g4+ ♔h8 21 ♖d7! fxe5 22 ♗xe5+ ♖f6 23 ♖xb7 ♕f7 can only give Black winning chances.

3) 12...g6 13 ♕d4 f6 is provocative, but White retains compensation after 14 ♗g4 (following 14 ♖xe6+?! ♔f7 15 ♗g4 ♖d8 16 ♕c4 ♗d6 White's pieces get tangled up and he will soon have to shed material) 14...e5 15 f4.

13 ♖xe6

Other moves simply allow Black to continue his development and keep the extra pawn. Kasparov rightly feels the consistent text-move will cause Black more practical problems.

13 ... g6 *(D)*

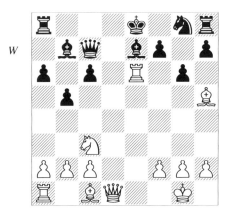

14 ♖e1

14 ♕d4? fxe6 15 ♕xh8 0-0-0 threatens both ...gxh5 and ....♗f6.

14 ... ♖d8?

Polugaevsky stumbles at the very start of the complications. After this move Black can't claim an advantage any more. The natural and best move is 14...gxh5. Now 15 ♕xh5? 0-0-0 shows one of the benefits of leaving the rook on a8, so White must first of all prevent queenside castling. 15 ♗g5 c5 also gets White nowhere. 15 ♘e4 is more plausible, but also insufficient: 15...♔f8 (15...♖d8 and 15...c5!? are worthy alternatives; in both cases Black has good chances to convert his extra piece into victory) 16 ♕d4?! (16 ♕xh5 is better, although even here after 16...h6 White is struggling to keep the game going) 16...f6 17 ♘c5 ♗c8 18 ♗f4 ♕d8 19 ♕e3 ♕d5 20 b4 ♗xc5 21 bxc5 ♗d7 22 ♕g3 ♖e8 23 ♖xe8+ ♗xe8 24 ♖e1 ♔f7 25 ♗d6 ♗d7 26 h3 ♗e6 and Black consolidated his position and won in Wojtkiewicz-Ionov, USSR 1980. Kasparov's own recommendation was

15 ♕d4!? f6 16 ♕d1, but after 16...♔f8 17 ♕xh5 b4!? despite all Black's technical problems White's compensation remains nebulous.

15 ♕f3   c5

After 15...gxh5 16 ♗f4 ♕d7 *(D)* (16...♕c8? loses to 17 ♗e5 c5 18 ♘e4!; 16...♕b6 is stronger, when 17 ♕g3 can transpose into the game after 17...c5, which is the best move) White must make a decision:

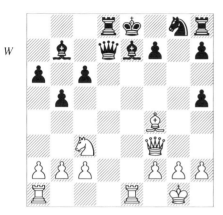

1) Black wants to exchange queens at any cost, and after 17 ♘e4 ♕g4! 18 ♕c3 (18 ♘d6+ ♖xd6 19 ♕xg4 hxg4 20 ♗xd6 ♗c8 is also insufficient for White) 18...♕xf4 19 ♕xh8 ♔f8 20 ♕xh7 c5, he is better.

2) 17 ♗e5 f6!? (17...c5 18 ♘e4 f6 19 ♗xf6 ♗xe4 20 ♖xe4 ♘xf6 21 ♕xf6 ♖f8 22 ♕g7 ♕d1+ 23 ♖e1 ♕d6 24 ♕xh7 and without his kingside pawns Black might even be worse) 18 ♗xf6 ♘xf6 19 ♕xf6 ♖g8 and White has nothing concrete; for example, 20 ♖e3 ♕d6 21 ♖e6 ♖f8!.

3) The most demanding is 17 ♕xh5!, threatening ♗e5:

3a) 17...♔f8? loses to 18 ♗h6+ ♘xh6 19 ♕xh6+ ♔g8 (19...♔e8 20 ♘e4) 20 ♖e3.

3b) 17...♘f6 18 ♕g5 ♔f8 19 ♕h6+ ♔g8 20 ♗e5! ♕f5 21 ♖e3 ♕xf2+ 22 ♔xf2 ♘g4+ 23 ♔e2 ♘xh6 24 ♖g3+ and White remains an exchange up.

3c) 17...c5 18 ♗e5 ♕c6 19 f3 ♘f6 20 ♕h6 ♔d7 (20...♖g8? 21 ♗xf6 ♖xg2+ is parried by 22 ♔h1 ♖e2 23 ♘e4! and White wins) 21 ♕h3+ ♔e8 and White can choose between repetition with 22 ♕h6 and the more ambitious 22 ♘e4!? ♘xe4 23 ♗xh8.

16 ♗f4!   ♕b6 *(D)*

16...♗xf3 17 ♗xc7 ♗xh5 18 ♗xd8 ♔xd8 19 f3 cuts off the bishop, and the endgame after 19...g5 20 ♖ad1+ ♔c8 21 ♘d5 ♗d6 22 ♖e8+ ♔b7 23 ♘c3!? (23 ♘f6 ♘xf6 24 ♖xh8 ♗e5 is not so clear either) guarantees White at least a draw.

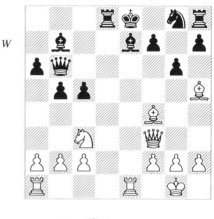

17 ♕g3   gxh5
18 ♗c7

A solid move. Instead, 18 ♗e5 ♘f6 (18...f6? 19 ♗c7) 19 ♗c7 (19 ♕f4 ♔d7 20 ♗c7 ♕c6 gets White nowhere) 19...♕c6 20 ♗xd8 ♖g8! and 18 ♕g7 ♕g6 19 ♖xe7+ (19 ♗e5? f6 is bad for White) 19...♘xe7! (19...♔xe7?! 20 ♗g5+ ♘f6 21 ♕xf6+! ♕xf6 22 ♖e1+ gives White a slightly better endgame) 20 ♕xh8+ ♔d7 21 ♖d1+ ♗d5 22 ♕xd8+ ♔xd8 23 ♘xd5 ♘c6!? both promise Black winning chances.

18 ...   ♕g6

Black on the other hand has no choice; otherwise White's attack quickly breaks through.

19 ♗xd8   ♕xg3
20 hxg3   ♔xd8
21 ♖ad1+   ♔c7
22 ♘d5+   ♗xd5
23 ♖xd5   h6

Black is going to lose another pawn anyway, and this move at least enables him to improve his rook's position.

24 ♖xh5   ♖h7 *(D)*

A series of more or less forced moves has led to a balanced endgame. Black still enjoys a slight material superiority, but his pieces are not coordinated well enough and White can keep the equilibrium by harassing his weak pawns.

25 ♖he5   ♔d7

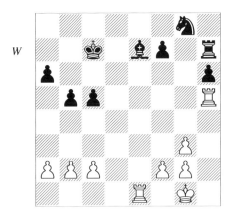

26	R5e3	Rg7
27	Rd3+	Kc7
28	Ra3	Rg6

28...Kb6 29 Rd3 is similar and can also lead to repetition.

29	Rf3	Bf6?!

To fight for an advantage Black must activate his minor pieces, but this is difficult to achieve without concessions. The prudent course is 29...Rg7 30 Ra3 Rg6 with a draw.

30 c3

The immediate penetration by 30 Re8 Bxb2 31 Rxf7+ Kd6 32 Ra7 Kd5 could only favour Black. Re8 can't be prevented anyway.

30	...	Kd7 (D)

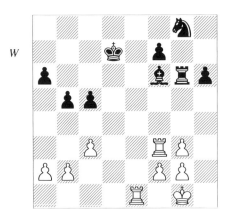

31	Rd3+	Kc7
32	Re8	

Now Kasparov spurns the repetition.

32	...	Ne7?

It's move 32 and Black finally decides to develop his knight. However, this error will cost him dearly. After 32...Bc7 33 Rf3 Rg7 Black's forces are passive, but it's difficult to find any inroads for White's second rook.

33 Red8 (D)

Now Black is paralysed. 33 Rf8 is weaker due to 33...Rg7.

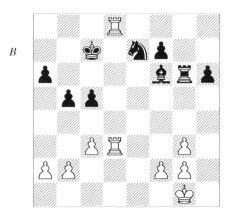

33	...	Nc6

Polugaevsky is mainly concerned about his king and gives a pawn away without a fight. This is a practical decision; after other moves Black is also in serious trouble; e.g., 33...Bg5 34 f4 Bf6 35 R8d7+ Kc8 (35...Kb8 36 Re3 is weaker) 36 Ra7.

34	R8d7+	Kb6
35	Rxf7	Be7
36	Re3	

36 Rd7 Re6 37 Kf1 c4 gives Black more play. In the final phase of the game White is much better, but still far from clearly winning.

36	...	Bd6 (D)

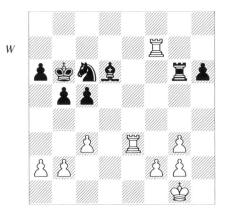

37	f4	c4
38	Kh2	Bc5

| 39 | ♖e2 | b4!? |

The only way to create counterchances.

| 40 | ♖e4 | |

Now White has some problems activating his king. The technical 40 ♔h3 ♖d6 41 ♔h4!? may be simpler; White wants to advance his kingside pawns and 41...♖d3 runs into 42 ♖e6!.

| 40 | ... | bxc3 |

40...b3 is worse, as after 41 ♖xc4 bxa2 42 ♖a4 ♗f2 43 ♖xa2 ♗xg3+ 44 ♔h3 White retains a compact pawn-chain without weaknesses.

| 41 | bxc3 | ♗f2 (D) |

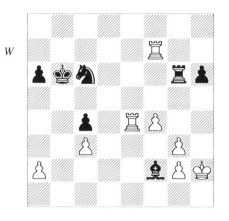

42	♖xc4	♗xg3+
43	♔h3	♗e1
44	a4! (D)	

Restricting Black's king. 44 g4 ♔b5 45 ♖e4 ♗xc3 is far from clear.

| 44 | ... | ♘a5 |

After 44...♖g3+ 45 ♔h2 ♖xc3 (weaker is 45...♖d3 46 g4! with the idea 46...♗xc3 47

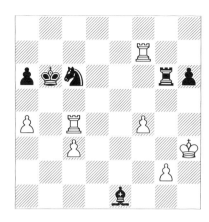

♖h7) 46 ♖xc3 ♗xc3 47 ♖h7 ♘b4 48 ♖xh6+ ♔a5 49 f5 White's pawns are too fast. However, 44...h5!? is an interesting alternative. After 45 ♖e4 (45 ♖h7 ♖g3+ 46 ♔h2 ♖e3! also isn't too convincing for White) 45...♗xc3 46 ♖h7 ♘b4 47 ♖xh5 (47 ♖c4 ♘d3!) 47...♘d3 Black's forces are finally cooperating and he is still fighting.

| 45 | ♖b4+ | ♔c5? |

This loses on the spot. 45...♔c6 is necessary. Then:

1) 46 ♖f5?! allows 46...♖g3+ (46...♗xc3? loses to 47 ♖xa5) 47 ♔h2 ♖xc3! (47...♗xc3? 48 ♔xg3 ♗xb4 49 ♖f6+ is hopeless for Black) with the point 48 ♖xa5 ♗g3+ 49 ♔h3 ♗e1+ 50 ♔g4 ♖g3+ and Black draws.

2) Stronger is 46 ♖b1 ♖g3+ (weaker is 46...♖e6 47 f5 ♖e3+ 48 ♔g4 ♗xc3 49 ♖a7) 47 ♔h2 ♖e3 48 g4!? and White should gradually win.

| 46 | ♖f5+ | 1-0 |

Game 8
Garry Kasparov – Josef Přibyl
European Team Ch, Skara 1980
Grünfeld Defence, Exchange Variation [D85]

1	d4	♘f6
2	c4	g6
3	♘c3	d5
4	cxd5	

The sharpest lines of the Exchange Variation were for many years Kasparov's main weapon against the Grünfeld. Only recently has he started to prefer the Russian System with 4 ♘f3 and 5 ♕b3.

4	...	♘xd5
5	e4	♘xc3
6	bxc3	♗g7
7	♘f3	

This logical but long-neglected knight move became very popular in the late 1970s. At the time our game was played it had practically pushed 7 ♗c4 and 8 ♘e2 off the scene.

| 7 | ... | b6?! |

The Grünfeld requires Black to take energetic action against White's centre, so this passive move (and also 7...0-0 8 ♗e2) is considered inferior. For the strongest move, 7...c5, see Kasparov-Romanishin, Moscow tt 1981 (Game 11).

| 8 | ♗b5+! *(D)* | |

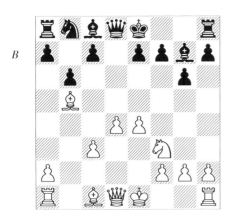

This check either disrupts Black's development (if he interposes with a piece), or forces the unwanted ...c6, which robs the knight of its most natural square and also closes the long diagonal for the c8-bishop. Later White even started playing 7 ♗b5+, and we can find a similar motif in other openings too (see Kasparov-Åkesson, Dortmund jr Wch 1980, Game 10).

| 8 | ... | c6 |

8...♗d7 9 ♗e2 (9 ♗c4!?) is also pleasant for White. If Black plays 9...c5, we transpose into a position from the line 7 ♗b5+ ♗d7 8 ♗e2 c5 9 ♘f3, where 9...b6?! is pointless.

| 9 | ♗c4 | |

White has stopped ...c5 for the time being and has an advantage.

9	...	0-0
10	0-0	

White could have prevented the following move with 10 ♕e2!?, but preferred straightforward development.

| 10 | ... | ♗a6 |

Although exchanges usually help the defence, this move also has a drawback – Black's knight will be misplaced on the edge of the board.

| 11 | ♗xa6 | ♘xa6 *(D)* |

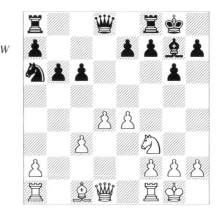

| 12 | ♕a4 | |

Kasparov criticized this move as artificial. The simple 12 ♗g5 ♕d7 13 ♕d2 promises White a permanent advantage. He has a mobile pawn-centre and after centralizing his rooks may turn his attention to the kingside with ♗h6.

12	...	♕c8
13	♗g5	♕b7

The typical break 13...c5 doesn't solve all Black's problems. White can choose between the patient 14 ♖ac1, intending to play d5 (14 d5 ♗xc3 15 ♗xe7 ♕e8!? 16 ♕xa6 ♕xe7 is unconvincing for White), and the more direct 14 ♗xe7!? ♖e8 15 ♗d6 ♖xe4 16 ♖fe1 with a promising initiative. Přibyl rightly decides to keep the position closed and only gradually prepare his counterplay.

| 14 | ♖fe1 (D) | |

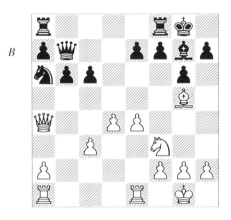

By protecting the e4-pawn, White creates the threat of ♗xe7.

| 14 | ... | e6 |

Kasparov mentions 14...♖fe8!? and this alternative is perhaps an improvement, as after the analogous 15 ♖ab1 c5 16 d5 ♗xc3 17 ♖ed1 ♗g7 White doesn't have a passed pawn yet and his compensation is not as concrete as in the game.

| 15 | ♖ab1 | |

The rook leaves the long diagonal, thus preparing 16 c4. At the same time White's move stops ...b5 in some lines; e.g., after 15 ♖ad1 c5 (15...h6 16 ♗f4!? c5 17 ♗e5 is unpleasant) 16 d5 ♗xc3 17 ♖e2 ♗g7 (the immediate 17...b5!? 18 ♕b3 ♗g7 19 a4 h6 is also far from clear) 18 dxe6 fxe6 19 ♖d7 Black has 19...b5!? with approximate equality.

| 15 | ... | c5 (D) |

Black can't allow White a broad centre and must act now, because after 15...h6?! 16 ♗e3 it's already too late for ...c5.

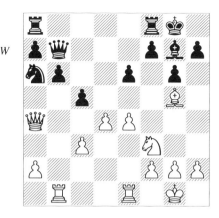

16 d5!

If a sacrifice is necessary to maintain the initiative, Kasparov rarely hesitates – he intuitively feels the need to act. The preparatory move 16 ♖ed1 cxd4 (even the sharper 16...h6 17 ♗h4 f5!? deserves attention) 17 cxd4 ♖ac8 promises White little.

16	...	♗xc3
17	♖ed1	exd5?!

Opening the position is risky, as it increases White's attacking chances. 17...♗g7 is more circumspect:

1) 18 dxe6 fxe6 19 ♖d7 ♕c8! (here 19...b5? 20 ♕xb5 ♕xb5 21 ♖xb5 leads to a miserable endgame for Black) 20 ♖bd1 c4 21 ♖d8 ♘c5 and although White regains his pawn, his edge is minimal at best.

2) 18 d6!? f6 19 ♗e3 is more ambitious. Now knight moves cost Black the c5-pawn. However, 19...♖ac8 with the idea 20 ♕c4 ♘b8! 21 ♕xe6+ ♕f7 is far from clear.

| 18 | exd5 | |

The positional factors justifying White's minor investment are his strong passed pawn and Black's offside knight.

| 18 | ... | ♗g7 |

After 18...f6? 19 ♗h6 Black's bishop remains cut off from the kingside. Activating the knight with 18...♘c7 or 18...♘b8 allows White to regain the pawn with a clear advantage after 19 ♕c4 ♗g7 20 ♕xc5.

| 19 | d6 | f6 (D) |
| 20 | d7! | |

After the solid 20 ♗f4 White has a promising position, but still nothing decisive after 20...♘b8!? (20...♖ad8 21 ♖e1! is worse for Black). Kasparov increases the tension with a

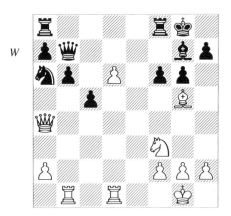

further sacrifice, and afterwards he freely admitted he was led more by intuition than pure calculation. Analysis proves him right – although Black could have played better at more than one point, the sacrifice is correct.

20 ... fxg5?

This is consistent, but very risky. Let's look at the less greedy alternatives:

1) 20...♔h8 gives White a choice between 21 ♕c4, when 21...♖ad8 transposes into line '2' (21...fxg5? is the game), and the less forcing, but interesting 21 ♗f4!?.

2) 20...♖ad8 forces White to act with 21 ♕c4+ (21 ♗f4? fails to 21...♖f7 22 ♕c4 ♖dxd7! 23 ♖xd7 ♕xd7 24 ♕xa6 ♕f5) 21...♔h8 22 ♘e5! *(D)* (otherwise ...♘b8 picks up the pawn), when Black has a choice:

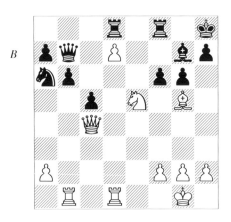

2a) After 22...fxe5?! 23 ♗xd8 ♖xd8 24 ♕e6! ♘c7 (24...♕b8 25 ♖b3 threatens ♖h3 with a mating attack and forces Black to play 25...♘c7 anyway) 25 ♕e7 ♕b8 26 ♖b3 Black's forces are limited to passive defence and White has more than one way to improve his position (♖f3-f7, ♕f7 and ♖h3, etc.)

2b) Safer is 22...fxg5! 23 ♘f7+ ♖xf7 24 ♕xf7 ♕c6! (24...♕b8? loses to 25 ♖e1) 25 ♖b3! (25 ♖e1 ♕xd7 26 ♕xd7 ♖xd7 27 ♖e8+ ♗f8 28 ♖xf8+ ♔g7, followed by ...♘b4, leaves Black with nothing to fear) 25...♕f6 26 ♕e8+ ♕f8 27 ♖e3 ♘c7 28 ♖de1. White will win one piece back and retain some winning chances in the endgame, but the game is far from over; e.g., 28...♗f6 (28...♔g8? 29 ♕xd8!) 29 ♕xf8+ ♖xf8 30 ♖e8 ♔g7 31 ♖c8.

3) 20...♘b4!? is also possible. 21 ♕b3+ ♔h8 22 ♘e5 (22 ♗f4!? retains the passed pawn and definitely deserves a closer look) 22...fxe5 23 d8♕ ♖axd8 24 ♖xd8 ♖xd8 25 ♗xd8 e4 (weaker is 25...♕d5 26 ♕xd5 ♘xd5 27 ♖d1) 26 ♖d1! (26 ♕e6 ♕d5 gets White nowhere) 26...♕c6!? (26...♘d3 27 ♕e6 gives White good winning prospects after 27...♗d4 28 ♗f6+ ♗xf6 29 ♕xf6+ ♕g7 30 ♕d8+ ♕g8 31 ♕xg8+ ♔xg8 32 f3!) 27 ♕f7 ♘d3 28 ♕xa7 b5. Black's active pieces and dangerous passed c-pawn give him real compensation for the exchange.

21 ♕c4+ ♔h8
22 ♘xg5 ♗f6

Forced. The threat was d8♕ and 22...♗d4? loses on the spot to 23 ♖xd4 cxd4 24 ♕xd4+ ♔g8 25 ♘e6.

23 ♘e6 *(D)*

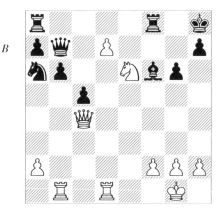

23 ... ♘c7

Again practically forced. After 23...♘b4 24 ♕f4 ♖f7 (24...♘d5 25 ♕d6 and 24...♘c6 25 ♘xf8 ♖xf8 26 d8♕! ♘xd8 27 ♖xd8 both lose immediately for Black) White has 25 ♘g5! (25 ♕xf6+ ♖xf6 26 d8♕+ is unconvincing due to

26...♖f8!) 25...♗xg5 (25...♖ff8 again allows 26 d8♕!) 26 ♕xf7 ♖d8 27 ♖b3 and Black is helpless against all the threats (f4, h4, ♖h3). 23...♖ad8 24 ♘xf8 ♖xf8 25 ♕f4 (or 25 ♖d6) 25...♔g7 26 ♖d6 is similar to the game, only Black's knight still doesn't help out from a6.

24 ♘xf8 ♖xf8
25 ♖d6!

White now wants more than the promising endgame after 25 ♕xc5 ♕xg2+ 26 ♔xg2 bxc5 27 ♖b7 ♘e6 28 ♖d6 ♘f4+ 29 ♔f1 ♗d8 30 ♖xa7.

25 ... ♗e7 (D)

This allows a tactical solution. However, one can't really call this move a mistake, as the alternative 25...♕b8 26 ♖bd1 ♕d8 27 ♖c6 ♗g7 28 h4 practically places Black in zugzwang. 25...♗d8 26 ♖e1 is similar. Black's queen remains offside even after 26...♕a6 27 ♕c3+ ♔g8 28 ♕c2 and White should gradually win by increasing his pressure against g6.

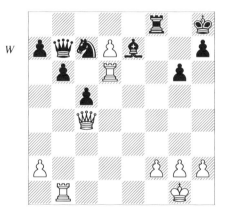

26 d8♕!

White sacrifices the d-pawn, his pride and joy, to exploit the temporary disharmony in Black's camp.

26 ... ♗xd8

26...♖xd8?! is hopeless: 27 ♖xd8+ ♗xd8 28 ♖d1! and Black loses a piece without any counterplay after 28...♕c8 29 ♕f7 ♗g5 30 ♖d7.

27 ♕c3+ ♔g8
28 ♖d7 ♗f6
29 ♕c4+ ♔h8
30 ♕f4 (D)

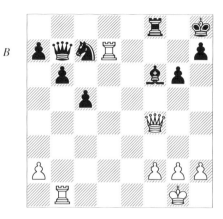

The clever queen manoeuvre nets White a piece.

30 ... ♕a6?

Black, exhausted after a long and demanding defence, commits suicide. After 30...♗g7 31 ♕xc7 ♕xc7 32 ♖xc7 ♗d4 33 ♖f1 a5 (33...a6 34 ♖c6 is no improvement, as 34...♖f6?! 35 ♖xf6 ♗xf6 36 ♖e1 costs Black a pawn) 34 a4 Black still has some practical chances, but White should win the endgame. Because of this line Black wants to get rid of White's a-pawn. Now 31 ♕xc7? ♕xa2 32 ♖xh7+ ♔g8 favours Black, but...

31 ♕h6 1-0

Mate is unavoidable.

Game 9
Garry Kasparov – Maia Chiburdanidze
Baku 1980
King's Indian Defence, Classical Line [E92]

Although Kasparov was making rapid progress and his Elo rating was nearing the 2600 mark, only the tournament victory in his home-town Baku formally confirmed his GM title. This game indicates he achieved his goal with consummate ease.

1	d4	♘f6
2	c4	g6
3	♘c3	♗g7

The Ladies World Champion shows considerable courage by playing one of Kasparov's own main openings – his theoretical prowess was already becoming his trademark. Even later in his career his opponents only relatively rarely dared to play the King's Indian against him.

4	e4	d6
5	♘f3	0-0
6	♗e2	e5
7	♗e3	

Together with the Sämisch Variation, this line still remains Kasparov's main choice against the King's Indian.

7 ... ♕e7 *(D)*

Later Kasparov had to defend this position in the 1990 title match against Karpov. He tried not only the text-move, but also just about every other possible option: 7...♘a6, 7...exd4 and 7...c6. For the most common reaction, 7...♘g4 8 ♗g5 f6, see Speelman-Kasparov, Madrid rpd 1988 (Game 52).

8 d5

8 dxe5 dxe5 9 ♘d5 ♕d8!? 10 ♗c5 ♘xe4 11 ♗e7 ♕d7 12 ♗xf8 ♔xf8 13 ♕c2 (13 ♕d3!? was tried later and is stronger) 13...♘c5 14 ♖d1 ♘c6! 15 0-0 ♘e6 16 ♘b6 axb6 17 ♖xd7 ♗xd7 was played in Karpov-Kasparov, New York/Lyons Wch (3) 1990. With only two minor pieces and a pawn for the queen, Black has reasonable compensation due to his solid centre and good piece-play and later was even close to winning. However, Kasparov never dared to repeat this bold concept later. Ten years earlier

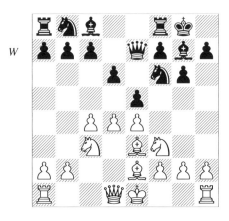

with opposite colours he adopts a different strategy and blocks the centre.

8	...	♘g4
9	♗g5	f6
10	♗h4	h5

Nowadays Black often prefers to do without this move and plays 10...♘h6 11 ♘d2 a5!?. The game will show that in certain favourable circumstances White can exploit the weakening of Black's kingside.

11 h3

Chasing the knight to a square it wants to go to anyway. Later White started to prefer the more flexible 11 ♘d2. After 11...c5 (11...a5!? is probably stronger) 12 dxc6 bxc6 13 b4 ♗e6 14 0-0 ♘d7 (14...♘h6 allows 15 f3) 15 ♘b3 White was somewhat better in Kasparov-Morrison, Graz U-26 Wcht 1981, where the misguided 15...♘xh2? 16 ♔xh2 g5 17 ♘a5 ♘b8 18 ♗g3 h4 19 ♗g4! ♗xg4 20 ♕xg4 hxg3+ 21 fxg3 gave White a strategically won position.

11	...	♘h6
12	♘d2	c5!?
13	♘f1	

White doesn't change the structure of the position and continues manoeuvring. 13 g4?! is premature, since after 13...hxg4 14 hxg4 ♘f7 followed by ...♗h6, Black activates his bishop, and White's kingside advance has only created targets for Black. If White by analogy with the previous note plays 13 dxc6 bxc6 14 b4 (after 14 f3 White's h3 remains just a wasted move), then 14...g5!? 15 ♗g3 h4 16 ♗h2 f5 gives Black good counterplay, as the h2-bishop is temporarily inactive.

13 ... ♘f7?

Black quickly wants to transfer the knight from the rim, but in this concrete position this basically sound endeavour is a serious positional mistake. Also 13...g5 14 ♗g3 h4 15 ♗h2 f5 16 ♘e3 is not ideal. Compared with the note above White is better, as the centre is closed and he can activate his bishop after f3 and ♗g1 without serious consequences. Better was the patient 13...♘a6 14 ♘e3 ♗d7 (14...♘c7!?) with complicated play; then the direct 15 g4 hxg4 16 ♘xg4 ♘xg4 17 ♗xg4 ♗h6 leads to unclear play.

14 g4! *(D)*

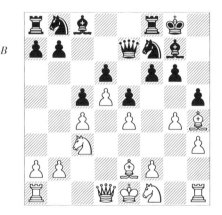

White immediately makes use of the changed situation to grab the initiative on the kingside.

14 ... hxg4

One may ask what kingside play White has after 14...g5 15 ♗g3 h4 16 ♗h2. Nevertheless the full blockade would play into White's hands, as he has a space advantage and can develop his queenside play without any disturbance on the opposite side of the board. Chiburdanidze understandably wants to avoid a position without any strategic prospects, but this gives White attacking chances.

15 ♗xg4!

This is the difference: without the knight on h6 White opens the g-file against Black's king. The direct threat is ♗xc8 and ♕g4.

15 ... g5?!

Black punches further holes into her already compromised kingside. 15...♘a6 16 ♖g1 and 15...♗xg4 16 ♕xg4 also allow White to force this advance; in the second case 16...g5 17 ♘e3 ♘h6 18 ♕h5 (Kasparov prefers the direct 18 ♘f5!? ♘xf5 19 exf5 gxh4 20 ♖g1 with a strong attack) 18...♕f7 (18...gxh4? loses immediately to 19 ♖g1) 19 ♕xf7+ ♖xf7 20 ♗g3 gives White a permanent strategic advantage. Therefore the best chance was 15...♘h6!? 16 ♗xc8 ♖xc8 17 ♖g1 ♔h7 with a passive, but still defensible position.

16 ♗xc8 ♖xc8
17 ♘e3!! *(D)*

An excellent positional sacrifice. Kasparov doesn't want to allow any possible complications after 17 ♗g3 f5!? 18 exf5 e4. Nor would he be content with 17 ♕g4!?, when 17...♖f8 transposes into the previous note.

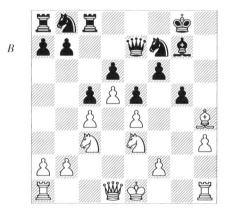

17 ... gxh4

Now Black will be reduced to a passive wait for the final blow. However, even after the less cooperative 17...♘h6 18 ♗g3 the extra knight moves favour White and the desperate liberating attempt 18...f5 19 exf5 e4 20 h4! leads to a hopeless position.

18 ♘f5 ♕d8

18...♕f8 19 ♕g4 ♘g5 20 ♘xh4 ♘a6 enables Black to activate her b8-knight, something she will be unable to do for the rest of the game. However, this is also insufficient: after 21 ♘f5 ♘c7 22 h4 ♘h7 (22...♘f7 23 h5 is similar, as 23...♔h8? loses outright to 24 h6 ♘xh6 25 ♕g6) White can simply regain the sacrificed piece with 23 h5 ♘g5 24 h6. Now 24...♔h8? 25

h7+ ♔f7 26 ♕h5# ends Black's suffering, while otherwise White retains a decisive positional advantage.

19	♕g4	♘g5
20	♘xh4!	

White has all the time in the world to take the impeding pawn, return with the knight and completely tie Black up in knots by tripling on the g-file. The rest of the game, although it lasts until the time-control, requires little comment.

20	...	♖c7
21	♘f5	a6

21...♘a6 22 h4 ♘h7 23 ♖g1 ♕f8 gives White the extra resource 24 ♘b5. The text-move prevents this, and Black also opens her 2nd rank for her rooks so as not to get overrun on the g-file.

22	h4	♘h7
23	♖g1	♕f8
24	♔e2	♖a7
25	a4	b6 (D)

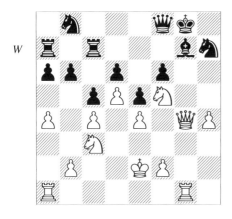

Black has been able to stave off the first wave of the attack, so White regroups.

26	♕h5	♔h8
27	♖g6	♖d7
28	♖ag1	♖ab7
29	♕g4	♖bc7
30	♖g2!	

30 h5 ♘g5 31 h6 ♗xh6 32 ♖xh6+ ♖h7 doesn't satisfy White. He first moves his king to safety to disarm any attempts connected with ...b5 and then transfers the c3-knight to the kingside.

30	...	♖b7
31	♔f1	♖a7
32	♔g1	♖f7
33	♘e2	♕c8

Otherwise ♘g3-h5 ends the game. After 33...♕g8 34 h5 ♘f8 35 ♕h4! the threat of h6 is decisive. We'll also see this motif in the game.

34 f4

Kasparov takes away the g5-square from Black's knight and renews the threat h5-h6. However, even the consistent 34 ♘eg3 wins readily enough, as 34...♘f8 loses to 35 ♕h5+ ♘h7 36 ♘xd6, followed by ♘xf7+ and ♘f5.

34	...	b5

34...exf4 35 ♘xf4 ♘f8 leads to mate after 36 ♖h6+ ♔g8 (36...♘h7 37 ♘g6+ ♔g8 38 ♘fe7+) 37 ♕h5.

35	axb5	axb5
36	cxb5	♖ab7
37	h5	♘f8 (D)

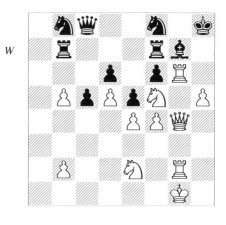

38 ♕h3

White naturally ignores material gains such as 38 ♘xd6 and goes for the quickest kill by threatening h6.

38	...	♘xg6

38...♕d8 39 ♖6g3! ♔h7 (39...♘h7 40 h6 ♗xh6 41 ♕xh6 ♕f8 42 ♕g6) 40 h6 ♗h8 41 ♖g7+ mates.

39	hxg6+	♔g8
40	gxf7+	

40 ♕h7+ is quicker.

40	...	♔f8

40...♖xf7 loses to 41 ♘h6+.

1-0

Black didn't wait for 41 ♖xg7.

Game 10
Garry Kasparov – Ralf Åkesson
World Junior Ch, Dortmund 1980
Queen's Indian Defence [E12]

In 1980 Kasparov gained his first world title by convincingly winning the World Junior Championship.

1	d4	♘f6
2	c4	e6
3	♘f3	b6
4	a3	

This system bears the name of 9th World Champion Petrosian and is quite typical of the Armenian's prophylactic style – by preventing ...♗b4 White wants to get a stronger grip on the centre with ♘c3, possibly followed by d5 and e4. Kasparov adopted it successfully in his first international tournament in Banja Luka in 1979 and it brought him a long string of impressive victories in the first half of the 1980s.

4	...	♗b7

On a rare occasion when Kasparov sat on the other side of the board, he preferred the Benoni-like 4...c5. The game Gelfand-Kasparov, Novgorod 1997 in Volume 2 shows he managed to enrich even Black's resources in the Petrosian.

5	♘c3	d5
6	cxd5	♘xd5 *(D)*

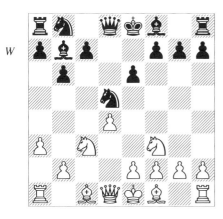

7	e3	

Kasparov also played the more topical alternative 7 ♕c2 with considerable success (see Kasparov-Gheorghiu, Moscow IZ 1982 and Kasparov-Karpov, Moscow Wch (32) 1984/5, Games 20 and 26 respectively).

7	...	♗e7

At the time this game was played, this was Black's usual reaction. However, against Kasparov in the first game of their Candidates semi-final in 1983, Korchnoi successfully employed 7...g6!? and this more ambitious move quickly became popular. The position after 8 ♗b5+ c6 9 ♗d3 ♗g7 10 e4 ♘xc3 11 bxc3 c5 has a Grünfeld Defence character, with Black exerting more pressure against White's pawn-centre than in our game.

8	♗b5+	c6
9	♗d3	♘d7

After 9...0-0 Black has to reckon with 10 ♕c2!?, which forces a kingside concession. From d7 the knight can later more easily take part in the defence of the king; on the other hand White's centre will be under less pressure than after 9...♘xc3 10 bxc3 c5 11 0-0 ♘c6. Also with the knight on c6 White doesn't have chances to play on the queenside with a4-a5.

10	e4	♘xc3
11	bxc3	c5
12	0-0	cxd4?!

More flexible is 12...0-0 13 ♕e2 ♖c8, postponing the central exchange until White develops his c1-bishop. If it goes to b2 anyway, Black can consider maintaining the central tension.

13	cxd4	0-0
14	♕e2	♖c8
15	♗b2 *(D)*	

Now this move doesn't require a second thought – once the centre opens up White's bishops eyeing the kingside will become a major attacking force.

15	...	♕c7
16	♕e3	

White prevents the sortie ...♕f4, but the developing 16 ♖ad1 ♕f4 17 ♖fe1, with d5 in the

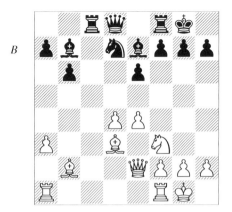

air, was a valid alternative. The queen on f4 will hardly stop White's attacking plans single-handed and may become exposed itself.

16 ... ♘f6

This allows White to activate his knight. After 16...♕b8 he may consider turning his attention to the queenside with 17 a4!?, while neutral moves like 16...♖fd8 17 ♖ad1 (17 h4!?) don't change the evaluation of the position: White is somewhat better.

17 ♘e5 b5!?

An attempt to get rid of the centralized knight with 17...♘d7 allows White to avoid exchanges by 18 ♖ac1 (18 f4 ♘xe5 19 fxe5 ♕d7 is unconvincing; the central pawns lose their flexibility) 18...♕d6 19 ♘c4 ♕b8 20 d5!? with a dangerous initiative, as Black's kingside is insufficiently defended.

18 f4 ♕b6
19 ♔h1!

A useful prophylactic move. Immediate activity by 19 f5 leads only to simplification and approximate equality after 19...♗d6 20 ♖ae1 exf5!? 21 ♖xf5 ♗xe5 22 dxe5 ♕xe3+ 23 ♖xe3 ♘d7 24 ♗xb5 ♘c5.

19 ... b4
20 axb4

After 20 ♘c4 ♕c7, neither 21 axb4 ♗xe4 nor 21 e5 ♘d5 22 ♕h3 g6 gets White anywhere.

20 ... ♗xb4
21 ♖ab1!? *(D)*

Directed against a possible ...♗c3. Although Black can't exchange the bishops immediately, it's difficult to point out any other useful move. After the immediate 21 f5 exf5! (21...♗c3? 22 ♗xc3 ♖xc3 23 ♖fb1 costs Black at least a pawn and 21...♗d6?! 22 ♖ab1 ♗xe5 23 ♗a1! also spells big trouble) 22 ♖xf5 ♗c3 23 ♗xc3 ♖xc3 White's central pawns are very vulnerable.

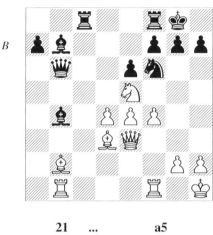

21 ... a5
22 ♕e2

A multi-purpose move, which unpins the d-pawn and also avoids exchanges after 22 f5 ♗a6 23 fxe6 fxe6, which would help the defence.

22 ... ♕a7

Black intends to attack White's centre, but the drawback of this move is that his queen will be sidelined. Kasparov shows Black could have insisted on exchanging the bishops with the consistent 22...♖a8!?. After 23 f5 ♗a6 24 fxe6 fxe6 the direct 25 ♖xf6 gxf6 (similar is 25...♖xf6 26 ♘d7 ♗xd3 27 ♘xf6+ gxf6 28 ♕xd3) 26 ♘d7 ♕d6 27 ♘xf8 ♗xd3 28 ♕xd3 ♖xf8 gives White perhaps an infinitesimal edge due to his safer king, but in a very simplified position. Better is 25 ♘c4!?; with more pieces on the board White can claim some advantage.

23 f5 ♕a8 *(D)*
24 d5?!

This hasty decision costs White at least a part of his admittedly rather volatile advantage. More promising was 24 fxe6 fxe6 and now:

1) The energetic 25 d5 exd5 26 ♘g4 ♘xg4 (26...♘xe4? 27 ♘h6+ ♔h8 28 ♘f7+ ♔g8 29 ♗xe4! dxe4 30 ♕g4 ♖xf7 31 ♖xf7 ♔xf7 32 ♕d7+ ♗e7 33 ♖f1+ and White's attack breaks through) 27 ♕xg4 ♖c7 (27...♖xf1+? 28 ♖xf1 ♗c3 loses a piece and the game after 29 ♗xc3 ♖xc3 30 ♕e6+ ♔h8 31 ♕e7 ♖c8 32 ♖f7 dxe4 33 ♗f1!) 28 e5, followed by e6, opens the

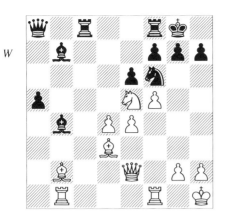

diagonals for the bishops. However, although White's attack is dangerous, Black still retains defensive resources.

2) If White wants to keep all his trumps, he has 25 ♖f4 ♗d6 26 ♖a1 (or 26 ♗a1) with an edge.

3) Another way to retain the initiative is 25 ♘c4!?. The threat is ♘b6, so e4 is taboo. After 25...♖ce8 (25...♖cd8 26 d5! exd5 27 ♘b6, followed by ♗xf6, and 25...♕a7 26 e5 ♘d5 27 ♕h5 are both dangerous for Black) 26 e5 (26 ♖f4 is also interesting; then 26...g5?!, provoking the sacrifice 27 ♖xf6! ♖xf6 28 d5, leads to trouble) 26...♘e4 (26...♘d5? 27 ♕h5 g6 28 ♗xg6 hxg6 29 ♕xg6+ ♔h8 30 ♕h6+ ♔g8 31 ♖f3! mates) 27 ♔g1 White is better. The e4-knight is vulnerable.

24	...	exd5
25	♘g4	♘xg4

25...♖xe4? 26 ♗xe4 dxe4 27 ♘h6+ ♔h8 28 ♗xg7+! ♔xg7 29 f6+ ♔xh6 (or 29...♔h8 30 ♕g4) 30 ♖f5 mates.

26	♕xg4	f6 (D)

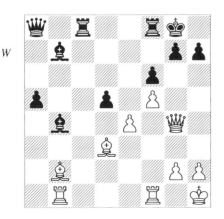

27 ♗xf6?!

Kasparov played this move after 45 minutes of thought. This intuitive sacrifice is typical for his maximalist attitude and creates a complex tactical landscape where the utmost accuracy is required. Objectively, however, after this move it's White who is fighting for a draw. The 'natural' 27 e5 ♗c3 28 e6 gives White a protected passed pawn and compensation, but no real advantage after 28...♗a6 or 28...d4.

27	...	♖xf6
28	e5	♖h6?

Åkesson stumbles right away. He should have played 28...♖f7 (protecting g7) 29 f6. White threatens e6, and Black must choose between:

1) 29...♗c3 allows White to bail out immediately with a perpetual: 30 ♗xh7+ (Black is better after 30 e6 ♖xf6 31 e7 ♗a6 32 ♖xf6 ♗xf6 33 ♕e6+ ♔h8 34 ♗xa6 ♖e8; 30 ♗f5 ♖c6!? is unclear) 30...♔xh7 31 ♕h3+ ♔g8 32 fxg7 ♖xg7 33 ♕e6+.

2) More ambitious is 29...♖cf8! 30 ♖f3!. White threatens ♖h3, so Black must avoid 30...♔h8? 31 ♖h3 gxf6 32 ♕g6, mating, and after 30...d4 31 ♖g3!, White wins by ♕h5 or e6. Therefore Black must play 30...♗c8! 31 ♕g5 (D). Now:

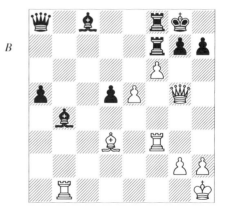

2a) 31...♗e6 32 ♖g3 g6 33 ♕h6 ♔h8 34 ♗xg6 ♗d2!? (34...♖c7? loses to 35 f7!) 35 ♕xd2 (35 ♕h5 ♖c7 is unconvincing for White) 35...hxg6 36 ♖xg6 ♖h7 37 ♖g7. White has sufficient compensation for the piece, but no more than that.

2b) 31...♔h8 32 ♖xb4! (32 fxg7+ ♖xg7 33 ♖xf8+ ♗xf8 34 ♕d8 ♗b7 35 ♕xa8 ♗xa8 36 ♖b8 ♖a7 37 ♖xf8+ ♔g7 gives Black a large endgame advantage) 32...gxf6! 33 ♕h6 axb4 34 ♗xh7 ♗g4! and now the simplest way to a draw is 35 ♖xf6 (35 ♗b1+ ♔g8 36 exf6 ♖c8 37 ♖f1!? ♗e6 38 ♖e1! ♕a6 39 ♕g6+ ♔f8 40 ♕h6+ is also good enough) 35...♗h5 (35...♖g7? 36 ♖xf8+ ♕xf8 37 ♗c4+) 36 ♖xf7 ♖xf7 37 ♗g6+ ♔g8 38 ♗xf7+ ♔xf7 (38...♔xf7 39 ♕f6+! ♔g8 40 ♕g5+) 39 ♕g5+ ♔f8 40 ♕h6+ ♔e7 41 ♕f6+ with a perpetual.

2c) The best is 31...♕a7 32 ♖bf1 g6! (avoiding 32...♗e6 33 fxg7 ♖xg7 34 ♖xf8+ ♗xf8 35 ♖xf8+! ♔xf8 36 ♕d8+ with a perpetual) 33 ♕h6 ♔h8! (33...♗e6 is worse, since after 34 ♖g3 ♔h8 35 ♗xg6, 35...♖g8? 36 ♗xf7 ♕xf7 loses to 37 ♖g7!) 34 ♗xg6 ♖g8!. Control over the light squares is more important than the exchange. Now after 35 ♗xf7 (35 ♖g3 is speculative) 35...♕xf7 36 ♖c1 ♗e6 Black consolidates his position and has winning chances.

29　f6　　　　♖c7 (D)

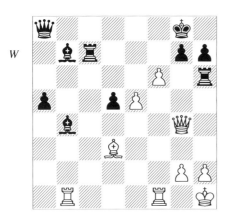

30　e6

Straightforward and logical. Kasparov rightly refrains from 30 ♖bc1?! ♕d8 31 ♕e6+ ♖f7 32 ♗b5 gxf6! 33 ♗e8 ♕e7 34 ♗xf7+ ♕xf7 35 ♕xf7+ ♔xf7 36 ♖c7+ ♔e6; e.g., 37 ♖xf6+? ♖xf6 38 exf6 d4! 39 ♖xb7 d3 and Black's pawns suddenly turn the tables completely.

30　...　　　　♕d8!

This is best. Black returns a whole rook, but avoids losing prettily after 30...♕f8 31 f7+ ♔h8 32 ♖xb4! axb4 33 ♕xb4! or 30...♔h8 31 ♕g3! ♕c8 32 ♖bc1! ♗d6 33 fxg7+ ♔g8 34 ♕xd6.

Also hopeless is 30...♕b8 31 ♕g3! (after 31 h3, 31....♗c8? loses to 32 ♖xb4!, but 31...♔h8!? 32 ♖xb4 ♖xf6 is less clear-cut) 31...♗d6 (the threat was e7) 32 ♕xd6 ♖xf6 33 ♗b5! and the passed pawn will promote shortly.

31　e7　　　　♖xe7
32　fxe7　　　♕xe7
33　♖bc1 (D)

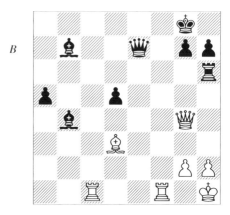

Despite material equality, Black is in trouble, as his forces are uncoordinated and he has back-rank problems.

33　...　　　　♕d8?

This loses by force. Although 33...♕e6 exchanges queens, it costs Black more material after 34 ♕xe6+ ♖xe6 35 ♖c7 ♖e7 36 ♖fc1 (36 ♗xh7+!? ♔xh7 37 ♖xe7 ♗xe7 38 ♖f7 is also very close to winning) 36...♔f7 (the only move; otherwise White wins a piece) 37 ♖xe7+ ♗xe7 38 ♖c7 ♗a8 39 ♗xh7, followed by ♖a7 with a technically won position. Even after 33...♖d6 34 ♕f4 g6 35 ♗b5! White threatens ♖c7 and his attack after the forced 35...g5 36 ♕g3 is very dangerous.

34　♕f5　　　　♕b8

Kasparov was looking forward to the pretty line 34....♗d6 35 ♕f7+ ♔h8 36 h3 (36 ♕xb7 ♖xh2+ 37 ♔g1 ♖h1+! only complicates matters and prolongs the game) 36...♗c8 37 ♖c7! and White forces mate. 34...♔h8 fails to 35 ♖c7 ♖xh2+ 36 ♔g1! and White wins a piece.

35　♕f7+　　　♔h8
36　♖c7　　　　1-0

Game 11
Garry Kasparov – Oleg Romanishin
Quadrangular Team Tournament, Moscow 1981
Grünfeld Defence, Exchange Variation [D85]

1	d4	♘f6
2	c4	g6
3	♘c3	d5
4	cxd5	♘xd5
5	e4	♘xc3
6	bxc3	♗g7
7	♘f3	c5

For 7...b6?! see Game 8.

8	♗e3	♕a5

The move-order is important. 8...♘c6?! 9 ♖c1 cxd4 (9...♕a5 10 d5!) 10 cxd4 ♕a5+ 11 ♗d2! is inferior for Black. 8...0-0 9 ♖c1 ♕a5 10 ♕d2 cxd4 11 cxd4 ♕xd2+ 12 ♘xd2 is playable, but somewhat passive and rarely appears in current practice. The text-move remains by far the most popular option.

9	♕d2	♘c6 *(D)*

Later Kasparov himself played the ambitious but risky 9...♗g4. However, this move practically disappeared from the scene after his match with Kramnik in London 2000.

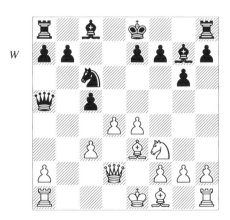

W

10	♖c1	cxd4
11	cxd4	♕xd2+
12	♔xd2	0-0

Black has forced White to give up his castling rights, which in turn makes it more difficult for him to keep his pawn-centre intact.

13	d5 *(D)*	

At the time our game was played this was a novelty. After 13 ♗b5 f5! Black gets excellent counterplay, mainly due to White's exposed king.

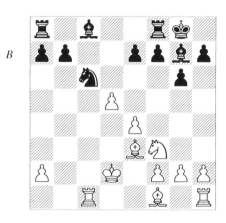

B

13	...	♖d8
14	♔e1!	

The point of Kasparov's idea. Meeting the threat of ...e6 with 14 ♔c2 ♘a5 is weaker, as the king is less safe on the queenside, and we'll also see White needs the c-file for his rook. Although White's set-up with the undeveloped h1-rook seems disharmonious, he in fact needs only two moves (♗d3, ♔e2) to coordinate his forces. Meanwhile Black's knight faces a tough decision.

14	...	♘a5!

After long thought Romanishin plays what even now is considered to be the main move. Surprisingly the weakest option is the centralizing 14...♘e5 15 ♘xe5 ♗xe5 16 f4, followed by ♔f2 – White's pawn-centre gives him space and a permanent advantage. Matters are less clear after 14...♘b4!? 15 ♗d2 ♘a6; Black prepares ...e6 and just as in the game he doesn't mind if White doubles his a-pawns, because the active bishop-pair gives him sufficient counterplay.

15	♗g5 *(D)*	

With the breaks ...e6 or ...f5 looming, White's centre might become a liability; e.g., 15 ♗d2 b6 16 ♗b4 runs into 16...e6! 17 ♗e7 ♖d7 18 d6 a6 and White has problems generating sufficient play to meet ...♗b7 and ...♘c6, Cyborowski-Krasenkow, Polish Ch (Warsaw) 2002. More to the point is 15 ♗d3!? f5 (tempting but weaker is 15...e6 16 ♗g5 f6 17 ♗d2 b6 18 ♗xa5 bxa5 19 ♗c4; 15...♗d7 16 ♔e2 e6 17 ♖c5! b6 18 ♖c7 exd5 19 exd5 is also better for White) 16 ♖c7 with complicated play.

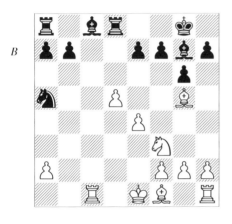

15 ... ♗f6

Times change and 20 years later Kasparov had to defend against his own idea, refined mainly by the efforts of Kramnik. He preferred a better move, known as early as 1981: 15...♗d7! 16 ♗d3 (16 ♗xe7 ♖e8 17 d6 ♘c6 18 ♗b5 ♗f8 gets White nowhere) 16...♖dc8 17 ♔e2 e6 18 ♖xc8+ (more ambitious is 18 ♗e3, but even here after 18...exd5 19 exd5 b5!? 20 ♘d2 a6 recent practice indicates Black is OK) 18...♖xc8 19 ♖c1 ♖xc1 20 ♗xc1 exd5 21 exd5 b5 22 ♗f4 ♘c4 23 ♗xc4 bxc4 24 ♗e5 ♗f8! 25 ♘d2 ♗b5 26 ♘e4 f5 27 ♘c3 ♗d7 28 ♔e3 ♗c5+ 29 ♗d4 ♗b4 30 ♗e5 and a draw was agreed in Kramnik-Kasparov, Astana 2001. However, we'll see it's very difficult to claim a concrete advantage even after the relatively weaker text-move.

16 ♗d2 b6

White has won some time to consolidate his position, as ...f5 is stopped. Due to the bishop being misplaced on f6, Black must also think twice about playing ...e6, which could run into the e5 advance.

17 ♖c7! (D)

With normal moves White can't use the respite he has been granted; e.g., 17 ♗b5 ♗g4 18 ♔e2 e6 practically forces simplification with approximate equality after 19 ♗xa5 bxa5 20 ♗c4 ♖ab8.

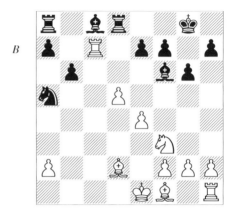

17 ... ♗g4

Romanishin strives for active counterplay. Less enterprising ideas such as 17...♗d7 18 ♗d3 or 17...♖d7 18 ♖xd7 ♗xd7 19 ♗a6 ♗c8 20 ♗b5!? a6 21 ♗d3 don't threaten White's centre, and give him a pleasant edge.

18 ♗a6 e6!?

The logical follow-up of Black's plan to blast open the centre while the h1-rook still remains passive. 18...♗xf3?! 19 gxf3 ♗e5 20 ♖c2 ♖ab8 21 f4 gives White an ideal position, but a more plausible way to avoid the following complications was 18...♗c8 19 ♗d3 (19 ♗b5 ♗g4 20 ♔e2 ♗e5 is similar) 19...♗g4!? 20 ♔e2 ♗e5 21 ♖c2 (21 ♖xe7!? ♗d6 22 ♗g5 is interesting, but far from clear) 21...♘b7 and White's advantage is only minimal.

19 ♘g5!

From now on White's four active pieces cooperate ideally, creating dangerous tactical threats.

19 ... ♗e5!

The only way to meet the threats of ♘xf7 and h3. After 19...exd5?! 20 ♘xf7 ♖d7 (20...♗c8 21 ♗b5! is no improvement) 21 ♘h6+ ♔g7 22 ♖c8! White wins at least an exchange.

20 ♖xf7! exd5

The best reaction. After 20...h6 21 ♘f3 ♗xf3 (weaker are 21...♔g7? 22 ♖xg7+ ♔xg7 23 ♘e5 and 21...♗b2 22 dxe6) 22 ♖xf3 exd5 23 exd5 ♖xd5 White has 24 ♖d3! with a pleasant endgame advantage thanks to the active bishops (instead, after 24 ♗xh6 ♖e8 White's lag in development gives Black enough counterplay: 25 ♖e3 b5! or 25 ♗e2 ♗d4).

21 f4!

Both 21 ♖xh7 dxe4 22 ♖h4 ♗c8 and 21 f3 ♗c8! 22 ♗xc8 ♖axc8 23 ♖xa7 dxe4 give Black too much play against White's king.

21 ... ♗g7! *(D)*

Romanishin also makes the best choice. 21...h6? 22 fxe5 hxg5 23 ♖f6 gives White a raging attack, while 21...♗d4 is also inferior: 22 ♖xh7 ♘c4 (22...dxe4? now fails to 23 ♗xa5 bxa5 24 ♗c4+) 23 e5. Kasparov gives the sample line 23...♖e8 (with the idea ...♗xe5) 24 h3! ♗xe5 (24...♗f5 25 ♖c7!? and after 25...♘xe5 26 fxe5 ♗xe5 27 ♖c6 the discovered check achieves nothing) 25 fxe5 ♖xe5+ 26 ♔f2 ♖f8+ 27 ♔g3 ♘xd2 28 hxg4! and White wins, as the h1-rook joins the fray just in time.

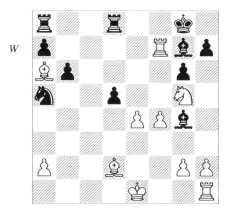

22 f5!

The most consistent move. Kasparov recommends instead 22 h3, but Black seems OK after 22...♗c8!? (22...h6 23 hxg4 hxg5 24 ♖c7 gxf4 25 exd5 ♗e5 26 ♖e7 ♖e8 27 ♖xe8+ ♖xe8 28 ♔f2 ♖d8 29 ♗xa5 bxa5 30 ♖e1 and White retains some winning chances) 23 ♗xc8 ♖dxc8, with ...h6 in the air.

22 ... dxe4?

Black buckles under the tension and commits a tactical mistake. He should have played 22...gxf5! 23 h3! (weaker is 23 exf5 ♘c4, threatening ...♖e8+) 23...♗h5 24 ♖xg7+ (24 ♖xf5 dxe4 can only be dangerous for the white king) 24...♔xg7 25 ♘e6+ ♔f6 26 ♘xd8 (26 exf5 ♖e8 27 g4 is best met by 27...♖xc6+! 28 fxe6 ♗g6, when Black wins a pawn, although a draw is the most probable result) 26...♖xd8 27 exf5 ♘c4 28 g4 ♖e8+ (or 28...♗f7) 29 ♔d1 ♗f7 with approximate equality. White's kingside pawns are not sufficiently supported by his pieces.

23 ♗xa5 bxa5

23...e3 is refuted by 24 ♖xg7+! ♔xg7 25 ♗c3+ ♔h6 26 ♘f7+ ♔h5 27 ♘xd8 ♖xd8 28 ♔f1! ♖d1+ 29 ♗e1, and White will gradually convert his extra piece.

24 ♗c4 ♗c3+

Black loses immediately after 24...♖ac8 25 ♖c7+ or 24...♖d4 25 ♖xa7+, while 24...♖d1+ 25 ♔f2 e3+ 26 ♔g3! (26 ♔xe3 ♖e8+ is less convincing) 26...♗e5+ 27 ♔xg4 ♖d4+ transposes into the game.

25 ♔f2 *(D)*

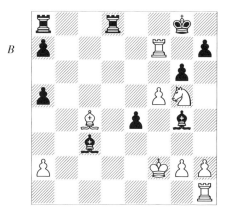

25 ... e3+
26 ♔g3

26 ♔xe3? ♗d2+.

26 ... ♗e5+
27 ♔xg4!

27 ♔h4? only leads to a perpetual after 27...♖d4 28 ♖xa7+ ♖xc4 29 ♖xa8+ ♔g7 30 ♖a7+ ♔g8!.

27 ... ♖d4+
28 ♔h3 ♖xc4
29 f6 *(D)*
29 ... ♗xf6

White had to exchange his proud bishop, but the threat of ♖g7+ nets a piece, as 29...♖c7 30 ♖xc7 ♗xc7 31 f7+ ♔h8 32 ♘c6 ♗d6 33 ♖e1 fully paralyses Black's position.

30 ♖xf6 ♖e8
31 ♖e1

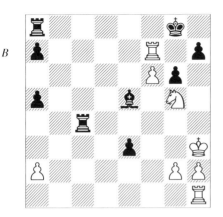

White finally develops his rook and is completely winning. However, in Romanishin's time-trouble Kasparov wants to end the game beautifully and comes very close to squandering a half-point.

31	...	e2
32	♔g3	

32 ♖e6 ♖xe6 33 ♘xe6 ♖c2 34 a4 is a simpler win.

32	...	♖a4
33	♔f2	♖xa2
34	♘e6	a4
35	♖b1?	

Playing for an illusory mate. 35 ♘d4 picks up the e2-pawn and still wins readily enough.

35 ... a3

Now the position should be drawn.

36 ♖b7 e1♕+

Black had a choice: 36...♖b2 37 ♖g7+ ♔h8 38 ♖e7 ♖bb8 39 ♖xa7 ♖a8 40 ♖xa8 ♖xa8 41 ♘d4 a2 42 ♘b3 ♖b8 43 ♖a6! and 36...♖a1 37 ♔xe2 a2 38 ♖g7+ ♔h8 39 ♖xa7 ♖g1 40 ♖f1!

♖xe6+ 41 ♔f2 both force White to liquidate the a-pawn to hold the game.

37	♔xe1	♖xg2
38	♖g7+	♔h8
39	♖gf7	h5?!

39...h6 is better. White must then give a perpetual.

40 ♔f1 (D)

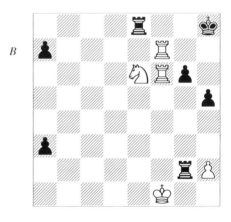

40 ... ♖xh2?

The fateful 40th move! With the flag on his clock hanging Romanishin inadvertently turns White's mating intentions into cruel reality. The correct 40...a2 41 ♖xa7 ♖xh2! (41...♖b2? loses to 42 ♘g5!, as White threatens mate in three and 42...♖e7 43 ♖f8+ ♔g7 44 ♘e6+ doesn't help) 42 ♖xg6 a1♕+ 43 ♖xa1 ♖h1+ would still have saved the game.

41 ♖xg6! ♖xe6

41...a2 42 ♖h6+ ♔g8 43 ♖g7#.

42	♖xe6	♔g8
43	♖xa7	1-0

Game 12
Alexander Beliavsky – Garry Kasparov
Moscow 1981
King's Indian Defence, Sämisch Variation [E83]

1	d4	♘f6
2	c4	g6
3	♘c3	♗g7
4	e4	d6
5	f3	0-0
6	♗e3	♘c6
7	♕d2	a6
8	♘ge2 *(D)*	

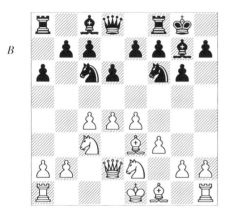

8 ... ♖e8?!

Kasparov readily admits this move is weaker than the usual continuation 8...♖b8. However, after Beliavsky inexplicably spent 40 minutes on his last two moves, an attempt to leave the beaten theoretical track has its practical logic. Apart from this the text-move also has objective merits. Now after ♗h6 Black can avoid the exchange of his dark-squared bishop. In Game 2 (see move 14!) we also saw that ...♖e8 can create hidden tactical opportunities for Black.

9 ♘c1

Basically White has two possible approaches. Beliavsky chooses the positional one. 9 ♖b1 followed by 10 b4 is similar in spirit and also promising. However, the sharper attacking continuations 9 0-0-0 and especially 9 h4!? are probably even more dangerous for Black.

9 ... e5

10 d5

Allowing ...exd4 would justify Black's 8th move.

10 ... ♘d4 *(D)*

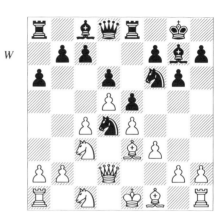

11 ♘1e2

White clearly has to get rid of the centralized knight as soon as possible. As the knight left e2 just two moves ago, 11 ♘b3 seems a more logical option: 11...c5 (after 11...♘xb3 12 axb3 White intends b4, and 12...c5 runs into 13 b4! cxb4 14 ♘a4 when Black, contrary to the 8...♖b8 line, doesn't have ...b5 and is clearly worse) 12 dxc6 bxc6 (12...♘xc6 13 ♖d1 is advantageous for White; he can finish his development much faster than in the game) 13 ♘xd4 exd4 14 ♗xd4 d5 (the only consistent move) 15 cxd5 cxd5 16 ♗xf6 ♗xf6 17 ♘xd5 ♖b8 18 ♖b1. White is just two moves away from castling and Black cannot claim sufficient compensation for the sacrificed material.

11 ... c5
12 dxc6 ♘xc6!?

Now Black isn't immediately forced to go for murky sacrifices. Although after Beliavsky's strong reply he decides to invest material anyway, his compensation will be more concrete than in the note above.

13 ♘d5!

By creating the threat of ♗b6, White wants to induce Black to close the position, so that he can finish his development and enjoy his spatial advantage without disturbance. Less demanding is 13 ♖d1 ♗e6 14 ♘d5 (or 14 b3 b5!?) 14...♘d7 with good counterplay.

13 ... b5!

Kasparov was never one to shy away from a sacrifice in the interests of activity. Here it took him over an hour to convince himself that more sedate moves lead to a passive position without prospects; e.g., 13...♘xd5 14 cxd5 ♘e7 15 ♘c3.

14 ♗b6

Beliavsky accepts the challenge only to sink into deep thought after three forced moves. An attempt to stabilize the position with 14 ♘ec3!? deserved serious attention. After the natural 14...♘d4 15 cxb5 axb5 Black threatens ...♘b3, but 16 ♗xb5! ♘xd5 (or 16...♘b3 17 ♗b6) 17 ♗xd4! exd4 18 ♘xd5 gives White an advantage.

14	...	♕d7
15	♘c7	♖b8
16	♘xe8	♕xe8 *(D)*

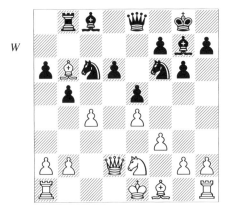

W

17 ♗e3?!

Although at first Black's compensation seems rather vague, White's task is in fact quite difficult. First of all it's not easy to evaluate and choose from the various options. The sole aim of Beliavsky's unambitious move is to evacuate the king from e1 as quickly as possible, but this half-measure doesn't curb Black's activity and can't refute Kasparov's concept. Therefore once White spurned 14 ♘ec3!?, he should have shown more consistency (and greed!):

1) 17 ♗c7 ♖b7 18 ♗xd6 bxc4 and the threat of ...♖d7 forces White to lose another tempo and gives Black the initiative after 19 ♗c5 ♗e6.

2) 17 c5 is well met by 17...♖b7! and now after 18 ♕xd6 ♖d7!? (interesting but speculative is 18...♗f8 19 ♕d2 ♗e6 20 ♘c3 ♖d7 21 ♕f2 b4 22 ♘a4) 19 ♕xc6 ♗b7 White will formally have enough material for the queen, but his lag in development gives Black excellent counterchances.

3) Kasparov himself argued for 17 cxb5 and this does seem best. After 17...axb5 (17...♖xb6 18 bxc6 d5 19 exd5 e4 20 ♖c1 is insufficient) 18 ♗e3 d5 19 exd5 ♘d4 20 ♘c3!? b4 21 ♘e4 ♘xd5 22 ♗d3 White is on the verge of castling and Black must still prove he has sufficient play for the exchange.

17	...	bxc4
18	♘c3 *(D)*	

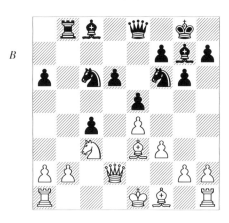

B

18	...	♗e6
19	♗e2	

Another move in a similar spirit to 17 ♗e3?! hands the initiative to Black. The most principled option is 19 ♘d5 (19 b3!? cxb3 20 axb3 ♘d4 21 ♖xa6 d5!? is also unclear), when the best chance to retain the initiative is the further sacrifice 19...♘xd5!? 20 exd5 e4 21 dxe6 ♕xe6 22 ♖c1 d5, when Black's excellent piece coordination compensates for White's extra rook.

19	...	♘d4!
20	0-0	

Weak is 20 ♗xd4? exd4 21 ♕xd4 ♘d5 and Black wins material, since 22 ♕d2? fails to 22...♖xb2.

20	...	d5
21	exd5	

The threat was ...♘xe2+ and ...d4. 21 ♗xd4? exd4 22 ♕xd4 (22 ♘xd5 ♘xd5 23 exd5 ♗xd5 is no better) 22...♘xe4 23 ♕e3 ♘d6 is out of the question; once the d-pawn starts rolling, White's position collapses.

21 ... ♘xd5
22 ♘xd5 ♗xd5 *(D)*

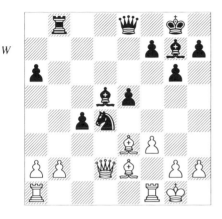

The tactical phase is over and Black's minimal material disadvantage is more than compensated by the activity of his forces. Especially strong is the centralized knight, which can't be dislodged by normal means. The following play revolves around this piece and White's possible liberating advance f4, with Black's edge still small and rather volatile.

23 ♖f2

As yet White can't undermine Black's central bastions. Both 23 b3? c3 24 ♕e1 e4! and 23 f4? ♘xe2+ 24 ♕xe2 exf4 are weak.

23 ... h5
24 ♖c1

White could have tried playing 24 f4, but after 24...♘xe2+ (a more demanding but possibly promising alternative is 24...♘f5!? 25 ♗a7 ♖d8) 25 ♖xe2 ♗e4 26 fxe5 ♗d3 27 ♗d4 Black has the *zwischenzug* 27...♖d8! with a slight advantage.

24 ... ♕e6
25 ♗f1 h4

The complications of the opening have left both players short of time, and mutual errors mar the final part of the game. Here or on the following move the flexible retreat 25...♘f5 would have kept White under pressure.

26 ♖e1 ♕c6 *(D)*
27 ♗h6?

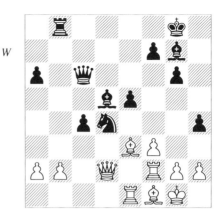

Now it's White's turn to go wrong. He misses an excellent chance to free his position by returning the extra material with 27 f4! ♘f5 28 fxe5 ♘xe3 29 ♖xe3 (29 ♕xe3 ♗f8 30 ♕f4 ♗c5 31 ♖ee2 is also playable). Now after 29...♗h6 White has a choice – he can continue the struggle in an equal position with 30 ♕d4 ♗xe3 31 ♕xe3 or immediately force a draw by perpetual check with 30 e6! fxe6 (30...♕c5 31 exf7+ ♗xf7 32 ♖e8+ is also equal, as 32...♗xe8 33 ♕xh6 ♖xb2? fails to 34 ♗xc4+ with mate) 31 ♕c2 ♗xe3 32 ♕xg6+.

27 ... ♗h8
28 f4?

Beliavsky finally plays this move, but only at the most unsuitable moment when it ruins his position beyond repair. 28 h3 is necessary, preventing ...h3; then the final outcome still remains open.

28 ... e4 *(D)*

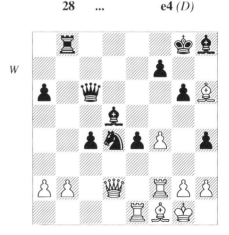

Now Black retains his d4-knight, while the h6-bishop remains sidelined.

| | 29 | ♖d1 | ♗e6 |

29...e3! 30 ♕xe3 ♘f5 31 ♕d2 ♗d4 is even more forceful.

| | 30 | f5 | |

Desperation, but 30 ♗g5 ♘f5 (30...♕a4 31 ♖e1 is less convincing) 31 ♕a5 ♔h7 wouldn't have saved the game either.

| | 30 | ... | ♘xf5 |

The rest of the game took place in sharp time-trouble and requires little comment.

| | 31 | ♕f4 | ♖e8 |

Avoiding the simple trap 31...♖xb2? 32 ♖d8+ ♔h7 33 ♖xh8+.

| | 32 | ♖fd2 | |

White would have lost the bishop even after the more resilient 32 ♗g5 e3 33 ♖e2 f6 34 ♗xh4 g5.

	32	...	♕c5+
	33	♔h1	♗e5
	34	♕g5	♔h7 (D)

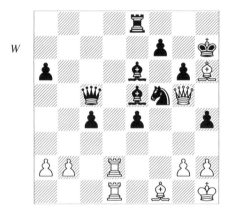

| | 35 | ♖d8 | |

Both players were down to their last seconds; otherwise White would have probably resigned instead.

| | 35 | ... | ♖xd8 |
| | 36 | ♖xd8 | ♕f2 |

36...♘xh6 is simpler.

| | 37 | ♖d1 | ♘xh6 |

37...♗d4 or 37...e3 is stronger.

| | 38 | ♕xe5 | e3 |
| | 39 | ♕c3 | |

Black also wins after 39 h3 ♗xh3! followed by ...♗g4.

| | 39 | ... | h3 |
| | 40 | ♕e1 | ♘g4 (D) |

40...e2 wins immediately, but with the time-control reached, even the text-move is more than enough to force resignation.

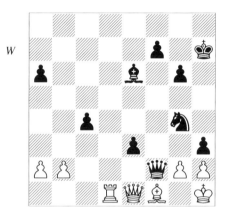

0-1

After 41 ♖c1 Black mates his paralysed opponent with 41...♗d5! 42 ♕xf2 exf2 43 ♖d1 ♗e4 and ...♘e3.

Game 13
Anatoly Vaiser – Garry Kasparov
USSR Team Ch, Moscow 1981
King's Indian Defence, Four Pawns Attack [E77]

1	d4	♘f6
2	c4	g6
3	♘c3	♗g7
4	e4	d6
5	f4	0-0
6	♘f3	

Vaiser has remained faithful to the Four Pawns Attack for more than 30 years and is probably the world's greatest expert on this sharp line.

6	...	c5
7	d5	e6
8	♗e2	exd5
9	e5?! *(D)*	

Objectively this move doesn't promise White an advantage, but one has to know the psychological background of the game to appreciate its merits. Kasparov mentions that three years earlier, at the USSR Championship qualification tournament in Daugavpils, he played an informal blitz match with Vaiser and in those games Vaiser always chose 9 cxd5, achieving excellent positions from the opening. Vaiser undoubtedly realized that Kasparov would be fully prepared for 9 cxd5.

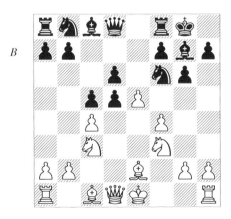

9	...	♘g4

Although later improvements of Black's play have been found, this move, at the time of our game considered an adequate reply, is surprisingly risky. Vaiser knew that 9...dxe5 10 fxe5 ♘g4 11 ♗g5 f6 12 exf6 ♗xf6 13 ♕xd5+ ♕xd5 14 ♘xd5 ♗xg5 15 ♘xg5 ♘c6 leads to rather sterile equality, but he rightly judged this was something Kasparov wouldn't strive for. Currently the whole line has a bad reputation due to 9...♘e4! 10 cxd5 (10 ♘xd5 ♘c6 11 ♗d3 f5 is also very good for Black) 10...♘xc3 11 bxc3 ♘d7 12 e6 fxe6 13 dxe6 ♘b6! and Black wins material for little or no compensation.

10	cxd5	

Weak is 10 h3? d4 11 ♘e4 ♘xe5! 12 fxe5 dxe5 and as the c5-pawn is taboo, Black's pawn-centre will sweep White off the board.

10	...	dxe5
11	h3	e4
12	hxg4	

For Kasparov this natural move was a novelty, although Vaiser had played it four years earlier against Shashin. After 12 ♘xe4 both 12...♘f6 and maybe even 12...♖e8!? give Black a good position.

12	...	exf3 *(D)*

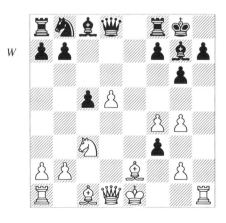

13	gxf3	

The aforementioned game went 13 ♗xf3 ♘d7 14 ♔f2 with unclear play. The text-move is stronger, as White's king is less exposed and this in turn increases his own attacking chances. Now Kasparov had his first long think. Superficially Black's position looks promising due to the strong g7-bishop and White's ragged pawns and unsafe king, but a closer look reveals a less appealing picture. Black must hurry up and effectively deploy his queenside pieces, as White, left to his own devices, will play f5, ♗h6 and whip up a vicious attack along the semi-open h-file. Kasparov's following actions are directed against this straightforward plan.

13 ... ♖e8

The radical 13...f5?! stops White's main idea, but seriously weakens the a2-g8 diagonal. After 14 ♗e3 ♖e8 15 ♕d2 White is better.

14 f5! *(D)*

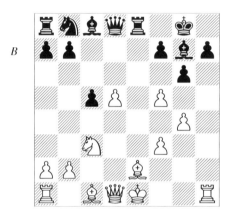

14 ... ♕b6?

This is a mistake, as the b2-pawn is insignificant and Black doesn't address his main problem – development. Subsequent practice saw Black test three alternatives:

1) 14...♘d7 15 ♗h6 ♗xh6!? (15...♗d4 16 ♕d2 followed by 0-0-0 was pointed out by Kasparov as unsatisfactory for Black) 16 ♖xh6 ♘e5 17 ♔f2 gxf5 18 ♕c2 ♕g5 and now Ravisekhar's recommendation 19 ♖h5!? ♕f4 20 ♖g1 seems to give White an advantage; e.g., 20...c4 (20...♘xg4+ 21 ♖xg4+ fxg4 22 ♕xh7+ ♔f8 23 ♕h8+ ♔e7 24 ♖e5+ ♗e6 25 ♕g7 is clearly better for White) 21 gxf5+ ♔h8 22 ♘d1! stops ...♘d3+ and threatens f6.

2) 14...b6 toys with the idea ...♗xc3+ and ...♗a6, but after 15 fxg6 (15 ♘e4?! gxf5 16 gxf5 ♗xf5 17 ♗g5 ♕d7 18 ♘f6+ ♗xf6 19 ♗xf6 ♕d6 favours Black; this line shows he can afford to exchange his strong dark-squared bishop and thus gain tempi for the defence) 15...fxg6 16 ♔f1 ♗a6 17 ♘e4 White is slightly better, J.Fries Nielsen-Mortensen, Esbjerg 1985.

3) Black's best way to implement the idea from line '2' is 14...gxf5 15 ♗h6 ♗xc3+! (15...♗xh6 16 ♖xh6 ♕g5 runs into 17 ♕d2! and despite the exchange of queens, White's attack is overwhelming, as Black's queenside is still completely asleep), keeping the crucial h-file closed by White's own bishop. After 16 bxc3 fxg4 17 ♕d3 ♕f6 18 ♖h5 ♖e5 19 ♖xe5 ♕xe5 (Belin-Kalinin, USSR 1987) 20 0-0-0 ♗f5 21 ♕d2 ♘d7 22 fxg4 ♗g6 the position is unclear.

15 ♗h6!?

Consistent and strong, but also quite committal. Vaiser points out the less incisive 15 ♕c2 c4 16 ♗g5 ♘a6 17 0-0-0 is also better for White.

15 ... ♕xb2

Black hardly has any alternative. 15...♗xh6 16 ♖xh6 ♕xb2 17 ♘e4 is probably even more dangerous.

16 ♗xg7 ♔xg7 *(D)*

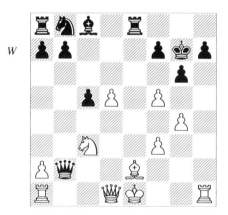

The critical position. White must decide how to continue his kingside assault.

17 f6+?

17 ♘e4?, contrary to the note above, allows 17...gxf5 18 gxf5 ♗xf5 and the bishop effectively joins the defence. However, the text-move also isn't ideal, as in his haste to decide the game White limits his options to the h-file. The seemingly slow 17 ♖c1! is correct. White threatens ♖c2 followed by ♕d2, and Black's counterplay with only two active pieces lacks punch; e.g., 17...gxf5 18 ♖c2 ♕b4 (18...♕b6

19 d6 ♖e6 20 ♘d5 ♕xd6 21 gxf5 with a strong attack for White) 19 ♕c1 f4 20 ♔f1. White has unpinned both his minor pieces, creating dangerous threats.

17 ... ♔g8!

Kasparov doesn't panic and correctly feels the turning tide allows this 'impossible' move. He is in no hurry to liquidate the advanced pawn – this task is reserved for the still inactive b8-knight. After 17...♔xf6?! 18 ♘e4+ ♖xe4 (18...♔g7 19 ♖b1 ♕e5 20 ♕d2 and the attack decides; e.g., 20...♔g8 21 ♕h6 ♕g7 22 ♕xh7+! ♕xh7 23 ♘f6+) 19 fxe4 White is better.

18 ♕c1!

Vaiser relied on this seemingly paradoxical move, considering the exchange of queens forced. Black easily parries the attempt 18 ♘e4 ♘d7! (18...♗xg4 19 ♖b1 ♕xa2!? 20 ♖xb7 ♘d7 21 fxg4 ♖xe4 22 ♖xd7 ♕a3! is also interesting, but after 23 0-0!? Black only has a perpetual check) 19 ♖b1 ♕e5 (19...♕xa2!? with the idea 20 ♕c1 ♖xe4 deserves attention) 20 ♕d2 ♘xf6 21 ♕h6 ♘xd5! (21...b6 22 g5 ♘xe4 23 ♕xh7+ ♔f8 24 ♕h8+ leads to an endgame in which White has reasonable drawing prospects) 22 ♕xh7+ ♔f8 and White's attack peters out.

18 ... ♕b4! *(D)*

Once again Black shows admirable *sangfroid* and keeps his counterattacking chances alive. 18...♕xc1+? 19 ♖xc1 leads to a bad endgame for Black, as the powerful f6-pawn remains alive and cramps Black's position. Also after 18...♖xe2+ 19 ♘xe2 ♕xf6 20 ♕c3 White is somewhat better.

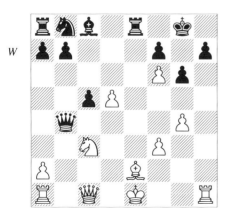

19 ♔f1?

White is still optimistic about his chances, but this mistake puts him on the verge of defeat. It was time to adapt to the changed situation and try to bail out; there were two possible alternatives:

1) 19 ♕d2 ♘d7 (19...♕d4!?) 20 ♖b1 ♕d4 21 ♕xd4 (21 ♘e4 allows 21...♖xe4 22 fxe4 ♕xe4 23 0-0 ♘xf6) 21...cxd4 22 ♘e4 d3! 23 ♗xd3 ♘xf6 24 ♔f2 leads to an approximately equal endgame, as 24...♘xd5? runs into 25 ♖b5!.

2) 19 ♖b1 ♕d4 20 ♘e4 ♘d7 21 ♕h6 ♘xf6 22 ♖d1 (luring the queen to an undefended square; 22 g5? ♘xe4 23 ♕xh7+ ♔f8 24 ♕h8+ fails to 24...♔e7!) 22...♕e5 23 g5 ♘xe4 24 ♕xh7+ ♔f8 25 ♕h8+ and again the endgame should be tenable for White despite the minus pawn.

19 ... ♘d7
20 ♗b5

This was Vaiser's idea: White once again renews the mating threat of ♕h6 in connection with ♗xd7. However, Black's reply once and for all stops these ambitions. Thus 20 g5 is a better fighting chance.

20 ... ♕d4! *(D)*

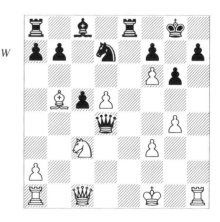

Black threatens ...♖e3; e.g., 21 ♖h3 ♖e3 22 ♘e2 ♕xf6.

21 ♔g2

The direct 21 ♕h6? loses quickly: 21...♘xf6 22 ♗xe8 ♕xc3 23 ♔g2 ♕b2+ 24 ♔g3 ♕e5+.

21 ... ♖e3!

Again Kasparov prefers activity. The materialistic 21...♕xf6 22 ♕h6 ♕g7 23 ♘e4! is considerably less convincing.

22 ♘e2

Other moves are even worse: 22 ♘d1 ♖xf3! or 22 ♖e1 ♖xe1 23 ♕xe1 ♕xf6 leads to a lost position.

22	...	♕e5
23	♔f2	♖xe2+
24	♗xe2	♘xf6 *(D)*

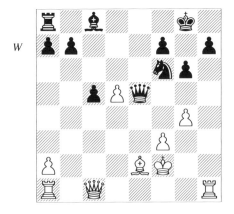

The dust has settled and Black has emerged clearly on top. He has two pawns for the exchange and White's d5-pawn is bound to fall shortly. Moreover, his king is much safer than White's.

25 ♕xc5

The threat was ...♗xg4 and ...♘e4+, and 25 g5?! ♘h5! gives Black a winning attack.

25	...	♗xg4
26	♕e3	

White decides to simplify into an endgame, shedding another pawn in the process. 26 ♖ae1 ♖e8! is even more dangerous, especially in a mutual time-scramble.

26	...	♕xe3+
27	♔xe3	♘xd5+
28	♔f2	♗e6
29	♖ab1	

Even after 29 ♗c4!? ♖c8 30 ♗b3 (30 ♖ac1? ♘f4!) 30...♔g7 31 ♖hc1 ♖xc1 32 ♖xc1 ♔f6 patience and technique should bring Black victory.

29	...	b6
30	♖bc1	♘f4

31 a3?!

The final mistake. Black has pawn-majorities on both flanks and the bishop is an ideal minor piece both to support the pawns and also to fight against them. Thus White's last chance to struggle on was 31 ♗c4 with the idea 31...♖c8 32 ♗a6! (32 ♗xe6 ♘d3+ 33 ♔e3 ♖xc1 34 ♖xc1 ♘xc1 35 ♗d5 ♘xa2 and four pawns against the bishop win easily) 32...♖xc1 33 ♖xc1 ♗xa2 34 ♖c7.

31	...	♘xe2
32	♔xe2	b5
33	♖c7	a5
34	♖b1	♗c4+
35	♔f2	a4! *(D)*

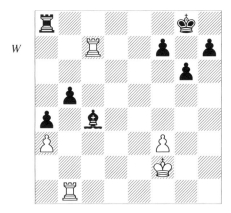

An instructive moment. Black stops a4 and all his pawns are unassailable. The activation of the rook will lead to a technically won position.

36	♖e1	♖d8
37	♖e3	♖d2+
38	♔g3	♔g7
39	f4	♖b2
40	♖c5	h5
41	♔h4	

White sealed this move, but resigned without resuming play.

0-1

Black has more than one way to win. A clean solution is 41...♗e6, followed by ...b4 and a combined advance of his passed pawns.

Game 14
Garry Kasparov – John Fedorowicz
World Student Olympiad, Graz 1981
Queen's Indian Defence [E12]

1	d4	♘f6
2	c4	e6
3	♘f3	b6
4	a3	c5

A sharp and double-edged reply, which leads to positions characteristic for the Modern Benoni. A safer choice is the more usual and popular 4...♗b7 5 ♘c3, featured in five games in this book, starting with Game 10.

5 d5   ♗a6

The Modern Benoni is in itself a difficult opening and the insertion of a3 and ...b6 only slows down Black's queenside counterplay in most of the main lines. Therefore he strives for a position where the extra move can be useful.

6 ♕c2   exd5

In the same event Kasparov faced the extravagant 6...♕e7?! and reacted with the energetic 7 ♗g5 exd5 8 ♘c3! ♗xc4 9 e4! h6 10 ♗xf6 ♕xf6 11 exd5 ♗xf1 12 ♔xf1 and White had a lead in development and excellent attacking chances, Kasparov-Van der Wiel, Graz tt 1981.

7 cxd5   g6 (D)

7...d6 8 ♘c3 ♘bd7 is less accurate because after 9 ♗f4! Black can't develop his f8-bishop to the long diagonal, Kasparov-Browne, Banja Luka 1979.

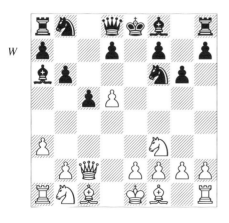

8 ♘c3   ♗g7

9	g3	0-0
10	♗g2	d6
11	0-0	♖e8

11...♘bd7 is perhaps more flexible; sometimes Black finds it useful to leave the e8-square free for his knight. An illustrative line is 12 ♗f4 ♕e7 13 ♖fe1 h6 and now 14 ♕a4?! ♗b7 15 ♘b5 ♘e8 is fine for Black, but circumspect prophylaxis with 14 h3 followed by e4 is more accurate and gives White an edge.

12 ♖e1 (D)

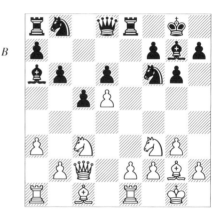

12 ...   ♕c7

This rather passive move has fallen into oblivion since. One of the reasons is that it's still difficult to say what is the best place for Black's queen. Currently the main options are 12...b5 and 12...♘bd7, but in recent practice the whole line isn't doing too well for Black.

13 ♗f4

Kasparov wants to exploit the position of the black queen on c7 to hamper Black's normal development. However, consistent central expansion with 13 e4!? is more promising: 13...♘bd7 14 ♗f4 ♘h5 15 ♗e3 ♖ac8 (15...c4 16 ♕a4 ♕b7 17 ♘b5!? ♗xb5 18 ♕xb5 c3 19 ♗d4 is also pleasant for White) 16 g4 ♘hf6 17 h3 b5 18 ♗f4 and White is better, A.Petrosian-O.Foisor, Baile Herculane 1984. His central pressure is more concrete than Black's vague queenside ambitions.

13 ... ♘h5

Necessary, as the immediate 13...♘bd7? runs into 14 ♕a4.

14 ♗d2 ♘d7 *(D)*

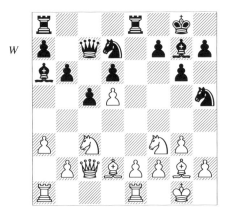

15 ♕a4!?

Both sides have finished their development and will start implementing their respective strategic plans. In Black's case it's simpler: his next moves will be ...c4 and ...♘c5, possibly followed by ...b5, ...♕b6, etc. White can't really stop the gradual queenside expansion, which will give Black good counterplay. After 15 a4 c4 16 ♗e3, even 16...♖xe3!? 17 fxe3 ♖e8 deserves serious attention, while 15 e4 c4 16 ♗e3 leads to a position from the sideline of the note to White's 13th move, only with Black to move, and 16...♘c5 leads to unclear play. After long thought, Kasparov chose a provocative plan – he abandons his queenside and concentrates his forces on the opposite flank, starting with his strongest piece. His concept is very risky, as initially Black's queenside play will develop very smoothly. On the other hand, to increase his pressure Black will in turn have to desert his kingside, thus giving White attacking chances. In the end Kasparov reaps rewards for his far-sightedness, but only after a complicated fight.

15 ... ♗b7
16 ♕h4 a6
17 ♖ac1?!

White continues the plan indicated in the previous note. However, 17 a4 is more circumspect, and gives White chances for an edge after 17...♘hf6 (17...c4 18 ♘d4 ♘hf6 19 ♘c6 ♘e5 20 ♗g5! ♘fg4 21 ♘xe5 ♘xe5 22 ♗f6 is similar) 18 e4 c4 19 ♗e3 ♘c5 20 ♗d4.

17 ... b5
18 b4

White limits Black's activity, but also weakens the c4-square.

18 ... ♕d8

The queen on h4 makes Fedorowicz nervous and he decides to chase it away. This move is not an error, but more direct was 18...♘b6!? 19 g4 ♘f6 20 e4 ♘c4 21 ♗g5 ♘d7 and Black's queenside play seems more potent than White's attacking chances.

19 ♗g5

19 ♘e4 ♘df6 gets White nowhere.

19 ... f6

Although this move weakens the e6-square and the kingside, it's the most consistent continuation. After 19...♗f6?! 20 ♗xf6, 20...♕xf6? fails to 21 ♘e4! and 20...♘hxf6 21 e4 allows White to consolidate his central bastions and start concentrating his forces against Black's vulnerable king.

20 ♗d2 *(D)*

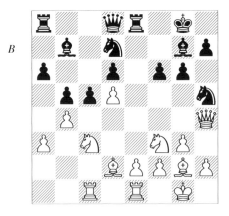

20 ... f5
21 ♗g5 ♕b6

This abandons the kingside, which only emphasizes the weaknesses created by the advance of the f-pawn. However, 20...f5 also has its pluses, namely the control of the e4-square. Thus after the more prudent 21...♗f6! the line from the previous note is not possible any more and the position remains balanced; e.g., 22 e4 cxb4 23 axb4 ♖c8.

22 e4! *(D)*
22 ... cxb4?

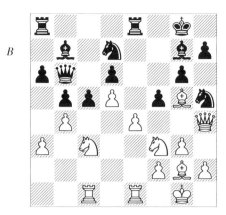

Only this is a serious error. Black hastens to open the c-file, but opening the g1-a7 diagonal for White will prove to be more potent factor in the following tactical phase. After 22...fxe4 23 ♘d2 (23 ♘xe4 ♗xd5 gets White nowhere, and 23 ♖xe4 ♘hf6 is playable for Black) 23...♘hf6 24 ♗h3!? White holds the initiative, but Black has counterchances.

    23   axb4   ♖ac8

Here 23...fxe4 runs into 24 ♗e3! ♕d8 25 ♘xe4 and White is better. The text-move leads to a tense critical position. White's knight is *en prise* and his centre is crumbling, so he has to act.

    24   ♗e3?

This hesitant move should have cost White his advantage. Luckily for Kasparov, he gets a chance to demonstrate the right continuation two moves later.

    24   ...   ♕d8
    25   ♗g5 *(D)*

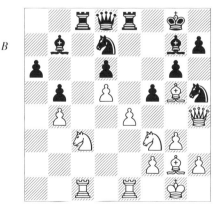

    25   ...   ♕b6?

Fedorowicz is obviously satisfied with a repetition, but Kasparov now took his time to penetrate to the heart of the matter. 25...♗f6! is necessary; this position was mentioned in the note to Black's 21st move as roughly balanced.

    26   exf5! *(D)*

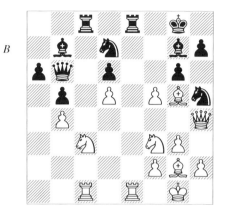

The culmination of White's long-term plan, initiated by the aggressive queen manoeuvre 11 moves ago. The main motif of Kasparov's combination is the distance of Black's major pieces from the kingside and their inability to return in time to the defence, or create effective counter-threats. This enables White to ignore the hanging piece and concentrate on his attack.

    26   ...   ♖xe1+
    27   ♖xe1   ♗xc3

27...♖xc3 keeps the c-file open for Black's rook, but weakens the back rank. After 28 ♖e8+ (28 ♗d8 is less incisive, as after 28...♕a7 29 ♖e8+ ♘f8 30 f6 Black has the defence 30...♖c2 31 ♘d4 ♖c1+ 32 ♗f1 ♘xf6 33 ♗xf6 ♗xd5! 34 ♖e7 ♖c7) the tactics favour White. Especially beautiful is the line 28...♘f8 (28...♗f8 29 fxg6 hxg6 30 ♕g4 creates numerous threats such as ♕xd7, ♕e6+ or ♗d2, overloading Black's defences; e.g., 30...♘g7 31 ♗d8! ♕a7 32 ♕xd7 ♘xe8 33 ♘g5) 29 f6 ♖c2 (29...♗xd5 30 fxg7 ♘xg7 runs into 31 ♗h6! ♘xe8 32 ♕e7, winning) 30 ♘d4 ♖c4 (30...♘xf6 is now insufficient due to the simple 31 ♗xf6 ♖c1+ 32 ♗f1 ♗xd5 33 ♗xg7) 31 ♘e6!! with a mating attack.

    28   ♖e7   ♖c4

Not only Black's king, but also his queen is under attack. If the d7-knight moves, 29 ♗e3 wins back material with a decisive advantage.

The line 28...♗f6 29 ♖xd7 ♖c1+ (29...♖c2 30 g4 doesn't help) 30 ♗xc1 (30 ♗f1!?) 30...♗xh4 31 ♗e3 shows this even more clearly. White retains a strong attack even after 28...♗xd5!? 29 fxg6 hxg6 30 ♖xd7 ♕c6 31 ♕g4 ♕c4 32 ♗f4!?.

29 ♕h3! *(D)*

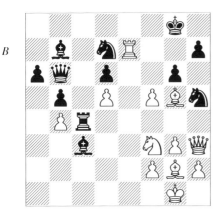

Here the queen is only seemingly passive, as it eyes the e6-square.

29 ... ♗c8?

This loses by force. After 29...♘df6, 30 ♗e3 regains the piece, but much more incisive is 30 fxg6! with lines similar to those in the game: White mates after 30...♗xd5 31 gxh7+ ♔h8 32 ♘h4! or 30...hxg6 31 ♕e6+ ♔h8 32 ♕f7. The only way to continue the game and put up some resistance was 29...♘f8 30 ♗e3 ♕d8 31 ♖xb7 ♖xb4, although White retains a large advantage after 32 fxg6 or 32 ♗f1!?.

30 fxg6 ♘df6

30...hxg6 31 ♕e6+ ♔h8 32 ♖e8+ mates, and just as hopeless is 30...♘f8 31 gxh7+ ♔h8 32 ♕xh5.

31 ♗xf6 ♘xf6

31...♗xf6 32 ♕xh5.

32 gxh7+ *(D)*

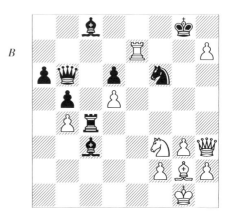

Kasparov's attack has crashed through.

32 ... ♔f8

After 32...♔h8 both 33 ♕h6 ♕xf2+ 34 ♔h1 and 33 ♘h4! force mate.

33 h8♕+ ♔xe7
34 ♕g7 1-0

Game 15
Garry Kasparov – Ulf Andersson
Tilburg 1981
Queen's Indian Defence [E12]

1	d4	♘f6
2	c4	e6
3	♘f3	b6
4	a3	♗b7
5	♘c3	♘e4

Especially in the opening, latent control of central squares is usually preferable to their direct occupation. Therefore a more effective way of preventing d5 and e4 is 5...d5, as in Games 10, 20, 24 and 26.

| 6 | ♘xe4 | ♗xe4 |
| 7 | ♘d2 *(D)* | |

The most ambitious continuation: White strives for a broad pawn-centre. 7 e3 or 7 ♗f4 promises only a small edge at best.

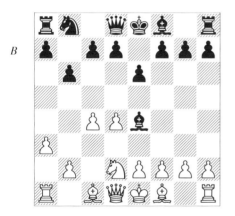

7 ... ♗g6?!

At the time of our game this was a novelty, but not a very successful one. Although time and again people return to Andersson's move, voluntarily leaving the long diagonal doesn't make a good impression. 7...♗b7 is more natural. Now after 8 e4 ♕f6 (the passive 8...d6 9 ♗d3 gives White a space advantage and a pleasant edge) 9 d5 ♗c5 10 ♘f3 ♕g6 White's best is the enterprising 11 b4!? ♕xe4+ 12 ♗e2 ♗e7 13 0-0 with a promising initiative for the sacrificed material. In the game he achieves this for free.

8 g3!

Although later White was also successful with 8 e4 ♘c6 9 d5 ♘d4 10 ♗d3, allowing Black's knight to occupy the protected central outpost on d4 seems to be an unnecessary concession. Kasparov's move is more solid and logical: White immediately wants to control the freshly deserted h1-a8 diagonal with his own bishop.

8 ... ♘c6 *(D)*

Played in a similar extravagant spirit as the previous move; placing a knight in front of the c-pawn is somewhat unusual in closed games. However, after 8...c5 9 d5, followed by e4, Black's g6-bishop remains passive and White is clearly better. Recent attempts to rehabilitate the line were connected with 8...♗e7, but the energetic 9 ♗g2 d5 10 e4! favours White. Now 10...♘c6? doesn't work since after 11 cxd5 the d4-pawn is taboo, while 10...c6 11 exd5 cxd5 12 cxd5 exd5 13 ♕a4+ shows how vulnerable Black's queenside is due to the absence of the g6-bishop from its usual place. Black is practically forced to give up a pawn for insufficient compensation after 13...♕d7 14 ♕xd7+ ♘xd7 15 ♗xd5. Finally, taking on c4 or e4 gives White more space and central control.

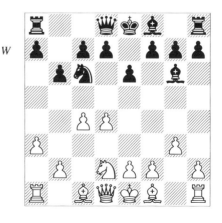

9 e3 a6?!

9...e5 10 d5 ♘b8 11 h4! h5 12 e4 a5 13 b3 ♘a6 14 ♗h3 ♘c5 15 ♕c2 ♗e7 16 ♗b2 d6 17 0-0 ♗f6 18 ♖ab1 ♘d7 19 b4 gave White a clear advantage in Psakhis-Gurgenidze, USSR Ch (Riga) 1985. The idea behind Black's move is to prepare ...d5 without having to fear a pin on the a4-e8 diagonal (9...d5? loses on the spot: 10 ♕a4 ♕d7 11 cxd5 ♕xd5 12 ♖g1). However, it is too passive. 9...a5 10 b3 ♗e7 is somewhat better, although even here 11 ♗b2 or 11 h4!? is good for White.

10 b4! *(D)*

Kasparov is his usual energetic self. 10 b3 d5 11 ♗b2 ♗e7 12 ♖c1 ♕d7 also leaves White better, but the text-move is more ambitious.

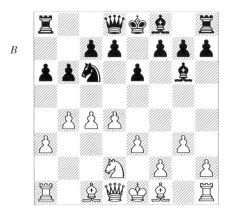

10 ... b5

White's 10th move not only increased his space advantage, but had additional and more concrete intentions. If Black plays as in the above note 10...d5 11 ♗b2 ♗e7 12 ♖c1 ♕d7, then after 13 ♗g2 the threat of ♕b3 forces further positional concessions.

11 cxb5

11 ♗b2 is also strong. The threats of cxb5 and d5 more or less force 11...bxc4 12 ♗xc4 d5 13 ♗e2 with a permanent positional advantage for White.

11 ... axb5
12 ♗b2

Weak is 12 ♗xb5? ♘xb4.

12 ... ♘a7

Now if Black manages to play ...d5 and finish the development of his kingside, he will be quite OK. White's advantage is dynamic, and not permanent, so he must act fast.

13 h4! h6?

It was not easy to foresee at this moment, but this seemingly solid move is a serious and probably decisive mistake. Black should have ventured 13...h5!?. Although the pawn is exposed on the light square, the position after 14 ♗e2 d5 remains closed and it's difficult to exploit this. Therefore Kasparov probably would have continued as in the game: 14 d5! exd5 15 ♗g2 c6 16 0-0 f6 17 ♖e1 (17 e4 dxe4 18 ♘xe4 d5 is less convincing) 17...♗e7. Now the important g4-square is inaccessible for White's queen and although he retains pressure and the initiative with 18 e4 dxe4 19 ♘xe4 0-0 20 ♘c5!, Black can still fight. In the game it will be far worse.

14 d5!

Maybe Andersson reckoned only with 14 e4?! d5!. The pawn sacrifice opens the long diagonal and Black won't get any respite until the end of the game.

14 ... exd5
15 ♗g2 c6
16 0-0 *(D)*

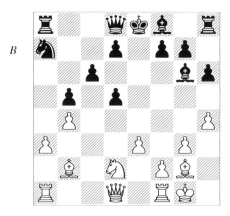

Suddenly White not only has a large lead in development, but also intends to open the position with e4.

16 ... f6

Black at least wants to develop his f8-bishop. The only way to prevent the aforementioned central thrust was 16...f5, but this creates dark-square holes all over Black's position. After 17 ♘f3 ♕e7 (17...d6 18 ♘d4 ♕d7 19 a4! is similar) 18 ♘e5 ♕e6 19 a4! White breaks through on the queenside while his opponent's kingside is still fast asleep.

17 ♖e1!?

Kasparov is patient. After 17 e4 dxe4 18 ♗xe4, 18...♗f7 avoids the exchange of the important light-squared bishop. Although White's attack is still very dangerous after 19 ♖e1 ♗e7 20 ♕g4 0-0 21 ♕f5 g6 22 ♕f4, at least Black has managed to castle.

17 ... ♗e7

Now 17...♗f7 18 e4 dxe4? 19 ♘xe4 loses immediately for Black, but in view of what happened in the game, 17...♔f7!? is somewhat more resilient.

18 ♕g4

By this point Andersson must definitely have been regretting 13...h6?. The following series of moves is forced.

18	...	♔f7
19	h5	♗h7
20	e4	dxe4
21	♗xe4	♗xe4
22	♘xe4	♘c8

Black would like to castle by hand, but after both 22...♖f8 23 ♖ad1 d5 24 ♘xf6! and 22...♖e8 23 ♕g6+ ♔f8 24 g4!, followed by ♘g3-f5 or g5, he loses on the spot. Also 22...d5 23 ♘c5! ♗xc5 24 ♕e6+ ♔f8 25 bxc5 is hopeless: Black can't untangle his forces and White can calmly transfer the a1-rook over to the kingside.

23 ♖ad1 ♖a7 (D)

23...d5 24 ♘c5 (24 ♘xf6 is probably also good, but more complex) is similar to the above note.

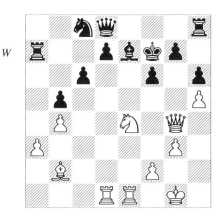

W

24 ♘xf6!!

White's army is fully mobilized and well coordinated, while Black's rooks are still unconnected, he has glaring light-square weaknesses and his king is vulnerable. In such a situation a tactical solution is the logical outcome.

24 ... gxf6

The pretty point of White's idea is 24...♗xf6 25 ♕g6+ ♔f8 26 ♗xf6 gxf6 27 ♖e6!, winning.

25 ♕g6+ ♔f8

26 ♗c1!

Kasparov plays for mate, but even the endgame after 26 ♖xe7 ♕xe7 27 ♗xf6 ♕h7 28 ♗xh8 ♕xg6 (28...♕xh8 loses to 29 ♖e1 ♘e7 30 ♕d6) 29 hxg6 is hopeless for Black; e.g., 29...♘e7 30 ♗d4 and ♗c5.

26 ... d5

26...♕e8 27 ♗xh6+ ♖xh6 28 ♕xh6+ ♔f7 (28...♔g8 also loses: 29 ♖e4 f5 30 ♕g5+!) doesn't help. After 29 ♕h7+ ♔f8 30 h6 ♕f7 31 ♕f5 ♘d6 32 ♕f4 ♘e8 the double attack 33 ♕e3! hits both rook and bishop and wins.

27 ♖d4!

This wins by force. 27 ♗xh6+?! ♖xh6 28 ♕xh6+ ♔g8! is unconvincing.

27	...	♘d6
28	♖g4	♘f7 (D)

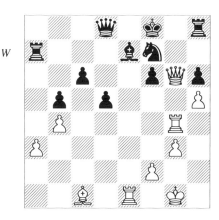

W

29 ♗xh6+! ♔e8

29...♘xh6 loses both the rook and the knight: 30 ♕g7+.

30 ♗g7 1-0

After 30...♖g8 (30...f5 31 ♖f4 doesn't help) 31 h6 the passed pawn promotes.

Game 16
Garry Kasparov – Artur Yusupov
USSR Ch, Frunze 1981
Bogo-Indian Defence [E11]

1	d4	♘f6
2	c4	e6
3	♘f3	♗b4+
4	♗d2	a5

For 4...♕e7 see Kasparov-Petrosian, Bugojno 1982 (Game 18).

5 g3 0-0

Taimanov and especially Smyslov made 5...d5 popular in the 1980s. The more modern approach is different: after 5...d6 followed by ...♘bd7 and ...e5 Black sets up his central pawns on the dark squares.

6	♗g2	b6
7	0-0	♗a6 *(D)*

After the seemingly more natural 7....♗b7 8 ♗g5 ♗e7 9 ♕c2 White has more chances to gain an advantage out of the opening. Therefore Black aims to disrupt his normal development by attacking the c4-pawn.

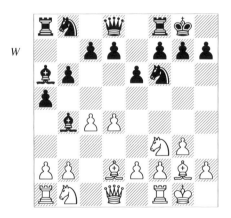

8 ♗g5!?

Kasparov reacts in his typical style, offering an unclear pawn sacrifice. Another tactical attempt, 8 ♘e5 ♖a7 9 ♗xb4 axb4 10 a3 d6 11 axb4! dxe5 12 dxe5, leads after 12...♘g4 13 b5 ♘xe5 14 b3 ♕e7 15 ♕d4 f6!? 16 bxa6 ♖d8 17 ♕e3 ♖xa6 18 ♘c3 ♖xa1 19 ♖xa1 ♘bc6 to a simplified position in which Black can gradually fully equalize, Hjartarson-Yusupov, Reykjavik 1985. However, even nowadays it's not easy to say how White should fight for an edge. The solid 8 ♕c2 d5 also gives Black reasonable counterplay.

8 ... ♗e7

This is a concession. The principled continuation is 8...♗xc4!. Now 9 ♘fd2 ♗d5 10 e4 ♗b7 11 e5 ♗xg2 12 ♔xg2 h6 13 ♗xf6 can lead to a draw by repetition after 14 ♕g4+ ♔h8 15 ♕f4 ♔g7, while if White wants to fight, he has 14 ♘e4!? or 9 ♘e5 ♗d5 10 e4 ♗b7 11 ♘g4 ♗e7 12 ♘xf6+ ♗xf6 13 ♗xf6 gxf6 14 ♘c3 with compensation for the pawn, but no real advantage.

9 ♕c2 ♘c6?!

In most closed openings putting the knight in front of the c-pawn is inflexible, and here this maxim is valid. After 9...h6 10 ♗xf6 ♗xf6 11 ♖d1 (11 ♘g5? hxg5 12 ♗xa8 c6 followed by ...♕c7-a7 is bad for White, while 11 e4 d5 gives Black counterplay) and e4 White is only slightly better.

10 a3

Stopping the unpleasant sortie ...♘b4.

10 ... h6 *(D)*

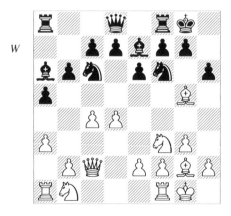

11 ♗xf6

Kasparov values time more highly than the bishop-pair, but even the retreat 11 ♗f4 gives

White a permanent pull after 11...b5 12 cxb5 ♗xb5 13 ♘c3 ♗a6 14 ♖fd1.

11	...	♗xf6
12	♖d1	♕e7
13	e3!	

After 13 e4?! e5 14 d5 ♘d4 15 ♘xd4 exd4 Black is OK thanks to the tactical trick 16 f4 d3! 17 ♖xd3 ♕c5+. Therefore White is patient and rightly so. His pawns cramp Black's minor pieces and after suitable preparation he may expand in the centre, or shift his attention to the kingside (as in the game). Note the unhappy placement of the c6-knight – any counterplay with ...c5 or ...d5 is impossible and repositioning the knight costs a lot of time.

| 13 | ... | ♖ae8 *(D)* |

Immediate activity is counterproductive, because 13...e5? 14 dxe5 costs Black material and 13...b5?! 14 d5 only worsens the situation. Yusupov at least removes his rook from the long diagonal.

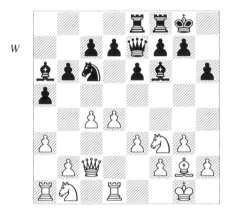

| 14 | ♘fd2 | |

By protecting the c-pawn White can finally develop the b1-knight to its most natural square. Kasparov indicates this goal could have been achieved by 14 ♕a4 ♗b7 (the complications after 14...e5 15 d5 e4 16 ♘fd2 ♘e5 17 ♕c2 c6 18 dxc6 dxc6 19 ♘c3! favour White) 15 ♘c3, but even here White will have to lose time to recentralize his queen. The simple 14 b3!? e5 15 ♘c3 exd4 16 exd4 also gives White a nagging pull.

| 14 | ... | g5!? |

In the King's Indian pawn-structure arising after 14...e5 15 d5 ♘b8 16 ♘c3 d6 17 b4 White is miles ahead with his queenside play, so Yusupov seeks activity by preparing the march of his f-pawn.

| 15 | ♘c3 | ♗g7 *(D)* |

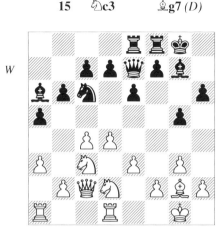

| 16 | ♘b5? | |

This tempting move is inaccurate, because the insecurity of the knight's outpost allows Black to win time for his counterplay. White could have preserved his advantage with the circumspect 16 f4!?. Now the game becomes messy.

| 16 | ... | ♕d8 |
| 17 | f4 | ♘e7! |

Black's pawns are finally ready to join the fight for the centre.

| 18 | ♘f3 | ♘f5 |

Natural, but even 18...gxf4 19 gxf4 d5!? deserved attention.

| 19 | ♕f2!? | |

White could have maintained material equality with 19 ♕e2, but after 19...d5 or 19...c6 (followed by ...d5) he would have quite a lot of trouble defending c4 anyway. Therefore, just as 11 moves earlier (8 ♗g5!?), Kasparov decides to invest a pawn.

| 19 | ... | c6 |
| 20 | ♘c3 | gxf4 |

Black opens the g-file; from now on control of this file will be the central theme of the game. Black could have avoided this by 20...♗xc4 21 e4 ♘e7!? 22 fxg5 hxg5 23 ♘xg5 ♘g6, returning the pawn with an unclear position. However, there is nothing wrong with accepting the sacrifice.

21	gxf4	♗xc4
22	e4 *(D)*	
22	...	♘d6?!

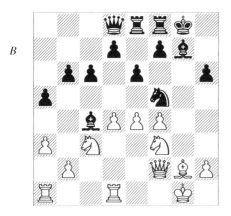

This, however, is a mistake. Misplacing the knight considerably furthers White's attacking plans. Much better is 22...♘e7!, when 23 ♘e5?! ♗b3 followed by ...d6 shows the main difference between the knight moves – here Black quickly chases away the intruding e5-knight. Stronger is 23 ♔h1 d6, but it's probably Black who can claim an advantage.

23 ♘e5! f5

Getting rid of the powerful knight requires concessions and exchanging the dark-squared bishop is out of the question. After 23...♗a6 24 ♔h1 f5 25 ♖g1 fxe4 26 ♗xe4 White has a dangerous attack, while 23...f6 gives him a choice between 24 ♘g6 and 24 ♘xc4 ♘xc4 25 b3, which is similar to the game.

24 ♘xc4 ♘xc4
25 b3

This side-tracks the knight. Less accurate is 25 e5 b5!? followed by ...♘b6 and possibly ...♘d5.

25 ... ♘d6
26 e5 *(D)*

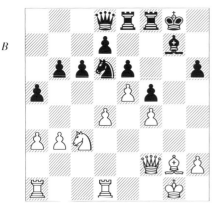

26 ... ♘c8

After 26...♘f7? 27 ♗f3 Black's pieces are hopelessly tangled up.

27 ♗f3

A practical decision. 27 ♔h1 ♘e7 28 ♗f3 is also strong, but the text-move has the extra virtue of preventing ...♘e7 altogether.

27 ... ♔h7
28 ♗h5 ♖e7
29 ♔h1 ♖g8?

Of course Black can't allow White to triple his major pieces on the open file, but deserting the f-file allows a powerful and more or less decisive tactical solution. The right move was 29...♗h8! 30 ♖g1 ♖g7 31 ♖xg7+ ♗xg7 32 ♖g1 ♕e7 33 ♕g3 ♖g8 34 ♘b1 ♕f8 and although Black's position is extremely cramped, there is still no decisive blow in sight.

30 ♖g1 ♗h8 *(D)*

After 30...♗f8 31 ♖xg8 (31 ♕h4 ♖e8 32 ♕h3 ♖e7 forces White to transpose to the main line anyway) 31...♔xg8 32 ♕h4! White has a strong attack, as Black can't oppose on the g-file any more.

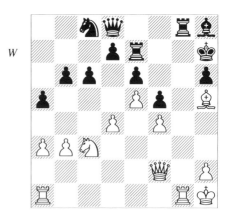

However, now the black queen is protected and there seems to be no way White can prevent ...♖eg7. The exchange of all rooks would mean the end of the attack, so Kasparov must quickly bring over the reserves...

31 ♘e4!!

Beautiful, energetic and above all effective. The threat is ♘f6+, so Black is forced to accept.

31 ... fxe4

The immediate acceptance is forced. After 31...♖xg1+? 32 ♖xg1! (32 ♕xg1? ♖g7 33 ♘f6+ ♕xf6 is not so convincing) 32...fxe4 White forces mate with the spectacular 33 ♗g6+ ♔g8 34 ♗f7++! ♔xf7 35 ♕g3.

32 f5 *(D)*

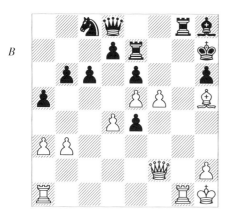

32 ... ♖g5?

Black cracks under the pressure. This move loses quickly, and the same goes for 32...e3? 33 ♕c2 or 32...♖eg7? 33 ♗g6+. The only way to continue the resistance is 32...♕f8:

1) 33 ♖xg8?! ♔xg8 34 f6 ♗xf6! (34...♖g7?! 35 ♕e2 ♖g5 36 h4 ♗xf6 37 hxg5 ♗xg5 38 ♖f1 and White should win) 35 exf6 ♖g7 is unclear to say the least.

2) Stronger is the immediate 33 f6! ♗xf6 (after the weaker 33...♖eg7 34 ♖xg7+ ♖xg7 {or 34...♗xg7 35 f7} 35 ♕e2 ♖g5 36 ♕xe4+ ♔g8 37 h4 ♗xf6 38 hxg5 White is close to winning) 34 ♕xf6 (34 exf6 ♖eg7! is again unconvincing for White) 34...♖eg7 35 ♗g6+ ♖xg6 36 ♖xg6 ♕xf6 37 ♖xf6 and White should be able to convert the extra exchange.

33 ♖xg5 hxg5
34 f6 ♔h6

Black is forced to give up a whole rook, as 34...♖e8 35 ♕e2 ♖g8 (35...♗xf6 36 ♗f7! ♔g7 37 ♕h5! doesn't help) 36 ♗f7 g4 37 ♕xe4+ ♔h6 38 ♕e3+ ♔h7 39 ♕d3+ ♔h6 40 ♕g3 mates or wins even more material.

35 fxe7 ♕xe7 *(D)*

Or 35...♘xe7 36 ♕f7 with a winning attack.

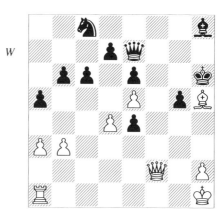

36 ♗f7 d6

After 36...g4 the most convincing is 37 h4!, followed by ♖g1 or ♖f1 and ♕g3xg4, trapping Black's king in a mating-net.

37 ♖f1 g4

The threat was ♕e2.

38 ♗xe6! ♕xe6
39 ♕h4+ ♔g7

1-0

Black resigned before Kasparov could play the decisive 40 ♖f6.

Game 17
Vladimir Tukmakov – Garry Kasparov
USSR Ch, Frunze 1981
King's Indian Defence, Averbakh Variation [E74]

Before this last-round game, Kasparov was trailing Psakhis by a half-point and only a win would give him chances to catch up with the leader. As he had nothing to lose and was already guaranteed at least a silver medal, even as Black he decided to go all-out for a win.

1 d4 ♘f6
2 c4 g6
3 ♘c3 ♗g7

Although in the previous 16(!) rounds of the national championship Kasparov had avoided the King's Indian, when spoiling for a fight he returned to his trusted weapon.

4 e4 d6
5 ♗e2 0-0
6 ♗g5

The Averbakh system is a solid choice, fitting Tukmakov's ambitions in this game: he was in clear 3rd place and a draw would have practically clinched the bronze medal for him.

6 ... c5

Nowadays Black more often opts for 6...♘a6 7 ♕d2 e5.

7 d5 *(D)*

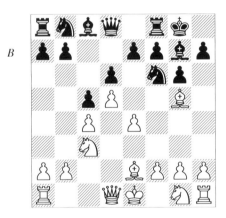

7 ... b5?!

Kasparov freely admits this pawn sacrifice is dubious, but he was striving for complications from the very start. Moreover, he had a recent previous experience with this line (albeit with opposite colours!) against Spassky and was familiar with its nuances. The approved continuation is 7...h6 8 ♗f4 e6 9 dxe6 ♗xe6 10 ♗xd6 ♖e8 11 ♘f3 ♘c6 (or 11...♕b6) with sufficient counterplay, but the resulting positions had already been deeply analysed by the time our game was played, and promise Black no winning chances whatsoever.

8 cxb5 a6
9 a4!

Holding on to the outpost on b5 makes it much more difficult for Black to achieve the typical Benko Gambit play on the semi-open queenside files.

9 ... h6 *(D)*

After 9...♕a5 10 ♗d2, 10...♘bd7? 11 ♖a3 gave White a large advantage in the aforementioned game Kasparov-Spassky, Tilburg 1981. Although 10...♕b4!? is a better try, White still remains on top after 11 ♕c2. Instead of playing on the queenside, Kasparov shifts his attention to the centre.

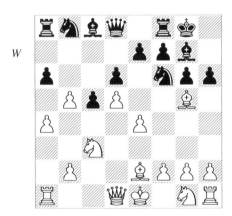

10 ♗d2

On e3 the bishop might later run into ...♘g4, while 10 ♗f4 g5 11 ♗d2 e6 gives Black a better version of the game position.

10 ... e6

11	dxe6	♗xe6
12	♘f3	axb5
13	♗xb5	

White would certainly like to keep a pawn on b5 to limit the b8-knight, but after 13 axb5? ♗b3! 14 ♕c1 ♖xa1 15 ♕xa1 ♕e7 the e4-pawn falls.

13	...	♘a6

Development comes first. After 13...d5 14 exd5 ♘xd5 15 0-0 White is clearly better.

14	0-0 *(D)*	

14	...	♘c7

The previous note has indicated that Black plans to open the centre with ...d5. However, 14...d5?! is still premature due to 15 exd5 ♘xd5 16 ♘xd5 and ♗c3, while after 14...♘b4 15 ♗e3 the pawn advance is stopped and White has a distinct advantage.

15	♖e1	

A debatable decision, as even after the somewhat passive 15 ♗e2 d5 16 exd5 ♘fxd5 17 ♘xd5 ♘xd5 18 ♕c1 Black finds it hard to claim full compensation. Tukmakov doesn't want to lose time to retain his bishop-pair and makes a more useful move instead. Despite its objective merits, it also spells a minor psychological victory for Kasparov. His provocative opening play gave White higher ambitions and in a few moves the game becomes a fierce fight. Black was ready for this from the very start, while Tukmakov had to adapt to the rising tension underway and this change negatively influenced his play. Even in his teens, Kasparov was experienced enough to sense such subtleties and profit from them.

15	...	♘xb5
16	♘xb5!?	

The point of the previous move. The weaker 16 axb5 ♖xa1 17 ♕xa1 d5 leads to a drawish position.

16	...	d5
17	exd5	♘xd5
18	♘e5!	

This is best. White activates his knight and threatens ♘xg6. 18 ♕c2?! ♘b4! 19 ♗xb4 cxb4 hands the initiative to Black and 18 ♖c1 ♘b4 doesn't promise any advantage either.

18	...	♖e8
19	♖c1?!	

Black has a pair of strong bishops and active piece-play, but only after this inaccuracy will he be able to balance the position. In an earlier game A.Petrosian-Arbakov, USSR Cht (Moscow) 1981 White got the upper hand after 19 ♕c1, but Kasparov was undoubtedly prepared for this and probably would have played 19...♗f5!? with an unclear position. He also indicated that the right continuation is 19 ♘c4!. Black must reckon with ♘d6; e.g., 19...♘b4 20 ♘cd6 ♖e7 21 ♗c3, and left to his own devices White will consolidate his advantage with ♖c1 and b3.

19	...	♗f5! *(D)*

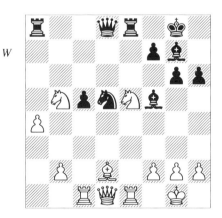

Black starts disrupting the coordination of his opponent's forces by forcing them away from their natural squares.

20	♘c6	

20 ♘c4 was ideal one move earlier, but now it allows Black a dangerous initiative after 20...♖xe1+ 21 ♗xe1 ♘f4! 22 ♕xd8+ ♖xd8. The tactical 20 ♗a5?! is not good either: 20...♖xa5 21 ♘c6 ♖xe1+ 22 ♕xe1 ♕g5! 23 ♘xa5 (23

h4? is even weaker, as 23...♕g4 gives Black a raging attack after 24 ♕xa5 ♗e4 25 f3 ♗xf3 or 24 f3 ♕f4 25 ♘xa5 ♗c5 26 g3 ♕xf3 27 ♕f2 ♕g4; defending the kingside against the pressure of all Black's pieces is impossible) 23...♘f4 24 g3 ♘e2+ 25 ♕xe2 ♕xc1+ 26 ♔g2 ♗c6! and White's knights remain offside and he is in trouble. The only alternative to the text-move was 20 f4, but one can hardly blame White for refraining from such a committal move, leading to a messy position after 20...g5!?.

20 ... ♕d7!

In keeping with the spirit of the previous move, Black sacrifices a second pawn. The seemingly more natural 20...♕b6 would misplace the queen and allow White's knight to reach its ideal square via a5.

21 ♖xc5 ♖xe1+
22 ♕xe1 (D)

This is forced. After 22 ♗xe1? ♖e8! White has no effective defence against the back-rank threats, starting with ...♘f4.

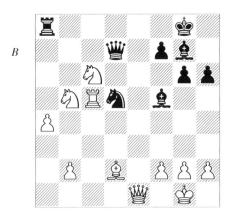

22 ... ♖e8?!

As Kasparov vigorously pursues his initiative, Tukmakov doesn't get time to create some desirable *luft* for the rest of the game. However, we'll see from the note to White's 25th move that the modest 22...♖xa4 was objectively better; here a draw would be the most likely result.

23 ♕c1 ♘b6
24 b3

White could have bailed out with 24 ♘c3 ♖e6 (24...♗f8 25 ♘e5 ♕d6 26 ♗e3! gets Black nowhere) 25 a5, returning one of the extra pawns to simplify the position. However, there is nothing wrong with the greedy text-move, although it allows Black to activate his rook.

24 ... ♖e2 (D)

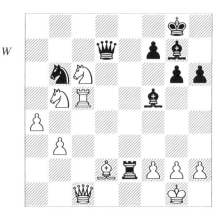

Black continues to pose direct threats and by giving White a wide choice of plausible options increases his chances to profit from a tactical error.

25 ♗a5?!

This wins a tempo by attacking the knight, but on the other hand the bishop deserts the kingside, which will quickly become the main theatre of action. Better moves would have allowed White to fight for an advantage:

1) Kasparov condemns 25 ♗e3 because of 25...♗b2 (increasing the tension by 25...♗e4!? deserves attention, as 26 ♘e5 ♕e7 leads to a murky position) 26 ♕f1 ♗d3, but after the strong 27 ♗d4! ♖d2 (27...♕e6? runs into 28 ♘e5!) 28 ♕e1 ♖e2 29 ♕d1!? ♗xb5 30 ♖xb5 ♗xd4 31 ♕xe2 ♕xc6 32 h3 White retains an edge.

2) 25 ♗c3 seems even stronger, although after 25...♖c2 26 ♕e1 ♗xc3 (26...♗e4 27 ♘cd4 ♕g4 28 g3 ♕h3 29 ♕xe4 ♖c1+ 30 ♕e1! ♖xe1+ 31 ♗xe1 leaves Black struggling for a draw) 27 ♘xc3 ♕e6! the position is full of back-rank tricks:

2a) 28 ♘e5? loses to 28...♘d7! 29 ♖c8+ ♔h7.

2b) After 28 ♕e3 ♘d7 neither side has anything better than 29 ♖c4 (29 ♘d4? ♕xe3 30 ♖c8+ ♘f8!) 29...♘b6 (29...♗d3? 30 ♘d4! ♕xe3 31 ♖c8+) 30 ♖c5 with a draw by repetition.

2c) Kasparov gives the line 28 ♕f1 ♗d3 29 ♕d1 ♕f6 30 ♕e1 ♕d6! (30...♕e6? allows 31

♕e3! ♘d7 32 ♘d4! ♕xe3 33 ♖c8+) 31 b4, which still requires accuracy from White after the pretty 31...♘xa4! (31...♘d7? 32 ♘b5 ♗xb5 33 ♖xc2 is bad for Black) 32 ♘xa4 ♖e2 33 ♕f1 (33 ♕c1? loses to 33...♕f4 34 ♕f1 {or 34 f3 ♕h4} 34...♕d2 35 ♘b2 ♗a6! 36 b5 ♖e1) 33...♖d2 34 ♕e1! (34 ♕c1? ♕f4 35 ♔h1 ♗e4! 36 f3 ♗xf3 37 ♕xd2 ♕xd2 38 gxf3 ♕d1+ gives Black winning chances) 34...♖e2 35 ♕f1 with a repetition.

2d) However, Black faces a more difficult task after the clever 28 ♕d1 ♗g4 29 ♕b1!? (29 ♕f1 ♗e2 30 ♕e1 is also possible, as now 30...♗d3 31 ♕e3! transposes into line '2c'); e.g., 29...♖b2 30 ♕a1 ♕xb3 (after 30...♖xb3 31 ♘d4 ♖a3 32 ♕c1 ♕e7 33 ♖c6 White wins more material) 31 ♖b5 ♕xc3 32 ♘e7+ ♔h7 33 ♖xb2 ♗d1 34 h3 ♕e1+ 35 ♔h2 ♕xe7 36 ♖xb6 ♕c7+ 37 ♔g1 ♕xb6 38 ♕xd1 with very good winning chances for White.

25 ... ♗e4!

Black continues to concentrate his forces for the attack. His initiative peters out after the weaker continuation 25...♗b2 26 ♕f1 ♗d3 27 ♘b4!.

26 ♘e5

White rightly feels he needs more pieces to defend his king. This is well illustrated by the line 26 ♗xb6? ♕g4 27 ♕f1 ♗xg2! and Black wins. 26 ♕f1 has similar ideas to the text-move: after 26...♖b2 27 ♗xb6, 27...♗xg2 forces a draw. Kasparov would have chosen 27...♗xc6!? to keep the game going; Black retains the initiative and good compensation.

26 ... ♕e7 *(D)*

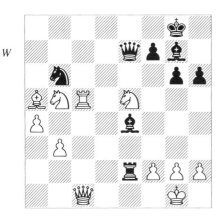

27 ♘d4?

Tukmakov falters under the continual harassment and commits a serious mistake. Bringing another piece closer to the kingside is the right idea, but the only safe way to do this was 27 ♕f1!, when Black is practically forced to give a perpetual after 27...♖a2 (27...♖b2? loses to 28 ♗xb6 ♗xe5 29 ♖xe5! ♕xe5 30 ♗d4) 28 ♗xb6 ♗xe5 29 ♘c3 ♗xh2+! (29...♗xc3? is bad due to 30 ♖xc3 ♕f6 31 ♗a5 ♕g5 32 ♖c8+ and ♗c3) 30 ♔xh2 ♕h4+ 31 ♔g1 ♗xg2! 32 ♔xg2 ♕g4+.

27 ... ♖a2
28 ♗xb6

This allows the g7-bishop to enter the fray with great effect, but even after 28 ♘df3 ♘d5! (28...♗xf3?! 29 ♘xf3 ♖a1 30 ♗xb6 is drawish) White is in trouble. A sample line is 29 ♘c6 ♕f6 30 ♘d2 ♖a1 31 ♘xe4 ♕b2! 32 ♗d2 ♘c3, winning.

28 ... ♗xe5

Now with all Black's tremendously coordinated pieces in attacking positions, the numerous threats (...♗xh2+, ...♕h4, etc.) are visible to the naked eye.

29 ♕e3?

Panic, time-trouble, last-round jitters... there are many possible explanations for this blunder, after which the game ends abruptly. An attempt to lessen Black's attacking potential by 29 ♖xe5 ♕xe5 doesn't help; the threats now are ...♕f6 and ...♕g5, and after 30 f3 ♗d3 there is no effective defence against ...♖b2-b1. Kasparov indicated that 29 ♕e1! is most resilient, and best met by 29...♕f6! (29...♕d6 is unconvincing: 30 ♘e2 ♗xh2+ 31 ♔h1) 30 ♘e2 (30 ♘f3? ♖a1 31 ♖c1 ♖xc1 32 ♕xc1 ♗xf3 costs White a piece and even after 30 ♖xe5 ♕xe5 31 f3 ♕g5 he should lose in the long run) 30...♖a1 31 ♖c1 ♕g5 32 ♕f1!? (32 g3 ♕f6! and the threat of ...♕f3 nets Black a piece; after 32 f3 ♗xf3 33 g3 ♖a2 he has a huge attack) 32...♖xc1 33 ♘xc1 ♕f4 34 f3 ♕xh2+ 35 ♔f2 ♕g3+ with a strong attack, but still no forced win for Black.

29 ... ♕xc5!
0-1

The back rank finally decides! Some 15 minutes later the game Psakhis-Agzamov was drawn and Kasparov became champion of the USSR for the first time.

Game 18
Garry Kasparov – Tigran Petrosian
Bugojno 1982
Bogo-Indian Defence [E11]

Chance had it that in all of his encounters against 9th World Champion Tigran Petrosian, Kasparov was White. After a quiet draw in Banja Luka 1979 Kasparov achieved promising attacking positions in the following two games (Moscow 1981; Tilburg 1981). However, his opponent's trademark cold-blooded defence, combined with his own time-trouble, resulted in two painful defeats. Kasparov eventually equalized their personal score with a different approach – patient but persistent positional pressure, typical for Petrosian himself. His first win against the Armenian, as well as their final game in Nikšić 1983, shows Kasparov was making progress towards a more universal style.

	1	d4	♘f6
	2	c4	e6
	3	♘f3	♗b4+
	4	♗d2	♕e7
	5	g3	♗xd2+

As has already been said in the notes to Game 16, currently a more popular set-up for Black is to place his central pawns on the dark squares. Therefore nowadays he more often plays 5...♘c6 with the possible follow-up 6 ♗g2 ♗xd2+ 7 ♘bxd2 d6 and ...e5. The c6-knight exerts pressure against d4 and forces White to clarify the central tension. He usually does so by playing d5, which gives him a pleasant space advantage, but on the other hand limits his own bishop.

	6	♕xd2	0-0
	7	♗g2	d5

Petrosian opts for a different and rather passive strategy by placing his central pawns on the light squares. This leaves White with the better bishop, but his advantage is rather ephemeral and can quickly dissipate if Black manages to finish his development and prepare an effective resolution of the central tension.

| | 8 | 0-0 | dxc4?! *(D)* |

This is quite committal and not too consistent with the strategy outlined above. If Black fails to get his pieces out in time, opening the long h1-a8 diagonal for the 'Catalan' bishop will favour White. Therefore subsequent practice preferred developing moves such as 8...b6, 8...♘bd7 or 8...♖d8!?.

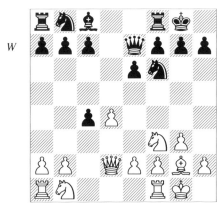

	9	♘a3	c5

Our game was played in round 6 of the tournament. Petrosian's preparation undoubtedly centred on improving Black's play from the following round 1 encounter: 9...♖d8!? 10 ♕c2 c5 11 dxc5 ♕xc5 12 ♖fd1 ♘c6 13 ♕xc4 ♕xc4 14 ♘xc4 ♔f8 15 ♘fe5 (15 ♖xd8+!? ♘xd8 16 ♘fe5 is a more demanding line) 15...♖xd1+ 16 ♖xd1 ♘xe5 17 ♘xe5 ♔e7 18 ♖d3 ♖b8 19 f4 ♘d7 20 ♖a3 ♘xe5 21 fxe5 a6 and although in Ivkov-Andersson, Bugojno 1982 careful defence earned the Swede a draw, White could certainly have posed him more problems. However, the text-move is no better, as in our game Black doesn't even get a chance of easing his task by exchanging queens. A further indication that the opening of the centre was premature was that Ulf Andersson himself later abandoned the line in favour of the more solid 4...♗xd2+ 5 ♕xd2 0-0 6 g3 d5.

| | 10 | dxc5 | |

Stronger than 10 ♘xc4 ♖d8, which doesn't promise White much.

10	...	♕xc5
11	♖ac1	♘c6
12	♘xc4 (D)	

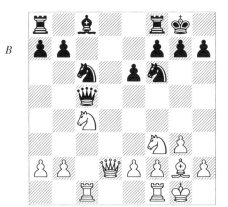

12 ... ♕e7?

The centre is wide open and White's lead in development gives him a nagging initiative despite the symmetrical character of the position. Neutralizing it requires patience, good nerves and the ability to judge correctly the concessions Black may still afford. Right now the most pressing problem is the development of the queenside, and the text-move doesn't address this concern. As both the a8-rook and c8-bishop won't move until the very end, this error decides the game. Black had two possible alternatives:

1) The simple 12...♗d7 leads to an unpleasant but defensible position after 13 ♘d6 ♕b6 or 13 ♘ce5 ♕e7.

2) More or less the same goes for 12...♖d8 13 ♕f4 (after 13 ♕c2 ♗d7 14 ♕b3 ♘a5! 15 ♕e3 ♕xe3 16 ♘xe3 ♖ac8 Black is close to full equality) 13...♘d5 (13...♕e7 14 ♖fd1 ♗d7 15 ♘fe5 ♘xe5 16 ♕xe5 ♖ab8 17 ♘d6 ♗e8 18 ♖d3 b6 19 ♖cd1 with increasing pressure, Izoria-Kholmov, Moscow 2000) 14 ♕h4 ♗d7!? (after 14...♕e7 15 ♕xe7 ♘dxe7 16 ♖fd1 Black has an inferior endgame: compared with Ivkov-Andersson above Black doesn't have the comfortable e7-square for his king). White is better, but he still has nothing direct; for example, 15 ♘g5 ♘f6.

| 13 | ♘fe5 | ♘xe5 |

It's already too late for 13...♗d7 14 ♘xd7 ♘xd7 15 ♘d6.

| 14 | ♘xe5 | |

White's centralized knight now dominates the position. Kasparov will prevent any attempts to dislodge it while preparing the invasion of Black's position via the central files.

| 14 | ... | ♘d5 |

14...♖d8 15 ♕a5 ♘d5 16 ♖fd1 is not much better; a sample line is 16...f6 17 e4 ♘b6 18 ♘c4!, when 18...♖xd1+ 19 ♖xd1 ♘xc4? runs into 20 ♖d8+ ♔f7 21 ♕h5+ with mate.

| 15 | ♖fd1 | ♘b6 (D) |

Relying on having no weaknesses, Black leaves the knight on e5. 15...f6 is a serious concession, and is met by 16 ♘d3, intending ♘c5 and ♘xe6.

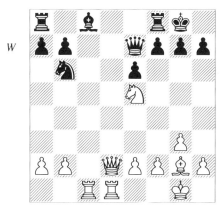

| 16 | ♕a5 | |

Immobilizing Black's rook. 16 ♕d6!? is probably just as strong, but for the time being White avoids simplification.

| 16 | ... | g6 |

White's last move was directed against possible liberating attempts such as 16...♖d8 17 ♘c4 or 16...f6 17 ♘c4 ♘xc4 18 ♖xc4 b6 19 ♕c3 with penetration to the 7th rank.

| 17 | ♖d3! | |

Once again clever prophylaxis by White.

| 17 | ... | ♘d5 |

17...♖d8?! fails to 18 ♕c5! ♕xc5 (18...♕f8 19 ♖xd8 ♕xd8 20 ♕c7 is similar) 19 ♖xd8+ ♕f8 20 ♖xf8+ ♔xf8 21 ♖c7, invading decisively.

| 18 | e4 | ♘b6 |

18...♕b4? loses on the spot: 19 ♖xd5.

| 19 | ♗f1! (D) | |

White had to chase away Black's only active piece. Now the bishop leaves the closed diagonal.

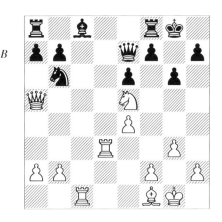

19 ... ♖e8

White's last move also had another hidden point, which shows after 19...f6 20 ♘c4: if Black plays 20...♘xc4?! 21 ♖xc4 b6 22 ♕c3 ♗a6 23 ♖c7, then he can't take on c7 any more, as the d3-rook is protected. The more resilient 20...♗d7 21 ♘xb6 axb6 22 ♕xb6 ♗c6 23 a3 is also hopeless in the long run.

20 ♖dd1!?

White wants to control both open files; slightly less incisive was 20 ♖dc3 f6 21 ♖c7 ♕f8 22 ♘c4 ♘xc4 23 ♖1xc4 b6.

20 ... ♖f8

Black has no constructive moves whatsoever. 20...f6 21 ♘c4 ♗d7 22 ♘xb6 axb6 23 ♕xb6 ♗c6 doesn't help, as after 24 a3 ♗xe4 25 ♖c7 ♕f8 26 ♗b5, White's victory is just a matter of technique. Petrosian decides to wait, but White has a clear-cut plan of further action.

21 a3

First he places the pawn on a secure square...

21 ... ♔g7
22 b3!

Kasparov has learned the lesson from his previous games with Petrosian and is in no hurry to force matters. White gradually prepares a4-a5.

22 ... ♔g8

Black is helpless.

23 a4 ♖d8

This oversight only shortens Black's suffering, but one can hardly recommend any improvement. 23...f6 24 ♘c4 ♘xc4 25 ♖xc4 b6 26 ♕c3 ♗d7 27 ♖c7 ♖ac8 28 ♗b5 loses material and 23...♔g7 24 ♕c3 f6 25 ♕c7! is hopeless as well.

24 ♕c5! *(D)*

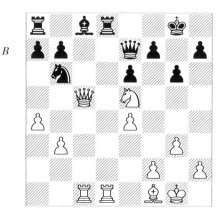

1-0

White breaks through: 24...♕xc5 (24...♕e8 25 ♘g4 penetrates on the dark squares) 25 ♖xd8+ ♕f8 26 ♖xf8+ ♔xf8 27 ♖c7 is crushing.

Game 19
Lubomir Kavalek – Garry Kasparov
Bugojno 1982
King's Indian Defence [E90]

1	d4	♘f6
2	c4	g6
3	♘c3	♗g7
4	e4	d6
5	♘f3	0-0
6	h3	

The most obvious idea behind this move is that White prepares ♗e3 by stopping ...♘g4. However, that's not his only intention, as we'll see later. Vladimir Makogonov from Baku introduced the whole system into practice and Kasparov himself employed it with White. He was well versed in its nuances, as Makogonov was his trainer in the 1970s.

6 ... e5

A typical King's Indian reaction. Instead, 6...c5 7 d5 e6 leads to Benoni-like positions. Kasparov later tried the flexible 6...♘a6!?.

7 d5 ♘a6

Black's region of activity should be the kingside and he naturally intends to play ...f5. However, he can't realize his plans too directly. After the simplistic 7...♘e8?!, 8 g4! restricts Black to passivity, because opening the kingside would only make his own king a welcome target. More refined is 7...♘h5, but this is well met by the subtle 8 ♘h2!. Yet another idea behind the seemingly innocuous 6 h3 is that if Black now insists on playing ...f5 with 8...♕e8 9 ♗e2 ♘f4 10 ♗f3 f5, White has the strong pawn sacrifice 11 g3! ♘xh3 (11...fxe4 12 ♘xe4 ♘h5 13 ♘g4 ♘d7 14 ♗e3 ♘hf6 15 ♘gxf6+ ♘xf6 16 ♘xf6+ ♖xf6 17 ♗e4 ♕f8 18 g4! ♗d7 19 ♕d3 c5 20 a4 b6 21 ♔e2 dooms Black to passivity, Kasparov-Lanka, Leningrad 1977) 12 ♗g2 fxe4 13 ♗e3 ♕e7 14 ♕d2! and to save his knight Black will have to return the pawns with an inferior position. With the text-move Kasparov masks his intentions for the time being.

8 ♗e3 *(D)*

In the 1990s the active 8 ♗g5 became the main move.

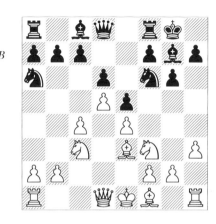

8 ... ♘h5!?

An alert reaction. Kasparov realizes the extra moves ...♘a6 and ♗e3 give Black a better version of the lines mentioned in the note to move 7. Nevertheless this aggressive plan is rather committal; we'll see later that the development of Black's initiative often requires material investment. A playable alternative is the more restrained 8...♘c5 9 ♘d2 a5 10 g4 c6!?.

9 ♘h2

Here 9 ♘d2 isn't ideal any more, as after 9...♕e8 10 ♗e2 ♘f4 the natural reply 11 ♗f3 would cost White his castling rights.

9 ... ♕e8
10 ♗e2 ♘f4

Later, in the game Cu.Hansen-Kasparov, Tåsinge (2) 1990, the World Champion came up with 10...f5!? 11 exf5 ♘f4!. The main point of Black's new idea was that 12 ♗xf4?! exf4 13 fxg6 ♕xg6 would give him a dangerous initiative for the pawn.

11 ♗f3 f5
12 h4

Here the analogy with the 7...♘h5 line breaks down, as 12 g3? ♘xh3 13 ♗g2 runs into 13...f4. Kavalek insists on chasing away the annoying f4-knight, but leaving the king in the centre can be dangerous. Nowadays White mostly plays 12 0-0 with an unclear position.

| 12 | ... | ♕e7 |

The less direct 12...♗d7!? with the similar idea 13 g3 ♘b4! was possibly a better choice, but perhaps Kasparov didn't want White to change his mind and castle after all.

| 13 | g3 *(D)* | |

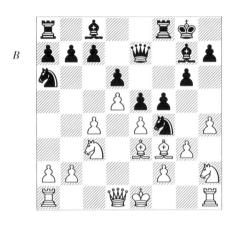

| 13 | ... | ♘b4! |

This attractive sortie is also the best move, as after 13...♘h3 14 ♖f1 Black's offside knight doesn't support his attack and White's king can still find a safe haven on the queenside.

| 14 | ♕b3? | |

Confused by Black's burst of activity, Kavalek commits a serious error by exposing his king. Let's look at the better options:
1) Taking the knight is perhaps possible, but very risky. After 14 gxf4 fxe4! (14...exf4? fails to 15 ♗xf4 fxe4 16 ♗g5!; this line wouldn't be possible if Black had played 12...♗d7!?) White has two moves:
1a) 15 fxe5?! gives Black a pleasant choice. After 15...♘d3+!? 16 ♔d2 ♖xf3! 17 ♘xf3 ♗g4 18 ♘xe4 ♘xe5 he has a powerful attack, while 15...exf3 16 a3 ♘a6 17 e6 ♕xh4 is also promising.
1b) The stronger 15 ♘xe4 exf4 16 ♗d2 ♘d3+ 17 ♔f1 (after 17 ♔e2? ♘c5 Black wins the pinned knight) 17...♘xb2 (17...♘h3+ 18 ♔g1 ♗d4 19 ♗e1! gets Black nowhere) 18 ♕c2 ♘xc4 19 ♗c3 ♗f5 is not quite clear, but with three pawns for the piece Black has little to fear.
2) The real test of Black's concept is the calm 14 0-0!. Now the knight is genuinely *en prise* and there is no way back, only forward. Kasparov recommends 14...g5!? (14...♘fd3 15 a3 ♘xb2 16 ♕e2 ♘1d3 17 ♗c1! costs Black material; this line wouldn't work for White if Black had played 12...♗d7!?), but after 15 exf5 (15 gxf4 gxf4 {or even 15...exf4!?} is quite dangerous for White) 15...♗xf5 16 ♗e4 (16 gxf4!?) White is better.

14	...	♘fd3+
15	♔e2	f4
16	♗d2 *(D)*	

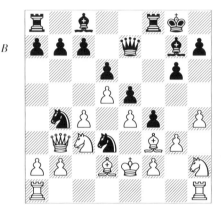

| 16 | ... | fxg3?! |

Black has obviously achieved a promising attacking position and could have maintained pressure with the patient 16...a5!?. However, this is not in Kasparov's nature and he looks for an immediate solution. His intuition didn't let him down, but the chosen method was insufficient and should have squandered Black's advantage. The energetic 16...♘xf2! is correct: 17 ♔xf2 (17 ♕xb4? ♘xh1 {or 17...fxg3} is hopeless for White) 17...♘d3+ 18 ♔g2 (18 ♔e2? loses to 18...♘c5 followed by ...fxg3 and ...♕f6) 18...fxg3 19 ♔xg3 ♖f4! with a raging attack *(D)*:

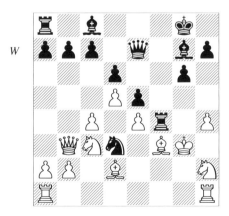

1) White's position crumbles after 20 ♘f1 ♖xf3+ 21 ♔xf3 ♕f6+ 22 ♔e2 ♘c5! 23 ♕c2 ♗g4+ 24 ♔e1 ♕f3 25 ♖g1 ♘d3+ 26 ♕xd3 ♕xd3 27 ♖xg4 ♖f8.

2) The same goes for 20 ♗g4 ♗xg4!? 21 ♘xg4 h5 22 ♘e3 ♖af8 23 ♖af1 ♘f2.

3) 20 ♘g4 h5 21 ♘e3 ♗f6! costs White the important h-pawn, as 22 ♘g2 is insufficient due to 22...♗xh4+! 23 ♖xh4 ♕g5+.

4) 20 ♗xf4 (probably best) 20...exf4+ 21 ♔g2 ♕xh4 22 ♖hf1 ♗h3+ 23 ♔h1 ♗xf1 24 ♖xf1 ♘f2+ 25 ♖xf2 ♕xf2 26 ♕xb7 ♖f8 lands White on the brink of defeat; e.g., after 27 ♘e2! g5 28 ♕xc7 g4! 29 ♗xg4 f3 30 ♘xf3 (30 ♗xf3? ♗e5) 30...♖xf3 (30...♕xe2!?) 31 ♗xf3 ♕xf3+ 32 ♔g1 ♕xe2 33 ♕d8+ ♗f8 34 ♕g5+ ♔f7 35 ♕f5+ ♔e8 36 ♕c8+ ♔e7 Black escapes the checks and remains a piece up.

| 17 | fxg3 | ♖xf3 |

Even now 17...a5!? deserved attention, but Kasparov consistently implements his idea.

| 18 | ♘xf3 | ♗g4 |
| 19 | ♖af1 | ♖f8 (D) |

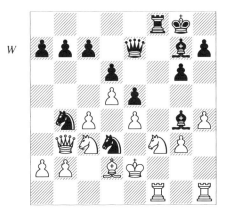

Now first of all Black threatens to take on f3, followed by a decisive penetration by the queen on the f-file. White's task is to prevent the invasion, while also taking into account Black's second idea to increase pressure against the pinned knight.

| 20 | ♘d1? |

Once again Kavalek goes astray in the critical position, this time with deadly consequences. 20 ♗e3! is necessary, which not only controls the f2-square, but also frees d2 for White's king. Now Black has nothing better than a pretty draw by 20...♗h6! (although Black scrapes some compensation for the exchange after 20...♕f7 21 a3! ♗xf3+ 22 ♔d2 ♕d7 23 ♖hg1 ♘c5!? 24 ♕xb4 a5 25 ♕b5 c6, it's clear that only White can claim any winning ambitions) 21 ♗xh6 (21 ♘d1? loses to 21...♖xf3 22 ♖xf3 ♕f8! 23 ♖hf1 ♗xe3 24 ♘xe3 ♗xf3+ 25 ♖xf3 ♘c1+) 21...♖xf3 22 ♖xf3 ♗xf3+ 23 ♔xf3 ♕f6+ 24 ♔g2 ♕f2+ 25 ♔h3 ♕f3 26 ♖h2 g5! 27 ♗xg5 (27 ♖d2? ♘f2+ 28 ♖xf2 g4+ 29 ♔h2 ♕xf2+ 30 ♔h1 ♕f1+ 31 ♔h2 ♘d3! and ...♘e1 mates) 27...♕f1+ 28 ♔g4 (28 ♖g2? ♘f2+) 28...h5+! 29 ♔xh5 ♕f3+ 30 ♔h6 ♕f8+ with a perpetual.

| 20 | ... | ♕f7! |

The winning move. White's knight falls and the b4-knight is taboo due to the fork on c1. Two moves later we will see why Kasparov's choice is better than 20...♕f6.

21	♗e3	♗xf3+
22	♔d2	♕d7!
23	♖hg1

Now Kasparov wraps the game up with a series of forceful moves. However, 23 ♖xf3 ♖xf3 24 a3 ♘c5 is also hopeless for White, and after 23 a3 Black can choose between 23...♗xe4 with a won endgame and 23...♗xh1 24 ♖xh1 ♘c5!? 25 ♗xc5 dxc5 26 axb4 ♕g4 with a decisive attack.

23	...	♕h3
24	a3	♗xe4
25	♖xf8+	♗xf8
26	axb4	♕h2+
27	♔c3	♘c1! (D)

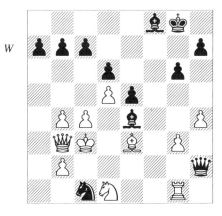

0-1

After 28 ♗xc1 Black can even force mate with 28...♕e2! 29 b5 (29 ♘f2 ♕f3+) 29...a5 30 bxa6 c5! 31 dxc6 d5!.

Game 20
Garry Kasparov – Florin Gheorghiu
Interzonal, Moscow 1982
Queen's Indian Defence [E12]

This win clinched Kasparov's victory in his first (and last as well!) Interzonal tournament.

1	d4	♘f6
2	c4	e6
3	♘f3	b6
4	a3	♗b7
5	♘c3	d5
6	cxd5	♘xd5 *(D)*

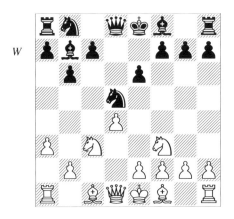

7 ♕c2!?

This is now the main line, but in 1982 it was only a new and fashionable alternative to the previously universally played 7 e3 (see Game 10). White intends to play e4 in one move and in the early days of 7 ♕c2!? he often managed to profit from the position of his queen, which is otherwise rather exposed on the c-file.

7 ... c5

Then the most usual reaction. However, practice has shown this logical move to be rather risky. 7...♘d7?! 8 ♘xd5 exd5 9 ♗g5 lost its appeal after Kasparov-Karpov, Moscow Wch (32) 1984/5 (see Game 26). Currently the topical continuation is 7...♘xc3 (7...♗e7 can lead to the same position after 8 e4, but Black also has to reckon with 8 ♗d2) 8 bxc3 (8 ♕xc3 ♘d7 9 ♗g5 ♗e7! 10 ♗xe7 ♔xe7 is satisfactory for Black) 8...♗e7 9 e4 0-0 10 ♗d3 c5 11 0-0 ♕c8! 12 ♕e2 ♗a6. Black has safeguarded his king and forced the white queen to make another move, while at the same time managing to exchange the potentially dangerous d3-bishop. Nevertheless, White has a strong pawn-centre and retains kingside attacking chances in a complicated position.

8	e4	♘xc3
9	bxc3	♗e7?!

It's only natural Gheorghiu didn't want to repeat the risky 9...♘c6 10 ♗b2 ♖c8 11 ♖d1! cxd4 12 cxd4 a6? (12...♗d6 is best, but White retains an edge after 13 ♕d2 0-0 14 ♗d3) 13 ♕d2 ♘a5 14 d5! exd5 15 exd5 ♗d6 16 ♗xg7 ♕e7+ 17 ♗e2 ♖g8 18 ♕h6 f5 19 ♗f6 ♕f8 20 ♕xh7, when Black was routed in Kasparov-Murei, Moscow IZ 1982. This game was played in round 3 and it was clear to Kasparov that in round 12 he was in for an opening surprise. However, it turned out to be a pleasant one. Arguably the best move is 9...♘d7, which became popular later. After 10 ♗f4 Black can choose between 10...♖c8 and 10...♗e7!?.

10 ♗b5+!

Once again we see the motif from Games 8 and 10; this clever check disrupts Black's piece coordination.

10 ... ♗c6

10...♘c6? 11 ♕a4 costs Black at least a pawn and as giving up castling rights is also out of the question, the text-move is forced.

11 ♗d3 *(D)*

Now the c6-bishop is misplaced; the reasons are clear from the note to Black's 7th move: it will take him longer to free the c-file for effective counterplay, and the exchange of the d3-bishop (by ...♗a6) is also impossible for the time being.

11 ... ♘d7

After 11...0-0 12 0-0 Black also has to cope with the impending d5 advance. 12...♗b7 either now or a move earlier means admitting 9...♗e7?! has cost him a whole tempo.

12 0-0 h6?!

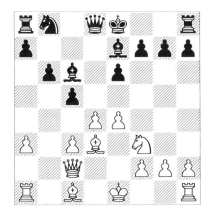

It's not easy to recommend a satisfactory continuation, but a further loss of time, weakening the kingside to boot, certainly isn't ideal. After 12...cxd4 13 cxd4 ♖c8 14 ♕e2 ♗b7 15 ♗b2 0-0 we suddenly have a position from Kasparov-Åkesson (Game 10), only with White to move. This naturally only enhances his advantage. Black should try to keep the position closed for as long as possible, so 12...♗b7 is preferable, or even the immediate 12...0-0!?, when the direct 13 d5 exd5 14 exd5 ♗xd5 15 ♗xh7+ doesn't promise White too much after 15...♔h8 16 ♗e4 ♘f6. However, calm moves such as 13 ♖d1 or 13 ♗f4!? give him a pleasant edge.

13 ♖d1!

Everything revolves around the central thrust d5. Kasparov prefers a preparatory move to the tempting, but less convincing, 13 d5!? exd5 14 exd5 ♗xd5 15 ♖d1 and now:

1) 15...♕c8? 16 ♗f5 g6 (16...♕b7? loses to 17 ♖xd5 ♕xd5 18 ♗e4) 17 ♖xd5 gxf5 18 ♗f4 is hopeless for Black: all White's pieces will pounce on Black's vulnerable king.

2) 15...♗c6 16 ♗f4! and as Black can't castle due to 17 ♘e5, he is in great trouble; for example, 16...♖c8 17 ♕e2 with a vicious attack for White.

3) 15...♗e6 loses an exchange: after 16 ♗c4 ♖c8 17 ♗f4 0-0 18 ♗b7 White has reasonable chances to convert his advantage, despite the technical problems.

4) However, Black has the paradoxical idea 15...♗xf3 16 gxf3 a6!? (16...♕c7?! is weaker due to 17 ♗b5; a sample line is 17...0-0-0 18 ♕e4 ♘e5 19 ♗f4 f6 20 ♕a8+ ♔b8 21 ♗d7+!, winning an exchange) 17 ♗f5 ♖a7 and the defences still seem to hold; e.g., 18 ♕e4 g6 19 ♗h3 ♔f8 20 ♕c6 ♖c7 21 ♕a4 f5.

13 ... ♕c7?!

This third mistake renders Black's position untenable. 13...cxd4 allows the surprising 14 ♘xd4!, when after the forced 14...♕c7 15 ♘xc6 ♕xc6 16 ♕e2 ♕c7 17 ♗b5 Black's king can choose only between two evils – staying in the centre or facing a strong queenside attack after 17...0-0-0 18 a4. Thus Black's safest option was 13...0-0 14 d5 exd5 15 exd5 ♗b7 16 c4, although this gives White a considerable and permanent advantage.

14 d5! (D)

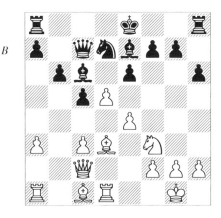

Kasparov's patience has expired and it's time to act!

14 ... exd5
15 exd5 ♗xd5
16 ♗b5 a6

16...♗e6 17 ♕e4 ♖d8 18 ♗f4 ♕c8 19 ♘e5 is hopeless for Black, as 19...0-0? 20 ♘xd7 ♗xd7 21 ♗d3 costs him a piece. The most natural defence was 16...♗c6, but after 17 ♗f4 ♕b7 18 ♗xc6 ♕xc6 19 ♖e1! Black is in grave trouble. His rooks are unconnected and dreams of castling unrealistic, as 19...♘f8? runs into 20 ♘e5 ♕b7 21 ♕b3. Kasparov gives an unforced but characteristic line: 19...♔f8 20 ♖ad1 ♖e8 21 ♕f5 ♘f6 22 ♘e5 ♕c8? 23 ♘d7+! ♖xd7 24 ♕xd7 ♕xd7 25 ♖xd7 and there is no defence against ♖xe7 and ♗d6.

17 ♗f4!

Gheorghiu relied upon 17 ♗xd7+? ♕xd7 18 c4 ♗e4!, but now Black's king remains in the line of fire until the bitter end.

17 ... ♕xf4

Even worse is 17...♕b7 18 ♗xd7+ ♕xd7 19 c4 ♕g4 20 ♖xd5 ♕xf4 21 ♖e1 ♖a7 (21...♕f6 22 ♖f5 ♕d6 23 ♖xe7+! ♕xe7 24 ♖e5 is just as hopeless) 22 ♘e5 and Black's position quickly collapses after 22...♖c7 23 ♕a4+ b5 24 ♕a5 ♖c8 25 ♘c6!.

18	♗xd7+	♔xd7
19	♖xd5+	♔c7

Black instinctively tries to keep his rooks connected and loses quickly. However, even 19...♔c8!? isn't much better. Black's a8-rook won't have time to join the game via a7 and White is winning after 20 ♖f5 ♕c4 21 ♖e1! ♖a7 (21...♗f6? loses immediately to 22 ♖xf6! gxf6 23 ♕f5+ ♔b8 24 ♕xf6) 22 ♘e5.

20	♖e1	♗d6 (D)

Black has no choice. 20...♗f6? 21 ♖e4 traps the queen and the pin after 20...♖he8 21 ♖de5 is decisive.

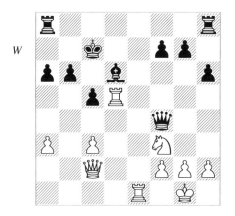

21	♖f5	♕c4
22	♖e4!	

The last moment when care is still required from White; Black turns the tables after 22 ♘d2? ♖he8!.

22	...	♕b5
23	♖xf7+	♔b8
24	♖e6	♖d8 (D)

24...♗c7 25 c4 ♕a5 26 ♕e4 with decisive threats.

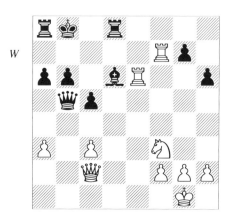

25 c4!

The most direct move. Surprisingly, this position also arose in the game Yakovich-Åkesson, Stockholm 1998/9, where Black resigned out of frustration following 25 ♕e4 ♗c7 26 g3.

25 ... ♕c6

White mates after 25...♕a5 26 ♕e4 ♗c7 27 ♖e8 ♖a7 28 ♘e5!.

26	♘e5	♕c8
27	♕b1	1-0

Now Black has no way to protect the b6-pawn, but 27 ♕e4 would have done the job as well.

Game 21
Viktor Korchnoi – Garry Kasparov
Olympiad, Lucerne 1982
Modern Benoni [A64]

Korchnoi, world champion challenger in 1978 and 1981, and Kasparov, the rapidly rising star, had previously met over the board only in a clock simul (see the note to move 7 in Game 2) and both had high ambitions in this game. They pursued their goals in ways typical for their respective styles. Korchnoi intended to draw out his opponent and punish any premature activity, and Kasparov responded with his typical resourceful attacking play, peppered with intuitive sacrifices. The tension inexorably grew and despite the mutual mistakes this game became one of the highlights of the Lucerne Olympiad.

1	d4	♘f6
2	c4	g6
3	g3	♗g7
4	♗g2	c5
5	d5	d6
6	♘c3	

6 ♘f3 makes it more difficult for Black to reach the Benoni positions from the game, as 6...0-0 7 0-0 e6 8 dxe6!? ♗xe6 9 ♘g5 ♗xc4 10 ♗xb7 ♘bd7 11 ♘a3! is advantageous for White. However, Black has other playable options, starting with 6...b5!?.

6	...	0-0
7	♘f3	e6
8	0-0	

8 dxe6 ♗xe6 9 ♘g5 ♗xc4 10 ♗xb7 ♘bd7 would have suited Kasparov's mood, as taking either the pawn or the exchange gives Black attacking chances. Korchnoi declines the offer.

8	...	exd5
9	cxd5	a6

Later Black started to prefer the more flexible 9...♖e8 or 9...♘bd7.

10	a4	♖e8
11	♘d2	

At the time of the game this was the main line. Now 11 ♗f4!? has a good reputation, especially due to the efforts of Nikolić.

11	...	♘bd7

12	h3	

Useful prophylaxis: taking away the g4-square from Black's pieces allows White to expand in the centre with f4. Although h3 makes White's kingside slightly more vulnerable, he often needs this move later on even in other lines such as 12 ♘c4 and 12 ♕b3!?.

12	...	♖b8

The immediate 12...♘h5!? is an interesting alternative.

13	♘c4 (D)	

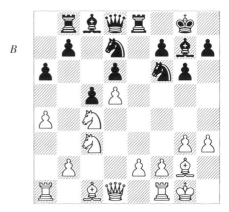

13	...	♘e5

Black must both protect the d6-pawn and challenge White's c4-knight, and the character of the game depends on how he does it. 13...♘b6 14 ♘a3 ♗d7 15 e4 ♕c7 16 ♗e3 ♘c8 17 ♕d3 ♘a7 leads to a balanced position, where most of the action takes place on the queenside. With the sharper text-move, Kasparov focuses his attention on the other flank.

14	♘a3	

White leaves the e5-knight as a target for his f-pawn. Too meek is 14 ♘xe5 ♖xe5 15 ♗f4 ♖e8 with equality.

14	...	♘h5

More or less forced: if Black wants to justify his previous move, he can't allow White to chase away the e5-knight without a fight. The following phase of the game revolves mainly around the centralized knight.

15 e4! *(D)*

Black's knights are real Trojan horses and attempts to dislodge them backfire: 15 g4? ♕h4! 16 ♘e4 h6 17 gxh5 ♗xh3 and 15 f4? ♘xg3 16 fxe5 ♗xe5!? both give Black a huge attack. On the other hand, less energetic moves allow 15...f5; after the text-move this typical advance is impossible without sacrifices.

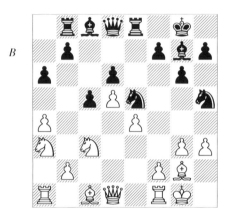

15 ... ♖f8?!

One can understand this 'mysterious rook move' only in the context of the alternatives:

1) The earlier violent attempt 15...f5 16 exf5 ♗xf5 17 g4 ♗xg4 18 hxg4 ♕h4 19 gxh5 ♖f8! 20 h6 ♗h8 is well met by 21 ♘c4! ♘g4 22 ♕xg4 ♕xg4 23 ♘xd6 ♗e5 24 ♘de4 ♖f3 25 ♘g5, V.Kovačević-Nemet, Karlovac 1979. Now 25...♖f5 (best) keeps the result of the game in doubt, but it's clear that White is on top and Black should definitely start looking for improvements. The text-move prepares all this by making Black's 19th move in advance.

2) However, obstinate insistence on enforcing ...f5 is probably not the best solution. Black can also turn his attention to the queenside once again; nowadays 15...♗d7!? is considered best. One can, however, hardly blame Kasparov, as this move appeared on the scene only about two months before the olympiad in a single game and its merits were still unclear. The critical continuation is 16 a5!? (...b5 was already in the air and it works quite well for Black after the immediate 16 g4 b5! 17 axb5 axb5 18 ♘axb5 ♗xb5 19 ♘xb5 ♖xb5 20 gxh5 c4!?) 16...♕xa5 17 g4 ♘f6 18 g5 (18 f4 ♘exg4! 19 hxg4 ♘xg4 and with three pawns for the piece Black has little to fear) 18...♘h5 19 f4 and now it's up to Black to choose between taking and sacrificing material. 19...♘c4 20 ♘xc4 ♕xa1 21 ♘xd6 ♗d4+ 22 ♔h2 was played in Hulak-Nunn, Toluca IZ 1982; although the position remains unclear, White has a dangerous initiative for the exchange. The most recent attempt to avoid this is 19...c4!? 20 ♗e3 ♘xf4 21 ♖xf4 ♕d8 and in Lacrosse-Marin, Cannes 2002 Black had ample compensation for the piece.

16 ♔h2

16 g4 ♕h4 17 gxh5 ♗xh3 is still very dangerous for White, so Korchnoi prepares f4.

16 ... f5

Even now Black can try 16...♗d7, but with the rook already on f8 White can stop ...b5 with 17 ♕e2! (17 f4 b5 18 fxe5 ♘xg3! 19 ♔xg3 ♗xe5+ followed by ...b4 is unclear; White's exposed king gives Black good tactical chances). After 17...f5 18 f4 fxe4 (18...♘f7 also loses material: 19 exf5) White can afford even 19 fxe5!; e.g., 19...♘xg3 20 ♖xf8+ ♕xf8 21 ♕e1 ♗xe5 22 ♘c4! with a clear advantage.

17 f4 b5! *(D)*

17...fxe4 18 fxe5 is similar to the previous note, so Black must try to create confusion.

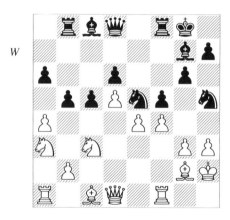

18 axb5

This interpolation is certainly the best option. Even if White decides to accept the piece sacrifice one move later, opening the a-file for the a1-rook can only be in his favour.

18 ... axb5
19 ♘axb5!

Korchnoi is not one to be intimidated. Taking the less valuable unit is the most practical solution, which enables White to avoid the unfathomable complications of 19 fxe5 ♘xg3! (the most principled continuation; 19...b4 20 ♘c4! favours White, but the as yet untested 19...♗xe5!? perhaps deserves attention – after 20 ♘e2 ♘xg3 21 ♘xg3 f4 Black's threats shouldn't be underestimated) 20 ♔xg3 (20 ♖f3 ♗xe5 was played in Van Wely-Timman, Wijk aan Zee 2002; now according to Ernst 21 ♖xg3 b4 22 ♕e1 is best, with an unclear position) 20...♗xe5+ 21 ♔f2 ♗d4+!? (21...♕h4+ 22 ♔g1 ♕g3 23 ♖f3 ♕h2+ 24 ♔f2!? ♗d4+ 25 ♕xd4! cxd4 26 ♗f4 fxe4 27 ♗xh2 exf3 28 ♗xd6 is good for White). Now attempts to avoid the perpetual lead to a murky position that is potentially dangerous for White; e.g., 22 ♗e3 ♕h4+ 23 ♔e2 ♗xe3 24 ♔xe3 b4.

19 ... fxe4 *(D)*

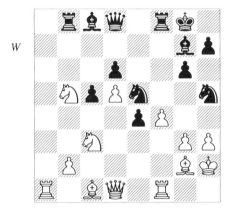

20 ♗xe4!

So far the players have followed in the footsteps of previous games, but finally Korchnoi comes up with a strong, albeit unintentional, novelty (in pre-Internet times, chess information travelled much more slowly). This natural move decides the theoretical duel (but not the game!) in White's favour. Other moves are weaker:

1) 20 fxe5?! ♗xe5 21 ♖xf8+ ♕xf8 and as White can't protect g3 effectively, his king will be subjected to a dangerous attack.

2) 20 ♘a7 was played in Alburt-H.Olafsson, Reykjavik 1982. Kasparov then recommends 20...♘f3+!? 21 ♗xf3 exf3 22 ♘c6 ♕d7, when Black has reasonable compensation for a minimal price.

3) The same goes for 20 ♘xd6 ♘xg3!? 21 ♔xg3 ♕xd6 22 ♘xe4 ♕b6 23 ♗e3 ♘d7, when White's vulnerable king gives Black counterchances.

20 ... ♗d7!

One has to admire the way Kasparov consistently ignores his attacked knight and resourcefully continues to increase the tension by creating new tactical problems for White. Weaker is 20...♘c4 21 ♕e2 ♘a5 22 ♘a7!? and White gradually consolidates.

21 ♕e2

21 ♘xd6 ♖b6! traps the d6-knight, forcing White to play 22 fxe5 ♗xe5. Now Black regains the piece, as after 23 ♘c4? ♗xg3+ 24 ♔h1 ♖bf6 25 ♖xf6 (25 ♗g2 runs into 25...♗xh3!) 25...♕xf6 the concentration of attacking forces around White's king is too dangerous. Korchnoi wants to keep his knight on b5 for as long as possible, but he had interesting alternatives in 21 ♘a3 and 21 ♘a7 ♖a8 22 ♖a2!? with ♘c6 in the air.

21 ... ♕b6
22 ♘a3 *(D)*

22 ♘a7? ♖a8 only spells trouble; e.g., 23 fxe5 ♖xf1 24 ♕xf1 ♗xe5 25 ♕a6 ♕b4!.

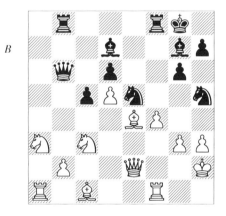

22 ... ♖be8!

Black's e5-knight still coolly remains *en prise*!

23 ♗d2

White prudently decides that winning material still isn't ideal and lines such as 23 g4?! ♘xg4+! 24 hxg4 ♕d8! or 23 fxe5 ♗xe5 24 ♘c4 ♗xg3+ 25 ♔g1 ♕d8 subject his king to a lot of dangerous harassment. Thus White's position requires further consolidation and Korchnoi decides to do something for his development. However, a better and definitely safer method was 23 ♕g2!. This multi-purpose move removes the queen from the gaze of the e8-rook, frees the important e2-square for the knight and overprotects the vulnerable kingside. Now 23...♘f7 24 ♘c4 ♕b3 25 ♗d3 ♗xc3? 26 ♖a3 is bad for Black, and White retains an advantage even after the superior 23...♕b3 24 ♗c2 ♕b4 25 ♗d2!, Sloth-Serud, corr. 1984.

23 ... ♕xb2! *(D)*

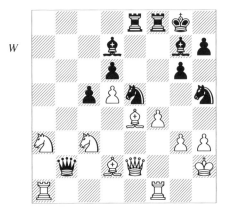

Retreat is out of the question, so Black continues the joyride.

24 fxe5?

Korchnoi buckles under the tension and finally decides to cash in, but this is a serious error. With time-trouble looming the probability of tactical miscalculations increases and this is the case. We can only presume White saw the line 24 ♖fb1? ♘f3+! one move too late and decided to abandon the idea of trapping the queen altogether. After 24 ♖a2 Black should play 24...♕b4!? (not 24...♕b8?! 25 fxe5 ♖xf1 26 ♕xf1 ♗xe5 27 ♕d3! ♘xg3 28 ♘c4!) 25 ♖b1 ♕d4 26 ♘ab5 ♗xb5 27 ♘xb5 ♕c4 28 ♕xc4 ♘xc4 29 ♗d3 with approximate equality.

The best move is 24 ♘c2!, threatening ♖ab1. Then:

1) 24...♕b8?! allows 25 fxe5 ♖xf1 (the alternative 25...♗xe5 26 ♖xf8+ ♖xf8 27 ♗e1 gets Black nowhere) 26 ♖xf1 ♗xe5 27 ♖f3 ♘f6 (27...♗f5 28 ♕d3 ♗xc3 29 ♗xf5 is hopeless for Black) 28 ♗g5! ♗xc3 29 ♗xf6 ♗xf6 30 ♖xf6 ♗f5 31 ♖e6! with a clear advantage.

2) 24...♘f7 25 ♖ab1 ♖xe4!? (25...♗b5 26 ♕f2 ♗xc3 27 ♖xb2 ♗xb2 28 ♖e1 is also better for White) 26 ♕xe4 ♘f6! 27 ♕d3 (27 ♕xg6?! is weaker: 27...hxg6 28 ♖xb2 ♘xd5) 27...♗f5

28 ♕xf5! ♕xb1 29 ♖xb1 gxf5 30 ♘e3 leads to a promising endgame for White.

3) 24...♘c4!? is probably best: 25 ♕xc4 ♗xc3 26 ♗xc3 (26 ♖fb1 ♗b5! 27 ♕xc3 ♕xc3 28 ♗xc3 ♖xe4 is only about equal) 26...♖xe4 27 ♕xe4 ♕xc3 28 ♕g2 (28 ♖a3?! ♘xg3 is OK for Black) 28...♗f5 29 g4 ♗xc2 30 gxh5 ♗d3 and Black retains reasonable drawing chances.

24 ... ♗xe5

White has chosen the least suitable moment to eliminate the irksome e5-knight. Now he can't protect the g3-pawn and his position falls to pieces.

25 ♘c4

25 ♔g2 ♘xg3 26 ♖xf8+ (or 26 ♘c4 ♕xa1!) 26...♖xf8 is no improvement.

25 ... ♘xg3!
26 ♖xf8+ ♖xf8
27 ♕e1!?

White is completely lost after 27 ♘xb2 ♘xe2+ 28 ♔g2 ♗xc3. Korchnoi finds the only way to cause Black any problems and his perseverance is nearly rewarded in the end.

27 ... ♘xe4+
28 ♔g2 *(D)*

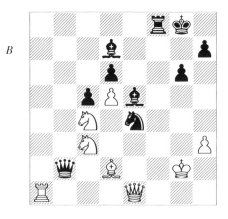

28 ... ♕c2

28...♕xa1 29 ♕xa1 ♖f2+ 30 ♔h1 ♘g3+ 31 ♔g1 ♗d4 32 ♗e3 ♖f1+ also wins, but the most attractive solution was 28...♖f2+! 29 ♕xf2 (after 29 ♔h1, Black wins by 29...♖h2+ 30 ♔g1 ♘xd2) 29...♗xh3+ 30 ♔f3 ♗g4+! 31 ♔g2 (31 ♔xe4 ♕c2+ 32 ♔e3 ♗d4+) 31...♕xa1 32 ♘xe4 ♗h3+! 33 ♔f3 ♕d1+ with a mating attack.

29 ♘xe5 ♖f2+?

With the full point within his grasp, Kasparov falters. Black retains a mating attack after

29...♘xd2! 30 ♘xd7 (30 ♖c1 ♘f3+!) 30...♘f3+ 31 ♕e2 ♘h4+ 32 ♔g1 (32 ♔g3 ♕xc3+ 33 ♔xh4 ♖f4+ is just as hopeless) 32...♕xc3.

30 ♕xf2! *(D)*

Black should gradually win after 30 ♔g1 ♖xd2 31 ♕xe4 (31 ♘xe4? ♖g2+ leads to mate) 31...♕xc3 32 ♖a8+ ♔g7 33 ♘f3 ♖d1+ 34 ♔g2 ♕f6 35 ♖a7 ♕f7, so White must sacrifice his queen.

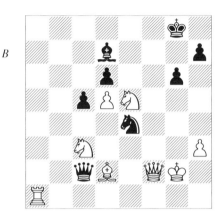

30 ... ♘xf2!?

An intuitive decision. With only five minutes left, Kasparov didn't have time for a closer look at 30...♗xh3+?!, by which Black snaps up a spare pawn but his forces lose coordination. After 31 ♔g1! (31 ♔h2? ♘xf2 32 ♖a8+ ♔g7 33 ♖a7+ ♔f6 34 ♖f7+ ♔xe5 35 ♖xf2 ♕d3 36 ♗g5 is best met by 36...♗f5 37 ♖e2+ ♗e4!) 31...♘xf2 32 ♖a2 ♕b3 (32...♕xa2 33 ♘xa2 ♘e4 34 ♘c4 and 32...♕f5 33 ♖a8+ ♔g7 34 ♖a7+ ♔f6 35 ♘d7+ ♕xd7 36 ♖xd7 ♗xd7 37 ♔xf2 lead only to drawish endgames) 33 ♖a8+ ♔g7 34 ♖a7+ ♔f6 (otherwise White has a perpetual) 35 ♘f3! it's suddenly White who is attacking. The main threat is ♗g5+ with mate in four and this will cost Black a piece, as 35...♘d3? 36 ♘e4+ ♔f5 37 ♘xd6+ ♔g4 38 ♘h2+ mates.

31 ♖a2 ♕f5

This move, which led nowhere in the previous note, is now possible.

32 ♘xd7 ♘d3 *(D)*

This should have led to a draw by force, but other winning attempts are also far from clear;

e.g., 32...♕xd7 33 ♔xf2 ♕xh3 34 ♘e4 ♕f5+ 35 ♔e3.

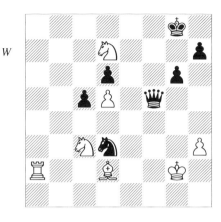

33 ♗h6?

Korchnoi squanders the unexpected chance Black's 29th move suddenly gave him. Necessary was 33 ♖a8+! ♔g7 34 ♖a7 ♕f2+ 35 ♔h1 and now either Black immediately gives a perpetual (35...♕f3+ 36 ♔h2 ♕f2+), or leaves it to White after 35...♕xd2 (35...c4? 36 ♘c5+! ♔g8 37 ♖a8+ ♔f7 38 ♘5e4 is dangerous only for Black) 36 ♘e5+ ♔f8 (after 36...♔h6?? 37 ♘g4+ Black loses his queen) 37 ♖a8+ ♔e7 38 ♖a7+ ♔d8 39 ♖a8+ because now 39...♔c7? 40 ♘b5+ ♔b7 41 ♖a7+ leads either to mate or the win of the queen.

33 ... ♕xd7
34 ♖a8+ ♔f7
35 ♖h8?!

In mutual time-trouble White eases Black's task. 35 ♘e4 is more testing, as White creates fork tricks such as ♖b8-b7 and keeps the enemy king pinned to the 7th rank. However, even here Black wins after the strong 35...♕e7! 36 ♖f8+ (36 ♘g5+ ♔f6 37 ♖f8+ ♔e5 38 ♖f7 ♕e8 and Black finally activates his queen) 36...♕xf8 37 ♘g5+ (37 ♗xf8 ♔xf8 38 ♘xd6 ♘f4+ with two extra pawns) 37...♔g8 38 ♗xf8 ♔xf8 39 ♘xh7+ ♔g7 40 ♘g5 ♔f6.

35 ... ♔f6

Now Black's king escapes to safety and the following blunder doesn't change the outcome.

36 ♔f3? ♕xh3+

0-1

Game 22
Garry Kasparov – Alexander Beliavsky
Candidates Quarterfinal (game 5), Moscow 1983
Queen's Gambit Declined, Tartakower Defence [D58]

Just before this game, Beliavsky equalized the score in a tense encounter, so Kasparov naturally wanted to regain the initiative in the match. He managed to do this in a convincing manner, which, especially later, became typical for him: a well-prepared novelty decided the theoretical duel in his favour and gave him a distinct advantage right out of the opening.

1	d4	d5
2	c4	e6
3	♘c3	♘f6
4	cxd5	

In Game 3, we saw in the note to Black's 11th move that Kasparov had been successful against Beliavsky's Tartakower Defence in 1978, but this didn't endanger the solid reputation of his opponent's favourite line. For their match Kasparov prepared the Exchange Variation, which was to become an integral part of his repertoire later on.

4	...	exd5
5	♗g5	♗e7
6	e3 *(D)*	

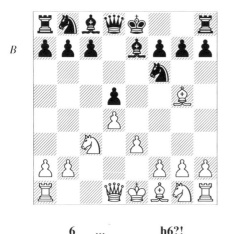

6	...	h6?!

Black usually postpones or omits this move altogether. The immediate 6...0-0 is more flexible. However, Black had a surprise of his own on his mind.

7	♗h4	0-0
8	♗d3	b6

Beliavsky transposes into Tartakower positions after all, but this concept isn't favoured by theory. In the match this position arose four times and Kasparov proved White has a promising initiative. The point is in lines with an early cxd5 Black usually recaptures with his knight, forcing an exchange of two pairs of minor pieces and easing his defensive task.

9	♘f3 *(D)*	

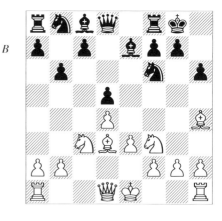

In game 1 of the match this natural move cost White a full 22 minutes. It indicates that it was Kasparov's intention to develop his knight to e2 after continuations such as 8...♘bd7. Instead of the queenside minority attack (♖b1, b4-b5), typical for this pawn-structure, White concentrates mainly on a gradual preparation of the central expansion with f3 and e4. For a convincing implementation of this strategy see Kasparov-Andersson, Belfort (World Cup) 1988 (Game 45).

9	...	♗b7
10	0-0	c5 *(D)*

In game 7 Beliavsky admitted this isn't ideal and tried a different approach with 10...♘e4 11 ♗xe7 ♕xe7, but even here after 12 ♘e5! (12 ♕b3 ♖d8 13 ♖ac1 also gives White an edge)

12...♘d7 13 f4 the centralized knight caused Black a lot of problems. Even 13...♘xe5 14 fxe5 c5 15 ♕e1 ♖ad8 16 ♖d1 ♕g5, as played, wouldn't have fully solved them, had White simply continued 17 ♕e2.

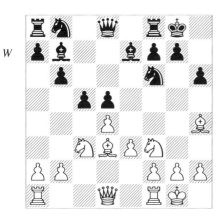

11 ♘e5!

Often played, but less demanding, is 11 ♖c1 ♘bd7. The text-move initiates Pillsbury's famous set-up: if left to his own devices, White will proceed to amass his forces against Black's already weakened kingside with f4, ♕f3, etc. The premature 6...h6?! makes the e5-knight even more powerful, as chasing the knight away with ...f6 would create gaping light-square holes around Black's king.

11 ... ♘bd7

The first game of the match saw Beliavsky play 11...♘c6?!. This is seemingly more logical, as Black attacks both e5 and d4 at once. However, White has the tactical shot 12 ♗a6!, and after 12...♕c8 13 ♗xb7 ♕xb7 14 ♗xf6 ♗xf6 15 ♘g4 ♗d8 16 ♘xd5 ♘xd4 17 ♘df6+ ♗xf6 18 ♘xf6+ gxf6 19 exd4 cxd4 20 ♕xd4 Kasparov had a large and permanent advantage due to Black's wrecked kingside.

12 ♗f5!

12 f4 allows welcome simplification with 12...cxd4 13 exd4 ♘e4. The text-move improves upon 12 ♕f3 from game 3, when Beliavsky equalized with the clever 12...cxd4 13 exd4 ♘xe5 14 dxe5 ♘d7 15 ♗xe7 ♕xe7 16 ♘xd5 ♕xe5 17 ♘e7+ ♔h8! 18 ♕xb7 ♘c5! 19 ♕f3 ♘xd3 20 ♘c6 ♕e6 21 b3 ♘e5.

12 ... ♘xe5

Black must somehow resolve the central tangle. The idea from the previous note, 12...cxd4, now leads after 13 ♘xd7! ♘xd7 14 ♗xe7 ♕xe7 15 ♕xd4 to an unpleasant position: Black has no active prospects to compensate for the isolated and blockaded d-pawn. A similar situation arises after 12...g6 13 ♗xd7 ♘xd7 14 ♘xd7 ♕xd7 15 ♗xe7 ♕xe7 16 dxc5; especially in the tense match atmosphere Beliavsky doesn't want to limit himself to passive defence yet.

13 dxe5 *(D)*

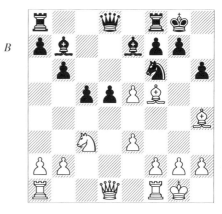

13 ... ♘e8?!

The typical freeing move 13...♘e4? runs into 14 ♘xd5!, winning a pawn. The same goes for 13...♘d7? 14 ♗xe7 ♕xe7 15 f4, but the text-move isn't ideal either, as the knight gets in the way on e8. The modest 13...♘h7 14 ♗g3 ♘g5 is somewhat better.

14 ♗g3 ♘c7?!

Naturally Black would like to play ...♘e6, but in fact his knight will only be able to leave the vulnerable c7-square 18 moves later. Weakening the kingside with 14...g6 15 ♗c2 ♘c7 (15...♘g7 16 ♕f3 and the d5-pawn is very weak) is a lesser evil, although after, e.g., 16 ♗f4 (16 ♕f3!?) 16...♗g5 17 ♕g4!? White has promising attacking chances.

15 ♕g4 ♕e8?

This move is connected with a tactical oversight and renders an already compromised position untenable. The only attempt to coordinate Black's forces was 15...♗c8 16 ♖ad1 ♗xf5 (16...♗e6? fails to 17 ♘xd5! ♗xd5 18 e4) 17 ♕xf5. Although now the d-pawn is defenceless, winning the simplified position after 17...d4 18 ♘e2 ♘e6 19 ♕e4 ♕d7 20 exd4 cxd4 21 ♘xd4 ♖ad8 will certainly require more than pure technique.

16 ♗d7! ♕d8

This is forced. Beliavsky realized too late that 16...♗c8 loses on the spot to 17 e6!.

17 ♖ad1 *(D)*

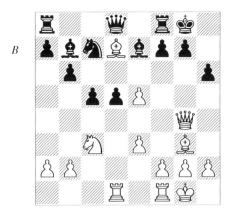

Kasparov's home preparation ended here. White's position is close to winning: the d7-bishop paralyses Black.

17 ... h5

Black doesn't relish the prospect of passively waiting (e.g., 17...♔h8 18 ♖d2!?, followed by ♖fd1 and a timely e6). Beliavsky's bid for counterplay is the best chance, requiring energetic play from White.

18 ♕h3 h4
19 ♗f4 ♗g5

This finally gives Black's queen some scope. Further weakening of the kingside with 19...g5? allows White a decisive attack by 20 ♕g4.

20 ♗f5!

The bishop is not needed on d7 any more. 20 e6?! ♗xf4 21 exf4 ♕f6 gets White nowhere, and 20 ♗xg5 ♕xg5 21 f4 ♕e7 is less convincing than the text-move.

20 ... g6

This natural reaction allows a tactical solution. However, even after 20...♕e7 White has 21 ♘e4! dxe4 (21...♗xf4? 22 ♘f6+! mates) 22 ♖d7 with a decisive advantage. No better is 20...♗xf4 21 exf4 d4 (21...♕e7 again runs into 22 ♘e4!, threatening ♘f6+) 22 ♘e4 ♗xe4 23 ♗xe4 ♖b8 24 f5 ♖e8 25 f4. Black's central pawns are going nowhere, while f6 is a strong threat. Kasparov continues the line with 25...f6 26 ♕xh4 fxe5 27 f6! and the attack breaks through.

21 ♘e4! ♗xf4

Black accepts the sacrifice, as after 21...♗e7 22 ♘d6!? ♗a6 23 ♗d3 White's d6-knight stops any meaningful counterplay.

22 exf4 gxf5
23 ♕xf5! *(D)*

Now Black must give up his queen. Instead, 23 ♘f6+?! is unconvincing: 23...♔g7 24 ♕xh4 ♖h8 25 ♕g5+ ♔f8.

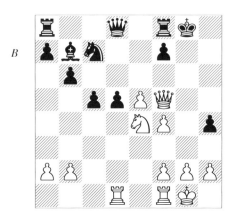

23 ... dxe4

The only move. 23...♔g7? 24 ♕g4+! ♔h8 25 ♘g5 is even more costly.

24 ♕g4+

This *zwischenzug* enables White to take the h4-pawn with check.

24 ... ♔h7
25 ♖xd8 ♖fxd8
26 ♕xh4+ ♔g8
27 ♕e7!

Despite approximate material equality, White is practically winning, as Black's king is permanently exposed and his pieces lack coordination. The accurate text-move is a necessary follow-up to the whole operation started on move 21, because 27 f5?! ♖d7! followed by ...♖e8 allows Black to connect his rooks and put up stiff resistance.

27 ... e3!

Black does his best to confuse the issue. After 27...♖ac8 28 f5 ♖d5 29 g4 the threat of e6 quickly decides.

28 ♖e1! *(D)*

Kasparov had enough time on the clock (he spent only 50 minutes on the entire game!) to find the best antidote to Black's last practical chance. White can't ignore the cheeky pawn: after 28 ♕xc7? e2 the deadly threat of ...♖d1 turns the tables. 28 fxe3!? is interesting, but still inferior to the text-move, as after 28...♖d2 29 ♖e1 (29 ♕xc7? even loses to 29...♖xg2+ 30 ♔h1 ♗e4!) 29...♖ad8!? (29...♖xg2+ 30 ♔f1 ♖c8 31 ♖e2! exchanges a pair of rooks and stops any possible tricks) 30 ♖e2 (30 e6 wins a piece, but after 30...♖xg2+ 31 ♔f1 ♘xe6 32 ♕xb7 ♖xh2 Black retains some drawing prospects) 30...♖8d7 Black's pieces cooperate much better than in the game, and the outcome still remains in doubt.

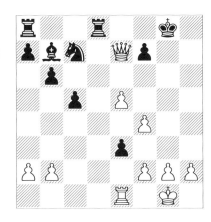

28 ... exf2+?!

Beliavsky on the other hand was in serious time-trouble and missed an opportunity to complicate matters. The trickier alternatives were:

1) 28...♖d2 29 f3! (weaker is 29 fxe3, transposing to the note to White's 28th move) 29...♖ad8 30 f5! (30 ♖xe3?! is unconvincing, as after 30...♖8d7 31 ♕g5+ ♔f8 Black intends ...♖xb2 and ...♖dd2 with counterplay), followed by ♕g5+ and ♕xe3, and the connected passed pawns should decide the game.

2) 28...e2 29 f3 ♖d1 30 ♔f2 ♗a6 is best met by 31 f5!? (31 ♕xc7 ♖ad8 32 ♕xa7 ♖xe1 33 ♕xa6 ♖ed1 34 ♔xe2 ♖8d2+ still gives Black some fighting chances) 31...♖ad8 (31...♘e8 32 e6 f6 33 g4 and the threat of g5 decides) 32 e6 ♘xe6 33 fxe6 fxe6 34 ♕xe6+ ♔f8 35 ♕f6+ ♔e8 36 ♕g6+ ♔f8 37 ♖xe2 and again the kingside phalanx is too strong.

29   ♔xf2

The e-pawn has been eliminated without any serious damage and Black's forces remain uncoordinated. The rest is quite simple.

29	...	♖d2+
30	♖e2	♖xe2+
31	♔xe2	♗a6+
32	♔f2	♘e6
33	f5 *(D)*	

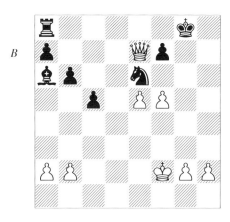

33   ...   ♘d4

33...♘g7 34 e6 ♖f8 35 ♕xa7 is just as hopeless.

34	e6	♖f8
35	♕g5+	♔h7
36	e7!	

White wants more than 36 exf7 ♘xf5 37 ♕xf5+ ♔g7.

36	...	♖e8
37	f6	♘e6
38	♕h5+	♔g8

1-0

Black resigned before White could choose from the various winning lines. The most convincing is 39 ♕g4+ ♔h7 40 ♕a4 ♘c7 41 ♕e4+ ♔h6 42 h4! and all the kingside pawns join the mating attack.

Game 23
Garry Kasparov – Mikhail Tal
USSR Team Ch, Moscow 1983
Queen's Gambit Declined, Semi-Slav Defence [D44]

1	d4	♘f6
2	c4	e6
3	♘f3	d5
4	♘c3	c6
5	♗g5	dxc4

In their previous encounter in the Moscow Interzonal in 1982, Tal opted for 5...h6 and the game went 6 ♗h4!? dxc4 7 e4 g5 8 ♗g3 b5 9 ♗e2 with a sharp position and good compensation for White – incidentally, this line is very popular nowadays.

6	e4	b5
7	e5	h6
8	♗h4	g5
9	♘xg5	hxg5
10	♗xg5	♘bd7
11	exf6	♗b7 *(D)*

The Botvinnik System started to appear in practice about 60 years ago and was one of the first lines symbolizing a new approach to opening theory. From the very beginning Black strives for active counterplay by creating an unbalanced – one could even say irrational – position, where both sides have their trumps on opposite sides of the board. Although various sidelines have been refuted in the course of time, the system as a whole has survived its inventor thanks to the complex nature of the arising positions.

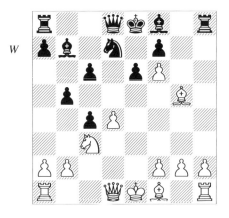

12	g3	c5
13	d5	♕b6

Currently this is still the most popular move, but continuations such as 13...♗h6 and recently even 13...♕c7!? 14 ♗g2 b4 are considered to be viable alternatives. Kasparov was always a staunch defender of White's cause in the Botvinnik and still continues to play it; Volume 2 will feature the game Kasparov-Ivanchuk, Linares 1994 with 13...♘xf6.

14	♗g2	0-0-0
15	0-0	b4
16	♘a4 *(D)*	

16 ♖b1!? was originally Uhlmann's idea, later revived in Kasparov-Kramnik, New York PCA rpd 1994. In the critical position after 16...♕a6 17 dxe6 ♗xg2 18 e7 Black is still fighting for equality.

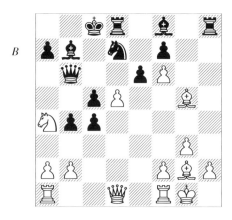

16	...	♕b5

The main move, but 16...♕a6 17 a3 ♗xd5 18 ♗xd5 ♘e5 19 axb4 ♖xd5 20 ♕e2 cxb4 21 ♘c3 ♖a5 22 ♖xa5 ♕xa5 23 ♘e4 ♘d3 is also playable and unclear.

17	a3	

Black has excellent piece-play for the pawn after 17 dxe6 ♗xg2 18 ♔xg2 ♕c6+ 19 f3 ♕xe6, so White ignores material and opens a file against the enemy king instead.

17 ... ♘b8?! *(D)*

More than 20 years later it's easy to condemn this move, which was Black's main continuation in those days but has been practically refuted since. Black should play 17...exd5 18 axb4 cxb4 (or even 18...d4!?) with unclear consequences.

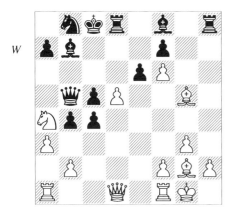

18 axb4 cxb4
19 ♗e3?!

Just as in the note above, the evaluation of this move is based on hindsight. White has stronger continuations which later forced 17...♘b8?! into oblivion: 19 ♕g4 ♗xd5 20 ♖fc1 ♘c6 21 ♗xd5 ♖xd5 22 ♖xc4 or the even more energetic 19 ♕d4!? ♘c6 20 dxc6! ♖xd4 21 cxb7+ ♔c7 22 ♗e3 e5 23 ♘c3! with a dangerous attack in both cases.

19 ... ♗xd5
20 ♗xd5 ♖xd5
21 ♕e2 ♘c6
22 ♖fc1 *(D)*

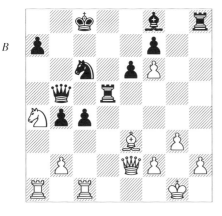

22 ... ♘e5!

This move occurred for the first time in the game Salov-Shabalov, Leningrad jr 1983, and we can presume that Tal knew about the idea of his talented junior compatriot from Riga. By powerfully centralizing his knight, Black overturns the evaluation of the whole line as advantageous for White. We'll see how Kasparov himself had significantly contributed to this verdict by examining the weaker alternatives:

1) 22...♔b7? 23 ♖xc4 ♘a5 24 b3! gives White a clear advantage, as 24...♘xb3? loses outright to 25 ♕c2.

2) 22...c3?! 23 ♕xb5 ♖xb5 24 ♘xc3! bxc3 25 ♖xc3 ♔d7 26 ♖a6 ♘d8 27 ♖xa7+ ♔e8 28 ♖c8 was played in Rashkovsky-Timoshchenko, Volgodonsk 1981. Preparing for his encounter with Timoshchenko in the USSR Championship in Frunze 1981, Kasparov analysed the aforementioned game and came to the conclusion Black was in trouble. Therefore he confidently repeated the first 22 moves, but...

3) Black came up with an interesting novelty 22...♘a5. However, despite the hunter becoming the hunted, Kasparov in turn proceeded to refute Black's idea over the board with the energetic 23 b3! c3 24 ♘xc3 bxc3 25 ♖xc3+ ♔d7 (25...♔b8 26 ♕c2 ♗d6 27 b4! with a raging attack) 26 ♕c2 ♗d6 27 ♖c1 ♕b7 28 b4 ♕xb4 (28...♖xh2? fails to the *zwischenzug* 29 ♕a4+!) 29 ♖b1 ♕g4 30 ♗xa7! *(D)*. This is only seemingly greedy, as the a7-pawn was important for the defence, preventing ♗b6+ in the line 30 f3 ♕f5! 31 ♕a4+ ♔d8.

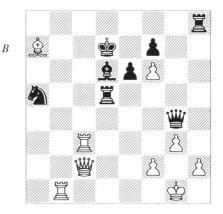

Now 31 f3 is a serious threat and it seems Black doesn't have a satisfactory defence:

3a) After 30...e5 31 ♕a2! ♖d1+ (31...♕f5 is somewhat more testing, but after 32 f3! ♕h7 33 ♗e3! White is ready to take on d5) 32 ♖xd1 ♕xd1+ 33 ♔g2 ♕h5 34 ♕a4+ ♔e6 35 h4 Black loses his knight and his king remains hopelessly exposed, Kasparov-Timoshchenko, USSR Ch (Frunze) 1981.

3b) This exciting game was followed by a lively post-mortem, in which the Botvinnik fans came up with 30...♗e5, which seemed to hold the position. Little did Kasparov know he was going to face this very move in the following round! However, this time he was fully armed, having found the decisive improvement the night before: 31 ♖c5! (31 f3? is wrong because of 31...♗d4+ 32 ♔h1 ♕xg3 33 ♕a4+ ♔d8) 31...♖xc5 32 ♗xc5! (weaker is 32 ♕xc5? ♘c6) 32...♘c6 (32...♕g6 loses by force: 33 ♕a4+ ♘c6 34 ♖d1+ ♔c7 35 ♖c1!) 33 ♕d3+ ♔c8 34 ♖d1 ♘b8 35 ♖c1! with a winning attack, Kasparov-Dorfman, USSR Ch (Frunze) 1981.

We return to the position after 22...♘e5! *(D)*:

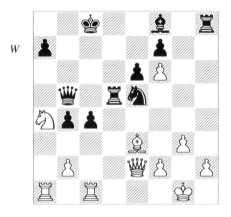

Over the board Kasparov has always been very consistent and principled, but one and a half years after the events described above he once again became the hunted. And the hunter was especially dangerous – the tactical magician Mikhail Tal.

23 b3!?

White's a4-knight is offside and after long thought Kasparov decided to sacrifice it in a similar fashion as in the above note. This is White's best chance, although here it's sufficient only for an uneasy sort of equality. The reason is Black's knight is now not only an object of attack, but a strong attacking piece itself.

The inferior alternatives demonstrate this even more clearly:

1) 23 ♗xa7?! ♔b7! 24 ♗e3 (24 ♘b6 c3! 25 ♕xb5 ♖xb5 26 bxc3 ♘c6 costs White a piece) 24...♖d3! is extremely dangerous for White. The main threat is ...♕c6 and after 25 f4 (25 ♘b6 loses material to 25...♖xe3! 26 ♕xe3 ♗c5) 25...♖xh2! 26 ♔xh2 ♖xe3 27 ♕d1 ♖e1! 28 ♕h5 ♕d5 Black wins White's queen with a huge advantage.

2) Also after 23 f4 ♘d3 24 ♖xc4+ ♕xc4 25 ♖c1 ♕xc1+ 26 ♗xc1 ♘xc1 27 ♕c4+ ♔b7 28 ♕xc1 ♗d6 Black's pieces are ideally coordinated and it's White who must be careful.

23 ... c3
24 ♘xc3 bxc3
25 ♖xc3+ ♔b8 *(D)*

This is best. 25...♔b7? loses on the spot to 26 ♕c2!, the point being 26...♗d6 (Black does not achieve a perpetual check after 26...♘f3+ 27 ♔g2) 27 ♖c7+!. 25...♔d8?! is also risky, as after 26 ♖xa7! the queen is taboo due to mate in three.

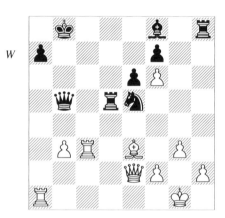

26 ♕c2

After the natural 26 ♗xa7+?! ♔b7 White has three pawns for the knight, but his own king is also in danger and he can hardly avoid the endgame: 27 ♕xb5+ (27 ♕c4 ♕b4! 28 ♕c2 ♗d6 gives Black the attack; Kasparov demonstrated the pretty line 29 ♖a4? ♘f3+!! 30 ♖xf3 ♕e1+ 31 ♔g2 ♖xh2+ 32 ♔xh2 ♖h5+ with mate) 27...♖xb5 28 ♗e3 ♗d6 with an edge for Black.

26 ... ♗d6!

Black must first consolidate his position. 26...♘f3+? fails to 27 ♔g2 ♖xh2+ 28 ♔xf3 ♖f5+ 29 ♔g4.

27 &xa7+

27 ♖xa7?? now runs into 27...♘f3+ 28 ♔g2 ♘e1+.

27 ... ♔b7 *(D)*

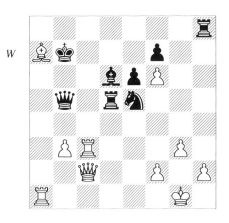

28 b4!

Black would come first after 28 ♗e3? ♘f3+ 29 ♔g2 ♖xh2+ 30 ♔xf3 ♖f5+ 31 ♗f4 (31 ♔g4 ♖f4+! mates) 31...♖xf4+ 32 gxf4 ♕h5+. Therefore White must keep f3 protected for the time being, and the seemingly weak and isolated b-pawn is in fact an important attacking tool.

28 ... ♘c6?!

A solid and natural move: Black attacks the bishop and prevents ♖a5. However, now White will be out of danger. More ambitious continuations:

1) 28...♖a8 29 ♖a5 ♕d7 30 ♗b6 ♗b8 (after 30...♖axa5 31 bxa5 ♘c6 32 ♖b3 White has enough play to hold the game) 31 ♖xa8 (31 ♕e4!?) 31...♔xa8 32 ♕e4 ♕b5!? with a slight edge for Black.

2) If Tal considered this too double-edged, the solid move 28...♖d3!? forces White to liquidate into an endgame with 29 ♖xd3 ♕xd3 (after 29...♘xd3 30 ♗c5!? White has sufficient counterplay against Black's exposed king) 30 ♕xd3 ♘xd3 31 ♖d1 ♗xa7 32 ♖xd3 ♖d8. Black still retains some winning chances, as White can't support his advanced f6-pawn yet (33 g4? ♗xh2+).

29 ♗e3 ♗e5 *(D)*

Tal decides to force matters, although now White will be the one to decide if he wants to fight for more than a draw. Therefore 29...♖c8 seems safer:

1) Kasparov's idea 30 ♖b1 is rather risky. After 30...♖c7 (30...♗e5!?) 31 ♖c5 ♕d3 32 b5 ♘e5 White must simplify into a worse endgame, because 33 ♖xc7+ ♗xc7 34 ♕a2?! runs into 34...♗a5! and the attack passes to Black.

2) Thus the best is 30 ♕h7! with the practically forced continuation 30...♗e5 (30...♘d8 31 ♖ca3 can be dangerous for Black) 31 ♕xf7+ (31 ♖xc6? ♕xc6 32 ♕xf7+ ♖c7 33 ♖a7+ ♔b8 and the weak back rank decides) 31...♖c7 32 ♕e8 ♖d8 33 ♕h5 (33 f7 ♗xc3 34 ♕xd8 ♘xd8 35 ♖a7+ ♔c8 36 ♖a8+! also draws) 33...♖d5 34 ♕e8 (34 f7? ♗xc3 35 f8♕ ♗xa1 gives Black a winning attack) with a repetition.

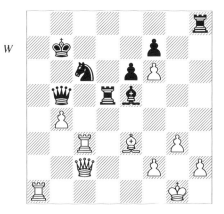

30 ♖xc6 ♗xa1
31 ♖c7+ ♔b8
32 ♗a7+

Weak is 32 ♖xf7? ♖d7 and after the exchange of rooks White's attack is over.

32 ... ♔a8
33 ♗e3

White repeats moves to win time on the clock, as Black's reply is forced.

33 ... ♔b8
34 ♗a7+ ♔a8
35 ♗c5 ♔b8

35...♗b2? loses a piece after 36 ♖a7+ ♔b8 37 ♗d4!.

36 ♖xf7! *(D)*

A dangerous winning attempt, which requires accurate defence.

36 ... ♗e5!

White's main threat was ♗d6+ and this also refutes the defence from the note to White's 32nd move: after 36...♖d7? 37 ♗d6+! ♔b7 38 ♕e4+ ♔a6 39 ♕xc6 ♖xf7 40 ♗c5+ ♔b7 41

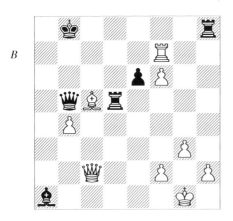

♕xf7+ Black is lost. Also 36...♗c3? 37 h4! only gives White's king more room; for example, 37...♖d3 38 ♖e7 ♖hd8 39 f7 ♖d1+ 40 ♔h2 ♕f1 41 ♗a7+ ♔a8 42 ♕e4+ and White wins.

37 ♗a7+

Other winning attempts are also insufficient due to White's vulnerable king:

1) 37 f4? is too risky due to 37...♖hd8 38 ♗a7+ ♔a8 39 ♗f2 ♖d1+ 40 ♔g2 ♕f1+! (40...♕d5+?! only leads to a draw after 41 ♔h3 ♗d4 42 ♗xd4 ♕h5+) 41 ♔f3 ♔b8! 42 fxe5 ♖c1 and the counterattack should decide the game.

2) After 37 ♖e7 ♖hd8! 38 f7 ♖d1+ 39 ♔g2 ♕c6+! (39...♕f1+? 40 ♔f3 ♕h1+ 41 ♔g4 and there is no defence against ♖e8) 40 ♔h3 ♕f3 41 ♕h7 ♗xg3! 42 fxg3 ♖1d5 (42...♕f1+ is a perpetual) 43 ♖b7+! ♔c8 44 ♖c7+ White has to give a perpetual.

37 ... ♔a8
38 ♗e3 ♖d7!

Tal remains alert. After 38...♔b8? 39 ♖e7 ♖hd8 40 f7 ♖d1+ 41 ♔g2 ♕d5+, unlike note '2' to White's 37th move, the white bishop covers d2 and he has 42 f3!, when Black is in trouble; e.g., 42...♖d3 43 ♖e8 ♗g7 44 ♕c5 ♕xc5 45 ♗xc5 with a won endgame.

39 ♕a2+

39 ♕e4+? ♕b7 costs White the f6-pawn.

39 ... ♔b8 (D)

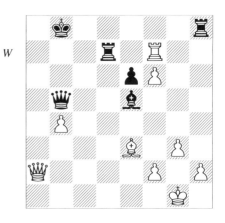

40 ♗a7+

40 ♕xe6 ♖d1+ 41 ♔g2 ♖d6! (hot pursuit of White's king by 41...♕f1+? 42 ♔f3 ♕h1+ 43 ♔g4 ♕e4+ backfires after 44 ♗f4! ♕g6+ 45 ♔f3) again picks up White's most advanced pawn and can only be good for Black.

40 ... ♔c8

After 40...♔b7? 41 ♕xe6 the f6-pawn stays alive and spells trouble.

41 ♕xe6 ♕d5
42 ♕a6+

Kasparov has had enough excitement and goes for repetition. After 42 ♕xd5?! ♖xd5 43 f4 (43 ♗c5 ♖h6 44 ♖f8+ ♔d7 45 f7 ♔e6 gets White nowhere) 43...♗d6 White can't connect his pawns and it's Black who can harbour ambitions.

42 ... ♕b7
43 ♕c4+ ♕c7

½-½

The last accurate move forces 44 ♕a6+ with a draw, as 44 ♕e6? ♗xg3! is advantageous for Black.

Game 24
Garry Kasparov – Lajos Portisch
Nikšić 1983
Queen's Indian Defence [E12]

1	d4	♘f6
2	c4	e6
3	♘f3	b6
4	♘c3	♗b7
5	a3	d5
6	cxd5	♘xd5
7	e3	♘xc3

7...♗e7 was played in Game 10, which also contains more notes about the opening phase. Portisch doesn't wait until White attacks the d5-knight with e4, but on the other hand the immediate exchange reinforces White's centre.

8	bxc3	♗e7
9	♗b5+	c6
10	♗d3	c5

After 10...0-0 Black has to reckon with 11 ♕c2. This also shows one of the reasons why 7...g6!? is a popular alternative – Black has no problems on the b1-h7 diagonal. In our game Black first develops his queenside: a quick ...♖c8 serves to discourage ♕c2 altogether.

| 11 | 0-0 | ♘c6 (D) |

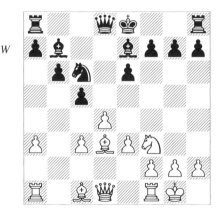

| 12 | ♗b2 | |

Earlier Kasparov used to play 12 e4. However, this is rather committal and after 12...♖c8 13 ♗b2 ♗f6!? White can retain the initiative only with the forceful 14 d5! exd5 15 exd5 ♕xd5 16 ♖e1+ ♔f8 17 ♕c2 ♘e5 18 ♗e4 ♘xf3+ 19 ♗xf3 ♕d7 20 ♖ad1 ♕c7 21 ♗xb7 ♕xb7 22 ♕a4 (22 ♖d6!? is perhaps stronger). In Kasparov-Ivkov, Bugojno 1982 White had good compensation for the pawn and went on to win, but the position is far from clear. The restrained text-move is more flexible.

12	...	♖c8
13	♕e2	0-0
14	♖ad1 (D)	

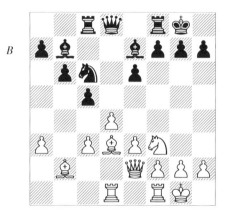

White wants to play in the centre and on the kingside, so his rooks belong on d1 and e1.

| 14 | ... | ♕c7? |

Black moves his queen out of harm's way, but in a higher sense this move can probably be labelled as the decisive mistake, as it is very difficult to find improvements in his subsequent play. After 14...♘a5 White could consider accepting the offer with 15 dxc5!?, but 14...cxd4 is better. Although in Game 10 we condemned a similar release of the central tension, there the situation was somewhat different, as White's pawn is not yet on e4 here. The difference will be apparent immediately after Kasparov's next move. Perhaps Portisch could have anticipated it, as the game Kasparov-Tukmakov, USSR 1982, which was published in *Informator*, went 15 exd4 (15 cxd4 is better; White can claim a slight advantage) 15...♗f6! 16 c4 ♘a5 17 ♘e5

♗xe5 18 dxe5 ♕c7 19 ♕h5 g6 20 ♕h6 ♕c6 21 f3 ♕c5+ 22 ♔h1 ♘xc4 23 ♗d4 ♕xa3 24 ♗f2 ♗d5 25 ♗h4 ♖fe8 26 ♗e4 and White had barely sufficient compensation for the pawns, and certainly no more than that.

We now return to the position after 14...♕c7? *(D)*:

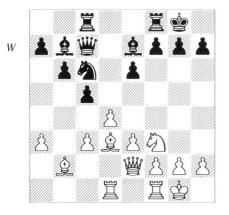

15 c4!

A strong and inspired novelty. Previous games featured the insipid 15 e4 ♘a5, which justified Black's strategy. However, it's far more logical to open the long diagonal for the b2-bishop than to close the b1-h7 diagonal. With both bishops targeting Black's king, White's hanging pawns will also become a dangerous attacking instrument.

15 ... cxd4

Black decides to open the position after all. An attempt to neutralize the b2-bishop with 15...♗f6? fails to 16 d5!, when the knight must retreat offside, as 16...♘e5 17 ♘xe5 ♗xe5 18 ♗xh7+! ♔xh7 19 ♕h5+ costs Black a pawn. Even after 15...♘a5 the energetic 16 d5! gives White a significant advantage. If Black continues analogously as in the game 16...exd5 17 cxd5 ♗xd5 (17...c4 18 ♗f5 and the mobile central pawns outweigh Black's passed c-pawn) 18 ♗xh7+ ♔xh7 19 ♖xd5, White gets an attack without having to reckon with counterplay on the c-file; the main threat is ♖h5+ and ♕c2. However, also after the text-move the central break is unstoppable.

16 exd4 ♘a5
17 d5!

Activating the b2-bishop. Contours of the famous games Em.Lasker-Bauer, Amsterdam 1889 and Nimzowitsch-Tarrasch, St Petersburg 1914 are starting to appear.

17 ... exd5

Other moves are no less dangerous. After 17...♕f4 18 ♘e5 White has a strong initiative, since 18...exd5?! loses material to 19 ♗c1!. 17...♘xc4 invites the forcing sequence 18 ♕e4 g6 19 ♗xc4 ♕xc4 20 ♘e5 f6 21 ♕xe6+ ♖f7 22 ♖c1 ♕a6 and now 23 d6 (Kasparov's subsequent recommendation 23 ♘d4!? also retains the pressure) forces 23...b5! (23...♗d8 loses to 24 ♘g5! fxg5 25 ♖xc8 ♗xc8 26 ♕e8+ ♖f8 27 d7; e.g., 27...♗xd7 28 ♕xd7 ♗f6 29 ♕e6+ ♔g7 30 ♖d1! and the attack breaks through). This resource was found by Volgin, but it still doesn't solve Black's problems after 24 ♖fd1 ♗f8 (24...♖xc1? 25 ♗xc1 ♗f8 26 ♕e8 ♕a4 27 ♖e1 and Black is lost, because attempts to parry the threat d7 allow ♖e7) 25 ♗e5!? and the passed d-pawn is a tower of strength.

18 cxd5 ♗xd5

Black can't afford to leave the d5-pawn alive, as 18...g6 19 ♖fe1 gives White a huge attack.

19 ♗xh7+

Compared with the games mentioned in the note to White's 17th move, this move is not a sacrifice, but just a standard exchanging manoeuvre.

19 ... ♔xh7
20 ♖xd5 *(D)*

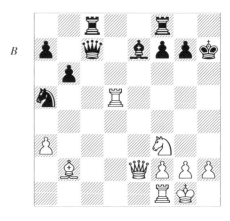

20 ... ♔g8

Black must spend a tempo safeguarding his king. The active try 20...♕c2 fails to 21 ♖d2 ♕c7 (21...♕c5 22 ♘e5 doesn't help) 22 ♕e4+ f5 23 ♕e6 with a winning attack.

21 ♗xg7!!

Two moves later White deals a deadly blow on the neighbouring square. This is a genuine sacrifice that permanently exposes Black's king. Kasparov wrote he felt this was the crucial moment when he had to play actively. However, 21 ♘e5 blocks the bishop and 21 ♘g5 ♗xg5 22 ♖xg5 f6 promises White only a slight edge. Then he started calculating the forceful game continuation and his intuition quickly told him he was on the right track.

21 ... ♔xg7
22 ♘e5

White's attacking trio cooperates excellently to create deadly threats; Black's extra piece is the offside a5-knight, which doesn't help the defence at all.

22 ... ♖fd8

The most resilient try: Black frees f8 for his king. Other moves lose even faster:

1) 22...f5 23 ♖d7 ♕c5 24 ♘d3 wins the e7-bishop.

2) 22...♕c2 23 ♕g4+ ♔h7 24 ♖d3 and as 24...♖c6 loses on the spot to 25 ♕f5+, Black must give up his queen.

3) 22...♖cd8 23 ♘d7 (23 ♕g4+ ♔h8 24 ♘d7 is also good enough) 23...♕c6 (23...f6 24 ♕g4+ ♔f7 25 ♖e1 doesn't help Black) 24 ♕e5+ ♔h6 25 ♖fd1 ♖fe8 26 ♕h5+ ♔g7 27 ♖5d3 and again the mating threats cost Black his queen.

4) After 22...♖h8 23 ♕g4+ ♔f8 24 ♕f5 f6 the quiet 25 ♖e1! creates decisive threats; e.g., 25...♖h6 26 ♕e6!, winning.

23 ♕g4+ ♔f8
24 ♕f5 (D)

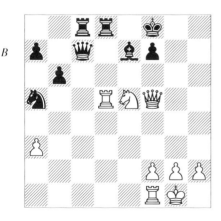

24 ... f6
Other moves were no better:

1) 24...♗d6 25 ♕f6 ♔g8 (the direct threat was ♘g6+) 26 ♕g5+ ♔f8 (otherwise 27 ♖d3 decides) 27 ♕h6+ ♔e8 (27...♔g8 28 ♖d4 mates) 28 ♖e1 and the discovered check can't be parried effectively; e.g., 28...♕c3 29 ♖d2 ♗xe5 30 ♕h8+!.

2) The computer-like 24...♗xa3 is met by 25 ♘d7+ ♖xd7 26 ♖xd7 ♕c4 27 ♖fd1! ♘c6 (27...♕e6 28 ♖xf7+ and 27...♗e7 28 ♕e5 ♕h4 29 ♖xe7 ♘c6 30 ♖xf7+ ♔xf7 31 ♕f5+ are also hopeless for Black) 28 ♕f6! ♔e8 29 ♖7d3 ♗f8 30 ♕f5 ♖c7 31 ♖d7 and White wins.

25 ♘d7+!

In his notes, Kasparov indicates that he had higher ambitions than a promising endgame with an extra pawn after 25 ♘g6+ ♔g7!? (not 25...♔e8? 26 ♕h5! ♖xd5 27 ♘e5+ mating, while 25...♔f7 26 ♘e5+ allows White to transpose back into the game) 26 ♘f4 ♖xd5 27 ♘xd5! (27 ♕g6+ ♔h8 28 ♘e6 ♖g5 is no good for White) 27...♕c5 28 ♘xe7 ♕xf5 29 ♘xf5+.

25 ... ♖xd7

Forced, as 25...♔f7? 26 ♕h7+ ♔e6 27 ♖e1+! ♔xd5 28 ♕e4+ mates and 25...♔g7? 26 ♖e1 also loses on the spot. However, now White has regained the sacrificed material with a continuing attack and Black's position is untenable in the long run, as his king is too vulnerable.

26 ♖xd7 ♕c5
27 ♕h7

An active move, creating the threat of ♖xe7, but 27 ♕h3 ♖c7 28 ♖d3 is a worthy alternative.

27 ... ♖c7 (D)

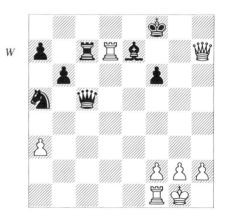

28 ♕h8+!

Contrary to the previous note, White now has to avoid the devilish trap 28 ♖d3? ♕xf2+!! 29

♔xf2 (29 ♖xf2? loses to 29...♖c1+) 29...♗c5+ and if anyone can claim an advantage, it's Black.

28	...	♔f7
29	♖d3	♘c4

Black finally gets a chance to move his knight closer to the scene of action, but it's too late. 29...♘c6? allows White to wrap up the game with 30 ♖g3 ♔e6 31 ♕g8+ ♔d7 32 ♖d1+ ♗d6 33 ♖gd3.

30 ♖fd1! *(D)*

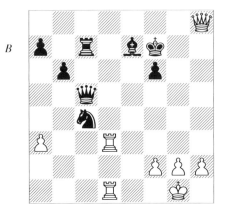

Kasparov patiently activates his last passive piece.

30 ... ♘e5?

Exhausted by the difficult defence, Portisch eases White's task. Now the attack wins by force, but even better moves wouldn't have changed the final outcome. After 30...♗d6 Nunn suggests 31 ♖h3!; e.g., 31...♖e7 32 ♖h5 ♕c6 33 ♖h6 and White wins the f-pawn. 30...♘d6 invites 31 ♖g3 ♔e6 32 ♕g7 ♘e4 33 ♕g8+, chasing Black's king out into the open.

31 ♕h7+ ♔e6

31...♔e8 32 ♕g8+ ♗f8 33 ♕e6+ mates.

32	♕g8+	♔f5
33	g4+	♔f4 *(D)*

33...♘xg4 34 ♖f3+ is no better.

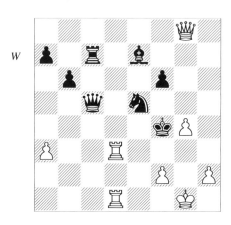

34	♖d4+	♔f3
35	♕b3+	1-0

Black's king will be mated after 35...♕c3 36 ♕d5+ ♔e2 37 ♕e4+.

Game 25
Garry Kasparov – Vasily Smyslov
Candidates Final (game 3), Vilnius 1984
Queen's Gambit Declined, Cambridge Springs [D52]

1	d4	d5
2	♘f3	♘f6
3	c4	c6
4	♘c3	e6
5	♗g5	♘bd7
6	e3	♕a5

By creating tactical threats along the e1-a5 diagonal Black wants to achieve a liberating central thrust (...c5 or ...e5), thus solving his most pressing long-term strategic problem in the Orthodox Queen's Gambit Declined – the development of the c8-bishop. The Cambridge Springs variation became a theoretical battleground in this match and although Kasparov did well to score 3 out of 4, the line has still retained its solid reputation.

7 cxd5

This ambitious and principled move fits Kasparov's style. Previously he had played the solid 7 ♘d2, but in Vilnius it brought him only two short draws (in the 7th and 13th games).

7	...	♘xd5
8	♕d2 *(D)*	

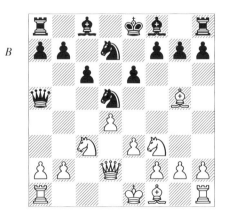

8 ... ♗b4

The older continuation 8...♘7b6 was once successfully adopted by Kasparov himself. The positions arising after 9 ♗d3 (the meek 9 ♘xd5?! ♕xd2+ 10 ♘xd2 exd5 11 ♗d3 a5 gave Black easy equality in Karpov-Kasparov, Moscow Wch (47) 1984/5; later Kasparov went on to score his first win ever with Black against Karpov) 9...♘xc3 10 bxc3 ♘a4!? 11 0-0 (11 ♖c1 ♘xc3 12 0-0 is similar) 11...♕xc3 12 ♕e2 promise White a lead in development and attacking chances for the pawn – this didn't suit Smyslov's classical style.

9 ♖c1 *(D)*

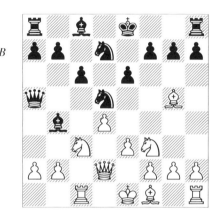

9 ... 0-0

Even a natural developing move can be inaccurate when realizing a complex strategic plan. Smyslov tried to improve his play in game 9 with 9...e5, but after 10 a3 ♗d6?! (10...♗xc3 11 bxc3 ♕xa3 is stronger, although 12 e4 gives White promising compensation) 11 dxe5 ♘xe5 12 ♘xe5 ♗xe5 13 b4! ♗xc3 14 ♕xc3 ♘xc3 15 bxa5 ♘e4 16 ♗f4 0-0 17 f3 ♘f6 18 e4 ♖e8 19 ♔f2 a6 20 ♗e2 White had a large and permanent positional advantage, which he convincingly converted into victory. It's interesting to note both Kasparov's white wins in the match were achieved in endgames with an active bishop-pair. Currently Black prefers a different treatment and he is quite successful with the topical alternative 9...h6 (interpolating this move is generally useful) 10 ♗h4 c5!? 11 a3 ♗xc3 12 bxc3 b6, followed by ...♗b7 or ...♗a6.

10 ♗d3

Kasparov's reaction, while natural enough, is perhaps not ideal either. White's pawn-centre after 10 e4 (the sacrificial 10 a3!? ♗xc3 11 bxc3 also deserves attention) 10...♘xc3 11 bxc3 ♗a3 12 ♖b1 e5 13 ♗d3 promises him some advantage.

10 ... e5
11 0-0 exd4

This was Black's last chance to flick in the move 11...h6!. After 12 ♗h4 exd4 13 exd4 ♖e8 White's best try to fight for an advantage is 14 a3!? (subsequent practice has shown Black is OK after 14 ♗b1 ♘f8 15 ♘e5 ♗e6), although here apart from accepting the pawn sacrifice Black can consider retreating his bishop.

12 exd4 (D)

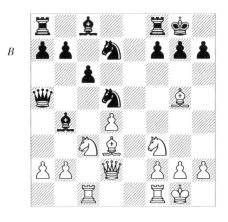

12 ... f6

Black's main problem is how to develop his queenside pieces without concessions. Smyslov's move softens the kingside, but 12...h6? runs into the decisive 13 ♗xh6! gxh6 14 ♕xh6 ♘5f6 15 ♘g5. After 12...♘7f6 13 a3 ♗xc3 (13...♗d6? 14 ♘xd5 costs Black material) 14 bxc3 followed by a timely c4 Black will have to relinquish his control of d5. 12...♘7b6!? might be a playable alternative, although cutting off the queen's retreat and deserting the kingside definitely looks risky.

13 ♗h4 ♖d8
14 a3!?

Given enough time, Black would consolidate his position with ...♘f8 and ...♗e6. 14 ♕c2 ♘f8 15 ♘xd5 cxd5 16 ♗g3 ♗d6 17 ♕b3 is pleasant for White, but Kasparov wants something more substantial than a slight pull in a symmetrical structure and strives for a more dynamic position.

14 ... ♗xc3

Forced. 14...♗f8? is weak due to 15 ♕c2 and 14...♗d6?! 15 ♘xd5 ♕xd2 16 ♘xf6+ ♗xf6 17 ♘xd2 ♗f4 18 ♖cd1 ♖xd4 19 ♘f3 only opens up the position, increasing Black's development problems.

15 bxc3 ♘f8!

Prudent; after 15...♕xa3 16 c4 both Black's king and queen would be in danger.

16 ♗g3 ♗e6

16...♕xa3?! 17 c4 is even more hazardous than in the previous note, as 17...♘b6? 18 ♗c7 ♖d7 19 ♖a1 costs Black material. However, 16...♗g4!? is a promising alternative. Kasparov was optimistic about his chances after 17 c4 ♕xd2 18 ♘xd2 ♘e7 (18...♘b6 19 ♘b3 ♘e6 20 c5 is advantageous for White, as the g4-bishop is misplaced) 19 ♘b3, but it seems 19...♘f5 (19...♘e6?! runs into 20 d5! cxd5 21 ♖fe1 ♔f7 22 cxd5 ♘xd5 23 f3 ♗h5 24 ♗c4 and Black with his uncoordinated pieces is in serious trouble) brings Black close to equality, as White loses his main trump – the bishop-pair.

17 ♖fe1! (D)

A useful preparatory move. 17 c4 ♕xd2 18 ♘xd2 ♘e7 19 ♘b3 ♘f5 leads to a similar position as in the previous note.

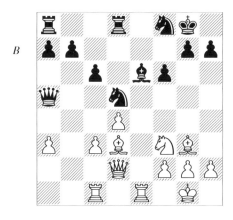

17 ... ♗f7

Black can't stop c4 forever:

1) 17...♘b6 18 ♕b2 ♖d7 (18...c5 19 ♗e4 is also good for White) 19 ♘d2 with pressure; White's knight is aiming for c5.

2) More radical is 17...b5 18 c4 (18 ♕b2!?) 18...♕xd2 19 ♘xd2 ♘b6 (19...bxc4 20 ♗xc4 is

simply good for White) 20 c5!? (20 d5 bxc4 21 dxe6 ♖xd3 22 e7 ♖xd2 is unclear), but even here White is better.

18 c4

18 ♕b2!? b5 19 c4 (19 ♘d2 followed by ♘e4 also deserves attention) is a promising alternative. Kasparov shows his style has become more universal and he is not reluctant to play a better endgame.

18 ... ♕xd2
19 ♘xd2 ♘b6
20 ♘b3 *(D)*

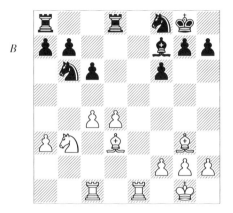

20 ... ♘a4

With his active bishops and central control, White holds the initiative. The main drawback of his position is the passive b3-knight and Smyslov puts his knight on the rim to limit its scope. 20...♘e6 is a tempting alternative, but White retains an edge with the simple 21 ♖cd1 (Kasparov recommends the committal 21 c5 ♘d5 22 ♘a5, but Black gets counterplay after 22...♘df4; for example, 23 ♗f1 ♖xd4 24 ♘xb7 ♘d3).

21 ♗f1 ♖d7?!

Smyslov begins to falter. The consistent follow-up to the previous move is 21...b6!, further limiting the b3-knight. Black's a4-knight remains invincible and White would have to improve his position on the kingside gradually, starting with 22 f3. Now he can activate his knight immediately.

22 ♘a5!

Now White intends to cut off Black's a4-knight with c5, whereas his own knight puts Black's queenside under strong pressure.

22 ... ♘e6

This allows a further opening of the position for White's bishops. However, 22...♖c8 23 c5 ♘e6 (23...♗d5 24 ♘c4 is no better) 24 ♖b1 (or 24 ♗d6) and 22...♖xd4!? 23 ♘xb7 c5 24 ♘d6 are also unpleasant for Black.

23 d5! ♘d4

Black tries to complicate the issue, because 23...cxd5 24 cxd5 ♖xd5 25 ♘xb7 gives White a clear advantage.

24 dxc6

24 ♖cd1?! c5 would close the position again.

24 ... ♘xc6

24...bxc6 25 c5 ♗d5 26 ♗a6 is hardly much better. The main drawbacks of Black's position are his uncoordinated and passive pieces; especially his rooks have no scope.

25 ♘xc6 bxc6
26 c5! *(D)*

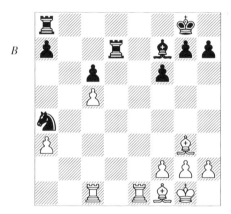

26 ... ♖e8

Left to his own devices, White would fully paralyse Black with ♗d6 and ♗a6. Smyslov at least simplifies the position and also lays a clever trap.

27 ♖xe8+ ♗xe8
28 ♗d6

Kasparov further cramps Black's forces and avoids the tempting 28 ♖c4? ♖d1! 29 ♖xa4 ♗g6, followed by ...♗d3, when White has squandered most of his advantage.

28 ... ♗f7

Black has a difficult choice between two evils. 28...♖b7 occupies the b-file, but Kasparov rightly shows that after 29 g3! Black can't activate his bishop and White will enter via the e-file.

29 ♖b1 ♗d5

Now White launches a mating attack, but even 29...h5 30 ♖b8+ ♔h7 31 ♗e2 wouldn't have saved the game; e.g., 31...♘c3 (31...g6 32 ♗f3 ♗d5 33 ♗xd5 cxd5 34 ♔f1 also wins for White) 32 ♗f3 ♘d5 33 h4 and Black has no sensible moves.

30	♖b8+	♔f7
31	♖f8+	♔e6

31...♔g6 loses to 32 ♗d3+ ♔h6 33 ♗f4+ ♔h5 34 ♗f5.

| 32 | g3 | |

The immediate 32 ♗a6 is more convincing.

| 32 | ... | g6 |

32...f5 avoids immediate losses and is more resilient, but after 33 ♗a6 ♖f7 34 ♖e8+ ♔f6 35 ♗e5+ ♔g6 36 ♗d4 ♖d7 37 ♗c8 Black remains passive and helpless.

| 33 | ♗a6 *(D)* | |

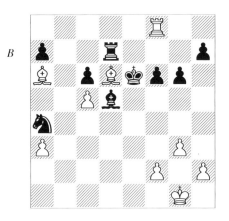

The threat of ♗c8 nets White at least an exchange.

33	...	♖xd6
34	cxd6	♔xd6

34...♘c5 35 ♗c8+ (or 35 ♗f1!? and ♔g2) is just as hopeless for Black.

35	♖xf6+	♔e5
36	♖f8	c5
37	♖e8+	♔d4
38	♖d8	♔e5
39	f4+	♔e4
40	♗f1	♗b3
41	♔f2 *(D)*	

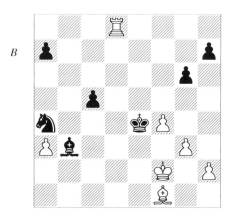

| 41 | ... | ♘b2 |

White is clearly winning even after the somewhat better 41...c4 42 ♗g2+ ♔f5 43 ♗d5. Smyslov played his knight to c3 and before letting it go realized White threatened ♗d3#. Thus the text-move was forced and Black didn't want to wait for 42 ♖b8 ♘d1+ (42...c4 43 ♗xc4) 43 ♔e2 ♗c4+ 44 ♔xd1 ♗xf1 45 ♖b7.

1-0

Game 26
Garry Kasparov – Anatoly Karpov
World Ch match (game 32), Moscow 1984/5
Queen's Indian Defence [E12]

Psychologically a very important game. In his rapid rise to the very top of world chess Kasparov had seemingly easily overcome all the obstacles but one. World Champion Karpov was an extremely tough nut to crack, and in 3 previous tournament games and 31 match games, the challenger still hadn't scored a single win. In their first annulled match Kasparov was trailing badly from the very beginning and after game 27 the score rose to 5-0. Now every game could be the last one, and in game 31 Karpov missed a golden opportunity. In the next game, Kasparov finally managed to turn the tide...

1	d4	♘f6
2	c4	e6
3	♘f3	b6
4	♘c3	

In their first match Kasparov played the Petrosian System only twice and concentrated more on the main alternative 4 g3. Karpov usually opted for 4...♗a6 5 b3 ♗b4+ 6 ♗d2 ♗e7 and despite being in serious trouble in games 6 and 16 managed to escape unscathed and even retain a +1 score in this line.

4	...	♗b7
5	a3	d5
6	cxd5	♘xd5 *(D)*

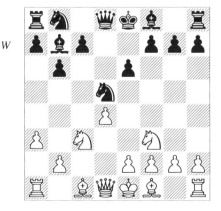

| 7 | ♕c2 | |

7 e3 ♘d7 8 ♗d3 c5 9 e4 ♘5f6!? 10 d5 (later practice has shown that 10 ♗f4! a6 11 d5 is more dangerous for Black) 10...exd5 11 exd5 ♗d6 12 0-0 0-0 13 ♗g5 ♕c7 14 ♗f5 a6 15 ♕d2 was played in Kasparov-Karpov, Moscow Wch (10) 1984/5. In this position Black has no problems whatsoever and Kasparov was probably quite pleased when Karpov accepted his draw offer.

7	...	♘d7?!

In the notes to Game 20 I mentioned that this is not the best reply.

8	♘xd5	exd5

Surprisingly enough, this position arose in Karpov's subsequent practice, albeit via the trickier move-order 6 ♕c2!? ♘bd7?! 7 cxd5 ♘xd5 8 ♘xd5. His reaction was even less convincing and in Gelfand-Karpov, Moscow 1992 after 8...♗xd5?! 9 e4 ♗b7 10 ♗b5! c6 11 ♗xc6 ♖c8 12 d5 ♕c7 Gelfand's suggestion 13 ♗e3! ♗xc6 14 ♖c1 would have given White a distinct advantage.

9	♗g5 *(D)*	

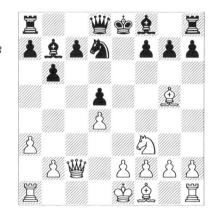

This forceful continuation highlights the drawbacks of Black's 7th move. Structurally there is nothing wrong with his position; even in other variations of the Queen's Indian or Queen's Gambit Declined the long diagonal of the b7-bishop is often closed by the d5-pawn. If he had time to play ...♗e7 and ...c5, he would achieve a both active and solid set-up. However, in this concrete situation White's slight lead in development gives him the initiative, which in turn allows him to force further positional concessions.

9 ... f6

An ugly move to make, but other moves have their drawbacks as well. After 9...♗e7 10 ♗xe7 ♔xe7 the exchange of the dark-squared bishops is strategically advantageous for White; moreover, Black will have to lose a couple of tempi to castle by hand. 9...♕c8 was tested in later games; after 10 g3 ♗d6 11 ♗h3 0-0 the most energetic is 12 ♗f4! ♗xf4 13 gxf4 ♕d8 14 ♕f5 ♘f6 15 ♖g1 ♘e4 16 ♕h5 ♕f6 17 ♗f5 g6 18 ♘e5 ♕g7 19 ♕h4 ♗c8 20 ♗xe4 dxe4 21 ♖c1 with a clear advantage in Akopian-Kacheishvili, Linares open 1996. White cleverly used the fact he hasn't castled yet to put Black under strong pressure on both flanks.

10 ♗f4 c5
11 g3! *(D)*

Just as after 9...♕c8, White's bishop will cause the most problems from h3. Less incisive is 11 e3, when Black can choose between 11...♖c8 and 11...c4!? 12 ♗e2 b5, keeping the position closed for the time being.

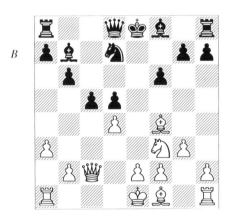

11 ... g6

Karpov decides to counter White's plan by preparing ...f5. After 11...♗e7 12 ♗h3 Black can't finish his development without further concessions, as 12...0-0?! 13 ♗f5 g6 14 ♗xg6 hxg6 15 ♕xg6+ ♔h8 16 ♘h4! gives White a strong attack. After 11...♕e7 12 h4! (12 ♗h3 allows 12...g5 13 ♗e3 ♕e4! with counterplay) 12...♕e4 13 ♕a4 ♕e6 14 ♗h3 ♕c6 15 ♕c2 White was also better in B.Lalić-Dizdarević, Pula 1996.

12 h4!

Black has weakened his position and Kasparov flexibly changes his plan.

12 ... ♕e7
13 ♗g2 ♗g7
14 h5 *(D)*

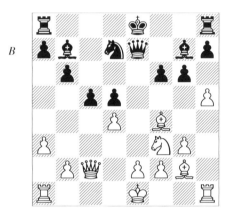

14 ... f5

Black activates his g7-bishop, but on the other hand this move further weakens the dark squares. The apparently unbecoming 14...g5!? was perhaps a better chance. Liquidating the kingside tension helps Black and although the g7-bishop remains passive and the f5-square vulnerable, White can't directly use this outpost to his advantage:

1) An ambitious attempt is 15 h6 gxf4 (the simple 15...♗f8!? improves the bishop and also deserves attention) 16 hxg7 ♕xg7 17 ♘h4!? fxg3 18 ♘f5 gxf2+ 19 ♔xf2 ♕f8 20 e4. White has attacking chances for the sacrificed pawns, but would Kasparov have gone for this double-edged continuation in his desperate match situation?

2) White retains an edge after the more sedate 15 ♗e3; e.g., 15...♖c8 16 ♕f5 ♕e4 17 ♗h3!, but the outcome of the game is still open.

15 ♕d2!

White naturally doesn't prematurely release the tension on the h-file and starts toying with the idea of ♗h6, which would be especially strong if Black decided to castle kingside.

15 ... ♗f6

After 15...♘f6 both 16 hxg6 ♘e4 17 ♕c2 hxg6 18 ♖xh8+ ♗xh8 19 ♘e5 and 16 h6 ♗f8 17 ♘g5 give White a dangerous initiative. In the latter case Black's best defence against the threat of ♗e5 is probably the awkward 17...♖g8.

16 ♖c1

Kasparov develops his last piece; his king is quite safe in the centre. This can't be said about its black counterpart, which soon becomes Karpov's main problem.

16 ... ♖c8

The only reasonable defence against the threat of ♖c3-e3.

17 ♖c3 ♖c6 (D)

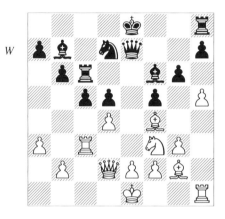

18 ♖e3

The consistent 18 ♗g5! is even stronger, highlighting the dark-square weaknesses and creating the threat of hxg6; e.g., 18...♖g8 19 hxg6 hxg6 20 ♖e3 ♖c6 21 ♗xf6 ♘xf6 22 ♖xe6 ♕xe6 23 ♘g5 (or 23 ♕f4) with a large advantage.

18 ... ♖e6
19 ♖xe6 ♕xe6
20 ♘g5 ♕e7!?

Karpov would rather sacrifice material than go for 20...♗xg5?! 21 ♗xg5 – a terrible concession, which would render Black's position strategically hopeless.

21 dxc5

White could have changed the move-order and resolved the position with 21 hxg6 hxg6 22 ♖xh8+ ♗xh8 23 dxc5 ♕xc5 (23...♘xc5?! 24 ♗xd5 gives White a healthy extra pawn) 24 ♘e6. Although this also gives him an advantage, there is no clear decision in sight after 24...♕a5! 25 ♘c7+ ♔d8.

21 ... ♘xc5
22 hxg6 d4!

Black grabs his only chance to complicate the issue. 22...hxg6? 23 ♖xh8+ and ♗xd5 transposes to the bad sideline from the previous note.

23 g7?

With mutual time-trouble looming, in his understandable search for a simple solution Kasparov squanders almost all of his advantage. Let's look at the other options:

1) 23 ♗d6? is also inferior. After 23...♗xg5 24 ♕xd4 ♗f6! 25 ♗xe7 (25 ♕xc5 bxc5 26 ♗xe7 ♔xe7 is similar) 25...♗xd4 26 ♗xc5 bxc5 (or 26...♗xg2) the extra pawn is not enough to win an opposite-coloured bishop endgame.

2) 23 ♘f7!? is stronger and maybe objectively best. After 23...♗xg2 24 ♖h2 ♖f8 (not 24...♗b7? losing to 25 ♘xh8 ♗xh8 26 ♖xh7 ♕f6 27 ♗g5) 25 ♖xh7! (25 ♗d6?! ♕e4 26 ♗xf8 ♔xf8 27 ♘d6 ♕b1+ 28 ♕d1 ♕xb2! 29 ♖xg2 d3! is dangerous only for White and 25 ♘d6+ ♔d8 26 g7 ♗xg7 27 ♖xg2 ♘e4 is inconclusive) 25...♕e6 26 ♘d6+ ♔d8 27 ♘b5! White doesn't risk anything and has a strong attack for the piece.

3) However, line '2' can hardly be called clear-cut. In this sense the most practical solution was indicated by Dorfman: 23 ♗xb7 ♕xb7 24 f3 hxg6 25 ♖xh8+ ♗xh8 26 b4 ♘d7 27 ♕a2 (27 ♘e6!?) 27...♘f8 28 ♘e6 with penetration via the a2-g8 diagonal; e.g., 28...♕d7 29 ♘c7+ ♔d8 30 ♕g8 ♗g7 31 ♘e6+! ♕xe6 32 ♕xg7 ♘d7 33 ♕xd4 and White should win this endgame in the long run.

23 ... ♗xg7

23...♕xg7!? 24 ♗xb7 ♕xb7 25 f3 ♕e7 is also possible. The resulting position is far from clear.

24 ♗xb7 ♕xb7
25 f3 ♕d5!?

Karpov seeks active counterplay. 25...d3? 26 b4 ♕e7 27 ♔f2! costs Black an important pawn, while 25...h6 26 ♘h3 followed by ♘f2 would give White an edge due to Black's isolated pawns.

26 ♖xh7

26 b4 h6 27 ♘h3 ♘a4 is unclear.

26 ... ♖xh7

26...0-0 27 b4! chases away the knight and stops tricks connected with ...d3.

27 ♘xh7 (D)

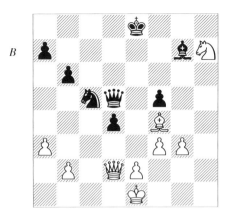

27 ... ♕b3?!

Black goes astray in time-trouble. Correct is 27...d3 28 b4 ♘e6 29 ♘g5 (after 29 ♕xd3 ♕xd3 30 exd3 ♘xf4 31 gxf4 b5! and ....♗b2 Black draws easily) 29...♘xf4 (29...♕d4 30 ♗c3! ♕a1+ 31 ♕c1 allows White to retain his extra pawn, but 29...♕b3!? deserves attention) 30 gxf4. Now White wants to take on d3 at a more suitable moment, possibly without exchanging queens. However, after 30...♔d7!? 31 exd3 ♕b3 the most plausible result is a draw.

28 ♗d6!

The only move to keep the tension. 28 ♘g5 d3 29 ♕e3+ ♔d7 30 ♗e5 gives Black sufficient counterplay after 30...♗xe5 31 ♕xe5 ♕c2!? 32 ♕xf5+ ♔c6 33 ♕c8+ ♔b5 34 ♕e8+ ♔c4 35 ♕e3 ♕xb2.

28 ... ♘e6?!

After 28...d3 the simplest continuation is 29 ♗xc5 bxc5 30 ♕xd3 ♕xd3 31 exd3 ♗xb2 32 a4 with good winning chances for White. However, 28...♕e6!? is better, because after 29 ♗xc5 bxc5 30 ♘g5 ♕g6 converting the extra pawn is still no easy task for White.

29	♘g5	♗h6
30	♗f4	♗xg5
31	♗xg5	♘xg5
32	♕xg5	♕xb2
33	♕xf5	♕c1+

This instinctive check saves time on the clock and also chases the king away from the queenside passed pawns. However, as the queen endgame will result in a pawn race, a more important consideration is to retain the chance of pawn promotion with check. In this respect 33...♕xa3!? is better, although after 34 ♕e5+ White should probably win anyway.

34	♔f2	♕e3+
35	♔f1	♕c1+?

35...♕xa3! is still stronger for the same reason as above. Now Black is irrevocably lost.

36	♔g2	♕xa3
37	♕h5+	

The naïve 37 ♕e5+? ♕e7 doesn't work, but White wins the d4-pawn anyway.

37 ... ♔d7

37...♔d8 38 ♕h8+.

38	♕g4+	♔c6
39	♕xd4	b5
40	g4	b4
41	g5 (D)	

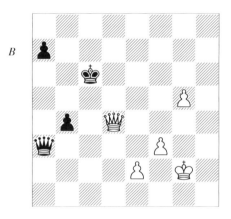

The sealed move.

1-0

Black resigned without resumption. After 41...b3 one way to win is 42 g6 (42 ♕e4+ ♔d6 43 ♕e8 ♕a2! is less convincing) 42...b2 43 ♕e4+ ♔d6 (43...♔c7 44 ♕c4+! ♔b6 45 g7 and with four queens on the board White's safer king will decide the issue) 44 g7 ♕a2 45 ♕g6+ ♔c7 46 g8♕ ♕xg8 47 ♕xg8 b1♕ 48 ♕f7+ and White will be faster in the second pawn race.

Game 27
Frank Behrhorst – Garry Kasparov
HSK-Kasparov simul, Hamburg 1985
Grünfeld Defence [D93]

This attractive tactical duel was played in a clock simultaneous against the German Bundesliga team HSK Hamburg. Later, such events became a standard part of Kasparov's calendar (see also Games 40 and 64 respectively).

1	d4	♘f6
2	c4	g6
3	♘c3	d5

Later, starting with the World Championship rematch in 1986, Kasparov also started using the dynamic Grünfeld against top-level opposition.

4	♘f3	♗g7
5	♗f4	0-0
6	e3	c5
7	dxc5	♘e4!? *(D)*

7...♕a5 8 ♖c1 dxc4 9 ♗xc4 ♕xc5 10 ♗b3 ♘c6 11 0-0 ♕a5 12 h3 ♗f5 is the solid main line, which also occurred in the aforementioned K-K match. Theory promises Black equality, but the resulting positions are rather sterile and in the current game Kasparov strives for a more complex struggle.

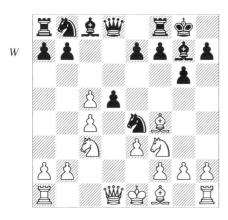

8 ♕b3?!

Behrhorst was probably surprised and reacted badly. 8 ♘xd5 ♗xb2 9 ♗c7 ♕d7 10 ♖b1 ♗c3+! is also not ideal and can only be dangerous for White, while 8 ♗e5 ♗xe5 9 ♘xe5 ♘xc3 10 bxc3 ♕a5 11 ♕d4 ♘c6!? promises Black easy equality at the least. The most testing continuation is 8 ♖c1 ♘xc3 (weaker is 8...♕a5 9 ♗e5) 9 bxc3 dxc4 (the sharper 9...♕a5 10 cxd5 ♘d7!? also deserves attention) 10 ♕xd8 ♖xd8 11 ♗xc4, but even here after 11...♘d7 12 ♗c7 ♖f8 13 c6 bxc6 14 ♘d4 ♘b6! 15 ♗xb6 axb6 16 ♘xc6 ♗f6 Black has enough compensation for the pawn to hold the game.

8 ... ♘a6!

Black has no problems even after 8...♕a5 9 ♖c1 dxc4, but Kasparov's ambitious continuation highlights the drawbacks of White's previous move even more clearly. By chasing the exposed queen, Black will increase his slight lead in development.

9 cxd5

It's hard to suggest a reasonable alternative. After 9 ♘xd5 ♕a5+! (9...e6 is also good) 10 ♔e2 ♘axc5 11 ♘xe7+ ♔h8 Black has a strong attack.

9 ... ♘axc5 *(D)*

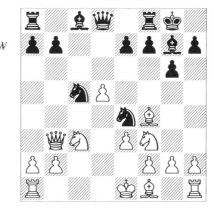

10 ♕c4?

White must tread with great care and this error puts him on the brink of defeat. 10 ♕c2? ♘xc3 11 bxc3 ♗f5 is no better than the text-move, so the queen must go forward. However, stronger was 10 ♕b4! ♘xc3 (10...a5 11 ♕c4 is not clear, because Black doesn't have the important a5-square for his queen) 11 bxc3 ♕xd5 (11...♘e4 12 ♖c1 ♕xd5 13 ♗c4 is playable for White; 11...♗f5!? is interesting but far from clear) 12 ♖d1 with approximate equality.

10 ... b5!

An energetic continuation. 10...♘xc3?! 11 bxc3 ♘a4 12 ♗e5 would be a relief for White.

11 ♘xb5?!

Now White is lost by force. The same goes for 11 ♕b4? a5 12 ♕xb5 ♗a6. However, even 11 ♕xb5 (best) is no bed of roses:

1) After 11...♘xc3 12 ♕xc5 ♘a4 13 ♕c2!? (weaker is 13 ♕c7 ♗xb2 14 ♕xd8 ♗c3+, but perhaps 13 ♕c6 ♕a5+ 14 ♘d2 is also playable) 13...♗xb2 14 ♖d1 ♕a5+ 15 ♘d2 ♗d7!? Black has the initiative, but still nothing concrete.

2) More dangerous is 11...♗a6! 12 ♕b4 ♗xf1 (12...♘xc3 13 ♕xc5 ♘e4 also gives Black an advantage; e.g., 14 ♕c7 ♗xf1! 15 ♕xd8 ♖fxd8 16 ♖xf1 ♖xd5) 13 ♔xf1 ♗xc3 14 bxc3 ♕xd5 15 ♕d4 ♕b7! with a strong attack.

11 ... ♗xb2
12 ♗c7 (D)

After 12 ♖d1? ♕a5+ (see the note to White's 10th move!) 13 ♘d2 a6 White's position collapses.

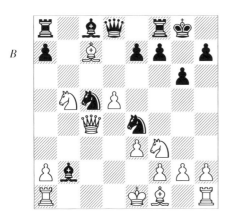

12 ... a6!?

The whole game is especially noteworthy thanks to this enterprising queen sacrifice. However, the mundane 12...♕d7! is simpler and objectively better: 13 ♗e5 (13 ♖b1 a6 costs White material, and 13 ♘e5 ♕f5 14 f3 ♗xa1 15 ♘c6 ♖e8 is also hopeless) 13...♗xa1 14 ♗xa1 ♗a6 15 ♕d4 (15 ♘fd4 loses quickly after 15...♖fc8 16 f3 ♘d6 17 ♕c3 ♘a4!) 15...f6 16 a4 ♕d8!

and once again Black's queen threatens to enter the fray via a5 with decisive effect.

13 ♗xd8 axb5
14 ♕c2

Forced. Hopeless is 14 ♕xc5 ♘xc5 15 ♗xe7 ♗xa1 16 ♗xc5 ♖d8 or 14 ♕xb5 ♗c3+ 15 ♔d1 ♖xd8! (even stronger than 15...♗xa1 16 ♕b6 ♘xf2+) 16 ♖b1 ♗d7 17 ♕e2 (17 ♕c4 loses to 17...♗e6) 17...♗a4+ 18 ♔c1 ♖xd5 with a decisive attack.

14 ... ♗c3+
15 ♕xc3!?

Behrhorst returns the queen immediately. Other moves are weaker:

1) 15 ♔d1? ♖xd8 16 ♖b1 ♗e6! followed by ...♗xd5 and ...♖xa2 is terrible for White.

2) Not much better is 15 ♔e2 ♖xd8 16 ♖c1 (16 ♖d1? is even weaker: 16...♗f5!) 16...♖xd5 (16...♗f5 17 ♘d4 still defends) 17 ♖d1 ♖xd1 18 ♔xd1 ♗e6 and Black is close to winning. In these lines White's extra material plays no role and Black's excellently coordinated forces dominate the board.

3) Even after 15 ♘d2 ♖xd8 (15...♗xd2+ 16 ♕xd2 ♘xd2 17 ♗xe7 ♘db3 18 ♗xf8 ♔xf8 19 ♖d1 ♖xa2 20 ♗xb5 is unconvincing) 16 0-0-0 ♗f6!? the initiative is in Black's hands; e.g., 17 ♘xe4 ♘xe4 18 ♕xe4 ♗f5 19 ♕xf5 gxf5 20 ♖d2 ♖dc8+ 21 ♔d1 b4!.

15 ... ♘xc3
16 ♗xe7 ♘b3 (D)

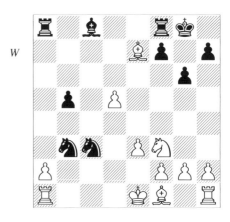

17 ♖d1?

White again strays from the right track and doesn't get a second chance. The most serious test of Kasparov's concept is 17 ♖b1! (after 17 ♗xf8, 17...♔xf8 18 ♖b1 transposes, but White has to reckon with 17...♘xa1) 17...♘xb1 18 axb3 ♖a1!? (18...♘c3 19 ♗xf8 ♔xf8 20 ♗d3! ♖a1+ 21 ♔d2 or 18...♖e8 19 ♗f6 can even be dangerous for Black) 19 ♗xf8 ♔xf8. Although Black risks little due to White's lag in development, the outcome still remains open.

17	...	♖xa2!
18	♗xf8	

Natural enough, because White's own rook is trapped. 18 ♗xb5 is best met by 18...♘xd1 (18...♘xb5?! 19 ♗xf8 is inferior and even 19...♘c3 {avoiding 19...♔xf8, which transposes to note '1' to White's 19th move} is not fully convincing due to 20 ♗b4 ♘xd1 21 ♔xd1 ♗a6 22 ♘d2!) 19 ♔xd1 (19 ♗xf8? ♘c3 costs White a piece) 19...♖a1+ 20 ♔c2 ♖xh1 21 ♔xb3 ♗b7 22 ♗xf8 ♗xd5+ 23 ♗c4 ♗xf3. Black wins another pawn and converting the extra exchange is only a matter of technique.

18	...	♔xf8 *(D)*

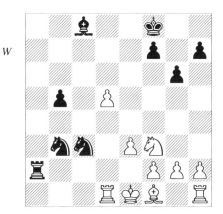

19	♘d4	

Now Black regains all the invested material with a huge positional advantage. The generous 19 ♗xb5!? is more interesting:

1) 19...♘xb5?! 20 0-0 (20 ♘d2!? ♘c5 21 0-0 with the idea 21...♘c3 22 ♖a1 ♖xd2 23 ♖a8 is also possible) 20...♘c3 21 ♖d3 ♖c2 22 d6 ♔e8 23 ♖e1 ♗e6 24 e4 saves the exchange and gives White good drawing chances.

2) Stronger is the materialistic 19...♘xd1 20 ♔xd1 ♖a1+ (20...♗f5? 21 ♖f1 and Black has no more than a perpetual) 21 ♔c2 ♖xh1 22 ♔xb3 ♖b1+! 23 ♔c4 (23 ♔a4 ♔e7!? is also good for Black) 23...♖f1 and Black should win this endgame.

19	...	♘xd1

20	♘xb3	

After 20 ♔xd1? ♘xd4 21 exd4 b4 22 ♔c1 ♗f5 the b-pawn is unstoppable.

20	...	♘xf2
21	♖g1	♘g4
22	d6	

22 ♗xb5? ♖b2 doesn't work for White, so he seeks counterplay. His attempt fails due to his passive pieces, but even after the slightly better 22 e4 ♖b2 Black will win by combining play against White's weak pawns with the advance of his own passed pawn.

22	...	♘xe3
23	♘c5	

23 ♗xb5 leads to a lost endgame for White after 23...♘xg2+ 24 ♖xg2 (24 ♔d1 ♗e6 is hopeless for White) 24...♖xg2 25 d7 ♗xd7 26 ♗xd7 ♖xh2.

23	...	♗g4
24	h3	♖c2! *(D)*

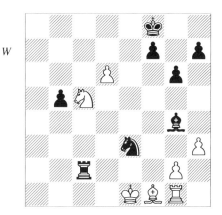

25	♘a6	

25 ♘b3 ♗e6 26 ♘d4 ♖c1+ is no better.

25	...	♗e6

Black has more than one way to win; e.g., 25...♘xf1 26 ♖xf1 (26 ♔xf1 ♗c8 also costs White the d-pawn) 26...♗e2+ 27 ♔d1 ♖e6+! 28 hxg4 ♖xd6+ with two extra pawns.

26	♗e2	♗c4
27	♗f3	♘f5

The time has come to take care of White's d-pawn.

28	d7	♔e7
29	♘b8 *(D)*	
29	...	♖c1+

Exchanging the active rook is not the best. After 29...♘d4 Black can quickly advance his

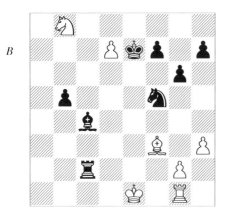

passed pawn. However, Kasparov's wish to simplify is understandable: he wanted to avoid any possible surprises and concentrate on the other games.

30	♔f2	♖xg1
31	♔xg1	♘d4
32	♗e4	f5
33	♗b1	

In a tournament game Behrhorst would have undoubtedly resigned, but once again let's not forget this was a clock simul. By playing on, he helped his team-mates, who incidentally managed to score an upset victory 4½-3½.

33	...	♗e6
34	♔f2	♗xd7

34...f4! is more accurate, but even after the move played White's desperate resistance can't change the final outcome.

35	♔e3	♘c6
36	♘xd7	♔xd7
37	g4	fxg4
38	hxg4	♔e6
39	♔f4	♔d5!

Kasparov simply calculates that White's kingside counterplay comes too late.

40	♗a2+	♔d4
41	♔g5	♘e5
42	♗g8	

The alternative 42 ♔h6 ♔e3! 43 g5 ♔f4, followed by ...♘g4+, is also hopeless for White.

42	...	b4
43	♗xh7	b3
44	♗g8	b2
45	♗a2	♔c3 (D)

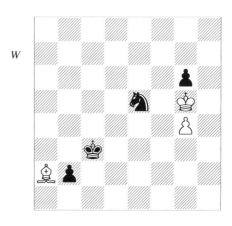

46	♗b1	

Black also wins after 46 ♔f6 ♘xg4+ 47 ♔xg6 ♔c2 and ...♘f2-d3-b4.

46	...	♔d2
47	♔f4	♔c1
48	♗e4	♘c4
49	♗xg6	♘a3

White has finally managed to level the material, but now the b2-pawn promotes.

50	g5	♘c2

0-1

Game 28
Robert Hübner – Garry Kasparov
Match (game 1), Hamburg 1985
English Opening [A21]

After the termination of their 48-game marathon, both Karpov and Kasparov had less than seven months to prepare for a new encounter. The challenger wanted to gain more match experience, and played two short 6-game training matches. Kasparov won the first training match against Hübner 4½-1½; the outcome was inevitably influenced by the following drastic game.

1	c4	e5
2	♘c3	d6
3	d4	exd4
4	♕xd4	*(D)*

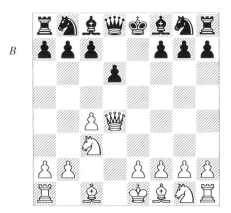

Hübner had successfully employed this line in the past. White controls the centre and left to his own devices, he will fianchetto both bishops, play ♘h3-f4 and enjoy a pleasant pull. On the other hand, as Kasparov elegantly and effectively demonstrates, by attacking the exposed queen Black wins tempi and can generate tactical threats.

4	...	♘f6!

Very concrete play by Black. After 4...♘c6 5 ♕d2 ♘f6 White can start with 6 b3!? first. Then 6...♗e6 (6...g6 7 ♗b2 ♗g7 8 g3 0-0 9 ♘h3! ♖e8 10 ♘f4 gives White a comfortable edge, but the immediate 6...a5!? is interesting) 7 e4 a5 (once White has played e4, 7...g6!? deserves more attention) 8 ♘ge2 a4 9 ♖b1 axb3 10 axb3 g6 11 g3 ♗g7 12 ♗g2 0-0 13 0-0 ♘d7 14 ♘d5 ♘c5 15 b4 ♘a4 16 ♕c2 ♘e5 17 ♘ef4 ♗d7 18 ♖e1 c6 19 ♘e3 led in Hübner-Balashov, Rio de Janeiro IZ 1979 to a complex position in which according to Hübner 19...b5!? promises Black reasonable counterplay.

5	g3?!	

A long-term aim such as consolidating a space advantage in a semi-open position with the king still in the centre requires great accuracy. As Black now develops an initiative by natural means, 5 b3 is more circumspect. The difference compared with the positions from the previous note is that Black doesn't have to develop his knight to c6, a square better left free for the c-pawn. As White's queen will have to retreat to d2 anyway, Black's knight is far better placed on c5, when the position resembles a Fianchetto King's Indian. Play can continue with 5...g6 6 ♗b2 ♗g7 7 g3 0-0 8 ♗g2 ♖e8 9 ♕d2 ♘bd7 10 ♘f3 ♘c5 11 0-0 and now the simplest is 11...♘fe4 (11...a5 is more ambitious) 12 ♘xe4 ♘xe4 13 ♕c2 ♗xb2 14 ♕xb2 ♕f6 15 ♕xf6 ♘xf6 16 ♘d4 a6 17 e3 ♖b8 18 ♖ac1 c5!, followed by ...b5 with equality, Smejkal-Mokry, Trnava 1989.

5	...	♘c6
6	♕d2	♗e6
7	♘d5	*(D)*

White must not only protect c4, but also stop ...d5. The other playable move is 7 e4, but after 7...♗e7 White still can't develop naturally, as 8 b3?! runs into the powerful 8...♘xe4! 9 ♘xe4 d5. Black then regains the piece with strong pressure, as 10 cxd5? ♗xd5 11 f3 ♗b4 12 ♘c3 ♕f6 13 ♗b2 0-0-0 is a complete disaster for White.

7	...	♘e5!
8	b3	♘e4

Black's concrete tactical harassment continues.

9	♕e3	

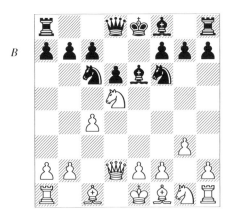

After 9 ♕d4 Black has not only 9...c6, but also the sharp 9...f5! 10 ♗g2 g6 (10...c6!?) with various lethal tricks in the air. A nice example is 11 ♗b2? c5! 12 ♕d1 ♗xd5 13 ♕xd5 ♕a5+ 14 ♔d1 ♘d3!! and Black was winning in J.Kristiansen-Reinert, Denmark 1985.

9 ... ♘c5!?

A fighting alternative to the equalizing 9...c6 10 ♕xe4 cxd5 11 cxd5 ♕a5+ 12 ♗d2 ♕xd5.

10 ♗b2

Kasparov recommends 10 ♗g2!, which stops the ideas from the game. However, after 10...c6 11 ♘c3 (11 ♘f4?! is weaker due to 11...♕f6) Black has more than one way to achieve an active position; e.g., 11...♕a5!? 12 ♗b2 ♗e7 with threats such as ...♗xc4 or ...♘a4.

10 ... c6 (D)

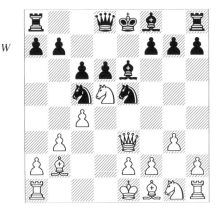

11 ♘f4?

Another step in the wrong direction gets White into real trouble. Safer is 11 ♘c3, although after 11...♕b6!? (11...♘g4 12 ♕d2 d5 13 cxd5 ♗xd5 14 f3! ♘f6 15 ♘xd5 ♘xd5 16

0-0-0 is unclear) White must lose further tempi and Black retains the initiative.

11 ... ♘g4
12 ♕d4

12 ♘xe6 ♘xe3 13 ♘xd8 ♘c2+ 14 ♔d1 ♘xa1 leaves White simply an exchange down and 12 ♕f3 ♘e4! is similar to the game.

12 ... ♘e4!! (D)

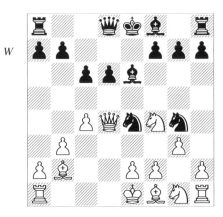

A real bolt from the blue! It's amazing how quickly, even with Black, Kasparov can get a world-class grandmaster on the ropes.

13 ♗h3!

Initially Hübner reacts well. Other moves are weaker:

1) The cheeky knight is taboo: 13 ♕xe4?? loses on the spot to 13...♕a5+.

2) 13 ♘xe6 fxe6! (better than 13...♕a5+?!, which is unconvincing after 14 ♗c3 ♘xc3 15 ♘c7+ ♔d8 16 ♗h3!) only helps Black; for example, 14 ♗h3 ♘gxf2 15 ♗xe6 ♗e7! 16 ♕xg7 ♖f8 and Black wins material with a continuing attack.

3) Passive defences of f2 fail as well: after 13 ♘gh3? ♕a5+ 14 ♔d1 d5 Black threatens ...♗c5 and White's king can't survive in the centre for long.

4) 13 ♘d3 f5 (13...d5!? is also promising for Black) 14 f3 c5 15 ♘xc5 ♕a5+ (15...dxc5!?) 16 ♗c3 dxc5 17 ♗xa5 cxd4 gives Black a clear advantage.

13 ... ♕a5+

This move-order aims to exclude the possibility of 13...♘gxf2 14 ♗xe6 fxe6 15 ♘xe6 ♕a5+ (15...♕e7 16 ♘h3! is probably enough to give White equality; an unforced sample line is 16...♘xg3 17 ♕xf2 ♘xh1 18 ♕e3!?

♔d7 19 ♘hg5 h6 20 ♕h3 hxg5 21 ♘xf8+ ♔c7 22 ♘e6+ and avoiding the perpetual with 22...♔b6?! 23 ♕e3+ c5 24 b4! is very dangerous for Black) 16 ♗c3!? (16 ♔f1 transposes into the game). Black's endgame advantage after 16...♕xc3+ 17 ♕xc3 ♘xc3 18 ♔xf2 ♔d7 is clear and permanent, but arguably less convincing than the attacking chances he retains in the game.

14 ♔f1 ♘gxf2

After 14...♘exf2? 15 ♗xg4! ♘xh1 16 ♘xe6 fxe6 17 ♗xe6 Black's knight remains trapped and the advantage changes hands.

15 ♗xe6

Capturing the other way by 15 ♘xe6? fxe6 16 ♗xe6 fails to 16...♗e7! 17 ♕xg7 ♖f8 and Black wins material.

15 ... fxe6
16 ♘xe6 ♔d7! *(D)*

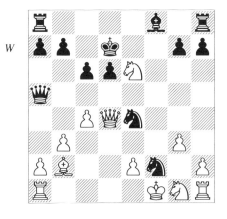

Kasparov also cedes his castling rights, as Black's king remains quite safe and this is the quickest way to connect his rooks.

17 ♘h3?

The losing move, as now Black can untangle his knights and continue the attack. White's e6-knight was *en prise* and 17 ♘f4 ♕b6 costs him an exchange. However, there was still a chance to hang on grimly with 17 ♘xf8+ ♖axf8 (17...♖hxf8 18 ♕xg7+ ♔e8 19 ♔g2 ♘xh1 20 ♔xh1 is unclear) 18 ♘f3! ♖e8 19 ♖g1 and although Black is much better, White can fight on.

17 ... ♘xh3
18 ♕xe4 ♖e8
19 ♘c5+

The only way for White to prolong the game. After 19 ♕g4?! ♖xe6 20 ♕xh3 the double attack 20...♕d2 wins on the spot.

19 ... ♕xc5

19...dxc5? 20 ♖d1+ ♗d6 21 ♗e5! would expose Black's king and turn the tables.

20 ♕g4+ ♔c7
21 ♕xh3 ♗e7
22 ♗xg7

Kasparov has finished his development and White's king has nowhere to hide against the concentrated final onslaught. The natural 22 ♔g2 fails to 22...♗f6!, winning a piece, while after 22 ♖g1 ♕e3 the king won't escape to h1 on time; e.g., 23 ♔g4 ♖ef8+ 24 ♔g2 h5!.

22 ... ♖hf8+! *(D)*

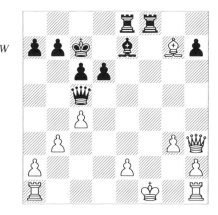

The last phase is pure calculation, something Kasparov excelled at from a very early age.

23 ♗xf8 ♖xf8+
24 ♔e1 ♕f2+
25 ♔d1 ♕d4+
26 ♔c2 ♕e4+
27 ♔d2

Black mates after 27 ♔b2 ♕xe2+ 28 ♔a3 (28 ♔b1 ♖f2 is even quicker) 28...d5+ 29 ♔a4 ♕d2 or 27 ♔c3 ♕e3+ 28 ♔b4 d5+. The text-move at least deflects the bishop from the a3-f8 diagonal.

27 ... ♗g5+
28 ♔c3 ♕e5+

0-1

After 29 ♔b4 (29 ♔c2 ♕xe2+ mates) even the king can lend a hand in the final attack with 29...♔b6! 30 a4 (30 ♔a3 ♗f6) 30...♗f6 31 a5+ ♔a6 and there is no defence against ...♕c5+.

Game 29
Garry Kasparov – Ulf Andersson
Match (game 5), Belgrade 1985
Catalan Opening [E06]

In the second training match (see also Game 28), against Andersson (4-2), Kasparov demonstrated good endgame technique.

1 d4 ♘f6
2 c4 e6
3 g3

In the Catalan, as opposed to the Queen's Indian, White aims to accentuate Black's problems with the development of the c8-bishop. This solid and risk-free opening had brought Kasparov success in the decisive phase of the 1983 Candidates semi-final against Korchnoi.

3 ... d5
4 ♗g2 ♗e7

4...dxc4 5 ♘f3 c5 6 0-0 ♘c6 7 ♘e5 ♗d7 8 ♘a3 cxd4 9 ♘axc4 ♘d5?! 10 ♘xc6 ♗xc6 11 ♕xd4 ♘b4 12 ♗xc6+ ♘xc6 13 ♕c3 f6 14 ♗e3 ♗e7 15 ♖fd1 ♕c7 16 ♕b3 was played in Kasparov-Andersson, Belgrade (3) 1985. Black didn't solve the opening problems satisfactorily and Kasparov proceeded to convert his advantage convincingly. Therefore Andersson goes for the main line, which was also Karpov's usual choice against the Catalan.

5 ♘f3 0-0
6 ♕c2!?

White chooses a less popular sideline, presumably expecting his opponent to be well prepared for the usual 6 0-0.

6 ... dxc4

This move is not ideal. Black obviously wants to play the Open Catalan and spurns 6...c6. However, his move gives White extra options and the standard reaction 6...c5 is better. Current theory promises Black equality after both 7 dxc5 ♕a5+ and 7 0-0 cxd4 8 ♘xd4 ♘c6.

7 ♕xc4

7 ♘bd2 is also promising. White retains an edge after 7...♘c6 (7...b5?! 8 a4 c6? fails to 9 axb5 cxb5 10 ♘g5!, winning material) 8 ♕xc4 ♕d5 9 0-0.

7 ... a6
8 ♗f4! *(D)*

This is the point of White's move-order. 8 ♕c2 b5 9 ♘e5 ♖a7 10 0-0 ♗b7 only yields equality, while 8 0-0 b5 transposes into the main line with 6 0-0.

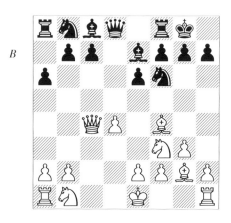

8 ... ♗d6

8...♘d5 is more natural, but after 9 ♘c3 Black faces a difficult decision:

1) 9...b5 10 ♕d3 ♗b7 11 ♘xd5 ♗xd5 12 0-0 (12 ♖c1!? is also interesting) 12...♘d7 13 ♖fd1 is advantageous for White. He is ready to occupy the centre with e4 and 13...♘f6 14 ♘e5! is also in his favour.

2) 9...♘xf4 10 gxf4 ♘d7 11 0-0 is more solid, and similar to the game. White retains a pleasant space advantage.

9 ♘e5!

9 0-0 b5 10 ♕c2 ♗b7 only helps Black.

9 ... ♘d5
10 ♘c3 ♘xf4
11 gxf4

A common motif in the Catalan: increased control over the important central outpost on e5 outweighs the disruption of White's pawn-structure.

11 ... ♘d7
12 e3

The careless 12 0-0? would lose a pawn after 12...♕h4! 13 e3 ♘xe5 14 fxe5 ♗xe5.

12 ... ₩e7

Later practice has seen an improved concept, starting with 12...♘f6! 13 0-0 ₩e7 14 ♖ac1 c6 15 ₩b3 (15 ₩e2 seems better) 15...♖b8 16 ♘a4 ♗d7 17 ♘c5 ♗e8 18 ♘cd3 ♘d7 19 ♖fd1 ♔h8 20 ♘c4 ♗c7 21 ₩a3 ₩d8 22 ♘c5 ♖g8! 23 ₩c3 ♘f6 24 ₩c2 ♘d5 25 ♘e5 ₩e7 26 ♔h1 f6 27 ♘ed3 and a draw was agreed in this unclear position in Vilela-Sieiro Gonzalez, Havana 1986. Although White can probably keep an edge with more accurate play, Black demonstrated he is not devoid of active prospects. Transferring the bishop to e8 makes it difficult for White to achieve the b5 advance, and from here it can later enter the fray via g6 or h5. In the final position, ...g5 with kingside play is on the cards. We'll see how Andersson gradually loses his active possibilities and falls deeper and deeper into full passivity, while Kasparov increases his pressure in an instructive manner.

13 0-0 *(D)*

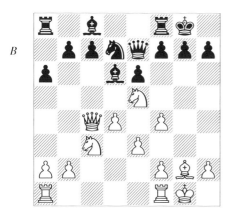

13 ... ♖b8?!

This error makes it easier for White to achieve his ideal set-up. 13...♘f6! transposes into the above note.

14 ♘e4 ♘f6
15 ♘c5 c6

Black's bishop-pair is a potential source of counterplay and especially exchanging the important unopposed d6-bishop would worsen his position. After 15...♗xc5?! 16 ₩xc5 ₩xc5 17 dxc5 White is clearly better.

16 b4 ♔h8

Chasing away White's annoying knights is not so easy: after 16...♘d5 17 a4 f6 18 ♘ed3 b6?! 19 ♘xa6 ♗xa6 20 ₩xa6 ♗xb4 21 ₩c4 White wins a pawn. However, Black could have played the stronger 16...♗d7!?.

17 a4 ♘d5
18 b5 f6
19 ♘ed3 axb5

The premature liberating attempt 19...e5?! 20 bxc6 bxc6 21 ♘e4! (21 fxe5 fxe5 22 ♘e4 is weaker due to 22...exd4 23 ₩xc6 ♖d8! with excellent counterplay) doesn't help Black.

20 axb5 *(D)*

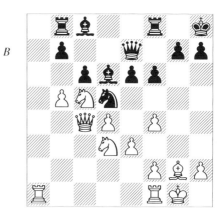

20 ... cxb5

Kasparov recommends 20...b6!? 21 ♘e4 cxb5 22 ₩xb5 ♗d7 23 ₩b3 ♗c6 24 ♖fc1 with an advantage for White. Black's pawns on e6 and b6 are vulnerable, but his position is certainly more active than later in the game.

21 ₩xb5 ♖d8?!

Another inferior move. The alternatives are:

1) 21...♘c7 22 ₩b6! (22 ₩b2 is weaker, as it allows 22...e5!) 22...♘d5 23 ₩b3 b6 24 ♘e4 gives White an extra tempo compared with the previous note, as Black's bishop is still on c8.

2) However, 21...b6!? is more testing. Now White has to choose between 22 ♘e4, transposing to the note to Black's 20th move, and the more ambitious, but also sharper 22 ♘xe6!? ♘xe3 23 fxe3 (after 23 ♘xf8?! ♘xg2! 24 ♔xg2 ♗b7+ White's wrecked kingside gives Black good compensation) 23...♗xe6 24 e4 ♖fc8. White's central pawns are mobile and dangerous, but on the other hand his king is less secure.

22 ♖a7

22 ♘xe6 ♗xe6 (22...♘xe3!? also deserves attention) 23 ♗xd5 ♗xd5 24 ₩xd5 ♗xf4 is hardly worth the trouble.

22 ... ♗xc5?

Three inferior and passive moves in a row are more than Black's position can stand. Kasparov indicates 22...e5!? (best) 23 fxe5 fxe5 24 dxe5 (24 ♗xd5 ♗xc5 gets White nowhere) 24...♗xe5 25 ♘xe5 ♕xe5 26 ♖d1 and now:

1) The tactical complications after 26...♗g4? 27 ♘xb7! ♗xd1 (27...♘xe3? loses a piece to 28 ♖xd8+ ♖xd8 29 ♕d3!) 28 ♘xd8 ♖xb5 (28...♖xd8 is no better in view of 29 ♕xd5!) 29 ♘f7+ lead to an endgame in which White should convert his extra pawn.

2) However, Black has the clever defence 26...♕e7!. Now the knight is protected indirectly (27 ♗xd5 ♕g5+) and as 27 ♘a6? fails to 27...♘c3, it remains an open question how large White's advantage is after, e.g., 27 ♕c4 ♘f6.

23 ♘xc5 ♗d7

It's now too late for 23...e5?, as 24 ♘a6! wins material.

24 ♘xd7 ♖xd7

24...♕xd7 25 ♖b1 would probably cost Black his b-pawn.

25 f5! (D)

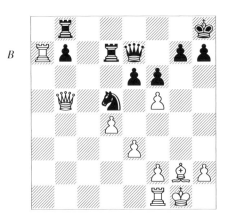

By exchanging both Black's bishops, White has both increased and stabilized his advantage. Undermining the position of the d5-knight is an important part of his plan.

25 ... g6

25...♘c7 26 ♕b1 is similar.

26 fxe6 ♕xe6
27 ♖fa1 ♔g7

27...♘xe3? loses to 28 ♕e2.

28 ♕b3 (D)

Exchanging queens stops any possible tactical tricks.

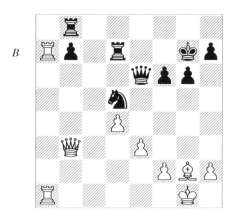

28	...	♘f4
29	♕xe6	♘xe6
30	♖b1	♘d8
31	♗f3	♖c8
32	♖a5	♖cc7
33	♖ab5	

White's main pluses in this endgame are his active pieces, especially the long-legged bishop, and better pawn-structure. They could probably be converted into a full point even after the best defence, but Andersson eases Kasparov's task.

33 ... f5?

We've criticized Black for passivity, but paradoxically in time-trouble he decisively compromises his position with a pseudo-active move. This advance weakens the kingside and also opens an inroad for White's king.

34	h4!	♔f7
35	h5	♔g7
36	♔g2	♖e7
37	♖b6	♖f7
38	♗d5	♖fd7
39	♖1b5 (D)	

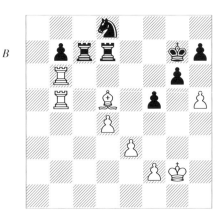

| 39 | ... | ♖e7 |

White has tightened the screws and even 39...♘f7 doesn't help much, as after 40 ♔g3 or 40 f3!? (only not 40 ♖xb7? ♖xd5!) Black can hardly move: 40...♘d6 loses a pawn to 41 ♖c5.

40	♔g3	♖ed7
41	hxg6	hxg6
42	♔f4 (D)	

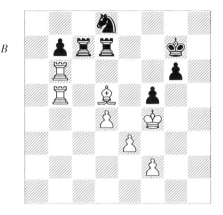

| 42 | ... | ♖c2 |

Black decides to lash out, as after 42...♔h6 43 f3 ♖e7 (43...♘c6 loses to 44 ♗xc6 bxc6 45 ♖c5 ♖d6 46 ♔e5) 44 ♖b1! (White's space advantage enables him to transfer his forces freely from one flank to another) 44...♔g7 (44...♘c6 doesn't help, as after 45 ♖c1 g5+? 46 ♔xf5 ♖xe3 47 ♔f6 White mates) 45 ♖g1 ♘c6 46 ♗b3 the passed d-pawn is ready to advance.

| 43 | ♔g5 | |

In accordance with his temperament Kasparov chooses an attacking continuation, but 43 f3 ♖e2 44 ♗c4! ♖c2 45 ♖d5 is probably a cleaner solution.

43	...	♖xf2
44	♖xg6+	♔f8
45	♗b3	♘f7+?!

45...♘c6!? is considerably more resilient; for example, 46 ♔f6 (46 ♖xf5+? only draws: 46...♖xf5+ 47 ♔xf5 ♘xd4+; the simplified nature of the position helps the defence) 46...♘e7 47 ♖g1 ♖h2! (47...f4? 48 ♖h5! mates) and White still has no direct win.

| 46 | ♔f6 | f4 |

The threat was ♖xf5 and 46...♖b2 is met by 47 ♗c6! ♖xb5 48 ♗xd7 ♖b6+ 49 ♗c6, winning.

| 47 | e4 | ♖b2 |

After 47...f3 48 ♖d5! Black loses a piece, as the black rook can't move due to ♖d8+!. Andersson prevents this, but now White's e-pawn rushes forward.

48	e5	f3
49	e6	f2
50	♗c4 (D)	

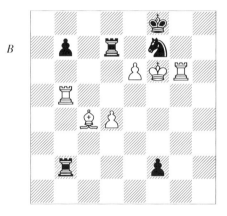

1-0

A pretty final line is 50...♖xb5 (50...f1♕+ 51 ♗xf1 ♖f2+ loses trivially to 52 ♖f5 ♖xf5+ 53 ♔xf5 ♖xd4 54 ♖f6) 51 ♗xb5 ♖c7 52 ♖g2 ♘d6 53 ♗d3 ♖c3 (otherwise White just takes the f2-pawn with an easy win) 54 e7+ ♔e8 55 ♔e6! and White mates.

Game 30
Garry Kasparov – Anatoly Karpov
World Ch match (game 1), Moscow 1985
Nimzo-Indian Defence [E20]

1	d4	♘f6
2	c4	e6
3	♘c3	

This was a minor surprise. Although in the first half of the 1980s Kasparov didn't always avoid the Nimzo-Indian Defence, his previous encounters with Karpov featured only 3 ♘f3 and 3 g3.

3	...	♗b4
4	♘f3	

While White's third move was not completely unexpected, this must have come as an unpleasant shock for Karpov. Firstly, Kasparov had never played this line before and preferred 4 e3 in the past, and secondly the World Champion realized the initial match-game was going to be no warm-up, but a tough and demanding fight.

4 ... c5

Glancing a bit forward, this line became a real nightmare for Karpov in the 1985 and 1986 K-K matches. He managed to score only 2 points out of 8 games from this position, and games 7 and 11 in 1985 convinced him 4...0-0?! 5 ♗g5 doesn't solve Black's opening problems.

5 g3 *(D)*

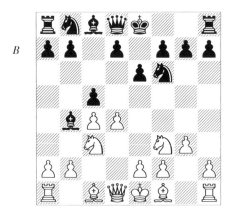
B

5 ... ♘e4

This was the first time Karpov had played this position, and he spent a full 50 minutes for his first five moves – a rare case in his practice. Later, satisfactory methods to fight White's set-up were found. Currently a popular alternative is 5...cxd4 6 ♘xd4 0-0 7 ♗g2 d5; see also Kasparov-Karpov, London/Leningrad Wch (4) 1986 (Game 34).

6	♕d3	♕a5

6...cxd4 7 ♘xd4 ♕a5 (7...♗xc3+!? 8 bxc3 ♘c5 is a sharper and possibly better option) 8 ♘b3 ♘xc3 9 ♗d2 ♘e4 10 ♕xe4 ♗xd2+ 11 ♘xd2 leads to a position that can also arise via an English Opening move-order. After 11...0-0 12 ♗g2 ♘c6 13 ♕e3 (or even 13 ♕c2!?) practice has shown White can claim a slight edge.

7	♕xe4	♗xc3+
8	♗d2	♗xd2+
9	♘xd2 *(D)*	

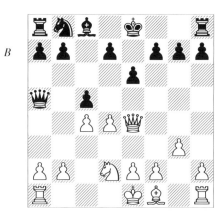
B

9 ... ♕b6?!

Just as in the Catalan, White's pressure on the h1-a8 diagonal hinders the activation of Black's c8-bishop. On the other hand, the pin of the d2-knight makes it difficult for White to keep his slight lead in development, so Black should maintain this pin instead of engaging in dubious pawn-hunting:

1) 9...cxd4?! isn't ideal: 10 ♕xd4 0-0 11 ♗g2 ♘c6 and now 12 ♕e3 transposes to the note to Black's 6th move, but 12 ♕d6!? ♕b4 13

♕xb4 ♘xb4 14 0-0 seems even stronger, when Black's problems persist.

2) 9...♘c6 is a more solid option. After 10 d5 (10 dxc5 b6! shows even White can have problems on the long diagonal; then 11 ♗g2 ♗b7 12 ♕f4 bxc5 leads to approximate equality) 10...♘d4 11 ♗g2 d6!? (this is the simplest solution; if Black wants to accept the offered pawn, the best way to do so is 11...♘b3 12 ♖d1 ♕xa2! with unclear consequences) 12 ♕d3 exd5 13 ♗xd5 ♗f5 14 ♗e4 ♗xe4 15 ♕xe4+ ♔f8 16 ♕d3 ♖e8 17 e3 ♘f3+ 18 ♔e2 ♕xd2+ with an equal endgame, Sapunov-Utemov, Briansk 1995.

10 dxc5!

After the timid 10 0-0-0 cxd4 11 ♘b3 ♕c6! 12 ♖xd4 b6 13 ♗g2 ♗b7 Black simplifies the position and equalizes.

10 ... ♕xb2
11 ♖b1 ♕c3!?

Until now Kasparov had played very quickly, but after this move it was his turn to think. Other queen moves are worse:

1) 11...♕xa2?! is extremely risky. After 12 ♕d4 0-0 13 ♕c3! (more convincing than 13 ♗g2 ♕a5 14 0-0 ♘c6) 13...♕a4 14 ♗g2 ♘c6 15 ♘e4 White's knight on d6 will have a paralysing effect on Black's position and there is little he can do against it; e.g., 15...b6 16 ♖a1! ♕b4 17 ♕xb4 ♘xb4 18 cxb6 ♘c2+ 19 ♔d2 ♘xa1 20 ♖xa1 ♗b7 21 ♘f6+ gxf6 22 ♗xb7 ♖ab8 23 ♖xa7 and White wins after his king marches to b5.

2) 11...♕a3 had been tested in earlier practice, but after 12 ♕d4! 0-0 13 ♗g2 ♘c6 14 ♕d6 b6 15 0-0 White retains strong pressure.

12 ♕d3!

White gets rid of the nagging pin, improving his pawn-structure in the process.

12 ... ♕xd3

Practically forced, as 12...♕a5 13 ♕d4 leads to positions similar to those from note '2' to Black's 11th move.

13 exd3 *(D)*

The b7-pawn is under both vertical and diagonal pressure and despite the exchange of queens Black must defend very accurately.

13 ... ♘a6

Black's main task is to get rid of the cramping c5-pawn, which hinders his development. 13...♘c6 14 ♗g2 b6 doesn't solve the problem,

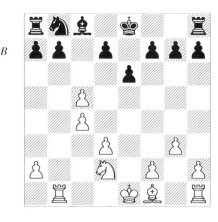

as apart from 15 d4 White has 15 ♘e4 ♔e7 (15...♖b8 16 ♔d2 is no improvement for Black) 16 ♔d2!?, followed by cxb6, and the pawn remains a serious weakness even on b6.

14 d4 ♖b8

14...e5!?, immediately breaking up White's pawn-chain, is more to the point:

1) Kasparov's recommendation 15 ♗g2 ♖b8 16 dxe5 ♘xc5 17 0-0 b6 18 ♗d5 ♗b7 19 f4 allows the liberating 19...d6!.

2) 15 dxe5 ♘xc5 16 ♘b3 ♘xb3 17 axb3 (17 ♖xb3 b6 18 ♗g2 ♖b8 is similar) 17...b6. White has a space advantage and is better, but at least Black's queenside is safe.

15 ♗g2 ♔e7? *(D)*

Karpov decides to activate his h8-rook first before undertaking any active measures, but this was the last suitable moment for 15...e5!, transposing to note '1' to Black's 14th move.

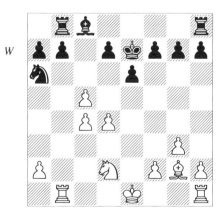

16 ♔e2

With only four pairs of pieces on the board, White wants to keep his king centralized, but 16

0-0 is also good. This stops 16...e5? due to 17 ♖fe1, while later in some lines White's king will be less exposed on g1, where it also protects the g2-bishop (e.g., see the note to White's 18th move).

16 ... ♖d8

After 16...b6 17 cxb6 axb6 18 ♖b3 ♗b7 19 ♗xb7 ♖xb7 20 ♖hb1 Black will lose his b-pawn and 16...e5 17 ♖he1!? exd4 18 ♔d3+ doesn't help much either.

17 ♘e4?!

This natural move surprisingly gives Black a chance to complicate the issue. White is clearly better after 17 ♔e3!: by protecting d4 he takes the sting out of 17...d6 (or 17...e5 18 ♘e4!?) due to 18 cxd6+ ♖xd6 19 c5.

17 ... b6!
18 ♘d6 (D)

Now after 18 cxb6 axb6 White doesn't have 19 ♖b3? any more due to 19...♗b7!, when the threats of ...f5 and ...d5 are annoying.

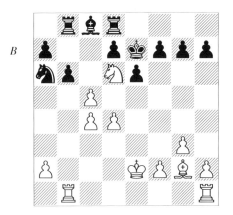

18 ... ♘c7?!

With time running short, Karpov continues to defend passively, but it was time to lash out with 18...bxc5!? 19 ♘xc8+! (19 ♖xb8 ♘xb8 20 dxc5 runs into the strong piece sacrifice 20...♘a6! 21 ♘xc8+ ♖xc8 22 ♗b7 ♖xc5 23 ♗xa6 ♖a5 24 ♗c8 ♖xa2+ 25 ♔e3 ♖c2 26 ♖d1 d5 with very real drawing chances – all this wouldn't be possible if White had played 16 0-0) 19...♖dxc8 20 ♗b7 ♖xb7 21 ♖xb7 cxd4 22 ♖xa7 ♘c5 (22...♘b4!?) 23 ♖b1 e5 and although White is better, Black's central pawns shouldn't be underestimated.

19 ♖b4 ♘e8
20 ♘xe8!?

It's counter-intuitive to exchange an enemy piece that hasn't moved yet, but in spite of this Kasparov recommended 20 ♘xc8+ instead:

1) 20...♖bxc8?! 21 cxb6 axb6 22 ♔d3 ♘d6 23 ♖c1 ♖b8 24 ♖cb1 ♖bc8 (24...♖dc8 25 a4 and Black has no defence against a5) 25 ♖a4! ♖b8 26 ♖a6 ♖dc8 27 ♖b4 b5 (otherwise White plays a4 and Black is practically in zugzwang, as king or rook moves run into c5) 28 c5 ♘e8 29 ♖a7 and with ♗b7 or ♖b7 in the air, the b5-pawn will soon fall.

2) However, stronger is 20...♖dxc8! 21 ♖hb1 ♖c7! (21...d6 is weaker due to 22 cxd6+ ♘xd6 23 c5 ♘f5 24 ♗e4) 22 ♔d3 ♖bc8 23 cxb6 axb6 24 a4 ♘d6 and Black is holding on.

20 ... ♔xe8?!

Even after 20...♖xe8!? 21 ♖hb1 ♗b7 (not 21...♗a6?, which now runs into 22 ♖a4! ♗b7 23 d5! and White wins material due to motifs with d6+) 22 d5! (22 ♗xb7?! ♖xb7 23 cxb6 axb6 24 ♖xb6 ♖a7 forces White into passive defence) 22...exd5 23 cxd5 ♔f8+ 24 ♔d2 ♖a8 25 f4!? (25 a4?! is weaker due to 25...♗a6) White retains pressure and a sizeable advantage; e.g., 25...♖ec8 (after 25...♗a6 26 ♗f3 Black still can't play 26...bxc5? 27 ♖a4) 26 ♖c1.

21 ♖hb1 ♗a6 (D)

21...♗b7? 22 d5 is hopeless for Black.

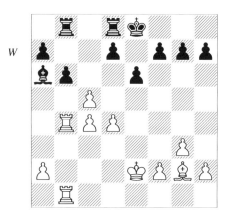

22 ♔e3

Now 22 ♖a4 ♗b7 gets White nowhere because 23 d5?! bxc5 24 ♖xa7? even loses to 24...♗xd5!. Therefore White improves his king, but 22 ♔d2! ♖dc8 23 a4 is even more accurate, with a large advantage.

22 ... d5?

This should have lost quickly. The only move is 22...♖dc8 23 ♗f1 (here 23 a4 e5! is less impressive) 23...♖a8! (the threat was ♖a4) 24 ♔d2! (24 ♖a4 ♗b7 25 cxb6 axb6 26 ♖xa8 ♖xa8 27 ♖xb6 ♗c6 28 ♖b2 ♖a3+ is probably insufficient to win, so White first prevents ...bxc5) 24...♗b7 25 ♖1b2. White has good winning chances, as he'll be the one to decide how and when to take the b-pawn.

23 cxd6!

Not 23 cxd5? exd5 24 cxb6 ♖xb6 25 ♖xb6 axb6 26 ♖xb6 ♗c4 and Black has good fighting chances.

23 ... ♖bc8 (D)

23...♖xd6? loses on the spot to 24 c5 ♖dd8 25 c6! with the double threats c7 and ♖a4.

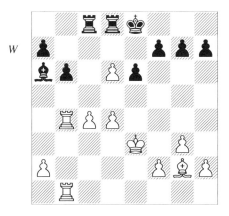

24 ♔d3

After this circumspect move White's advantage is sufficient to win the game, but he had two more incisive options:

1) 24 ♗f1!? ♖xd6 (24...♗b7 25 c5 is no improvement for Black) 25 ♖a4 rules out the game continuation and after 25...♗b7 26 ♖xa7 Black will shortly lose the weak b6-pawn as well.

2) 24 ♖a4 ♗xc4 25 ♗b7 b5 26 d7+! is even more convincing, netting an exchange with a quick win.

24	...	♖xd6
25	♖a4	b5
26	cxb5	♖b8
27	♖ab4	

Even after 27 ♔e3 ♗b7 (27...♖xb5? loses a piece to 28 ♖xa6) White remains only one pawn up. However, this is also sufficient, as in the double-rook endgame Black is devoid of effective counterplay.

27	...	♗b7
28	♗xb7	♖xb7
29	a4	♔e7
30	h4	h6
31	f3	

White's plan is to force an exchange of one pair of rooks, or otherwise invade via the c-file. This can't be prevented in the long run, so Kasparov doesn't force matters in Karpov's time-trouble.

31 ... ♖d5

After 31...♖c7 White can choose between 32 ♖c4 and 32 a5.

32 ♖c1 ♖bd7

Otherwise White plays ♖c5 and a5 anyway.

33 a5 g5

Black desperately seeks counterplay. 33...e5 doesn't help either: 34 ♖cc4 ♔d6 35 a6!? followed by b6.

34	hxg5	♖xg5
35	g4	h5
36	b6	axb6
37	axb6	♖b7
38	♖c5 (D)	

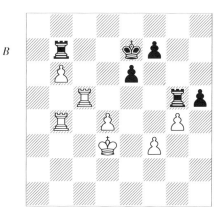

The last accurate move, which keeps Black's rook cut off from the queenside for long enough to allow White's king to support the b6-pawn.

38	...	f5
39	gxh5	♖xh5
40	♔c4	♖h8
41	♔b5	♖a8
42	♖bc4	1-0

The sealed move. Black resigned without resumption, as after ♖c7 or ♖c8 White forces the b-pawn through. What a start to an all-important match!

Game 31
Anatoly Karpov – Garry Kasparov
World Ch match (game 16), Moscow 1985
Sicilian Defence, Taimanov Variation [B44]

This was the key game of the 1985 World Championship match. An impressive win with Black not only gave Kasparov a lead that he didn't relinquish until the end, but was certainly worth more than that – it put him firmly in the driving seat.

| 1 | e4 | c5 |

So finally we have a Sicilian, which still remains a mainstay of Kasparov's repertoire (see also the note to move 9 in Game 5).

| 2 | ♘f3 | e6 |

Kasparov aims for the Scheveningen Variation, using a move-order designed to avoid the Keres Attack (2...d6 3 d4 cxd4 4 ♘xd4 ♘f6 5 ♘c3 e6 6 g4).

3	d4	cxd4
4	♘xd4	♘c6
5	♘b5	

5 ♘c3 d6 6 g4!? occurred in the game Karpov-Kasparov, Moscow Wch (14) 1985. Now the World Champion feels he is ready to continue the theoretical duel and plays his favourite move.

5	...	d6
6	c4	♘f6
7	♘1c3	a6
8	♘a3 *(D)*	

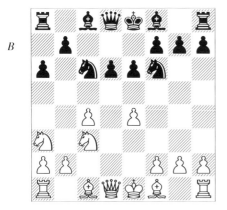

| 8 | ... | d5!? |

Earlier Kasparov used to play 8...♗e7 9 ♗e2 0-0 10 0-0 b6. Black's Hedgehog set-up is a typical representative of the 'coiled spring' opening strategy. Although White gains space, it's not easy for him to formulate a concrete plan, as Black's position lacks weaknesses. Later on Black can lash out with a flank (...b5) or central (...d5) thrust. However, after losing game 3 of the aborted 1984/5 match Kasparov came up with this immediate sharp liberating advance, which better suits his style. The move originates from Hungarian chess circles (it appeared for the first time in 1965!) and was suggested to the challenger by Adorjan, but Kasparov deserves full credit for using such a daring idea at the highest possible level.

| 9 | cxd5 | exd5 |
| 10 | exd5 | ♘b4 |

Black has sacrificed a pawn to open the centre and profit from the misplaced a3-knight before White manages to consolidate his space advantage. The main drawback of his plan is that he must still complete his own development and even regaining the d5-pawn is quite dangerous if Black's king is forced to stay in the centre.

| 11 | ♗e2!? | |

Karpov played this instantly, and nearly two decades later it still remains the main move. 11 ♗c4 ♗g4! had occurred a week earlier in Karpov-Kasparov, Moscow Wch (12) 1985. The most aggressive move is then the double-edged 12 ♕d4 (Karpov bailed out with 12 ♗e2 ♗xe2 13 ♕xe2+ ♕e7 14 ♗e3 ♘bxd5 and the game was quickly drawn) 12...b5 13 ♘cxb5!? (13 ♗b3?! ♗c5! 14 ♕e5+ ♔f8 is dangerous for White), but Black still has reasonable chances of beating off the onslaught after 13...axb5 14 ♗xb5+ ♗d7 15 d6! ♘c2+! 16 ♘xc2 ♕a5+ 17 ♗d2 ♕xb5 18 0-0-0 ♕d5.

| 11 | ... | ♗c5?! |

Kasparov also replied quickly, indicating he was still following his home analysis. By spurning the d5-pawn, Black continues his development and increases the tension. However, his concept has a tactical flaw and later practice concentrated on the more sedate 11...♘fxd5 12 0-0 ♗e6. After the enterprising 13 ♕a4+!? (13 ♘xd5 ♕xd5 14 ♗f3 ♕xd1 15 ♖xd1 ♗e7 only leads to equality) 13...b5 14 ♘axb5 axb5 15 ♗xb5+ ♔e7 16 ♘xd5+ ♘xd5 17 ♕e4 f5 18 ♕f3 ♔f7 19 ♖d1 Black's position admittedly hangs on a thin thread, but no one has yet refuted Galkin's recommendation 19...♗e7! 20 ♗c6 ♖a5 21 ♗e3 ♕d6 with unclear play.

12 0-0?!

A natural reply, but 12 ♗e3! ♗xe3 13 ♕a4+ is much stronger. Nowadays this is the first choice of *Fritz* in a few seconds and it more or less refutes Black's 11th move. In practice it appeared for the first time a few months later in Karpov-Van der Wiel, Brussels 1986. After 13...♗d7 (best) 14 ♕xb4 ♕b6 15 ♕xb6 ♗xb6 16 ♘c4 Black faces a tough uphill fight for a draw.

12 ... 0-0
13 ♗f3 *(D)*

Despite being, just as in game 12, on unknown territory, this time White feels obliged to accept the challenge and defends his extra pawn. One can understand Karpov, as Black's compensation is as yet far from obvious. However, surprisingly enough probably the last chance to fight for an advantage from the opening was 13 ♗g5!? ♘bxd5 (13...♗f5 is weaker due to 14 ♘c4!) 14 ♘xd5 ♕xd5 15 ♕xd5 ♘xd5 16 ♗f3 and with White's rooks occupying the central files first, Black still has some problems to solve, Barbulescu-Wirthensohn, Lucerne Wcht 1985.

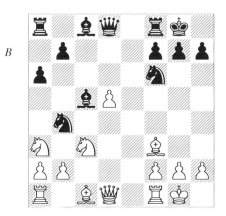

13 ... ♗f5!

This keeps the a3-knight offside and prepares to occupy the crucial d3-square, weakened by White's greedy 13 ♗f3. As we'll see, these two factors will effectively decide the game.

14 ♗g5

Again a natural move. After 14 ♘c4 ♗c2 (14...♘c2?! runs into the unpleasant 15 ♗e3!) 15 ♕d2 ♗d3 or 14 ♗e3 ♗xe3 15 fxe3 ♕b6 16 ♘c4 ♕c5 17 ♗e2 ♗g6 Black comfortably regains the pawn.

14 ... ♖e8!

Black's plan necessitates preventing ♗e4 or ♘e4.

15 ♕d2

After 15 ♘c4 ♗d3 16 a3 taking the exchange is dubious, but 16...♗xc4 17 axb4 ♗xb4 18 ♖e1 ♖xe1+ 19 ♕xe1 ♕b6 regains the pawn with an edge. 15 d6 gives Black a pleasant choice between 15...♖b8 and 15...♗d3!?.

15 ... b5 *(D)*

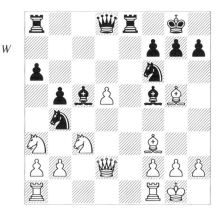

16 ♖ad1?!

Just as earlier (moves 12 and 13), Karpov chooses a natural continuation. However, this, together with further errors (once again 'non-committal' moves!) on moves 17 and 19, causes the rapid deterioration of his position, which after 21...g5!! is in a higher sense lost. How did all this come to be? First of all Karpov failed to realize that White's task here is not one of quiet consolidation and converting his extra pawn. Quite the opposite, as once Black achieves full coordination of his forces, White will be reduced to passivity and finally helplessness. Thus paradoxically enough White is the side that should try to lash out and get counterplay before it's too late. In this sense Kasparov's play is a great creative achievement – he found a specific situation in which 'normal' moves are simply not enough. Even much weaker players than Karpov know and can apply basic strategic rules, so beating a very strong opponent requires recognizing the value of an exceptional idea. The second consideration is psychological: after bailing out in game 12, Karpov badly wants to punish Black's audacious 8...d5!?, but his sense of danger deserts him. Objectively much stronger is 16 d6 ♖a7 17 ♖ad1, and now:

1) 17...♘d3?! 18 ♗e2! forces the knight away from d3, as 18...♘xf2? 19 ♖xf2 b4 runs into 20 ♕f4!; e.g., 20...♗d7 21 ♗c4 bxc3 22 ♗xf7+! and White is winning.

2) 17...♖e6 is a better try. After 18 ♘d5 Black has 18...♘bxd5 (18...♕xd6? 19 ♗xf6 ♘xd5 loses material after 20 ♕g5! ♖xf6 21 ♖xd5) 19 ♕xd5! ♘xd5 20 ♗xd8 ♖xd6! 21 ♖xd5 ♖xd5 22 ♗xd5 ♖d7 23 ♖d1 ♗g4 24 ♖d3 ♗f5 with a draw by repetition.

3) After 17...♖d7 18 ♕f4 ♗d3 (18...♗g6 19 ♗xf6 ♕xf6 20 ♕xf6 gxf6 21 ♘axb5! axb5 22 a3 ♘d3 23 ♗c6 could only be dangerous for Black) 19 ♗xf6 ♕xf6 20 ♕xf6 gxf6 21 ♖xd3!? ♘xd3 22 ♗c6 Black cannot expect any more than a draw, and the quickest way to force it is by 22...♘xf2 23 ♗xd7 ♘d3+ with a perpetual check.

16 ... ♘d3! (D)

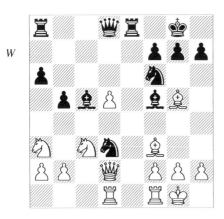

From now on the whole plot will revolve around this mighty knight. It practically paralyses all White's major pieces and when all attempts to remove it fail, 17 moves later it will cost Karpov his queen.

17 ♘ab1?

Here the knight will remain until the bitter end and from now on White will be fighting for his life.

17 ♗e2? fails to 17...♘xf2 18 ♖xf2 b4, but the active 17 d6 is more or less mandatory. Kasparov indicates the difference from the note to White's 16th move: now Black has 17...♕xd6! (17...b4? 18 ♗xa8 ♕xa8 19 ♘a4 bxa3 20 ♗xf6 gxf6 21 ♘xc5 passes the advantage to White) 18 ♗xa8 ♖xa8, threatening ...♘g4. After 19 ♗xf6 ♕xf6 the monster stays in place on d3, providing excellent compensation.

17 ... h6!

A well-timed nudge, which allows Black to expand on both flanks.

18 ♗h4

Exchanging the bishop would be a concession, while 18 ♗e3 ♗xe3 (18...♖xe3!? 19 fxe3 ♕b6 also deserves attention) 19 fxe3 ♕b6 wins back the pawn and keeps the pressure.

18 ... b4 (D)

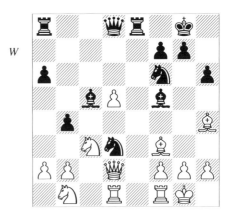

19 ♘a4?!

Sidelining the other knight is more than White's position can stand. Stronger was 19 ♘e2 g5 (19...♘e5!? 20 ♘d4 ♘xf3+ 21 ♘xf3 ♗e4 also deserves attention) 20 ♗xg5! ♘xf2 21 ♖xf2 ♗xf2+ 22 ♔xf2 hxg5 23 ♕xg5+ ♗g6 24 ♘d2 ♖c8. Although in the resulting position White's king is more vulnerable than its black counterpart, the outcome of the game remains undecided.

19 ... ♗d6 (D)

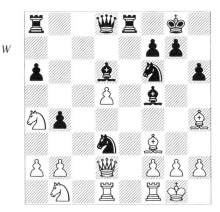
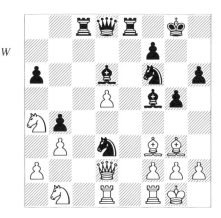

Black toys with the threat of ...♗f4, while White is starting to lack constructive ideas. Kasparov writes this position was still part of his home preparation! This only shows how well he came to know and understand his main rival during their first unlimited match.

20 ♗g3

The attempt to dislodge the d3-knight with 20 ♗e2? fails to the pretty 20...♗f4 21 ♕c2 ♖c8 22 ♘ac3 ♘g4!! (22...g5 23 ♗g3 is less convincing) 23 ♗xd8 (23 ♗g3 ♘e3! and 23 g3 ♕xh4! are no better) 23...♗xh2+ 24 ♔h1 ♘dxf2+ 25 ♖xf2 ♘xf2+ 26 ♔xh2 ♗xc2 and Black remains an exchange up. Another forced line is 20 ♕c2? ♖c8 21 ♕b3 ♘f4. The threat is ...♗c2 and 22 ♖c1 ♖xc1 23 ♖xc1 g5 24 ♗g3 g4 costs White a piece.

20 ... ♖c8

The premature 20...♘e4? allows White to unravel by 21 ♗xe4 ♗xe4 22 ♕e3!. Subsequently Kasparov analysed 20...♗xg3. Although this also promises Black an advantage, it simplifies the position and gives White a choice between two recaptures. The ambitious text-move aims for full control and is more thematic.

21 b3

Now 21 ♗e2? fails to 21...♘e4, while 21 ♗xd6 ♕xd6 22 ♗e2 also loses after 22...♘f4 23 ♗f3 ♖c2 24 ♕d4 ♘g4. Therefore Karpov prepares ♘b2.

21 ... g5!! (D)

A surprising but very effective piece of prophylaxis. By preventing White's only active idea, Kasparov tightens his grip on the position and accentuates Karpov's lack of moves. Moreover, we'll see in the next note that control of f4 is important for Black.

22 ♗xd6

Once again White plays the most natural move. The alternatives were:

1) 22 ♘b2? loses a piece after 22...♘xb2 23 ♕xb2 g4 24 ♗e2 ♖c2.

2) 22 h3 ♘e4 23 ♗xe4 ♗xe4 24 ♕e3 ♘f4 gives Black a huge advantage.

3) Lashing out with 22 h4 is more demanding, although it is insufficient after 22...♘e4 (22...g4? 23 ♗e2 ♘e4 runs into 24 ♕xh6, but 22...♘f4!? is interesting) 23 ♗xe4 ♗xe4 24 ♕e3 (both 24 hxg5 ♗xg3 25 fxg3 ♕xd5 26 gxh6 ♖e6! and 24 ♗xd6 ♕xd6 25 hxg5 ♘f4 26 ♖fe1 ♘xg2! 27 ♖xe4 ♖xe4 28 ♔xg2 ♖g4+ give Black a decisive attack) 24...♗f4 25 ♕b6 ♕xd5!?; e.g., 26 ♕xh6 ♗xg3 27 fxg3 gxh4 and after the position opens up White's king can't survive the absence of both knights.

22 ... ♕xd6
23 g3

23 ♗e2? again fails, this time to 23...♘f4 24 ♗c4 ♘g4 25 g3 ♖xc4! 26 bxc4 ♖c2 27 c5 (27 ♕d4 ♗e4 costs White his queen) 27...♘h3+ 28 ♔g2 ♗e4+ 29 ♔xh3 ♕g6! and Black mates. Karpov again intends ♘b2.

23 ... ♘d7!

As on move 21, Kasparov applies active prophylaxis.

24 ♗g2?!

Stopping halfway completely ruins White's position. 24 ♘b2 is more resilient, although after 24...♕f6! (24...♘7e5?! 25 ♗g2 ♕f6 26 ♔h1! only helps White) 25 ♘c4 (the beautiful main point is 25 ♘xd3 ♗xd3 26 ♕xd3 ♘e5! and White's queen is trapped) 25...♘7e5 26 ♘xe5 (26 ♗e2 ♗h3 forces 27 ♘xe5 ♘xe5 28 f4 ♕b6+ 29 ♖f2 ♘g4 30 ♗xg4 ♗xg4 31 ♖e1

Xe1+ 32 ♕xe1 gxf4 33 gxf4 ♗f3 and White's vulnerable king can't survive in the long run) 26...♘xe5 27 ♗g2 (27 ♗e2 ♖c2 28 ♕e3 g4 29 ♔h1 ♔f8!, followed by a knight move, nets Black a piece) 27...♗d3 28 ♕xb4! (28 f4 ♖c2 and 28 ♖fc1 ♘f3+! 29 ♗xf3 ♕xf3 30 ♖xe8+ ♖xe8 31 ♕xd3 ♖e1+ are both hopeless for White) 28...♗xf1 29 ♖xf1 ♖c2 Black should win after overcoming some technical obstacles.

24 ... ♕f6!

This stops ♘b2, leaving White paralysed and without any meaningful ideas. The rest is carnage.

25 a3 a5
26 axb4 axb4
27 ♕a2 ♗g6

Stopping ♘d2, but even the immediate advance 27...g4!? with the idea 28 ♘d2 ♖e2 is good enough.

28 d6

After 28 ♗h3 the simplest reply is 28...♖cd8, threatening ...♘7e5.

28 ... g4!

Kasparov is not interested in 28...♕xd6? 29 ♘d2, and continues to increase his domination of White's forces by denying them even more squares.

29 ♕d2 ♔g7

Black has no need to hurry; his following plan can be, e.g., doubling rooks on the e-file.

30 f3

With time running short Karpov desperately tries to break free, but only hastens the end. 30 f4 also doesn't help, as after 30...♗f5! Black will penetrate via e3.

30 ... ♕xd6

The position is opening up, so Black finally takes White's extra pawn to free his knight for the final attack.

31 fxg4

31 ♕b2+ ♘f6! 32 fxg4 ♕e7 is similar to the game and 31 ♘b2 provides no relief due to 31...♕d4+ 32 ♔h1 ♕xb2 33 ♕xb2+ ♘xb2 34 ♖xd7 ♖c2 35 fxg4 (35 ♖d2 ♖xd2 36 ♘xd2 ♖e2 also loses) 35...♖ee2 (or even 35...♘d3!?) and Black's attack continues even in the endgame.

31 ... ♕d4+
32 ♔h1 ♘f6! *(D)*

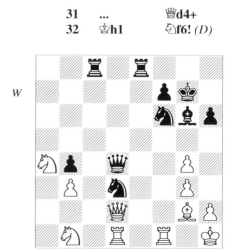

The threats of ...♘xg4 and ...♘e4 give Black a decisive attack.

33 ♖f4

After 33 h3 Black has a pleasant choice between 33...♖e3!? and the more forcing line 33...♘e4 34 ♕xd3 (34 ♗xe4 ♕xe4+ 35 ♔g1 ♖c6! with a decisive zugzwang) 34...♘f2+ 35 ♖xf2 ♗xd3 36 ♖fd2 ♕e3 37 ♖xd3 ♖c1! 38 ♖f1 ♕xd3 39 ♖xc1 ♕xb3 40 ♘b6 ♕e3, netting material.

33 ... ♘e4
34 ♕xd3 ♘f2+
35 ♖xf2

After 35 ♔g1 ♘h3+ 36 ♔h1 ♕xd3 37 ♖xd3 ♖e1+ 38 ♗f1 (38 ♖f1 ♖xf1+ 39 ♗xf1 ♗e4+ mates) 38...♗xd3 White loses everything.

35 ... ♗xd3
36 ♖fd2 ♕e3
37 ♖xd3 ♖c1!
38 ♘b2

Black's main threat was ...♖xd1+ followed by ...♕xb3, while 38 ♖f1 fails to 38...♕f2! and 38 ♖xe3 ♖xd1+ 39 ♗f1 ♖xe3 costs him another minor piece. After the text-move White gets mated.

38 ... ♕f2!
39 ♘d2 ♖xd1+
40 ♘xd1 ♖e1+

0-1

Game 32
Anatoly Karpov – Garry Kasparov
World Ch match (game 24), Moscow 1985
Sicilian Defence, Scheveningen Variation [B85]

The decisive game! Karpov was trailing by a point, and so a win was the only way to avoid losing the world title.

1 e4

Karpov admitted this move was his old love. However, his negative score in the Sicilian against Kasparov (see also Game 31) forced him to reconsider. This was the last match-game in which Karpov played 1 e4. Later on he switched to closed openings not only against his main rival, but also in general tournament practice.

1 ... c5

Kasparov decides to be true to himself and doesn't avoid possible complications and a principled fight.

2	♘f3	d6
3	d4	cxd4
4	♘xd4	♘f6
5	♘c3	a6

This is the first game in this book with the Najdorf move-order, which will be especially richly featured in Volume 2.

6	♗e2	e6
7	0-0	♗e7
8	f4	0-0
9	♔h1	♕c7
10	a4	♘c6
11	♗e3	♖e8 *(D)*

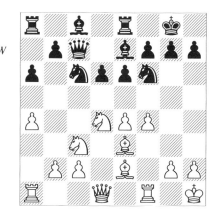

12 ♗f3

Although nowadays most of the theoretical development in the Scheveningen or Najdorf takes place in systems connected with ♗e3 and 0-0-0, this still remains one of the critical opening positions. Kasparov also defended Black's cause in his PCA World Championship match in 1995 against Anand, who apart from the text-move also tried 12 ♕d2 and 12 ♗d3.

12 ... ♖b8 *(D)*

This semi-waiting move used to be Kasparov's favourite, but currently it has faded from the limelight due to the reasons mentioned in the next note. Later practice concentrated more on the immediate 12...♗d7 13 ♘b3 b6 14 g4 ♗c8 15 g5 ♘d7 16 ♗g2 ♗b7. As long as Black doesn't intend to play ...♘a5, ...♖b8 is more or less superfluous. Another popular alternative is 12...♗f8!?: Black makes a useful and flexible move without committing his a8-rook or c8-bishop yet.

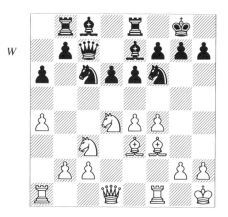

13 ♕d2

The critical continuation is 13 g4!?, as the complications after 13...♘xd4 14 ♗xd4 e5 15 fxe5 dxe5 16 ♗a7 ♖a8 17 g5! are in White's favour. If Black avoids simplification on move 13, then after a further g5 White's queen has a more direct road to the kingside via h5.

13 ... ♗d7

Considered mandatory at that time, but later Kasparov came up with 13...♘a5!? 14 ♕f2 ♘c4 15 ♗c1 e5 16 ♘de2 exf4 17 ♘xf4 ♗e6 18 b3 ♘e5 19 ♗b2 ♖bc8 20 ♖ac1 ♕c5 21 ♕g3 g6 22 ♘ce2 ♘xf3 23 gxf3 b5 with a complex and approximately equal position, Anand-Kasparov, Linares 1997.

14 ♘b3

The most consistent continuation. White avoids the exchange and pinpoints the main drawback of Black's last move – his d7-bishop takes away the most natural square for the f6-knight. 14 ♕f2 ♘xd4 15 ♗xd4 e5 16 ♗e3 was played in Karpov-Kasparov, Moscow Wch (2) 1985; now after 16...exf4 17 ♗xf4 ♗e6 followed by ...♘d7 Black has little to fear.

14 ... b6 *(D)*

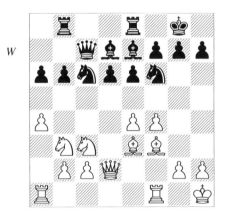

15 g4!?

The most aggressive and promising continuation, which also fits the match situation well. Yet considerations about objective strength of certain moves don't really apply with the tension running so high. One can't help feeling such do-or-die play doesn't suit Karpov. As World Champion, Kasparov found himself in the same situation two years later and despite his tactical capabilities and love for complications, he chose a completely different (and ultimately successful!) approach (see Kasparov-Karpov, Seville Wch (24) 1987, Game 42). The quiet 15 ♗f2 ♗c8 16 ♗g3 ♘d7 17 ♖ae1 ♗b7 18 e5 ♖bd8! 19 ♕f2 ♖f8 20 ♗e4?! dxe5 21 fxe5 ♘c5 22 ♘xc5 bxc5 23 ♗f4 led to a draw in Karpov-Kasparov, Moscow Wch (18) 1985. After 23...♘d4 Black is slightly better.

15 ... ♗c8
16 g5 ♘d7 *(D)*

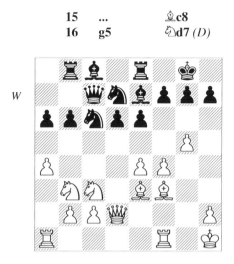

17 ♕f2

At the time our game took place, this position was still uncharted territory and had only one predecessor, which was played a few days earlier in the Candidates tournament and undoubtedly inspired both sides. There White went 17 ♗g2, which gives Black a choice:

1) 17...♘a5 was until then considered a typical method to create counterplay in similar positions. After 18 ♕f2, an interesting reply is 18...♘xb3!? (18...♗f8?! 19 ♖ad1 ♘c4 20 ♗c1 b5 21 axb5 axb5 22 ♖d3 g6 23 ♖h3 ♗g7 24 f5! gave White a strong attack in A.Sokolov-Ribli, Montpellier Ct 1985; the subsequently recommended 18...♘c4 19 ♗c1 keeps the a1-rook offside and is somewhat better, but it also enhances the strength of the follow-up ♘d4 and f5, possibly in connection with b3 and ♗b2) 19 cxb3 ♘c5 with chances for both sides.

2) Later Black started to prefer 17...♗f8 and the set-up introduced by Kasparov in our game became standard. Black fianchettoes both bishops and finishes his development; his c6-knight aims for b4, tying down one of White's major pieces to the defence of c2. Now 18 ♕f2 transposes, so later practice mainly featured the sharper 18 ♖f3!?. The immediate transfer of the rook to h3 is more effective, leaving White the option of deploying both his queen and the a1-rook depending on the circumstances.

17 ... ♗f8

Karpov's move-order has the advantage of disarming the ...♘a5-c4 idea: here 17...♘a5 is ineffective due to 18 ♖ad1 ♘c4 19 ♗c1.

18 ♗g2

18 h4 was tried in Beliavsky-Kasparov, Barcelona (World Cup) 1989. Then Kasparov recommends 18...g6!? 19 h5 ♗g7 with unclear play. Although it takes White longer to create threats on the h-file, on the other hand Black finds it much more difficult to lash out with ...f5 as in the game.

18	...	♗b7
19	♖ad1	g6
20	♗c1!? *(D)*	

After long thought Karpov returns to Sokolov's plan and clears the 3rd rank for his rook. More direct methods such as 20 f5?! ♘ce5 or 20 ♕h4 ♗g7 21 ♖f3 ♘b4 (or even 21...f5!?) promise White nothing.

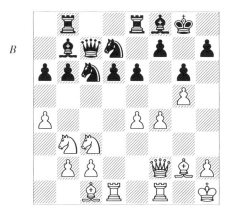

20 ... ♖bc8?!

Playing such a volatile position for the first time is always fraught with danger. Kasparov's move is positionally sound, but it loses a tempo and underestimates White's attacking potential. 20...f5?! 21 gxf6 ♘xf6 22 f5 is rather shaky for Black, and 20...♘b4 21 ♖d4! d5 (otherwise Black can't justify his previous move) 22 exd5 ♘xd5 23 ♘xd5 ♗xd5 24 ♗xd5 cxd5 25 f5 also gives White the initiative. Slowing down White's attack with 20...♘c5! is Black's best option, when after 21 ♘xc5 either recapture is playable. Black then plants his knight on d4 and meets White's play on the h-file by preparing a timely ...h5.

21	♖d3	♘b4
22	♖h3	♗g7? *(D)*

Once again a mistake in the same spirit as on move 20. This careless move fits Black's plans, but is tactically flawed. On the other hand 22...f5! is now not only playable, but also necessary. After 23 gxf6 ♘xf6 24 f5 (24 ♕d4?! e5 25 ♕xb4 d5 26 ♘b5 axb5 27 ♕xb5 ♘xe4 is fine for Black) 24...exf5 25 exf5 ♗g7 both kings are vulnerable and the position remains unclear.

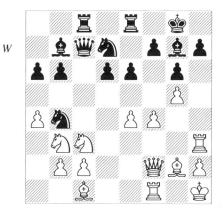

23 ♗e3?

A hesitant move, which partly confirms the reservations about Karpov's opening choice and strategy (see the notes to moves 1 and 15). White's whole set-up literally begged for immediate action, and the straightforward 23 f5 exf5 24 exf5 is very strong:

1) 24...♘e5? 25 ♕h4 ♕c4 runs into 26 ♖f4! ♗xg2+ (26...♘f3 was played in Timoshenko-Gorelov, Moscow 1988; now 27 ♖hxf3! ♗xf3 28 ♔g1 wins for White) 27 ♔xg2 ♕c6+ 28 ♔g1 gxf5 29 ♘d4 ♕c5 30 ♗e3 and the concentration of attacking forces is irresistible.

2) Kasparov recommends the stronger line 24...♗xg2+ 25 ♔xg2 ♕b7+ (25...♖xc3? fails to 26 fxg6!) 26 ♔g1 ♖c4 (after 26...gxf5? 27 ♕h4 ♘xc2 28 ♕xh7+ ♔f8 29 ♕xf5 White has a decisive attack, and even tactical tricks can't help Black as 29...♘c5 30 g6! ♗xb3 loses to the energetic 31 ♖h8+! ♗xh8 32 ♗h6+ ♗g7 33 ♗xg7+ ♔xg7 34 ♕f6+ ♔h6 35 gxf7+ ♔h7 36 ♕h4+ ♔g7 37 ♕g5+ ♔h7 38 ♕h5+) 27 fxg6 ♖g4+ 28 ♖g3 ♖xg3+ 29 hxg3 ♘e5 30 gxh7+ ♔h8 31 ♕f5 ♘xc2 32 ♕xc2 ♘f3+ 33 ♖xf3 ♕xf3 34 ♕f2 ♕d3, but after 35 ♗d2 White retains good winning chances.

23 ... ♖e7!

23...f5 24 gxf6 ♗xf6 is somewhat loose, but perhaps playable. However, Kasparov was justifiably proud of the stronger and highly original prophylactic text-move, which takes the sting out of White's attack.

24 ♔g1

Now it was Karpov's turn to sink into thought and after 30 minutes he came up with a useful move, safeguarding himself against back-rank surprises. The intended 24 ♗d4 now gets White nowhere due to 24...e5! 25 fxe5 ♗xe5, and the same goes for the direct 24 f5 exf5 25 exf5 ♗xg2+ 26 ♔xg2?!, as Black has 26...♗xc3! 27 bxc3 ♕xc3. Both lines clearly show the importance of overprotecting the f7-pawn.

24 ... ♖ce8

This seemingly mysterious doubling of rooks on a closed(!) file not only once and for all stops f5, but also prepares Black's own kingside counterplay.

25 ♖d1! *(D)*

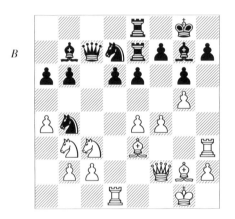

White flexibly changes his plan and turns his attention to the vulnerable d6-pawn. This requires immediate action.

25 ... f5
26 gxf6

Practically forced, as 26 ♕d2 e5! would unleash Black's dormant rooks.

26 ... ♘xf6!?

This pawn sacrifice is consistent with Black's previous moves. After 26...♗xf6 27 ♕d2 White can claim an edge; e.g., 27...e5 28 f5! gxf5 29 exf5 ♖g7 30 ♖g3.

27 ♖g3

Karpov understandably wants to maintain the tension. However, 27 ♗xb6 is objectively better: 27...♖g4!? (Kasparov's idea 27...♕b8 28 a5 e5 seems weaker due to 29 fxe5 ♖xe5 30 ♕d4!) 28 ♗xc7 ♘xf2 29 ♗xd6 (29 ♔xf2 ♖xc7 30 ♖xd6 ♘xc2 31 ♘a5 ♖f8 also gives Black counterplay) 29...♘xd1 30 ♗xe7 ♖xe7 31 ♘xd1 ♘xc2, when Lepeshkin proved Black should be able to hold the endgame; e.g., 32 e5 ♗xg2 33 ♔xg2 g5 34 fxg5 ♗xe5 35 ♘c5 ♗d4!.

27 ... ♖f7
28 ♗xb6 ♕b8 *(D)*

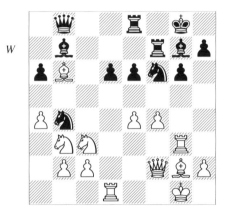

Now the circumstances are less favourable for White than in the above note, because Black intends to increase his pressure against f4 with ...♘h5, ...♗h6, ...♖ef8, etc.

29 ♗e3 ♘h5
30 ♖g4

After 30 ♖f3 Black can not only repeat moves (30...♘f6), but get more ambitious with 30...♗xc3!? 31 bxc3 ♘a2.

30 ... ♘f6
31 ♖h4!?

Only one result counts for Karpov... Although avoiding repetition leads to complications, the position still remains tense and balanced.

31 ... g5! *(D)*

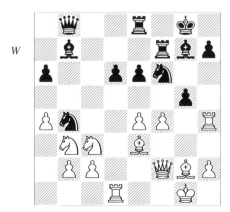

GAME 32: ANATOLY KARPOV – GARRY KASPAROV

32	fxg5	♘g4

A pragmatic decision. 32...♘xe4 is perhaps playable, but it would expose Black to unnecessary risk after 33 ♕xf7+! ♔xf7 34 ♘xe4.

33	♕d2	

Now the queen sacrifice is insufficient, as White's e4-pawn limits his own pieces.

33	...	♘xe3
34	♕xe3	♘xc2
35	♕b6!	

White must control the a7-g1 diagonal, as allowing ...♕a7+ followed by ...♘e3 would be playing with fire.

35	...	♗a8! *(D)*

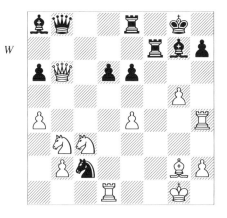

36	♖xd6?	

An oversight (or desperation?) in serious time-trouble, which loses material. White's uncoordinated forces and Black's active bishops indicate Kasparov holds the initiative, but after the correct 36 ♕xb8 ♖xb8 37 ♗h3! a draw would still be the most plausible result; e.g., 37...♖xb3 38 ♗xe6 ♗d4+! 39 ♔h1 ♖xb2 40 ♖f1 ♗xc3 41 ♖xf7 ♘d4 42 ♖a7+ ♘xe6 43 ♖xa8+ ♔g7 44 ♖a7+ ♔g8.

36	...	♖b7
37	♕xa6	♖xb3?

Black is impatient and allows White to get back into the game. 37...♘b4 wins on the spot.

38	♖xe6	♖xb2
39	♕c4	♔h8
40	e5?	

Karpov finally makes the time-control only to throw away the game for good. Although Black's piece is worth more than White's pawns, the position is very simplified and 40 ♖xe8+ ♕xe8 41 ♘d1 ♘a3 42 ♕d3 ♖a2 (42...♖b1 43 e5 h6 44 ♖d4 ♖b8 45 ♗xa8 is good enough for a draw) 43 g6! h6 (43...♖xg2+ 44 ♔xg2 ♕xg6+ 45 ♔f3 doesn't give Black realistic winning chances) 44 ♖xh6+! ♗xh6 45 ♕c3+ would regain the rook and liquidate Black's last pawn, saving at least the game, if not the world title.

40	...	♕a7+
41	♔h1	♗xg2+
42	♔xg2	♘d4+ *(D)*

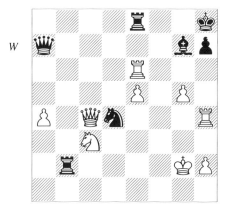

0-1

Winning the rook is the simplest. At this moment Kasparov became the youngest World Champion in chess history.

Game 33
Garry Kasparov – Jan Timman
Match (game 4), Hilversum 1985
Queen's Indian/Nimzo-Indian Hybrid [E13]

With the rematch against Karpov due in 1986, the new World Champion once again chose a combination of home and match preparation. Against Timman he tested some new opening ideas and won convincingly 4-2. The following exciting game was typical for the match.

1	d4	♘f6
2	c4	e6
3	♘f3	b6
4	♘c3	♗b4
5	♗g5	

Although Timman has side-stepped Kasparov's favourite Petrosian Variation (see Game 10, etc.), he can't and doesn't even want to avoid sharp play. This ambitious bishop sortie was featured in all the even-numbered match-games and still remains in Kasparov's repertoire.

5	...	♗b7
6	e3	

Later Kasparov started to prefer 6 ♘d2!?. This limits Black's options, as later on White may be able to play e4 in one go.

6	...	h6
7	♗h4 *(D)*	

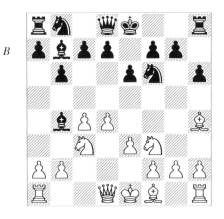

7	...	g5

Black gains space but also weakens his kingside, which will play a major role later on. In any case in the 1986 rematch a forewarned Karpov went for this position only once and chose the more restrained 7...♗xc3+ 8 bxc3 d6, by which Black just controls the centre rather than occupying it.

8	♗g3	♘e4
9	♕c2	

9 ♘d2!? ♘xc3 10 bxc3 ♗xc3 11 ♖c1 ♗b4 (11...♗a5!? 12 h4 ♖g8 with the intention of ...♕e7-a3 is the latest try) 12 h4 gxh4 13 ♖xh4 ♗d6 14 ♕g4 ♗xg3?! 15 ♕xg3 ♘c6 16 d5 ♘e7 17 ♗d3 d6 18 ♕g7 ♖g8 19 ♕h7 ♖f8 20 ♘e4 gave White a huge initiative in Kasparov-Timman, Hilversum (2) 1985. This time Kasparov refrains from the pawn sacrifice and goes for the main line.

9	...	♗xc3+
10	bxc3	d6
11	♗d3	f5?!

An ambitious but risky attempt to retain the central outpost. The last chance to keep the game in quiet waters was 11...♘xg3 12 fxg3 ♘d7 13 0-0 ♕e7 with a solid position where Black still retains both castling options.

12	d5! *(D)*	

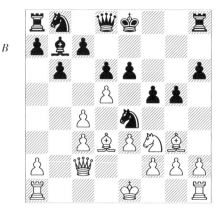

If Black catches up with his development, he might well end up being better, so opening up the position for the bishops is a must.

12	...	♘c5

Arguably the best reaction. Other moves:

1) 12...exd5?! isn't ideal. After 13 cxd5 Bxd5 14 Nd4 Qf6 15 f3 Nxg3 16 hxg3 White regains the pawn, highlighting Black's light-square holes.

2) 12...Qf6 13 Bxe4 fxe4 14 Qxe4 and now 14...Nd7 transposes into line '3', while 14...Qxc3+ 15 Ke2 Qb2+ 16 Nd2 Qf6 17 h4 g4 18 h5 is advantageous for White.

3) The former main move 12...Nd7 13 Bxe4 fxe4 14 Qxe4 Qf6 15 0-0 leads to a position in which Black has play for the pawn, but only White can have any ambitions after 15...0-0-0 16 Qxe6 Qxe6 17 dxe6 Nc5 18 Nd4 Rde8 19 f3 Ba6 20 Nb5 Rxe6 21 e4.

13 h4!

Previously White played only 13 Nd4. Kasparov's strong novelty further loosens Black's crumbling kingside.

13 ... g4

Black can't allow the opening of the h-file, but the drawbacks of the text-move will show clearly six moves later.

14 Nd4 Qf6
15 0-0 (D)

15 dxe6? is out of the question owing to 15...Bxg2 16 Rg1 Be4, and 15 Nxe6?! Nxe6 16 dxe6 Bxg2 17 Rg1 Bf3! 18 Bxf5 Nc6 is also premature and hands the advantage to Black.

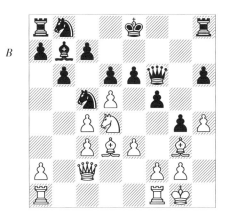

15 ... Nba6

A dissatisfied Timman tried 15...Nxd3?! 16 Qxd3 e5 17 Nxf5 Bc8 in game 6. Although White won, the beautiful refutation was demonstrated only later: 18 f4!! (Kasparov played the simpler 18 Nd4 exd4 19 cxd4, which would have led to an unclear position after 19...0-0) 18...Qxf5 19 e4 Qh5 20 fxe5 dxe5 21 c5! Kd8 22 d6 Qe8 23 dxc7+ Kxc7 24 Qd5 Nc6 25 Rf7+ Bd7 26 Raf1 and Black was completely helpless in Miles-Beliavsky, Tilburg 1986.

16 Nxe6

16 dxe6? Nxd3 17 Qxd3 Be4 and ...Nc5 suits Black, but White can't postpone taking on e6 any more.

16 ... Nxe6
17 Bxf5!

The piece sacrifice is the only consistent continuation, as the timid 17 dxe6?! 0-0 favours Black.

17 ... Ng7

Otherwise Black's king won't reach safety on the queenside.

18 Bg6+ Kd7 (D)

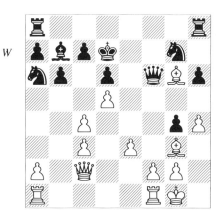

19 f3

This is the well-hidden idea behind 13 h4!. To prevent immediate disaster Black is forced to give up another pawn. Thus the resulting position will be materially equal, but White's more active forces (note Black's passive b7-bishop) and potentially dangerous kingside pawns promise him the initiative.

19 ... Raf8
20 fxg4 Qe7
21 e4 (D)

Should Black activate the knight, or safeguard his king first?

21 ... Kc8

Timman's solution is probably the best, as it enables Black's bishop to join in more effectively. 21...Nc5 22 Qe2 Kc8 23 e5 Ba6 24 e6 c6 25 Rxf8+ Rxf8 26 Rf1! Rxf1+ 27 Qxf1

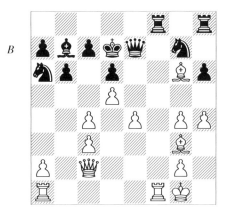
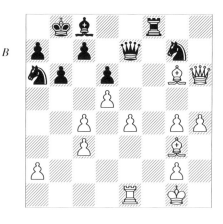

♔d8 28 ♕f4 ♗b7 was played in Ivanchuk-Anand, Monte Carlo rpd 1993. Now White would be virtually winning after 29 h5!. The main threat is ♕f2 and 29...cxd5 30 cxd5 ♗xd5 runs into 31 ♕d4. This example shows Black's knight is poorly placed on g7: even after a possible queen swap, a g5 break may leave it helpless against the passed h-pawn.

22 ♕d2 ♔b8!

The time is still not ripe for 22...♘c5?! 23 ♖xf8+ ♖xf8 24 ♕xh6 ♕f6 25 ♗f5+! ♘xf5 26 ♕xf6 ♖xf6 27 exf5, when the kingside pawns decided the issue in Miles-Timman, Tilburg 1986.

23 ♖xf8+?!

This is too greedy. The centralizing 23 ♕d4! is more critical; after 23...♘e8 24 ♖f7 (Kasparov's recommendation 24 ♖xf8 ♖xf8 25 ♖f1 is unclear due to 25...♖xf1+ 26 ♔xf1 ♘f6) 24...♖xf7 25 ♕xh8 ♖f8! (25...♕f8 leads to a lost endgame after 26 ♕xf8 ♖xf8 27 ♖f1!) 26 ♕xh6 ♘c5 27 h5 ♘d7 28 ♗f5 ♗c8 29 ♖f1 ♘e5 30 ♗xc8 ♖xf1+ 31 ♔xf1 ♔xc8 32 g5 White was better in Salov-Timman, Saint John Ct (5) 1988.

23 ... ♖xf8
24 ♕xh6 ♗c8!

Timman avoids the trap 24...♕f6? 25 e5! dxe5 26 ♖e1 and starts emphasizing the main drawback of White's position – his miserable pawn-structure.

25 ♖e1?! (D)

Now the advantage changes hands. One can understand White's reluctance to shut off his queen, but 25 g5 ♘c5 26 ♖f1 is stronger, with complex play.

25 ... ♗xg4

26 c5!

White is doing his best to confuse the issue. Possibly Kasparov originally planned 26 e5, but this is parried by the cold-blooded 26...dxe5 27 ♗xe5 ♘f5!. Black forces further exchanges and stands better, as 28 ♗xc7+? ♘xc7 hangs a piece.

26 ... ♕f6!

An excellent reaction: Timman ignores the pawn and pins White's pieces. 26...bxc5? 27 e5 doesn't work for Black and 26...♘xc5? 27 e5 dxe5 (27...♘d7 is even worse due to the pretty line 28 exd6 ♕f6 29 dxc7+ ♔b7 30 d6 ♘f5 31 ♕d2! ♕xg6 32 ♕d5+ ♔a6 33 ♕c4+ ♔b7 34 ♕e4+! ♔a6 35 c8♕+! ♖xc8 36 ♕a4+ ♔b7 37 ♕xd7+ ♔b8 38 ♖e8! and White wins) 28 ♗xe5 ♘f5 29 ♗xc7+! ♔a8 30 ♖xe7 ♘xh6 31 ♗e8 gives White a decisive advantage.

27 cxd6 (D)

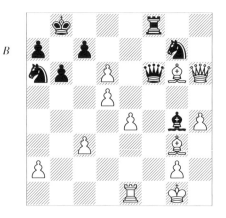

Further sacrifices are forced to keep the game going.

27 ... ♗h5

28 e5

28 d7 is a sharp idea: 28...♕xg6 (28...♗xg6 is weaker because of 29 h5! with the idea 29...♘xh5? 30 ♗h4!) 29 ♕xg6 ♗xg6 30 ♗e5 (30 e5 ♘c5! transposes into the game), winning back one piece. However, White is still fighting for equality after 30...♘h5 (30...♖d8!?) 31 g4 ♘c5.

28	...	♕xg6
29	♕xg6	♗xg6
30	e6	♘c5!
31	d7	

White's pawns are going nowhere after 31 dxc7+? ♔b7 32 ♗d6 ♖f5 33 ♗xc5 bxc5 34 d6 ♖d5.

31 ... ♘xd7

The move-order is important; after 31...♖d8?! 32 ♗e5 only White can be better.

32 exd7 ♖d8 *(D)*

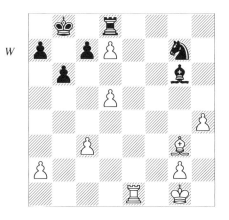

33 ♖e6

Only active play can save the game, but 33 ♖e7? is bad due to 33...♘f5. Possibly 33 ♗f4!?, followed by g4, is an interesting alternative.

33 ... ♗h5

After 33...♘xe6? 34 dxe6 Black has no defence against ♗f4-g5, but 33....♗f5!? 34 ♖h6 ♖xd7 35 ♗e5 ♘e8 is promising. This was actually played in Lerch-Helmreich, corr. 1986, and after 36 ♖h8 ♖e7 37 ♗f4 ♔b7 38 ♖f8 ♗b1 39 a3 ♗a2 40 g4 ♗xd5 41 ♔f2 ♗f7 42 h5 ♘f6 43 ♔g3 ♘xh5+ 44 gxh5 ♗xh5 Black's winning chances were far more realistic than later on in our game, because here White had two weak pawns on the queenside.

34	♗e5	♖xd7
35	♖h6 *(D)*	

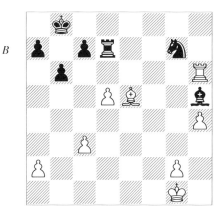

35 ... ♗f7?!

Only now does Timman squander his advantage. Kasparov pointed out that the clever 35...♗d1! is possible; following 36 g4 (after 36 ♖h7 ♖e7! 37 ♗xg7 ♔b7 Black regains the piece with ...♗c2) 36...♖e7 Black still retains winning chances.

36	♗xg7	♗xd5
37	♗e5	♗xa2
38	h5	♔b7
39	g4	♗c4
40	g5?!	

With the material again equal, White's united passed pawns seem to give him an edge. However, the outside a-pawn guarantees Black sufficient counterchances, as the long dark-squared diagonal is closed and White finds it difficult to stop its advance. The text-move even puts White in danger, whereas activating the rook first with 40 ♖f6 probably leads to a draw.

40 ... a5 *(D)*

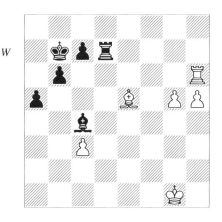

41 g6

Now it's too late for 41 ♖f6? ♖d5!.

41 ... ♖d5!

41...a4? 42 ♖h7 would justify White's 40th move. Timman correctly activates his rook first.

42 ♗f4 ♖f5 *(D)*

Another accurate move; after 42...a4 43 ♖h7 ♖c5 44 ♗c1! White stops the a-pawn.

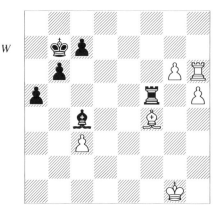

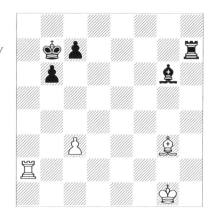

43	♗g3	a4
44	♖h7	♖c5
45	h6	a3
46	♖e7!	

White's rook must return to the back rank via a protected square. The difference is clear after 46 ♖d7? a2 47 ♖d1 ♖b5! 48 h7 ♖b1 and Black wins.

46	...	a2
47	♖e1	♖h5
48	h7	

48 ♗f4? again loses to 48...♖b5.

48	...	♗d3
49	♖a1	♗xg6
50	♖xa2	♖xh7 *(D)*

The adventures are finally over, the result being a prosaic endgame. White has good drawing chances due to simplification and the opposite-coloured bishops, but precision is still required.

51	♔f2	♖d7
52	♔e2	♖d5
53	♖a4	c5
54	♖f4	♗e8
55	♔e3	♖d1
56	♖e4	♗b5
57	c4!	*(D)*

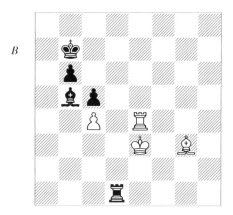

This required some calculation. Although the pawn becomes vulnerable, this move solves White's defensive task.

57	...	♗d7
58	♔e2	♖g1
59	♖e7!	♖xg3

The rook endgame is a dead draw, but after 59...♔c6 60 ♖g7 or 59...♔c8 60 ♗f4 Black can't improve his position either.

60	♖xd7+	♔a6
61	♔d2	♔a5
62	♖d6	½-½

Game 34
Garry Kasparov – Anatoly Karpov
World Ch match (game 4), London/Leningrad 1986
Nimzo-Indian Defence [E20]

1	d4	♘f6
2	c4	e6
3	♘c3	♗b4
4	♘f3	c5
5	g3	cxd4

The element of surprise from White's opening choice, mentioned in the notes to Game 30, had naturally disappeared. Nevertheless the character of the positions resulting from this line didn't suit Karpov, as he kept changing his reactions nearly all the time.

6	♘xd4	0-0
7	♗g2	d5
8	♕b3	

At the time our game was played this was the main try. Nowadays White mostly prefers 8 cxd5 ♘xd5 9 ♗d2. This continuation will be featured in Volume 2 in Kasparov-Short, Sarajevo 1999.

8	...	♗xc3+
9	bxc3 *(D)*	

Our game prompted some experiments with 9 ♕xc3 e5 10 ♘b3, but Black is doing fine after both 10...♘c6 and 10...d4 11 ♕a5 ♕e8!?.

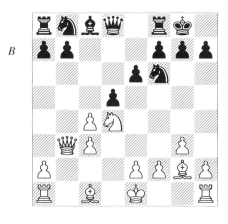

| 9 | ... | ♘c6! |

This strong novelty practically put the whole line out of business. Black's main task is neutralizing White's pressure on the h1-a8 diagonal and developing his queenside. Older options such as 9...dxc4 10 ♕a3!? (10 ♕xc4 e5 helps Black's development) didn't solve these problems satisfactorily.

| 10 | cxd5 | |

White has no other good way to meet the threat of ...♘a5, as 10 ♘xc6 bxc6 would only reinforce Black's centre.

| 10 | ... | ♘a5! |

This move is the point of Black's idea. After 10...exd5 11 0-0 his d5-pawn would become a welcome target.

| 11 | ♕c2 | ♘xd5 *(D)* |

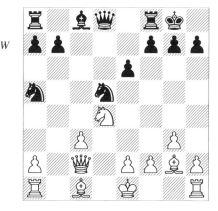

| 12 | ♕d3!? | |

Black has achieved an attractive position and White's slight lag in development disqualifies immediate attempts such as 12 ♗a3 ♖e8 13 c4? ♘xc4!. On the other hand White must act fast; otherwise he can end up saddled with his split queenside pawns and no activity to show in exchange. Therefore concrete play has priority over general considerations; the aforementioned Kasparov-Short game will illustrate this even more clearly. After the natural 12 0-0 Black has no problems whatsoever and a pleasant choice between 12...♗d7 and 12...♕c7.

| 12 | ... | ♗d7?! |

Just as in Game 31, both players were treading in virgin territory and Karpov, perhaps surprised by White's previous move, slips up first. Kasparov wrote that he anticipated Karpov's novelty and reached the game position in his pre-match preparation. However, he admitted both he and his team didn't seriously consider the strong 12...♕c7!. Here prudence is indicated; White's best course seems to be 13 ♘b5 (13 0-0 ♗d7 14 e4?! ♘b6 15 f4 was played in the game Kasparov-Suba, Dubai OL 1986, and now 15...♖ac8 would have given Black a distinct advantage) 13...♕c6 14 0-0 ♗d7 15 a4 a6 (15...♘c4!?) 16 e4. Now Black can choose between the drawish 16...axb5 17 exd5 ♕c4, or the more complex 16...♘b6!?.

13 c4

White doesn't give Black a second chance to stop the c-pawn in its tracks.

13 ... ♘e7 (D)

Other moves leave Black's knights in a tangle and give White the initiative; e.g., 13...♘b4 14 ♕c3 or 13...♘b6 14 c5 ♘bc4 15 0-0 ♖c8 16 ♘b3.

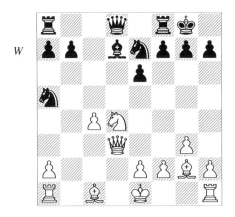

14 0-0!

Finally the time has come to castle. Kasparov avoids committing his bishop, as after 14 ♗a3 ♖e8 15 0-0 ♘ec6! Black forces exchanges and releases the tension.

14 ... ♖c8?!

In this position 14...♘ec6 15 ♘f3! doesn't solve Black's problems, as ♘g5 is in the air. However, the text-move isn't ideal either; Kasparov indicated the best continuation was the paradoxical 14...♗c6!?. Nevertheless White has an edge after 15 ♗a3! (15 ♘xc6 is tempting, but after 15...♘exc6 Black's forces are coordinated well enough to cope with the bishop-pair) 15...♗xg2 16 ♔xg2.

15 ♘b3!

This strong move decides the opening duel in White's favour. He gets rid off his weak c4-pawn, further opening the position for his bishop-pair. However, it's still surprising how quickly Kasparov increases his advantage – after all, the resulting pawn-structure is nearly symmetrical and Black's forces are reasonably active. Karpov probably relied on these factors and didn't realize he couldn't afford any further mistakes. On the other hand White's further play is a model of precision.

15 ... ♘xc4
16 ♗xb7 ♖c7 (D)

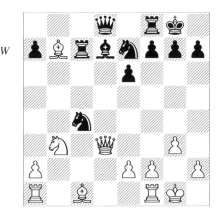

17 ♗a6!

White still hasn't consolidated his edge and chasing away the active c4-knight plays a key role. It's definitely more important than controlling the a1-h8 diagonal. Thus although 17 ♗e4?! also wins a tempo, it gets White nowhere after 17...h6.

17 ... ♘e5

This is best. 17...♘g6 is well met by the radical 18 f4!, further limiting Black's knights.

18 ♕e3!

White treads with care and doesn't want to expose his queen. After the tempting 18 ♕d6 ♘7g6! (Black loses material after 18...♖c8? 19 ♕xe5 ♗xa6 20 ♗b2 ♘f5 21 e4, while 18...♖c6 19 ♕xe5 ♖xa6 20 ♘c5 ♖c6 21 ♖d1 gives White a strong initiative) White must reckon with ...♖c6 or ...♗c8.

18 ... ♘c4

Black is understandably reluctant to weaken his pawn-structure, but 18...f6!? nevertheless deserves attention. Black intends ...♘d5 and after 19 ♗a3 ♗c8! 20 ♖fd1 ♘d5 21 ♗xc8 (21 ♗xf8 ♗xa6!?, followed by ...♕c8, is OK for Black) 21...♕xc8 22 ♖xd5 exd5 (or 22...♘c4) White's advantage is still not threatening.

19 ♕e4 ♘d6

Kasparov criticizes this move, but perhaps unjustly so. Instead 19...♕a8 20 ♕xa8 ♖xa8 21 ♗g5!, followed by ♖ac1, leads to an unpleasant endgame for Black.

20 ♕d3! *(D)*

The queen returns to the square where it was three moves ago, but White has made progress by denying Black the c4-square. 20 ♕b4 ♗c8 is unconvincing for White.

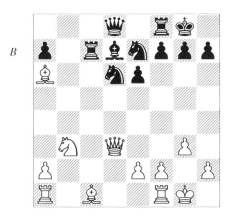

20 ... ♖c6?

Karpov still relies on his famed defensive technique, but refusing to accept any concessions only increases his problems. The immediate 20...♗c8 is stronger. Now 21 ♖d1 (21 ♗a3 ♗xa6 22 ♕xa6 ♘e4 gets White nowhere, while after 21 ♗f4 ♖c6 22 ♗xc8 ♘dxc8 White's f4-bishop is not too impressive and Black's position is defensible) 21...♘d5 22 ♗xc8 ♕xc8 23 e4 (23 ♗a3 ♖c3 24 ♕b1 ♖c6 is about equal) 23...♘xe4 24 ♕xe4 ♘c3 25 ♕f3 ♘xd1 26 ♕xd1 ♖d8 leads to a materially unbalanced position with reasonable drawing chances for Black, as it's not easy for White to coordinate his forces.

21 ♗a3 ♗c8

21...♕b6? loses material after 22 ♘d4!.

22 ♗xc8 ♘dxc8 *(D)*
23 ♖fd1!

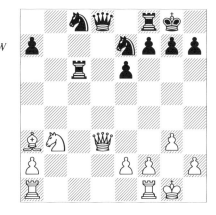

White's bishop-pair has been halved, but he has gained other advantages instead, most notably full control over the d-file. The text-move is more concrete than 23 ♕f3 ♕b6.

23 ... ♕xd3

23...♕b6 24 ♖ab1 is no improvement for Black.

24 ♖xd3 ♖e8

24...♖a6 25 ♘c5 ♖c6 26 ♖ad1 doesn't help much.

25 ♖ad1 f6

With ♖d8 looming, Black badly needs some *luft*. Other moves are also dreary: 25...h6?! 26 ♖d8 ♖xd8 27 ♖xd8+ ♔h7 28 ♗xe7 ♘xe7 29 ♖d7 costs Black a pawn, and 25...g6 26 ♗c5 a6 27 e4 keeps Black bottled up.

26 ♘d4 ♖b6 *(D)*

26...♖a6 27 ♘b5 is similar.

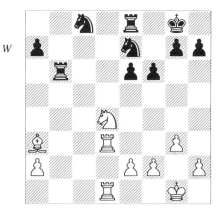

27 ♗c5 ♖a6?!

This passive continuation loses without a fight. 27...♖b2!? is somewhat more resilient although even here after 28 ♘xe6 ♘c6 (28...♖xe2

29 ♘c7 ♖f8 30 ♖d7 ♖f7 31 ♔f1 ♖e5 32 f4! ♖e4 33 ♘b5 is hopeless for Black) 29 ♖e3 ♖xa2 30 ♖d7 White's attack should decide the game.

| 28 | ♘b5 | ♖c6 |

28...♖xa2 loses on the spot to 29 ♘c7 ♖f8 30 ♘xe6 ♖e8 31 ♘c7 ♖f8 32 ♖e3.

| 29 | ♗xe7! |

Again a concrete solution, as on move 23.

| 29 | ... | ♘xe7 |

29...♖xe7? loses a piece: 30 ♖d8+ ♔f7 31 ♖xc8.

| 30 | ♖d7 *(D)* |

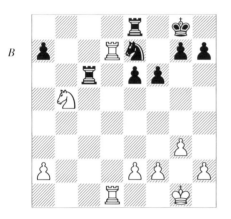

The threat of ♘d6 nets White a pawn and the rest is a matter of technique.

30	...	♘g6
31	♖xa7	♘f8
32	a4	♖b8
33	e3	h5
34	♔g2	e5
35	♖d3	

White exchanges a pair of rooks and his pieces remain more active than Black's.

| 35 | ... | ♔h7 |

35...♖bc8 allows 36 a5.

36	♖c3	♖bc8
37	♖xc6	♖xc6
38	♘c7	♘e6
39	♘d5	♔h6
40	a5	e4 *(D)*

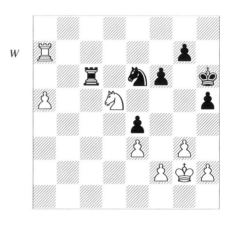

| 41 | a6! | 1-0 |

This, the sealed move, is the most incisive. Black's counterplay is ineffective: after 41...♖d6 (41...♘c5 42 ♖c7) 42 ♘e7 ♖d1 43 ♖a8 ♘c7 (43...♔h7 44 a7 ♖a1 45 ♘c6 and the a-pawn queens) 44 ♖h8+ ♔g5 White has the pretty 45 h4+ ♔g4 46 ♖c8! ♘xa6 47 ♖c4 and the mating threats decide.

Game 35
Garry Kasparov – Anatoly Karpov
World Ch match (game 16), London/Leningrad 1986
Ruy Lopez (Spanish), Zaitsev Variation [C92]

A real crown jewel of the rematch; this game is arguably the most tense and exciting of all the K-K encounters.

1	e4	e5
2	♘f3	♘c6
3	♗b5	a6
4	♗a4	♘f6
5	0-0	♗e7
6	♖e1	b5
7	♗b3	d6
8	c3	0-0
9	h3	♗b7

This system bears the name of GM Igor Zaitsev, who was for a long time on Karpov's team. It was an integral part of Karpov's repertoire for many years. In our game his choice to go for the Ruy Lopez was undoubtedly influenced by the fact that at this moment he was trailing by two points and even with Black he strove for more complex play – something difficult to achieve in the Petroff or the Caro-Kann.

10	d4	♖e8
11	♘bd2	♗f8
12	a4	h6 *(D)*

This useful move, which prevents ♘g5, is the main continuation. Earlier Karpov tried 12...♕d7, a move also played in Kasparov-Smejkal, Dubai OL 1986 (Game 37).

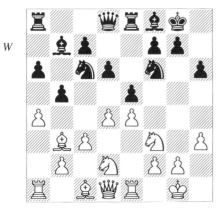

13	♗c2	exd4

The most principled option, which leads to a sharp and unbalanced position. Black gives up his central stronghold on e5 to start active counterplay on the queenside. Only once did Karpov venture 13...♘b8, transposing into the Breyer system. After 14 ♗d3 c6 15 ♘f1 ♘bd7 16 ♘g3 Black's position was solid, but rather passive, in Kasparov-Karpov, Moscow Wch (9) 1985.

14	cxd4	♘b4
15	♗b1	c5

Karpov stopped playing 15...bxa4 16 ♖xa4 a5 17 ♖a3 ♖a6 after Kasparov-Karpov, Lyons/New York Wch (1) 1990 (Game 60).

16	d5	

Black's forces are well prepared for an open struggle, so closing the centre is the only way for White to fight for the initiative.

16	...	♘d7
17	♖a3 *(D)*	

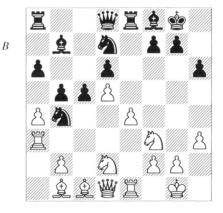

White's chances in the Benoni-like pawn-structure lie on the kingside, where he gradually starts concentrating his pieces.

17	...	c4

A crucial decision. With the text-move Black clearly intends to plant his knight on d3, stifling White's attacking ambitions. On the other hand the important d4-square becomes accessible for White's knight. The main alternative 17...f5!? blows up White's centre, but weakens the kingside and leads to an even more complex position. It was also tested in the K-K duel; see Kasparov-Karpov, New York/Lyons Wch (20) 1990 (Game 61).

18 ♘d4 *(D)*

Despite his success, Kasparov is the first to deviate from game 14 of the match, in which after 18 axb5 axb5 19 ♘d4 ♖xa3 (the recently tested 19...♘e5 20 ♖xa8 ♕xa8 21 ♘xb5 isn't quite sufficient for equality) 20 bxa3 ♘d3 21 ♗xd3 cxd3 22 ♗b2 (later practice featured mostly 22 ♖e3, when after 22...♘e5!? 23 ♘4f3 f5 24 ♘xe5 ♖xe5 25 ♗b2 ♖e7 26 exf5 ♖xe3 27 fxe3 ♗xd5 28 ♕g4 ♕g5! White is better, but Black should be able to hold the resulting endgame) 22...♕a5 23 ♘f5 (23 ♖e3 ♘e5 is unclear) 23...♘e5?! (Kasparov subsequently recommended the fearless 23...g6!; e.g., 24 ♘b3 ♕a4 25 ♕xd3 ♘e5! 26 ♗xe5 ♖xe5 27 f4 ♖e8 with good compensation for the pawn, or 24 ♘e3 ♘e5 with complex play) 24 ♗xe5! dxe5 25 ♘b3 ♕b6 26 ♕xd3 White was better, Kasparov-Karpov, London/Leningrad Wch (14) 1986. The line is nowadays not so topical, but the notes in the brackets indicate it's still alive and the current consensus is that it gives White more chances to fight for an advantage than the text-move. This is mainly due to the strength of Karpov's reply.

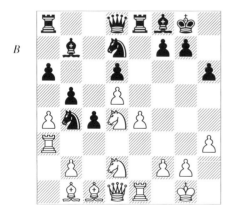

18 ... ♕f6!

A strong novelty, which surprised Kasparov. In general in 1986 Karpov was much better theoretically prepared than in their previous matches (see also the move 9...♘c6! in Game 34). 18...♘e5?! 19 axb5 ♕b6 was the continuation Kasparov considered at home and he had prepared the enterprising 20 ♘xc4! ♘xc4 21 ♖g3. This idea proved its worth in A.Sokolov-Portisch, Brussels (World Cup) 1988: after 21...♗c8 22 b3! ♘e5 23 ♗e3 ♘g6 24 f4 ♕d8 25 f5 ♘e5 26 ♕d2 a5 27 ♗xh6 White had a strong attack. However, 18...♘d3!? 19 ♗xd3 b4 also deserves attention, as White is practically forced to sacrifice an exchange with unclear consequences.

19 ♘2f3

After 19 ♘f5? ♘e5 Black conquers d3 for free, which spells positional bankruptcy for White, so he has to close the 3rd rank and for the time being Black's king can feel safe.

19 ... ♘c5

A positional pawn sacrifice. Karpov's knights revengefully aim for d3 – the very same square from which Kasparov's knight paralysed his position in game 16 of the previous match (see Game 31). Kasparov suggested the immediate 19...♘d3!? with similar ideas as on move 18. Although here White has the extra option 20 ♖xd3!? (20 ♗xd3 b4! 21 ♗xc4 bxa3 22 b3 ♘c5 is OK for Black), this is no refutation and after 20...cxd3 21 axb5 axb5 22 ♘xb5 ♖a1 Black has at least equality.

20 axb5 axb5
21 ♘xb5 *(D)*

Now the knight lands on the edge, but White must have at least some material to suffer for, and 21 ♖xa8? ♖xa8 22 ♘xb5 ♖a1 is just plain bad for him.

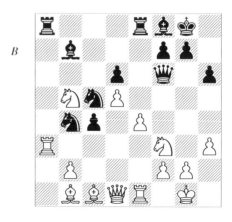

21 ... ♖xa3

22 ♘xa3

Black is better after 22 bxa3?! ♘bd3.

22 ... ♗a6!

The tension grows as Karpov calmly increases his pressure. A threat is often stronger than its execution; here after 22...♘bd3 23 ♗xd3 ♘xd3 (23...cxd3!? 24 b4 gives White a slight edge) 24 ♖e3 Black has to play 24...♗a6 anyway and White can lash out with 25 ♕a4! ♖a8 26 ♕c6! (26 ♗d2 ♕xb2 27 ♘xc4 ♕b1+ 28 ♗e1 ♘c5 and Black's activity compensates for the missing pawn) 26...♕d8 27 ♗d2 ♘xb2 28 ♘c2 ♘d3 29 ♘b4. The skirmish is over and so is Black's initiative; he must fight for equality.

23 ♖e3 (D)

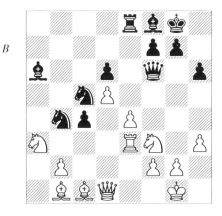

A move directed against ...♘d3; moreover, White's remaining rook has attacking potential, which will dramatically come to fruition 12 moves later.

23 ... ♖b8!?

An ambitious preparatory move in the same spirit as 22...♗a6!. Karpov played it without too much thought, conveying the message that he was still following his preparation. Another playable option is 23...♘bd3 24 ♕c2 (Kasparov points out that 24 ♗xd3 cxd3 25 b4 ♘xe4 26 b5 ♗b7 27 ♖xd3 ♖c8! is promising for Black; he is likely to win the d5-pawn in the near future) 24...♕g6!? 25 ♘xc4 ♖xe4 with unclear play.

24 e5!

Being about an hour down on the clock and plagued by rather sad associations with Game 31 (a well-prepared opponent, the knight coming to d3, the passive a3-knight – only this time on the receiving end), Kasparov correctly decides it's time to act. The passive 24 ♖c3 ♘bd3 25 ♗xd3 (25 ♘xc4? loses on the spot to 25...♕xc3!) 25...cxd3 26 ♗e3 ♘xe4 27 ♖c6 ♖a8 28 ♕a4 (28 ♖b6!? is better) 28...d2 29 ♘xd2 ♘xd2 30 ♖xa6 ♖xa6 31 ♕xa6 ♕xb2 gave Black a small edge in Anand-Timoshchenko, Frunze 1987.

24 ... dxe5
25 ♘xe5 (D)

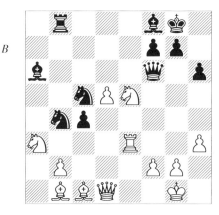

25 ... ♘bd3?

Suddenly Karpov sank into deep thought ... and committed a serious mistake. The most logical explanation seems to be that he underestimated White's 24th move at home. Thus from now on both players were on their own and Karpov, anxious to demonstrate the strength of his position, overlooked White's strong response. It's clear Black can't postpone jumping to d3 and the text-move has the extra benefit of opening the b-file for the rook. Nevertheless it has a serious tactical drawback, and 25...♘cd3! is necessary: 26 ♘g4!? (White aspires for more than 26 ♗xd3 ♘xd3 27 ♖xd3 cxd3 28 ♘d7 ♕d6 29 ♘xb8 ♕xb8 30 ♕a4, which is drawish) 26...♕d4! (here the analogy to the game with 26...♕b6? 27 ♖g3 is clearly in White's favour: his b2-pawn is not under attack and he can later win an important tempo with ♗e3) 27 ♘c2 (now 27 ♖g3?! is too optimistic; Kasparov gives the fantastic line 27...♗d6! 28 ♗e3 ♕xb2 29 ♘xh6+ ♔f8 30 ♕h5 gxh6 31 ♖f3! ♘e5 32 ♖f6 ♔e7 33 ♕xh6 ♘xd5 34 ♖xd6 ♘f3+!! 35 gxf3 ♘xe3 and Black is clearly better) 27...♘xc2 (27...♕xd5? runs into 28 ♘f6+! gxf6 29 ♖g3+ and 30 ♕g4, winning) 28 ♗xc2 ♗d6!. Now

White's attack is over, so he has to cope with the d3-knight and play 29 b3! ♕a1! (29...♗f4 is weaker due to 30 ♖e1!) 30 bxc4 ♗xc4 (30...♘xc1?! 31 ♖e1 is dangerous for Black) 31 ♗xd3 ♗xd3 32 ♖e1 (32 ♖xd3 ♖b1 33 ♘f6+ forces a perpetual, as king moves allow 34 ♖e3; the same goes for 32 ♘xh6+ gxh6 33 ♖xd3 ♖b1 34 ♕g4+) 32...♗g6. Black has full compensation for the pawn and in Dvoirys-Timoshchenko, USSR Cht (Naberezhnye Chelny) 1988 a draw was agreed shortly.

26 ♘g4?

26 ♘axc4?! ♕xf2+ 27 ♔h1 ♘f4 favours Black, but both players overlooked the clever multi-purpose move 26 ♕c2!. White pins the d3-knight and threatens to take on c4, and after 26...♘b3!? (relatively best; 26...♖b4 is weaker due to 27 ♘c6 ♖b7 28 ♖e8, when White's intention is ♗e3 and after 28...g5 29 f3! the counterplay against f2 is over and Black is in great trouble) 27 ♘axc4 ♘bxc1 28 ♘xd3 ♘xd3 29 ♖xd3!? (29 ♕xd3 g6 30 b3 ♗c5 makes White's life more difficult) the tactical trick 29...♗xc4?! 30 ♖b3! gives him time to play 30 b3 and he should be able to convert his extra material in the long run.

26 ... ♕b6

Played quickly and universally praised, but later on Black will miss his queen in the defence. 26...♕f5!? certainly deserves attention and presses White to prove he has sufficient counterplay. Kasparov condemned this move due to 27 ♖f3 (27 ♖g3 ♔h8 is unconvincing) 27...♕xd5 28 ♗a2, but after 28...♕d7 or even 28...♖d8!? Black threatens to play 29...♘e5 and White's minor pieces on the a-file create a sorry impression.

27 ♖g3 (D)

After a rocky interlude the exciting final phase of the game begins. The players are attacking on opposite flanks and although White's target is the enemy king, his task is not easy – only a part of his army is taking part in the onslaught, while his queenside is already collapsing.

27 ... g6!

Objectively the best move, as Black can't avoid the weakening of his kingside anyway:

1) 27...♔h8?! 28 ♘xh6! ♘e4 (28...gxh6? loses to 29 ♘xc4! ♗xc4 30 ♕g4 ♕g6 31 ♕xc4) 29 ♘xf7+ ♔g8 30 ♖e3! ♘exf2 (30...♔xf7? 31

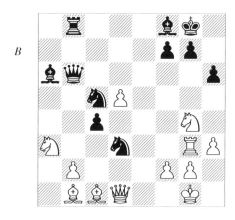

♗xd3 simply gives White extra material) 31 ♕h5 ♗c5 32 ♘g5! ♗xe3 33 ♕h7+ ♔f8 34 ♕h8+! (White wants more than a draw after 34 ♕f5+) 34...♔e7 35 ♕xg7+ ♔d6 36 ♕f6+ ♔xd5 (36...♔d7 37 ♕f7+ ♔c8 38 ♕e8+ ♔b7 39 ♕e7+ ♕c7 40 ♕xe3 gives White good winning chances) 37 ♕f3+ ♔d6 38 ♗xe3 ♕xb2 is perhaps not fully clear, but definitely dangerous for Black with his exposed king after 39 ♗c2!?.

2) 27...♘e4!? is interesting, when White's best chance is the complicated 28 ♘xh6+!? (inconsistent moves such as 28 ♖e3 ♗xa3 or 28 ♘xc4 ♗xc4 29 ♗xd3 ♘xg3 30 ♗xc4 ♘e4 promise Black an edge) 28...♔h7 29 ♗c3! (here after 29 ♖e3 ♘exf2 30 ♕f3 White has to reckon with 30...♗c5!? 31 ♘xf7 ♘d1!) 29...♕xb2 30 ♘xf7 ♘xg3 31 fxg3. Now Black's king is very vulnerable and despite his huge material advantage he should resign himself to forcing a draw after 31...♗xa3 (winning attempts may even cause Black some problems; e.g., 31...♗c7 32 d6 ♗f6 33 ♕h5+ ♔g8 34 d7! ♗b7 35 ♗c2) 32 ♗xd3+ cxd3 33 ♕h5+ ♔g8 34 ♘g5 and 35 ♕f7+.

28 ♗xh6

White needs to retain his knight; after 28 ♘xh6+? ♗xh6 29 ♗xh6 ♕xb2 30 ♗xd3 cxd3! (30...♘xd3?! is weaker due to 31 ♕a4!) Black is clearly on top.

28 ... ♕xb2

Now White loses material, while his own threats are still far from obvious. At this moment most of the commentators in the press-centre and almost certainly Karpov himself thought the game was over. However, even a thorough post-mortem didn't find any clear-cut win for

Black and one has to admire Kasparov's intuition and his readiness to go for the enormous complications. Objectively speaking the position is about equal, but by consistently avoiding draws or messy lines in the further course of the game, Karpov gradually gets into trouble.

29 ♕f3! *(D)*

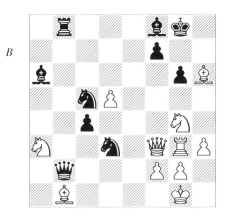

29 ... ♘d7?!

This move well illustrates Karpov's attitude described above. Kasparov's creative play demonstrates that its main drawback is weakening Black's control over d3. Black had some safer options:

1) 29...♕xa3 leads to a perpetual after 30 ♘f6+ ♔h8 31 ♕h5 ♖xb1+ 32 ♗c1+ (after 32 ♔h2? ♖h1+! 33 ♔xh1 ♕a1+! Black covers f6 and wins) 32...♔g7 33 ♘e8+.

2) Less clear is 29...♗d6!? 30 ♗e3! (after 30 ♗g5? the g-file is closed and Black has the strong 30...f5!) 30...♗xg3 (White is better after 30...f5?! 31 ♘h6+ ♔h7 32 ♘xf5! ♗xg3 33 ♘xg3) 31 ♘f6+! ♔g7 32 ♕xg3 ♖h8 (the circumspect 32...♔xf6 allows White to force a perpetual with 33 ♗xd3! ♘xd3 34 ♕h4+ ♔e5 35 ♕e7+ ♔xd5 36 ♕d7+) 33 ♘g4. Black's kingside is shaky, while White has pressure on the dark squares and various tactical chances compensate for his slight material disadvantage; for example, 33...♗b7 34 ♗xc5 ♘xc5 35 ♗xg6!.

30 ♗xf8 ♔xf8

Now the h6-square is inaccessible to White's knight. 30...♖xf8?! 31 ♘h6+ ♔g7 32 ♘f5+ ♔h7 33 ♕e3! gxf5 34 ♗xd3 (34 ♕g5? ♕c1+!) 34...cxd3 35 ♕g5 ♕f6 36 ♕h5+ ♕h6 37 ♕xf5+ ♔h8 38 ♕xd7 is still probably a draw after 38...♕c1+ 39 ♔h2 ♖g8!, but White is undoubtedly the active side.

31 ♔h2! *(D)*

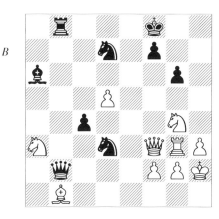

White calmly improves his king and gives his attack a fresh impetus. This move keeps the a3-knight alive by creating various threats, depending on Black's reaction.

31 ... ♖b3!

Karpov confidently played the best move and took a leisurely stroll. Black activates his rook, challenges White's major pieces along the 3rd rank and gets ready to take the piece under better circumstances. Other moves are weaker:

1) 31...♔g7? 32 ♘xc4! ♕xb1 33 ♘d6 ♖f8 (after 33...♘3e5 34 ♘xe5 ♘xe5, White wins with 35 ♕h5! followed by 36 ♘f5+) 34 ♕e3 ♘3c5 (or 34...♕c1 35 ♕e7 and the attack breaks through) 35 ♕c3+ ♔h7 (35...f6 doesn't help due to 36 ♕e3) 36 ♘f6+ ♘xf6 37 ♕xf6 and Black has no defence against both ♘xf7 and ♖g4. Note how quickly the a3-knight joined the attack!

2) 31...♕xa3?! 32 ♘h6 and now:

2a) 32...♕e7 33 ♖xg6 ♔e8 34 ♗xd3! cxd3 (34...♕e5+ 35 g3 fxg6 36 ♗xg6+ ♔e7 37 ♕a3+ and a knight fork wins the black queen) 35 d6 ♕e5+ 36 g3 fxg6 37 ♕f7+ ♔d8 38 ♕g8+, followed by the decisive 39 ♘f7+.

2b) 32...♘7e5 33 ♕f6 ♕b2! is more resilient, though White should win the endgame after 34 ♖xg6 ♔e8!? 35 ♖g3! (35 ♗xd3 is unconvincing due to 35...fxg6! 36 ♗xg6+ ♔d7 37 ♗f5+ ♔c7 38 ♕xa6 ♕d4) 35...♘g4+ 36 ♘xg4 ♕xf6 37 ♘xf6+ ♔e7 38 ♗xd3 cxd3 39 ♘e4.

3) 31...♕c1?! 32 ♗xd3 cxd3 33 ♘f6! ♘e5 (33...♘xf6 34 ♕xf6 ♔g8 35 ♖g4! and the mating threats force Black into passivity) 34 ♕e4 d2 35 ♕xe5 d1♕ 36 ♕xb8+ (36 ♘d7+!? is also possible) 36...♔g7 (36...♔c8 37 ♖e3 is similar) 37 ♘e8+ (37 ♖e3!?) 37...♔h7 38 ♖e3 and in this remarkable position White is better in spite of Black's two queens. He threatens 39 ♘f6+ and retains a powerful attack on the dark squares even after 38...♕d4 (best) 39 ♕d6.

32 ♗xd3! *(D)*

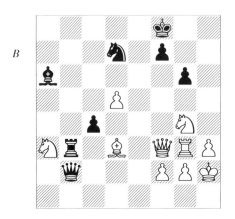

Finally White removes the nagging knight, and at the same time gives his queen access to the f4-square. Kasparov wrote that despite having less than 10 minutes on the clock, after the text-move he calmed down, intuitively feeling White had nothing to fear any more. On the other hand Karpov, who at this moment still had more than half an hour, sank into thought...

32 ... cxd3?!

Despite using up most of his remaining time, Karpov chose a very thorny path. He still probably didn't fully realize that it's now Black who is struggling for a draw. The text-move is very ambitious, but dubious. Safer options:

1) 32...♖xd3 33 ♕f4 ♕xa3 34 ♘h6 ♕e7! (34...♔e7 35 ♕xf7+ ♔d8 36 ♖xg6 gives White a huge attack) 35 ♖xg6 ♕e5 (with the rook on d3 White doesn't have the blow {d6+!} that decided the actual game) 36 ♕xe5 ♘xe5 37 ♖xa6 ♖xd5 and as White can't immediately activate his knight (38 ♘f5? ♘f3+!), the passed c-pawn gives Black reasonable counterplay.

2) 32...♖xa3!? is also possible. After 33 ♕f4 ♖xd3 (33...cxd3? loses – see note '1' to Black's 33rd move) 34 ♕d6+ ♔g7 (after 34...♔e8 35 ♕xa6 Black's king remains in the danger zone) 35 ♕xd7 ♖xg3 36 fxg3 (36 ♔xg3?! c3 37 ♘e5 ♕b7 gets White nowhere) White's pawns are split and Kasparov shows that the accurate 36...♗b7! (36...c3? is weak due to 37 ♕c7! c2 38 ♘e5) 37 h4 ♗a8! 38 ♕d8 ♕d4 should be enough for a draw.

33 ♕f4 *(D)*

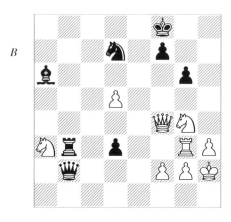

33 ... ♕xa3?

For five moves White's a3-knight has remained successfully taboo! Karpov's nerves finally snapped and he decided to cash in, but chose the least suitable moment to take it, as this move loses by force. Black still could have fought back, albeit only by letting the seemingly condemned knight play an important role, especially in the '2b' lines:

1) 33...♖xa3? is also bad, as after 34 ♖f3! ♕b8 (34...f5 35 ♕d6+ ♔e8 36 ♖e3+ ♔d8 37 ♘e5 ♗b5 38 ♘f7+ with a successful king-hunt) 35 d6 ♗c4 (after 35...♕e8 both 36 ♕d4 and 36 ♖e3 are winning for White) 36 ♕d4! f5 37 ♘h6 ♗g8 38 ♘xf5 White's attack breaks through.

2) 33...d2! is the only continuation consistent with Black's previous move. After 34 ♘h6 ♘f6! (34...♘e5? runs into 35 ♖xb3 ♕xb3 36 ♕xe5 d1♕ 37 d6 and White wins) White has two possible attempts:

2a) 35 ♕d6+ ♔e8 is the more romantic line. Now 36 ♖g5!? is interesting (Kasparov analyses the wild 36 ♕xa6 d1♕ 37 ♕c8+ ♔e7 38 ♕c5+ ♔d7!, where White has numerous perpetuals, but seemingly no win): 36...d1♕ (36...♘d7? leads to mate after 37 ♕xa6 d1♕ 38 ♕c8+ ♔e7 39 ♘g8+) 37 ♖e5+ ♕xe5+ 38

♕xe5+ ♔f8! (38...♔d7 is somewhat weaker: after 39 ♕xf6 ♕xd5 40 ♕xa6 ♕e5+ 41 g3 ♕c5! 42 ♕f6!? ♖xa3 43 ♕xf7+ followed by ♘g4 White has some winning chances due to his safer king, although a draw is the most likely result) 39 ♕xf6 ♕xd5 40 ♕xa6 ♕e5+ 41 g3 ♔g7! (now 41...♕c5? loses to 42 ♕f6) and as Black threatens both ...♔xh6 and ...♕a1, White should force a perpetual after 42 ♘c4 ♕e1 43 ♘g4 ♖b1 44 ♕f6+ ♔g8!.

2b) Somewhat more promising is 35 ♖xb3 ♕xb3 36 ♕xf6 ♕xd5 (D), and now:

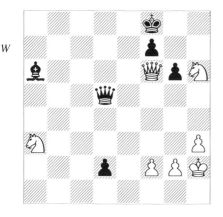

2b1) After 37 ♘xf7 d1♕ (37...♔e8? 38 ♘b1! d1♕ 39 ♘c3! with a decisive fork) 38 ♘d6+ ♔g8 39 ♕xg6+ ♔f8 40 ♕f6+ ♔g8 41 ♘f5 ♕xf5! 42 ♕xf5 ♕d6+ Black finally wins the hapless knight and should save the endgame.

2b2) 37 ♕h8+ ♔e7 38 ♘g8+ ♔d6 (after 38...♔e6!? 39 ♕f6+ ♔d7 40 ♕e7+ ♔c8 41 ♘f6 ♕d8 42 ♕c5+ ♕c7+! {but not 42...♔b7? 43 ♘b5!} Black also has good drawing chances) 39 ♘f6 (39 ♕f6+ requires some careful footwork by Black's king, but after 39...♔c7! 40 ♕c3+ ♔b7! 41 ♕b4+ ♔a8 42 ♘f6 ♕d8 43 ♕e4+ ♔a7 44 ♕e3+ ♔b8! White has only a perpetual) 39...♕e5+ 40 g3 ♕e2 41 ♕d8+ ♔e6 (41...♔c6? is weak, as after 42 ♕d7+ ♔b6 43 ♘d5+ ♔c5 44 ♘e3! ♕xf2+ 45 ♔g2 ♕e2 46 ♕c7+ ♔d5 47 ♘b1! White has safeguarded his king and retains his material advantage) 42 ♕b6+ ♔e7 43 ♘d5+ ♔f8 44 ♘b1! (44 ♘c3 is less impressive, since after 44...♕f3! White practically can't avoid an exchange of queens following, e.g., 45 ♕e3) 44...d1♕ 45 ♘bc3. White wins one black queen, but he will be unable to avoid the exchange of the remaining pair of queens due to the light-square vulnerability of his king. In the resulting minor-piece endgame Black should be able to hold the position. However, the complexity of all these lines indicates that the defence hangs on a very thin thread.

34 ♘h6 ♕e7

Other moves don't help: the attack breaks through after both 34...♔e7 35 ♖e3+! ♔d8 36 ♘xf7+ and 34...f6 35 ♖xg6.

35 ♖xg6 ♕e5

35...♔e8 loses on the spot to 36 d6, but Karpov relied on this pin.

36 ♖g8+ ♔e7
37 d6+! (D)

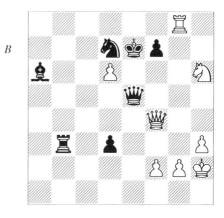

The pawn is taboo due to a knight fork, so Black loses his queen and the game.

37	...	♔e6
38	♖e8+	♔d5
39	♖xe5+	♘xe5
40	d7	♖b8
41	♘xf7	1-0

Game 36
Garry Kasparov – Anatoly Karpov
World Ch match (game 22), London/Leningrad 1986
Queen's Gambit Declined, Tartakower Defence [D55]

1 d4

After game 16 (see Game 35) Kasparov increased his lead in the match to 3 points, only to relax and lose 3 games in a row! Therefore, with the score equal again and the end so near, caution was indicated. Moreover, Karpov had shown that despite the result of games 14 and 16 he was well prepared for the Ruy Lopez. And indeed from game 18 onwards Kasparov as White refrained from 1 e4 altogether.

1	...	♘f6
2	c4	e6
3	♘f3	d5
4	♘c3	♗e7
5	♗g5	h6
6	♗xf6	♗xf6
7	e3	0-0
8	♖c1	

Kasparov opts for a safe system, in which accurate play is required to neutralize White's edge. Moreover the positions arising after move 13 suit his style – White's initiative stems from his active piece-play. This was also his choice in the 1985 match in game 23 in a very similar situation, when he wanted to put his opponent under some pressure without undue risk.

8	...	c6
9	♗d3	♘d7
10	0-0	dxc4
11	♗xc4	e5 *(D)*

This natural liberating move solves Black's typical problems with developing the c8-bishop, but it also has a drawback – it opens the a2-g8 diagonal for White's bishop.

12 h3!?

The insipid 12 ♘e4 exd4 13 ♘xf6+ ♘xf6 14 ♕xd4 ♕xd4 15 ♘xd4 ♖e8 leads to a sterile endgame. Thus to fight for an advantage White must let Black resolve the central tension, and make a move that is useful in positions with an isolated d4-pawn. The earlier choice was 12 ♗b3. The bishop leaves a vulnerable square, but after 12...exd4 13 exd4 ♖e8! followed by

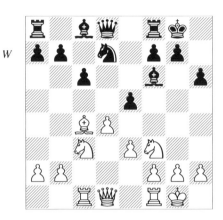

...♘f8 and ...♗e6 Black neutralizes the pressure against f7 and equalizes. On the other hand 12 ♖e1 allows 12...exd4 13 exd4 ♘b6 14 ♗b3 ♗g4, hence the refined text-move.

12	...	exd4
13	exd4	♘b6

Although 13...c5 leads to a symmetrical position, after 14 ♗b3 cxd4 15 ♘d5! b6 16 ♘xd4 ♗xd4 17 ♕xd4 ♘c5 18 ♗c4 ♗b7 19 ♖fd1 ♖c8 20 ♕g4 White's superior piece coordination gave him a long-term pull in Kasparov-Karpov, London/Leningrad Wch (10) 1986. The text-move is the most natural reaction, but, as indicated in the previous note, the ideal square for Black's knight is f8. Thus even investing a tempo with 13...♖e8!? 14 ♕b3 ♖f8! 15 ♕c2 (15...♘b6 was a positional threat) 15...♖e8 deserves serious attention; e.g., 16 ♖fe1 ♘f8 17 ♕b3 ♗e6! 18 ♗xe6 ♘xe6 19 ♕xb7 ♕b6 20 ♕xb6 axb6 and pressure against d4 will soon restore both the material and positional balance.

14	♗b3	♗f5

In 1985, 12 h3!?, although not completely unknown, took Karpov by surprise and after 14...♖e8 15 ♖e1 ♗f5 16 ♖xe8+ ♕xe8 17 ♕d2 ♕d7 18 ♖e1 ♖d8 (18...a5! is nowadays considered the most accurate road to equality; compared with the game Black has avoided a possible improvement by White on move 17 and now 19 a3 transposes into the line mentioned in the note to move 18; also other attempts don't promise White much) 19 ♕f4 ♘d5 20 ♘xd5 cxd5 21 ♘e5 ♗xe5 22 ♖xe5 ♗e6 23 ♕e3 ♔f8 24 ♕d3 f6?! 25 ♖e1 White had a permanent and nagging initiative in Kasparov-Karpov, Moscow Wch (23) 1985. Subsequently White's plan became universally popular and in 1986 Black was still searching for a reliable road to equality.

15 ♖e1   a5!?

Black seeks counterplay on the queenside. Although ...a4 is not an immediate threat, the implementation of White's set-up is complicated by this possibility. Moreover the text-move has a hidden tactical point, which will become apparent later.

16 a3   ♖e8 (D)

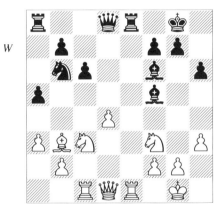

17 ♖xe8+

Later practice has shown that the only way to fight for an advantage is 17 g4!?, when Black can play 17...♗e6 only at the cost of a weak e6-pawn, while 17...♗g6 leaves White in full control of the a2-g8 diagonal. However, this move also weakens the kingside and as we have already observed, Kasparov wasn't too interested in such radical solutions.

17 ...   ♕xe8
18 ♕d2   ♘d7?!

The main reason why the whole 8 ♖c1 line is not too topical any more is 18...♕d7 19 ♖e1 ♖e8 20 ♖xe8+ ♕xe8 21 ♕f4 ♗e6!. This idea occurred for the first time only after our game in M.Gurevich-Van der Sterren, Baku 1986. Black solves his problems by tactical means: 22 ♗xe6 ♕xe6 23 ♕c7 (23 ♕b8+ ♕c8 24 ♕a7 ♘c4 gets White nowhere; note that without 15...a5!? this would net White a pawn) 23...♘c4 24 ♕xb7 ♗xd4! 25 ♘xd4 (25 ♕b8+ ♔h7 26 ♘xd4 ♕e1+ 27 ♔h2 ♕xf2 and the threat of ...♘e3 forces White to give a perpetual himself with 28 ♕c8!) 25...♕e1+ 26 ♔h2 ♕e5+ 27 g3 ♕xd4 with full equality. Karpov's decentralizing move is not ideal, but parrying the ideas ...♗e6, followed by ...♘f8, or ...♕d8-b6 requires resourceful play.

19 ♕f4!

The most accurate continuation. 19 d5 ♘c5 gets White nowhere and the tempting 19 ♖e1 gives Black a choice between 19...♕d8 and 19...♕b8!?, which prevents ♕f4 altogether.

19 ...   ♗g6 (D)

A difficult choice. Now Black's bishop can't oppose White's b3-bishop any more, but after 19...♗e6 20 ♗xe6 ♕xe6 21 ♕c7 ♕b3 the pawn sacrifice 22 ♘e4! ♕xb2 23 ♖e1 ♘f8 24 ♘xf6+ gxf6 breaks up Black's kingside and White retains good attacking chances with 25 ♕g3+ ♘g6 26 ♘h4.

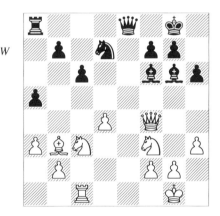

20 h4!

A seemingly mysterious move, which is not so much a prologue to a pawn-storm, as prophylaxis against Black's possible activity. Its strength is seen more clearly when compared with the natural alternative 20 ♖e1 ♕d8. Now the game continuation 21 ♘a4 allows 21...♗h5! 22 ♕f5 (22 g4 ♗g6 and it's not clear how White should proceed) 22...♗xf3 23 ♕xf3 ♘b6 with sufficient counterplay against the d4-pawn.

20 ...   ♕d8
21 ♘a4!

For now the knight prevents ...♕b6, and after suitable preparation (starting with ♖e1) it can quickly and effectively rejoin the fray. Black has only limited chances to exploit its temporary absence from the centre, as his own knight protects the c5-square.

21 ... h5?!

After 21...♕b8?! 22 ♕g4 ♘f8 23 h5 ♗h7 24 ♘c5 White has only increased his pressure, and lines like this convinced Karpov to prevent h5 for good. However, the radical text-move weakens not only g5, but also Black's whole kingside, as the possible fall of the f7-pawn would now give White a mating attack. The tactical chances combined with his strategic pluses will give White a permanent advantage. The provocative 21...♗h5!? 22 g4 ♗g6 23 h5 ♗h7 is interesting. Here Kasparov recommends the direct 24 ♘e5?!, but this is far from clear after 24...♗xe5!? (even 24...♘xe5 25 dxe5 ♕c7! is possible) 25 dxe5 (weaker is 25 ♗xf7+?! ♔h8 26 dxe5 ♕c7, followed by 27...♖f8) 25...♕e7 and White's loose kingside gives Black a lot of counterplay. The more circumspect 24 ♖e1 gives White an edge, but it's smaller than in the game.

22 ♖e1 b5!?

After 22...♕b8 23 ♕e3 ♕c7!? 24 ♗a2! followed by ♘c3-e4 White is better, so Karpov lashes out.

23 ♘c3 ♕b8 (D)

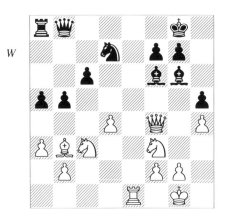

24 ♕e3!

Kasparov doesn't hurry and refrains from the tempting but committal 24 ♘e5. Then:

1) 24...♘xe5 25 dxe5 b4 26 axb4 ♕xb4 (weaker is 26...axb4 27 ♘d1!, when the direct threat is 28 ♕g3 and White prepares ♘e3-f5 too) 27 ♗c4 (the only way to fight for the initiative is to keep the queens on the board) 27...♕xb2 28 ♖e3 ♗e7. Although White has attacking chances, Black seems to be able to hold his own; e.g., 29 e6 ♕c1+ 30 ♔h2 fxe6 31 ♗xe6+ ♔h8.

2) Another playable option is 24...♗xe5 25 dxe5 ♘c5 26 ♗a2 b4! (26...♘d3?! gives White a raging attack after 27 ♕g3! ♘xe1 28 ♕xg6 ♕xe5 29 ♘e4! ♖a7 30 ♘g5) 27 ♕g5 ♔h7 (after 27...b3 28 ♗b1 ♗xb1 29 ♘xb1 ♘d3 30 ♖e3 ♘xb2 31 ♖g3 ♕f8 32 ♘d2! White's attack outweighs Black's queenside play) 28 ♘e2 ♕d8! (after 28...♘d3 29 ♘f4 the greedy 29...♘xe1? 30 ♘xg6 fxg6 31 ♗f7 ♔h8 32 ♗xg6 ♔g8 33 ♕xh5 gives White a winning attack; note that all the lines in the brackets are possible only due to 21...h5?!) 29 ♕e3 b3 30 ♗xb3 ♘xb3 31 ♕xb3 ♖b8 with counterplay.

24 ... b4

24...a4 25 ♗a2 b4 26 ♘e4 b3 27 ♗b1 only helps White, as Black's counterplay is over and he can fully concentrate on the kingside.

25 ♘e4 bxa3

The light-squared bishop is crucial for the defence and the short line 25...♗xe4? 26 ♕xe4 bxa3? 27 ♕xc6 axb2 28 ♕d5! provides ample tactical proof – Black loses at least a piece.

26 ♘xf6+ ♘xf6
27 bxa3 (D)

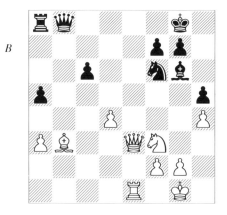

The time has come to take stock. White has managed to halve Black's bishop-pair and his remaining minor pieces are more active than their black counterparts. The a5- and c6-pawns are also more vulnerable than White's pawns.

All this indicates that Kasparov has gained a sizeable long-term advantage. However, the game still is far from over.

27 ... ♘d5!

Kasparov praises this decision, and rightly so. Simplification helps the defence and exchanging the powerful b3-bishop is certainly more to the point than 27...♘g4 28 ♕c3 ♕d6 29 g3 ♕f6 30 ♔g2!?. Black already can't play 30...a4? due to 31 ♗xa4! and his temporary activity gradually peters out, leaving the c6-pawn permanently vulnerable.

28 ♗xd5 cxd5
29 ♘e5 ♕d8

One of Black's major pieces should guard the back rank. Weaker is 29...♕d6 30 ♖c1 with the idea 31 ♖c6, when Black's rook remains passive.

30 ♕f3

30 ♕f4 is a natural alternative, but White wants to keep an eye on both his a3-pawn and Black's d5-pawn.

30 ... ♖a6

30...♖c8 is more accurate. Then Black remains clearly worse, but finding inroads for White is more difficult.

31 ♖c1 (D)

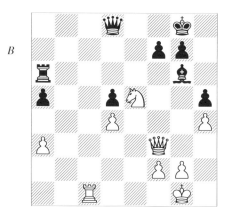

B

31 ... ♔h7

White's strategic assets (dominating knight, more active major pieces and safer king) indicate that it's in Black's interest to seek complications to turn the course of the game. Kasparov recommends 31...♕xh4!? 32 ♕xd5 ♔h7 (after 32...♕f6 33 ♖c5! Black is too passive). Although this drops a pawn after 33 ♘f3 ♕g4! (33...♕f6? loses on the spot to 34 ♘g5+ ♔h6 35 ♖c8!) 34 ♘g5+ ♔h6 35 ♘xf7+ ♗xf7 36 ♕xf7 ♖f6 (not 36...♕xd4? 37 ♖c8 and White has a decisive attack) 37 ♕c4, converting it into a win requires much more than just pure technique after 37...♖d6.

32 ♕h3!

Kasparov targets c8 and doesn't give Black a second chance to take on h4.

32 ... ♖b6

After 32...♖e6 33 ♖c5 White's forces dominate the position.

33 ♖c8 ♕d6
34 ♕g3 a4?

This loses a pawn. Karpov's position was already very difficult, but after the more resilient 34...♕e7!?, intending to chase away the huge e5-knight with ...♗e4 and ...f6, Black can still fight on.

35 ♖a8! (D)

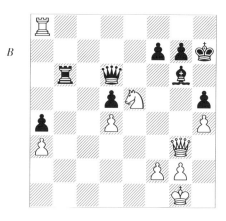

B

35 ... ♕e6

35...♖b3? 36 ♖h8+! ♔xh8 37 ♘xf7+ and 35...♖a6? 36 ♘xf7! ♗xf7 37 ♕d3+ lead to heavier losses for Black.

36 ♖xa4

36 ♕g5!? is also strong. Black can't avoid losing the a4-pawn anyway, as after 36...♖a6 White can simplify into a won queen endgame with 37 ♘xg6 fxg6 38 ♖xa6. However, Kasparov has more ambitious plans with his knight than simply exchanging it.

36 ... ♕f5
37 ♖a7

Already envisaging the final combination. First of all White needs his rook on the 7th rank.

37 ... ♖b1+

After 37...f6 38 ♘d7 ♖b1+ 39 ♔h2 ♗f7 40 ♘f8+ ♔g8 41 ♕c7 ♔h8 42 f3! Black has no effective defence against 43 ♕g3 ♔g8 44 ♖a8.

38 ♔h2 ♖c1

Karpov was already desperately short of time and missed 38...♖b2!? with the idea 39 ♘f3 (39 f3 ♖d2 and with the rook on a7 the game continuation doesn't work) 39...f6 40 ♕c7 ♗f7!, which would have forced White to work harder for his point. Now White has a beautiful forced win.

39 ♖b7 ♖c2
40 f3 (D)

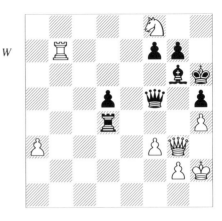

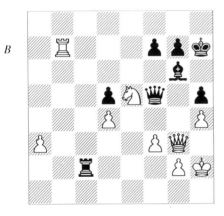

40 ... ♖d2

40...f6 41 ♘d7 is also hopeless for Black.

41 ♘d7!

The sealed move, which cost Kasparov 17 minutes. However, it was a wise investment, as he worked out the final phase of the game over the board. The passive 41 ♖b4? f6 would have given Black excellent drawing chances.

41 ... ♖xd4
42 ♘f8+ ♔h6 (D)
43 ♖b4!!

The fabulous point of 41 ♘d7!. White would like to play 43 ♖b8, but this achieves nothing after 43...♕f4. However, he can afford this quiet move, as after the exchange of rooks Black's king can't escape the mating-net. Finding such an idea after five hours of a gruelling fight deserves full admiration.

43 ... ♖c4

43...♖d3 can even be met by the cheeky 44 a4!, when Black is defenceless: 44...f6 45 ♖f4, 44...♖a3 45 ♖d4! and 46 ♖xd5, or 44...♖e3 45 ♖b8 ♗h7 46 ♕g5+, winning a piece. However, an even prettier line is 43...♖xb4 44 axb4 d4 45 b5 d3 46 b6 d2 47 b7 d1♕ 48 b8♕ ♕c1 49 ♘xg6 ♕xg6 50 ♕h8+ ♕h7 51 ♕gxg7#, a finish reminiscent of Capablanca-Alekhine, Buenos Aires Wch (11) 1927.

44 ♖xc4 dxc4
45 ♕d6 c3
46 ♕d4 1-0

The only defence against immediate mate is 46...♗h7, but in the endgame after 47 ♕xc3 ♗g8 (47...f6 48 ♕e3+ g5 49 ♘xh7 swaps even the queens) 48 ♕e3+ g5 49 ♕xg5+ Black will lose both his remaining pawns.

Game 37
Garry Kasparov – Jan Smejkal
Olympiad, Dubai 1986
Ruy Lopez (Spanish), Zaitsev Variation [C92]

1	e4	e5
2	♘f3	♘c6
3	♗b5	a6
4	♗a4	♘f6
5	0-0	♗e7
6	♖e1	b5
7	♗b3	d6
8	c3	0-0
9	h3	♗b7
10	d4	♖e8
11	♘bd2	♗f8
12	a4	♕d7 *(D)*

Smejkal is a lifelong Closed Ruy Lopez devotee and he naturally closely followed the K-K matches. One can understand he is reluctant to go for the complications after 12...h6 13 ♗c2 exd4 (see Game 35), justifiably feeling he would be entering Kasparov's home turf. He chooses another option, which was also tried by Karpov and brought him success. Nowadays, however, the text-move has gone out of fashion.

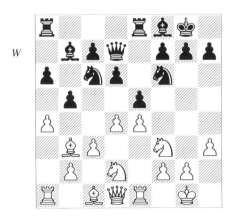

13 axb5

White is running out of suitable waiting moves, so his best chance to fight for an opening edge is to close the centre and, relying on his space advantage, start playing on one of the flanks. His region of activity depends on the route Black's c6-knight will take. Apart from the text-move, the only ambitious option is 13 d5 ♘e7 14 ♘f1 (practice has shown that even in positions with a blocked centre after 14 c4 ♘g6! 15 ♗c2 c6 16 b3 ♕c7 Black can hold his own) 14...h6 15 ♘3h2 c6 16 dxc6 ♘xc6!? with complex play. The text-move leads to positions of a similar type.

13	...	axb5
14	♖xa8	♗xa8

In principle exchanges favour the defence, but the main point behind 13 axb5 is that White intends to profit from the temporary displacement of Black's bishop to a8. In the game it will take Smejkal one extra move (see move 19) to activate his bishop and thus fight for the open a-file. Right now the seemingly logical 14...♖xa8? fails tactically to 15 ♘g5 ♘d8 16 ♘df3! and the pressure against e5 and f7 causes Black huge problems. Even 16...c5 (relatively best; 16...h6? runs into 17 ♘xf7! ♔xf7 18 dxe5 and 16...exd4 17 e5! gives White a raging attack) costs him a pawn after 17 dxe5 dxe5 18 ♕xd7 ♘xd7 19 ♘xf7! ♔xf7 20 ♗e6!.

15 d5 *(D)*

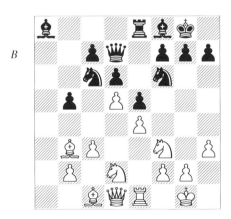

15	...	♘b8 *(D)*

Smejkal doesn't follow in Karpov's footsteps and is the first to introduce a novelty. However, later Black spends a lot of time coordinating his pieces, and undermining White's centre with the natural ...c6 will take him another six moves. This warrants a look at the alternatives:

1) Karpov's initial try was 15...♘d8?!, but here the knight is misplaced and after 16 ♘f1 h6 17 ♘3h2 ♘b7 (17...c6 also doesn't solve Black's problems after 18 ♘g4 ♘xg4 19 hxg4 cxd5 20 exd5) 18 ♗c2 ♘c5 19 b4 ♘a6 20 ♘g4 ♘h7 21 ♘g3 c6 22 dxc6 ♗xc6 23 ♗b3 ♘c7 24 ♕f3 ♘e6 25 h4 ♕d8 26 ♖d1 White built up a nice attacking position in Kasparov-Karpov, Moscow Wch (46) 1984/5.

2) A later attempt was 15...♘e7 16 ♘f1 h6 17 ♘g3 c6 18 dxc6 ♗xc6, but after 19 ♘h2! d5?! 20 ♘h5! ♘xe4 21 ♘g4 ♕f5, as played in Timman-Karpov, Kuala Lumpur Ct (7) 1990, White missed the promising 22 ♖xe4! dxe4 23 ♘g3 ♕c8 24 ♘xe5 with more than sufficient attacking chances for the exchange.

3) 15...♘a5!? is arguably best. One of the rare recent top-level games went 16 ♗a2 (16 ♗c2!? deserves attention) 16...c6 17 b4 ♘b7 18 ♘f1 (18 c4 ♖c8! 19 dxc6 ♕xc6 20 c5?! ♘d8 21 ♗b2 dxc5 22 bxc5 ♕xc5 23 ♗xe5 ♘d7 and in Kasparov-Karpov, Moscow Wch (5) 1985 it was already White who had to fight for equality) 18...cxd5 19 exd5 ♖c8 20 ♗g5 ♘e8 21 ♕d3 f6 22 ♗d2 ♘d8 23 ♘e3 ♘f7 24 c4 g6! and after ...f5 Black got active counterplay in Leko-Nikolić, Bled OL 2002.

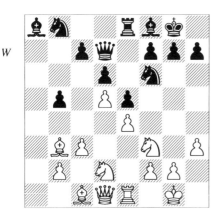

16 ♘f1

White continues analogously to note '1' to the previous move. Shifting the attention to the queenside with 16 c4 is less effective, as after Gutman's prophylactic move 16...♖c8! (16...c6 gives White the initiative after 17 dxc6 ♗xc6 18 cxb5 ♗xb5 19 ♘g5) Black will gradually prepare the liberating ...c6 with good counterplay.

16 ... ♘a6

Smejkal improves his knight first. Closing the centre with 16...c5 favours White, as it not only frees his hands on the kingside, but also gives him a chance to change his mind and play on the other flank with 17 c4!?. The main alternative 16...c6?! is premature as well, since after 17 ♗g5 ♗e7 18 dxc6 ♗xc6 19 ♘g3 g6 (19...h6 20 ♗xf6 ♗xf6 21 ♘f5 and play on the light squares gives White an advantage) 20 ♗h6 White has a promising attacking position.

17 ♗g5 ♗e7
18 ♘g3 *(D)*

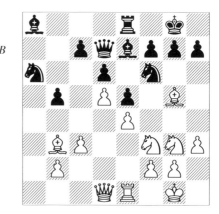

18 ... g6?!

Black radically prevents ♘f5, but is White's threat really worth a permanent kingside weakness? In the final phase of the game Smejkal will suffer heavily on the dark squares, so this seems like a moment to look for improvements. 18...h6!? 19 ♗e3 (after 19 ♗d2 ♗f8 the knight sortie to f5 is ineffective) 19...c6 gives Black reasonable counterplay.

19 ♕d2 ♗b7

White is clearly better after 19...c6 20 dxc6 ♗xc6 21 ♗xf6 ♗xf6 22 ♖d1 ♖d8 23 ♘g5!? ♗xg5 24 ♕xg5, so Black keeps the position closed for the time being.

20 ♖a1

A subsequent attempt to improve Kasparov's play was 20 ♗a2 ♘c5 21 b4 ♘a4 22 c4! bxc4 23 ♗xc4 ♘b6 24 ♗b3 ♖a8 25 ♖c1 ♘e8 26 ♗h6 and in Svidler-Zhang Zhong, Shanghai 2001 White had a pleasant position. Black must passively defend the c7-pawn, while White has active options on the kingside.

20	...	♖a8
21	♗c2	

This removes the bishop from a vulnerable square, but on the other hand now the opening of the a2-g8 diagonal will not be so dangerous for Black. 21 ♗e3!? is interesting, and gives White an advantage. He has prevented both 21...♘c5 and 21...c6?! as well, as the latter move would give him heavy pressure after 22 dxc6 ♗xc6 23 ♘g5 d5 24 ♖d1 ♘c7 25 ♗b6.

21	...	c6

Weaker is 21...♘c5 22 ♖xa8+ ♗xa8 23 ♗e3.

22	dxc6	♗xc6
23	♖d1	♖d8?! *(D)*

After this mistake Black's position starts sliding downhill rapidly. Kasparov points out the stronger 23...♕e6!, by which Black prevents the bishop from returning to b3 and will activate his a6-knight via c5 or c7, depending on the circumstances. White's edge would then have been only minimal at best.

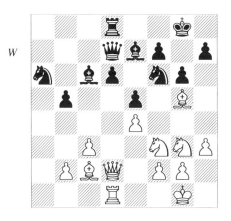
W

24	♕e3!	

Kasparov takes control of the g1-a7 diagonal and renews the threat of ♘xe5.

24	...	♕b7

24...♕c7 25 b4!, followed by ♗b3, keeps the a6-knight sidelined. Even after 24...♕e6 25 b4! (the immediate 25 ♕b6 is weaker, as Black has 25...♘b8 26 ♗d3 ♖c8!, defending the b5-pawn indirectly) White has a sizeable advantage, as the possibility ♕b6 ties Black's hands.

25	♗h6!	♘c7

Black finally activates his knight. The other route, 25...♘c5?, is out of the question due to 26 ♘xe5!. However, the text-move allows White's main and most dangerous idea. Although the alternatives 25...♘e8 26 b4! ♘ac7 27 ♗b3 and 25...♘d7 26 ♘f5 ♗xf5 27 exf5 are unattractive, they are probably more resilient.

26	♘f5	

In his notes Kasparov also mentions 26 ♖a1 ♖a8 27 ♖xa8+, followed by ♘f5, but keeping pieces on the board is more natural.

26	...	♘e6

26...♘ce8 is no better: 27 ♘xe7+ ♕xe7 28 ♗g5.

27	♘xe7+	♕xe7
28	♘g5	

The unopposed h6-bishop rules supreme on the weak dark squares.

28	...	♘c5 *(D)*

After 28...♘xg5? 29 ♗xg5 Black can't disentangle from the pin, so he must live with another attacking piece in the vicinity of his king.

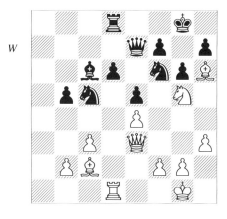
W

29	b4	♘a4
30	♗b3	♗e8

Black's centre would have been very vulnerable after 30...d5 31 ♖e1!. After the passive text-move White increases his pressure in straightforward positional fashion.

31	♖d2!	

White prevents ...♘b2 and keeps the knight offside.

31	...	♖c8
32	♖c2	♘d7
33	♘f3	♘db6

After 33...♘ab6 White sidelines Black's queen and invades via the queenside with 34 ♗g5 ♕f8 35 ♖a2!. The text-move keeps the a-file closed.

34 ♗g5! *(D)*

34 ... ♕c7?!

In time-trouble Smejkal strays with his queen too far from his king, moreover to a vulnerable square. However, even after the better 34...♕f8 35 ♘d2 Black's position is untenable in the long run.

35 ♘d2 ♔g7

35...♘xc3? 36 ♘b1 and 35...♘c4? 36 ♗xc4 bxc4 37 ♗f6 lose on the spot, while after 35...♕b7 36 ♗f6 ♘d7 37 ♗e7! Black has no good moves; e.g., 37...♘dc5 38 ♗xd6 ♘xb3 39 ♘xb3 ♕c6 40 ♖d2! ♕xc3 41 ♕h6 ♗d7 42 ♗e7.

36 c4 h5

White mates after 36...bxc4 37 ♘xc4 ♘xc4 38 ♖xc4 ♕b7 39 ♗h6+ ♔g8 40 ♕g5.

37 cxb5 ♕d7
38 ♕f3

38 ♗h6+ ♔h7 (38...♔g8 39 ♕g5 is similar) 39 ♗f8 would have won immediately.

38 ... ♖xc2
39 ♗xc2 *(D)*

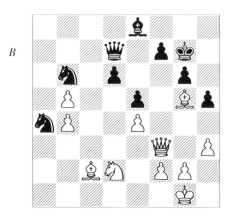

39 ... ♔g8
40 ♗b3 ♕xb5

After 40...♔h7 41 ♕f6 Black has no good defence against 42 ♗h6! with a mating attack.

41 ♕f6 1-0

The threats of ♗h6 and ♕xg6+ can't be parried.

Game 38
Robert Hübner – Garry Kasparov
OHRA, Brussels 1986
Grünfeld Defence, 5 ♕a4+ [D90]

1	d4	♘f6
2	c4	g6
3	♘c3	d5
4	♘f3	♗g7
5	♕a4+	

Kasparov's Grünfeld suffered rather badly in his 1986 match against Karpov, the main culprit being the Russian System, 5 ♕b3. In our game Hübner strives for a similar position, albeit with a slight twist.

5	...	♗d7
6	♕b3	dxc4
7	♕xc4	0-0
8	e4	

In the basic position of the Russian System both sides have one move less and Black's bishop is on c8 instead of d7. Seemingly this limits Black's options, as now for example after 8...♘a6 9 e5! his knight doesn't have the d7-square and the queen sacrifice 9...♗e6 10 exf6! is advantageous for White. Naturally Black can transpose into normal Smyslov lines with 8...♗g4, but this is not everyone's cup of tea. However, Kasparov shows there is another option, by which Black makes full use of his extra ...♗d7 move. The following thrust took Hübner by surprise, even though it had occurred in previous practice and found its way into *Informator*.

8	...	b5! *(D)*

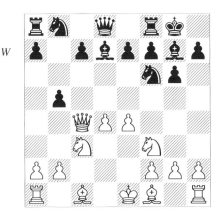

Quite in the spirit of the Grünfeld, Black attacks White's centre from the flank. One also has to bear in mind White is at least two moves away from castling – and in the game it will actually take him much longer!

9	♕b3?	

White's reaction is too soft and he will remarkably quickly find himself with his back against the wall. The only principled way to deal with the gambit was to accept it with 9 ♘xb5 ♘xe4 10 ♕xc7! (White has to get the queens off as fast as possible; lines such as 10 ♕d5 c6 11 ♕xe4 ♗f5! and especially 10 ♘xc7 ♘c6 11 ♘xa8 ♕a5+ 12 ♗d2 ♘xd2 13 ♘xd2 ♘xd4 spell danger for his centralized king) 10...♘c6 11 ♕xd8 ♖axd8 12 ♗d3 ♘b4! 13 ♗xe4 ♗xb5 14 ♗d2 ♘d3+ 15 ♗xd3 ♗xd3 16 ♗c3 ♗e4. In the resulting endgame Black has enough play for the pawn and a draw is the most likely result.

9	...	c5!

Blasting open the centre is the best way to profit from a lead in development.

10	e5	

Also this move isn't ideal, although even after other continuations White is fighting for equality:

1) 10 ♗xb5 ♗xb5 11 ♘xb5 ♘xe4 12 0-0 cxd4 13 ♕c4 ♘d6 14 ♕d5 ♘d7! 15 ♘bxd4 ♘b6 16 ♕b3 ♘bc4 and in Anikaev-Malishauskas, USSR 1983 Black's central pawn-majority and queenside pressure gave him an advantage.

2) Probably the lesser evil was 10 dxc5!? ♘a6 11 e5 ♘g4! 12 ♗xb5 (12 e6 ♗xe6! 13 ♕xb5 ♘c7 14 ♕a5 ♘d5! is a line given by Kengis; White's uncoordinated forces can hardly hope to survive Black's pressure) 12...♘xc5 13 ♕c4 ♖c8 (13...♗xb5 14 ♕xc5 ♗a6 15 h3 is less clear). Black advantageously wins his pawn back, but at least after 14 0-0 White's king is safe.

10	...	♘g4
11	♗xb5	

Further ignoring development and hunting for material with 11 ♕d5?! doesn't help, as after 11...cxd4! 12 ♘xd4 (12 ♕xa8 dxc3 gives Black a raging attack) 12...♕b6 or even 12...♗xe5!? with the threat of ...♕b6 Black is clearly on top. After 11 dxc5 Black can transpose into note '2' to White's 10th move with 11...♘a6, but 11...b4!? 12 ♕xb4 ♘c6 is even more dangerous for White.

11	...	cxd4
12	♘xd4	♗xb5!?

After 12...♗xe5 13 ♘f3!? (complications after 13 ♕d5 ♕b6 or 13 ♗xd7 ♘xf2! favour Black as the better developed side) 13...♕b6 (13...♗xc3+!? 14 bxc3 ♕b6 15 ♘d4 ♗xb5 16 ♕xb5 ♕c7 is good for Black, but certainly not more so than in the game) 14 0-0 ♗xc3 15 ♗xd7 ♗xb2 16 ♗xb2 ♕xb3 17 axb3 ♘xd7 18 ♖a4 realizing the extra pawn would be very difficult. Kasparov decides the time is not yet ripe for material gains and aims for a clear-cut positional advantage.

13	♘dxb5	a6
14	♘a3	♕d4! *(D)*

Powerful centralization. 14...♘xe5? 15 0-0 would have been a relief for White.

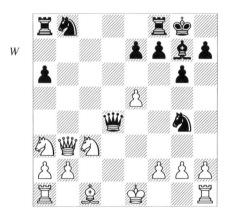

15 ♕c2

White would have liked to castle, but after 15 0-0?! ♕xe5 16 g3 ♕h5 17 h4 ♘c6 his kingside is full of holes and Black has a strong attack.

15 ... ♘c6

The threat of ...♘b4 forces White to lose another tempo.

16 ♕e2 ♕xe5

16...♘gxe5!? 17 0-0 ♕d3 is perhaps more accurate. Then 18 ♕xd3 ♘xd3 transposes into the game and even after other moves White can't avoid a highly unpleasant endgame.

17 ♕xe5

Hübner moves his queen for the third time in a row; didn't White have any more useful moves? 17 ♘c4?! ♕xe2+ 18 ♘xe2 ♘b4 and ...♖ac8 spells big trouble, but 17 ♘c2!? is interesting. White activates his knight, something he managed to do in the game only on move 33! Protecting the d4-square enables his king to save time and go directly to e2 in the coming endgame. Now stranding the knight with 17...♘xh2 18 ♕xe5 ♗xe5 19 f3 is far from clear, while after other moves Black's pressure is also not as strong as in the game.

17	...	♘gxe5
18	0-0	♘d3 *(D)*

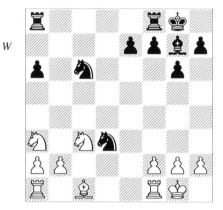

As in Game 31, Kasparov lands a mighty knight on d3. The following phase of the game revolves around this square.

19	♖b1	♖ab8
20	♖d1	♖fd8
21	♔f1	

As indicated in the note to move 17, White's king aims for e2. How does Black maintain his outpost?

21	...	f5!
22	♔e2	♘ce5 *(D)*

Mission accomplished. The tempting alternative 22...♘cb4 achieves the same goal, but limits Black's b8-rook.

23 ♘a4!

The main point of Black's 21st move was to prevent the development of White's bishop: now 23 ♗g5?! h6 24 ♗e3 (24 ♗xe7? loses a piece: 24...♖d7 25 ♗h4 g5) runs into 24...f4 25

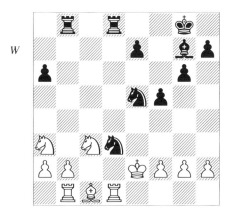
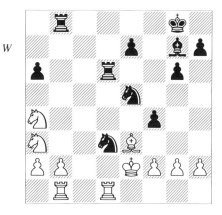

♗a7 ♖b7 26 ♗c5 f3+! 27 gxf3 ♘f4+ 28 ♔f1 (28 ♔e3 ♘ed3 and the threats of ...♗xc3 and ...♖bd7 in connection with ...♘g2+ are decisive) 28...♖xd1+ followed by 29...♘xf3 with a won endgame. Black will win the h-pawn and his pieces are far more active than White's. On the other hand Black threatened to win material with ...♘xc1+ and ...♘d3, so Hübner's move, which covers b2, is best.

23 ... ♖d6

Black's task is to keep White's forces bottled in as long as possible and penetrate into his position. Kasparov suggests 23...♖bc8 is a worthy alternative. Then Black readily deals with White's most obvious freeing attempts such as 24 b3 ♘b4 25 ♗d2 ♘ec6!, 24 f4 ♖xc1 25 ♖bxc1 ♘xc1+ 26 ♖xc1 ♘d3 27 ♖c4 e5! or 24 ♘b6 ♖c6 25 ♘bc4 ♘xc4 26 ♘xc4 ♖xc4 27 ♖xd3 ♖c2+ 28 ♗d2 ♖b8!. All these lines cost White at least a pawn, while Black doesn't have to relinquish much of his positional advantage. Finally, 24 ♗e3 f4 25 ♗b6 f3+! 26 gxf3 ♘f4+ 27 ♔e3 ♖f8 is similar to the game and gives Black a strong attack.

24 ♗e3

Other moves are no better:

1) 24 f4 ♖d4! 25 ♘c5 (after 25 fxe5 ♘xc1+ and 26...♖xa4 Black wins a pawn) 25...♘xc1+ 26 ♖dxc1 ♖xf4 27 ♘xa6 ♖b6 28 ♘c5 ♘g4 and Black's attack will net him material.

2) 24 b3 ♘b4! 25 ♖xd6 exd6 and again White can't avoid losses; e.g., 26 ♘c3 ♖e8 27 ♔f1 ♘g4.

3) 24 ♘c4 ♘xc4 25 ♖xd3 ♖xd3 26 ♔xd3 ♘a3 27 ♖a1 e5! and the marching e-pawn paralyses White's pieces.

24 ... f4 (D)

25 ♗c5 f3+!

Kasparov transforms his advantage into a direct attack.

26 gxf3 ♘f4+
27 ♔e3

The passive move 27 ♔f1?! is weaker. After 27...♖xd1+ 28 ♖xd1 ♘xf3 Black's knights keep the white king trapped in a mating-net and as White's h-pawn will fall, Black's own passed pawn will become very dangerous; e.g., 29 h3 ♗xb2 30 ♗xe7 ♖e8! and Black is close to winning.

27 ... ♖f6 (D)

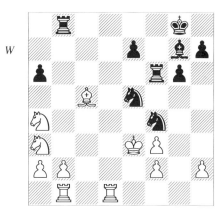

28 ♗xe7?

A serious error, which greatly increases the force of Black's superbly coordinated army. 28 ♔e4? ♖f5 only further exposes the king, but 28 ♗d4! is stronger. After 28...♖f5 29 ♗xe5 ♗xe5 Black is much better, but exchanging one of the menacing knights enables White to fight on.

28 ... ♘g2+
29 ♔e2 ♖xf3

| 30 | ♗d6 |

30 ♗g5?! fails to 30...♖bf8 31 ♖f1 ♘g4, and 30 ♖d8+ ♖xd8 31 ♗xd8 ♘f4+ 32 ♔f1 ♘g4 33 ♗b6 ♘xf2! doesn't help either.

| 30 | ... | ♘f4+ |
| 31 | ♔f1 | ♘g4! |

Compare the activity of Black's and White's knights!

| 32 | ♖d2 |

32 ♗xb8? ♖xf2+ 33 ♔g1 ♖g2+ leads to mate.

| 32 | ... | ♖e8 *(D)* |

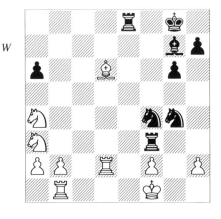

| 33 | ♘c4 |

It's now too late for exchanges: after 33 ♗xf4 ♖xf4 34 ♘c5 (34 ♘c3 ♘xh2+ {or 34...♖ef8} is lost for White) 34...♖e5! 35 h3 (Black mates after 35 ♖d8+ ♗f8 36 ♘d7 ♘xh2+ 37 ♔g2 ♖g5+!) 35...♘e3+ 36 ♔g1 ♖g5+ 37 ♔h1 ♖f3 38 fxe3 ♖xh3+ 39 ♖h2 ♖xh2+ 40 ♔xh2 ♖xc5 the united kingside passed pawns will decide this technical endgame.

| 33 | ... | ♘xh2+ |

33...♗d4 is less convincing: 34 ♗xf4 ♖xf4 35 ♔g2.

| 34 | ♔g1 | ♘g4 |
| 35 | ♖f1?! |

Hübner was by now in heavy time-trouble and missed the more resilient 35 ♗c5!. Nevertheless after 35...h5 White's position is untenable in the long run.

| 35 | ... | ♗d4! *(D)* |

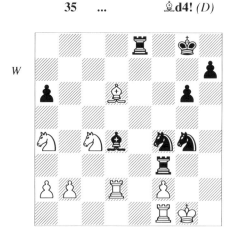

The last piece joins the attack with great effect.

| 36 | ♗c5 |

36 ♘c5? allows mate after 36...♗xf2+! 37 ♖dxf2 ♖g3+ 38 ♔h1 ♘xf2+. The only way to prolong the game was 36 ♗xf4 ♖xf4 37 b3, but after 37...♖ef8 the f-pawn falls and the attack will break through.

36	...	♖g3+
37	♔h1	♖h3+
38	♔g1	♘h2! *(D)*

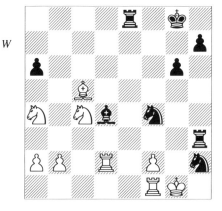

0-1

Preventing ...♘f3# will cost White too much material.

Game 39
Garry Kasparov – Mikhail Tal
SWIFT, Brussels 1987
Nimzo-Indian Defence, Rubinstein Variation [E48]

1	d4	♘f6
2	c4	e6
3	♘c3	♗b4
4	e3	

This was the last round of the tournament and the situation was critical. After a flying 4/4 start, Kasparov slowed down considerably and in the penultimate round was even overtaken by Ljubojević. Therefore only a win could satisfy the World Champion and to further his ambitions, he refrains from 4 ♘f3 (see Games 30 and 34) and returns to a favourite of his junior years. The battle plan was an opening surprise followed by sharp and complex play, something that Tal, who played very peacefully in Brussels, found difficult to cope with.

4 ... 0-0

The magician from Riga learned his lesson and a few weeks later in Moscow the 45-minute TV exhibition game Kasparov-Tal went 4...c5 5 ♗d3 d5 6 cxd5 ♘xd5 7 ♘e2 cxd4 8 exd4 ♘c6. Later Black managed to solve his opening problems.

5 ♗d3 d5
6 cxd5

A clever solution. Kasparov aims for a position resembling the Exchange Variation of the Queen's Gambit Declined. As he will develop his knight to e2 and intends to play in the centre (f3, e4), the c1-bishop will probably be locked behind the pawn-chain only temporarily (see also the note to move 9 in Game 22, and Games 45 and 51).

6 ... exd5

Weaker is 6...♘xd5 7 ♕c2.

7 ♘e2 *(D)*
7 ... c5

7...♘bd7?! 8 0-0 c6 9 f3 c5 10 a3 cxd4 11 exd4 ♗e7 12 ♘f4 ♘b8 13 g4! ♗d6?! 14 ♔h1 ♖e8 15 g5 ♗xf4 16 ♗xf4 ♘h5 17 ♗xb8 ♖xb8 18 f4 g6 19 ♕f3 b6 20 f5 ♖b7 21 f6 ♗e6 22 ♖ae1 gave White a decisive positional advantage in Kasparov-Yurtaev, Moscow 1981 mainly

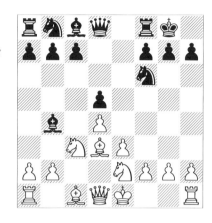

due to the offside h5-knight. This game shows traces of the strategy Kasparov intended to follow if Tal hadn't played 10...♗xc3?. However, a more popular and better option than the text-move is 7...♖e8!? 8 0-0 ♗d6. Black wants to create counterplay on the kingside and only after 9 f3 plays 9...c5, intending to release the central tension only at a suitable moment.

8 0-0

This natural move conceals a fine nuance. After 8 a3 cxd4 9 exd4 Black can already consider 9...♗xc3+ 10 bxc3 b6! followed by ...♗a6 with counterplay.

8 ... ♘c6

8...b6 9 a3 ♗xc3 10 bxc3 is somewhat better for White; this has been known since the famous game Botvinnik-Capablanca, Rotterdam (AVRO) 1938.

9 a3 cxd4
10 exd4!?

At the time this game was played, the most popular choice was 10 axb4 dxc3 11 b5 ♘e5 12 ♘xc3 ♗g4 with complications. Kasparov opts for a seemingly innocuous older option, injecting it with new ideas.

10 ... ♗xc3?

It's surprising how quickly Black is routed after this serious positional error. The bishop was a valuable piece, worth keeping alive, so

10...♗d6 is stronger. Nevertheless, by 11 f3! White limits the active prospects of both the c8-bishop and the f6-knight and is slightly better despite the symmetrical pawn-structure. ♗g5 is in the air and at a suitable moment he can even play g4 as in Kasparov-Yurtaev. Tal was sufficiently impressed to play the whole line with White against Sax later in the same year!

11 bxc3! *(D)*

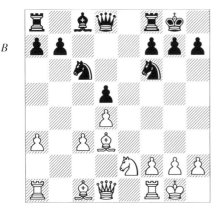

A novelty. In an endgame such a capture would be suspect, creating a weakness on an open file. However, Kasparov rightly feels that lending support to the d4-pawn will considerably increase his attacking prospects.

11 ... ♘e7?!

Black has problems with White's bishops. The d3-bishop is obviously a strong attacking piece, and setting up a barrier on the b1-h7 diagonal with 11...♘e4 has only a temporary effect due to 12 ♕c2, forcing the knight back to f6. The dark-squared bishop has no black counterpart and can exert strong pressure from g5. An attempt to prevent this sortie with 11...h6 only creates a further target on the kingside and gives White a clear attacking plan after 12 f3 followed by g4, ♔h1, ♖g1, etc. Slightly better is 11...♖e8, although this doesn't really address Black's problems and White is better after 12 f3. After Tal's somewhat unnatural move, Black's pieces start getting in each other's way; in particular the c8-bishop will play a sorry role later on. Thus Nikitin's suggestion 11...♗g4!? may be best, when the bishop aims for g6. Although 12 ♗g5 (12 f3 ♗h5 13 ♘f4 is also pleasant for White) 12...♕d6 (weaker is 12...♗h5 13 ♕b3) 13 f3 ♗h5 14 ♕b1 nets White a pawn, turning it into a full point is going to be no mean feat after 14...♗g6.

12 ♕c2

White prevents ...♗f5 and in turn threatens ♗g5; his queen on c2 is well sheltered by the c-pawn. The immediate 12 ♗g5 ♘e4 is unconvincing for White.

12 ... ♗d7

By this point Black has no time for queenside manoeuvres, and now Kasparov quickly builds up a raging attack with a few pointed moves. However, suggesting an improvement is not easy; e.g., 12...♗g4 13 f3 ♗h5 14 ♗g5 and White breaks up Black's kingside.

13 ♗g5 ♘g6
14 f4!

Now the f-pawn gets a more active role than just protecting the e4-square.

14 ... h6

After 14...♖e8 15 f5 ♘f8 16 ♘f4 ♗c6 17 ♘h5 ♘8d7 18 ♖f3 White's pressure will quickly overload Black's defences.

15 ♗xf6 ♕xf6
16 f5! ♘e7
17 ♘g3 *(D)*

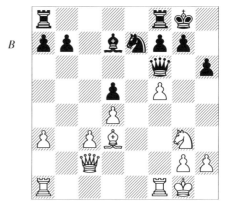

Very concrete play. Although White has exchanged one of his bishops and voluntarily closed the b1-h7 diagonal, the misplaced queen on f6 causes Black great problems.

17 ... ♘c8

The queen certainly isn't an ideal blockading piece, but after 17...♕g5 18 ♖f3! White has everything ready for the f6 break. The attempt to consolidate the position with 17...♔h8 followed by ...♘g8 is too slow: 18 ♘h5 ♕g5 19 f6! ♕xh5 20 fxe7 ♖fe8 21 ♖ae1 and Black has no defence against ♖e5, as 21...♗e6? loses on the spot to 22 ♖xe6! fxe6 23 ♗g6.

18 ♖f4!

Again concrete play: with the rook on the 4th rank White will be able to create the threat of ♘h5 faster than after 18 ♖f3?!.

18 ... ♘d6 *(D)*

The tactical justification for White's last move is 18...♕d6 19 f6! and the rook is taboo: 19...♕xf4 20 ♗h7+ ♔h8 21 fxg7+ ♔xg7 22 ♘h5+. After 18...♔h8 White has a choice between 19 ♖g4 and 19 ♘h5 ♕g5 20 ♕e2, followed by h4 and f6.

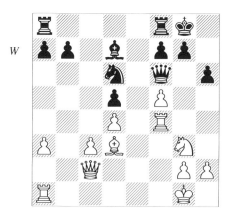

19 ♕f2!

Finishing the last preparations for driving the black queen out of f6.

19 ... ♖fe8

Now White wins by force, but Black's position was most probably already beyond saving:

1) 19...♘e8 20 ♘h5 ♕g5 21 h4! is hopeless for Black, as 21...♕xh5 22 g4 traps the queen.

2) White has a very strong attack even after the better 19...♕d8!? 20 f6 g5 (20...g6 21 ♖h4 and the h-pawn falls) 21 h4!, as taking the rook by 21...gxf4? leads to mate after 22 ♕xf4 ♘e8 23 ♕xh6 ♘xf6 24 ♘h5.

20 ♘h5 ♕d8

20...♕g5 21 h4! only postpones the inevitable.

21 ♘xg7! *(D)*

The winning blow. Black can't take the knight and his kingside is ruined.

21 ... ♘e4

21...♔xg7? 22 f6+ and 23 ♕h4 mates.

22 ♗xe4 ♖xe4

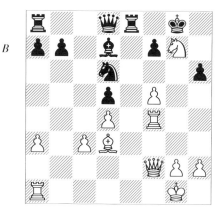

23	f6	♔h7
24	♖xe4	dxe4
25	♕f4	♗c6
26	♖e1	

Tal has staved off an immediate disaster, but the relief is only temporary. White is a healthy pawn up and winds up his attack by activating his rook. 26 ♕f5+ ♔h8, followed by ...♕d5, is less convincing for White; the f5-square is needed for the knight.

26 ... ♕f8 *(D)*

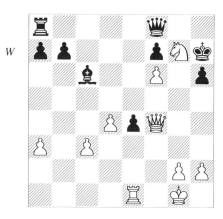

27 c4!

Kasparov avoids the last pitfall: after 27 ♖e3? ♕xa3 28 ♖h3? ♕a1+ Black survives. Now everything is ready for ♖e3 or d5.

27	...	♕xa3
28	♘f5	♕f8
29	♖e3	♗d7
30	♖g3	♗xf5
31	♕xf5+	1-0

31...♔h8 32 ♖g7 costs Black his queen.

Game 40
Beat Züger – Garry Kasparov
Switzerland-Kasparov simul, Zurich 1987
Queen's Gambit Declined, Tarrasch Defence [D34]

1	c4	♘f6
2	♘c3	c5
3	g3	e6
4	♘f3	d5
5	cxd5	exd5
6	d4	♘c6
7	♗g2	♗e7
8	0-0	0-0 *(D)*

The popularity of the Tarrasch Defence declined in the second half of the 20th century, with only two World Championship contenders breaking this tendency. There was, however, a notable difference between their use of the system. While in 1969 Spassky took Petrosian by surprise and the Tarrasch played a major and positive role in his fight for the title, Kasparov had already used it successfully in his Candidates matches against Beliavsky, Korchnoi and Smyslov. In the first aborted 1984/5 K-K duel he used it twice and after losing both games against a well-prepared opponent gradually excluded it from his repertoire altogether. However, in a clock simul against lesser opposition Kasparov had no qualms in playing this strategically risky defence. Black intends to prove that the weakness of his isolated d-pawn is sufficiently compensated by active piece-play – an imbalance quite typical for Kasparov's practice (see also Game 36).

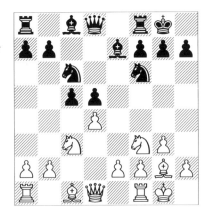

9 ♗g5

White's most ambitious continuation, also played by Kasparov himself on the rare occasions he has had to face the Tarrasch.

9	...	cxd4
10	♘xd4	h6
11	♗e3	♖e8
12	♖c1	

In the aforementioned games Karpov continued with direct pressure against d5 by 12 ♕b3 ♘a5 13 ♕c2 ♗g4 14 ♘f5 ♖c8 (14...♗b4!? is currently the main move, although the pawn sacrifice 15 ♗d4! requires accurate defence from Black). Now 15 ♗d4! ♗c5 16 ♗xc5 ♖xc5 17 ♘e3 ♗e6 (17...♗h5!?) 18 ♖ad1 ♕c8 (18...♕d7!?) 19 ♕a4 gave White a nagging edge, which he brilliantly converted in Karpov-Kasparov, Moscow Wch (9) 1984/5. Although recently the Russian GM Bezgodov was successful with the interesting improvements mentioned in the brackets, this line still remains one of White's main attempts. Züger's move is even more popular and indicates White is ready to change the pawn-structure with ♘xc6 at a suitable moment.

12	...	♗g4

Black's main alternative is 12...♗f8. Then 13 ♘xc6 bxc6 14 ♘a4 ♗d7 15 ♗c5 forces a strategically desirable exchange of the dark-squared bishops, but after 15...♗xc5 16 ♘xc5 ♗g4 17 ♖e1 ♕a5! 18 h3 ♗f5 19 ♕d4 ♖ab8 20 a3 ♕b5 21 b3 Black can get sufficient pressure against b3 with 21...a5! (instead of the inferior 21...♘e4? 22 b4!, when White was better in Kasparov-Illescas, Linares 1994).

13	h3	♗e6

13...♗h5?! is weaker due to 14 ♘f5, so Black must present White's d4-knight with a choice.

14	♔h2 *(D)*	

Züger postpones any possible captures and makes a useful waiting move instead. If White wants to take on e6, it's best to do so immediately. However, 14 ♘xe6 fxe6 15 f4 ♗b4!? 16

♗f2 ♕e7 followed by ...♖ad8 leads to an unclear position, as the scope of White's bishops is limited.

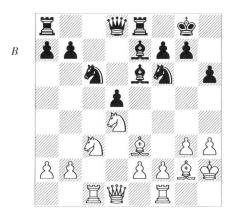

14	...	♕d7
15	♘xc6	

Natural enough, but practice has shown White has more chances for an advantage after quiet moves such as 15 ♘a4 or 15 ♕c2 followed by ♖fd1.

15	...	bxc6
16	♘a4	♗f5
17	♗c5	

17 ♘c5 deserves attention, although after 17...♗xc5!? (weaker is 17...♕c8 18 ♗d4) 18 ♗xc5 ♘e4 Black has reasonable counterplay.

17	...	♗d8!

Contrary to the note to Black's 12th move, Kasparov can now retain his dark-squared bishop, which will play a star role later on. 17...♗e4 18 ♗xe7 ♗xg2 19 ♔xg2 ♕xe7 20 e3 ♕e4+ 21 ♔h2 ♖ac8 22 ♘c5 ♕f5 23 ♔g2 h5 24 ♕f3 gives White a pleasant edge in a simplified position, Seirawan-Piket, Merrillville 1997.

18	♗d4	♘e4
19	f3!?	

White embarks on an ambitious plan. This move wins tempi and chases away Black's pieces, but on the other hand weakens the king's shelter. The immediate 19 ♘c5 ♘xc5 is harmless, as now White must retake with the bishop and 20 ♗xc5 ♗f6 21 ♕d2 a5 leads to an equal position. The solid 19 e3 ♗e7 20 ♘c5 ♗xc5 21 ♗xc5 ♕b7 22 ♗d4 a5 23 ♕a4 ♗d7 24 ♕c2 ♖ac8 25 f3 was played in M.Gurevich-Ponomariov, Belfort 1998, when after 25...c5! 26 ♗xg7 ♘xg3 Black would have been OK.

19	...	♘g5
20	♘c5	♕e7?!

Kasparov also increases the tension, but this risky retreat practically loses material by force. The modest 20...♕c8 is fully playable and leads to a somewhat passive, but balanced, position after 21 h4 ♘e6 22 e4 ♘xd4 23 ♕xd4 dxe4 24 fxe4 ♗g6.

21 e4!

White changes the move-order from the previous note. Now 21 h4 ♘e6 22 e4?! runs into the strong *zwischenzug* 22...♗c7!. An interesting alternative is 21 ♕a4, but after 21...♕xe2 22 ♖ce1 ♕xe1 23 ♖xe1 ♖xe1 24 ♕xc6 ♗e2! Black's counterplay should be enough to hold the game.

21	...	dxe4
22	fxe4	♗g6

22...♗xe4?! is best refuted by 23 ♘xe4 (23 ♖e1 f5 24 h4 ♗c7 25 ♕b3+! is also strong) 23...♘xe4 24 ♕g4 (24 ♖f4? fails to 24...♘xg3! 25 ♕g4 ♘h5!) and Black loses material; e.g., 24...♕g5 25 ♖ce1 ♕xg4 26 hxg4 ♗f6 27 ♖xe4 ♖xe4 28 ♗xf6.

23 e5 *(D)*

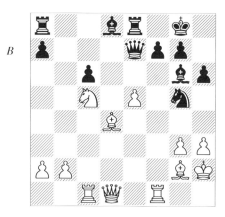

Now Black's position looks very dismal indeed and a real tightrope act is required to keep the game going.

23	...	♗b6!

The only playable move. 23...♖c8 24 h4 is passive and hopeless for Black.

24 h4!

White reacts well and refuses to be tempted by 24 ♗xc6? ♖ad8! (24...♗xc5 is unconvincing due to 25 ♗xc5 ♕e6 26 ♗d7) 25 ♗xe8 (25 h4 ♘e6! and Black is better) 25...♗xc5! (25...♕xe8

26 ♕g4 ♗xc5 {or 26...♘e4!?} is also interesting, but less incisive) 26 ♖xc5 (26 ♗xc5? ♖xd1 27 ♗xe7 ♖d2+ leads to mate, and 26 ♗xf7+ ♗xf7 27 ♖xc5 ♕d7 is dangerous for White) 26...♕xe8, when the only move that barely holds White's position together is 27 ♖f4! (not 27 ♕g4? ♘e6 28 ♖c4 ♗d3 29 ♖fc1 h5 30 ♕h4 f6! and the threat of ...g5 decides).

24 ... ♖ad8!?

Kasparov ups the stakes. Objectively the text-move is a gamble, but the 'solid' 24...♘c6 25 ♘xe6 fxe6 26 ♗xb6! (26 ♗xc6 doesn't win an exchange, as after 26...♗xd4 27 ♗xe8? ♗xe5 the mating threat ...♕xh4+ turns the tables) 26...axb6 27 ♖xc6 ♖xa2 28 ♖xb6 gives White great winning chances in a quiet technical position.

25 hxg5 ♕xg5 (D)

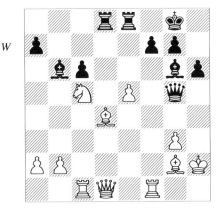

26 ♕a4?!

Züger impatiently unpins his bishop, but his queen wanders too far from the kingside and this will greatly complicate his defensive task. White had better options:

1) 26 e6! ♖xe6! 27 ♘xe6 fxe6 28 ♕e2 might promise White some edge, but is hardly a refutation – his material advantage is small and his king exposed.

2) 26 ♖e1! is stronger. The important e5-pawn is protected and White is ready to consolidate his position further with b4 or ♕a4, not to mention possible activity with e6. After 26...♗c7 (26...♖a5 27 ♘e4 ♕e7 28 ♘d6! ♗xe1 29 ♕xe1 is bad for Black, as the d6-knight is taboo) 27 ♕a4 (27 ♘b7?! ♖xe5 28 ♘xd8 runs into the surprising 28...♕h4+!, and after the forced 29 ♔g1 ♖xe1+ 30 ♕xe1 ♕xd4+ Black has the safer king and counterchances as in line '1') 27...♖xe5 28 ♗xe5 ♗xe5 29 ♖xe5 ♕xe5 30 ♕b4! Black's activity should gradually peter out.

26 ... ♕h5+
27 ♔g1 (D)

After 27 ♔h3? ♖xe5! White can't take on e5 and his position is crumbling; e.g., 28 g4 ♕h4.

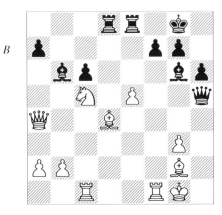

27 ... ♖xe5!

The dark-squared bishop (in this case both White's and Black's!) is worth at least a rook.

28 ♗xe5

Forced. 28 ♗f3? loses at once to 28...♖xd4! 29 ♕xd4 ♖xc5 and after 28 ♘b3 ♕g4 Black will gain the important g3-pawn without sacrifices.

28 ... ♕xe5
29 ♕b4?!

Another important moment. While 29 b4 ♕xg3 leaves the queen offside and is obviously dangerous for White, a much stronger move is 29 ♕c4!. This retains the important option of b4 and also eyes f7, giving White chances to convert his material advantage; e.g., 29...♗d3 30 ♕xf7+ ♔h8 31 b4 ♗xf1 32 ♔xf1 and ♖e1.

29 ... ♖d3!

After 29...♕xg3? 30 ♕f4 Black must disrupt his piece coordination in order to avoid a queen swap.

30 ♖f2

White's king can't retain his shaky pawn-cover with 30 g4?!, since the flexible reply 30...♕g5! (30...♖g3 31 ♖f2 ♕g5 32 ♖c4 ♗d3 33 ♘xd3 ♖xd3 34 ♖cf4 is insufficient) and after 30...♗c7 White can, apart from 31 ♖f2, even simplify the position with 31 ♕f4!?) 31 ♖c4 (after 31 ♕c4 ♖g3 32 ♖f2 ♖xg4 33 ♕c3 Black has 33...♗a5! with a huge attack) 31...♖d2!, with threats of ...♗d3 and ...♖c2, causes him serious problems.

30 ... ♖xg3 *(D)*

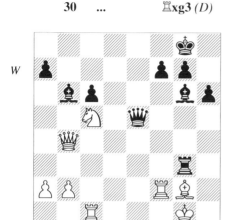

31 ♕f4!?

Prudently returning most of the extra material. After 31 ♕c4 Black has the surprising 31...a5!. This move creates the threat of ...♖g5 and also prevents 32 b4? due to 32...axb4 33 ♕xb4 ♖xg2+! 34 ♔xg2 ♕g5+ 35 ♔h3 ♗c7! 36 ♖c3 ♕g1 37 ♖f4 ♗f5+! 38 ♖xf5 ♕h2+ 39 ♔g4 ♕g2+ with a mating attack.

31 ... ♖xg2+!
32 ♔xg2 ♕d5+
33 ♔g3

33 ♕f3? loses to 33...♕g5+.

33 ... ♗xc5

The final metamorphosis. Although White still has two extra exchanges, his material advantage is negligible and it's clear he is fighting for survival. Once Black fully coordinates his forces, the active bishops will make life hell for the naked white king, not to mention the possible advance of the connected passed pawns.

34 ♖d2 ♕h5
35 ♕g4?

In view of the above note Züger should have grabbed his chance to repeat moves with 35 ♖h2, as 35...♗d6?! 36 ♖xh5 ♗xf4+ 37 ♔xf4 ♗xh5 38 ♖xc6 will cost Black another pawn and can only be better for White.

35 ... ♕e5+
36 ♕f4 ♕e7!

White has missed his chance and now the bishops rule supreme.

37 ♖c3 ♗b6

37...♗b4? is weak due to 38 ♖e3!.

38 ♔g2

White would be glad to give up an exchange for a bishop and a pawn, but now 38 ♖xc6 ♕e1+ 39 ♖f2 fails to 39...♗xf2+ 40 ♕xf2 ♕e5+ 41 ♕f4 ♕xb2 with a won endgame.

38 ... ♕e1

Black's attack plays itself.

39 ♖c1 ♕e6!
40 ♕g3

40 ♖c3 already doesn't help due to 40...♗e4+ 41 ♔f1 (41 ♔h2 ♕e7! threatens both ...♗c7 and ...♗a5) 41...g5 and 40 ♖f1 ♗e4+ 41 ♔h2 ♗d5 is similar.

40 ... ♗e4+
41 ♔h2

41 ♔f1 ♕f5+ 42 ♔e1 ♗f3 43 ♔f1 (43 ♖dc2 ♕e4+ 44 ♔f1 ♗c2+! leads to mate) 43...♗e3 44 ♖d8+ ♔h7 leaves the white king defenceless.

41 ... ♕f5 *(D)*

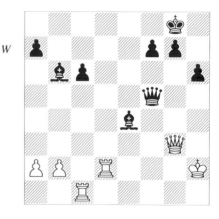

0-1

White lost on time, but there is no effective defence against the main threat 42...♕h5+. After 42 ♕h4 (42 ♖c3 ♕f1 43 ♕e5 f5 with a mating attack) 42...♗c7+ 43 ♔g1 g5! he'll lose too much material.

Game 41
Garry Kasparov – Anatoly Karpov
World Ch match (game 8), Seville 1987
English Opening [A36]

1 c4

Seville was Kasparov's fourth title match against the same opponent in quick succession. He admitted he was suffering from a lack of motivation and also his form was far from ideal. This might explain his deliberate abstention from the sharp opening duels of the previous matches after 1 e4 (see Game 35) and 1 d4 (see Games 30 and 34). 1 c4 was featured in most of the even-numbered games, and Kasparov showed he had grown to become at least Karpov's equal in a manoeuvring struggle, as well as in technical positions (see also Game 42).

1 ... e5

Karpov on the other hand didn't avoid complex play. In his matches with Korchnoi he often transposed into a QGD with 1...e6 or 1...♘f6, but in Seville he played the Reversed Sicilian no fewer than five times and achieved an equal score.

2 ♘c3 d6
3 g3 c5

A very rare guest in Karpov's practice. He played this system for the first and only time in this game. The whole set-up was introduced into practice by Botvinnik, albeit against the Closed Sicilian, when White's pawn is on e4, not c4. However, even against the English it's viable despite the major difference – White's fianchettoed bishop controls the vulnerable light squares. This is usually compensated by Black's central control and if he retains the right minor pieces (e.g., *not* a g7-bishop against a d5-knight!), the hole on d5 doesn't play a major role. This system occurs quite often, only the move-order is different. Black usually plays 1...c5, first fianchettoes his king's bishop and plays ...e5 later on. In our concrete situation Karpov is somewhat behind in development, which gives White an interesting extra option.

4 ♗g2 ♘c6
5 a3! *(D)*

A clever idea: White's flank action is more effective before Black fully consolidates his position. The less enterprising 5 ♘f3 g6 6 0-0 ♗g7 leads to normal English Opening positions.

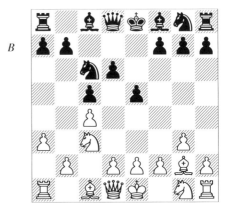

5 ... g6

In similar situations Black usually prefers the prophylactic 5...a5, but here Karpov had to reckon with 6 e3 g6 7 ♘ge2 ♗g7 8 d4!, when White has the initiative thanks to his lead in development and the weakness of the b5-square. However, 5...♗e6!? 6 d3 ♘ge7, fighting for the d5-square, is an interesting alternative.

6 b4 ♗g7

Developing pieces and keeping the position closed is a prudent choice. After 6...cxb4 7 axb4 ♘xb4 8 ♕a4+ ♘c6 9 ♗xc6+ bxc6 10 ♕xc6+ ♗d7 11 ♕b7 (11 ♕a6!?) 11...♖c8 12 ♖xa7 ♖xc4 13 ♘f3 White has a dangerous initiative. 6...♘ge7 avoids the line in the next note and can transpose into the game after 7 ♖b1 (the direct 7 bxc5 dxc5 8 ♘e4 ♗g7 9 ♘xc5 ♕d4 10 ♘b3 ♕xc4 gets White nowhere).

7 ♖b1

Dorfman suggests 7 bxc5 dxc5 8 ♗xc6+ bxc6 9 ♖b1. Black's c-pawns are weak and if White gets to play d3 and ♗e3, he can claim an advantage. However, after the reply 9...f5! his development is slowed down and the position is unclear to say the least. Kasparov spurns such committal options and is satisfied with a small edge.

7	...	♘ge7
8	e3	0-0
9	d3	♖b8

A more active continuation is 9...f5. Now 10 ♘ge2 (after 10 b5 White must reckon with the tactical 10...e4!?) 10...g5 11 b5 ♘b8 12 f4 gxf4 13 exf4 ♘d7 14 0-0 ♘f6 15 ♔h1 ♔h8 16 ♗e3 gave White a pull in Kasparov-Wendt, Frankfurt simul 2000, but Black was not without counterplay and went on to draw the game.

10	♘ge2	♗e6 (D)

10...a6 11 b5!? (11 0-0 cxb4 12 axb4 b5 is less clear) 11...axb5 12 ♖xb5 is also better for White, but 10...f5!? was still an option.

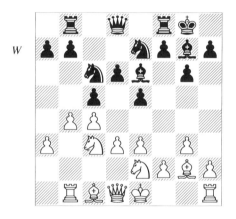

11 b5!

This releases the queenside tension, but misplaces Black's knight. Later this will become a permanent feature of the position.

11	...	♘a5
12	♗d2	

12 e4 f5 13 ♗g5 (13 f4!? is better) 13...h6?! (too cooperative; 13...f4! equalizes) 14 ♗xe7 ♕xe7 15 exf5 gxf5 16 ♘d5 ♕d7 17 0-0 b6 18 ♕c2 ♘b7 19 f4 ♘d8 20 ♖f2 ♔h8 21 ♖bf1 ♗g8 22 ♔h1 ♘e6 23 ♕d2 ♗h7 24 a4 ♖be8 25 a5 gave White a clear advantage in Miles-Bellon, Malmö 1996. The significance of this instructive example will become clear later.

12	...	b6

12...d5?! 13 cxd5 ♘xd5 14 ♘xd5 ♗xd5 15 ♗xd5 ♕xd5 16 0-0 b6 (16...♕d8 17 ♕c2 is no better) 17 ♗xa5 bxa5 18 ♘c3 ruins Black's pawn-structure and leaves White with the already-mentioned ideal knight vs bishop position. However, 12...f5!? is interesting: 13 ♕a4 b6 14 0-0 g5 15 ♘d5 ♘xd5 16 ♗xd5 (16 cxd5! is better) 16...♗xd5 17 cxd5 f4!? with counterplay, Marin-Campora, Andorra open 2000.

13	0-0	♘b7?!

Black gradually slips into a passive position. This was the last chance to play 13...f5! effectively.

14 e4! (D)

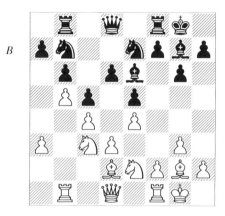

Kasparov radically prevents ...d5 and stabilizes his edge, based on the inability of Black's b7-knight to take part in the fight for the centre.

14	...	♔h8

More or less pointless. 14...h6 prepares ...f5 and is better.

15	♕c1	f5?!

This is another inaccuracy. Once Black has decided to postpone any activity, it was better to play the patient 15...♕d7, followed by ...♖be8, ...♘d8 and possibly a later ...f5.

16	♗g5	♕e8

Black doesn't dare to exchange the important defensive bishop: after 16...♗f6 17 ♗xf6+ ♖xf6 18 f4 White has good attacking chances.

17 ♗xe7!

On the other hand Kasparov has no qualms about exchanging his g5-bishop. With the disappearance of the e7-knight the weakness of d5 becomes apparent and White can realize his plan of light-square domination.

17	...	♕xe7
18	exf5	♗xf5

This was a widely criticized decision, but Miles-Bellon (see the note to White's 12th move) shows that 18...gxf5 19 f4 also gives White a perceptible initiative. In the game the f4 advance is at least not immediately effective and it will take Kasparov a full 24 moves to prepare it properly.

19	♘d5	♕d7
20	♕d2	♘a5?!

A crucial moment. After this move Black will soon be reduced to full passivity. Did Karpov really believe in the absolute invincibility of his position? This is unlikely, so a more complex explanation comes to mind. At the time our game was played Kasparov was trailing by one point and in the long adjournment session of the previous game Karpov missed a good chance to increase his lead. This undoubtedly preyed on his mind and the resulting indecision had serious consequences. Objectively stronger was 20...♘d8 21 a4 ♘f7 22 a5 ♗h6 followed by ...♘g5; although White is undoubtedly better, Black still has chances to make a fight of it.

21	♘ec3	♖be8
22	♘e4	♘b7
23	a4	♘a5
24	h4 *(D)*	

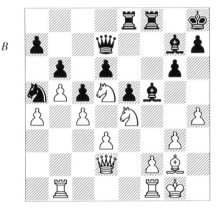

Black has missed the right moment and as his knight has to remain on the queenside, Kasparov starts to concentrate his forces against Black's king.

24	...	♘b7
25	♔h2	♖b8
26	♖a1	♘a5
27	♖a3	

27 ♕c3 or 27 ♕d1!? could have saved White tempi, but Black can only mark time anyway. Therefore Kasparov unhurriedly improves his position and wisely postpones decisive action until after the adjournment.

27	...	♖f7
28	♕c3	♖d8
29	♖a2	

The best square for the rook: from here it pins Black's knight to a5 and can be quickly transferred to the opposite flank – a natural consequence of White's space advantage.

29	...	♗h6
30	♘g5!	♖ff8
31	♖e2	

31 f4? is premature due to 31...♗g7, so White first improves his queen and later returns his rook to the ideal a2-square.

31	...	♗g7
32	♕c2	♖de8
33	♘e3	♗h6
34	♗d5	♗g7

Just as on move 30, the exchange 34...♗xg5?! 35 hxg5 weakens the dark squares. In the long run Black can't withstand the pressure against e5 after f4, ♕c3, ♖fe1, etc.

35	♕d1	h6

The first concession, but otherwise Black would always have to reckon with h5.

36	♘e4	♕d8
37	♖a2	♗c8 *(D)*

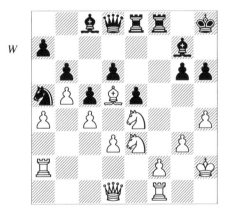

38	♘c3!	

Kasparov has found the most effective set-up: his minor pieces will change places in the centre.

38	...	h5!?

Although this move further weakens the kingside, it at least frees h6 for the bishop and allows Black to prevent, or at least lessen the effect of, the f4 break.

39	♗e4	♖e6
40	♘cd5	♗h6
41	♘g2!	♔g7?!

Despite White's adroit manoeuvring, Black could still have fought on after 41...♗b7!. White's strategic pluses can be realized only by opening the position. Here the direct 42 f4 ♗xd5 43 ♗xd5 ♖ef6 44 ♖af2 retains an advantage, but it's still not decisive after 44...♕d7!?; given the opportunity, Black's knight may re-enter the game via b7 or b3.

42 f4! *(D)*

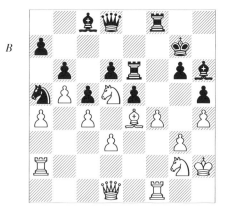

The final phase of White's powerplay begins. Karpov now had the unpleasant duty to seal a move. The swift assault against Black's king will be successful mainly because the a5-knight will remain offside until the bitter end.

42 ... exf4

It's already too late for 42...♗b7 43 f5 and even after the slightly more resilient 42...♖ee8 43 ♖af2 Black can't prevent the opening of the position (f5 or fxe5) for long; for example, 43...♗f5 44 ♗xf5 ♖xf5 45 ♘ge3 (or even 45 g4!?).

43 ♘gxf4 ♖e5

43...♗xf4 44 ♘xf4 ♖ef6 45 ♖af2 is no actual improvement for Black: g6 is under fire and after 45...♗g4 46 ♕c2 ♕e8 47 ♔g2! (47 ♘xg6?! is premature: 47...♖xf2+ 48 ♖xf2 ♖xf2+ 49 ♕xf2 ♘xc4) everything is ready for ♘xg6.

44 ♘xg6!

44 ♗xg6?! ♖xd5! is not so clear, but a good alternative is 44 ♖af2 with the idea 44...♗g4 45 ♘e6+! ♖xe6 46 ♖xf8 ♕xf8 47 ♕a1+. However, the text-move is even more energetic. Kasparov had undoubtedly worked out all the details of the final attack at home.

44	...	♖xf1
45	♕xf1	♖xe4
46	dxe4	♔xg6
47	♖f2	♕e8 *(D)*

47...♕d7 runs into 48 ♖f6+ ♔g7 49 ♖xh6! ♔xh6 50 ♕f6+ ♔h7 51 ♕g5! and Black loses his queen. After 47...♔g7 48 ♖f7 the main threat is ♘e7+ and 48...♗e6 gives White a choice between 49 ♖e7 and 49 ♘e7+ ♔h7 50 ♕f6!, winning.

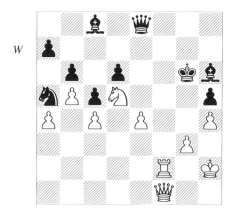

48 e5!

Stronger than 48 ♖f6+ ♔g7 49 ♖xd6 ♕e5.

48 ... dxe5

After 48...♕xe5 49 ♖e2 or 48...♗g7 49 ♕d3+ ♔h6 50 ♘f6 ♗xf6 51 ♖xf6+ ♔g7 52 ♕e3! Black loses immediately.

49	♖f6+	♔g7
50	♖d6	1-0

Defending against the mating attack with 50...♕f7 leads to a lost endgame after 51 ♕xf7+ ♔xf7 52 ♖xh6.

Game 42
Garry Kasparov – Anatoly Karpov
World Ch match (game 24), Seville 1987
Réti Opening [A14]

Just as two years earlier, the fate of the title was going to be decided in the last game after more than two months of a tense match. In both cases the defending champion faced a must-win situation. The most notable difference in Kasparov's predicament was that just one day earlier he lost the penultimate game, his protracted and resourceful defensive effort coming to nought after a gross tactical error. However, the World Champion managed to cope even with this extra psychological burden.

1	c4	e6
2	♘f3	♘f6
3	g3	d5
4	b3	

Compared with Game 32, Kasparov chooses a completely different approach. He avoids forcing opening lines and early tactical complications, intending to keep the pieces on the board and increase the tension only gradually by slow manoeuvring. The double fianchetto system fits this purpose well; Kasparov's early mentor Botvinnik often played it, especially in the last phase of his active career.

4	...	♗e7
5	♗g2	0-0
6	0-0	b6
7	♗b2	♗b7
8	e3 *(D)*	

| 8 | ... | ♘bd7 |

Although 8...c5 is more popular, Black's choice at this point is still a matter of taste. There is nothing wrong with Karpov's more restrained approach; White's quiet handling of the opening gives Black more than one way to achieve a balanced position.

| 9 | ♘c3 | |

9 ♕e2 is slightly more flexible. This often leads only to a transposition of moves after a later ♘c3, but has the merit of avoiding the game continuation.

| 9 | ... | ♘e4 |

Black wants to neutralize White's pressure on the long dark-squared diagonal. Otherwise after 9...c5 White might change his mind and prevent this sortie with 10 d3.

| 10 | ♘e2!? *(D)* | |

An interesting idea. Kasparov avoids the exchange of his knight and opens new vistas for it on the kingside. 10 cxd5 ♘xc3 11 ♗xc3 ♗xd5 12 ♕e2 c5, possibly followed by ...♗f6, is relatively sterile – here it's difficult for White to avoid further simplification.

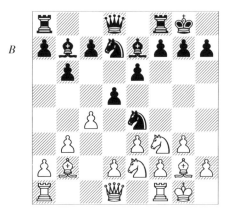

| 10 | ... | a5 |

This move is not so bad in itself, but it doesn't fit in too well with Black's plans and especially his ambitions. More consistent is 10...c5 11 d3

♗f6 12 ♕c2 ♗xb2 13 ♕xb2, when practice has shown Black can gradually achieve full equality after 13...♘d6 and even the untested 13...♕f6!? deserves attention. 10...♗f6 is similar; if White doesn't transpose into the above line with 11 ♕c2 c5 12 d3 and plays 11 d4 instead, then 11...dxc4!? 12 bxc4 ♘d6 followed by ...c5 gives Black definite central pressure and a promising position.

11	d3	♗f6
12	♕c2	♗xb2
13	♕xb2	♘d6

Now 13...♕f6?! 14 ♕c2 isn't ideal, as the knight can't retreat harmoniously to d6 any more.

    14   cxd5   ♗xd5?! *(D)*

Although we have already mildly criticized Black's decisions, objectively speaking only this is Karpov's first minor inaccuracy. More in keeping with 10...a5 is 14...exd5!? 15 d4 c5 with complex play; after 16 dxc5 bxc5 Black's hanging pawns are well supported by his minor pieces. Black aims for a simpler position, but this makes his 10th move not only superfluous, but also potentially weakening.

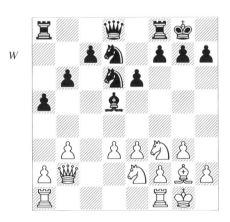

    15   d4!

A flexible move. Kasparov doesn't commit his e2-knight, and occupies the centre first. The tempting 15 ♘f4 is weaker: 15...♗b7 16 d4 (16 ♘h5 f6 17 ♘f4 ♕e7 and White can't effectively prevent ...e5) 16...c5.

    15   ...   c5

Black finally makes a move he could have played much earlier. However, now his minor pieces will start feeling the pressure on the d-file; moreover, his queenside structure becomes vulnerable (b6-pawn, b5-square). The patient alternative 15...♗b7 deserved attention: Black will first finish his development with ...♕e7, ...♖ac8 and ...♖fd8 before undertaking any central activity.

    16   ♖fd1   ♖c8?!

Again a second-rate move. Despite the nearly symmetrical pawn-structure Karpov feels surprisingly insecure. The alternatives were:

1) 16...c4 releases the central tension, but after 17 ♘c3!? (17 ♘f4 b5 18 ♘xd5 exd5 19 ♘e5 ♘f6 is unclear) White is better; e.g., 17...b5 18 bxc4 ♘xc4 19 ♕e2! b4 20 ♘xd5 exd5 21 ♘e5!.

2) The most natural move is 16...♕e7!, when after Kasparov's recommendation 17 ♘c3 ♗b7 18 ♘a4 the advance 18...c4!? is more justified and leads to an unclear position.

    17   ♘f4   ♗xf3

This concession is forced, as 17...♗e4? loses to 18 dxc5 ♘xc5 19 ♕e5 ♘cb7 20 ♘h5, and after 17...c4?! 18 ♘xd5 exd5 19 bxc4 dxc4 20 a4! Black's queenside is in tatters.

    18   ♗xf3 *(D)*

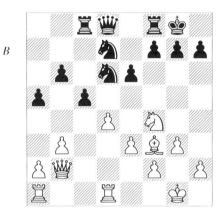

The unopposed bishop on the long diagonal is White's first permanent positional plus and gives him a slight but nagging initiative.

    18   ...   ♕e7
    19   ♖ac1

The decentralizing 19 ♘h5 is best parried by 19...♘e8 and 19 dxc5 ♘xc5 20 ♕e5 ♖fd8 21 ♘d5 ♕a7 also promises little, so White activates his rook first.

19	...	♖fd8
20	dxc5	♘xc5
21	b4!?	

Kasparov realizes the only way to increase his pressure is to open the queenside. 21 a3 is also interesting.

21	...	axb4
22	♕xb4	♕a7
23	a3 *(D)*	

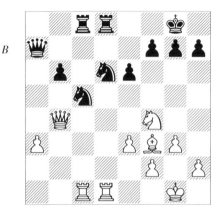

23 ... ♘f5

White's pull stems from his better piece coordination, and also Black's b-pawn is weaker than the a3-pawn (23...b5? fails to 24 ♗e2). In any case Black's knight has to leave d6. 23...♘e8 24 ♘d3!? (24 ♖xd8 ♖xd8 25 a4 ♘f6 26 a5 ♘cd7 only leads to equality) is similar to the game, and after 24...♘f6 25 ♘xc5 ♖xd1+ 26 ♗xd1 bxc5 27 a4! White is somewhat better.

24	♖b1	♖xd1+
25	♖xd1	

After 25 ♗xd1 ♖d8 26 ♗c2 ♖d6 Black consolidates his position.

25 ... ♕c7

The active 25...♕a5!? is also possible. After 26 ♖c1 ♘d6 White's edge remains minimal.

26 ♘d3!

To succeed on the queenside, White must exchange or undermine the c5-knight. After 26 ♖b1 ♖b8 27 a4 ♘d6!? the defence holds, as 28 a5 b5 followed by ...♘c4 or ...♘a6 gives White nothing.

26 ... h6

26...♘xd3 27 ♖xd3 h6 28 ♔g2! (28 ♖b3? is premature, because 28...♕c1+ 29 ♔g2 ♖c2! turns the tables) prepares ♖b3 and forces Black into passivity. Creating some *luft* for the king is natural enough and at this point it's difficult to say if 26...g6 was any better.

27	♖c1	♘e7

Black's position is still solid, but the text-move is rather pointless. Stronger is 27...♘d6!, by which Black prepares ...♘xd3 and after 28 ♘xc5 (28 ♕b1 ♕a7 with equality) 28...bxc5 his passed pawn gets ample support.

28	♕b5	♘f5

Karpov admits his previous move wasn't ideal. After 28...♕a7?! 29 ♘xc5 bxc5 30 a4 ♘f5 31 a5 ♘d6 32 ♕d3! (32 ♕b6? ♕xb6 33 axb6 ♖b8 34 b7 c4! and Black is ready to play ...♘xb7 with a draw) White is clearly better.

29	a4	♘d6
30	♕b1	♕a7

Black must cope with the concrete threat of 31 a5. After 30...♕d8?! 31 ♘xc5 bxc5 (the alternative 31...♖xc5 32 ♖xc5 bxc5 33 a5 is no better) 32 ♖d1 White's passed pawn is decidedly stronger than Black's.

31 ♘e5!? *(D)*

A clever move in the opponent's time-trouble. White abruptly changes the direction of his attack, creating the threat of ♘c6. After 31 ♘xc5 ♖xc5! (weaker is 31...bxc5 32 ♕d3 ♖d8 33 ♕a3!) 32 ♖xc5 bxc5 33 ♕d3 (33 a5? fails to 33...♘c4) 33...♕c7 Black should be able to hold the game.

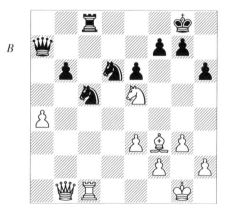

31 ... ♘xa4?

Karpov is disoriented and commits a losing blunder. Black definitely had better moves:

1) After 31...♕xa4? 32 ♕xb6 ♕a3 33 ♖d1 White gains material and retains winning prospects; e.g., 33...♘ce4 (33...♘de4? is weak, as after 34 ♗h5! Black can't play 34...g6? due to 35 ♗xg6 fxg6 36 ♖d8+ with mate; 33...♘e8 34 ♖d8 ♖xd8 35 ♕xd8 ♕a1+ 36 ♔g2 ♕xe5 37 ♕xe8+ leads to a similar ending as in the game)

34 ♖d4!? (34 ♘xf7 ♕a2 35 ♖f1 is possible as well) 34...♕c5 (34...♕c1+ 35 ♔g2 ♕c2 is worse due to 36 ♘d3!) 35 ♕xc5 ♖xc5 36 ♘xf7 with an extra pawn.

2) 31...♘f5 is better, as after 32 ♘c6 ♕xa4 33 ♕xb6 ♘d3 White has no direct win.

3) However, the safest and best defence is 31...♕c7!. Black parries the main threat and White has yet to prove he has anything concrete.

32 ♖xc8+   ♘xc8
33 ♕d1?

The tension shows on White as well, as with enough time on the clock he misses a relatively simple defence. Subsequently Kasparov showed two stronger continuations:

1) 33 ♗h5 f6!? (Black loses quickly after both 33...♘d6? 34 ♕d1 and 33...g6? 34 ♗xg6!) 34 ♗f7+ ♔f8 35 ♗xe6 fxe5 36 ♕f5+ ♔e8 37 ♕xe5! (37 ♗xc8 ♕e7 38 ♗a6 ♘c5 39 ♕g6+ also wins a pawn) is very promising for White. He wins the piece back with an extra pawn, as 37...♘e7? loses to 38 ♕xg7 ♘c6 39 ♕g6+ ♔d8 40 ♗b3.

2) 33 ♕b5! is more complicated, but objectively even stronger: 33...♔h7 (both 33...♘d6? 34 ♕c6 and 33...♔f8? 34 ♘c6 ♕a8 35 ♕d3! g6 36 ♕d4! are hopeless for Black) 34 ♘c6 ♕a8 35 ♕d3+! f5 (35...g6 36 ♕d7 and White's attack breaks through) 36 ♕d8 ♘c5 (the only defence against the threat of ♘e7) 37 ♔g2 and Black is lost even after the tricky 37...♕a2! (37...♕b7 38 ♘e5 ♕b8 39 ♘f7 ♔g6 40 ♕g8 ♔f6 41 ♘h8! and Black's king can't escape after 41...♔e7 42 ♕xg7+ ♔e8 43 ♘g6 followed by ♘e5) 38 h3! (not 38 ♕xc8? ♘d3, when White even loses, while the direct 38 ♘e5 ♕b2 39 ♘f7 fails to 39...♘e7! 40 ♕h8+ ♔g6 41 ♕e8 ♔h7 with a draw) 38...b5 (38...♕a6 allows 39 ♗h5 g6 40 ♗xg6+!) 39 g4. White prepares to take on c8 after gxf5 and Black is more or less in zugzwang.

33 ...   ♘e7?

Karpov overlooks it too! 33...♘c5! forces White to fight for a draw after 34 ♕d8+ ♔h7 35 ♔g2!? (35 ♗d1 f5! gives Black more winning chances) 35...f6 36 ♘c6 ♕d7 37 ♕xd7 ♘xd7 38 ♘d8 ♘c5 39 ♘xe6 ♘xe6 40 ♗g4 ♘c5.

34 ♕d8+

Kasparov decides to play it safe and therefore spurns the attacking continuation 34 ♗h5!?

♘c5 (34...g6? loses to 35 ♕d8+ ♔g7 36 ♘d7!) 35 ♗xf7+.

34 ...   ♔h7
35 ♘xf7

Now 35 ♗h5 ♘c5! 36 ♘xf7 ♘g8 is not so incisive any more.

35 ...   ♘g6
36 ♕e8

After 36 ♘d6 ♘c5 Black's position holds. The text-move is better and wins a pawn by force.

36 ...   ♕e7

Forced, as after 36...♘c5? 37 ♗h5 Black is in terminal trouble; e.g., 37...♕a4 38 ♕xa4 ♘xa4 39 ♗d1! ♔g8 40 ♘xh6+ with a won endgame.

37 ♕xa4   ♕xf7
38 ♗e4   ♔g8

38...e5 is no better: 39 ♕c6 (39 h4 h5 40 g4!? is also promising) 39...♕f6 40 ♕e8.

39 ♕b5

White wants to win the pawn without exchanging minor pieces, as his centralized bishop dominates the board.

39 ...   ♘f8
40 ♕xb6   ♕f6
41 ♕b5   ♕e7
42 ♔g2 (D)

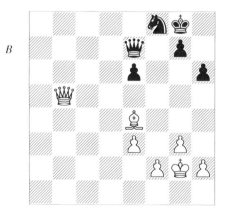

At this point the game was adjourned and Kasparov sealed the text-move. Black's chances to save the game derive from the limited material and space – the play is concentrated solely on one flank. However, White has both a material and a positional advantage and can definitely subject the defence to more or less endless torture. After painstaking analysis Kasparov evaluated his winning chances at 50% and although academically this might be so, Karpov's more pessimistic appraisal (70%) seems closer to the mark, bearing in mind the enormous practical difficulties facing the defender.

42 ... g6

Black's first problem is how to place his kingside pawns. Allowing the cramping h4-h5 is hardly possible, as then by combined play against the two weaknesses on e6 and g7 White can gradually advance his pawns and maybe even activate his king. Thus Black should move his g-pawn, but after 42...g5 43 f4 ♕f6 44 ♔h3! the threat of fxg5 and ♔g4 forces the new weakening 44...gxf4 45 exf4. Now by further advancing his pawns White can create a tandem of united passed pawns. After 42...♕f6 43 h4 g5 Kasparov intended to avoid exchanges and further limit Black with 44 h5!. Therefore Karpov chooses the more passive, but solid, alternative.

43 ♕a5 ♕g7
44 ♕c5 ♕f7
45 h4 h5?

Although now it's difficult for White to advance his own pawns, this move has a major and decisive drawback. As now the weakness on g6 is fixed, White can afford a queen exchange and this enables him to paralyse Black's position completely. Marking time with 45...♔g7 was indicated.

46 ♕c6 ♕e7
47 ♗d3 ♕f7
48 ♕d6 ♔g7
49 e4 ♔g8

More resilient is 49...♕b7, when the e-pawn requires protection.

50 ♗c4 ♔g7
51 ♕e5+ ♔g8

White's last move was just a test; in the endgame after 51...♕f6 52 ♕xf6+ ♔xf6 53 f4 e5 54 ♔f3 ♘d7 55 ♔e3 ♘c5 56 ♗d5 Black can't hold both e5 and g6, as the white king penetrates further.

52 ♕d6 ♔g7
53 ♗b5 ♔g8
54 ♗c6

Kasparov methodically squeezes his opponent.

54 ... ♕a7

55 ♕b4!

55 e5?! ♕a5! ties White to the e-pawn and significantly complicates his task.

55 ... ♕c7
56 ♕b7!

The decisive penetration.

56 ... ♕d8

56...♕e5 57 ♗e8 ♔h8 58 f3 ♕f6 59 ♕f7 doesn't help either.

57 e5! *(D)*

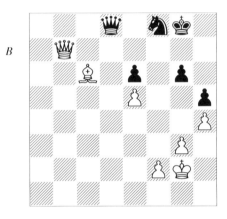

Black is in zugzwang and must allow ♗e8, ♕f7, or a queen swap.

57 ... ♕a5

57...♕d3 58 ♗e8 ♕f5 is just as hopeless due to 59 ♕f3!.

58 ♗e8 ♕c5
59 ♕f7+ ♔h8
60 ♗a4 ♕d5+
61 ♔h2 ♕c5

61...♘h7 loses to 62 ♗c2!.

62 ♗b3 ♕c8
63 ♗d1 ♕c5
64 ♔g2 1-0

After White gets his bishop to e4, Black will be in another zugzwang and even stalemate tricks are insufficient: 64...♕b4 (64...♕a3 65 ♗c2 ♕b4 66 ♗d3 leads to the same position) 65 ♗f3 ♕c5 66 ♗e4 ♕b4 67 f3! (a necessary precaution; White would dearly regret the hasty 67 ♗xg6?? ♘xg6 68 ♕xg6 ♕b7+ 69 ♔h2 ♕g2+!) 67...♕d2+ 68 ♔h3 ♕b4 (68...♕h6 69 f4 ♕g7 70 ♕xg7+ ♔xg7 71 ♗c6 and White's king penetrates via d6) 69 ♗xg6 ♘xg6 70 ♕xg6 ♕xh4+ 71 ♔g2! and White wins.

Game 43
Garry Kasparov – Anatoly Karpov
Optiebeurs, Amsterdam 1988
Caro-Kann Defence [B17]

1	e4	c6
2	d4	d5
3	♘d2	dxe4
4	♘xe4	♘d7
5	♘g5	

Currently this is still the most topical line. In Seville Kasparov didn't cause Black any problems whatsoever with the rather insipid 5 ♘f3 ♘gf6 6 ♘xf6+. Their previous Amsterdam game featured 6 ♘g3 e6 7 ♗d3, and later White obtained a promising attacking position, mainly because Black refrained from the usual 7...c5.

5	...	♘gf6
6	♗d3	

For 6 ♗c4 see Kasparov-Karpov, Linares 1992 (Game 65).

6	...	e6
7	♘1f3 *(D)*	

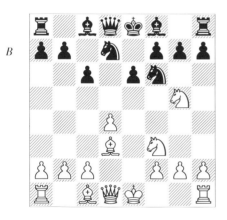

7	...	♗d6

The popularity of 5 ♘g5 rose rapidly when White managed to prove that the piece sacrifice 7...h6 8 ♘xe6! ♕e7 9 0-0 fxe6 10 ♗g6+ ♔d8 11 ♗f4 (or 11 c4!?) gives him rich attacking chances and excellent compensation. The text-move is safer and nowadays Black hardly plays anything else.

8	0-0	

8 ♕e2 has become the modern main line. It's more flexible than the text-move, as White retains the option of castling queenside. Kasparov put it to good use in his subsequent practice; Volume 2 will feature Kasparov-Anand, Linares 1998.

8	...	h6
9	♘e4	♘xe4
10	♗xe4 *(D)*	

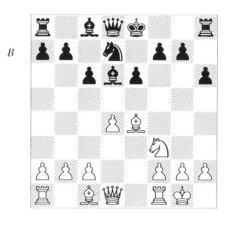

10	...	0-0

A very natural and logical move, but it's not ideal, as Black commits his king a bit too early. In his later games with the 4...♘d7 Caro-Kann, Karpov often successfully left it on e8 or even e7. Winning a tempo with 10...♘f6 11 ♗d3 lessens Black's control over e5, but the most flexible continuation is 10...♕c7!?, followed by ...b6 and ....♗b7, possibly even ...c5. Black can choose from both castling options after White clarifies his plans.

11	c3!	

White prepares a safe retreat for his bishop, indicating he might line up on the b1-h7 diagonal with ♗c2 and ♕d3. Kasparov's move is more accurate than the pseudo-active 11 c4 e5. Here White is a tempo down on a line of the Semi-Slav and the c4-pawn only limits his pieces by closing the a2-g8 diagonal. Also after

11 b3 e5 12 dxe5 ♘xe5 13 ♗b2 ♕c7 Black gradually equalizes.

11 ... e5 *(D)*

Black aims for symmetry, but despite the high drawish tendencies this is exactly the type of position in which the active side can retain and nurse a small edge despite possible simplification. 11...♘f6 12 ♗c2 c5 (or 12...b6 13 ♕d3 c5) is perhaps riskier, but on the other hand it promises Black realistic chances for fully-fledged counterplay.

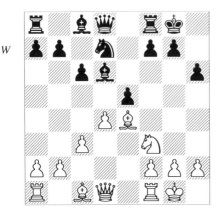

12 ♗c2 ♖e8
13 ♖e1

With his last move Black parried the threat of ♕d3, and by renewing it White forces a release of the central tension.

13 ... exd4
14 ♖xe8+ ♕xe8
15 ♕xd4 ♕e7

Other options don't change the character of the position:

1) 15...♕e2 16 ♗d2 (after other moves Black has nothing to fear; e.g., 16 ♕xd6 ♕xc2 17 h3 ♕g6) 16...♗c5 17 ♕h4 ♕e7 18 ♕g3 (18 ♗g5 ♕e2 only repeats moves) 18...♗d6 19 ♗f4 leads to the game position with three extra moves, which might be useful in time-trouble.

2) 15...♗c5 16 ♕h4 ♕e7 (or 16...♕e2, but not the weaker 16...♗e7?! 17 ♕g3) is the same as in line '1'.

3) 15...♗e7!? is an independent move, deserving attention. After 16 ♗f4 (Karpov suggests he was worried about 16 ♗xh6 gxh6 17 ♖e1, but after 17...♘f8 18 ♕e3 ♗e6 19 ♕xh6 ♕d8 Black intends ....♗f6-g7 and White's attacking chances are too vague) 16...♗f6 17 ♕d3 ♘f8 18 ♖e1 ♗e6 19 ♘d4 ♖d8 20 ♕g3 ♗xd4 21 cxd4 ♔h8 (or 21...♘g6) White has some initiative, but still nothing concrete.

16 ♗f4 ♗xf4
17 ♕xf4 ♘f8 *(D)*

17...♘f6?! is weaker, as after 18 ♖e1 Black can develop his bishop only at the cost of creating a permanent weakness. White is clearly better after 18...♗e6 19 ♘d4 or 19 ♗b3.

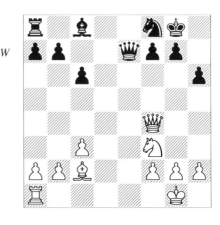

18 ♖e1 ♗e6

Black can't well avoid remaining with his knight against White's active bishop, as e6 is the only suitable square for the c8-bishop.

19 ♘d4 ♖d8

After 19...♖e8!? White must avoid the trap 20 ♘f5? ♗xf5! 21 ♖xe7 ♖xe7, when the back-rank mating threat costs him material. However, 20 h4 leads to a similar position as in the game.

20 h4 ♕c5

Black can play 20...♕d6 immediately. This recommendation of Karpov's was tested in a later game. After 21 ♘xe6 ♘xe6 22 ♕e4 ♘f8 (22...♔f8? 23 g3 ♕c5 24 ♗b3 ♖d2 25 ♖e3 ♕e7 26 ♖f3 ♔g8 27 ♖xf7! ♔xf7 28 ♕f4+ netted White a pawn in Ulybin-Georgadze, Simferopol 1988) 23 ♗b3 (23 h5 ♕e6 24 ♗b3 ♕xe4 25 ♖xe4 ♘e6! is less impressive) White for the time being avoids simplification and keeps Black under slight pressure.

21 ♖e3 ♕d6
22 ♘xe6 fxe6? *(D)*

This inexplicable move was probably based on an oversight. After the natural 22...♘xe6 23 ♕e4 ♘f8 White's advantage remains only minimal.

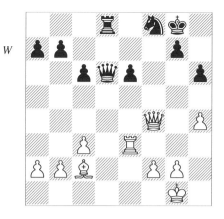 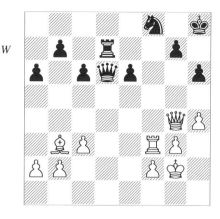

23 ♕g4!

23 ♕a4? ♕d2 leaves White too passive, while after 23 ♕e4 ♕d5 he finds it difficult to prevent a queen swap. The text-move avoids exchanges, as keeping both major pieces on the board is ideal for the active side.

23	...	♕d2
24	♗b3!	

24 ♖c2 ♕c1+ 25 ♔h2 ♖d2 trades rooks and helps the defence.

24	...	♔h8

Perhaps Karpov hadn't realized that after 24...♕xb2 25 ♖g3 Black has to defend g7 passively with 25...♕b1+ 26 ♔h2 ♕h7, when after 27 ♗xe6+ ♘xe6 28 ♕xe6+ ♔h8 29 ♕f7 White wins a pawn. He also has the more active pieces and good winning chances.

25	♖e2	♕d6
26	g3	

26 ♗xe6? is premature due to 26...♘xe6 27 ♕xe6 ♕xe6 28 ♖xe6 ♖d1+ 29 ♔h2 ♖d2 with a drawn endgame. The text-move consolidates White's advantage. He has the better minor piece, Black's knight is tied to the defence of e6 and moreover his kingside is seriously weakened. It's interesting to note the parallel between this game, especially its final phase, and the endgame from Game 42 against the same opponent.

26	...	a6
27	♔g2	♖e8

Black's rook must leave the open file, as White was ready take on e6. The pseudo-active 27...e5?! 28 ♕f5 would only be a further concession.

28	♖e3	♖e7
29	♖f3	♖d7 (D)

30 ♕h5

White could have played 30 ♖f4 (with the idea of ♕f3) immediately, but Kasparov knows only too well that he won't win the game on the kingside alone – the position is too simplified for this. White starts probing on both flanks to increase the pressure and create new weaknesses.

30	...	♕e7

Understandably enough, Black doesn't let White's queen invade via e8 or f7.

31 ♕e5 (D)

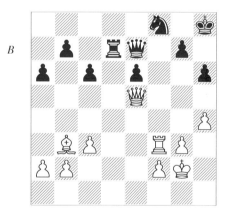

31	...	♖d8
32	a4!	

Left to his own devices, White could gain more space and continue a5, ♗c4, b4, etc. With the b7-pawn fixed on a light square, Kasparov could later even exchange a pair of major pieces at a suitable moment and try to penetrate with his king to the queenside via the weak dark squares.

32	...	b5

Black plays actively to avoid the scenario from the previous note, but this move gives White new potential targets.

33 ♕e4 ♕c7

After 33...c5?! 34 ♕c6 c4 35 ♗c2 Black's queenside is crumbling.

34 ♖f4

34 ♗xe6? is premature and throws away White's advantage after 34...♖e8 35 ♗d5 ♕d8!. However, more incisive is 34 axb5 cxb5 (34...axb5? is weaker due to 35 ♕b4!, when Black has to give up material to prevent a decisive invasion on the 7th rank) 35 c4!? (35 ♗xe6 ♖e8 36 ♗d5 ♖xe4 37 ♖xf8+ ♔h7 38 ♗xe4+ g6 is not too convincing; e.g., 39 ♖f6 ♕e5! 40 ♗xg6+ ♔g7 41 ♖xa6 ♕d5+ with a draw by repetition or 39 ♖a8 ♕c4 40 ♔f3 ♕f7+ 41 ♔e3 ♕f6), when White opens the position and starts playing against the weak a-pawn as well.

34	...	c5
35	♕f3	♕d6
36	axb5	axb5
37	♖f7	♖b8?! *(D)*

Black also misses a better defence. 37...c4 38 ♗c2 ♔g8 is more resilient, with the tactical point 39 ♖b7 ♕d7! and 40 ♖xb5? runs into 40...♖f7 41 ♕e4 ♕d2, turning the tables. Karpov didn't want to commit his queenside pawns to the light squares, but now White's control of the 7th rank will be uncontested.

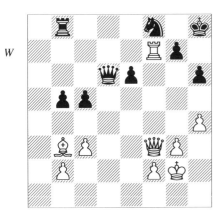

38 ♖a7

38 ♗c2!? is perhaps even stronger.

38	...	b4
39	♗c2	bxc3
40	bxc3	♕e5
41	♖f7	

41 c4! is technically cleaner. The pawn leaves a vulnerable square and White can concentrate on attacking its black counterpart with ♕f7-c7.

41 ... ♘h7

41...♔g8 42 ♖e7 transposes to the position after move 44.

42 ♕g4 *(D)*

42 c4 with the idea 42...♕d4 43 ♕d3 still deserved attention.

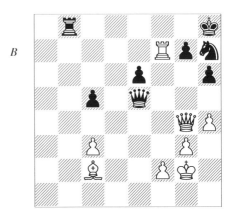

42 ... ♔g8

42...♕xc3? loses on the spot to 43 ♕e4 ♔g8 44 ♖f3, and Karpov does his best to avoid the dreary endgame after 42...♘f8 43 ♕e4 ♕d5 (43...♕xe4+ 44 ♗xe4 ♖c8 45 ♖e7 with a zugzwang) 44 c4 ♕xe4+ 45 ♗xe4 ♖d8 46 ♗c6, when Black will lose his c-pawn after ♖c7 and ♗b5.

43	♖e7	♘f8
44	♕f3	c4!?

Although now the c-pawn can also be attacked with the bishop, this move gives Black more chances to exchange the queenside pawns and ease his defence. 44...♕f6 45 ♖c7 is similar to the previous note, as 45...♕e5 46 ♕f7+ ♔h8 47 c4! doesn't help.

45	♗e4	♔h8
46	♗c6	♘h7

Black can't activate his knight as 46...♘g6 leads to a hopeless queen endgame after 47 ♖e8+ ♖xe8 48 ♗xe8 ♔h7 49 ♗xg6+ ♔xg6 50 ♕g4+.

47 ♕f7 ♘f8

The best move. 47...♕f6 48 ♖e8+ ♖xe8 49 ♕xe8+ ♘f8 50 ♗b5 is untenable for Black.

48	♖e8	♖xe8
49	♗xe8	♘h7! *(D)*

Trying to keep material equal as long as possible would leave Black paralysed after 49...♕d5+ 50 ♔g1 ♕c5 51 ♗a4. White will transfer his bishop back to e4, improve his king and prepare ♕e8-c6 with a won minor-piece endgame.

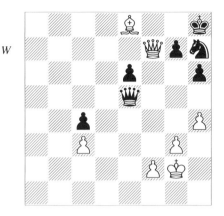

W

| 50 | ♗d7 | ♘f6 |
| 51 | ♗xe6 | h5 |

Black needs some space for his king. The immediate 51...♕e4+ 52 ♔h2 ♕c2 (52...♕f3? loses the queen to 53 ♕f8+ ♔h7 54 ♗g8+! ♔g6 55 ♕f7+ ♔f5 56 ♗h7+ ♔e5 57 ♕e7+ ♔d5 58 ♕b7+) 53 ♕f8+ ♔h7 54 ♕c5! ♕xc3 55 ♗f5+ is hopeless for Black.

| 52 | ♗xc4 | ♕e4+ |

Karpov does his best to complicate the issue. After 52...♕xc3 53 ♕f8+ ♔h7 54 ♕c5! ♕d2 (54...♔h6 55 ♕g5+ ♔h7 56 ♗f7 doesn't help) 55 ♕f5+ ♔h8 56 ♗f7 ♕e2 57 ♗g6 ♕g4 58 ♕d3 ♘d5 (58...♕c8 59 ♕f3 is similar) 59 ♔g1 White wins a second pawn in a technically straightforward endgame.

| 53 | ♔h2 (D) | |

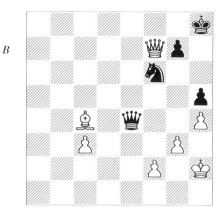

B

| 53 | ... | ♔h7?! |

Black's last hope was 53...♕f3 54 ♕f8+ (54 ♔g1 ♕xc3 and with his king on g1 White can't concentrate his pieces against the h5-pawn as in the previous note) 54...♔h7 55 ♕c5 ♘e4 56 ♗d5 ♕xg3+ 57 fxg3 ♘xc5 58 ♔g2 (or 58 ♗f3). This ending should be won for White, but he must still show some care, as he has the 'wrong' bishop for his h-pawn.

| 54 | ♕e6 | ♕f3 |
| 55 | ♕e1 | ♘g4+ |

Now after 55...♘e4 the simplest is 56 ♗e2.

| 56 | ♔g1 | |

The rest is easy. White has two extra pawns for nothing.

56	...	♕c6
57	♗d3+	g6
58	♕e7+	♔h6
59	♗e4	♕b6
60	♕f8+	♔h7
61	♕f7+	♔h6
62	c4	♕a6
63	c5	1-0

The c-pawn is unstoppable.

Game 44
Ljubomir Ljubojević – Garry Kasparov
World Cup, Belfort 1988
Sicilian Defence, Scheveningen Variation [B81]

1	e4	c5
2	♘f3	e6
3	d4	cxd4
4	♘xd4	♘f6
5	♘c3	d6
6	g4	♘c6!?

Only rarely did Kasparov allow the dangerous Keres Attack in his practice. Here he even spurns the safer option 6...h6, which he played in his very first match-game against Karpov. The text-move, recommended as logical by Kasparov in his book on the Scheveningen Sicilian, is nevertheless risky, as it gives White a free hand to develop a dangerous kingside initiative. Black's choice can be explained by the tournament situation – at this moment Kasparov was trailing the leader Ehlvest by a half-point and had to score even with Black to keep in contact. Glancing a bit forward, he managed to solve his task in great style: this game was the first of a series of five wins, which decided the tournament in his favour.

| 7 | g5 | ♘d7 *(D)* |

| 8 | ♖g1 | |

Basically White can attack Black's kingside with his own pawns, or his pieces; e.g., ♖g1-g3 and ♕h5. The best method appears to be a combined one and the whole line is currently in disrepute mainly due to the more flexible 8 ♗e3. After 8...♗e7 9 h4 0-0 White doesn't need his rook on g1 at all and can play the dangerous 10 ♕h5! instead. A nice sample line is 10...a6 11 0-0-0 ♘xd4 12 ♗xd4 b5 13 ♗d3 ♘e5 (13...b4 14 ♘d5! exd5? loses quickly to 15 ♗xg7!) 14 f4 ♘xd3+ 15 ♖xd3 ♗b7 16 ♖g1 b4 17 ♘d5 exd5 18 ♖dg3! and Black has no good defence against the threat of ♕h6, Movsesian-Cvitan, Bundesliga 1997/8.

| 8 | ... | ♗e7 |
| 9 | ♗e3 | 0-0!? |

Kasparov castles into it, this time spurning his own double-edged recommendation 9...♘b6 with the idea ...d5.

| 10 | ♕d2 | |

10 ♕h5 is now less impressive and leads to an unclear position after 10...g6 11 ♕h6 ♘de5 12 0-0-0 f6! 13 gxf6 ♗xf6. Therefore White often prefers to start the piece attack with 10 ♖g3. With the text-move Ljubojević indicates he wants to return to the pawn-storm plan after tucking away his king.

10	...	a6
11	0-0-0	♘xd4
12	♗xd4	

The other recapture 12 ♕xd4 is unclear after 12...b5 13 f4 ♕a5.

| 12 | ... | b5 *(D)* |

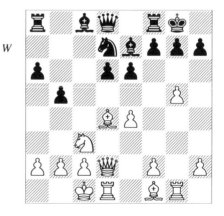

13 f4?!

This move gives Black's counterplay a further impulse, as White can now become active both on the queenside and in the centre. The prophylactic 13 a3! is stronger, as it slows Black down considerably. After 13...♖b8 14 ♖g3 there is not enough time for ...♗b7-c6 and ...a5, so Black should play some prophylactic moves of his own with 14...♖e8 15 h4 ♗f8. Nevertheless it seems White's chances in the upcoming struggle are better.

13 ... b4
14 ♘e2

White chooses the more logical and safer centralizing route for his knight. After 14 ♘a4?! it slows down Black's impending counterattack, but doesn't help out in the centre and becomes vulnerable itself: 14...e5 (the more restrained 14...♕a5!? 15 b3 ♗b7 is fully playable as well; Black retains the choice between ...e5 and ...♗c6) 15 ♗e3 exf4 (15...♕a5!? 16 ♕d5 ♕xa4 17 ♕xa8 ♕xa2 is also good for Black) 16 ♗xf4 ♕a5 more or less forces the rather speculative piece sacrifice 17 ♗xd6!? (17 b3?! is too passive; Black is better after 17...♘c5). After 17...♗xd6 18 ♕xd6 ♕xa4 19 ♗c4 ♕a5 20 g6 ♕e5! 21 gxf7+ ♔h8 22 ♕xb4 (22 ♕h6 ♗b7! gets White nowhere) 22...♖b8 Black has reasonable chances to consolidate his position fully.

14 ... ♕a5
15 ♔b1

15 a3? only weakens the queenside; after 15...♖b8 16 ♔b1 ♘c5 Black is better.

15 ... e5! (D)

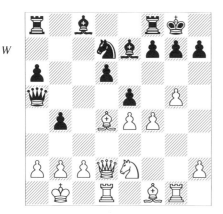

16 ♗f2?!

16 ♗e3 ♘c5 appears more natural, when White's best is 17 ♗g2 (17 ♘g3 exf4 18 ♗xf4 ♗e6 with the idea 19 b3 ♘a4! gives Black a dangerous initiative; 17 ♗xc5 dxc5 18 f5 ♖d8 is also pleasant for Black) 17...♗e6 18 b3 exf4 19 ♗xf4. This position arose in Dvoirys-Scherbakov, Cheliabinsk 1989; now 19...♖ac8 20 ♘d4 ♔h8!? is difficult to evaluate unequivocally.

16 ... ♘c5
17 ♕e3

Here after 17 ♗g2 ♗e6 (or 17...exf4) White's pieces are not as well coordinated as in the previous note.

17 ... ♗e6 (D)

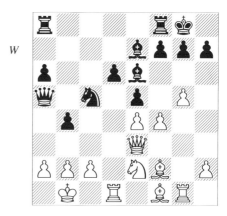

18 ♘c1

Ljubojević was reluctant to move a pawn in front of his king and preferred a safe but passive move. Instead, 18 b3 keeps the knight in touch with the kingside. White ruthlessly pursues his own ambitions and Black can't very well ignore the threat of f5-f6:

1) 18...exf4 19 ♘xf4 is good for White: compared with Dvoirys-Scherbakov quoted above, his f1-bishop can quickly land on c4.

2) 18...♖ac8?! 19 f5 d5 is a wild tactical attempt, which Kasparov refutes with 20 fxe6 (20 ♗g2? d4 21 ♕g3 d3! turns the tables) 20...♘xe4 21 ♗e1!? ♗c5 (21...♖xc2 is insufficient due to 22 a4) 22 exf7+ (22 ♖xd5 ♗xe3 23 ♖xa5 ♖fd8 24 ♖g4 is probably good for White as well) 22...♖xf7 23 ♕h3 ♕c7 24 g6! hxg6 25 ♖xg6 ♗e3 26 c4 bxc3 27 ♔c2. Black's attack is over and the counterattack is coming fast after, for example, 27...d4 28 ♗g2 ♘f6 29 ♗h4.

3) However, the issue is unclear if Black reacts in kind and stops the immediate threat with the prophylactic 18...g6!. From d2 White's queen helped the defence as well, and moving it too far away from the queenside may lead to trouble; e.g., 19 ♕f3?! d5! 20 exd5 ♗f5 with a strong attack.

18	...	exf4
19	♕xf4	♖ac8
20	♗d4 (D)	

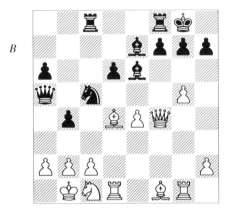

20 ... ♖fe8

This prophylactic move frees f8 for the bishop and takes the sting out of ♗f6. A worthy alternative was 20...♕c7!? with a small edge. The direct threat is ...♘b3, and later Black can transfer his knight to e5 via d7.

21 ♘b3!?

21 h4 ♕c7 is comfortable for Black, so Ljubojević tries to throw a spanner in the works.

21 ... ♕a4

Kasparov indicates that 21...♕c7!? was still playable; after 22 ♗xc5 dxc5 23 ♕xc7 ♖xc7 24 ♗xa6 ♖a8 25 ♗b5 g6! followed by ...♔g7 and ...h6 the active bishop-pair and better pawn-structure give Black full compensation.

22 ♗f6?

This sortie is pointless and loses valuable time. White can't accomplish anything with piece-play and should have tried to get his pawns going with 22 h4. Black can't allow h5 and g6 without a fight:

1) 22...♕c6 23 ♗xc5 dxc5 24 ♘a5 ♕c7!? (24...♗xa2+? 25 ♔xa2 ♕a4+ 26 ♔b1 ♕xa5 27 ♗c4 is out of the question and 24...♕a4 25 ♘c4 is slightly worse for Black) 25 ♕xc7 ♖xc7 26 ♗c4 ♗f8 with approximate equality.

2) More ambitious is 22...♘d7!? 23 h5 ♘e5 24 h6!? (24 ♗xe5 dxe5 25 ♕xe5 ♗f8 with good compensation) 24...♕c6 25 ♖g2 with an unclear position.

22	...	♗f8
23	♖g3	

It was more prudent to admit the mistake with 23 ♗d4!?, although after 23...♕c6 or 23...a5 Black is better.

23 ... ♕c6 (D)

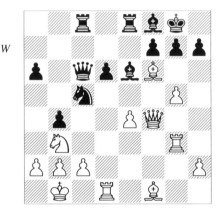

24 ♘xc5

The double attack on c2 and e4 forces this serious concession. Now Black's pawns start rolling.

24	...	dxc5
25	♗e5	

The attempt to stop the phalanx with 25 c4? fails to 25...bxc3 26 ♗xc3 ♗xa2+!, while after 25 e5 c4 26 ♗g2 ♕a4 the f6-bishop is cut off from the defence and the threats of ...b3 and ...c3 decide.

25	...	c4
26	♗d6?	

Black's pawn-storm is far more effective than any attempts White might undertake on the kingside. Therefore Ljubojević at least tries to close the d-file by creating an outpost on d6, but his attempt fails tactically. 26 c3 is more resilient, although after 26...♖cd8 27 ♖xd8 ♖xd8 28 ♗e2 ♕a4 Black retains a strong attack.

26	...	b3
27	c3	

White wants to prevent the deadly opening of queenside files after 27 cxb3 cxb3 28 ♖c3 ♕a4! or 27 ♗xf8 bxc2+ 28 ♗xc2 ♕a4+ 29 ♔c1 c3! 30 ♖xc3 ♖xf8!. The logical follow-up to 26 ♗d6? at least gives him the consolation of losing brilliantly.

27	...	♖cd8
28	e5	♗xd6

28...♗d5 was also good enough, but Kasparov has something far more concrete on his mind.

| 29 | exd6 *(D)* | |

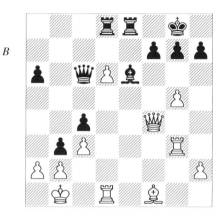

Can White generate some counterplay with his passed pawn?

| 29 | ... | ♖xd6!! |

A real hammer-blow based on White's back-rank weakness.

| 30 | ♖c1 | |

The rook was taboo:

1) 30 ♖xd6 ♗f5+ 31 ♔c1 (31 ♕xf5 ♖e1+ mates immediately) 31...bxa2 and the pawn queens with a quick mate.

2) 30 ♕xd6 ♗f5+ 31 ♔c1 bxa2 32 ♕a3 ♕e4 33 ♖gd3 (33 ♗d3 loses quickly to 33...♕f4+) 33...cxd3 34 ♕xa2 d2+! 35 ♖xd2 ♕f4 and Black wins.

| 30 | ... | ♕c5 |

The rest is simple. White's back rank is chronically weak and Black's major pieces can invade via the open central files.

31	♔a1	♖ed8
32	♖e3	

32 ♗e2 ♖d2 doesn't help.

32	...	♖d1
33	♖e1	♖xe1
34	♖xe1	♕a5
35	a3	♕d5
36	♗e2	g6
37	h4	♕d2 *(D)*

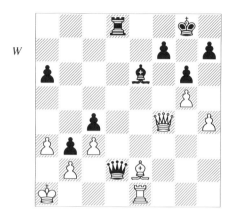

| 38 | ♕f1 | |

After 38 ♕xd2 ♖xd2 39 ♔b1 ♔g7 White's king remains trapped and his pieces paralysed, while Black creates a passed pawn on the kingside. Ljubojević doesn't want to prolong his suffering.

38	...	♗h3
39	♕g1	♖e8

0-1

After 40 ♕f2 ♗g4 41 ♖f1 ♗f5! 42 ♖e1 ♗d3 43 ♖f1 ♖e7 Black wins a piece.

Game 45
Garry Kasparov – Ulf Andersson
World Cup, Belfort 1988
Queen's Gambit Declined [D36]

1	d4	♘f6
2	c4	e6
3	♘c3	d5
4	cxd5	exd5
5	♗g5	c6
6	♕c2	

The alternative move-order 6 e3 ♗e7 7 ♗d3 allows the simplifying 7...♘e4!?, something Kasparov was intent on avoiding.

6	...	♗e7
7	e3	♘bd7
8	♗d3	0-0

Andersson was sufficiently impressed to try 8...♘h5 in a later encounter. After 9 ♗xe7 ♕xe7 10 ♘ge2 g6 11 0-0-0 ♘b6 12 ♘g3 ♘g7! 13 ♔b1 ♗d7 14 ♖c1 0-0-0 15 ♘a4 ♘xa4 16 ♕xa4 ♔b8 17 ♖c3 b6 18 ♗a6 ♘e6 19 ♖hc1 ♖he8 20 ♕b3 ♕d6 21 ♘f1 ♖a8 22 ♘d2 ♘c7 23 ♗f1 he should have gone for the unclear 23...♕xh2! 24 ♘f3 ♕d6 25 ♘e5 ♖xe5. The passive 23...♘e6 24 g3 ♖c8 25 ♗g2 left Black under pressure in Kasparov-Andersson, Reykjavik (World Cup) 1988.

9	♘ge2	♖e8
10	0-0	♘f8 *(D)*

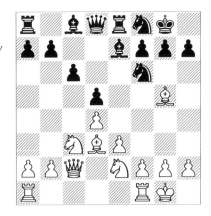

11 f3!

For a long time the queenside was considered White's natural region of activity in the Exchange Queen's Gambit. Black in turn tested and found satisfactory methods to counter the minority attack initiated by the advance of White's b-pawn. Kasparov employs a different strategy – White has an extra pawn in the centre and intends to make full use of it by pushing his e-pawn. These intentions are best furthered by White's text-move. Even here one can see the influence of Botvinnik, mentioned in the notes to Game 42. Botvinnik-Keres, USSR Ch (Moscow) 1952 went 11 ♖ab1 ♗d6?! 12 ♔h1! ♘g6 13 f3 ♗e7 14 ♖be1 ♘d7 15 ♗xe7 ♖xe7 16 ♘g3 ♘f6 17 ♕f2 ♗e6 18 ♘f5 ♗xf5 19 ♗xf5 ♕b6 20 e4 dxe4 21 fxe4 ♖d8 22 e5 ♘d5 23 ♘e4 with a clear advantage for White. Another noteworthy example is 11 a3 g6 12 b4 ♘e6 13 ♗h4 a6 14 f3! ♘g7 15 ♗f2! h5 16 h3 and in Kasparov-Beliavsky, Moscow (exhibition game) 1987 White was better, as everything is ready for e4. One can see Botvinnik toyed with the idea of the minority attack and flexibly changed his mind only after Keres's dubious reaction, while Kasparov had other intentions and his queenside expansion was meant mainly as a prophylactic measure directed against Black's future counterplay with ...c5.

11 ... ♗e6

The most direct method to counter White's plans is 11...c5?!, but Kasparov has shown that even after exchanging on d4 Black can't reckon with full equality despite the symmetrical position (see the notes to Game 39). Moreover, in this concrete situation White has the strong 12 ♗xf6!? ♗xf6 13 dxc5 ♖xe3 14 ♖ad1 and Black's d5-pawn is too vulnerable. The text-move was relatively new at the time our game was played, but has become one of the main lines since. White has been doing fine after 11...♘h5 12 ♗xe7 ♕xe7 13 e4 dxe4 14 fxe4 ♗e6 15 ♖f2!. Another popular alternative is 11...♘g6. Now 12 ♖ad1 (or 12 e4 dxe4 13 fxe4 ♗e6 and now 14 h3 c5! or 14 ♖ad1 ♘g4 followed by a quick ...c5 gives Black sufficient counterchances) is most often met by 12...♗e6, transposing back into lines that can arise after 11...♗e6.

12 ♖ae1

Once again the immediate 12 e4 is slightly premature due to 12...dxe4 13 fxe4 ♘g4 14 ♗xe7 ♕xe7 15 ♕d2 c5 and Black either dismantles or advantageously blockades White's centre. Therefore the central push requires extra preparation, but instead of Kasparov's move more recent practice prefers 12 ♖ad1, which lends more support to White's centre. Black's best replies are 12...♘g6 or 12...♖c8 with complex play. The extra tactical point in comparison with the text-move becomes apparent after the weaker 12...♘6d7 13 ♗xe7 (13 ♗f4!? is also possible) 13...♕xe7 14 e4 dxe4 15 fxe4 and here the typical 15...c5?! fails to 16 d5 and the d-pawn marches on, as 16...c4? is met by 17 ♗xc4 ♕c5+ 18 ♖d4.

12 ... ♖c8 (D)

Andersson plays the most common move, but the immediate 12...♘6d7!? deserves attention and is possibly stronger. Kasimdzhanov-Yusupov, Erevan Wcht 2001 continued 13 ♗xe7 ♕xe7 14 ♘f4 ♕d6 15 ♕f2 ♖ad8 16 ♔h1 ♘b6 17 b3 ♗d7 18 ♘ce2 and now Yusupov recommends 18...♕h6!?; countering the e4 thrust with the threat of ...g5 leads to approximate equality.

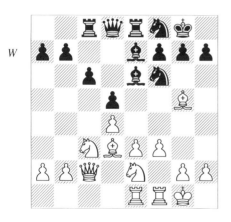

13 ♔h1

A useful multi-purpose move: White sidesteps any possible checks on the a7-g1 diagonal and frees g1 for other pieces, should the necessity or opportunity (♖g1, g4, etc.) arise.

13 ... ♘6d7

13...c5 hasn't been tested yet. Kasparov indicates White can not only hold the tension, but also play 14 dxc5!? followed by ♘d4 with an edge.

14 ♗xe7 ♖xe7

Later Black tried the more active 14...♕xe7!? with success. After 15 ♕d2 (15 e4 dxe4 16 fxe4 c5 17 d5 c4! 18 dxe6 ♕xe6 is only equal and 15 ♘f4 ♕d6 16 ♕d2 ♖cd8 is very similar to Kasimdzhanov-Yusupov above) 15...♘b6 16 b3?! (16 e4 is more consistent and the only way to fight for an edge) 16...♖cd8 17 a4 ♕b4 18 ♘e4 ♕xd2 19 ♘xd2 ♗d7 20 ♘g3 a5 21 ♖e2 ♘c6 White lacks a constructive plan and his position is already somewhat uncomfortable, Lutz-Yusupov, Tilburg 1993.

15 ♘f4

Kasparov is patient. After 15 e4 Black again has 15...dxe4 16 fxe4 c5 17 d5 ♘e5! with good counterplay. The same goes for 15 f4 ♘f6 16 f5 ♗d7.

15 ... ♖c7?! (D)

The start of an artificial plan that allows White's pull to take a more concrete shape. 15...♘f6 16 ♕d2 ♖d7 is stronger, as Black has managed to prevent e4, though after 17 b4 White retains an edge.

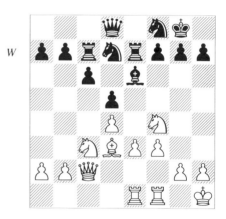

16 ♕f2!

White is still in no hurry. After 16 e4 dxe4 17 fxe4 Black's knight may choose a different route than in the game: 17...♘b6!? 18 ♘ce2 ♗g4 keeps White's central pawns in check.

16 ... ♘f6?!

Even here 16...♘b6! is better. Then 17 e4 dxe4 18 fxe4 ♖cd7 19 d5 cxd5 20 ♗b5 ♖c7 21 exd5 ♗f5 is not so convincing, as contrary to the game the a7-pawn is not *en prise*. Probably it is more promising to keep the tension and continue the preparations with 17 ♖d1, retaining the initiative.

17 e4 dxe4

Allowing e5 would mean suffering without counterplay.

18 fxe4 ♖cd7 *(D)*

18...♘g4 19 ♕g1 (see the note to 13 ♔h1) doesn't improve Black's chances at all. Andersson's idea was to put White's centre under pressure. However, he underestimated the dynamic potential of White's position.

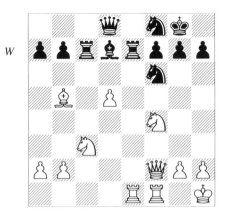

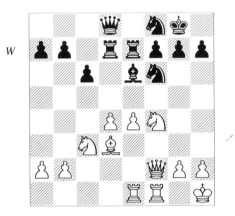

19 d5! cxd5

Otherwise Black loses quickly; for example, 19...♗g4? 20 h3 ♗h5 21 e5 or 19...♘g6? 20 dxe6 ♘xf4 21 exf7+!.

20 ♗b5!

The real point of the central break. 20 exd5? ♘xd5 leads only to simplification and squanders White's advantage.

20 ... ♖c7

Black's rook must abandon the d-file. After 20...dxe4 21 ♗xd7 ♕xd7 (21...♗xd7? is even more costly due to 22 ♘fd5 ♖e6 23 ♘xe4!) 22 ♘xe4 White has an exchange for a single pawn and very good winning chances.

21 exd5 ♗d7!? *(D)*

This is Black's best chance. 21...♘xd5? loses material after 22 ♘fxd5 ♗xd5 23 ♖d1 ♖e5 24 ♗c4! ♖xc4 25 ♖xd5, and other bishop moves cost Black at least the a7-pawn.

22 ♗e2!

22 d6? is weak due to 22...♖xe1 23 ♕xe1 ♖xc3! 24 ♗xd7 ♖c4, and 22 ♕xa7?! ♖xc3 is also a bad idea for White. 22 ♖xe7 ♕xe7 is unconvincing as well, because after 23 ♗xd7 ♖xd7 24 ♕xa7 g5 Black regains the pawn. White's surprising retreat is in fact a double attack, as the threats of d6 and ♕xa7 can't both be parried. Thus Black loses material and the game is more or less decided. One can only wonder how Kasparov's creative play often quickly gets the otherwise ultra-solid Swedish grandmaster into big trouble (see also Games 15 and 29).

22 ... ♖c8 *(D)*

22...♘e4 is no better, because after 23 ♕xa7, 23...♘xc3? is out of the question due to 24 d6. 22...♗f5 gives White a choice between 23 ♕xa7 and 23 d6 ♕xd6 24 ♘b5, so Black moves his rook out of the possible forks.

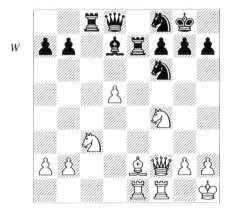

23 ♕xa7

White cashes in. A tempting alternative is 23 d6 ♖e5 (Black can't defend the f6-square satisfactorily; after 23...♖e8 24 ♘h5 ♖e6? White has the decisive 25 ♘d5!) 24 ♘fd5, but after 24...♘g6!? (24...♘xd5? is weak owing to 25

♘xd5!) immediate material gains give Black some counterplay and otherwise White can claim only a large positional advantage.

23 ... b6

If White manages to consolidate his position, his victory should be a matter of technique. This goes for 23...♘e4 24 ♕d4! (24 ♘xe4 ♖xe4 25 ♘d3 allows 25...♗b5! 26 ♕xb7 ♕d7!? with complications), so Andersson prefers to cut off White's queen.

24 ♕a6 *(D)*

The passive 24 ♕a3?! ♕e8 causes White problems on the e-file, but the more direct 24 d6!? ♖e5 25 ♗f3 ♖a5 26 ♕b7 deserved attention. Black can't hurt White's queen, which in turn lends support to the passed d-pawn.

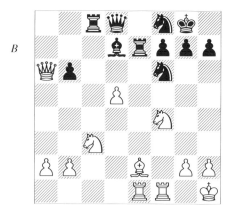

24 ... ♘e4?

After more resilient continuations such as 24...♘g6 25 ♘xg6 hxg6 26 ♗f3 and 24...♖e3 25 ♗f3 (or 25 ♖d1) White retains a healthy extra pawn, which he can gradually convert into victory. The weak text-move allows White to increase and transform his advantage by tactical means.

25 d6!

This blow stops any possible play on the e-file and wins the b6-pawn.

25 ... ♘xd6

25...♖e5 26 ♘xe4 ♖xe4 27 ♘d5 is hopeless for Black.

26 ♘fd5 ♖e5 *(D)*

26...♖e6 27 ♕xb6 ♕g5 would have at least kept the queens on the board.

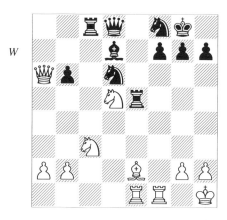

After the move played White forces an easily won endgame.

27	♕xb6	♘f5
28	♕xd8	♖xd8
29	♗d3	

The queenside passed pawns will decide the game, and further exchanges limit any possible counterplay. The rest is trivial.

29	...	♖xe1
30	♖xe1	♘g6
31	a4	♘d4
32	a5	♔f8
33	♗xg6	

As more pieces disappear from the board the pawns become unstoppable.

33	...	hxg6
34	♖d1	♘e6
35	♘b6	♗c6
36	♖xd8+	♘xd8
37	b4	♘e6
38	b5	**1-0**

Game 46
Garry Kasparov – Andrei Sokolov
World Cup, Belfort 1988
English Opening [A19]

1	c4	♘f6
2	♘c3	e6
3	e4	

Despite a one-point lead before the last round, Kasparov was in an aggressive mood. With the text-move he avoids the more sedate Queen's Gambit or one of the Indian defences and prefers one of the sharpest lines of the English Opening.

| 3 | ... | c5 |

This game started a turn of the tide in the favour of 3...d5 4 e5 d4 5 exf6 dxc3 6 bxc3 ♕xf6 7 d4 (or 7 ♘f3!?). Although this alternative also gives White some chances to fight for the initiative, it's safer than Sokolov's choice.

| 4 | e5 | ♘g8 |
| 5 | ♘f3!? | |

Early pawn sacrifices for the initiative have always belonged to Kasparov's arsenal, one of the most striking examples being Game 31. The less enterprising 5 d4 cxd4 6 ♕xd4 ♘c6 7 ♕e4 d6 8 ♘f3 dxe5 9 ♘xe5 ♗d7! makes life easier for Black and only leads to equality.

| 5 | ... | ♘c6 |

Black in turn does best to accept the challenge, as after 5...d6 6 exd6 ♗xd6 7 d4 White has a pleasant edge for free.

| 6 | d4 | cxd4 |
| 7 | ♘xd4 | ♘xe5 (D) |

| 8 | ♘db5 | |

The most popular continuation. 8 ♗f4 increases White's lead in development, but doesn't promise anything concrete after 8...♘g6 9 ♗g3 a6 or even 8...d6!?.

| 8 | ... | a6 |

White's previous move guarantees him at least the bishop-pair and chances to play on the dark squares, as the direct way to prevent ♘d6+, 8...d6?, leads to big trouble after 9 c5!. White regains the pawn with a large advantage, as 9...dxc5? loses on the spot to 10 ♗f4. 8...f6 often transposes into the game after 9 ♗e3 a6, as 9...b6?! 10 f4 ♘c6 11 f5 with the idea 11...exf5 12 ♘d5 gives White a dangerous attack.

9	♘d6+	♗xd6
10	♕xd6	f6
11	♗e3	♘e7

Black naturally wants to chase White's queen away from its outpost. However, after 11...♘f7 12 ♕g3 White forces a concession – Black either weakens his kingside, or returns the pawn.

| 12 | ♗b6 | ♘f5 |
| 13 | ♕c5! (D) | |

This move and White's whole plan was not new at the time our game was played, but Kasparov deserves credit for recognizing its merits. Being a pawn down it's only natural to avoid an exchange of queens, but surprisingly enough previously the main line went 13 ♗xd8 ♘xd6 14 ♗c7 ♔e7 15 c5 ♘e8 16 ♗b6 d5 17 cxd6+ ♘xd6 18 0-0-0 (or 18 ♗c5). Here White has enough compensation to hold the balance, but not more.

| 13 | ... | d6 |

Subsequent practice also featured 13...♕e7. Paradoxically enough, here White can flexibly change his mind and play 14 ♕xe7+! (also 14 ♕a5 ♘c6 15 ♕a4 ♕d6!? 16 c5 ♕e5+ 17 ♕e4 d5 18 cxd6 ♘xd6 19 ♕xe5 ♘xe5 20 0-0-0 is playable; White gets a better version of the above line) 14...♔xe7 (weaker is 14...♘xe7 15

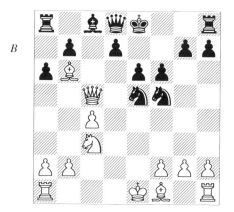

c5! and Black's queenside remains immobilized) 15 f4 ♘g6 16 g3. As White hasn't played c5 yet, Black can't free himself with a timely ...d5 and remains under heavy pressure after 16...d6 17 ♗h3! ♗d7 18 0-0-0 ♗c6 19 ♖he1 ♔f7 20 ♘d5!, Bacrot-Dorfman, French Ch (Marseilles) 2001.

14 ♕a5

14 0-0-0 is interesting, but unclear after 14...0-0 (14...♕e7 is not ideal, because 15 ♕a3 leaves White a tempo up on the game) or even 14...♕d7!? followed by ...♕c6.

14 ... ♕e7

Later Kasparov had to face 14...♕d7. After 15 f4 ♘c6 16 ♕a3 e5?! (16...♘ce7! 17 0-0-0 ♕c6 is more consistent and better; and although White has attacking chances after both 18 ♕b3 and 18 ♕a5!?, the position remains unclear) 17 ♗d3 0-0 18 0-0 White had more than enough for the pawn and the misguided 18...exf4? 19 ♖xf4 ♘fe7 20 ♖d1 ♘g6 21 ♖ff1 ♘ge5 22 ♗e4 ♕f7 23 b3 enabled him to equalize material and retain a huge positional advantage in Kasparov-Beliavsky, Linares 1991.

15 0-0-0

Aggressive and very natural. However, the previous note indicated White also has a less committal alternative in 15 f4 ♘c6 16 ♕a3 0-0 17 ♗d3!? followed by 0-0. Black has fewer tactical counterchances with the white king on g1 and faces similar problems as Beliavsky did in the above game.

15 ... 0-0
16 f4 ♘c6?!

16...♘f7?! is too passive and gives White a free hand both in the centre and on the kingside, which he can exploit by 17 ♗d3 or 17 g4.

However, Black still could have fought for dark squares: the more energetic 16...♘d7!? 17 ♗c7 b6 18 ♗xb6 ♘xb6 19 ♕xb6 ♗b7 leads to an unclear position.

17 ♕a3 e5 *(D)*

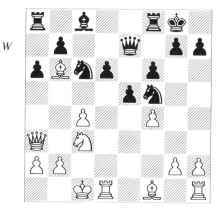

Although this move weakens the light squares (especially d5), it gives Black control over d4 and is the only chance to lash out before White fully mobilizes his whole army.

18 g4!

The only predecessor to our game went 18 c5 ♕f7! 19 cxd6 ♘fd4 20 ♗d3 ♗c6 21 fxe5 ♘b5! 22 ♕c5 ♘xc3 (22...♘xe5!? is playable as well) 23 ♕xc3 ♘xe5 and in R.Hernandez-Am.Rodriguez, Havana 1980 Black had more than enough queenside play to hold the balance. Amador Rodriguez even gave the text-move in his notes, but underestimated its strength.

18 ... ♘fd4

A natural reaction. Rodriguez recommended 18...♘h6?!, but this is too passive. After 19 ♘d5 followed by h3 Black remains under heavy pressure.

19 ♘d5 ♕f7

19...♕d7?! is weaker. After 20 f5 Black's development is a problem and threats such as ♗c7 or ♗g2, followed by ♗xd4 and ♘b6, are in the air.

20 f5 g6! *(D)*

Sokolov finds the only chance to enliven his cramped position. Despite the obvious risk his decision deserves praise.

21 ♖g1!?

21 fxg6 hxg6 (21...♕xg6?! is weaker due to 22 ♗xd4 exd4 23 ♖xd4! with a strong attack) 22 h3 ♗e6 23 ♗g2!? (23 ♕xd6 ♖ad8! 24 ♗xd8

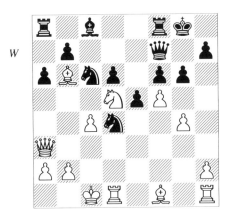

♖xd8 gives Black real compensation) 23...♕d7 24 ♕e3 retains the pressure, but Black at least gets some breathing space in a simpler position. Instead Kasparov increases the tension. The text-move leads to great tactical complications, but up to a certain point Sokolov defends well.

21	...	gxf5
22	g5!	♔h8!

After 22...fxg5 23 ♖xg5+ ♔h8 24 ♕xd6 White has the direct threat of ♖xd4! and after 24...♘e6 25 ♖g2 he has a strong attack. Black's queenside pieces are still undeveloped and moving the central pawns only opens diagonals against his own king.

23 gxf6

23 ♘xf6 ♗e6 24 ♕xd6 ♗xc4 is unclear, while 23 ♕xd6 ♗e6 can transpose either into the above line, or the game.

23 ... ♗e6 *(D)*

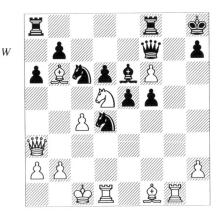

24 ♕xd6

The immediate 24 ♖g7 ♕h5 gets White nowhere, as after 25 ♕xd6? ♗xd5 26 ♕xd5 (26 cxd5 runs into 26...♕h6+ and ...♖xf6) 26...♖xf6 27 ♖xb7 ♘b4! it's suddenly Black who has a decisive attack.

24 ... ♗xd5

Black logically gets rid of an important attacking unit. ♖g7 was already a serious threat and 24...♖g8? 25 ♗xd4 exd4 26 ♖g7! (26 ♖xg8+ ♖xg8 27 ♖e1 is probably also sufficient) wins for White; e.g., 26...♖xg7 27 fxg7+ ♔xg7 28 ♘c7 ♗xc4 29 ♗xc4! ♕xc4+ 30 ♔b1 with a winning attack.

25 cxd5 ♕xf6!

This tactical trick justifies Black's previous move. 25...♖ad8? 26 ♗xd8 ♖xd8 fails to the heavy blow 27 ♖g7!.

26	♕xf6+	♖xf6
27	♔b1!	*(D)*

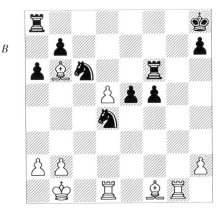

27 ... ♘d8!?

Black's central outpost is crumbling and it's not easy to wade through all the alternatives:

1) Weak is 27...♘e7? 28 ♗c7 ♘f3 29 ♖g3 and the d-pawn is ready to rush forward.

2) 27...♘b4 28 ♗xd4 (28 ♗c7!? ♖e8 29 ♗c4 is also promising) 28...exd4 29 ♖xd4 a5 30 a3 leaves White distinctly better even though he no longer possesses the bishop-pair.

3) 27...♘b8 28 ♗xd4 exd4 29 ♖xd4 ♘d7 30 ♗h3 is a similar story to line '2'.

4) 27...♘a7 28 ♗c7 ♖e8 29 d6! (here regaining the pawn with 29 ♗xe5 ♖xe5 30 ♖xd4 ♘c8 gets White nowhere, as Black's knight is well placed) 29...♖f7 30 ♗b6 (30 ♗c4!? ♖d7 31 ♖g2 is also interesting) 30...♘ac6 31 ♗g2 ♖d7 32 ♖ge1 gives White compensation and pressure, so Sokolov's choice was probably the right one.

28 ♗c5!?

28 ♗c7 ♘f7 and 28 ♗xd4 exd4 29 ♖xd4 ♘f7 followed by ...♘d6 both get White nowhere. Instead Kasparov keeps his bishop and creates the threat of ♖xd4.

28 ... ♖c8

An ambitious alternative is 28...b6!? 29 ♗e7 ♖f7 30 d6 (30 ♗d6?! ♘f3 31 ♖g3, by analogy to the game continuation, runs into 31...♘b7!) 30...♘8c6 31 ♗c4 ♖xe7 32 dxe7 ♘xe7 33 ♖ge1. The resulting position is far from clear, but White holds the initiative. Black's forces are uncoordinated and his pawns are not yet sufficiently advanced to pose serious threats.

29 ♗e7 ♖f7 *(D)*

Black's king is in danger after 29...♖h6 30 d6 ♘8c6 31 ♗c4; e.g., 31...♖g6 (31...♘xe7? loses to 32 dxe7; the threats of ♖g8+ and ♗f7 decide) 32 ♖xg6 hxg6 33 ♗f6+ ♔h7 34 ♖d3 with an ongoing attack.

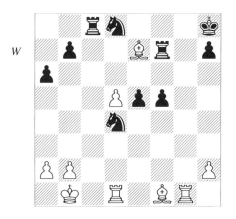

30 ♗d6 ♘f3
31 ♖g3 e4

Black is still doing his best. The weaker 31...♖d7? would cost him a pawn after 32 ♖xf3 ♖xd6 33 ♖xf5.

32 ♗e2 ♖f6?!

After defending resourcefully, Sokolov slips and allows White to increase his pull.

1) 32...♖g7?! also isn't ideal, as 33 ♗xf3 ♖xg3 34 ♗xe4! is similar to the game. Black can't retain the extra exchange; e.g., 34...♖g5 35 ♗c7 ♖h5? 36 ♖g1! gives White a decisive attack.

2) 32...♖d7 is better. After 33 ♗f4 ♘f7 34 ♗xf3 exf3 35 ♖xf3 ♔g7 (35...♖cd8?! is weaker due to 36 ♗d2!) Black's pieces are well placed to fight the passed pawn and White has only a small edge.

33 ♗f4 ♖g6

The rook is misplaced on f6, and the comparison with the line '2' above after 33...♘f7 34 ♗xf3 exf3 35 d6 (or 35 ♖xf3) is definitely in White's favour.

34 ♗xf3 ♖xg3? *(D)*

Black's attempt to simplify the position is understandable, but the text-move loses practically by force. He should have opted for 34...exf3 35 ♖xf3, although White is clearly better thanks to the stronger minor piece and dangerous d5-pawn.

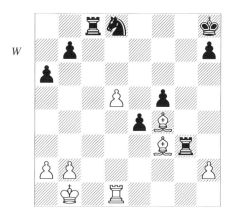

35 ♗xe4! fxe4

Black can't keep the extra material; due to the threats ♗xf5 and ♗e5(+) his rook has no safe escape.

36 hxg3

White has regained the sacrificed pawn with a decisive positional superiority.

36 ... ♔g7

The weak e-pawn is lost anyway. 36...♘f7 37 d6 ♔g7 38 d7 ♖a8 39 ♗c7 e3 40 ♖e1 is hopeless for Black.

37 ♖d4 ♘f7
38 ♖xe4 ♖d8
39 ♖e7 ♖xd5

39...b5 40 d6 ♔f8 is more resilient.

40 ♖xb7

Now the a-pawn can't survive for long.

40 ... h5
41 ♖a7 a5
42 a4! 1-0

There is no good defence against ♗c7, which wins after almost all reasonable moves.

Game 47
Garry Kasparov – Vasily Ivanchuk
USSR Ch, Moscow 1988
English Opening [A29]

1	c4	♘f6
2	♘c3	e5
3	♘f3	♘c6
4	g3	♗b4

Nowadays the Reversed Dragon with 4...d5 has become more popular. Kasparov hasn't had the position after 4...♗b4 on the board too often, but his contribution to White's cause has certainly played a role in the shift of trends.

5	♗g2	0-0
6	0-0	

White spurns the more direct continuations 5 ♘d5 and 6 ♘d5, giving Black a chance to double the c-pawns. In the Seville title match Kasparov had this position three times with White and gained a meagre point despite achieving promising positions, so one can easily understand his eagerness to 'rehabilitate' himself.

6 ... e4

Ivanchuk chooses the sharpest option. 6...♖e8 7 d3 ♗xc3 8 bxc3 e4 9 ♘d4 h6 was played in Kasparov-Karpov, Seville Wch (16) 1987, and here White came up with the surprising novelty 10 dxe4! ♘xe4 11 ♕c2 d5 12 cxd5 ♕xd5. Now the best continuation is 13 ♖d1 ♗f5 14 ♕b2! ♘xd4 15 cxd4 ♕d7 16 ♗f4 with a permanent advantage for White, Portisch-Salov, Tilburg 1994. A solid, if somewhat passive, alternative is to keep the pawn-structure unchanged with 6...d6.

7 ♘g5

7 ♘e1 ♗xc3 8 dxc3 h6 promises White little chance to fight for an advantage. The text-move is more enterprising.

7	...	♗xc3
8	bxc3	♖e8 *(D)*
9	f3	

It's obvious that White must remove Black's e4-pawn to fight for the initiative. With the text-move he strives for an asymmetrical position, as this promises his bishops more scope. In this sense his sharp choice is more logical than the less aggressive line 9 d3 exd3 10 exd3

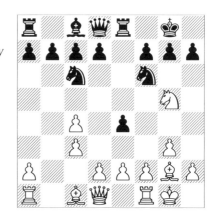

h6 11 ♘e4 b6 12 ♗f4 ♗b7 with approximate equality.

9 ... exf3

The whole drama in Seville began with the surprising novelty 9...e3!?. Kasparov invested a lot of time and found a good reaction: 10 d3 d5 11 ♕b3!. After 11...♘a5 12 ♕a3 c6 13 cxd5 cxd5 14 f4 ♘c6 (later Black's play was improved by 14...♗g4! 15 ♘f3 ♘c6 16 h3 ♗d7 with complex play, but this was only in the mid-1990s) 15 ♖b1 ♕c7 16 ♗b2 ♗g4 and now in Kasparov-Karpov, Seville Wch (2) 1987 the patient 17 ♖fe1! would have given White an edge. Kasparov played the dubious 17 c4?! and later mishandled the resulting complications in time-trouble. In any case he was willing to repeat this line against Ivanchuk and Karpov himself, but they both thankfully declined the offer and chose the older text-move instead.

10 ♘xf3 d5

10...♕e7?! 11 e3 ♘e5 12 ♘d4! ♘d3 13 ♕e2 ♘xc1 14 ♖axc1 d6 15 ♖f4 c6 16 ♖cf1 ♕e5 17 ♕d3 ♗d7?! (17...♖f8! is stronger) 18 ♘f5 ♗xf5 19 ♖xf5 ♕e6 20 ♕d4 ♖e7 21 ♕h4! gave White a crushing attack in Kasparov-Karpov, Seville Wch (4) 1987. However, why did Karpov avoid the official theoretical recommendation? Ivanchuk is curious and decides to find out, and Kasparov gladly obliges...

11 d4!

Black's previous move is seemingly illogical, as it opens the position for White's bishops. However, passive play would allow White to build up a strong pawn-centre and the long-term factors would start working in his favour. Therefore Black wants to remind White that 9 f3 has its drawbacks as well, namely the weakening of the kingside. The previously played 11 cxd5 ♕xd5! 12 ♘d4 (even after other moves Black plays ...♕h5) 12...♕h5 13 ♘xc6 bxc6 14 e3 ♗g4 demonstrates this clearly and gives Black good attacking chances. With the text-move Kasparov prevents such activity and starts energetically fighting for the centre, while developing his own kingside initiative.

11 ... ♘e4 *(D)*

A logical reaction. 11...dxc4?! is inferior due to 12 ♗g5, while after 11...h6 12 ♕c2 dxc4 13 ♗f4 Black won't be able to prevent e4 for long, and White's strong centre will give him attacking chances.

12 ♕c2!

As in Game 46, Kasparov improves upon an earlier example. However, there is little doubt that both 11 d4! and this move were part of his preparation for Karpov. 12 cxd5 ♘xc3 13 ♕d2 ♘xd5 (13...♘e4!? seems even better) 14 e4 ♘f6 15 e5 ♘e4 led to an unclear position in Vaiser-Dzhandzhgava, Uzhgorod 1988.

12 ... dxc4

12...♗f5!? was an interesting later try to hold on to the central outpost. After 13 ♘h4 ♗g6 14 ♘xg6 hxg6 15 ♗f4 (or 15 ♕d3) Black controls the light squares and his position remains solid, but White's play on the semi-open files and his active bishops give him a slight edge.

13 ♖b1!

White fights for the centre from the flank. The rook move makes it difficult for the c8-bishop to control e4, and it also takes the sting out of possible tactics in some lines; e.g., 13 ♘h4 ♕d5 14 ♖f4?! f5 and now 15 g4? runs into 15...♘xd4!. Kasparov also mentions the more forcing alternative 13 ♘e5 – even here White can claim good compensation after 13...♘xe5 14 ♕xe4 ♘g6 15 ♕d5 ♕e7 16 e4.

13 ... f5

Black fortifies his centralized knight, but Kasparov energetically demonstrates that the e4-outpost remains vulnerable. However, even after other moves the defence is not easy:

1) 13...♖b8?! is too passive and the c6-knight becomes a tactical weakness. After 14 ♘h4 ♕d5 (14...♕e7? fails to 15 ♖f4) 15 ♖f4 f5 16 g4! g5 17 ♖xf5! ♗xf5 18 ♘xf5 White has a strong attack for the exchange.

2) After 13...h6?! Black wants to play ...♗f5, but now White can change tack and 14 ♘e5! (here the tactics after 14 ♘h4?! ♕d5 15 ♖f4 f5 16 g4 g5 17 ♖xf5 work in Black's favour owing to 17...♘xd4! 18 cxd4 ♕xd4+ 19 e3 ♕d3) 14...♘xe5 15 ♗xe4 followed by ♗h7+ gives him a large advantage.

3) 13...f6 is also insufficient: after 14 ♘e5! ♘xe5 (14...fxe5? 15 ♗xe4 is even more dangerous for Black) 15 ♗xe4 ♘g6 16 ♖f2 White is better.

4) 13...♕e7 14 ♘d2! ♘g5 15 e4 resolved the question of central control in White's favour in Hodgson-Naumkin, Amantea 1995.

14 g4! *(D)*

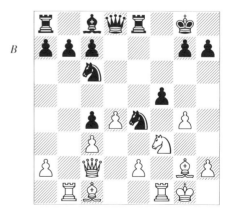

This mighty blow creates new problems for Black.

14 ... ♕e7?!

The text-move is not ideal, but White holds the initiative even after other continuations:

1) After 14...♘d6 15 ♗g5 ♕d7 16 ♗f4! with the idea ♘e5 White is fully developed, while Black has trouble getting his pieces out.

2) 14...g6 15 ♗f4 ♗e6?! (15...♘f6 16 ♕a4 ♘xg4 17 ♘g5! is dangerous for Black, but 15...♘d6!? is somewhat better) 16 ♖xb7 ♗d5 17 gxf5! ♘xd4 18 cxd4 ♗xb7 19 fxg6 hxg6 20 ♘e5 and Black's position is on the verge of collapse, Smirin-Avrukh, Groningen open 1996.

3) The principled 14...fxg4! is more testing: 15 ♘e5 ♘xe5 (15...♘d6 16 ♘xc6 bxc6 17 e4! is very good for White; his g2-bishop is worth more than the a8-rook and Black's extra c-pawns present a sorry picture) 16 ♗xe4 ♘g6 17 ♗xg6 hxg6 18 ♕xg6 ♕d7 (the only move; otherwise ♖b5-h5 quickly decides). Now Da Costa Junior recommends 19 ♖f2!? (19 d5 a5! 20 ♖f6 ♖a6 and 19 ♖b5 ♖e6! 20 ♕h5 ♕e8 both get White nowhere). White plans ♗a3, or ♗f4-e5 and has an edge because of the opposite-coloured bishops – his is the more active one.

15 gxf5 (D)

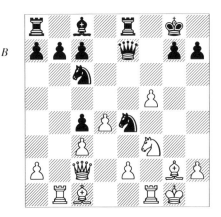

15 ... ♘d6?

Ivanchuk is shell-shocked and succumbs quickly. 15...♗xf5 is practically the only move, when Kasparov intended 16 ♘g5! (16 ♘e5 ♘xe5! 17 ♖xf5 ♘g4 promises Black distinct counterplay) 16...g6 (16...♗g6 17 ♘xe4 ♗xe4 18 ♗xe4 ♕xe4 19 ♕xe4 ♖xe4 20 ♖xb7 ♖c8 21 ♗a3!? with the threat of ♖xc7 is similar) 17 ♗xe4 ♗xe4 18 ♘xe4 ♕xe4 19 ♕xe4 ♖xe4 20 ♖xb7 ♘e7 (otherwise White plays ♗h6) 21 ♖xc7 ♖xe2 22 ♖xc4 with a clear endgame advantage. The united passed pawns, supported by the bishop, will be very strong.

16 ♘g5 ♕xe2

This loses by force, but allowing an advance of the e2- or f5-pawn would give White an overwhelming position; for example, 16...♘d8 17 ♗d5+ ♔h8 18 f6! gxf6 19 ♖xf6.

17 ♗d5+ ♔h8
18 ♕xe2 ♖xe2
19 ♗f4 (D)

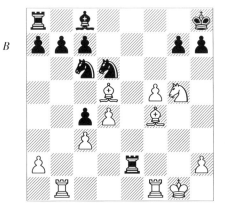

Black's queenside pieces are completely offside and he can't prevent a decisive invasion via the recently opened e-file.

19 ... ♘d8

This allows a mating attack. 19...♗xf5? 20 ♗xd6 ♗xb1 loses on the spot to 21 ♘f7+ ♔g8 22 ♘d8+. After 19...♘xf5 20 ♘f7+ ♔g8 21 ♘d8+ and ♘xc6 Black loses a piece, and the same goes for 19...♘e7 20 ♗f3 ♖xa2 21 ♗xd6 cxd6 22 ♖be1. 19...h6 is slightly more resilient, but after 20 ♗xd6 hxg5 (20...cxd6 21 ♘f7+ ♔h7 22 ♘xd6 is no better) 21 ♗xc7 Black is lost, as he still can't finish his development.

20 ♗xd6 cxd6
21 ♖be1 ♖xe1
22 ♖xe1 ♗d7
23 ♖e7 ♗c6

23...h6 24 f6! is similar.

24 f6! 1-0

White forces mate after 24...♗xd5 25 ♖e8+ ♗g8 26 f7.

Game 48
Garry Kasparov – Ilia Smirin
USSR Ch, Moscow 1988
King's Indian Defence, Classical Main Line [E97]

1	♘f3	♘f6
2	c4	g6
3	♘c3	♗g7
4	e4	d6
5	d4	0-0
6	♗e2	e5
7	0-0	

Kasparov only exceptionally reaches this position with White. In Game 9 we saw him play 7 ♗e3.

7	...	♘c6
8	d5	♘e7
9	♘d2	

This move was the height of fashion in the late 1980s and early 1990s. One of its main practitioners was Karpov. Kasparov had already to face it once in this tournament and decided to give this solid line a try from the opposite side of the board. Despite this fine effort he never returned to 9 ♘d2 again and proceeded to develop the theory of the line for Black.

9	...	a5

After the weaker 9...♘d7 10 b4 f5 11 c5! White's knight quickly comes to c4 and his queenside play usually develops much faster than Black's kingside attack. On the other hand, while the knight remains on d2 it somewhat impedes the deployment of the queenside forces, so slowing down White's build-up makes good sense. Thus 9...c5 and especially the text-move have become the main continuations.

10	a3	

The slower 10 b3 gave Black approximate equality after 10...c5!? 11 a3 ♘e8 12 ♖b1 f5 13 b4 axb4 14 axb4 b6 15 ♕b3 ♘f6 16 ♗d3 ♗h6 17 ♖b2 ♖a1 18 ♕c2 ♗f4 in Karpov-Kasparov, Seville Wch (17) 1987. While in positions of this type White doesn't have any targets on the queenside, he is usually the first to occupy the open files with his major pieces. Thus the d6-pawn becomes vulnerable and Black's chances for a successful kingside attack are minimal. Bearing this in mind, in his later games against 9 ♘d2 Kasparov avoided the set-up with ...c5 and strove for more full-blooded counterplay.

10	...	♘d7

Black again turns his sights to the kingside. A possible alternative is 10...♗d7 11 b3 c6!? with central counterplay. 10...c5, with similar ideas as in the above note, is also playable.

11	♖b1	f5
12	b4 *(D)*	

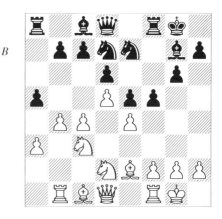

12	...	b6?!

This piece of prophylaxis seems excessive. It has the further drawback that Black can't play ...c6 later on. It soon disappeared from tournament practice and 12...♔h8 13 ♕c2 (13 f3 c6 14 ♔h1!? is the latest hit), as played in Gavrikov-Kasparov, USSR Ch (Moscow) 1988, became the main line. Nowadays Black mostly prefers 13...♘f6 (Kasparov's games featured 13...♘g8 14 f3 ♘gf6; Black aims for kingside piece-play with ...♘h5 and ...♘df6, but 15 ♗d3!? forces him to close the position with 15...f4 and this gives White an edge) 14 f3 c6, combining kingside and central counterplay.

13	f3	

White fortifies the e4-pawn, thereby preventing Black's possible plan ...fxe4 and ...♘f5-d4.

13	...	f4

As we have already seen in the note to move 12, this typical advance is rather committal in the 9 ♘d2 line. However, even after 13...♗h6 14 ♘b3 ♗xc1 15 ♕xc1 White quickly plays c5 with an advantage.

14 ♘a4

14 ♘b3 is less incisive, as in this line the knight belongs on c4. Another promising option is 14 ♕c2!? g5 15 ♘b5 ♘g6 (15...axb4 is better) 16 c5! bxc5 17 bxc5 ♘xc5 18 ♘b3 ♘xb3 19 ♖xb3 and White's queenside play came first in Ftačnik-Peshina, Pardubice 1992.

14	...	axb4
15	axb4	g5

Looking as far ahead as move 21, 15...h5!? might be an improvement.

16 c5

Black has slightly slowed down this inevitable advance, but the fact that he hasn't yet created any kingside play is more important. For the next few moves Smirin is limited to defending the opposite flank.

16	...	♘f6
17	cxd6	

White can't achieve any progress without releasing the tension, but 17 c6? is too committal. The time needed to occupy the a-file and create threats against the c7-pawn is probably more than the white king can afford to survive the onslaught after 17...h5.

17	...	cxd6
18	b5	♗d7
19	♘c4	♘c8
20	♗a3	♘e8 (D)

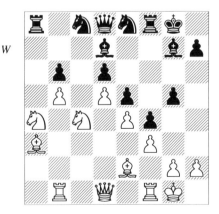

Until now most of the action has taken place on the queenside, where White has created targets for his pieces and tied down a substantial part of Black's forces. However, now the time is ripe for Kasparov to turn his sights to the opposite flank...

21 g4!

This strong move is in fact a prologue to the kingside attack that will decide the game 20 moves later. The logic behind Kasparov's idea requires some explanation. Black's impending pawn-storm with ...h5 and ...g4 would inevitably complicate matters, had White continued his ruthless piece concentration on the queenside. Of course 21 g4! doesn't directly threaten the black king; in first place it's mainly prophylaxis. However, the severe limitation of Black's chances on 'his' flank practically forces Smirin to open the position. This in turn will create kingside holes and White can profit from his space advantage and try to exploit them.

21	...	fxg3

We have already discussed why this is the best move. After 21...h5?! 22 h3 Black has no constructive plan, as the weakness of the b6- and d6-pawns makes it impossible for him to prepare his only counterchance – a piece sacrifice on g4. On the other hand, White can make progress on the queenside unhampered; e.g., transfer his knight or rook to c6, occupy the a-file, etc.

22	hxg3	g4! (D)

Smirin refuses to go down without a fight. Given the time, White would have stopped any counterplay with ♘e3 and g4. 22...♗h3 23 ♖f2 g4 24 ♗c1 is weaker, as Black has committed his bishop too early.

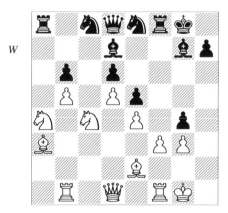

23 ♗c1!

White's pieces are beginning to change their direction. The bishop aims for e3 and prevents Black's queen from entering the fray via g5. The greedy 23 fxg4?! ♖xf1+ 24 ♔xf1 (24 ♗xf1 ♘f6 regains the pawn immediately) 24...♕f6+ 25 ♔g1 ♕g6 26 ♗f3 ♘f6! opens the play prematurely in Black's favour; White needs more forces on the kingside.

23 ... gxf3

23...♘f6 24 ♗g5 would most probably transpose into the game, while after other moves Black would have to reckon with f4.

24 ♗xf3 ♘f6

Black's queen must stay put for the time being, so he takes control of the g4-square. This is important, as given the chance, White would play 25 ♗e3 ♖b8 26 ♗g4! and gain control over the light squares in the vicinity of Black's king. After 24...♘c7 25 ♘axb6 (25 ♘c3 ♘a7!? 26 ♘xb6 ♘axb5 may lead to the same position) 25...♘xb6 26 ♘xb6 ♘xb5 27 ♘xa8 ♘c3 28 ♕c2 (or 28 ♕b3) Black will have more problems with his misplaced knight than White.

25 ♗g5 ♖a7

25...♖b8 26 ♖b3 (or even 26 ♖f2!?) is similar to the game. Smirin keeps the a4-knight under attack, but White has enough useful moves to improve his position, and the b6-pawn will soon require protection anyway.

26 ♖f2 ♖b7!

Black would like to get his queen to g6 via e8, but the immediate 26...♕e8? fails to 27 ♘axb6 ♘xb6 28 ♘xb6 ♗xb5 29 ♗xf6! ♖xf6 30 ♗h5 and White wins.

27 ♖b3!

Kasparov is alert and stops Black's idea by indirectly protecting the g3-pawn.

27 ... ♖a7

The point of White's previous prophylactic move becomes clear after 27...♕e8 28 ♗xf6! ♖xf6 29 ♗h5 ♕f8 30 ♖xf6 ♕xf6 31 ♗g4. Now 31...♕g6 gets Black nowhere, so White achieves the strategically advantageous bishop exchange and remains with much the better minor pieces.

28 ♖b1 ♖b7
29 ♖b3 ♖a7
30 ♖b4!

By repeating moves White has gained some time on the clock before the decisive phase of the game.

30 ... ♔h8 (D)

30...♕e8? is still impossible, for the reason indicated in the note to move 26. The text-move gives White tactical chances, but the passive 30...♖b7 31 ♗h5 is not too enticing either.

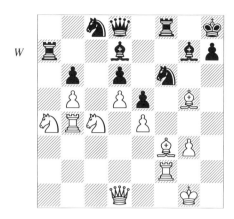

31 ♕f1?!

A good positional move. From f1 the queen lends protection to the b5-pawn, should Black's queen try to move in the direction of the kingside. White also increases his pressure against the pinned f6-knight and this second factor will soon play an important role. However, 31 ♕f1?! also has one major drawback – the full implications of the tactical complications it unleashes were practically impossible to foresee. The more circumspect 31 ♗h5 or 31 ♗e3 ♖b7 32 g4!? would have kept Black under pressure without allowing him too much counterplay.

31 ... ♗xb5!

Lashing out is Black's best chance. 31...♖b7 32 ♗h5! is hopeless for him; the follow-up will be ♘e3-f5 or ♖b3-f3.

32 ♖xb5 ♖xa4
33 ♗g2! h6

The deadly pin can be broken only if Black's queen attacks the loose b5-rook, but it's necessary to free some space around the king first. After 33...♕e8? 34 ♗xf6 ♖xf6 35 ♖xf6 Black loses on the spot, because 35...♕xb5 36 ♖f8+ mates.

34 ♗h4 ♕e8!

The only move. 34...♕c7? loses a piece after 35 ♘b2 and 34...♘a7? 35 ♖b3! b5 36 ♘e3 is also bad for Black; White's main threats are ♘g4 and ♘f5, and the pressure on the f-file will sooner or later decide the game in his favour.

35 ♗xf6

35 ♘xb6 ♘xb6 36 ♗xf6 ♖a1!? gives Black good drawing chances. A sample line is 37 ♕xa1 ♕xb5 38 ♕c1 ♔g8 39 ♗xg7 ♖xf2 40 ♔xf2 ♔xg7 41 ♕c7+ ♘d7 42 ♕xd6 ♕c5+.

35 ... ♖xf6

35...♕xb5? leads to mate after 36 ♗xg7+ ♔xg7 37 ♖xf8.

36 ♖xf6 ♕xb5
37 ♖e6!

Kasparov pursues his ambitions. 37 ♖f8+ ♗xf8 38 ♕xf8+ ♔h7 only draws, as after 39 ♗h3? ♕c5+ 40 ♔h1 ♖a1+ White's bishop doesn't get a chance to join the attack.

37 ... ♔g8!

Still on the right track. After 37...♖xc4? 38 ♕f7, followed by ♖e8(+), Black will have to give up his queen to postpone mate. The passive 37...♖a7 is also inferior due to 38 ♕f2!?. White intends ♘e3-f5 with domination on the light squares and 38...♖e7 39 ♖xe7 ♘xe7 40 ♘xd6 leads to a difficult endgame.

38 ♗h3 *(D)*

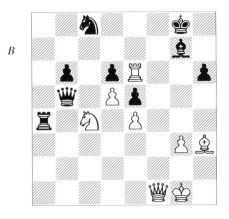

38 ... ♖xc4?

Smirin misses Kasparov's brilliant idea and throws the game away. Strictly the only defence was the computer move 38...h5!, by which Black frees some more space for his king and prevents White's main threat. Kasparov didn't mention this resource in his notes and it would have severely tested his creativity:

1) 39 ♗f5 ♖xc4 forces 40 ♔h1! (40 ♗g6? fails to 40...♕c5+ 41 ♔h1 ♖c1! 42 ♖e8+ ♗f8) 40...♖c5 41 ♕xb5 ♖xb5 42 ♖e8+ ♔f7 43 ♖xc8 with a drawish endgame.

2) 39 ♖g6 ♕c5+!? (39...♕xc4?! 40 ♗e6+ ♔h8 is also possible, but after 41 ♕f3 ♖a1+ 42 ♔h2 ♕c2+ 43 ♔h3 ♕d1 44 ♕xd1 ♖xd1 45 ♗xc8 it's still Black who has to fight for a draw) 40 ♔h2 ♖a2+ 41 ♔h1 ♖f2 beats off the attack.

3) The only way to retain at least some slim chances seems to be 39 ♘e3!? ♕xf1+ 40 ♗xf1! and White's piece activity is dangerous despite the queen swap; e.g., 40...♖xe4 41 ♘f5 ♗f8 (41...♔f7? loses to 42 ♗a6) 42 ♖e8 ♘e7! 43 ♘xe7+ ♔f7 44 ♖xf8+ ♔xf8 45 ♘f5. However, one can be almost sure of one thing – had Kasparov seen 38...h5! beforehand, he would have refrained from 31 ♕f1?!.

39 ♖xh6!!

This beautiful blow crowns White's light-square attack. Black can't pin White's queen, as he must respect the direct threat ♗e6#. Therefore the cheeky rook must be taken, but this also leads to a forced mate.

39 ... ♗xh6
40 ♗e6+ ♔h8
41 ♕f6+ *(D)*

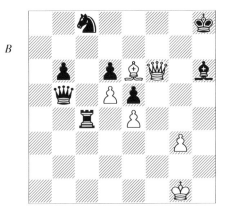

1-0

It's mate in another five moves: 41...♔h7 (41...♗g7 42 ♕h4+ is quicker) 42 ♕f7+ ♗g7 43 ♗f5+ ♔h8 44 ♕h5+ ♔g8 45 ♗e6+.

Game 49
Jan Timman – Garry Kasparov
World Cup, Reykjavik 1988
King's Indian Defence, Sämisch Variation [E88]

1	d4	♘f6
2	c4	g6
3	♘c3	♗g7
4	e4	d6
5	f3	0-0
6	♗e3	e5
7	d5	

White can also keep the central tension; for 7 ♘ge2 c6 8 ♕d2 see Shirov-Kasparov, Dortmund 1992 and Karpov-Kasparov, Linares 1993 (Games 67 and 71 respectively). Even Timman himself played this line against Kasparov in Amsterdam 1996.

7 ... c6

This is the modern treatment: by opening the c-file Black aims to discourage White from queenside castling. Somewhat later Kasparov tested even the older continuation 7...♘h5 8 ♕d2 f5 9 0-0-0 ♘d7.

8 ♗d3 b5!? *(D)*

In the fight for the tournament lead Kasparov direly needed a full point, so he essayed an experimental gambit. The fact that Timman himself introduced the idea into practice (in the game Spassky-Timman, Amsterdam 1973) gave his choice a further psychological twist. The less adventurous alternative is 8...cxd5 9 cxd5 ♘h5 10 ♘ge2 f5 11 exf5 gxf5 12 0-0 ♘d7 13 ♖c1 ♘c5, although this also led to complex play in Karpov-Kasparov, Reggio Emilia 1991/2.

9 cxb5

The insipid continuation 9 dxc6 bxc4 10 ♗xc4 ♘xc6 11 ♘ge2 ♗e6 allows Black to equalize with ease. The same goes for 9 ♘ge2 b4, followed by ...c5. Accepting the sacrifice is the most principled option, but White can also fight for an advantage with the quiet 9 a3!?. The point is that after 9...bxc4 10 ♗xc4 c5 the energetic 11 b4! gives White an edge and reminds Black that his 8th move weakened the queenside.

9	...	cxd5
10	exd5	e4!

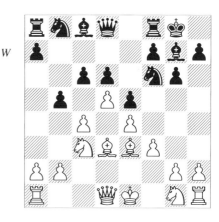

This game was played before the age of huge databases, which makes Kasparov's claim of playing a novelty understandable – he was simply unaware of the predecessors and invested 40 minutes of precious time to make sure the daring idea was viable. Timman wrote he had indeed intended to try out the second pawn sacrifice himself in the aforementioned game against Spassky, had his opponent not played 9 ♘ge2 instead. However, in a later game he was on the other side of the board: Timman-Quinteros, Bled/Portorož 1979 went 10...♗b7 11 ♘ge2! ♘bd7 (11...♘xd5 12 ♘xd5 ♗xd5 13 ♘c3 followed by ♗e4 is clearly better for White) 12 ♗c2 (Kasparov prefers 12 0-0 ♘b6 13 ♗g5; White again advantageously returns the pawn) 12...a6 13 bxa6 ♖xa6 14 b4! ♘b6 15 ♗b3 and Black had no compensation for the pawn. This example shows the crux of the position is not the weakness of the d5-pawn, as White is only too willing to sacrifice it for a central blockade on the light squares. Black must strive for piece activity and especially free his g7-bishop. Thus the text-move is the only consistent continuation.

11 ♘xe4

The most prudent option. Accepting the offer is possible, but certainly riskier and not too practical:

1) 11 fxe4 ♘g4 12 ♕d2 (12 ♗f4 ♕b6 is risky for White) 12...f5 13 ♘ge2 (13 ♘f3 ♘xe3 14 ♕xe3 f4 followed by ...♘d7-e5 gives Black full dark-square control) 13...♘xe3 14 ♕xe3 fxe4 15 ♗xc4 a6!?. The white king has no safe hideout and despite the extra pawns White must be careful.

2) More interesting is 11 ♗xe4 ♘xe4 12 ♘xe4 (12 fxe4 ♕h4+ 13 g3 ♗xc3+ 14 bxc3 ♕xe4 15 ♕f3 ♕c4!? might be dangerous for White) 12...♖e8 13 ♘e2 f5 (13...♗f5!?) 14 ♗g5 ♕a5+ 15 ♘4c3 (15 ♕d2 ♕xb5 is OK for Black, as after 16 ♘xd6?! he has 16...♖xe2+! 17 ♕xe2 ♕b4+) 15...a6!?. Here Black wins one of the pawns back, but contrary to line '1' White can tuck away his king and fight for an edge with 16 0-0.

11	...	♘xd5
12	♗g5 *(D)*	

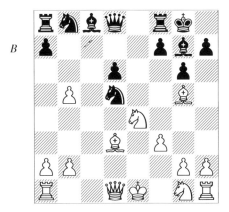

| 12 | ... | ♕a5+ |

In 1988 Kasparov considered this the only move and criticized 12...♕b6!? 13 ♕d2 as insufficient. However, two years later he changed his mind, only after 13...♘d7 14 ♗c4 ♘5f6 15 ♘xf6+ in Gulko-Kasparov, Linares 1990 he should have played 15...♘xf6! 16 ♘e2 ♖e8 17 ♗h4 d5 18 ♗d3 ♗b7! 19 ♗f2 d4 20 0-0 ♘d5 with compensation for the pawn. This variation certainly seems playable for Black, perhaps even more so than the queenless middlegame in current game.

13	♕d2	♕xd2+
14	♗xd2	

Weaker is 14 ♔xd2 h6; there are still too many pieces on the board for the king to find a safe haven in the centre.

14	...	♗xb2
15	♖b1	

Although the subsequent try 15 ♖d1!? might be stronger than the natural text-move, even here after 15...♘d7 16 ♘e2 ♘7b6 17 ♘xd6 ♗e6 18 g4 ♘f6 19 ♗c3 ♘a4 20 ♗a5 ♗e5 Black's piece activity allowed him to hold the balance in Razuvaev-Lautier, Paris 1989.

15	...	♗g7
16	♘e2	

White is in no hurry to take the indefensible d-pawn and continues his development. 16 ♘xd6 ♗e6 17 ♘e2 ♘d7 is similar to the previous note and gives Black tactical chances.

| 16 | ... | ♘d7!? *(D)* |

16...♗e6 could transpose into the previous note by 17 ♘xd6, as Black need not fear 17 ♗g5 ♘d7 18 ♘xe6 fxe6 followed by ...♘c5 or ...♘e5 with a complex position. Black's move avoids immediate simplification and is more interesting. Psychologically it proves to be a good choice, as it induces Timman to become overconfident.

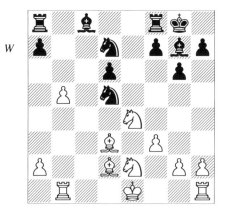

| 17 | ♘xd6 | |

Timman's 9 cxb5 has already indicated he is playing for a win and now to fight for an advantage he is more or less forced to take the bait on d6. While the text-move is still alright, his subsequent stubborn clinging to the extra material is not and we'll see how it will finally cause White's downfall. Moves such as 17 ♘f4 ♘xf4 18 ♗xf4 ♘e5 and 17 ♔f2 ♘e5 18 ♗c2 ♘c4 19 ♖bd1 ♗e6 are comfortable for Black, but the prophylactic 17 ♗c2!? deserves more attention. Nevertheless after 17...♘e5 (17...♘c5 allows 18 ♘f4! ♘xf4 19 ♗xf4, when White is better) 18 ♘xd6 ♗e6 the position remains sharp; e.g., 19 ♘d4 ♘d3+! 20 ♗xd3 ♗xd4 and White's king is trapped in the middle.

17	...	♘c5
18	♗c2	

White still needs his light-squared bishop. 18 ♗c4?! is weaker due to 18...♘b6. However, Timman's proposal 18 ♗e4 is worth considering. This was the first possibility to return the pawn to reduce the tension after 18...♗e6 19 ♖c1 ♘xe4 20 fxe4 ♘b6 21 ♗c3 ♗xa2 with a probable draw.

18	...	♗e6
19	♘e4 (D)	

Again a characteristic moment, illustrating White's maximalist approach. After 19 0-0 ♖fd8 20 ♘e4 ♘xe4 21 ♗xe4 f5 22 ♗c2 ♘b6 White can achieve approximate equality with 23 ♗c3!? (23 ♗g5 ♖e8 24 ♖fe1 h6 is less convincing) 23...♗xa2 24 ♗b3+. This was obviously still not enough for Timman, but if he had higher ambitions, 19 a4!? would have been a more suitable move – White removes the a-pawn from a vulnerable square.

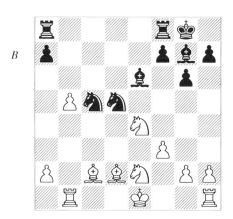

19	...	♖ac8

Black had another option in 19...♘xe4 20 ♗xe4 (20 fxe4 ♘b6 21 ♗b3 ♖fe8 with good compensation) 20...♖ac8, which prepares ...f5 and can still transpose into the game. This would have avoided White's chance to deviate on the following move.

20	0-0?!	

Timman regretted having missed 20 ♘g5!. While this move is somewhat stronger, Black nevertheless retains undeniable pressure after 20...♗d7 (20...♖fe8 is unconvincing due to 21 ♘xe6 ♘xe6 22 ♗e4 ♘f6 23 ♗c6!?) 21 0-0 ♖fe8 22 ♖fe1 ♘e3.

20	...	♘xe4
21	♗xe4	f5
22	♗d3? (D)	

This is a serious mistake. White continues to overestimate his chances and his forces lose co-ordination. Necessary was 22 ♗xd5 ♗xd5 23 ♖bc1 (23 a4 ♖c2 24 ♖fd1 ♗a2 25 ♖bc1 ♗b3 is similar: Black regains the pawn with a more active position) 23...♗xa2 24 ♗e3. Although Black has a slight edge, he can hardly prevent the liquidation of the queenside (or win the b5-pawn only at the cost of an opposite-coloured bishop endgame) with a drawish position.

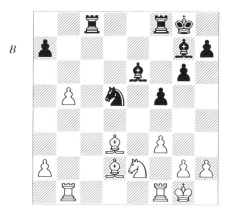

22	...	♘b6!

This targets the a-pawn and, more importantly, White's misplaced bishops on the d-file. From now on the initiative is firmly in Kasparov's hands.

23	♘c1	

Forced, as after 23 ♖bc1? ♖cd8 24 ♘f4 ♗f7 White loses material; for example, 25 h4 (25 ♗b4 doesn't help due to 25...♖fe8 26 ♗c2 ♗d4+ 27 ♔h1 ♗e3) 25...♗e5 26 ♖fd1 ♘a4! 27 ♖c2 ♘b2 28 ♖e1 ♗xf4 29 ♖xb2 ♗g3.

23	...	♖fd8

Both Black's bishops and rooks now have full scope, while the unhappy c1-knight prevents White from connecting his rooks.

24	♗g5	

The threat was ...♖xc1 and the following moves are practically forced.

24	...	♖d7
25	♖e1	♔f7
26	♗e2	

After 26 ♗f1 h6 27 ♗e3 ♗c3! 28 ♘d3 (28 ♖e2?! ♖d1 is even worse) 28...♗xa2 29 ♖bd1 ♘c4! Black wins an exchange.

26	...	h6
27	♗h4	♘d5!

The knight returns to the centre and joins the rest of Black's army in piling up the pressure.

28 ♗d1? *(D)*

White is still unwilling to cede the extra pawn, but the text-move leads to even heavier losses. 28 ♗f2 ♘c3 29 ♖b4 ♘d1! gives Black a strong attack, as 30 ♗xd1? ♗c3 nets material. However, 28 b6!? axb6 29 ♗b5 is more resilient. Although here White won't be able to liquidate the queenside as on move 22 and after 29...♖dc7 or 29...♖a7 will probably soon lose the a-pawn, it was his last chance to stay in the game.

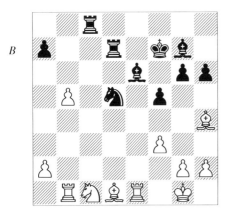

28 ... ♗d4+!

This refutes White's idea. Timman only reckoned with 28...♗c3?!, when 29 ♖xe6! ♔xe6 30 ♗b3 gives White counterchances. However, Black could have also inverted the move-order: 28...♘c3 29 ♗b3 ♗xb3 30 ♖xb3 ♗d4+! wins the exchange just as in the game after 31 ♔f1 g5.

29 ♗f2

This is best. 29 ♔h1 g5 30 ♖xe6 ♔xe6 31 ♗e1 ♔f6 loses even faster, as White remains passive.

29	...	♗xf2+
30	♔xf2	♘c3 *(D)*

The double attack nets Black an exchange and gives him a sufficient advantage to win with relative ease.

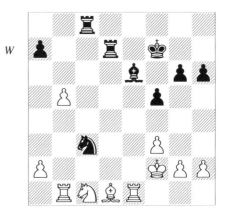

31	♗b3	♗xb3
32	♖xb3	♘d1+
33	♖xd1	♖xd1
34	♘d3	

34 ♘e2 ♖d2 also costs White more material.

34	...	♖d2+
35	♔e3	

35 ♔g3 ♖cc2 36 ♘e1 ♖xa2 37 b6 axb6 38 ♖xb6 ♖d1 traps the knight.

35	...	♖xg2

35...♖xa2! is a cleaner solution; White will lose at least one of his kingside pawns in any case.

36	♖a3	♖e8+
37	♔d4	♖e7

White has managed to generate some counterplay, but it's not enough to change the issue.

38	♘e5+	♔f6
39	♘c6	

39 ♖a6+ ♖e6 doesn't help, as after 40 ♘d7+ ♔e7 41 ♖xa7? Black has 41...♖d6+.

39	...	♖d7+
40	♔c4	♖c2+
41	♔b4	♖xh2
42	♖a6	

42 ♘xa7 h5 43 b6 h4 is hopeless for White: the h-pawn is too fast. In the game it won't be much different.

42	...	♔g5
43	a4	h5
44	♖xa7	♖xa7
45	♘xa7	0-1

White resigned, not waiting for 45...h4 46 ♔c3 (46 b6 ♖b2+ 47 ♔a5 h3 48 ♘b5 ♖d2 is similar) 46...♖e2 47 b6 ♖e8, stopping the b-pawn and queening the h-pawn.

Game 50
Jaan Ehlvest – Garry Kasparov
World Cup, Reykjavik 1988
English Opening [A28]

1	c4	♘f6
2	♘c3	e5
3	♘f3	♘c6
4	e3	

Presumably fearing Kasparov's expertise in the 4 g3 line (see Game 47), Ehlvest chooses a different system.

4	...	♗b4
5	♕c2	0-0
6	d3	

This allows Black to finish his development comfortably. White can fight for an opening advantage with the more ambitious 6 ♘d5 ♖e8 7 ♕f5!?, a line that had appeared in Kasparov's practice in his junior years. In Kasparov-Romanishin, USSR Ch (Tbilisi) 1978 he came close to scoring a full point.

| 6 | ... | ♖e8 *(D)* |

| 7 | ♗d2 | |

A rather risky, but more enterprising, approach is 7 a3!? ♗xc3+ 8 ♕xc3. White would like to fianchetto his queen's bishop with b4 and ♗b2, aiming for a better version of the Sicilian-like position from our game. After 8...d5 9 cxd5 ♕xd5!? (9...♘xd5 10 ♕c2 a5 11 b3 fits White's plans) 10 e4 (10 ♗e2 e4 is not ideal; due to Black's lead in development White should keep the position closed) 10...♕d6 11 ♗e3 ♗g4 12 ♘d2 ♘d4!? 13 ♘c4 ♕c6 a sharp and complex position arose in Ljubojević-Illescas, Groningen (PCA qualifier) 1993.

| 7 | ... | ♗xc3!? |

7...a5 and 7...♗f8 8 a3 d6 are viable alternatives, but Black has higher ambitions and wants to play ...d5 in one go. Exchanging the bishop voluntarily may seem strange, but after 7...d5 8 cxd5 ♘xd5 9 ♗e2 White can later on retake on c3 with the b-pawn.

| 8 | ♗xc3 | |

Now after 8 bxc3? e4 White's pawns are a mess.

| 8 | ... | d5 |
| 9 | cxd5 | ♘xd5 |

Contrary to the note to White's 7th move, this recapture is now more accurate than 9...♕xd5 10 ♗e2. Here the bishop-pair has more potential than in the game and the impetuous 10...e4?! 11 ♗xf6! exf3 12 ♗xf3 ♘b4 13 ♕c3 ♕a5 14 ♗xg7 ♘c2+ 15 ♔d2 ♕xc3+ 16 bxc3 ♘xa1 17 ♗d4 gave White a large endgame advantage in Ribli-Kavalek, Manila IZ 1976.

| 10 | ♗e2 | ♗f5! *(D)* |

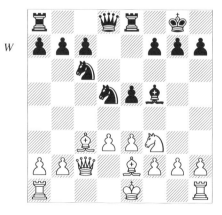

Kasparov has actively placed his pieces and the first threats are already in the air. Black certainly has no problems whatsoever.

| 11 | ♖d1 | |

Ehlvest parries ...♘db4, but commits the rook too early – usually it belongs on c1. Better moves were:

1) The direct 11 e4 leads to approximate equality after 11...♘xc3, but Kasparov indicated he wanted to try the sacrificial 11...♘f4!? 12 exf5 ♘d4 13 ♗xd4 exd4 14 ♘g1 ♕d5 15 0-0-0 ♕xa2. White's forces are uncoordinated and his king is vulnerable, so if Black manages to mobilize his rooks quickly his attack may become decisive. However, White's defensive resources are not exhausted and after 16 ♗f3 (16 g3 ♕a1+ 17 ♔d2 ♕a5+ is similar: Black has a perpetual and can maybe aspire for more following 18 ♔c1 ♘d5!?) 16...♕a1+ (after 16...♖e5? White frees himself with 17 ♕c4) 17 ♕b1 ♕a5 18 ♕c2 (18 g3? ♖e5! is too dangerous) a draw by repetition seems the most probable result.

2) A more circumspect alternative is the natural 11 0-0, when Black can achieve sterile equality with 11...♘cb4 12 ♗xb4 ♘xb4 13 ♕c3 ♘xd3 14 ♖fd1 e4 15 ♘e1 ♕e7, or opt for a fighting continuation such as 11...♕d6!?.

| 11 | ... | a5 |
| 12 | 0-0 | |

Black's last move has enabled him to meet 12 e4?! advantageously with 12...♘db4, so White leaves the central situation unchanged and safeguards his king.

| 12 | ... | ♕e7 |
| 13 | a3 | a4 (D) |

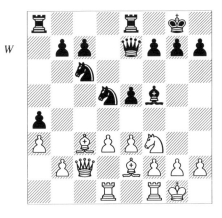

14   ♗e1?!

Inconsistent. After a passively played opening, Ehlvest suddenly remembers his bishop-pair and decides to retain it. However, there is little use for the bishop on e1 and moreover it disrupts the coordination of White's rooks. The typical manoeuvre 14 ♘d2? runs into the piece of tactics 14...♘xc3 15 ♕xc3 ♘d4!, while after 14 e4?! ♘xc3 15 bxc3 ♗e6 Black has a small advantage due to the weakness on a3. The patient 14 ♖fe1 is better, when Black's edge is at best only minimal.

| 14 | ... | ♗g6 |
| 15 | ♕c4 | |

15 ♘d2?! again fails, this time to 15...♘f4!. The text-move is not ideal either, as it doesn't reduce Black's tactical chances. 15 ♖c1!? (see the note to move 11) is somewhat better, with ideas like ♘d2 or ♕c5.

| 15 | ... | ♖ed8 (D) |

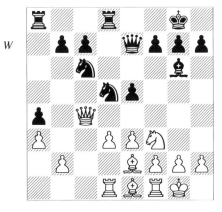

16   ♘d2?

Just as on earlier occasions, this move is flawed tactically, only this time the refutation is far more spectacular. In the phase of the game from move 10 onwards Ehlvest hasn't done too well and several inaccuracies have given Kasparov a solid position with prospects to develop his initiative. Now 16 d4 e4 17 ♘d2 ♘b6 leads to a pleasant space advantage for Black, but his pull would have still remained within limits after 16 ♕h4 or 16 ♗c3.

| 16 | ... | ♘d4!! |

Knight sacrifices on d5 or f5 are typical in the razor-sharp lines of the Sicilian, like the Velimirović Attack. Although our position has Sicilian contours, Black's blow is unexpected and based on different considerations – Kasparov forcefully exploits the congestion in White's camp caused by 14 ♗e1?! and especially 16 ♘d2?.

| 17 | exd4 | |

White has no choice, as after 17 ♗f3 ♘b6 18 ♕c3 ♘b5 he simply loses material.

17 ... ♘f4
18 ♗f3 ♖xd4 *(D)*

Black tightens the screws. 18...♗xd3?! 19 ♕c5 is weaker and unclear.

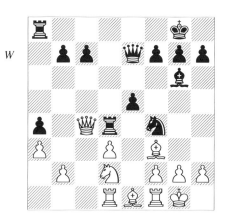

19 ♕b5?

The psychological effect of 16...♘d4!! is just as powerful as its chess strength and Ehlvest quickly buckles under the strain. White had more resilient alternatives:

1) 19 ♕a2?! puts White's queen offside and 19...♗xd3 20 ♗xb7 ♖ad8! (less convincing is 20...♖b8 21 ♗f3 e4 22 ♘xe4 ♖xe4 23 ♗b4!) gives Black a very strong attack. The advance of the e-pawn is a serious threat and White can't unravel his forces, as after 21 ♘f3 ♗xf1 22 ♘xd4 Black has the decisive 22...♗xg2! 23 ♘f5 ♘h3+! 24 ♔xg2 ♕g5+ 25 ♘g3 ♘f4+ 26 ♔f1 ♖xd1.

2) 19 ♕c3 is stronger, although after the simple 19...♗xd3 (Kasparov's preference was the interesting 19...♖ad8!?, piling up the pressure) 20 g3 ♘e2+ 21 ♗xe2 ♗xe2 Black has a clear advantage.

19 ... c6

Now Black regains the sacrificed piece with a decisive positional advantage, as White still can't coordinate his misplaced forces.

20 ♗xc6

20 ♕b6? loses on the spot to 20...♖a6.

20 ... bxc6

21 ♕xc6 *(D)*

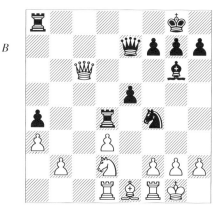

21 ... ♕d8!

Black removes the queen from a potentially vulnerable square. 21...♖ad8 22 ♘f3 ♗e4 23 ♗b4! ♕a7 (or 23...♗xc6 24 ♗xe7) 24 ♕xe4 was not enough for Kasparov, who wanted to crush his opponent quickly.

22 ♘f3

22 g3 ♗xd3, with the idea 23 gxf4 ♖a6, is also hopeless for White.

22 ... ♖d6!

White could still fight on after 22...♗e4 23 dxe4 ♖xd1 24 g3.

23 ♕b5

White's queen has no safe squares. 23 ♕c5 ♖d5 is similar to the game.

23 ... ♖d5
24 ♕b4

After 24 ♕b7 Black has, among other replies, 24...♗h5!? and the threats ...♗xf3 and ...e4 will cost White a piece.

24 ... e4

Taking on d3 was also sufficient, but Black prefers playing for the attack.

25 ♗c3

In time-trouble White loses immediately, but there was no effective defence against ...♘e2+ or ...♘xd3 anyway. After 25 ♘d2 ♕h4! Black has a mating attack; e.g., 26 ♘xe4 ♘e2+ 27 ♔h1 ♕xh2+!.

25 ... ♘e2+

0-1

Game 51
Garry Kasparov – Daniel Campora
Olympiad, Thessaloniki 1988
Queen's Gambit Declined [D35]

1	c4	♘f6
2	d4	e6
3	♘c3	d5
4	cxd5	exd5
5	♗g5	♗e7

In Game 45 we saw 5...c6. For the time being Campora omits this natural move and chooses a slightly different plan. He wants to keep the option of playing ...c5 in one go until White commits his king, as after queenside castling this advance is one of Black's most natural methods of achieving counterplay. This is in fact exactly what happens in the game on move 14.

6	e3	0-0

Game 22 shows us why the seemingly innocuous 6...h6?! is inaccurate.

7	♗d3	♘bd7
8	♘ge2	♖e8
9	♕c2	

Kasparov keeps both castling options open. In his later practice he started to prefer 9 0-0. If Black continues as in the game with 9...♘f8, he runs into the strong 10 b4! a6 (after 10...♗xb4 11 ♗xf6 gxf6 12 ♘xd5! ♕xd5 13 ♕a4 White regains the pawn with a clear advantage) 11 a3 c6 12 ♕c2 g6 13 f3 ♘e6 14 ♗h4 ♘h5 15 ♗xe7 ♖xe7 16 ♕d2 b6?! 17 ♖ad1 ♗b7 18 ♗b1 ♘hg7 19 e4 ♖c8 20 ♗a2 ♖d7 21 ♘f4 ♘xf4 22 ♕xf4, when White had a substantial advantage in Kasparov-Short, London PCA Wch (15) 1993; his 10th move had seriously limited Black's possible counterplay. Therefore the solid 9...c6 is objectively better, although after 10 f3 ♘f8 White doesn't have to develop his queen to c2 any more and can play the interesting 11 ♗h4!? instead.

9	...	♘f8
10	0-0-0!? *(D)*	

Kasparov was in a belligerent mood; this still remains the only example in his practice when he castled queenside in the Exchange Variation of the Queen's Gambit Declined. White could have still transposed into Game 45 with the less aggressive continuation 10 0-0 c6 11 f3.

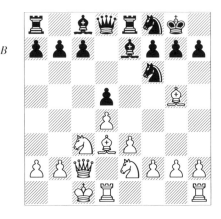

10	...	♗e6

Campora continues the plan indicated by his 5th move. However, Black more often plays the consolidating 10...c6. This not only makes the sortie ...♘e4 possible, but also prepares the advance of Black's queenside pawns against White's king (...a5-a4 and ...b5).

11	♔b1	

This side-step is a necessary follow-up to 10 0-0-0!?. White's king must sooner or later leave the semi-open c-file. However, the question of the right timing is a difficult one. The immediate 11 f3 a6!? followed by ...c5 or ...♖c8 leads to an unclear position, but 11 ♘f4 deserves attention.

11	...	♘g4?!

Not an ideal reaction, as Black's knight will have to return with a loss of time. Preferable was 11...♘e4 (the preparatory 11...♖c8!? is also interesting) 12 ♗xe7 ♘xc3+ (12...♕xe7 13 ♘xe4 dxe4 14 ♗xe4 ♗xa2+ 15 ♔xa2 ♕xe4 16 ♕xe4 ♖xe4 17 ♘c3 or 17 d5!? gives White central control and a very pleasant endgame) 13 ♘xc3 ♕xe7 14 f4 ♖ad8. Black has simplified the position and will soon be ready to launch his own play with ...c5.

12	♗xe7	♕xe7
13	♘f4	♘f6
14	f3!	

Kasparov's trademark move in this pawn-structure. White takes the e4-square under control, while even more important is the preparation of g4.

14	...	c5

A logical reaction. Black strives for active counterplay, because defensive measures such as 14...♘g6 15 g4! ♘xf4 16 exf4 don't help – White's advancing pawns will open up Black's kingside.

15	g4 *(D)*	

Consistent. 14 f3! also had one drawback – namely the e3-pawn has become slightly vulnerable. This would be more apparent if White changed his mind and switched to play against the isolated d5-pawn with 15 dxc5?!, as after 15...♖ac8 (15...♕xc5?! 16 ♘cxd5! gives White a long-lasting endgame advantage) the position is unclear.

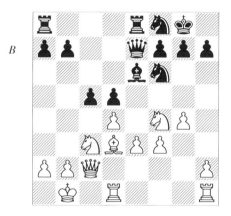

15	...	cxd4?

It's very difficult to point out where exactly Black went wrong and even Kasparov didn't use a single question mark in his notes. Nevertheless, Campora's last move is dubious, as now Black's pawn-storm is over before it even began and White can easily defend his d4-pawn. On the other hand Kasparov gets enough time to improve his position and although it will take a full nine moves before he advances another kingside pawn, the delayed effect will be devastating. Black probably should have tried the double-edged 15...c4 16 ♗f1 ♕d6!? (16...♕d7?! allows the strong 17 e4!). After the plausible continuation 17 h4 ♖ab8 18 g5 ♘6d7 19 h5 b5 20 g6 White has a lead in the coming pawn-storm race, especially as 20...b4? runs into the tactical blow 21 ♘cxd5!. Nevertheless the outcome remains undecided, as the position is still volatile.

16	exd4	♕d6
17	♕d2	a6
18	♘ce2	

Kasparov considers 18 h4 weaker due to 18...b5 19 g5 ♘6d7 20 h5 ♘b6. Although White keeps an advantage after 21 ♕h2!? with the threat h6, he is basically right – by moving his forces to the main theatre of action White increases his attacking chances.

18	...	♖e7

Black's counterplay on the e-file is non-existent (see also move 21), so 18...b5!?, in the spirit of the previous note, was worth trying.

19	♘g3	♘g6 *(D)*

After 19...♖ac8 White can play either 20 h4, or transform his advantage with 20 ♘xe6!? fxe6 (20...♖xe6 21 ♘f5 is no better) 21 g5 ♘6d7 22 f4. In both cases he has a strong attack.

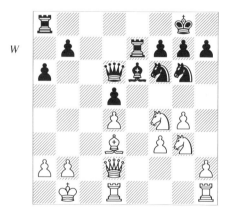

20	♘g2!	

Kasparov starts an impressive regrouping of his attacking forces. The text-move both prevents ♘h4 and avoids exchanges, which would help the defence.

20	...	♘d7
21	♖hg1	♖ee8
22	♖df1!	♘gf8

Black is limited to passivity. Relinquishing control of f4 seems to be a concession, but 22...♖ac8 allows 23 f4! ♗xg4 24 f5 ♘gf8

(24...♘e7 25 ♕g5 ♘f6 26 ♘e3 h6 27 ♕h4 and the attack breaks through) 25 ♘f4 or even 25 ♕f4!? with a large advantage.

23 ♘e3

Afterwards Kasparov indicated the alternative solution 23 ♘h5!? ♘g6 (23...f6 24 ♘e3 with the idea ♘f5 is similar) 24 h3 and there is no effective defence against f4-f5; for example, 24...f6 25 ♘e3 and Black can't prevent ♘f5.

23 ... ♔h8
24 ♘h5!

White doesn't want to give Black even the slightest whiff of counterplay after 24 f4 ♘f6!?, followed by ...♘e4. The text-move is a prelude to the final attack.

24 ... g6

Practically forced, as after 24...f6? 25 ♘f5! ♗xf5 26 gxf5 White breaks through via the g-file.

25 f4! (D)

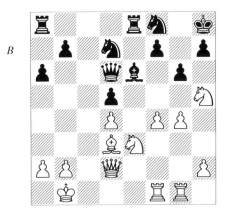

The preparations are over and it's time to act!

25 ... gxh5

Black can't open the g-file: 25...♗xg4 26 ♘xg4 gxh5 27 ♘e5 and 25...f6 26 f5 gxh5 27 gxh5! with the pretty idea 27...♗f7 28 ♘c4! ♕e7 29 ♘d6! are both hopeless for Black.

26 f5 h4

The only way to keep the position closed for a while. After 26...hxg4? 27 ♘xg4 White's attack is decisive; the main threat is ♘h6.

27 fxe6 fxe6
28 g5

The winning move. White frees the road for his knight to Black's vulnerable kingside and all his pieces will participate in the final attack.

28 ... ♖e7

28...♘g6 29 ♗xg6 hxg6 30 ♕f2 ♖e7 31 ♘g4 ♖h7 32 ♘h6 doesn't help much. In the long run Black can't prevent an invasion via the f-file.

29 ♘g4 ♖g7
30 ♘h6 ♕b6

30...♕e7 is slightly more resilient, but after 31 ♖e1 (31 ♖g4 followed by ♖gf4 is also good enough) White threatens ♘f5, forcing Black's queen to leave the kingside again.

31 g6! (D)

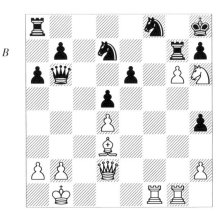

White finally opens the g-file and wins by force.

31 ... hxg6

31...♕xd4? loses on the spot to 32 ♘f7+ ♔g8 33 gxh7+, and 31...♘xg6 32 ♗xg6 ♖xg6 33 ♖xg6 hxg6 34 ♘g4! (34 ♘f7+ ♔g8 35 ♕h6 ♕xd4 36 ♕xg6+ ♖g7 37 ♕xe6 ♖f8 is less convincing) 34...♔g8 35 ♕h6 ♕xd4 (35...e5 loses to 36 ♘f6+!) 36 ♕xg6+ ♖g7 37 ♕xe6+ followed by ♖f7 doesn't help either.

32 ♘f7+ ♔g8

White mates after 32...♖xf7 33 ♖xf7 ♕xd4 34 ♖xg6!.

33 ♕h6! ♖h7

33...♖xf7 34 ♗xg6 ♖xf1+ 35 ♖xf1 ♘f6 gives White a pleasant choice between 36 ♖xf6 ♕c7 37 ♕h5! or 36 ♗f7+!. After the text-move White forces mate.

34 ♖xg6+ ♘xg6
35 ♕xg6+ ♖g7
36 ♕h6 1-0

Game 52
Jonathan Speelman – Garry Kasparov
Rapidplay, Madrid 1988
King's Indian Defence, Classical Line [E92]

This is one of the few games in this book played with a shortened time-limit. Even in rapid chess Kasparov has no qualms about demonstrating some of his interesting new ideas, and this encounter is a typical example.

1	c4	g6
2	e4	♝g7
3	d4	d6
4	♘c3	♘f6
5	♘f3	0-0
6	♗e2	e5
7	♗e3	

This line has occurred in Kasparov's games with both colours and underwent its most serious practical test in the last K-K match in 1990.

7 ... ♘g4

Although this is generally the most popular continuation, Kasparov has usually avoided it in favour of lesser common alternatives. His initial preference was 7...♕e7, played earlier in 1988 against Vaganian and also in Game 9, in which Kasparov was White. Later he turned his attention to 7...c6!? and in the position after 8 ♕d2 exd4 9 ♘xd4 ♖e8 10 f3 d5 11 exd5 cxd5 12 0-0 ♘c6 13 c5 came up with the surprising positional sacrifice 13...♖xe3!? 14 ♕xe3 ♕f8! 15 ♘xc6 (15 ♘cb5 later became the main line and was played in Gelfand-Kasparov, Linares 1992; nevertheless even here Black's play on the dark squares keeps the position balanced after 15...♕xc5 16 ♕f2 ♗d7) 15...bxc6 16 ♔h1 ♖b8! 17 ♘a4 ♖b4 18 b3 ♗e6 19 ♘b2 ♘h5 20 ♘d3 ♖h4 21 ♕f2 ♕e7 22 g4 ♗d4! 23 ♕xd4 ♖xh2+! and Black forced a perpetual in Karpov-Kasparov, New York/Lyons Wch (11) 1990.

8	♗g5	f6
9	♗h4	

9 ♗c1 is less consistent. White avoids later problems with his bishop, but Black gets an active position with 9...♘c6 10 0-0 f5.

9 ... g5

Even here Kasparov shies away from the main line 9...♘c6.

10 ♗g3 ♘h6

Black can't leave his knight exposed on g4, as 10...♘c6?! 11 d5 ♘e7 12 ♘xg5! ♘xf2 13 ♗xf2 fxg5 14 ♗g4 gives White a long-lasting advantage.

11 h3

Left to his own devices, Black would get an active position with ...g4 and ...♘c6. Speelman wants to maintain the central tension, but White can fight for an opening advantage even by resolving it with 11 d5 or 11 dxe5!?, followed by h4.

11 ... ♘c6

The direct 11...exd4?! 12 ♘xd4 ♘c6 is suspect due to the energetic 13 h4! (13 0-0 f5 gives Black reasonable counterplay), when Black's kingside is crumbling. However, a playable alternative seems to be 11...♘d7!?, preparing ...f5; then 12 d5 f5 transposes into lines from the above note.

12 d5 (D)

The text-move is more ambitious than 12 dxe5 dxe5! (12...fxe5?! is weaker due to 13 c5!), when Black has sufficient central control to claim equality.

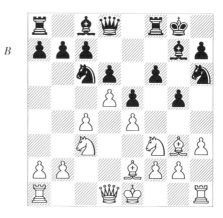

12 ... ♘d4!?

An enterprising pawn sacrifice for a dark-square bind. Although the idea of forcefully opening the a1-h8 diagonal is fairly typical for the King's Indian in general (for example see Game 49), in this concrete position it's new. Objectively, Kasparov's novelty is quite risky and probably no better than the sedate 12...♘e7 13 ♕d2!? (13 ♘d2 f5 14 f3 ♘g6 followed by ...♘f4 gives Black enough counterplay), when White has temporarily prevented ...f5 and is slightly better. However, one has to take into account the surprise and psychological value of 12...♘d4!?; moreover, in a rapid game it's even more difficult to refute such a daring concept.

13 ♘xd4   exd4
14 ♕xd4

White must accept the challenge. The weaker 14 ♘b5?! f5 hands the initiative to Black.

14 ...   f5
15 ♕d2   f4

A further benefit of the pawn sacrifice is that White's bishop will be shut out for the next few moves. Regaining the pawn with 15...♗xc3 16 ♕xc3 fxe4 (Jakubiec-Acs, Polish Cht (Lubniewice) 2003) is less consistent. Then 17 0-0 ♘f5 18 ♗h2 ♕f6 19 c5 gives White the initiative.

16 ♗h2 (D)

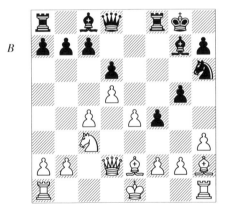

16 ...   ♘f7

Black's knight aims for e5; moreover, this natural move takes the sting out of the h4 break. 16...♗e5!? was an interesting subsequent try, preventing White's next move altogether by protecting the f4-pawn. After 17 ♗g1 ♕f6 18 f3 c5! (much stronger than 18...b6?! 19 0-0-0 a6 20 ♔b1 ♗d7 21 ♗d4 ♘f7 22 ♗xe5 ♘xe5 23 ♕d4 h5 24 ♖dg1 h4 25 ♖c1 and Black was reduced to passivity in Avrukh-Efimenko, Biel open 2001) 19 dxc6 bxc6 20 ♗f2 White is

perhaps slightly better, but it's not easy for him to place his king and the position remains sharp.

17 h4

White was successful with 17 0-0-0 c5 18 dxc6 bxc6 19 h4 h6 20 hxg5 hxg5 21 f3 ♕a5 22 g3 fxg3 23 ♗xg3 ♖b8 24 f4 in Shulman-Fedorov, Vladivostok 1995, but opening the h-file against Black's king immediately can't be a bad idea.

17 ...   h6
18 hxg5   hxg5
19 g3? (D)

This direct attempt to blast open Black's kingside is in fact a serious positional error with grave consequences. 19 f3 would have been a serious test of Black's concept. White intends to play g3 or ♗g1-d4 and Kasparov would have had to work hard to prove he has sufficient compensation for the pawn. Now it will all be different...

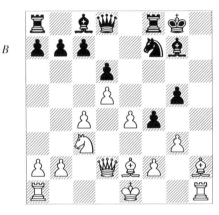

19 ...   f3!
20 ♗xf3   ♘e5

20...g4 21 ♗e2 ♗h6!? 22 ♕c2 ♘e5 keeps White's king in the centre, but Black's position is impressive enough even without this refinement.

21 ♗e2   g4

Black's three previous moves have clarified the situation – the temporarily entombed h2-bishop is now buried permanently, as the immediate f4 advance is out of the question and even later White has no effective way to prepare it. Thus Kasparov is practically a piece up and although converting the advantage is not so easy, White's defensive task in a rapid game is much more difficult.

GAME 52: JONATHAN SPEELMAN – GARRY KASPAROV

| 22 | ♗g1 | c5! |

Another energetic move, which further limits White by denying him the d4-square. Moreover Black prepares the opening of the queenside with ...a6 and ...♗d7 in case White keeps the position closed.

| 23 | dxc6 | |

The other liberating attempt 23 f4? is completely hopeless due to 23...gxf3 24 ♗d1 (24 ♗f1? loses on the spot: 24...f2+!) 24...♘xc4 25 ♕h2 ♕g5. Although the text-move further activates Black's forces and his powerplay becomes more distinct, passively waiting for the inevitable with 23 0-0-0 a6 was even less enticing.

23	...	bxc6
24	0-0-0	♗e6
25	♕xd6 (D)	

Speelman tries to take as many pawns as possible to compensate for his horrible g1-bishop. However, the immediate 25 ♖h5!? is stronger, as now Black activates his queen.

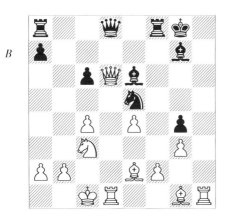

25	...	♕g5+
26	♔b1	♕g6
27	♔a1	♖ab8
28	♖h5?!	

Desperation, but despite the three(!) extra pawns it is difficult to find a good defence against the impending doubling of rooks on the b-file. Lashing out with 28 f4! gxf3 29 ♗f1 is better, but after 29...♖bd8!? 30 ♕xd8 ♖xd8 31 ♖xd8+ ♔f7 White's pieces are uncoordinated and the passed f3-pawn is dangerous.

28	...	♕xh5
29	♕xe6+	♔h8
30	♕e7	♘f3!

Black once and for all stops any tricks with f4. White's bishop remains incarcerated and the attack on the long dark diagonal decides the game.

| 31 | ♗xf3 | ♖xf3 |
| 32 | ♘a4 (D) | |

32 ♕xa7 ♕e5 and 32 ♖d7 ♕h6 33 ♖d8+ ♖xd8 34 ♕xd8+ ♔h7 are both hopeless for White. The rest requires little commentary, as the blitz phase of the game has already started.

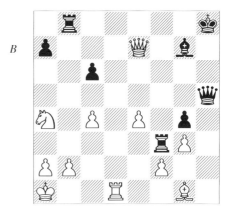

| 32 | ... | ♖e8 |
| 33 | ♕xa7 | |

33 ♖d8 loses quickly to 33...♖ff8! 34 ♖xe8 ♖xe8, followed by ...♖xe4 or ...♕h1. 33 ♕d7 ♖xe4 34 ♕xc6 ♕e5 doesn't help either.

33	...	♕e5
34	♕b6	♕xe4
35	♕b4	♕c2
36	♖b1	♖d3
37	♕c5	♖e2

Kasparov avoids the simple trap 37...♕xa4? 38 ♕h5+ and in turn sets a pitfall of his own. However, 37...♖e1! forces mate even faster.

| 38 | ♕h5+ | ♔g8 |
| 39 | ♕xg4 | ♕xb1+! |

0-1

Game 53
Artur Yusupov – Garry Kasparov
World Cup, Barcelona 1989
King's Indian Defence, Petrosian System [E92]

Kasparov could have been justifiably proud of this game. However, when the finishing touches to his brilliant concept required only a few simple moves, he completely lost his way and went horribly astray...

1. ♘f3 ♘f6
2. c4 g6
3. ♘c3 ♗g7
4. e4 d6
5. d4 0-0
6. ♗e2 e5
7. d5

A former favourite of Petrosian, especially in connection with the following sortie ♗g5. This system has lately been far less popular than the main line with 7 0-0, but its strategic complexity from time to time attracts strong players. For example in the mid-1990s Kasparov had to defend Black's cause more than once in a heated theoretical duel against Kramnik.

7. ... a5

This move starts the most topical plan, originally devised by Stein and Geller. Black will develop his b8-knight without obstructing the important c8-h3 diagonal; his next moves will not only further his own kingside ambitions, but slow down White's queenside play as well. Kasparov later tried the older continuation 7...♘bd7 as well, but two painful defeats against Kramnik in 1994 caused him to reconsider.

8. ♗g5

Just as Black's previous move, this pin has prophylactic purposes. Now Black finds it much more difficult to launch his typical counterplay, connected with ...f5.

8. ... h6
9. ♗h4 ♘a6
10. ♘d2 ♕e8

The key move of Stein's plan. Black unpins his knight and by moving it to h7 frees the road for the f-pawn. However, he needn't hurry with this standard manoeuvre, as 10...♗d7 11 0-0 ♘c5 is another interesting idea. The game Kramnik-Kasparov, Munich blitz 1994 in Volume 2 will show Black can still put his queen to good use from d8.

11. 0-0 ♘h7
12. a3 *(D)*

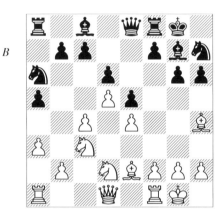

12. ... ♗d7

The most flexible continuation. Black makes a useful developing move and postpones the choice between ...h5 and ...f5. The immediate advance 12...f5?! is inferior due to 13 exf5! ♗xf5 (13...gxf5 14 ♗h5 ♕d7 is perhaps somewhat better, but compared with the game Black's forces lack coordination) 14 g4!? (14 f3 is pleasant for White and less committal) 14...♗d7 15 ♘de4 a4 16 f3 b6 17 ♗d3 ♗f6 18 ♘xf6+! ♘xf6 19 ♕d2 ♘c5 20 ♗c2 and White was better in Veingold-Kasparov, USSR Cht (Moscow) 1979.

13. b3

At the time our game was played, the text-move was considered more or less mandatory. Later White realized that the unprotected c3-knight increases Black's tactical chances and he needn't fear the ...a4 advance. The joint efforts of Kramnik and Illescas produced 13 ♔h1!?, which is nowadays considered to be the best try to fight for an edge.

13. ... f5!?

The former theoretical recommendation was 13...h5 14 f3 ♗h6. Here Black often activates his g7-bishop via e3, but his kingside dark squares can become vulnerable in the process. However, Kasparov had already shown (against Veingold in 1979) an inclination toward this natural King's Indian pawn thrust.

14 exf5 gxf5! *(D)*

Here White's 13th move makes 14...♗xf5 more attractive in comparison with the note to move 12, as after 15 g4 he gets reasonable counterplay with 15...e4! 16 ♖c1 e3. However, Kasparov's surprising novelty is more enterprising and shows that he is willing to make material sacrifices to keep his central pawns mobile with this positionally desirable recapture.

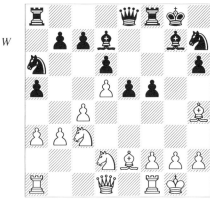

15 ♗h5 ♕c8

The idea of Black's previous move was definitely not to clutter up his queenside with his major pieces after the fainthearted 15...♕b8 16 ♗e7 ♖c8 (better is 16...♖e8!?, transposing into the game).

16 ♗e7 ♖e8!

Black wants the light-squared bishop, as its colleague will remain offside on h4 after White takes the offered exchange.

17 ♗xe8

Yusupov accepts the challenge. The inconsistent 17 ♗h4 gives Black a choice between repeating moves with 17...♖f8, or the more ambitious 17...e4!?.

17 ... ♕xe8
18 ♗h4 e4

The g7-bishop is free, the a6-knight is aiming for d3 and White must now defend carefully, as otherwise Black's initiative might quickly reach alarming proportions.

19 ♕c2

White would gladly return the exchange to take the sting out of Black's play by controlling f4, but unfortunately 19 ♘e2? loses a piece to the double attack 19...♗xa1 20 ♕xa1 ♕h5. Yusupov's move connects his rooks, but White doesn't get time to play ♖ae1 anyway, while now Black activates his queen with tempo. Later practice concentrated on the slightly stronger 19 ♖c1!? ♘c5 20 ♖c2, although even here Black seems to have sufficient compensation after, e.g., 20...♘f8 21 ♘e2 ♘g6 22 ♗g3 ♘d3.

19 ... ♕h5
20 ♗g3 *(D)*

The seemingly ugly move 20 g3 is perhaps no worse than the text-move, although after 20...♘f8 21 ♖ae1 ♘g6 22 ♕d1 ♕xd1 23 ♘xd1 ♘c5 Black has a clear-cut initiative despite the exchange of queens.

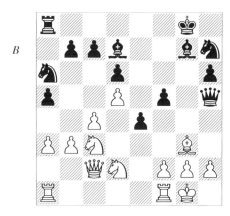

20 ... ♖f8

The rook joins the fray with a direct threat. Although the text-move is natural, later Black will invest a tempo to play ...♔g8, and moreover White could have consolidated his position on the very next move. Therefore Kasparov's suggestion 20...♘c5!? deserves attention. White's best bet is to lash out: 21 f3 e3 22 b4! leads to an unclear position.

21 ♗f4?

Kasparov's dynamic play has forced his opponent to solve concrete problems and it's no surprise that Yusupov is the first to commit a serious error. Although the text-move looks natural enough, the further course of the game will prove that retaining an effective piece blockade on f4 is very difficult. 21 f4! is necessary, denying the knight the g5-square. Another idea behind this move is that after 21...♘c5 White has the manoeuvre 22 ♖fd1 ♘d3 23 ♘f1! with a fully defensible position, the follow-up being ♖xd3.

21	...	♕g4
22	g3	♘g5!

Already the first drawbacks of 21 ♗f4? are clear enough – White's kingside light squares are dangerously vulnerable.

| 23 | ♔h1?! | |

This half-measure allows Black to tighten his grip on the position. It was safer to get rid of the menacing knight with 23 ♗xg5 hxg5 24 f3. After 24...♕h3 25 fxe4 f4! 26 e5!? ♗f5 27 ♘de4 ♗xe5 28 ♕d2 (weaker is 28 ♕g2 ♕xg2+ 29 ♔xg2 f3+!) 28...♘c5 29 ♖ae1 despite Black's dangerous attack White has more counterplay than in the game.

23	...	♘f3
24	♖ac1	

After 24 ♖ad1 ♕h5 25 h4 ♕g4 Black's attack breaks through. 24 ♔g2 ♘c5 25 h3 ♕h5 is no better; the threats are ...♘d3 and especially ...♘xd2, followed by ...f4. The text-move at least allows White to take on f3.

24	...	♘c5
25	♘xf3	

Forced. After 25 ♕d1 ♘d3 Black wins the exchange back with a continuing attack, as 26 ♖c2 runs into the pretty 26...♘fe1!.

25	...	♕xf3+
26	♔g1	♘d3 (D)

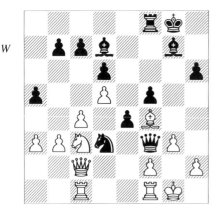

| 27 | ♕d2 | |

White's bishop must obviously remain on f4, but this move is rather passive. He had better options:

1) 27 ♘e2 prevents Black's following move, but after the simple reply 27...♘xc1 followed by 28...a4 Black breaks up White's queenside with a permanent advantage.

2) Therefore White should try to challenge Black's threatening queen. One way to do this is 27 ♕d1 ♘xf4!? (27...♘xc1 28 ♕xf3 leads to line '3') 28 gxf4 (28 ♕xf3? ♘h3+ 29 ♔g2 exf3+ 30 ♔xh3 f4+ 31 g4 h5 lands White's king in a desperate predicament) 28...♕xf4 29 ♔h1 ♗e5. Black has more than enough for the exchange, but White still retains defensive chances after 30 ♕h5.

3) 27 ♕e2!? is possibly best. Following 27...♘xc1 (after 27...♘xf4 28 gxf4 ♕xf4 29 ♕e3! White has a better version of line '2') 28 ♕xf3 (after 28 ♖xc1 ♕xe2 29 ♘xe2 ♗b2 White has problems with his vulnerable queenside) 28...exf3 29 ♖xc1 ♖e8 30 h3 White's position seems very passive, but it's not easy to break and he has counterplay connected with ♘b5.

| 27 | ... | ♗d4!? |

Kasparov is still not interested in material and continues to pile up the pressure.

| 28 | ♖c2 | |

After 28 ♕e2 Black has a choice between 28...♘xf4 (similar to line '2' above) or 28...♘xc1 (an improved version of line '3' above), but 28 ♘b5 is interesting.

28	...	♔h7
29	h3?	

It's already too late for 29 ♕d1? ♘xf4 30 ♕xf3 ♘h3+, but this was White's last chance to play 29 ♘b5!?. Driving the bishop away from the long diagonal helps; for example, after 29...♗c5 30 ♕d1 ♘xf4 31 ♕xf3 ♘h3+ 32 ♔g2 exf3+ 33 ♔xh3 f4+ 34 ♔h4 ♖g8 35 ♖e1 Black has no more than a perpetual.

29	...	♖g8
30	♔h2	♕h5! (D)

Kasparov still had four minutes on his clock and was objectively right to spurn the technical 30...♘xf4 31 ♕xf4 ♕d3 32 ♘e2! ♗c5!. Here White's queenside is crumbling and Black's passed pawns will be amply supported by his bishop-pair, but the attacking text-move should have decided the game much faster.

| 31 | ♘d1 | |

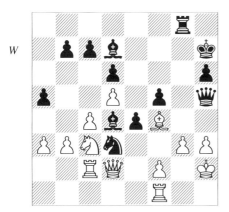
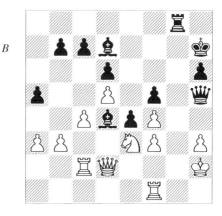

31 ♕d1 is slightly more resilient, but after 31...♘xf4 32 gxf4 ♕h4 33 ♕d2 ♗c5 White's position is untenable. Black's main threat is the direct ...e3, while ....♗e8-h5 is also in the air and 34 ♖g1 ♖xg1 35 ♔xg1 ♕g3+ 36 ♔f1 ♕xh3+ doesn't help.

31 ... ♘e5?

The tragedy begins. By now Kasparov was down to his last minute and missed the first forced win with the relatively simple 31...♘xf4! 32 ♕xf4 (32 gxf4 ♕g6 33 ♘e3 ♗xe3 mates) 32...♗e5, followed by 33...f4 and Black's attack breaks through.

32 f3!

This trick shouldn't have saved the game, but it's White's best resource. Black's attack plays itself after 32 ♗xe5 ♗xe5 33 ♕e2 ♕g6 34 ♔h1 f4.

32 ... ♘d3?

After overlooking White's last move Kasparov continues to falter. 32...♕xf3! 33 ♗xe5 (33 ♖xf3 ♘xf3+ with a healthy extra pawn in the endgame) 33...♕xf1 34 ♗xd4 f4 35 g4 ♗xg4! 36 hxg4 ♖xg4 37 ♕f2 ♕xd1 should still have won for Black.

33 ♘e3?

Yusupov returns the favour. 33 fxe4 fxe4 34 ♕g2 was definitely stronger. After 34...♘xf4 35 ♖xf4 ♗e5! (35...♕xd1? loses to 36 ♕xc4+ ♖g6 37 ♖f7+ ♔h8 38 ♖g2! ♖g7 39 ♖xd7!) 36 ♕xc4+ ♔h8 37 ♘f2 Black retains an edge thanks to the trick 37...♖xg3! 38 ♔xg3 ♗f5, but White still has reasonable drawing chances.

33 ... ♘xf4
34 gxf4 (D)

34 ... ♗b6??

A serious error, which leads to a total turnaround. 34...♕h4! 35 ♕xd4 ♖g3! forces mate.

35 ♕f2

White covers the vital h4-square and puts an end to Black's attack. Although with the strong b6-bishop Kasparov still could have fought on tenaciously and possibly even saved the game, time-trouble and understandable dejection shorten his resistance.

35 ... ♕g6

Both 35...exf3 and 35...♖e8!? are more resilient.

36 ♖e2

Yusupov is reluctant to open the position prematurely. 36 fxe4 fxe4 37 f5 ♕g5 38 ♖e2 ♗d4 gives Black counterchances.

36 ... ♗c5?

36...♖e8! was still better. Now White frees his f-pawn and with his 39th move prevents Black's bishop from rejoining the fray via d4.

37 fxe4 fxe4

37...♖e8 38 ♖g1 ♕f7 39 exf5 is also insufficient.

38 f5 ♕h5
39 ♖d2! ♖g5
40 ♕f4 ♕e8?!

40...♗xe3 41 ♕xe3 ♗xf5 42 ♖df2 is hopeless for Black in the long run, but the text-move loses immediately.

41 ♘g4 1-0

Black has finally made the time-control, but his position is completely ruined. With a hanging flag, differences in class tend to disappear and we all become only too human...

Game 54
Viktor Korchnoi – Garry Kasparov
World Cup, Barcelona 1989
King's Indian Defence, Classical Main Line [E97]

1	♘f3	♘f6
2	c4	g6
3	♘c3	♗g7
4	e4	d6
5	d4	0-0
6	♗e2	♘c6
7	0-0	e5
8	d5	♘e7 *(D)*

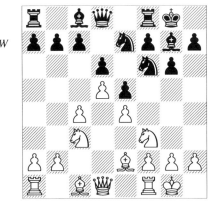

9 a4!?

At the moment this game was played Kasparov was lagging behind on –1 (see Game 53) and he still desperately needed to score his first win. His sharp opening choice suits the situation, but Korchnoi had ambitions of his own and was the first to come up with a big surprise. Unexpected as it seems, the text-move has its logic. White intends to proceed with his usual queenside play only after gaining space by playing a5 first. In 1987 Korchnoi had introduced a very similar idea in his favourite line 9 ♘e1 ♘d7 10 ♗e3 f5 11 f3 f4 12 ♗f2 g5, namely 13 a4 (for 13 b4 see Piket-Kasparov, Tilburg 1989, Game 56). This later became a standard continuation and White's most popular choice, and Korchnoi essayed it against Kasparov himself in Amsterdam 1991. Here 13...a5!? is again considered a good option for Black; our game could have transposed into this variation later on by 12...f4.

9 ... a5!

Just as in the line from the above note, Black has to decide what to do with White's a-pawn, only here this moment came four moves earlier. Kasparov's reaction, which cost him 30 minutes on the clock, sins against the principle "avoid unnecessary pawn moves on the flank where you are under attack". However, modern chess is a concrete game and especially in such a strategically difficult opening as the King's Indian Black can't rely solely on general considerations. Practice has shown the text-move is the best. For a similar example see the note to move 9 in Game 48.

10	♘e1	♘d7
11	♗e3	f5
12	f3 *(D)*	

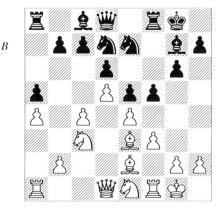

12 ... ♘c5!?

Facing an opening surprise as early as move 9 has always been an unusual experience for Kasparov, but his understanding of the King's Indian allows him to pass such tests. He is reluctant to close the position mainly because this would reduce his chances to activate the g7-bishop in the near future. Although 12...f4 13 ♗f2 g5 leads to a fully playable position, it usually arises from the different line, mentioned in the note to White's 9th move. The more flexible text-move retains the central tension and is a critical test of White's opening concept. A telling fact is that Korchnoi never returned to 9 a4!? in his subsequent practice.

13 ♘d3 b6

13...♘xd3?! 14 ♕xd3 b6 is weaker, and after 15 ♘b5 ♔h8 16 ♗d2! followed by b4 White gets a pleasant edge.

14 b4!

Now Korchnoi had his first longer think and realized that further preparation of this important advance would be too time-consuming. The temporary pawn sacrifice is the most consistent continuation.

14 ... ♘xd3

An important moment. Kasparov opts for a straightforward plan, but 14...axb4 15 ♘xb4 ♖a5!? also deserved attention. In the lines with 12...f4 Black's knight usually goes to f6 instead of c5, thus furthering his typical kingside play. On the other hand here it's not so easy for White to make progress on the opposite flank and the position remains unclear.

15 ♕xd3 axb4
16 ♘b5 ♔h8 (D)

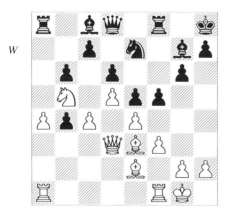

A consistent follow-up to moves 12-14; Black redeploys his passive knight via g8.

17 ♕b3?!

The note to move 13 indicates 17 ♗d2! as an alternative. White plans ♗xb4 followed by a quick a5. This is indeed stronger and gives White chances to fight for an edge even after the most active reaction, 17...c5!? 18 dxc6 ♘xc6 19 ♕d5! (19 ♘xd6?! is weaker, because after 19...♗e6 Black comfortably finishes his development and secures a slight advantage).

Now:

1) 19...♗b7 20 ♘xd6 ♕e7 (20...♘d4?! 21 ♘xb7 ♘xe2+ 22 ♔f2 gets Black nowhere) 21 ♘xb7 (21 c5? is weak due to 21...bxc5 22 ♕xc5 ♖fd8!) 21...♕xb7 22 ♗xb4 ♖fd8 23 ♗d6 ♕d7 (after 23...♖a5 24 c5 ♖xc5 25 ♗xc5 ♖xd5 26 exd5 bxc5 27 dxc6 the passed a-pawn can become very dangerous) 24 c5 bxc5 25 ♗b5! (25 ♗xc5 ♕xd5 26 exd5 ♖xd5 followed by ...e4 or ...♘d4 gives Black enough activity to hold the position) 25...♕xd6 26 ♗xc6 and Black still hasn't fully equalized.

2) Kasparov's preference was 19...♗d7 20 ♕xd6 ♘d4! and here Black indeed has good counterplay. A plausible line is 21 ♘xd4 exd4 22 ♗xb4 ♖e8 23 a5 bxa5! 24 ♗xa5 ♖xa5 25 ♖xa5 ♕xa5 26 ♕xd7 ♖d8 27 ♕e7 d3!? 28 ♗xd3 ♗f8 29 ♕f6+ ♗g7 drawing by repetition.

17 ... ♘g8

Here White's minor pieces are more active and 17...c5?! is inferior in view of 18 dxc6 ♘xc6 19 ♖ad1.

18 ♕xb4 ♘f6? (D)

Inconsistent. Kasparov could have played 18...♗h6, which would have been a logical follow-up of the manoeuvre started with 16...♔h8. It seems even better to play the preliminary exchanges 18...fxe4!? 19 fxe4 ♖xf1+, followed by 20...♗h6, activating Black's minor pieces. This would have justified his decision to refrain from 12...f4 and given him a slight edge, as White still hasn't achieved anything significant on the queenside.

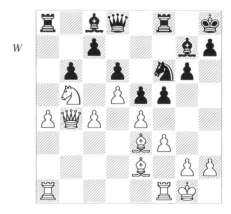

19 exf5

Korchnoi doesn't stubbornly insist on defending e4. This simple capture leads to a sharp position in which White's queenside ambitions slightly outweigh Black's less clearly defined counterplay.

| 19 | ... | gxf5 |
| 20 | ♗g5 | |

20 a5? is premature due to the simple trick 20...bxa5 21 ♖xa5? c5!. However, Black will soon have to play ...♗d7 anyway, so Korchnoi improves his pieces, knowing he will get a better opportunity for this key advance.

| 20 | ... | h6 |

20...♗d7!? is probably more accurate.

| 21 | ♗h4 | ♗d7 (D) |

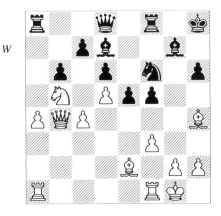

| 22 | ♖a3 | |

White refuses to commit himself. The more energetic alternatives were:

1) 22 f4 e4!? is not ideal for White. A transfer of White's minor pieces to better squares with ♗e1-c3 and ♘d4 requires preparation (the immediate 23 ♘d4? runs into 23...♘xd5!) and the invested time can be used by Black to play ...♕c8, possibly followed by ...♗e8 and ...♘d7-c5.

2) However, this was a good moment for the consistent 22 a5!. White has the initiative, and the drawbacks of 20...h6 are seen in the line 22...bxa5 (22...♗xb5 23 ♕xb5 bxa5 24 ♖xa5 ♖b8 25 ♕a4 doesn't fully solve Black's problems either; his light squares are vulnerable) 23 ♖xa5 c5 24 ♖xa8 ♕xa8 25 ♕d2!. Now after 25...♗xb5 26 ♗xf6 White forces the undesirable 26...♖xf6 27 cxb5 and is better.

| 22 | ... | ♕b8 |

Now the a5 advance again requires preparation.

| 23 | ♗f2 | ♖g8 |

The blockade 23...♖a5? fails tactically to 24 ♘xc7!, but Black could have played 23...♘h5!? immediately, limiting White's options.

| 24 | ♖b1 | |

24 a5 is possible, but after 24...♗xb5 25 ♕xb5 bxa5 26 ♖xa5 ♕xb5 27 ♖xb5 ♖a2 Black has sufficient counterplay. However, here 24 f4!? ♘e4 25 ♗e3 deserved serious attention.

| 24 | ... | ♘h5 |
| 25 | ♔h1!? | |

White still aspires for more than 25 a5 ♗xb5 26 ♕xb5 bxa5 27 ♖xa5 ♘f4 28 ♗f1 e4!? (the alternative 28...♕xb5 29 ♖axb5 e4 is also playable), when Black activates his forces with approximate equality.

| 25 | ... | ♕d8 |
| 26 | a5 | |

Although further prophylaxis with 26 ♗f1!? was possible, Korchnoi's decision to act is logical enough and was criticized unjustly.

| 26 | ... | ♗xb5 |

With time running low, Kasparov opts for simplification. The more complex 26...♘f4 27 ♗f1 bxa5 28 ♖xa5 gives White an advantage.

| 27 | ♕xb5 | bxa5 |
| 28 | g3?! | |

Only this panicky move is an error, after which White starts losing control over the game. The natural 28 ♖xa5 ♖b8 (28...♕g5!?) 29 ♕xb8 ♕xb8 30 ♖xb8 ♖xb8 31 ♖b5 ♖xb5 (Kasparov's notes indicate both players overlooked that after 31...♖a8? 32 ♗d3 it's not White, but Black who has problems with his back rank) 32 cxb5 ♘f6 33 ♗c4 leads to an endgame in which Black still has to tread with care to earn a draw.

| 28 | ... | f4! |
| 29 | g4 | e4! (D) |

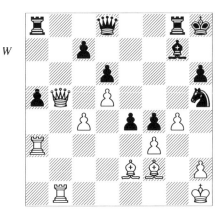

After two sharp blows it's clear that 28 g3?!, instead of limiting Black's possibilities, has achieved quite the opposite – Kasparov's forces are coming alive with a vengeance and it's White who has to be on his toes.

30 fxe4?

The radical change of the situation has its psychological effect. The text-move weakens the dark squares and White's position slides further downhill. Other moves:

1) Kasparov sacrificed the piece practically instantly and his intuition proved right. After 30 gxh5?! e3 White must play 31 ♗g1 (31 ♗e1? ♕g5 gives Black a decisive attack; for example, 32 h4 ♕f5! 33 ♗f1 ♕xh5 34 ♗e2 ♗f6 or 32 ♗d3 ♕xh5 33 ♗e4 ♖ae8! followed by ...♖xe4) 31...♕g5 32 ♗d3 ♕xh5 33 ♖f1. Here it's not necessary to delve much deeper: White's extra bishop is trapped on g1 and Black's full control of the g-file gives him a large advantage. White will have to defend g2 and g1 passively and even the passed a-pawn may play a major role yet. Probably best is 33...♕h3, when the natural 34 ♖a2? loses beautifully to 34...♖ab8 35 ♕a4 e2! 36 ♗xe2 ♖b1!! 37 ♖xb1 ♗b2! and Black mates.

2) However, White still could have held the balance with the cold-blooded 30 ♖xa5! ♖xa5 31 ♕xa5 ♗c5 (31...e3 32 ♗e1 gets Black nowhere). Now the most practical is 32 gxh5 e3 33 ♕a7! with a draw.

30 ... ♘f6 (D)

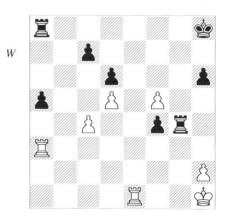

31 ♗h4

White will regret this sortie four moves later, but 31 ♗f3 ♘d7! is no real improvement for White. Black threatens ...♖b8 and his knight will exert strong pressure from e5.

31	...	♕e7
32	♗f3	♕e5
33	♖e1	

The e4-pawn was not so important, but it's not easy to find a constructive alternative. With 33 ♔g2 White keeps an eye on b2 (see the following note) and prepares ♖xa5 (the immediate 33 ♖xa5? loses to 33...♕c3), but must reckon with the dangerous reply 33...h5!. Now Kasparov cleverly increases his control of the dark squares.

33	...	♘h7!
34	♕d7	♗f6
35	♗xf6+	

This ugly exchange is forced, as 35 ♗f2? loses on the spot to 35...♕b2.

| 35 | ... | ♘xf6 |
| 36 | ♕f5 | |

36 ♕e6 is not much better due to 36...♕g5!? (36...♕xe6 37 dxe6 ♘xg4 38 ♗xg4 ♖xg4 39 e5 gives White good drawing chances).

| 36 | ... | ♕xf5 |
| 37 | exf5 | |

A debatable decision, but Korchnoi was already short of time as well and prefers sacrificing a pawn for active counterplay to suffering with his passive bishop after 37 gxf5 ♘d7 38 ♖f1 ♖gb8. However, even the text-move doesn't eliminate the main drawback of White's position – his cornered king.

| 37 | ... | ♘xg4 |
| 38 | ♗xg4 | ♖xg4 (D) |

39 ♖h3?!

Korchnoi's flag was about to fall and after this final mistake Black wins practically by force. However, it may well be that White's position was already beyond saving. In the post-mortem the players considered 39 ♖e6 the best chance, but even here after 39...♖ag8!? 40 ♖xh6+ ♔g7 41 ♖e6 (41 ♖g6+? ♖xg6 42 fxg6 ♖a8! is hopeless for White) 41...♔f7 42 ♖e1 ♔f6! 43 ♖xa5 f3 44 ♖a2 ♖xc4 White's pawns are weak and Black should win. Perhaps 39 f6!? is more resilient.

39 ... ♔g7!
40 ♖e7+ ♔f6

With his 39th move White has only enhanced the strength of the a-pawn, while allowing Black to activate his king.

41 ♖e6+

The lesser evil. After 41 ♖xc7 ♖ag8! 42 ♖xh6+ ♔xf5 43 ♖f7+ ♔e4 the mating threats force 44 ♖e7+ ♔f3 45 ♖e1 ♔f2 46 h3 ♔xe1 47 hxg4 f3 48 ♔h2 f2 49 ♖e6+ ♔f1 and Black will quickly queen his f-pawn.

41 ... ♔xf5
42 ♖hxh6 (D)

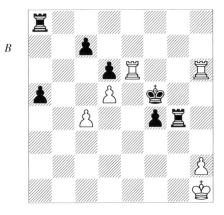

42 ... ♖f8!

Black prevents the threatened perpetual and simultaneously supports the f-pawn, thereby forcing White to exchange a pair of rooks.

43 ♖h5+ ♖g5
44 ♖xg5+ ♔xg5
45 c5 a4!

Seventeen moves earlier White spurned this pawn and now it decides the game. 45...dxc5?! 46 ♖a6 ♖f5 47 ♖xa5 ♖xd5 48 ♔g2 is less convincing.

46 cxd6 cxd6
47 ♖xd6 ♖a8
48 ♖e6 a3

49 ♖e1 ♔f5

49...f3 wins as well; e.g., 50 ♔g1 a2 51 ♖a1 ♔f4 52 ♔f2 (52 ♔f1 ♔e3 53 ♖e1+ ♔d4 54 ♖a1 ♔xd5 is hopeless for White) 52...♖g8! 53 d6 ♖g2+ 54 ♔f1 ♖xh2 55 d7 ♖h1+! 56 ♔f2 ♖xa1 57 d8♕ ♖f1+ and Black mates. With the text-move Black threatens to annihilate the d-pawn, thereby forcing White to move his h-pawn; this will allow the king to penetrate via g3.

50 h4

After 50 ♔g2 a2 51 ♖a1 ♔e5 52 ♔f3 ♖a4 Black gradually deals with both White's pawns.

50 ... f3 (D)

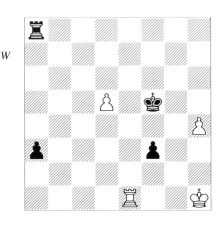

51 d6

We already know Black wins after 51 ♔g1 ♔f4 52 ♔f2 a2 53 ♖a1 ♖g8!.

51 ... a2

51...f2 52 ♖a1 ♖e8 is even simpler.

52 ♖a1 ♔f4

52...♔e6 53 h5 ♔xd6 54 h6 ♖a7 55 ♔g1 ♔d5 56 h7 ♖g7+! followed by ...♖xh7 also wins, but Kasparov plays for mate. The threat is ...♔g3 followed by ...♖b8.

53 ♔h2 f2
54 d7

After 54 ♔g2 ♔e3 55 d7 ♖g8+ 56 ♔h3 ♖d8 Black first takes White's d-pawn and then queens one of his own pawns.

54 ... ♔f3
55 ♖c1 a1♕

0-1

Korchnoi was not interested in getting mated after 56 ♖xa1 (56 d8♕ ♕e5+ 57 ♔h1 ♕e1+ is no better) 56...♖xa1 57 d8♕ ♖h1+!. A tremendous fight!

Game 55
Garry Kasparov – Valery Salov
World Cup, Barcelona 1989
English Opening [A34]

Kasparov won a brilliancy prize for this spectacular game.

1	♘f3	♘f6
2	c4	b6
3	♘c3	c5
4	e4	

After 4 d4 cxd4 5 ♘xd4 ♗b7 White can reach a Hedgehog-type position with 6 f3 followed by e4. However, Kasparov had something else in mind.

4 ... d6

This move is slightly passive, as it limits the options of Black's f8-bishop. A good illustration of this is a sample line after the more enterprising 4...♘c6. Then 5 d4 cxd4 6 ♘xd4 ♗b7 7 ♗g5 e6 8 ♘xc6 ♗xc6 9 ♗d3 ♕b8 10 ♕e2 allows 10...♗d6!?, when active development promises Black good counterplay.

5	d4	cxd4
6	♘xd4	♗b7
7	♕e2!?	*(D)*

7 f3 leads to the type of positions mentioned in the note to White's 4th move. White chooses a less played, but more aggressive alternative. He will fianchetto his king's bishop and in some lines he might even contemplate queenside castling.

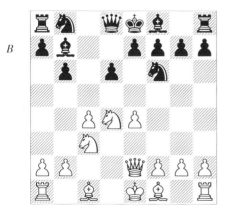

7 ... ♘bd7

Other moves:

1) 7...♘c6?! is not ideal. 8 ♘xc6 ♗xc6 9 ♗g5 e6 10 0-0-0 shows one of the ideas behind 7 ♕e2!?, and White's lead in development gives him a nagging initiative.

2) 7...g6 is possible, but has one serious drawback – to chase away White's knight from d5 Black will later have to play ...e6 anyway, thus weakening both the d6-pawn and the kingside dark squares. After 8 g3 ♗g7 (the weaker 8...♘bd7 9 ♗g2 ♖c8 10 0-0 a6?! 11 ♖d1 ♕c7 12 b3 e6 was played in Salov-Yudasin, St Petersburg 1997; Salov put his bitter experience to a good use and got a clear advantage after the energetic 13 ♗a3! ♘c5 14 ♖ac1 ♗e7 15 b4 ♘cd7 16 ♘d5! exd5 17 cxd5 ♕b8 18 ♘c6 ♗xc6 19 dxc6 ♘e5 20 f4! b5!? 21 fxe5 dxe5 22 ♗b2 0-0 23 ♔h1 ♕c7 24 a3) 9 ♗g2 0-0 10 0-0 ♘c6 11 ♗e3 White has a slight but pleasant edge.

3) Arguably the safest continuation is 7...e6. Now 8 g4!? is a sharp idea, but Kasparov's next move indicates he probably would have preferred the less committal 8 g3 ♗e7 9 ♗g2 a6 (9...0-0 10 0-0-0 is less comfortable for Black, as the natural 10...a6? loses material after 11 e5! ♗xg2 12 exf6 ♗xf6 13 ♔xg2 ♗xd4 14 ♕e4!) 10 0-0 ♕c7, which leads to a typical Hedgehog position with chances for both sides.

8 g3

Black's previous move took away the most natural retreat-square for the f6-knight. A double-edged attempt to profit from this is 8 g4!?, but the position after 8...h6 9 h4 g6!? is anything but clear.

8 ... ♖c8

Again the immediate 8...e6 is more circumspect, but Salov obstinately refrains from this natural move until it's too late...

9	♗g2	a6
10	0-0	♕c7?

This was Black's last chance to play 10...e6 in relative safety. Only after 11 ♖d1 (here 11 ♘d5?! is dubious, as after 11...exd5 12 exd5+

♕e7!? White's compensation is very vague) Black parries the threat of e5 with 11...♕c7 12 b3 ♗e7, finishing his development with a playable position.

11 b3 e6 *(D)*

Salov has been trying to postpone this move for as long as possible, but now with ♘d5 in the air he has no choice. Black can't afford 11...b5? since after 12 ♘d5 ♕c5 13 ♗e3 his position is falling apart; e.g., 13...bxc4? 14 b4 ♕a7 15 ♘b5 ♕b8 16 ♗a7 and White traps the poor queen. However, even the text-move can't stop the powerful knight jump.

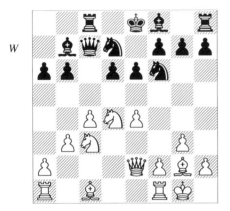

12 ♘d5!

After a poor start, Kasparov became his usual energetic self in the second half of the tournament. This typical Sicilian sacrifice punishes Black for neglecting his development and starts a powerful attack against the king stuck in the centre (see an interesting parallel, albeit with different motifs, in Game 50). 12 ♗d2 transposes to a position that had arisen in earlier practice; after 12...♗e7 or even 12...g6!? White can at best claim only a slight edge. The same goes for 12 ♗b2 ♗e7.

12 ... ♕b8

Black decides to ignore the knight and this is the safest way to do it (his position rapidly collapses after 12...♕d8? 13 e5! or 12...♕c5?! 13 ♗e3 exd5 14 exd5). Accepting the sacrifice gives White a powerful attack: 12...exd5 13 exd5+ and now:

1) 13...♗e7 14 ♘f5! (14 ♖e1? lets Black's king escape with 14...0-0!, as after 15 ♕xe7? ♖fe8 White's queen is trapped) 14...♘e5 15 ♘xg7+ ♔d8 (15...♔f8 16 ♗h6 {or 16 ♘f5} is even more dangerous) 16 ♘f5. Black's forces are uncoordinated, his pawns on both flanks are vulnerable and with two pawns for the piece White has numerous ways of developing his initiative.

2) 13...♔d8 is somewhat stronger, but even here 14 ♖e1 (Kasparov's recommendation 14 ♗b2!? is a worthy alternative and leads to a similar position) 14...♘e5 15 f4 ♘g6 16 ♗b2 gives White permanent pressure and more than sufficient compensation.

13 ♖d1! *(D)*

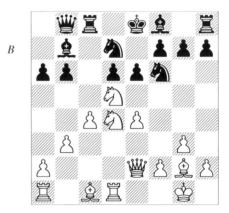

White calmly leaves the knight *en prise* and makes a useful attacking move without prematurely committing his c1-bishop.

13 ... g6

After 13...exd5 14 exd5+ ♔d8 15 ♘c6+ ♗xc6 16 dxc6 ♘c5 17 b4 ♘e6 18 ♗e3 White threatens c5 and the black king has only minimal chances to survive in the middle. 13...e5 closes the position, but on the other hand this positional concession gives White a clear and permanent advantage after 14 ♘xf6+ ♘xf6 15 ♘f5 g6 16 ♘h6 (or 16 ♗g5). Although his position is under heavy fire, Salov indicates he would still like to finish his development. Given the time, Black would play ...♗g7 and seriously intend to take the Trojan horse on d5.

14 ♗g5!

Kasparov will have none of this. This energetic move is stronger than 14 ♗h3 ♗g7 15 ♗xe6 (15 ♘xe6!? fxe6 16 ♗xe6 is perhaps more dangerous for Black) 15...fxe6 16 ♘xe6 ♔f7 17 ♘g5+ ♔f8, when it's not clear if White has more than a draw by repetition.

14 ... ♗g7 *(D)*

It's now too late for 14...exd5? 15 exd5+ ♗e7 16 ♘c6 ♗xc6 17 dxc6 ♘e5 18 f4 and White wins the piece back with an overwhelming position, as 18...♘eg4 19 ♗h3 h6 20 ♖e1 doesn't help.

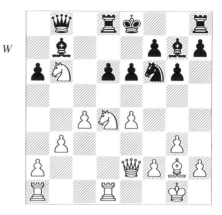

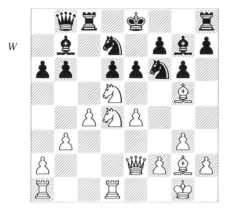

15 ♗xf6 ♘xf6

A difficult decision. The text-move costs Black a pawn without much compensation, but the materialistic 15...♗xf6 is hardly any better and definitely riskier. After 16 ♘xf6+ ♘xf6 17 e5! ♗xg2 (17...dxe5? loses quickly: 18 ♗xb7 ♕xb7 19 ♕xe5 ♔e7 {or 19...♕e7 20 ♘c6!} 20 ♘xe6! fxe6 21 ♖d6) 18 exf6 ♗h3 (forced, as 18...♕b7? fails to 19 ♘xe6 fxe6 20 ♕xe6+ ♔f8 21 ♖e1!, winning) 19 ♕e4! Black is in big trouble. His king can't leave the centre (19...0-0? loses a piece to 20 ♕h4), and 19...♕a8?! 20 ♕xa8 ♖xa8 21 ♘c6 also costs him material. Meanwhile White can calmly improve his position by doubling rooks on the d-file.

16 ♘xb6 ♖d8? *(D)*

The final mistake, which gives Kasparov a welcome chance to wind up his attack combinatively. After the stronger 16...♖c7 17 ♘a4 0-0 he would still have to show good technique to realize his material advantage.

17 e5! ♗xg2

After 17...dxe5?! 18 ♘c6 ♗xc6 (18...♖xd1+ 19 ♖xd1 ♗xc6 20 ♗xc6+ ♔f8 21 c5 is hopeless for Black) 19 ♗xc6+ ♔e7 20 c5 ♕c7 21 ♕xa6! (even the less forceful 21 ♗g2 ♕xc5 22 ♕xa6 is sufficient) 21...♕xc6 (after 21...♖xd1+ 22 ♖xd1 ♕xc6 23 ♕a7+ ♔e8 24 ♘c4! White's attack breaks through quickly, as Black's king can't castle any more) 22 ♕a7+ ♘d7 23 ♖d6 ♕xc5 24 ♖xd7+ ♖xd7 25 ♕xd7+ ♔f6 26 ♘c4

or 26 ♕b7!? Black can't survive for long with his exposed king.

18 exf6 ♗xf6

What now? Has Kasparov miscalculated?

19 ♘xe6!

Another typical Sicilian sacrifice. This time it has a concrete and deadly effect, especially in connection with White's 21st move. White should avoid 19 ♔xg2? ♕xb6, while 19 ♘d5 ♗xd5 20 cxd5 gives him an edge, but is unconvincing compared with the text-move.

19 ... fxe6

19...♗xa1 20 ♘xd8+ ♔xd8 (20...♗e5 21 ♘d7! ♔xd7 22 ♘xf7 and Black's position disintegrates) gives White a choice between the technical 21 ♔xg2 and the more forceful 21 c5!? with a decisive advantage in both cases.

20 ♕xe6+ ♗e7 *(D)*

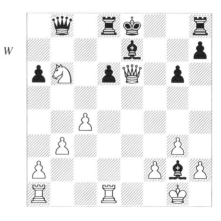

21 c5!!

The real point of 17 e5!. This powerful blow shattered Salov's futile hopes for 21 ♖e1 ♕b7 22 ♕xe7+ ♕xe7 23 ♔xg2 ♕xe1 24 ♖xe1+

♔f7, when Black has good chances to hold this slightly inferior endgame.

| 21 | ... | ♗b7 |

After 21...♗c6 22 ♖ac1 Black has no effective defence against cxd6. Just as hopeless is 21...♗f3 22 ♖d3 ♕b7 23 ♖e1, when White threatens both cxd6 and ♖xf3.

| 22 | ♖e1 | ♕c7 (D) |

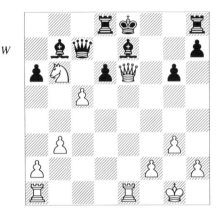

| 23 | c6! | ♗xc6 |

23...♗c8 loses immediately to 24 ♘d5.

| 24 | ♖ac1 | ♖d7 |

This sad move is the only defence against ♖xc6.

| 25 | ♘xd7 | ♕xd7 |
| 26 | ♕c4! (D) | |

Kasparov gives Black no respite. The rook endgame after 26 ♖xc6 ♕xe6 27 ♖xe6 ♔d7 28 ♖xe7+ ♔xc6 or 26 ♕xe7+ is also won for White, but the text-move is far more incisive.

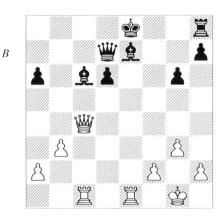

| 26 | ... | ♗b7 |

After 26...♗b5 the simplest is 27 ♕e4!? and the threats ♖c8+ and a4 net White at least a piece. Other bishop retreats allow the decisive ♕c8+.

| 27 | ♕c7 | ♖f8 |

The threat was ♕b8+ and even putting the rook on a protected square doesn't help.

| 28 | ♕b8+ | ♔f7 |
| 29 | ♖c7! | 1-0 |

White wins one of Black's bishops.

Game 56
Jeroen Piket – Garry Kasparov
Tilburg 1989
King's Indian Defence, Classical Main Line [E99]

1	d4	♘f6
2	♘f3	g6
3	c4	♗g7
4	♘c3	0-0
5	e4	d6
6	♗e2	e5
7	0-0	♘c6
8	d5	♘e7
9	♘e1	♘d7 *(D)*

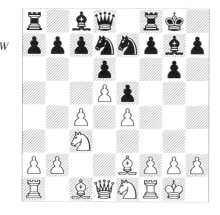

10 ♗e3

White's most enterprising choice. From the g1-a7 diagonal the bishop exerts considerable pressure against Black's queenside, at the same time helping out with the defence. However, all this comes at a certain price. First of all Black wins a tempo by advancing his f-pawn, which is always an important consideration in complex positions with attacks on opposite flanks. Another drawback of the text-move becomes clear when one compares it with White's main alternative 10 ♘d3 f5 11 ♗d2 ♘f6 12 f3. As the reader has already seen in Game 5, in this line the f2-square is reserved for the knight instead of the bishop and it's more difficult for Black to continue his assault with ...g4. After 10 ♗e3 Black mostly has no problems with implementing this key advance and the outcome of the game depends on the extent of the positional or material gains White meanwhile achieves on the queenside. The value of every move increases considerably and hidden tactical nuances often decide heated theoretical duels (just as in our game). Thus it's no wonder the whole line has experienced rather wild swings in popularity in the past 50 years.

10	...	f5
11	f3	f4
12	♗f2	g5 *(D)*

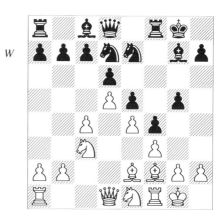

13 b4

This is an important moment and White's choice greatly influences the further course of the game. This warrants a short look at the alternatives:

1) The oldest and most natural way to prepare the c5 advance with 13 ♘d3 has had a bad reputation for more than 50 years. Even the few recent outings by Korchnoi, the main guru of the 10 ♗e3 line, have shown its main drawback – the knight is often needed on e1 to protect g2 and contrary to the 10 ♘d3 variations it can't take part in the defence of the king. Black gets a dangerous attack by regrouping his forces just as in our game.

2) Thus the whole line started falling into oblivion and the revival came only in the 1980s, when White found more accurate and forceful

methods to pursue his goals. In 1987 Korchnoi came up with the direct 13 ♘b5!?, starting a hunt for Black's important attacking bishop. However, subsequent practice proved that the time invested into this sortie gives Black sufficient counterplay after 13...b6! 14 b4 a6 15 ♘c3 ♘g6.

3) White often plays 13 a4, intending a5 and increasing the effect of a possible ♘b5. Another motif is that in some lines he might do without the rather superfluous text-move; for example, after 13...♘g6 14 a5 ♖f7 the pawn sacrifice 15 c5! ♘xc5 16 ♗xc5 dxc5 17 ♗c4 ♔h8 18 a6 gives White promising compensation. However, as has already been mentioned in the notes to Game 54, he must seriously reckon with 13...a5!?.

4) Finally, a different version of the above idea occurred in a later game between the same players, namely 13 ♖c1 ♘g6 14 c5!? ♘xc5 15 b4 ♘a6 16 ♘d3 h5 17 ♘b5 ♗d7 18 a4 ♗h6 19 ♖c3 b6!? 20 ♗e1 ♖f7 21 ♘f2 ♘h4 22 ♘xd6 cxd6 23 ♗xa6 ♕e8 24 ♕e2 g4! 25 fxg4 and now the energetic 25...♘xg2! 26 ♔xg2 hxg4 would have given Black the initiative in Piket-Kasparov, Linares 1997.

13	...	♘f6
14	c5	♘g6
15	cxd6	cxd6 (D)

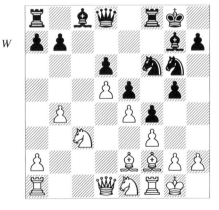

16 ♖c1

This move is a necessary part of White's set-up. Now ♘b5 will create the threat of ♘c7-e6. Keeping a distant eye on the c8-bishop is also important for the defence (see the following note). To be more concrete, after 16 a4?! Black can do without the subtleties and play 16...h5 17 a5 (17 ♖c1 g4 18 ♘b5 g3! 19 ♗xa7? ♗d7 simply loses a piece for White) 17...g4 18 ♘b5 g3!. Now this typical pawn sacrifice is very dangerous, as White has no time for 19 ♗xa7 ♘h7 20 ♔h1? due to 20...♖xa7 21 ♘xa7 ♕h4.

16	...	♖f7
17	a4 (D)	

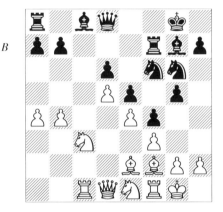

17 ... ♗f8!?

Piket had recently scored five wins in this line, so Kasparov could have been reasonably sure he would get a chance to demonstrate his preparation. Weaker is 17...b6 18 a5!; after the queenside opens up completely it's difficult for Black to continue his kingside attack. However, the main line until this game was 17...h5 18 a5 ♗d7 (18...g4 19 ♘b5 g3 20 ♗xa7 ♘h7 21 ♔h1! works for White; after 21...♖xa7 22 ♖xc8! ♕xc8 23 ♘xa7 ♕d8 24 h3 ♘g5 25 ♕d2 he has chances to convert his extra pawn) 19 ♘b5 ♗xb5 20 ♗xb5 g4 21 ♔h1 g3 22 ♗g1 gxh2 23 ♗f2 h4?! (23...a6!? was a subsequent improvement, but even here White can aspire for an edge) 24 ♔xh2 ♘h5 25 ♖g1 ♘g3 26 a6! bxa6 27 ♗xa6 ♗f8 28 ♘d3 ♖h7 29 ♗e1. White prepares ♘f2 and is in full control, Piket-Paneque, Adelaide jr Wch 1988. Here a number of things have gone wrong for Black: he has exchanged his strong light-squared bishop; moreover, the advance of the h-pawn has deprived his pieces of important squares – first his knight couldn't go to h5, and solving this with ...h4 limited his queen. Although Kasparov's move is in itself fairly typical, it's connected with an impressive and ambitious plan. Black intends to achieve all his goals – keep his attacking bishop, leave h5 free for his knight and above all get in the ...g4 advance by simply making useful preparatory moves! The point is that once White's c3-knight stops protecting the e4-pawn, the g-pawn doesn't need the support of the h-pawn to move forward.

18 a5 ♗d7! *(D)*

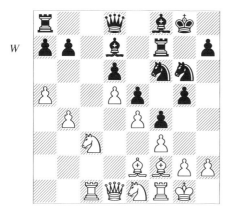

19 ♘b5?!

Piket is curious (or rather reckless?), but this straightforward continuation allows Kasparov to realize his idea. Even objectively the text-move is barely playable, and entering such a volatile position in a practical game without preparation is extremely risky. White shouldn't have been so cooperative, and should have searched for useful moves of his own:

1) After 19 ♗b5 Black can retreat his bishop with 19...♗c8, when 20 ♗e2 prevents ...g4 and repeats the position. However, even 19...g4!? 20 ♗xd7 ♕xd7 is playable, despite the exchange of the light-squared bishops, as Black's attacking chances shouldn't be underestimated.

2) A plausible try is 19 ♘c2. White aims for b5 with his other knight, if he gets a chance. The drawback of this otherwise interesting idea is that it's rather slow; moreover the knight deserts the kingside (see the note to move 13). Black may possibly even return to the original attacking pattern with 19...h5 20 ♘b5 (20 ♘a3?! g4 enables Black to open up the kingside with ...g3 in any case; this is especially dangerous after the greedy 21 ♘cb5 g3 22 ♗xa7 ♖xa7!? 23 ♘xa7 ♘xe4! with a strong attack) 20...g4 21 ♘xa7 g3 (21...gxf3?! is weaker, as after 22 gxf3 ♗h3 23 ♔h1! White will have more than enough for the exchange) 22 ♗b6 gxh2+ 23 ♔h1 (23 ♔xh2? runs into 23...♘g4+! 24 ♔g1 ♕h4) 23...♕e8 and Black's attacking chances are definitely more real than in the aforementioned game Piket-Paneque.

3) The previous line as well as the above notes have repeatedly indicated the most expedient is 19 ♔h1!?. This was briefly suggested by Kasparov. White frees g1 for his bishop and also a later ...gxh2 will be without a check. Black's best is 19...♖g7 (after 19...♕e8?! 20 ♘c2 the queen runs into a possible fork from c7), and here again 20 ♘c2 is interesting and leads to a very complicated position.

19 ... g4! *(D)*

19...♗xb5?! devalues Black's previous play. After 20 ♗xb5 g4 21 fxg4! ♘xe4 22 ♗d3 White gains control over the light squares and an advantage.

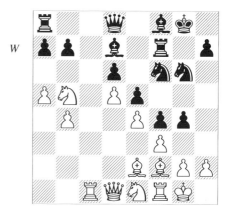

20 ♘c7

The most principled option. Other moves make life easier for Black:

1) After 20 ♘xa7 g3 21 ♗b6 ♕e7! (after 21...gxh2+? 22 ♔xh2 ♕e7 White can regroup advantageously with 23 ♖h1 ♘h5 24 ♔g1) White can't blockade the kingside successfully. 22 h3? loses more or less by force to the immediate sacrifice 22...♗xh3! 23 gxh3 ♕d7; for example, 24 ♗b5 ♕xh3 25 ♖c2 ♘h4 26 ♖e2 ♖g7 27 ♕c2 ♖g6!, followed by ...♖h6. Thus White can't prevent Black's attacking mechanism (...♘h5 and ...gxh2) from getting going by normal means and his only chance to throw a spanner in the works is a half-desperate measure like 22 ♘c6!?.

2) 20 fxg4 ♘xe4 21 ♘c7 ♗a4 (21...♖c8 is less incisive, and is met by 22 ♘e6) 22 ♕xa4

♖xc7 is pleasant for Black. Contrary to the line after 19...♗xb5?! he has more central control and with ...♘d2 in the air White finds it difficult to fight for the light squares and stabilize his position.

20 ... g3! *(D)*

Kasparov consistently continues his attack. Giving up the light-squared bishop is again dubious, as here White retains his central pawn-chain and is better after 20...♗a4?! 21 ♕xa4 ♖xc7 22 ♖xc7 ♕xc7 23 ♕c2.

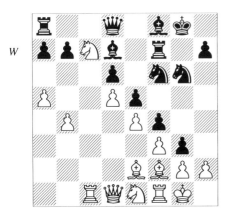

21 ♘xa8?

The tension has reached breaking point and it's no wonder that Piket panics. White hopes that a slight material sacrifice will keep his king relatively safe and slow down Black's attack considerably. However, quite the opposite proves to be the truth and the text-move virtually loses by force. No matter how great the danger, White should have gone for 21 hxg3 fxg3 (21...♘h5?! is unconvincing due to 22 g4! ♘g3 23 ♘xa8, when Black has no obvious way to continue the attack; e.g., 23...♕h4 24 ♗xa7 or 23...♕xa8 24 ♘d3 ♕d8 25 ♗xa7 ♕h4 26 ♘f2) 22 ♗xg3 ♗h6!? (after 22...♘h5 23 ♗f2 ♘gf4 taking the rook {24 ♘xa8} gives Black attractive attacking alternatives to the main line, such as 24...♕g5! with the threat of ...♘xg2; the problem is White can re-route his knight and play 24 ♘e6! instead, because the follow-up 24...♘xe6 25 dxe6 ♗xe6 26 ♗c4 enables him to exchange most of Black's attacking pieces with a satisfactory position) and now:

1) Here 23 ♘e6 is a half-measure. After 23...♗xe6 24 dxe6 ♖g7 Black has activated the f8-bishop and 25 ♖c3 ♘h5 (or 25...♘f4) gives him an attack for a minimal investment.

2) More testing is 23 ♘xa8 ♘h5 24 ♗f2 (24 ♗h2? loses quickly to 24...♗e3+ 25 ♖f2 ♕h4 26 ♘d3 ♘gf4, when White's king is trapped in a mating-net and apart from ...♘xd3 Black also threatens ...♘xg2 and ...♘h3+!) 24...♘gf4. Taking material is useful mainly because White may be forced to return it to survive the menacing concentration of Black's attacking forces against his king:

2a) 25 ♖c7? runs into 25...♗a4!, forcing the humiliating 26 ♖c2 (26 ♕xa4 ♘xe2+ leads to mate by force; especially pretty is 27 ♔h2 ♘hg3! 28 ♗xg3 ♗f4!) 26...♖g7 with a decisive attack.

2b) 25 ♘d3!? is much better. Kasparov considers this the best defence and gives the line 25...♖g7 (25...♘xg2 26 ♔xg2 ♖g7+ 27 ♔h2 ♘g3! 28 ♗xg3 only leads to a draw by perpetual after 28...♖xg3, since 28...♕g5? is insufficient due to 29 ♖g1 ♕h5+ 30 ♔g2 ♗e3 31 ♘f2, when White beats off the attack) 26 ♘xf4 ♗xf4 27 g4! (otherwise ...♘g3 or even ...♖xg2+!, followed by ...♕g5+ and ...♘g3+, forces mate) 27...♗xc1 28 ♕xc1 ♘f4 29 ♕e3 h5! 30 ♖c1 ♘xe2+ 31 ♕xe2 hxg4 32 fxg4 ♗xg4 33 ♕e3. White's defence is holding and the outcome remains open.

2c) 25 ♖c3!? *(D)* is an interesting computer suggestion.

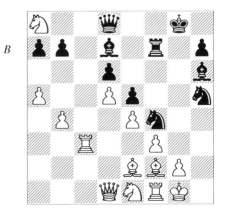

Contrary to line '2b', with two minor pieces on the h-file it's difficult to break up the kingside with ...h5 after Black forces g4. White has also removed the rook from a vulnerable square and in some variations it might effectively join the defence after f4. This is well illustrated by the sample line 25...♗a4 (possibly the simple 25...♕xa8!? is best, with an unclear position) 26 ♘c2 ♘xg2 27 f4! (27 ♔xg2? is weak, as after the accurate 27...♖g7+ 28 ♔h1 ♗f4! 29 ♖g1 ♗g3! 30 ♔g2 ♕h4 31 ♔f1 ♕h3+ 32 ♔e1 ♗xf2+ 33 ♔xf2 ♕h2+ 34 ♔e3 ♖xg1 Black's attack should triumph) 27...♖g7 28 ♔h1 and Black's attack grinds to a halt.

21 ... ♘h5! *(D)*

Kasparov finally makes full use of his access to the h5-square. Piket expected to get a break after the less incisive 21...gxf2+ 22 ♖xf2 ♕xa8, but the energetic text-move continues the attack and shatters his hopes.

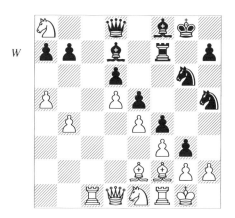

22 ♔h1

Now Black will gain a few tempi in comparison with the immediate 21...gxf2+. The only alternative, 22 ♗xa7 ♕h4 23 h3 ♗xh3 24 gxh3 (24 ♖f2 is perhaps more resilient, but after 24...♗d7 Black will have an overwhelming attack for only a single pawn) 24...♕xh3 25 ♖f2 gxf2+ 26 ♔xf2 (26 ♗xf2? ♖g7 mates) 26...♘h4 27 ♗f1 (after 27 ♘d3 ♕g3+ 28 ♔f1 ♘g2! Black's pieces gradually close in on the helpless white king; e.g., 29 ♕d2 ♕h2 30 ♗g1 ♘g3+ 31 ♔f2 ♘xe4+! 32 fxe4 ♕g3+ 33 ♔f1 ♘e3+ mates) 27...♕h2+ 28 ♘g2 ♖g7 29 ♔e2 ♘xg2, allows Black to regain all the material and continue the assault.

22 ... gxf2

23	♖xf2	♘g3+!
24	♔g1	♕xa8
25	♗c4	

Black's knight was taboo for the last two moves, so Piket tries to free some space around his king.

25 ... a6! *(D)*

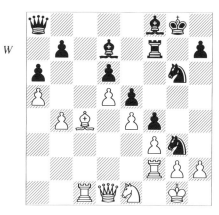

A surprising but very effective solution. Black quickly activates his queen and the pin on the a7-g1 diagonal will be decisive.

26 ♕d3

This loses quickly, but the alternatives were just as bleak:

1) 26 ♘d3 ♕a7 27 ♘c5 ♗b5! 28 ♗xb5 axb5 29 hxg3 fxg3 30 ♖fc2 dxc5 31 bxc5 ♘f4 and sooner or later Black's queen will find its way to White's king.

2) 26 hxg3 fxg3 27 ♖fc2 doesn't help either. Black has a pleasant choice between 27...♕d8 and 27...♖f4!?, when he might yet use the dark diagonal; e.g., 28 ♔f1 ♖h4 29 ♔e2 ♗h6 30 ♘d3 ♖h2 31 ♕e1 ♕a7! 32 ♕g1 ♗e3! and Black wins.

| 26 | ... | ♕a7 |
| 27 | b5 | |

27 ♖cc2 ♗e7 followed by ...♗h4 only postpones the inevitable.

| 27 | ... | axb5 |
| 28 | ♗xb5 | ♘h1! |

0-1

Black will come out a piece up.

Game 57
Ljubomir Ljubojević – Garry Kasparov
Belgrade 1989
Sicilian Defence, Najdorf Variation [B96]

1	e4	c5
2	♘f3	d6
3	d4	cxd4
4	♘xd4	♘f6
5	♘c3	a6
6	♗g5	

In the 1990s the English Attack with 6 ♗e3 or 6 f3 became highly fashionable on all levels. After starting with Kasparov-Kamsky, Linares 1993 (Game 72) we'll see much more of it in Volume 2, with Kasparov playing both colours. The text-move, on the contrary, has a more peaceful reputation despite the highly tactical positions it leads to. This apparent paradox stems from the fact that a lot of the thoroughly explored main lines lead to forced draws. However, in our game neither of the players was in a peaceful mood and they leave the well-trodden paths soon enough.

6	...	e6
7	f4	♕c7

Somewhat later Kasparov started to prefer 7...♕b6, which still belongs to his repertoire; see also Ivanchuk-Kasparov, Linares 1990 (Game 58).

| 8 | ♕e2!? | *(D)* |

White's main try is 8 ♕f3 b5 9 0-0-0 b4 (or 9...♘bd7) with a lot of sharp theory. Ljubojević opts for a less common sideline. White toys with the idea of a quick e5 advance, while sometimes the queen might be useful on e2 in case of a standard ♘d5 sacrifice. On the other hand the text-move obstructs the natural development of White's kingside.

| 8 | ... | ♘c6! |

Now a standard reaction, at the time of our game this strong idea was still relatively fresh, being introduced into high-level practice by Kasparov himself only in Tilburg 1989. Black immediately attacks the centralized knight; this move is less effective against the more usual 8 ♕f3, because then White can develop faster and more harmoniously. After 8...b5, 9 e5 forces a

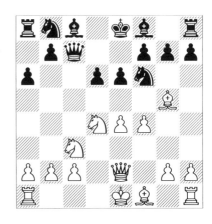

transposition into the extremely risky Polugaevsky Variation (introduced by 7...b5) with 9...dxe5 (9...b4?! 10 ♘cb5! axb5 11 exf6 gives White a clear advantage) 10 fxe5 ♘fd7 11 0-0-0, which is hardly to everyone's taste. Also 8...♘bd7 9 0-0-0 b5 (after 9...♗e7 Black must reckon with 10 ♘f3!?) 10 g4 ♗b7 11 ♗g2 is quite dangerous; ♘d5 is already seriously in the air.

| 9 | 0-0-0 | |

With his knight on c6 instead of d7 Black doesn't have to fear 9 ♘f3 ♗e7 10 0-0-0 0-0, while 9 ♘xc6 ♕xc6! 10 0-0-0 ♗e7 11 g3 (11 e5 dxe5 12 fxe5 ♘d5 is about equal) also achieves little; after 11...♕c7 12 ♗g2 ♗d7 Black develops as in the game.

| 9 | ... | ♘xd4 |

Black can play also 9...♗e7, when the reasonable continuations transpose either to the game, or to the previous note. After 10 ♘xc6 he should avoid 10...bxc6?! 11 e5 dxe5 12 ♕xe5!, when his split queenside pawns offer White an object of attack.

| 10 | ♖xd4 | ♗e7 |
| 11 | g3 | |

11 e5 dxe5 12 fxe5 ♘d5 13 ♗xe7?! (13 ♗d2 is roughly equal) 13...♘xe7 14 ♘e4 0-0 15 ♕h5 ♘g6 (15...♘f5!? is also possible) 16 ♘g5 h6 17 ♘f3 was played in the aforementioned

game Ivanchuk-Kasparov, Tilburg 1989. Now the strong 17...♖d8! would have challenged White's active rook, underlined the vulnerability of the e5-pawn and given Black an advantage. Ljubojević's novelty aims to finish development before starting central action. 11 g4?! has similar ideas but is weaker due to 11...h6 12 ♗h4 g5! 13 fxg5 ♘d7, when Black regains the pawn with firm control of the e5-square. Kasparov's interesting suggestion 11 ♗h4 still remains untested; by moving the bishop to a less vulnerable square White enhances the effect of e5. However, after 11...0-0!? 12 e5 dxe5 13 fxe5 ♘d5 14 ♘xd5 exd5 15 ♗xe7 ♕xe7 16 ♖xd5 ♗c6 Black has sufficient compensation, so perhaps 11 ♔b1!? deserves more attention.

11 ... ♗d7!

The typical Sicilian thrust 11...b5 12 ♗g2 ♖b8!? (12...♗b7 is weaker, because after the natural 13 ♖hd1 0-0 14 ♗xf6! Black is forced to recapture with the pawn due to 14...♗xf6? 15 e5!) has also been tested subsequently, but modest development is more flexible – Black still retains the option to castle queenside, should it become necessary.

12 ♗g2 (D)

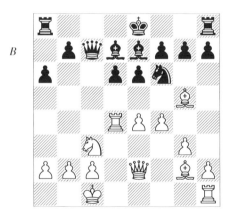

12 ... h6

Flicking in this move limits White's options. After 12...♗c6 Black has to reckon with 13 ♖hd1 h6 14 ♗xf6 ♗xf6 15 e5!? (15 ♖xd6 ♗xc3 16 bxc3 0-0 can only be better for Black), although this probably just leads to a repetition after 15...dxe5 16 ♗xc6+ bxc6 17 ♖d7 ♕a5 18 ♘e4 ♕xa2!? (18...exf4 19 ♘d6+ ♔xd7 20 ♘c4+ ♕d5 21 ♘b6+ ♔c7 is also possible; even after the queen sacrifice Black doesn't risk losing) 19 ♕h5 0-0 20 ♘xf6+ gxf6 21 ♕g4+ ♔h7 22 ♕h5 ♔g7.

13 ♗h4 ♗c6 (D)

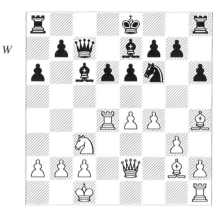

14 f5

A sharp and committal move: White abandons his central strategy and turns his sights to the kingside instead. The immediate 14 e5?! ♗xg2 15 ♕xg2 dxe5 16 fxe5 is premature, as Black has a pleasant choice between 16...♗c5 and the simple 16...♕xe5!? 17 ♕xb7 0-0 with an edge in both cases. Ljubojević's move was also designed to take the motif 14 ♖hd1 g5!? 15 fxg5 hxg5 16 ♗xg5 ♖xh2 out of the position, as this gives Black good counterplay. However, the Yugoslav GM was not satisfied with his idea and later came up with 14 ♖c4!?. With this refinement White renews the threat of e5, but it only proved enough for equality after 14...♕b6 15 a3 (15 e5 ♗xg2 16 ♕xg2 dxe5 17 fxe5 ♘d5! gets White nowhere, as he has to take into account the ...g5 threat) 15...♖d8 (15...0-0 is even better) 16 ♗f3 0-0 17 ♖f1 ♖d7 18 e5 ♗xf3 19 ♕xf3 dxe5 20 fxe5 ♘d5 21 ♘xd5 exd5 22 ♗xe7 dxc4 in Ljubojević-Xu Jun, Novi Sad OL 1990.

14 ... 0-0

Kasparov keeps the tension. It's too early for 14...e5?! 15 ♖d3.

15 ♖hd1

Playing 15 g4 immediately allows 15...♘xe4! (15...e5 is weaker: 16 ♖d3 ♘xe4 17 ♘xe4 ♗xh4 18 ♘xd6) 16 ♗xe4 (Black is better after 16 ♘xe4 ♗xh4 17 fxe6 ♖ae8!) 16...♗xh4 17 fxe6 ♗f6 18 ♖c4 ♗xc3 19 ♖xc3 d5! and it's White who must fight for equality. Also 15 fxe6 isn't ideal, as apart from accepting the piece sacrifice with 15...g5 Black can simply play 15...fxe6 and renew the threat.

15 ... **b5!** *(D)*

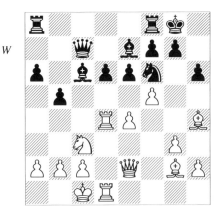

16 g4?!

The critical position. As the text-move tips the scales in Black's favour, White should consider other options:

1) 16 a3 prevents the game continuation, but does little for White's position. By 16...♖ab8 Black prepares ...a5 and can claim an edge.

2) Kasparov indicates White should have entered the complications with 16 fxe6!?, letting Black make a difficult decision. True to his style, he would have preferred the more active continuation 16...fxe6 (even the greedy 16...g5 can't be discarded outright, although it's not without danger for Black after 17 ♘d5 ♗xd5 18 exd5 gxh4 19 ♖xh4 or 19 gxh4!?) 17 ♗xf6 ♗xf6! (17...♖xf6?! is inferior due to 18 e5! dxe5 19 ♖4d3 and White's knight will occupy a beautiful outpost on e4) 18 ♖xd6 b4 19 ♖xc6! (simplification is necessary; the weak 19 ♕c4? bxc3 gives Black a strong attack) 19...♕xc6 20 e5 ♗g5+ 21 ♔b1 ♕c7 22 ♗xa8 bxc3 White's king is somewhat more vulnerable than Black's, but the position is not clear.

16 ... e5!

Now Black doesn't have the tactic from the previous note (16...♘xe4? drops material after 17 ♗xe7 ♘xc3 18 bxc3), so he chooses the most suitable moment to stabilize the centre.

17 ♖4d3? *(D)*

The most natural square for the rook. However, now Black gets a practically winning advantage by simple and straightforward means,

so the text-move can be described as a decisive error. The time has come for White to be generous, but the immediate sacrifice 17 ♗xf6?! exd4 18 ♗xd4 b4 doesn't give him sufficient compensation. This leaves only 17 ♖4d2 b4 18 ♘d5!? (the passive 18 ♘b1 is unattractive due to 18...♖fc8) 18...♘xd5 19 exd5 ♗xh4 20 dxc6 ♗g5 21 ♔b1 (or 21 h4). For the exchange White gets a strong bind on the light squares and realizing the extra material will be far from easy.

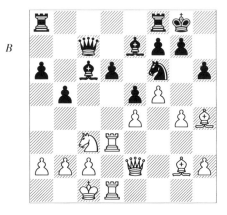

17 ... b4
18 ♗xf6

Now White has no choice: knight moves lose an exchange for nothing after ...♗b5.

18 ... bxc3

Kasparov naturally isn't interested in playing 18...♗xf6? 19 ♘d5, when the opposite-coloured bishops can only favour White. The text-move exposes White's king and this permanent drawback will cost Ljubojević the game.

19 ♗xe7 cxb2+
20 ♔b1

A typical motif – the king seeks shelter behind the enemy pawn. The problem is that the seemingly insignificant b2-pawn will become a major source of tactical chances for Black and White will manage to take it only seven moves later, when his position is on the verge of collapse. However, after the immediate 20 ♔xb2 ♕xe7 21 ♖xd6 ♖fc8 Black's attack on the open queenside files practically plays itself. The main threat is ...♗a4, and a sample line is 22 c4 ♗a4 23 ♖1d2 ♖ab8+ 24 ♔a1 ♗c2!, when Black wins material.

20 ... ♕xe7

21 ♖xd6

Both players must have seen this position when White played 16 g4?!, but they evaluated it differently. Ljubojević hoped the tempo gained by attacking the c6-bishop would enable him to break up Black's kingside with f6. However...

21 ... ♖fc8

After this calm move, White must have realized it's Black who has all the attacking chances. His king is much safer than its counterpart, and the difference in the scope of the bishops is obvious (the g2-bishop won't even get a chance to rejoin the fray). In a Sicilian, losing the thread (on moves 16 and 17) can cost one dearly and lead to grave trouble.

22 ♖1d2

Ljubojević admits that something has gone wrong. As 22 f6 gxf6 gets White nowhere, he passively parries the threat of ...♗a4.

22 ... ♗b5
23 ♕e3

Kasparov condemned this as the decisive mistake and recommended 23 ♕d1 ♖ab8 24 ♗f1 as slightly more resilient. However, although White solves the problem of his passive bishop, he runs into the strong blow 24...♗xf1 25 ♕xf1 (25 f6 gxf6 doesn't change the issue) 25...♖xc2!, winning an important pawn and further exposing White's king. Now 26 ♔xc2? loses immediately to 26...b1♕+ 27 ♕xb1 ♕c7+! and even other moves can't hold the position in the long run.

23 ... ♖ab8
24 ♖b6

It's already too late for 24 f6 ♗c4! 25 ♖b6 (25 fxe7? ♗xa2+ mates) 25...♕a7 26 ♖dd6 (26 ♖xb8 ♖xb8 27 ♕e1 ♕c5) 26...♕c7! and White has no good defence against both ...♕xd6 and ...♗xa2+.

24 ... ♗c4
25 ♖d1 (D)

This loses by force, but White's position was beyond saving. The nagging b-pawn is taboo: 25 ♔xb2? ♕g5! loses White at least a rook and 25 ♖xb2 ♖xb2+ 26 ♔xb2 ♕b4+ 27 ♔c1 ♖b8 (27...♗xa2!?) 28 ♖d7 ♕b5! costs material as well. Another way to go down fast is 25 c3? ♕a3 26 ♖dxb2 ♖xb6 27 ♕xb6 ♗d3+ 28 ♔a1 ♕xc3. Ljubojević at least tries to solve his back-rank problems, which are apparent in the line 25 ♖dd6? ♕xd6! 26 ♖xd6 ♗xa2+.

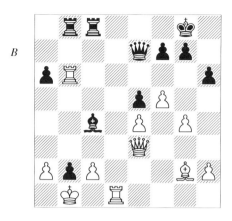

25 ... ♖xb6

After 25...♕c7?! 26 ♖xb8 ♖xb8 White could still plod on with 27 ♕a3, whereas the text-move simplifies into an easily won rook endgame.

26 ♕xb6 ♕a3
27 ♕xb2 ♗xa2+!
28 ♔a1

Both 28 ♕xa2? ♖b8+ 29 ♔a1 ♕c3+ and 28 ♔c1? ♕e3+ 29 ♖d2 ♖d8 lose immediately.

28 ... ♕a4
29 ♕xa2

Now at least White doesn't get mated. After 29 ♖c1 ♗c4+ 30 ♔b1 ♖c5 or 29 ♖d2 ♕a5! his exposed king wouldn't survive for long.

29 ... ♕xa2+
30 ♔xa2 ♖xc2+
31 ♔b3 ♖xg2

The series of forced moves is over and White is hopelessly lost, as he will drop more pawns.

32 ♔c4 ♖xh2
33 ♔d5 f6
34 g5

Ljubojević tries the last trick...

34 ... hxg5
35 ♔e6 g4
36 ♖d8+ ♔h7
37 ♔f7 ♖h5

Black parries the threat of ♖g8 and leaves White with nothing to play for. 37...♖b2 would have also done the job.

0-1

Game 58
Vasily Ivanchuk – Garry Kasparov
Linares 1990
Sicilian Defence, Najdorf Variation [B97]

1	e4	c5
2	♘f3	d6
3	d4	cxd4
4	♘xd4	♘f6
5	♘c3	a6
6	♗g5	e6
7	f4	♕b6

The notorious Poisoned Pawn Variation, which despite some early attempts in the 1950s by Tolush will always be connected with the name of Bobby Fischer. The idea of the queen sortie, attacking both b2 and d4 is quite common in the contemporary Sicilian, but especially in this version it leads to great complications, as White's lead in development enables him to sacrifice a pawn for a dangerous initiative. Prior to this game, Kasparov had only gone in for this line once as Black, and used to prefer 7...♕c7 (see Game 57).

| 8 | ♕d2 | |

The main move. White can play the modest 8 ♘b3 as well, but he won't be able to avoid a sharp struggle after 8...♗e7 9 ♕f3 ♘bd7 10 0-0-0 ♕c7 anyway – the tempo invested into the manoeuvre ...♕b6-c7 is compensated by the poorly placed knight on b3.

| 8 | ... | ♕xb2 *(D)* |

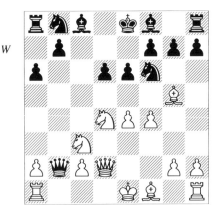

| 9 | ♖b1 | |

The most natural and popular option. With 9 ♘b3 ♕a3 10 ♗xf6 gxf6 11 ♗e2 Spassky inflicted upon Fischer his only defeat in the 7...♕b6 line, but Kasparov successfully coped with Short's subsequent attempts to revive this line.

| 9 | ... | ♕a3 |
| 10 | f5 | |

Best by test. Fischer's games showed that Black has little to fear after the other direct attempt, 10 e5 dxe5 11 fxe5 ♘fd7, while 10 ♗e2 ♘bd7 11 0-0 ♕c5 is nowadays considered too slow.

10	...	♘c6
11	fxe6	fxe6
12	♘xc6	bxc6
13	♗e2 *(D)*	

The straightforward 13 e5 dxe5 14 ♗xf6 gxf6 15 ♘e4 ♗e7 (or even 15...♕xa2!?) leads to complications which mostly peter out into forced draws. Ivanchuk strives for more, and chooses the fashionable line of the moment.

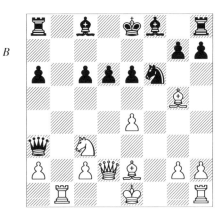

| 13 | ... | ♗e7 |
| 14 | 0-0 | |

14 ♖b3 ♕a5 15 ♗h5+!? (after 15 0-0 ♖a7! Black is OK) 15...g6 16 0-0 gives Black a choice between a safe and equal endgame after 16...♘xe4, or the more enterprising 16...♕c5+

17 ♔h1 gxh5! 18 ♗xf6 ♖f8 19 ♕h6 ♕c4 20 ♖bb1 ♖b8 21 ♖bd1 ♖xf6 22 ♖xf6 ♕xc3 23 ♕xh5+ ♔d8 24 ♖f7 ♖b7 25 ♖df1 ♖d7!? with an unclear position.

14	...	0-0
15	♖b3	

The less concrete 15 ♔h1 promises White little after 15...♖a7! 16 ♕e3 ♖d7.

15	...	♕c5+

15...♕a5?! is weaker due to 16 ♘d5 ♕d8 (16...♕xd2 17 ♘xe7+ ♔f7 18 ♗xd2 ♔xe7 19 e5 gives White a large advantage) 17 ♘xe7+ ♕xe7 18 ♖d3 ♕a7+ 19 ♔h1 with a dangerous attack, as Black's queenside forces are asleep.

16	♗e3	♕e5 *(D)*

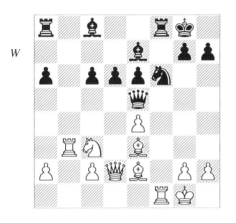

17	♗f4	

Here (and one move later as well) White can repeat moves with 17 ♗d4 ♕a5 18 ♗b6, but we have already mentioned above that Ivanchuk had no intention of bailing out.

17	...	♕c5+

17...♘xe4 is tactically sound, but after 18 ♘xe4 ♕xe4 19 ♗xd6 ♖xf1+ 20 ♔xf1 ♗f6 21 ♗a3 White's activity fully compensates for the missing pawn and he retains chances for a slight edge even after 21...c5! (best) 22 ♗f3 ♕c4+ 23 ♕d3!?.

18	♔h1	♘g4!

Now Black does best to rely on tactics. 18...d5 19 e5 ♘d7 doesn't solve his development problems and White got a strong attack after 20 ♘a4 ♕a7 21 ♕c3! ♘c5 22 ♘xc5 ♗xc5 23 ♕h3 in Am.Rodriguez-Ernst, Subotica IZ 1987.

19	h3	

19 ♗xg4 e5 only releases the tension, and gets White nowhere.

19	...	e5

Black frees the c8-bishop. 19...♘e5 is weaker due to 20 ♘a4! (20 ♗e3? ♖xf1+ 21 ♗xf1 ♘c4 is good for Black).

20	♘a4	♕a7
21	♗c4+	♔h8
22	hxg4	exf4
23	♘b6 *(D)*	

A refinement compared with 23 ♖xf4 ♗d7 24 ♘b6 (24 ♖bf3 ♖xf4 25 ♕xf4 ♕d4 might even be dangerous for White) 24...♖xf4 25 ♕xf4 ♖f8 26 ♕g3 a5 27 ♘xd7 ♕xd7 and Black had full equality in Balashov-Pigusov, Sverdlovsk 1987.

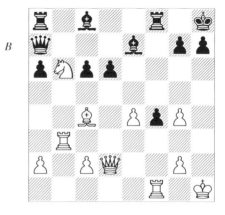

23	...	d5!

And this is Kasparov's improvement, after which the popularity of 13 ♗e2 declined rapidly. The text-move is much more convincing than the seemingly forced 23...♖b8 24 ♖xf4! ♗d7 (24...♖xb6? 25 ♖xf8+ ♗xf8 26 ♕f2 and 24...♖xf4 25 ♕xf4 ♖xb6? 26 ♕f7 both lose on the spot; these characteristic lines indicate Black's back-rank problems are of a permanent nature) 25 ♘xd7 ♕xd7 26 ♖f5!?. This position arose in Spraggett-A.Sokolov, Saint John Ct (5) 1988, a game that Black went on to lose. White has more active pieces; moreover, Black's king is dangerously cornered and his pawns are more vulnerable than their white counterparts. The presence on the board of opposite-coloured bishops enhances rather than neutralizes these factors. Although subsequently Black's play was improved upon and in practice he managed to hold most of the later games after 26...♕a7, the whole line seemed to offer White a practically risk-free small plus and required accurate and tenacious defence from Black.

24 exd5 cxd5
25 ♗xd5

25 ♕xd5 ♗b7 enables Black to retain his active bishop-pair with an excellent position, while 25 ♘xd5 ♗xg4 forces White to fight for equality.

25 ... ♖b8
26 ♘xc8

The first tactical consequences of 23...d5! are already evident: 26 ♖xf4? ♖xb6 27 ♖xf8+ ♗xf8 28 ♕f2 doesn't work due to the reply 28...♖h6+.

26 ... ♖bxc8 *(D)*

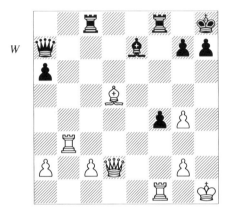

In comparison with 23...♖b8 the position is more open. This favours Black and gives him active counterplay against White's king, which is now no less vulnerable than his black counterpart on h8. The further course of the game will amply prove this.

27 ♖h3!

Ivanchuk rightly ignores the f4-pawn and pursues his own ambitions; in such positions the initiative is more important. After 27 ♖xf4 ♖xf4 28 ♕xf4 ♖f8 29 ♖b7 (29 ♕c1 ♕f2 30 ♖f3 ♕h4+ is similar) 29...♕c5! 30 ♖b8 ♗d8 White can't retain his material advantage (31 ♖c8? ♕e7! 32 ♕g3 ♕d7 33 ♖c5 ♗e7 is too costly) and the open b8-h2 diagonal makes his king feel uncomfortable.

27 ... ♕b6

Black starts playing on the dark squares. Kasparov suggests 27...♕c7 as a possible alternative.

28 ♖e1

The pawn is still taboo: after 28 ♖xf4? ♕b1+ 29 ♔h2 ♗d6 30 ♖xh7+ ♔xh7 31 ♗e4+ ♔h8 32 ♕xd6 ♖xf4 33 ♕xf4 ♕b8 Black swaps queens and is close to winning. Ivanchuk tries to keep Black's queen away from the kingside; if he doesn't succeed, this might have serious consequences: 28 ♕d3 h6 29 c4 ♖ce8 30 ♖b1?! ♕f6 31 ♖h5 ♗c5 32 ♗e4 ♖e5 33 ♖xe5 ♕xe5 34 ♗f5 f3! 35 gxf3 ♕g3 36 ♕f1 ♖e8 gave Black a strong attack in Oorebeek-Noomen, corr. 1992.

28 ... ♗g5
29 ♖e6 ♕d8! *(D)*

Black's queen shouldn't abandon its king; 29...♕b1+? is a serious error, and after 30 ♔h2 the initiative passes to White. The immediate threat is ♖xh7+ and ♕d3+, and after 30...♕xc2 31 ♕xc2 ♖xc2 32 ♗e4 White's attack persists into the endgame.

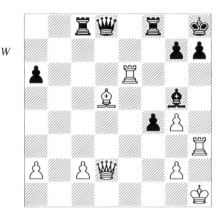

30 c4?!

Ivanchuk continues playing for a win, but he overestimates and thus endangers his position. Kasparov indicates two alternative roads to clear equality:

1) 30 ♕d3 ♗h4! 31 ♗e4 (31 ♖xa6 ♖e8 {or even 31...♕g5!?} can only be risky for White, while 31 c4 ♖b8 transposes into the game) 31...♕xd3 32 ♗xd3 g5 (32...♗g3 33 ♖xh7+ ♔g8 34 ♖e7 ♖f7 35 ♖xf7 ♔xf7 36 ♔g1 is drawish as well) 33 ♖c7 ♖fe8 34 ♖xh7+ ♔g8 and now the safest is 35 ♖3xh4 gxh4 36 ♖xh4 and Black doesn't have enough resources left to win this endgame.

2) Even more clear-cut is 30 ♖d6!? ♕xd6 31 ♖xh7+ ♔xh7 32 ♗e4+ ♕g6 33 ♗xg6+ ♔xg6 34 ♕d3+ ♔h6 35 ♕h3+ with a perpetual check.

30 ... Rb8

Kasparov starts toying with back-rank motifs. The premature 30...f3?! 31 Qd3 fxg2+ 32 Kxg2 would only give White's king more breathing space.

31 Qd3 Bh4!

In the spirit of the previous move. Although the bishop's outpost is shaky, it creates threats against White's king. Weaker is 31...h6?! 32 Qg6, which forces 32...Bh4 (32...Rf6? loses at once to 33 Qxg5) anyway in a far less attractive situation.

32 Be4

White has no time for 32 Rxa6? Re8, when he is forced to give up an exchange with 33 Re6 Rxe6 34 Bxe6 Qxd3 35 Rxd3 Rb1+ 36 Kh2 and fight for bare survival after 36...Bg3+ 37 Rxg3 fxg3+ 38 Kxg3 g5!.

32 ... Qg5!? (D)

32...Qxd3 33 Bxd3 g5 is a more promising version of note '1' to White's 30th move, but now it's Kasparov's turn to display his ambitions. Objectively he risks little and keeping the queens on the board is more unpleasant for an opponent who is plagued by time-trouble.

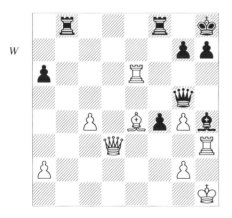

33 Bxh7

Although after the text-move defending both the back rank and the errant bishop will be a difficult task, White's counterplay on the open h-file should still be enough to save the game. 33 Qd5?! is not ideal due to 33...Qxg4 with the threat of ...Qe2, but after the less committal alternative 33 Bf5 the outcome of the game remains open, as 33...g6? runs into 34 Be4! (34 Bxg6 is less convincing due to 34...f3!) and White threatens Qd4+ followed by Bd5.

33 ... Rfd8

Kasparov points out 33...f3!? is a viable alternative. The difference between the immediate sacrifice and the text-move is that here Black threatens not only ...f2 or ...fxg2+, but ...Qc1+ as well. White must be extremely careful, as the cheeky pawn is poisoned:

1) 34 gxf3? Rfd8 35 Qe2 Kxh7 36 Qf2 (36 f4 Qxf4 37 Rxh4+ Kg8 and White loses quickly) and after 36...Rb1+ 37 Kg2 Kg8! 38 Rxh4 Rd2 39 Re2 Rbb2 Black wins material.

2) 34 Rxf3? Rxf3 35 gxf3 (35 Qxf3 is also insufficient, since after 35...Kxh7 36 g3 Qc1+ 37 Kg2 Rb2+ 38 Kh3 Bf6 39 Qe4+ g6! the mating threat ...Qh6# decides) 35...Bg3!, followed by ...Qh4, and Black's attack nets him an extra piece.

3) However, White still has the paradoxical 34 Be4!, when Black has no clear win. After 34...f2 (34...Qc1+ 35 Kh2 Qf4+ 36 Kh1 is only a perpetual) 35 Qf1 Qxg4 36 Kh2! White threatens g3 and he will manage to surround and disarm the dangerous passed pawn; e.g., 36...Rbd8 37 Bd5 Rde8 38 Rf3! and a draw is the most likely result.

34 Qc2

A natural reaction, but 34 Qe2!? is also playable. After 34...Kxh7 (34...f3? is bad due to 35 Qxf3! Kxh7 36 Qg3) 35 Re5! (White loses after both 35 Qf2? Kg8 36 Rxh4 Rb2! and 35 Qe1? Kg8 36 Rxh4 Rb1 37 Qxb1 Qxh4+ 38 Kg1 f3!) Black should be glad he has 35...Qh6! 36 Rh5 Rb1+ 37 Kh2 Rdd1 38 Rxh6+ (38 Qxd1? Bg3+) 38...gxh6, forcing White to give a perpetual with 39 Qe4+ Kg7 40 Qe5+.

34 ... f3! (D)

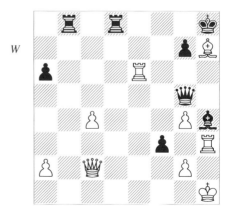

35 ♖xf3?

35 gxf3? is also insufficient: after 35...♖d2 36 ♕xd2 ♕xd2 37 ♖xh4 ♕f2 White is lost. However, there still was the paradoxical 35 ♗f5!. Now Black should content himself with a draw after 35...♖b2! (pursuing the attack with 35...♖d2? 36 ♕b3! fxg2+ 37 ♔g1 turns the tables, as White both attacks the b8-rook and threatens ♕g3) 36 ♕xb2 ♖d1+ 37 ♔h2 ♕f4+ 38 g3 ♖d2+ 39 ♔h1 ♖d1+.

35 ... ♖d2
36 ♕e4

After 36 ♕g6 ♖d1+ 37 ♔h2 ♕c1! White has nothing better than 38 ♖e8+ ♖xe8 39 ♕xe8+ ♔xh7 40 ♕h5+ ♕h6 41 ♕f5+ g6 42 ♕f7+ ♕g7 and Black will gradually convert his extra bishop; e.g., 43 ♕e6 ♕c7+ 44 g3 ♔g7.

36 ... ♖d1+
37 ♔h2 (D)

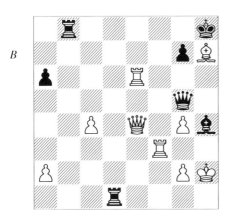

37 ... ♖e1?

Kasparov was also short of time; this error once again puts Black's victory in jeopardy. 37...♕c1 forces 38 ♖e8+, transposing into the note to White's 36th move.

38 ♕f5 ♖xe6
39 ♕xe6 ♔xh7
40 ♕e4+! g6 (D)

The only move to retain the extra material. 40...♔g8? 41 ♖f5! gives White a decisive attack and 40...♕g6?! 41 ♕f4 followed by ♖h3 nets him the bishop.

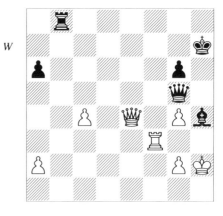

41 ♖h3?

The last mistake in the tumultuous final phase, after which Black disentangles himself. Although the time-control had been reached, Ivanchuk didn't find the relatively simple 41 ♖f7+ ♔g8! (41...♔h6? 42 ♕d4 ♖g8 43 g3 favours White; after 43...♕d8 44 ♖d7 ♕b8 he has the deadly 45 ♕d2+! ♗g5 46 ♕g2 ♗h4 47 g5+! ♔xg5 48 ♕d2+ with a successful king-hunt) 42 ♕e6 ♔h8 43 g3 ♕h6 44 ♔g2 ♗g5 45 ♕e5+ ♔g8 46 ♕d5 ♔h8 with a forced repetition.

41 ... ♔g7
42 ♕d4+ ♔g8
43 ♕e4

After 43 g3, Black's simplest response is 43...♕d8.

43 ... ♕f6!

0-1

Perhaps White resigned slightly prematurely, but his position is certainly lost after 44 ♖f3 (44 ♕d5+ ♔g7 45 ♕d7+ ♕e7 is hopeless for White) 44...♕d6+ 45 ♔h3 (after 45 g3 the cleanest solution is again 45...♔g7!) 45...♔g7!. Black has parried the threat of c5 and consolidated his position, as the bishop is taboo – 46 ♔xh4? g5+! leads to a quick mate.

Game 59
Lev Psakhis – Garry Kasparov
Match (game 5), La Manga 1990
English Opening [A26]

Another encounter with Karpov was approaching fast and Kasparov resorted to his trusted method of preparation – a short training match. In La Manga he showed good form and trounced Psakhis, his former USSR co-champion from 1981, by the score of 5-1.

    1   c4   g6
    2   ♘c3   ♗g7
    3   g3

The sharp Sämisch Variation against the King's Indian had brought Psakhis more trouble than joy in the previous odd-numbered games and he managed to score only a meagre half-point. One can understand his attitude – he intends to use his last white game to reach a peaceful position with less tension on the board.

    3   ...   ♘c6
    4   ♗g2   d6
    5   ♘f3   e5 *(D)*

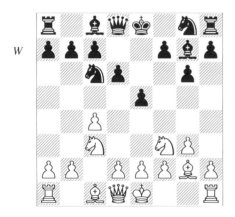

On the other hand Kasparov is his usual aggressive self. After spurning symmetrical lines such as 3...c5 he goes for one of the most double-edged lines of the English Opening – a Closed Sicilian with colours reversed. Although with White it's difficult to gain a workable advantage with this set-up, Black, as the side with less ambitious opening goals, usually achieves good counterplay despite being a tempo down. Here White has already committed his knight to f3 and although it exerts more influence on the centre than from e2, this comes at a price: Black gets more realistic attacking chances by advancing his f-pawn.

    6   d3   f5

As explained above, this is the most logical and enterprising reaction to 5 ♘f3.

    7   0-0   ♘f6
    8   ♖b1

The alternatives 8 ♗g5 and 8 ♘d5!? also deserve attention, but the text-move is the most natural and popular continuation.

    8   ...   h6 *(D)*

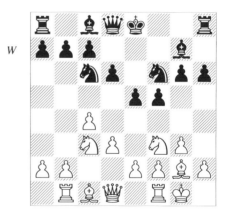

This move serves the double purpose of furthering the advance of the kingside pawns, as well as preventing the possible bishop sortie. Now White will have to find another way to deploy his c1-bishop.

    9   b4   0-0

An important moment: Kasparov decides not to open the a-file. An equally popular option is 9...a6 10 a4 0-0 11 b5 axb5 12 axb5 ♘e7 13 ♗b2. This position can also arise after 8...a5 9 a3, etc., and it's difficult to compare it with the game continuation. Black usually has to concede the open file after ♖a1 anyway, but with the a-pawns gone White has fewer targets on the queenside and the future invasion via a7 often doesn't bring anything tangible.

10 b5 ♘e7 *(D)*

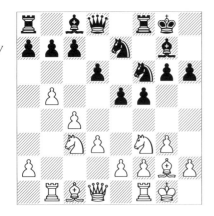

11 a4

Compared with the lines after 8...a5 or 9...a6 White has a wider range of attacking options. This is not necessarily an advantage, as choosing the ideal and most flexible way to develop his queenside play is more difficult. The text-move is played often enough, but in some lines the a4-square may be useful for White's queen; also in the further course of the game the a-pawn will remain on a4 until the very end. 11 c5 ♗e6! 12 ♗a3 ♖c8 13 ♕a4 allows Black to resolve the tension advantageously with 13...b6!, but 11 ♘d2 and 11 ♘e1 also deserve attention. By opening the long light diagonal White slows down Black's play.

11 ... ♗e6!?

Kasparov knows well enough that an all-out attack like 11...g5 12 ♗a3 f4 13 c5 is unlikely to be successful without the participation of his whole army. Therefore he strives to finish his development first.

12 ♗a3

12 c5? is now out of the question, as 12...dxc5 13 ♘xe5 ♘e8 costs White material. 12 ♘e1 ♖b8 13 ♘c2 can be parried by 13...♕d7 14 ♘b4 c5! and as the a4-square is inaccessible to White's queen, Black takes over the initiative. However, the immediate 12 ♘d2!? is somewhat better, as it forces 12...♖b8 (12...d5 13 cxd5 ♘exd5 14 ♘xd5 ♗xd5 15 e4 is good for White).

12 ... ♖c8!

Black safeguards his queenside by playing ...b6 and ...♖c8; this manoeuvre has been known since 1968, when Spassky used it against Geller in their Candidates match, playing White in a Closed Sicilian. However, here the move-order is crucial: 12...b6? is a serious tactical mistake due to 13 ♘xe5!.

13 ♘d2

13 c5 b6 14 cxd6 cxd6 15 ♕d2 ♕d7 gives Black at least equality; given the chance, he might even become active in the centre with a later ...d5. However, if White wanted to proceed with his queenside activity, 13 ♘e1 b6 14 ♘c2 followed by ♘b4 deserved attention; White can always meet ...f4 with e3.

13 ... b6
14 e3!?

Psakhis sensibly shifts his attention from the queenside to the centre, as after 14 a5 g5 15 axb6 axb6 occupying the a-file would cost precious time and allow Black to develop his own attack.

14 ... g5 *(D)*

Possibly 14...♕d7 is more accurate, as by protecting the e6-bishop Black prevents the possibility from the following note.

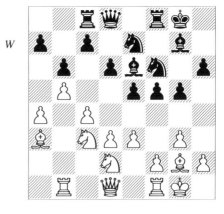

15 d4

A typical move is these positions is 15 f4!?, blocking Black's pawn advance. Here it would have worked both strategically and tactically, as after 15...♘g4 (White is better after 15...♘g6 16 fxe5 ♘xe5 17 ♘b3 followed by ♘d4) 16 ♕e2 exf4 17 exf4 White has nothing to fear.

15 ... exd4!?

A tough decision, as opening the centre diminishes Black's attacking chances. However, after 15...e4 White achieves the same with 16 f3! exf3 17 ♕xf3 under even better circumstances.

16 exd4 f4!
17 ♖e1

White refrains from the risky 17 gxf4 ♘g6! 18 fxg5 hxg5 (after the wild 18...♘g4 Black has to reckon with 19 ♗d5!? ♗xd5 20 ♕xg4 ♖f4 21 ♕g3 ♗e6 22 gxh6 ♖g4 23 hxg7 and White has more than enough for the queen) and the extra pawn makes no big difference, while White's king will start feeling uneasy after Black's knight comes to f4 or h4.

17 ... ♗g4

17...♗f5 18 ♘de4 favours White; for example, 18...g4 19 ♘xf6+ ♗xf6 20 ♗e4!. The text-move attempts to bring some disharmony into White's camp.

18 ♘f3

18 ♕b3?! ♘f5 and 18 f3 ♗f5 are both OK for Black; in the latter case after 19 ♘de4 he has the tactical shot 19...♘xe4 20 fxe4 (20 ♘xe4 c5! also works fine for Black) 20...♗g4!. However, instead of the somewhat unnatural self-pinning text-move a viable alternative was 18 ♗f3 with approximate equality.

18 ... ♕d7
19 c5 (D)

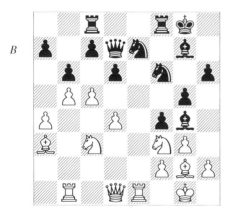

Although Kasparov has actively deployed his forces, White retains considerable counterplay and the position is still highly unclear.

19 ... ♖ce8
20 ♖c1

Once again 20 gxf4?! ♘h5 leaves White's kingside vulnerable, so Psakhis keeps the tension and makes a useful move instead.

20 ... ♘f5

Natural, but the immediate 20...♔h8!? might be more accurate.

21 ♕d3 ♔h8!

Thanks to the position of the king on g8 Psakhis was able to unpin his knight without harm. 21...dxc5?! 22 ♕c4+ would only have opened the centre for White.

22 cxd6

White starts to lose the thread. This premature exchange makes life easier for Black. More testing is 22 ♕c4 with complex play.

22 ... cxd6
23 ♖xe8

Giving up the open file is also debatable. There was nothing wrong with 23 ♘d2!?.

23 ... ♕xe8!? (D)

With White's time running low, Kasparov spurns the more cautious recaptures 23...♖xe8 or 23...♘xe8 and concentrates his forces against White's king – his queen aims for h5 and the rook remains on the f-file.

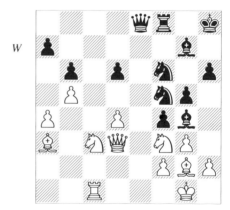

24 ♖f1?

This passive move is a big step in the wrong direction. White should have radically fought against the growing concentration of enemy forces against his kingside with the unprejudiced 24 h3!. Then:

1) 24...fxg3 25 hxg4!? (25 ♖e1? ♕h5 26 hxg4 gxf2+ gives Black's attack a crucial extra tempo, while 25 fxg3 ♗xf3 is similar to line '2') 25...gxf2+ 26 ♔xf2 ♘xg4+ 27 ♔g1 ♘xd4!? (after other moves Black still has to prove he has enough for the piece; for example, 27...♕h5 28 ♘e2 ♘ge3 29 ♘h2) 28 ♘xd4 (28 ♗xd6 ♕d8! 29 ♗xf8 ♘xf3+ 30 ♕xf3 ♗d4+ 31 ♔h1

♘f2+ also leads to a perpetual) 28...♕e5 29 ♘f3 ♖xf3! 30 ♕xf3 ♕d4+ 31 ♔h1 ♘f2+ draws.

2) 24...♗xf3 25 ♗xf3 ♘d7 26 ♗e4!? (26 ♘e2 allows the tactical shot 26...fxg3 27 fxg3 ♘xd4!, but even here after 28 ♘xd4 ♘e5 29 ♕b3 ♘xf3+ 30 ♘xf3 ♕e2 White has 31 ♖e1! with a drawish endgame) 26...♘xd4 27 ♗xd6 ♘c5 is about equal.

24 ... ♕h5
25 ♘e4?

The second mistake in a row will have grave consequences. White must seek activity, and Psakhis himself suggests 25 ♘e5!? as a better option. Although after 25...dxe5 26 ♗xf8 ♗xf8 27 dxe5 ♘e8 (27...f3?! runs into 28 ♗xf3) Black is slightly better, the game is far from decided.

25 ... ♘xe4
26 ♕xe4 ♗h3! *(D)*

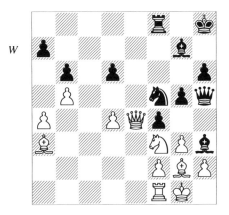

Now Black's pawns are ready to move on and drive away the defending pieces. It's surprising how rapidly White's seemingly solid position has deteriorated.

27 ♘e5

Black's kingside initiative puts the defence under great strain and it's only natural that Psakhis tries to gain some counterplay at any cost. The text-move loses almost by force, but White had no effective defence against ...g4 anyway. After 27 ♗xh3 ♕xh3 28 ♘e5 (28 gxf4 g4 is no better) 28...♗xe5 29 dxe5 fxg3 Black wins at least a piece, the point being 30 fxg3 ♕xf1+!. Also the ugly 27 gxf4 ♕g4 (27...♗xg2

28 ♔xg2 g4 29 ♘g1 is less incisive) 28 ♘e1 ♘h4! 29 ♗xd6 (after 29 f3 ♗xg2 or 29 ♔h1 ♖xf4 White loses simply) 29...♖d8 30 ♗c7 (30 ♗e5 ♗xg2 31 ♘xg2 ♘f3+ 32 ♔h1 ♗xe5 and the threat of ...♕h3 decides) 30...♖c8 31 ♗d6 ♗xg2 32 ♘xg2 ♘f3+ 33 ♔h1 ♘d2 doesn't help, as Black wins material and his attack continues.

27 ... ♗xg2

Certainly not 27...dxe5? 28 ♗xf8 ♗xf8 29 ♕xe5+ ♗g7 30 ♕e6, when it's White who is attacking; the threats are ♗d5 and ♖c1.

28 ♔xg2 g4! *(D)*

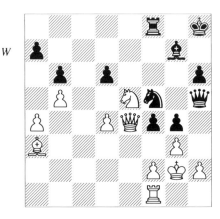

Kasparov first of all prevents g4 and creates numerous and decisive threats of his own, ...f3+ and ...fxg3 being the most obvious ones.

29 ♗xd6

The last attempt to confuse the issue. 29 ♕xf4? loses on the spot to 29...♘h4+. 29 ♔g1 is slightly more resilient, but then the materialistic 29...♖e8! wins a piece.

29 ... ♖f6

Black naturally doesn't fall for the simple trap 29...♕h3+ 30 ♔g1 f3? 31 ♘g6+ ♔h7 32 ♘f4, but the fork motif from the note to move 27 is even more convincing, namely 29...fxg3! 30 hxg3 ♕h3+ 31 ♔g1 ♕xf1+!.

30 ♗b8

30 ♘xg4!? was the only way to prolong the game.

30 ... ♕h3+
0-1

31 ♔g1 f3 32 ♘xf3 gxf3 33 ♕xf3 ♘h4 costs White his queen.

Game 60
Garry Kasparov – Anatoly Karpov
World Ch match (game 2), New York/Lyons 1990
Ruy Lopez (Spanish), Zaitsev Variation [C92]

1	e4	e5
2	♘f3	♘c6
3	♗b5	a6
4	♗a4	♘f6
5	0-0	♗e7
6	♖e1	b5
7	♗b3	d6
8	c3	0-0
9	h3	♗b7
10	d4	♖e8
11	♘bd2	♗f8
12	a4	h6
13	♗c2	exd4
14	cxd4	♘b4
15	♗b1	bxa4!?

After a break in the 1987 Seville title match, the Ruy Lopez is back from the very start and both players are eager to continue the theoretical duel from Leningrad 1986. See Game 35 for more notes about the opening phase; in that exciting fight Karpov chose the more usual 15...c5, a move to which he was later to return (see Game 61). Meanwhile the challenger decides to trust a sideline that had brought him success in the Candidates cycle over the previous two years. The text-move opens the queenside, a natural area of Black's future counterplay. On the other hand with 13...exd4 Black has already given up the centre, and now he further compromises his pawn-structure – such drawbacks can be compensated only by active piece-play.

16	♖xa4	a5
17	♖a3	♖a6

17...♕d7 is weaker, as it allows 18 ♘h4! and the a3-rook can join the attack, while after 17...g6 Black must seriously reckon with the straightforward advance of the e-pawn. The text-move, introduced into practice by Karpov himself, is directed mainly against this idea. Given the chance, Black may also at a suitable moment activate the rook, which is quite often a serious headache in this line (see also Game 61, where it perished on a8). However, as Timman succinctly pointed out, Black still lacks a more concrete active plan and Kasparov will cleverly profit from this.

18 ♘h2

Here 18 ♘h4? is tactically flawed, as it allows 18...♘xe4! 19 ♘xe4 ♗xe4 20 ♗xe4 d5, when Black can claim a slight advantage, Timman-Karpov, Kuala Lumpur Ct (1) 1990. Therefore Timman prepared the knight manoeuvre with 18 ♖ae3 a4 19 ♘h4!? and gained an edge after 19...c5 20 dxc5 dxc5 21 ♘f5 ♗c8 22 e5 ♘fd5 23 ♖g3 ♘f4 24 ♕f3 ♗xf5 25 ♗xf5 in Timman-Karpov, Kuala Lumpur Ct (5) 1990. Presumably here Karpov had an improvement ready (possibly 18...g6!? or 21...g6!?), but Kasparov had other ideas...

18 ... g6 (D)

A necessary precaution. 18...♕a8?! 19 ♖ae3 ♕a7 misplaces the queen and gave White a huge attack after 20 e5! in Sax-Banas, Balatonbereny 1984.

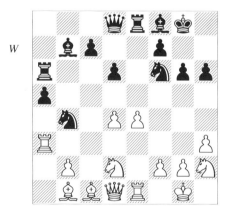

19 f3! (D)

A surprising novelty. Although closing the road to the kingside for both the rook and the queen inevitably postpones White's attacking ambitions, the text-move fortifies his main asset – the strong pawn-centre. Kasparov intends to put pressure on the other flank first with

♘c4 and finish his development harmoniously. Meanwhile, Karpov faces the question indicated in the note to move 17: "What can you do (about it)?". If instead White acts immediately, Black is well prepared:

1) 19 e5 dxe5 20 dxe5 ♘h7 (20...♖ae6!?) 21 ♘c4 ♕d5 22 ♕xd5 ♗xd5 led to an equal endgame in J.Horvath-Razuvaev, Sochi 1987.

2) 19 ♘g4 ♘xg4 20 ♕xg4 allows 20...c5!? 21 dxc5 dxc5 22 e5 ♕d4 23 ♕g3 ♖ae6 24 ♖ae3 c4 25 ♗f5 ♘d3! with good counterplay for Black, Hjartarson-Karpov, Seattle Ct (5) 1989.

3) 19 f4 enhances the strength of another typical motif: Black plays 19...d5! 20 e5 ♘e4! 21 ♘g4 (after 21 ♘xe4 dxe4 22 ♗xe4 ♗xe4 23 ♖xe4 c5 White will soon be forced to return the extra material with, e.g., 24 d5!? to avoid a central blockade) 21...c5 22 ♘xe4 dxe4 23 dxc5 ♗xc5+ 24 ♗e3 ♗f8 25 ♘f6+ ♖xf6 26 ♕xd8 ♖xd8 27 exf6 ♘d3, winning back the exchange with full equality, Ivanchuk-Karpov, Linares 1989.

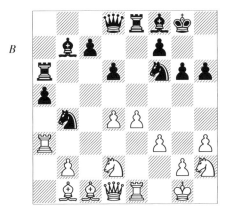

19 ... ♕d7?!

Karpov's play in the following phase creates an awkward impression. However, let's not forget that facing a new idea is always difficult, especially if the usual methods of developing counterplay are ineffective. Both 19...c5?! 20 d5 and 19...d5 20 e5 ♘d7 21 f4 are positional concessions; in the latter case White can again dangerously turn his sights to the kingside after 21...c5 22 ♖g3. Thus Black has to be patient. Seirawan's recommendation 19...c6 is interesting, as it takes the sting out of the prepared ♘c4. Kasparov himself indicated 19...♗g7!? as a better move and his suggestion later underwent a practical test. After 20 ♘c4 ♕a8 21 d5 ♖d8! 22 ♗d2?! (22 ♘e3 and 22 ♕a4!? are possible improvements) 22...c6 23 dxc6 ♘xc6 24 ♖d3 d5 25 exd5 ♘b4! Black had an excellent position in Liss-Shvidler, Tel-Aviv 1991.

20 ♘c4 ♕b5

Transferring the queen to b5 will only help White's initiative to grow, but Black is worse even after 20...a4 21 ♘e3!?.

21 ♖c3! ♗c8

21...d5?! now runs into 22 ♘a3 followed by 23 e5. Karpov doesn't want to move his queen again, as after 21...♕d7 22 ♘e3 White stops ...d5 with an advantage. However, 21...♗g7 is a logical alternative.

22 ♗e3

This threatens ♕c1 with a double attack on the h6- and c7-pawns (in connection with ♘a3).

22 ... ♔h7

The radical 22...h5 would limit White's h2-knight, but one can understand Karpov's reluctance to weaken his kingside.

23 ♕c1 c6?!

Karpov prepares ...♗e6 followed by ...♗xc4 and ...d5, but the text-move gives White a welcome tactical opportunity. According to Kasparov 23...♕b8 is safer, when Black has a passive but defensible position.

24 ♘g4! *(D)*

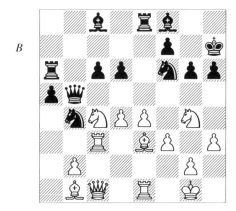

24 ... ♘g8?!

A sad retreat, but choosing between two evils is always tough. Opening the h-file against his own king would have seriously compromised Black's position: after 24...♘xg4 25 hxg4 d5 (Black has no time for 25...♗e6 due to 26 ♘a3

♕b8 27 ♔f2 ♗g7 28 ♕d2 and the h6-pawn is about to fall) 26 ♘e5! (now 26 ♘a3 ♕b8 27 e5 c5 is unclear) 26...dxe4 (passive defence with 26...♗e6 gives White a huge attack after 27 ♔f2 ♕b6 28 ♕d2 ♗g7 29 f4!) 27 ♘xf7 the h6-pawn is *en prise* and the vulnerable kingside can't withstand the onslaught in the long run. In fact, to avoid losing immediately Black should play 27...♘d3! (Kasparov gives the pretty line 27...exf3 28 gxf3 ♘d5 29 ♗xh6! ♖xe1+ 30 ♕xe1 and Black is helpless against all White's threats; for example, 30...♘xc3 31 ♕e8! ♘e2+ 32 ♔f2 and ♘g5+ decides, or 30...♕xb2 31 ♗xf8 ♕xc3 32 ♕h4+ ♔g8 33 ♕h8+ ♔xf7 34 ♗xg6+! with mate), although after 28 ♗xd3 exd3 29 ♖d1 White is much better. However, in retrospect this seems to offer Black more chances than the text-move. From now on until the end Karpov could have improved his play, but hardly saved the game any more.

25 ♗xh6!

White has a pleasant space advantage and he could have increased his pressure by quiet means, 25 ♗f4 being the most obvious alternative. Kasparov, however, opts for a more radical solution. For a minimal material investment he opens the position and starts a direct attack. His idea is not only objectively very dangerous, but makes practical sense as well – Karpov was approaching time-trouble and the sudden switch from a positional massage to a sharp assault causes the defender additional problems.

25 ... ♗xh6

Forced, since after 25...♘xh6? 26 ♘f6+ and 25...♗xg4? 26 ♗xf8 Black loses quickly.

26 ♘xh6 ♘xh6
27 ♘xd6 ♕b6
28 ♘xe8

The sacrificial 28 ♖c5 ♖d8 29 e5 is far less clear: after 29...♕c7 Black's queen returns to the defence, at the same time preparing the right moment for ...♖xd6.

28 ... ♕xd4+

This natural move cost Karpov a full 20(!) minutes – presumably only now he understood the extent of the problems he would be facing in the position after move 31. An attempt to keep the centre closed with 28...♕d8 can be met by 29 d5 or 29 ♖c5 ♕xe8 30 ♕g5, when White enjoys both a material and a positional advantage.

29 ♔h1 ♕d8
30 ♖d1 ♕xe8
31 ♕g5! *(D)*

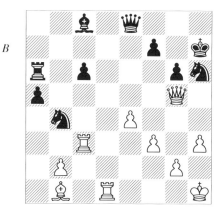

This is the position Kasparov was striving for with his 25th move. White controls the only open file and this makes his rook a more valuable unit than Black's uncoordinated minor pieces. All White's forces are aimed at Black's vulnerable kingside and once he can get his central pawns moving, the attack will become decisive. This is in fact exactly what happened in the game.

31 ... ♖a7

Black's problem is that most of his pieces are misplaced and he can only improve their positions one at a time. Karpov concerns himself with the rook first, but in the end it won't get involved in the defence as intended for tactical reasons. Other attempts to restore the piece coordination are:

1) 31...♘g8 fails to 32 ♕h4+! (Black's idea was 32 ♖d8?! ♕e7) 32...♔g7 33 ♖d8 ♕e6 (33...♕e7? now loses to 34 ♖xg8+) 34 f4 and the f-pawn marches on decisively – 34...♖a8 35 f5 ♕e5 36 f6+! and White mates or wins the queen.

2) 31...♗d7 prevents the penetration by the rook, but otherwise does little for the defence. After 32 ♖c5 or Kasparov's 32 f4!? Black's misery continues.

3) 31...♕e6 intends to chase away White's queen, but after 32 ♖d8 f6 (32...♖a7 transposes into the game, while after 32...♖a8 33 f4 Black's main idea is stopped, as 33...f6 fails to 34 f5! ♘xf5 35 ♕xg6+! ♔xg6 36 exf5+ ♕xf5 37 ♖g3+) 33 ♕g3 ♖a8 34 ♕c7+ ♘f7 35 ♗d3!

♘xd3 36 ♖cxd3 Black is practically paralysed and ♖3d6 will quickly decide the issue.

32	♖d8	♕e6
33	f4	

The pawns start rolling. White also finally frees the 3rd rank for his rook.

| 33 | ... | ♗a6?! |

Probably only now did Karpov realize that 33...♖d7 runs into the powerful 34 f5! gxf5 (34...♕d6 35 ♖xc8 ♕d1+ 36 ♔h2 ♕xb1 37 ♖h8+ mates as well) 35 exf5 with a mating attack; e.g., 35...♕e1+ 36 ♔h2 ♕xb1 37 ♖h8+!. After the text-move the queen doesn't have to defend the bishop any more, but 33...f6!? is more resilient: 34 ♕c5 (34 ♕h4?! now allows the unclear 34...♖d7! 35 f5 ♕e5) 34...♖d7. Nevertheless even here after 35 ♕xa5 ♖xd8 36 ♕xd8 both White's attack and Black's coordination problems persist despite the slight simplification.

| 34 | f5 | |

The greedy 34 ♕xa5?! is weaker due to 34...♕e7.

| 34 | ... | ♕e7 (D) |

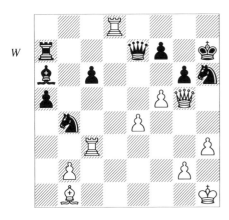

| 35 | ♕d2! | |

Kasparov naturally avoids the exchange and continues his attack. The white queen heads for d4.

| 35 | ... | ♕e5 |

After 35...♘d5 the simplest is 36 fxg6+ fxg6 37 exd5! ♕xd8 38 ♗xg6+!, when the attack breaks through. Karpov feels he should try to prevent the e5 advance. This is clear from lines such as 35...♗e2 36 e5! ♘xf5 37 ♗xf5 gxf5 38 ♖g3 and the threats ♖h8+ and ♕h6+ decide, and 35...f6 36 e5! ♘d5 (36...fxe5 37 ♖g3 and White crashes through) 37 ♖d6!? with an irresistible attack. The problem with the text-move is that Black can't keep his queen on e5 long enough.

| 36 | ♕f2 | ♕e7 |

With his flag about to fall, Karpov eases White's task, but his position was already beyond saving anyway. 36...♖e7 37 ♖c5 ♕c7 (37...♕f6 38 e5! doesn't help either) is hopeless; the prettiest solution is Byrne's 38 fxg6+ fxg6 39 ♕f8 ♘f7 40 ♖h5+! gxh5 41 e5+ ♗d3 42 ♖xd3 with mate. After 36...♕f6 37 fxg6+ ♔g7 White has 38 ♕xf6+ ♔xf6 39 g7! ♔xg7 40 e5 and the mating attack will cost Black at least a piece.

| 37 | ♕d4 | ♘g8 |

Even 37...f6 38 fxg6+ ♔g7 can't stave off the attack for long due to 39 ♖e8! ♕d7 40 ♕c5.

| 38 | e5 (D) | |

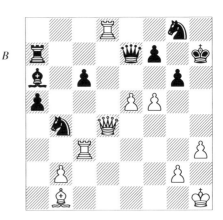

The final blow. Now Black's position collapses.

| 38 | ... | ♘d5 |

The main threat was f6 with a quick mate, while after 38...c5 White wins with 39 fxg6+ fxg6 40 ♗xg6+.

39	fxg6+	fxg6
40	♖xc6	♕xd8
41	♕xa7+	

The time-control has been reached and Kasparov opts for a prosaic solution. 41 ♖xg6! is more energetic, but the text wins easily enough.

41	...	♘de7
42	♖xa6	♕d1+
43	♕g1	♕d2
44	♕f1	1-0

Game 61
Garry Kasparov – Anatoly Karpov
World Ch match (game 20), New York/Lyons 1990
Ruy Lopez (Spanish), Zaitsev Variation [C92]

	1	e4	e5
	2	♘f3	♘c6

In the numerous K-K encounters 1 e4 became Kasparov's most successful weapon and the only opening in which his main rival was able to hold his own was the Petroff Defence. However, Karpov once again decides to trust the sharp Zaitsev Variation despite the previous severe defeats, although it fits his opponent's style better than his own. His reasoning was presumably twofold: in their previous Ruy Lopez games, with the notable exception of Game 60, Kasparov never outplayed Karpov in the opening and from a theoretical viewpoint Black mostly achieved satisfactory positions. Another fact one has to take into account is the match score – Karpov was trailing and the end was close, so even with Black he had higher ambitions than just peaceful equality (a similar situation also arose in Game 35).

	3	♗b5	a6
	4	♗a4	♘f6
	5	0-0	♗e7
	6	♖e1	b5
	7	♗b3	d6
	8	c3	0-0
	9	h3	♗b7
	10	d4	♖e8
	11	♘bd2	♗f8
	12	a4	h6
	13	♗c2	exd4
	14	cxd4	♘b4
	15	♗b1	c5
	16	d5	♘d7
	17	♖a3	f5!? *(D)*

This move was unknown four years earlier, but from 1987 onwards it superseded 17...c4 (see Game 35) as the main move in a line that still remains very much alive. From now on the main theme becomes White's kingside initiative against Black's central control. Although the holes around the black king indicate the attacking chances can become very real, once Black's pawns get moving White's pieces may find themselves cut off from their main target.

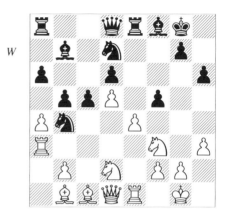

18 ♖ae3 *(D)*

White's first attempts were connected with the natural 18 exf5, but here Karpov has shown that Black even has a choice. After 18...♘f6 (18...♗xd5 19 ♘e4 gives Black the option of transposing into the main line with 19...♘f6, but he can also try the more enterprising 19...♗f7!? 20 axb5 d5! 21 ♘c3 ♖xe1+ 22 ♘xe1 d4 23 ♘a2 ♘xa2 24 ♗xa2 c4! 25 ♖xa6 ♘c5 26 ♖xa8 ♕xa8 27 ♗b1 d3 and despite the extra pawns it's White who has to be careful, Kasparov-Karpov, New York/Lyons Wch (22) 1990) 19 ♘e4 ♗xd5 20 ♘xf6+ ♕xf6, when the solid 21 ♖ae3 leads to a complicated but balanced position. 21 ♗d2?! proved too risky in Kasparov-Karpov, New York/Lyons Wch (4) 1990, and after 21...♕xb2 22 ♗xb4 ♗f7! 23 ♖e6 ♕xb4 24 ♖b3 ♕xa4 Black was better. Gradually White realized that resolving the central tension is not ideal. Although the position opens up, the important b1-h7 diagonal remains closed; moreover, White's minor pieces are not yet ready to take part in the attack and Black can simplify the position and ease his defensive task by exchanging a pair of rooks on the e-file. On the other hand if White induces Black into playing

...fxe4 himself, he will activate his forces much faster, hence the text-move. However, further research in the 1990s has shown White can go about it even more accurately and the best move is 18 ♘h2! immediately. This frees the way for a direct rook-swing to the kingside, thereby saving time in comparison with our game (see move 24). It also leaves the a3-rook more options. Currently the closely scrutinized main lines are 18...♘f6 19 ♖f3 (or 19 ♖g3) 19...♖e5 20 ♖xf5 ♖xf5 21 exf5 ♗xd5 22 ♘g4 ♖a7!? with unclear play.

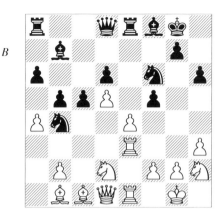

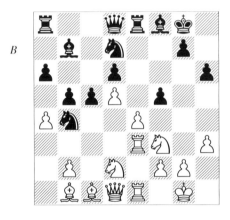

18 ... ♘f6

Also Black probably does the best to keep the status quo. Otherwise:

1) 18...fxe4 is risky and so far Black has only had the guts to try it in correspondence games. However, although after 19 ♖xe4 (19 ♘xe4 ♘xd5 20 ♖3e2 ♘e5! isn't fully clear either) 19...♖xe4 20 ♘xe4 ♘xd5 21 ♕e2 ♘c7!? 22 ♕c2 ♗xe4 23 ♕xe4 ♘f6 24 ♕g6 ♕d7 25 ♗xh6 ♕f7 White is perhaps slightly better, he will be forced to prove it in an endgame, Milos-Hybl, corr. 1999.

2) Blockading the centre with 18...f4 is also interesting: 19 ♖3e2 (19 ♖a3!? is perhaps stronger) 19...♘e5 20 ♘f1!? ♘xf3+ 21 gxf3 ♕h4 22 ♘h2 ♖e5 23 ♕d2. Although in Timman-Karpov, Kuala Lumpur Ct (9) 1990 Black won this complicated position after a fierce struggle, Kasparov undoubtedly had ideas about how to improve White's play.

19 ♘h2 *(D)*
19 ... ♔h8?!

Both sides still refrain from dissolving the tension, but Karpov's move is not ideal, as it doesn't improve his position. It's not clear h8 is a better place for the king than g8; once the position opens up mating threats on the b1-h7 diagonal may prove quite the opposite (see especially note '1' to Black's 20th move). 19...fxe4?! is now considerably weaker than on the previous move: after 20 ♘xe4 ♘bxd5 (20...♘fxd5 21 ♖g3 also gives White a huge attack) 21 ♘xf6+ ♘xf6 22 ♖xe8 ♘xe8 23 ♕d3 White invades via the light squares. However, the patient 19...♕d7 is stronger: 20 exf5 (20 b3 fxe4 21 ♘xe4 ♘bxd5 is not impressive any more, as after 22 ♖g3 Black can effectively simplify with 22...♘xe4 23 ♗xe4 ♖xe4! 24 ♖xe4 ♘c3) 20...♖xe3 21 fxe3 ♗xd5 22 ♘g4 ♗e7 23 e4 ♗f7 24 ♘f3 ♖d8 with approximate equality, Kasparov-Karpov, Amsterdam (Euwe mem) 1991.

20 b3!

This clever idea pinpoints the main drawback of 19...♔h8?!. White finds a way for another piece to join the attack before the centre opens up. The bishop will be very effective on the long dark diagonal.

20 ... bxa4!

A good decision. Karpov appreciates that 19...♔h8?! hasn't made the immediate 20...fxe4 21 ♘xe4 less risky:

1) 21...♘bxd5?! is the worst option. After 22 ♘xf6 ♖xe3 (22...♘xe3 23 ♕d3 wins for White) 23 ♖xe3 ♘xf6 (after 23...♕xf6 24 ♕c2 Black is defenceless) 24 ♘g4 White exchanges all the relevant defensive pieces and his queen will soon decisively invade via the weak light squares.

2) After 21...♗xd5 22 ♘xf6 ♖xe3 23 ♖xe3 ♕xf6 24 ♘g4 (24 ♗d2 ♗g8!? allows Black to

cover his main weakness on h7) 24...♕d4 25 ♗d2 Black faces a difficult defence. White threatens the direct ♘xh6, as well as the slower ♕c1 and ♗c3.

3) 21...fxd5 is similar to line '2': 22 ♖g3!? (22 ♖f3 is less convincing, since 22...♘f6 practically forces the unclear sacrifice 23 ♖xf6) 22...♘f6 23 ♘xf6 ♖xe1+ (23...♕xf6 24 ♘g4 ♕d4 25 ♗d2 again threatens ♘xh6) 24 ♕xe1 ♕xf6 25 ♗d2 with a dangerous attack.

| 21 | bxa4 | c4 |

The point of the pawn exchange: Black prepares to meet possible future threats on the b1-h7 diagonal with a timely ...♘d3.

| 22 | ♗b2 *(D)* | |

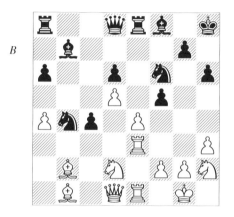

| 22 | ... | fxe4! |

The best available moment for this capture; further attempts to improve Black's position would only backfire. 22...♖c8?! 23 ♕f3! fxe4 (23...♕d7 24 ♗xf6 gxf6 25 ♖c1 and Black's weak pawns will soon start to drop) gives White the extra tactical motif 24 ♘xe4 ♘fxd5 (after 24...♗xd5 25 ♘xf6! ♗xf3 26 ♖xe8 Black loses his queen and White will remain a piece up) 25 ♘xd6!. Now 25...♘xe3 (25...♖xe3 26 ♘f7+ ♔g8 27 ♘xh6+! ♔h8 28 fxe3 gives White a winning attack; e.g., 28...♕h4 29 ♖f1 ♘d3 30 ♘f7+ ♔g8 31 ♘d6!) 26 ♘f7+ ♔g8 27 ♘xh6+! ♔h8 (27...gxh6? 28 ♗h7+! mates) 28 ♘f7+ ♔g8 29 ♗h7+! (29 ♕h5? is only good enough for a draw after 29...♘ec2 30 ♘h6+) 29...♔xh7 30 ♕h5+ wins the queen and White should gradually convert his material advantage.

| 23 | ♘xe4 | ♘fxd5 |

After 23...♘bxd5? 24 ♘xf6 the only way to stave off immediate defeat is the ugly 24...♖xe3 (after 24...♘xe3 25 ♕h5! Black has no defence against ♕g6) 25 ♖xe3 gxf6 (25...♗xf6 loses on the spot to 26 ♕c2 c3 27 ♘g4!) 26 ♕g4 ♗g7 27 ♖g3 ♕g8 28 ♕xc4 and White has a decisive positional advantage for free.

| 24 | ♖g3!? | |

The time is not ripe yet for tactical solutions: 24 ♘xd6? now fails to 24...♘xe3 25 ♘f7+ ♔g8 26 ♘xd8 ♘xd1 27 ♖xe8 ♘xb2. 24 ♕h5 is a tempting alternative, but Black can bail out into a slightly worse endgame with 24...c3 (24...♘xe3? loses material to 25 ♕xh6+ ♔g8 26 ♘g5!, while Kasparov's tricky suggestion 24...♖e5 25 ♗xe5 dxe5 also gives White an edge after 26 ♘g4 ♕e8!? 27 ♕xe8 ♖xe8 28 ♖f3) 25 ♗xc3 ♘xc3 26 ♘xc3 ♖xe3 27 ♖xe3 ♕g5. Kasparov strives for more and quietly piles up the pressure.

| 24 | ... | ♖e6! |

Karpov also keeps his cool and lends support to the vulnerable h6-pawn. Premature liquidation with 24...♘d3?! 25 ♗xd3 cxd3 26 ♕h5 ♖c6 27 ♖g6 ♖xg6 28 ♕xg6 would lose Black exactly this important defensive link and increase White's attacking chances (28...♕h4? 29 ♘f3 ♕f4 loses immediately to 30 ♘fg5!).

| 25 | ♘g4 *(D)* | |

25 ♘f3!? is interesting, as the knight heads for d4 and possibly even g5.

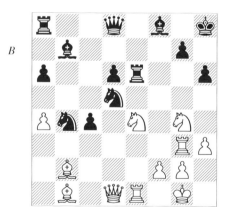

| 25 | ... | ♕e8? |

The alarming concentration of White's attacking forces requires Black to be on the lookout for tactical blows, which are literally hanging in the air. After his inferior 19th move Karpov has defended with great care, but the attempt to pin the e4-knight fails to keep his kingside intact. Other continuations illustrate the dangers Black is facing:

1) 25...♕d7?! 26 ♕c1! with a double attack against c4 and h6 regains the sacrificed pawn without allowing simplification and gives White a permanent advantage.

2) 25...♘f4? runs into the beautiful reply 26 ♘ef6!. White's main threats are once again directed against h6; e.g., 26...♖xe1+ (26...♗c8 27 ♖xe6 ♗xe6 28 ♕f3! ♘bd3 29 ♕e4 ♗g8 30 ♘xh6 doesn't help) 27 ♕xe1 ♘bd3 28 ♗xd3 cxd3 29 ♘xh6! ♘e2+ 30 ♕xe2 ♕xf6 31 ♕d2 with a winning attack.

3) It's not easy to return the booty at the right moment. Black should have been generous right now with 25...♘d3!. This is probably the only plausible move, as it exchanges at least one of the attacking pieces. After 26 ♗xd3 (26 ♖xd3 cxd3 27 ♕xd3 ♘b4 is inconclusive) 26...cxd3 White has no deadly tactics and 27 ♖xd3 (27 ♘xh6? ♖xh6 28 ♘g5 ♕d7 29 ♖e6 ♘f6 and White's compensation is too vague) 27...♕e8 gives Black enough counterplay.

26 ♘xh6! *(D)*

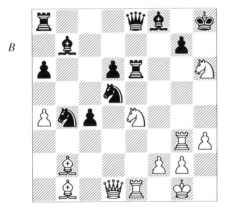

Although the underlying motifs are completely different, just as in Game 60 the dismantling of Black's defences starts with a sacrifice on h6. This chink in Black's armour proves decisive.

26 ... c3

This is more resilient than 26...♖xh6 27 ♘xd6, when even giving up the queen won't save Black's king; after 27...♕xe1+ (27...♕d7 loses quickly to 28 ♕g4! ♕xg4 29 ♘f7+ ♔g8 30 ♘xh6+ gxh6 31 ♖xg4+ ♔f7 32 ♗g6+, and the same goes for 27...♕h5 28 ♖g5! ♕xd1 29 ♘f7+ ♔g8 30 ♘xh6+ ♔h8 31 ♖xd1 c3 32 ♘f7+ ♔g8 33 ♗g6, when the threat of ♖h5 forces 33...♘f4 34 ♗xc3 ♘xg6 35 ♗xb4 ♔xf7 36 ♖d7+ ♔f6 37 ♖xg6+ ♔xg6 38 ♖xb7 and White is two pawns up in a simple rook endgame) 28 ♕xe1 ♖xd6 29 ♕e4 ♘d3 (29...♖h6 30 ♗c1 ♖h5 31 ♖g5 doesn't help) White winds up his attack with 30 ♕h4+ ♔g8 31 ♗xg7! ♗xg7 32 ♕g4.

27 ♘f5

There is no way back. As the long dark diagonal is now closed, White parts with the b2-bishop to achieve ideal coordination of his attacking forces.

27 ... cxb2

27...♖c8 28 ♕g4 forces 28...cxb2, transposing to note '3' to Black's 28th move. 27...♖e5 28 ♕g4 ♖xf5 29 ♕xf5 cxb2 30 ♖g4 is no improvement: White has a winning attack.

28 ♕g4! *(D)*

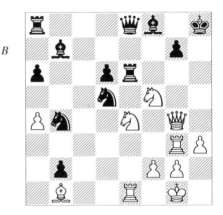

Black's kingside is now heavily compromised, and cannot withstand the onslaught from White's mass of attacking forces. Despite Black's extra piece, a substantial part of his army (the a8-rook, b7-bishop, b4-knight) exerts no influence on the part of the board where the action is taking place. In many lines White can even afford a preparatory king move to unpin his e4-knight.

28 ... ♗c8

Karpov tries to bring one of the aforementioned passive pieces into the fray. Other defensive attempts are also insufficient:

1) 28...♘c3 runs into 29 ♘f6! ♖xe1+ 30 ♔h2 with a quick mate.

2) 28...g6 29 ♔h2! creates the threat of ♘g5. After 29...♕d7 (29...♗e7 30 ♘xe7 ♕xe7 31 ♘xd6! and the attack breaks through) White has 30 ♘h4! ♗c6 (30...♘e7 loses to 31 ♘g5, as 31...♖xe1 32 ♕h5+! leads to a forced mate) 31 ♘xg6+ (or even 31 ♘c5) and the attack is irresistible.

3) 28...♖c8 intends ...♖c4 or ...♘c2, but White can again stop both ideas with 29 ♔h2!; e.g., 29...♘c2 (29...♖g6 30 ♘g5! and 29...♕g6 30 ♘g5 ♖xe1 31 ♘f7+! ♕xf7 32 ♕h4+ lead to a quick mate; the same goes for 29...♖c4 30 ♘xg7 ♖g6 31 ♕h5+ ♔xg7 32 ♘f6!) 30 ♕h4+ ♖h6 31 ♘xh6 gxh6 32 ♗xc2 ♖xc2 33 ♘xd6! and again the attack triumphs. We can safely conclude Kasparov hadn't seen everything beforehand, but he correctly felt that in such a position combinative solutions would come naturally.

29 ♕h4+

Avoiding the trap 29 ♘xg7? ♖g6! with an unclear position.

29 ... ♖h6

After 29...♔g8 30 ♔h2! the follow-up ♘g5 will quickly wrap up the game.

30 ♘xh6 gxh6 *(D)*

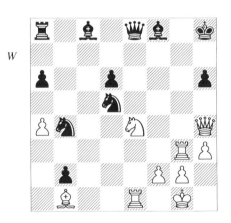

31 ♔h2!

Just as in the above notes, this key move wins. Premature is 31 ♘xd6? ♕xe1+ 32 ♔h2 ♕e6!, but now Black can't take the rook with check any more and he has no defence against the numerous knight jumps. An interesting parallel – in Game 35, 31 ♔h2! was also a strong (albeit not decisive) attacking move.

31 ... ♕e5

Neither 31...♖a7 32 ♘f6 ♕f7 33 ♖e8 nor 31...♗g7 32 ♘xd6 helps Black.

32 ♘g5 ♕f6
33 ♖e8! *(D)*

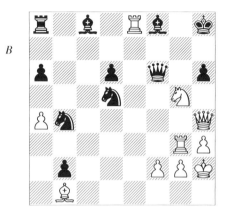

The defensive forces are completely outnumbered.

33 ... ♗f5
34 ♕xh6+

A queen sacrifice is always tempting, but in fact the prosaic 34 ♘f7+! ♕xf7 35 ♕xh6+ ♗h7 36 ♖xa8 leads to mate.

34 ... ♕xh6
35 ♘f7+ ♔h7
36 ♗xf5+ ♕g6
37 ♗xg6+

37 ♖xg6! is even more crushing, as the only way to prevent a quick mate is 37...b1♕ 38 ♗xb1 ♘f4. However, the text-move is more than sufficient, although Karpov continues until the time-control.

37 ... ♔g7
38 ♖xa8 ♗e7
39 ♖b8 a5
40 ♗e4+ ♔xf7
41 ♗xd5+ 1-0

Game 62
Garry Kasparov – Boris Gelfand
Linares 1991
Queen's Gambit Declined, Semi-Slav Defence [D46]

1	d4	d5
2	c4	c6
3	♘c3	♘f6
4	e3	e6
5	♘f3	a6 *(D)*

The usual Semi-Slav move is 5...♘bd7, when it's up to White if he wants to allow the Meran System or avoid it. Gelfand opts for a rare alternative, but his move is often useful in this type of position. However, it's more flexible to play it before ...e6 when Black retains the possibility of developing his bishop on the c8-h3 diagonal. The system with 4...a6 is currently very popular and even Kasparov has recently given it a try with Black.

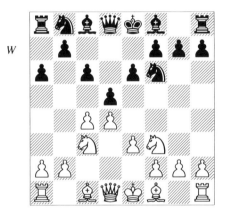

6 b3

After 6 ♗d3 Black can justify his previous move with 6...dxc4 7 ♗xc4 b5 followed by ...c5. The resulting position can also arise via a Queen's Gambit Accepted move-order and doesn't cause Black any serious worries. By giving the c4-pawn extra protection, Kasparov avoids transpositions into the Meran and tries to prove 5...a6 a loss of time. Another attempt to achieve this is 6 c5 ♘bd7 (6...b6 is stronger) 7 b4 a5?! 8 b5 e5 9 ♕a4 ♕c7 10 ♗a3 e4 11 ♘d2 ♗e7 12 b6 ♕d8 13 h3 0-0 14 ♘b3 and White was clearly better in Kasparov-*X3D Fritz*, New York (3) 2003, as the a5-pawn is about to fall. However, here one can clearly see traces of anti-computer strategy: in closed positions with pawn-chains even strong machines are sometimes surprisingly helpless.

6	...	♗b4
7	♗d2	♘bd7
8	♗d3	0-0
9	0-0	

Times certainly change and 12 years later we can find Kasparov sitting on the other side of the board. After 9 ♕c2 ♗d6 10 ♘e2 c5 11 0-0 b6 12 cxd5 exd5 13 ♘g3 ♗b7 14 ♘f5 ♗c7 15 dxc5 bxc5 16 b4 c4 17 ♗e2 ♘e4 Black had a satisfactory position in Khuzman-Kasparov, Rethymnon (ECC) 2003. The text-move is certainly more logical.

| 9 | ... | ♗d6 |

Now that White has castled, Black must parry the ♘xd5 threat, so he retreats the bishop to its most natural square. The manoeuvre ...♗b4-d6 can't be simply condemned as a waste of time, because White will later also have to invest tempi to reposition his d2-bishop. If Black wanted to prevent the following central advance, he could have played 9...♕e7 instead, but after 10 ♕c2 White retains a slight edge.

10 e4!? *(D)*

Left to his own devices, Black would free his position with ...e5. Kasparov therefore decides to act first, but his seemingly natural central thrust is in fact quite risky, since in the subsequent fight for the advantage he is more or less committed to a pawn sacrifice. The sedate alternative is 10 ♕c2 with the idea not so much to play against an isolated d5-pawn after 10...e5 11 cxd5 cxd5, but to open up the position with 12 e4! (12 dxe5 ♘xe5 13 ♘xe5 ♗xe5 is not too promising for White, as the d2-bishop is misplaced). This is a typical motif in the Anti-Meran systems: White's small lead in development gives him chances for an edge.

| 10 | ... | dxc4 |

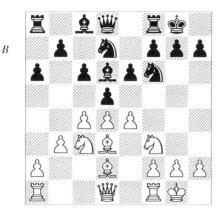
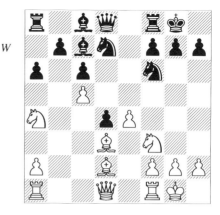

10...dxe4?! opens up the position prematurely: after 11 ♘xe4 ♘xe4 12 ♗xe4 e5 13 ♕c2 White's bishop comes to c3 and Black will soon be in serious trouble.

11 bxc4

11 ♗xc4 is inconsistent with White's 6th move and allows Black to solve his opening problems after 11...e5 12 ♗g5 ♕e7.

11 ... e5
12 c5!

This pawn push is more enterprising than stabilizing the centre with 12 d5, when both 12...♘c5 and 12...h6!? give Black a satisfactory position.

12 ... ♗c7

After 12...exd4? 13 cxd6 dxc3 14 ♗xc3 followed by e5 White's pawns are too powerful. The text-move is stronger than the passive 12...♗e7 13 ♕c2! (13 ♘a4? fails to 13...♘xc5!) 13...exd4 14 ♘a4 ♘g4 15 ♗f4, when White has more than enough compensation, as any move by the d7-knight invites White's knight to b6. Now, however, the centre is crumbling...

13 ♘a4

13 dxe5? ♘xe5 (or even 13...♘xc5) would really mean White's concept had failed, as the position would open up in Black's favour.

13 ... exd4 *(D)*
14 h3!

White's plan is getting clearer contours. For the time being Kasparov is not interested in the extra – but weak and unsupported – d4-pawn (14 ♘xd4? ♘xc5 is out of the question) and is content with blockading it. His last move plays an important role in this, as it prevents the manoeuvre ...♘g4-e5. (Kasparov indicates that another way to accomplish this was 14 ♗g5!?.)

In the following course of the game White's hopes lie in his kingside pawn-majority; especially if Black exchanges his f3-knight with ...♘e5 the central pawns can start rolling. Also after suitable preparation he can show interest in the d4-pawn after all (♖b1-b4, ♗c1-b2, etc.). Moreover, on the queenside Black is seriously limited by the c5-pawn; here 5...a6 plays a significant and negative role by taking the sting out of a possible ...b5 or ...b6 advance. All in all White has play for the pawn and Black must defend with care.

14 ... ♖e8

After 14...b5?! 15 cxb6 ♘xb6 16 ♘xb6 ♗xb6 17 ♕c2 followed by e5 White regains the sacrificed pawn advantageously, while 14...♘e5?! 15 ♘xe5 ♗xe5 16 ♘b6 ♖b8 17 f4 also favours White. However, 14...♕e7!? is a valid and perhaps more testing alternative. Kasparov intended to play 15 ♖e1 (15 ♕c2 keeps more tension, but the position remains unclear after 15...♘e5 16 ♘xe5 ♕xe5 17 f4 ♕h5) 15...♘xc5 (15...♘e5 16 ♘xe5 ♕xe5 17 f4 ♕h5 18 ♕xh5 ♘xh5 19 e5 cramps Black; despite the exchange of queens White's initiative is unpleasant) 16 ♗b4 ♘fd7 17 ♖c1 b6 18 e5, but Black can escape from the pins and retain a playable position with 18...♕d8; e.g., 19 ♘xd4 ♘xe5 20 ♘xc5 bxc5 21 ♗xc5 ♖e8 and White's piece activity is good enough for equality at best.

15 ♖e1 h6

A first step in the wrong direction. 15...♘e5 isn't ideal for Black for the same reason as in the above note, but neither is the text-move. Although sooner or later ...h6 will be forced anyway, right now Gelfand would have done better to address his main problem, namely the underdeveloped queenside. The subsequent games from this position continued 15...♘f8! 16 ♖b1 (the straightforward 16 e5?! ♘d5 17 ♗g5 ♕d7 18 ♖b1 h6 19 ♗h4 ♘f4 20 ♗f1 ♘8g6 21 ♗g3 ♖d8 22 ♖b4 ♘e6 23 ♖b3 ♕e7 24 ♕c2 ♖b8 25 ♖eb1 ♘g5 led to problems with the impetuous e-pawn in the game L.Lengyel-Godena, Budapest 1995) 16...♘e6 17 ♕c2 h6!? (17...♘d7 18 e5 h6 19 ♖b4 is less convincing, as White can defend c5 with ♖c4; the text-move waits for White to commit his rook). Now 18 ♗c4 or even 18 ♘b6!? ♗xb6 19 cxb6 leads to an interesting position, whereas 18 ♖b3 ♘d7 19 e5 ♕e7 20 ♗c4 ♘dxc5 21 ♗b4 b6 22 ♘xc5 bxc5 23 ♗a3 ♖b8 forced White to simplify in order to avoid trouble in Cvitan-Godena, Vienna open 1991.

16 ♖b1 ♘h7 *(D)*

Even here 16...♘f8 was possible, although White can target the weakness created by the previous move with the clever 17 ♕c1!. The idea is that once Black plays ...♘e6, White can launch a fierce attack with e5 and ♗xh6.

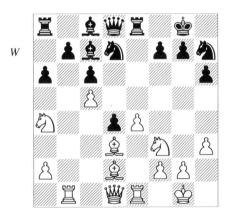

W

17 ♗c4

Targeting d4 with 17 ♖b4 gives Black counterplay after 17...♘g5!? (17...♘hf8 18 ♕c2 ♘e6 19 e5 leads to an advantageous position from the note to move 15) 18 ♘xg5 hxg5 19 ♖xd4 (weaker is 19 ♕h5 ♘f6! 20 ♕xg5 ♖e5) 19...♗e5 20 ♖b4 ♘xc5 21 ♘xc5 b6. Kasparov stops this idea, but only temporarily.

17 ... ♕f6

17...♘g5? now runs into 18 ♘xg5 hxg5 19 ♕h5 ♘e5 20 ♗xg5, when Black has only weakened his kingside.

18 ♖b3 ♘hf8?

Despite the criticism voiced in the notes above, White only truly gains the upper hand after this passive move. Gelfand should have insisted on his plan and precisely calculated the seemingly risky, but more active continuation 18...♘g5!?. After 19 ♘xg5 (19 ♗xg5 hxg5 20 ♕xd4 ♘e5 and the unopposed dark-squared bishop offers Black excellent counterplay) 19...hxg5 20 ♖f3 (20 ♕h5 ♗f4 gets White nowhere) 20...♗f4 21 ♘b6 (21 g3 ♘e5 22 gxf4 ♘xc4 can only be better for Black) 21...♘xb6 22 cxb6 the safest is 22...♗e6 23 ♗xe6 ♕xe6 24 ♗xf4 gxf4 with equality. Thus the best way to keep tension in the position seems to be 19 ♕c2!? with unclear consequences.

19 ♗c1 ♘g6

19...♘e5 20 ♘xe5 ♕xe5 21 f4 gives White the initiative and also after 19...♘e6!? 20 ♗xe6 ♕xe6 21 ♘xd4 his pieces are better coordinated; the knight comes to f5.

20 ♘xd4 ♘de5
21 ♗f1 *(D)*

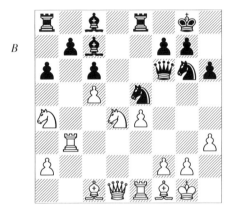

B

The strategic initiative is now clearly in Kasparov's hands. White has won back the pawn and retained his better pawn-structure. His pressure against b7 makes it difficult for the c8-bishop and the a8-rook to get out and although the remainder of Black's army is reasonably active, they can quickly be forced into passivity once White prepares the f4 advance.

21 ... ♖d8

Kasparov suggested lashing out by 21...♘f4 22 ♗b2 (22 ♕c2!? also looks good for White) 22...♗e6 was an improvement. After 23 ♖xb7 ♗a5 24 ♖c3 ♖ad8 (24...♗xa2? 25 ♘b6 eases White's task, as after 25...♖ad8 he has 26 ♕a4)

25 ♕c2 (25 ♕a1 ♗c8 is less clear) 25...♗xa2 Black's pieces are more active than in the game, but the problems remain; e.g., 26 ♖a3! ♗c6 27 ♘b6 ♗b4 28 ♘xc6 clearly favours White.

| 22 | ♗b2 | | ♘h4?! |

Following 22...♘f4 23 ♕c1, 23...♗e6?! is again insufficient, as after 24 ♘xe6 ♘xe6 25 ♖xb7 ♖ab8 26 ♖xb8 ♖xb8 27 ♗c3 White simply has an extra pawn. Therefore Black should prefer the modest 23...♖b8 or even, instead of the text-move, 22...♖b8!?, preparing ...♗e6 and keeping White's advantage within limits.

| 23 | ♖ee3! |

A strong prophylactic move: by overprotecting the f3-square White avoids the trap 23 g3? ♖xd4! and gets ready to play in the centre.

| 23 | ... | | ♕g5?! |

The ugly 23...g5 is the only way to prevent the decisive advance of the f-pawn, but after 24 ♕c2 or 24 ♘b6 White has a large advantage. The text-move only puts the queen in the way; now White is practically winning.

| 24 | g3 |

Kasparov's notes imply that 24 ♕c2 is also strong, but there is nothing wrong with the text-move, which directly threatens f4.

| 24 | ... | | ♘hg6 |
| 25 | ♕c2! |

White has time to side-step the pin and doesn't need to calculate moves such as 25 ♔h1.

| 25 | ... | | h5 |

Black doesn't have enough firepower to cause any confusion on the kingside. Thus 25...♘f4 is effectively parried by 26 ♘f5! ♗xf5 (26...♘d5 27 exd5 ♗xf5 28 ♕c2 doesn't help) 27 exf5 ♖d2 28 ♕e4!? with unavoidable losses, and after 25...♕h5 26 f4 ♗xh3 27 ♗xh3 ♕xh3 28 fxe5 ♗xe5 29 ♘f5 Black's tricks will soon be over as well.

| 26 | ♗g2 (D) |
| 26 | ... | | h4 |

The expulsion of Black's centralized pieces is imminent and as it means a failure of his whole set-up, Gelfand decides to sacrifice material instead of retreating. 26...♕e7?! 27 f4

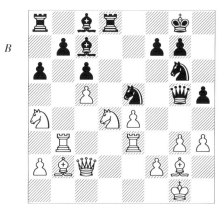

♘d7 28 ♘f5 is even more disgusting; Black pays a high price for ignoring the development of his queenside forces.

27	f4		♘xf4
28	gxf4		♕xf4
29	♘b6!

The most convincing: White exchanges one of the bishops that still might cause his king some awkward moments.

| 29 | ... | | ♘g4? |

29...♖b8 30 ♘xc8 followed by ♘f5 is hopeless for Black, as both Black's king and queen get into trouble. The text-move is sheer desperation, but even after 29...♗xb6 (relatively best) 30 cxb6 ♗e6 31 ♘xe6 fxe6 32 ♗c1 White will gradually consolidate his ranks and convert his extra piece.

30	hxg4		♗xg4
31	♘xa8		♕h2+
32	♔f1		♗g3
33	♖xg3

The body-count shows White is a rook and two minor pieces up, so it's worth giving something back to safeguard the king fully.

33	...		hxg3
34	♕d3		♗h3
35	♕xg3		♕h1+
36	♔f2		♗xg2
37	♕xg2		♕h4+
38	♔e2		1-0

Black, presumably short of time, has run out of ideas and resources.

Game 63
Garry Kasparov – Vishy Anand
Tilburg 1991
Sicilian Defence, Taimanov/Paulsen Variation [B48]

1 e4

In the 1980s Kasparov was mainly a 1 d4 player and went for the open games almost exclusively only in his matches with Karpov. This started changing in the following decade, when he considerably broadened his repertoire with White.

1 ... c5
2 ♘f3 ♘c6
3 d4 cxd4
4 ♘xd4 ♕c7
5 ♘c3 e6

Anand adopts a Taimanov/Paulsen move-order, which he trusts to this very day.

6 ♗e3

Kasparov alternates between the text-move and 6 ♗e2; for example, in his later games with Anand he preferred the second option. More details about this continuation will be featured in Volume 2 in the game Kasparov-Lautier, Cannes (rapid) 2001.

6 ... **a6** *(D)*

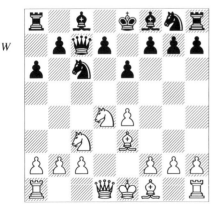

7 ♗d3

Nowadays it's very popular to use the aggressive English Attack set-up practically regardless of the system Black chooses. Even Kasparov isn't immune against fashion and gave 7 ♕d2 a try. After 7...♘f6 8 0-0-0 ♗b4 9 f3 ♘e5 10 ♘b3 b5 11 ♗d4 ♗e7 12 ♕f2 d6 13 ♔b1 0-0 14 g4 ♘fd7 15 ♖g1 ♗b7 16 g5 ♖fc8 17 a3 a complex position arose in Kasparov-Ye Jiangchuan, Bled OL 2002.

7 ... ♘f6
8 0-0 ♘e5

This move still enjoys the status of the main line, although lately Rublevsky has been reasonably successful with 8...b5, and 8...♗d6!? is also a playable alternative.

9 h3

The positional threat ...♘eg4 can't be ignored and the text-move is better than 9 ♗e2 b5 10 f4 ♘c4 11 ♗xc4 ♕xc4, when Black is doing fine. The difference between these two lines will become apparent from the following note.

9 ... **♗c5** *(D)*

Now 9...b5 10 f4 ♘c4 11 ♗xc4 ♕xc4 allows 12 ♕d3!, as ...♘g4 is stopped. Due to Black's vulnerable queenside White gets a pleasant endgame advantage after 12...♗b7 13 a4! ♕xd3 14 cxd3.

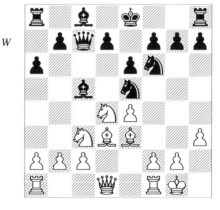

10 ♔h1

A positional alternative is 10 ♘a4 ♗a7 11 c4 d6 12 ♖c1 with typical Hedgehog characteristics – White has space, but Black's set-up is very solid. Prior to our game White usually preferred 10 ♕e2, but Black's good practical results after 10...d6 11 f4 ♘g6 prompted a search for a new approach. Kasparov comes up with an older but rare continuation. His move is both useful and flexible – the white queen may yet be developed more actively to f3 or h4 via e1. It's no surprise this game revived interest in 10 ♔h1, which is currently considered to be White's main option. One final remark – after 10 f4 Black can, apart from 10...d6, also play 10...♘c6!? 11 ♘f5 (here 11 e5? fails to 11...♘xe5!) and now choose between the solid 11...♗xe3+, or materialistic moves such as 11...♕a5 and 11...♘e7!?.

10 ... d6
11 f4

White regains the tempo he was forced to invest on move 9.

11 ... ♘c6?

Attacking the d4-knight is seemingly logical, but Kasparov shows that the insertion of ♔h1 and ...d6 completely changes the assessment of the text-move and proceeds to refute it. Black should retreat his knight (11...♘xd3?! 12 cxd3 is a concession, as the typical Sicilian counterplay on the semi-open c-file is now over; White has strengthened his centre and is slightly better). After 11...♘ed7 12 a3 b5 (12...0-0 13 ♕e1 b5 14 b4! gives White the initiative for free) Kasparov introduced the sharp 13 ♗xb5 axb5 14 ♘dxb5 against Lautier in Amsterdam 1995, but the sacrifice is far from clear after both 14...♕c6 and 14...♕b8!?. Black also has 11...♘g6, which is nowadays his main move.

12 e5! (D)

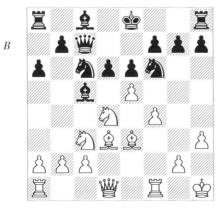

Black is one move short of castling, but he never makes it as Kasparov energetically opens the position. On the other hand this central thrust is not only natural and strong, but also practically forced and Anand must have reckoned with it. In the following note we'll see what the Indian GM overlooked.

12 ... ♘xe5?!

Black faces a bewildering choice of evils:

1) 12...dxe5? is weak: 13 ♘db5! axb5 14 ♗xc5 ♘d4 15 fxe5!? ♕xc5 16 exf6 g6 17 ♘e4 and Black's compromised position will soon collapse.

2) 12...♘d7 gives White a pleasant choice between the simple 13 exd6 and the more enterprising 13 ♘xe6!? fxe6 14 ♕h5+ ♔d8 (not 14...♔f8? losing quickly to 15 f5!) 15 ♕h4+ ♘e7 16 ♘e4 with a raging attack for the piece.

3) 12...♘xd4 13 exf6 gxf6 14 ♘e4!? (14 ♗xd4 ♗xd4 15 ♗b5+ axb5 16 ♕xd4 is also very good for White) spells big trouble for Black; his king has no safe hiding place and 14...f5 15 ♗xd4 costs him material.

4) Anand's original intention was 12...♗xd4 13 ♗xd4 dxe5 (13...♘xd4 14 exf6 gxf6 15 f5! gives White a dangerous attack) 14 fxe5 ♘d7 (14...♘d5 allows the analogous 15 ♘e4!; e.g., 15...♘xe5 16 ♕h5 ♘xd3 17 ♖xf7! or 15...0-0 16 ♘f6+! gxf6 17 ♗xh7+! and White's attack breaks through; also after 14...♘xe5 15 ♖xf6! gxf6 16 ♘e4 f5 17 ♘f6+ ♔e7 18 ♕e2 ♔xf6 19 ♖e1 Black's exposed king can't last for long) 15 ♘e4! ♘cxe5 (15...♘dxe5? loses to 16 ♗c5, while after 15...0-0 16 ♕h5! the threat of ♘f6+ is decisive), but he freely confessed he initially overlooked the powerful 16 ♕h5!, which traps Black's king in the centre. All this actually occurred in a later game and Black was duly crushed: 16...h6 (16...0-0? loses on the spot to 17 ♗xe5 ♕xe5 18 ♘f6+) 17 ♘g5 g6 18 ♘xe6! ♕d6 19 ♗xg6! fxg6 20 ♘g7+ ♔d8 21 ♕h4+ ♔c7 22 ♖ad1 g5 23 ♕g3 ♕e7 24 ♖fe1 ♔b8 25 ♖xe5 ♘xe5 26 ♗xe5+ ♔a7 27 ♕e3+ b6 28 ♗b8+! 1-0 Goloshchapov-Al.Kharitonov, Ekaterinburg 1999.

5) Arguably the safest option is 12...♘d5!? 13 ♘xd5 exd5 14 ♘xc6 ♕xc6 (14...♗xe3 15 ♘b4 ♕c5 16 ♕f3! is even more dangerous) 15 ♗xc5 dxc5 16 c3. Although White enjoys a significant positional advantage with his mobile kingside majority, simplification gives Black better chances to face the onslaught than in the game.

| 13 | fxe5 | dxe5 *(D)* |

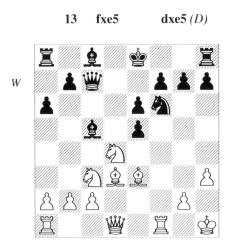

| 14 | ♗b5+!? | |

Kasparov was not pleased with this move and indicated that 14 ♘db5! is more forcing and gives White a powerful bind after 14...axb5 15 ♗xb5+ ♔e7 (15...♗d7 runs into 16 ♗xd7+ ♘xd7 17 ♗xc5 ♕xc5 18 ♖xf7 and White wins) 16 ♗g5 h6 17 ♗h4. White's main threat is ♕f3 and after 17...♗e3 18 ♘e4 ♗f4 the most convincing winning line is the beautiful 19 ♖xf4 exf4 20 ♕d4 e5 21 ♗xf6+ gxf6 22 ♕b4+ ♔e6 23 g4!! fxg3 24 ♖f1. While this is true and the game would possibly be over sooner, the text-move doesn't deserve such harsh criticism; even now White's attack is strong enough to be considered decisive.

| 14 | ... | axb5 |

14...♗d7? 15 ♗xd7+ ♘xd7 (15...♕xd7 16 ♘f5 retains the extra piece) 16 ♕f3 is completely hopeless for Black, but 14...♔f8!? is arguably somewhat more testing. 15 ♖xf6! (White has nothing better; 15 ♘f5 ♗xe3 16 ♘xe3 axb5 17 ♘xb5 ♕b6 is unclear) and now:

1) The rook is taboo: 15...gxf6? loses on the spot to 16 ♗h6+ ♔e7 17 ♘f5+!.

2) Therefore Black must take the knight. After 15...♗xd4 the most energetic continuation is 16 ♗h6! (Kasparov recommends the more "mundane" 16 ♖xf7+!? ♕xf7 17 ♗xd4 exd4 18 ♕xd4 ♕e7 19 ♖f1+, when Black will have a tough time with his disconnected rooks). White wants to pile up pressure on the f-file (♕h5, ♖af1) regardless of material and there is little Black can do against it:

2a) After 16...♗xc3 17 ♕h5! b6 the most convincing continuation for White is 18 ♗d7! ♕xd7 19 ♗xg7+! ♔xg7 20 ♕h6+ ♔g8 21 ♖f3 and White wins.

2b) 16...♕e7 17 ♘e4 doesn't help much either; e.g., 17...gxh6 18 ♕h5 ♖g8 19 ♖xh6! axb5 20 ♖xh7 ♗e3 21 ♘d6 and again the attack triumphs.

2c) 16...gxh6 17 ♕h5 ♖g8 (after 17...e4 18 ♕xh6+, 18...♔e7 19 ♖xf7+! leads to mate, while 18...♔g8 19 ♖d1! is also hopeless for Black; the same goes for 17...♗e3 18 ♖af1 ♗f4 19 g3 axb5 20 gxf4) 18 ♕xh6+ ♖g7 19 ♗e8! ♗e3 20 ♕xe3 ♔xe8 21 ♖af1. Although Black has beaten off the first wave of the attack, his pieces are still uncoordinated and White's onslaught (♕h6, ♘e4, etc.) will duly break through.

3) Black can also try 15...exd4 *(D)*.

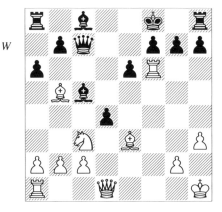

However, after 16 ♗h6! (16 ♗f4?! ♕e7 17 ♘e4 axb5 is more speculative; although White has a dangerous initiative after 18 ♗g5 or even 18 b4!? ♗xb4 19 ♕xd4, the outcome remains open) 16...dxc3!? 17 ♕f3! (stronger than 17 ♕h5? ♗d4!, as here 18 ♗xg7+ only leads to a perpetual) 17...♗d4 (after 17...axb5 18 ♖f1 ♔e8 19 ♖xf7 Black can't survive for long; e.g., 19...♕c6 20 ♕h5 g6 21 ♕e5 ♖g8 22 ♖xh7 with the threat of ♕f6) 18 ♗xg7+! (18 bxc3? ♗xf6 19 ♕xf6 ♖g8 20 ♖d1 gxh6 21 ♖d8+ ♕xd8 22 ♕xd8+ ♔g7 23 ♕d4+ f6 is unclear, as White's attacking forces have dwindled considerably) 18...♔xg7 19 ♖f1 the attack breaks through. The main threats are ♖xf7+ and ♕g4+, and 19...♖f8 (19...♗xf6 20 ♕xf6+ ♔g8?! 21 ♗e8 and White mates) loses to 20 ♗d3!.

| 15 | ♘dxb5 | ♕b6 |
| 16 | ♗xc5 | ♕xc5 |

Game 63: Garry Kasparov – Vishy Anand

17 ♘d6+ ♚e7 *(D)*

After 17...♚f8 White has the simple 18 ♘ce4 ♛d5 19 ♛f3 followed by ♖ad1, when his attack doesn't require any violent measures to succeed.

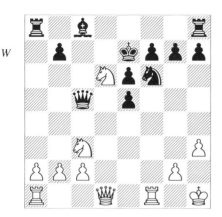

18 ♖xf6!

Now, however, it's different. The tame 18 ♘ce4? is bad due to 18...♛d4 19 ♛f3 ♘xe4, so Kasparov forcefully removes the important defensive piece.

18 ... gxf6
19 ♘ce4 ♛d4

Anand doesn't have much of a choice. 19...♛e3? 20 ♘f5+! mates directly, while after 19...♛c7 20 ♛h5 ♖f8 21 ♛h6 f5 (21...♖a4 is convincingly met by 22 ♛xf6+ ♚d7 23 ♛g7 ♚e7 24 ♖f1) the quiet 22 ♖d1! traps Black's king in a mating-net. ♛h5-h6 will also decide after any other reasonable queen moves.

20 ♛h5 ♖f8
21 ♖d1!

Kasparov doesn't content himself with 21 ♛h4 ♚d7. The rook joins the rest of his army to participate in the final assault.

21 ... ♛e3
22 ♛h4 ♛f4
23 ♛e1!

Black has managed to defend his f6-pawn, but now White's mobile queen strikes from the other flank.

23 ... ♖a4

This at least prevents ♛b4; for example, 23...f5 24 ♘xc8+ ♖fxc8 25 ♛b4+ followed by mate.

24 ♛c3 ♖d4

The main threat was ♛c7+, while 24...♖xe4 25 ♘f5+ and 24...♗d7 25 ♛c5! both lose immediately.

25 ♖xd4 ♛f1+

The queen must leave the vulnerable square due to 25...exd4 26 ♛c7+ ♗d7 27 ♘c8+.

26 ♚h2 exd4 *(D)*

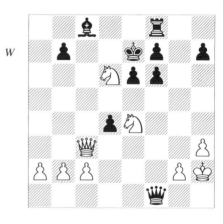

27 ♛c5!

27 ♛c7+ ♗d7 28 ♛c5 ♛f4+ 29 g3 ♛e5 30 ♘f5+ ♚d8 31 ♛xf8+ ♚c7 32 ♛c5+!? leads to a won pawn endgame, but Kasparov doesn't want to prolong the game unnecessarily.

27 ... ♚d7

This allows mate by force, but after 27...♛f4+ 28 g3 ♛e5 29 ♘xc8+ Black loses the house.

28 ♘b5! ♛f4+
29 g3 1-0

After 29...♛e5 30 ♘xf6+! ♛xf6 31 ♛c7+ (or 31 ♛d6+) White mates.

Game 64
Garry Kasparov – Matthias Wahls
Germany-Kasparov simul, Baden-Baden 1992
Pirc Defence [B07]

Kasparov has taken on national teams in simuls before (see Game 40), but this was the first time he had to face exclusively GM opposition. He won the closely contested event 3-1, when in the final game Lobron misplayed an advantage in time-trouble.

1	e4	d6
2	d4	♘f6
3	f3!?	

A flexible move. White spurns the usual 3 ♘c3 and by keeping the option to play c4 later on, postpones the fundamental decision – will Black have to face a semi-open (Pirc Defence) or closed (King's Indian Defence) opening?

3 ... e5

Black naturally also has a word in the opening 'fencing' and decides to avoid both options mentioned above. Hort, who faced the same problem on an adjacent board, decided to allow a transposition into a Sämisch King's Indian with 3...g6 4 c4 ♗g7 5 ♘c3. Wahls doesn't relish the fianchetto and his choice is best described as an Old Indian hybrid. Another interesting option is 3...d5 4 e5 ♘fd7 5 c4!? (more usual is 5 f4 c5 6 ♘f3 e6, transposing into the French(!) Defence) 5...dxc4 6 ♗xc4 e6 (6...♘b6 is stronger) 7 f4 c5 8 dxc5 ♗xc5 9 ♘f3 a6 10 ♘c3 b5 11 ♗d3 ♗b7 12 a3 ♘c6 13 ♘e4 0-0 14 h4! ♗e7 15 ♗e3 with attacking chances for White, Kasparov-Cu.Hansen, Tåsinge (1) 1990.

4 d5 c6

4...♘xe4?! would have perhaps been worth trying in a rapid game, but after 5 fxe4 ♕h4+ 6 ♔d2 ♕xe4 7 ♘c3 it's hard to believe Black has enough for the piece.

5 c4 ♕b6

Practice has shown that White, due to his space advantage, has good chances to emerge from the opening with an edge after the more solid but less enterprising 5...♗e7 6 ♗e3, so Black tries to create some confusion by complicating White's natural development.

6 ♘c3 ♗e7

Black can try to justify his queen sortie with 6...♗d7, but after 7 ♘a4!? ♕d8 (7...♕a6 8 b3 is similar; Black's queen will have to find its way back to c7 or d8 anyway) 8 ♗e3 cxd5 9 cxd5 even the tactical trick 9...♘xd5 10 ♕xd5 ♗xa4 11 ♕xb7 ♗c6 12 ♕b3 doesn't fully overcome his positional problems. Once White finishes his development with ♗c4 and ♘e2-c3, his better pawn-structure will give him a clear advantage; this is exactly what happened in Psakhis-Sturua, Biel open 1995. However, even the bolder 12...d5 13 exd5 ♗xd5 14 ♕b5+ ♕d7 15 0-0-0 gives White the initiative.

7 ♘ge2

Even here White can play 7 ♘a4, while another interesting method is Korchnoi's 7 ♕e2!? followed by ♗e3 and ♕d2.

7	...	0-0
8	♘g3 *(D)*	

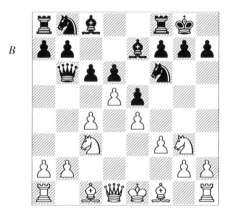

8 ... cxd5

Wahls wisely doesn't insist on retaining control over the a7-g1 diagonal with 8...a5?! 9 ♘a4 ♕a7. This attempt failed and led to Black's total passivity after 10 ♕b3! ♗d8 11 ♗e3 c5 12 ♗d3 ♘a6 13 a3 ♖b8 14 ♘c3 in Brennink-meijer-Van der Wiel, Dutch Ch (Eindhoven) 1991.

9 ♘a4!

The automatic 9 cxd5 ♗d7, followed by ...♖c8 and ...♘a6, eases Black's task and makes it more difficult for White to achieve his envisaged set-up.

9 ... ♕c7

The pseudo-active 9...♕d4?! 10 ♕xd4 exd4 11 cxd5 ♗d7 12 b3 only compromises Black's pawn-structure.

10 cxd5 ♗d7
11 ♗e3

Mission accomplished: White has taken control over the important diagonal.

11 ... ♖c8

The attempt to fight back with 11...♕a5+ 12 ♘c3 ♗d8?! is simply parried by 13 a3!, when Black has problems with his queen.

12 ♘c3 ♘a6
13 ♗e2 (D)

Kasparov points out 13 ♗xa6! bxa6 14 0-0 as a cleaner solution, leading to a small but permanent edge. True enough: White doesn't need his passive light-squared bishop; he can easily parry any play on the b-file and develop his own active plans on either of the flanks, depending on the circumstances.

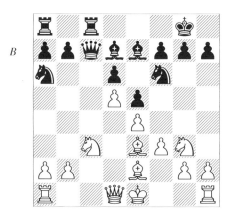

B

13 ... ♗d8?!

Wahls in turn wants to activate or exchange his own passive bishop, but this manoeuvre is rather cumbersome and turns out to be a loss of time (see Black's 18th move). If Black tries to achieve the same with 13...♕d8 14 0-0 ♘e8 15 ♕d2 h6, White may change his mind and return to the idea 16 ♗xa6!? bxa6 17 ♖ac1 with an advantage. Thus 13...♘c5 is more natural. Black intends ...♕a5 and ...♘a4 with counterplay and if White prevents this with moves such as 14 a3 or 14 ♖b1, he can consider the 14...♕d8 plan.

14 0-0 ♕a5
15 ♔h1 ♘c5

Wahls changes plan and activates his knight. Perhaps the consistent 15...♗b6!? 16 ♗d2 ♗c5 was better after all, although it temporarily leaves both the queen and the a6-knight out on the limb.

16 ♗d2?!

Now there was no need for this move. Kasparov admits that the immediate 16 f4!? is more energetic. If Black continues as in the game, White will have an important extra tempo.

16 ... ♘e8

The d6-pawn requires protection, which can be seen from the line 16...a6?! 17 b4! ♕xb4 18 ♘b5 with a clear advantage for White. Also 16...♘a4 17 ♘b5 ♕b6 18 ♕xa4 a6 doesn't solve Black's problems; after 19 ♕b3 axb5 20 a3 the vulnerability of the b5- and d6-pawns makes life difficult for him.

17 f4! (D)

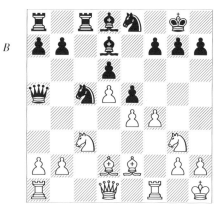

B

Kasparov plays flexible and concrete chess. The pawn-structure seems to indicate White's arena of activity should be the queenside due to the space advantage guaranteed by the d5-pawn. However, in reality most of Black's forces are concentrated in this region, minimizing the chances for any successful queenside play. Therefore White turns his sights to the opposite side of the board and there his attack can become dangerous, as Black's king has been deserted by almost all his pieces and coordinating the defence will take some time.

17 ... exf4

18	♗xf4	♗f6
19	♗g4!	

Once White's knight gains access to f5, it will become his main attacking force. Kasparov doesn't hesitate to sacrifice material to achieve this.

19	...	♕d8!? *(D)*

Black's defence needs reinforcement. This circumspect move is safer than the materialistic alternatives:

1) 19...♗xc3 20 bxc3 ♗xg4 (after 20...♕xc3 21 ♗xd7 ♘xd7 22 ♘f5 White both attacks the d6-pawn and threatens ♘e7+, and 22...♕f6 23 ♗g3 ♘e5 24 ♕h5! gives him unbearable pressure) 21 ♕xg4 ♕xc3 22 ♖ac1! (White needs this *zwischenzug*; after 22 ♘f5 Black complicates matters with 22...♘xe4!, the main idea being 23 ♘e7+ ♔f8 24 ♘xc8? ♘f2+!, winning) 22...♕f6 23 ♘f5 gives White a strong initiative.

2) 19...♗xg4 is risky, but perhaps playable: 20 ♕xg4 ♘d3 21 ♘f5! ♘xf4 (21...♘xb2? 22 e5 dxe5 23 ♘e4 {or 23 ♗xe5!?} gives White a huge attack) 22 ♕xf4 ♖c4!? (22...♕d8?! 23 ♘b5 forces the bishop back to e7, since the positionally desirable 23...♗e5? runs into 24 ♘h6+!). Now taking the pawn with 23 ♘xd6 ♘xd6 24 ♕xd6 ♖d8 25 ♕f4 ♕c7 gives Black dark-square play and reasonable compensation.

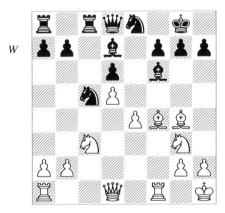

20	♗xd7	♕xd7

Black needs his pieces on the kingside. 20...♘xd7!? is more to the point and in the spirit of the previous move. This gives Black a playable position; the possible follow-up is ...♗e5 or ...♘e5.

21	♕f3	♖c7?!

Wahls still underestimates White's attacking potential and pursues his own ambitions. 21...g6! is necessary. Black has prevented ♘f5 and although his control of the e5-square is not as strong as in the above note, he is still only slightly worse; e.g., 22 ♖ae1 ♗e5!?.

22	♘f5	♗xc3
23	bxc3	♘a4?

A third careless move in a row is more than the position can stand. Kasparov now punishes Black's unfounded optimism and develops a strong attack. The most resilient continuation is 23...f6, although 24 ♖ae1 gives White a tangible advantage. He can transfer a rook to the kingside via the 3rd rank, combining his attacking ambitions with pressure against d6.

24	♕g3! *(D)*	

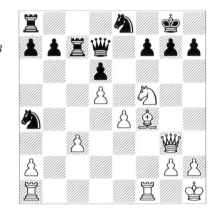

Suddenly the important d6-pawn is defenceless, as the e8-knight has to cover g7 as well.

24	...	♘xc3

After 24...♖xc3 25 ♕g4 the threat of ♘h6+ forces 25...♔h8, which is no less dangerous for Black. The best is now probably the simple 26 ♗xd6 (26 e5 is tempting and works nicely in a line like 26...g6?! 27 e6! fxe6 28 ♘xd6! ♘xd6 29 dxe6 ♕c6 30 e7! ♘f7 31 ♗h6 ♔g8 32 ♕d4 ♘xh6 33 ♕d8+! with mate, but is far less clear after 26...♘b6 or 26...♖d3!?) 26...♖c4 (after 26...f6 Black has to reckon with 27 e5! ♘xd6 28 e6 ♕c7 29 ♕xa4 and the central passed pawns will eventually decide the game), and after 27 ♗f8 or 27 ♕e2!? followed by e5, White's powerful mobile pawn-centre again greatly complicates the defence. The text-move at least activates the knight and postpones the fall of the d-pawn.

| 25 | ♖ae1 |

25 ♗xd6? loses material to 25...♘xe4. By protecting e4, White renews the threat of ♗xd6.

| 25 | ... | f6 |

Black has nothing better:

1) 25...♖c4?! 26 ♗xd6 forces 26...f6 anyway (26...♘xe4? loses outright: 27 ♖xe4 ♖xe4 28 ♘h6+) and after 27 e5 ♘e4 28 ♕h3! the exposed position of Black's queen gives White the tempo needed to push through his pawns.

2) 25...♘xe4 26 ♘h6+ ♔h8 27 ♖xe4 ♘f6 (27...gxh6 28 ♗xh6 f6 29 ♖fe1 and Black can't stand the concentrated pressure for long) 28 ♖d4 gxh6 (28...♘h5 29 ♕g5 ♘xf4 30 ♕xf4 and taking the knight leads to mate after 30...gxh6 31 ♕f6+ ♔g8 32 ♖d3) 29 ♗xd6 ♘h5 30 ♕e5+ f6 31 ♖xf6 ♘xf6 32 ♗xc7 and although Black has avoided losing immediately, his position is untenable due to his exposed king.

| 26 | ♗xd6 |

26 ♘xd6? ♘xd6 27 ♗xd6 ♖c4 is unconvincing.

| 26 | ... | ♘xd6 |
| 27 | ♘xd6 | ♔h8 (D) |

27...♖f8!? is slightly stronger, although even here White has a pleasant choice between 28 ♘f5 and the game continuation 28 e5!? ♘xd5 29 e6, with a dangerous attack in both cases.

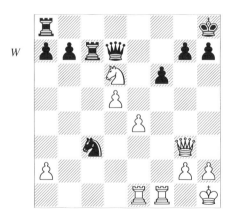

| 28 | e5! |

Now with the rook still passive on a8 there are no doubts about the strength of the central break.

| 28 | ... | ♘xd5 |

Black has no choice. Taking the other pawn, 28...fxe5?, loses on the spot to 29 ♖f7.

| 29 | e6 | ♕c6 |

After 29...♕e7 30 ♘f5 ♕f8 31 e7 ♖xe7 (31...♕g8 32 ♕d6 ♖e8 33 ♖d1 and the passed pawn will cost Black even more material) 32 ♘xe7 ♘xe7 33 ♕c7 White will gradually realize his extra exchange, as Black's pieces remain too passive.

| 30 | ♖d1 (D) |

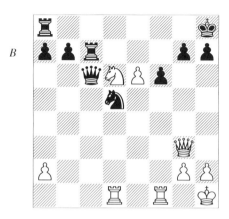

| 30 | ... | ♖f8?! |

Black's flag was rising and this costs him material. However, the e6-pawn was too strong and he had no effective defence anyway:

1) 30...♔g8 31 ♘f5 ♕xe6 (31...♕c4 32 ♖fe1 doesn't help) 32 ♖xd5 and White wins a piece.

2) 30...♘e7 allows the heavy blow 31 ♖xf6!; e.g., 31...♘g6 32 ♖xg6! hxg6 33 ♖e1 and the pawn marches on.

3) 30...♘c3 is a bit trickier, but after 31 ♖d3! (31 ♖c1? runs into 31...♘e2) 31...♘b5 White has 32 ♘f7+ ♔g8 33 a4! ♘c3 34 ♖c1 ♘e2 35 ♕xc7 ♕xc1+ 36 ♕xc1 ♘xc1 37 ♖e3 followed by ♘d6, and again the e-pawn decides the issue.

| 31 | ♘f7+ | ♔g8 |

Dropping a piece, but after 31...♖cxf7 32 exf7 White is winning anyway.

32	♖xd5	♕xd5
33	♕xc7	♕xe6
34	♘d6	♕xa2
35	♕xb7	♕e2?

35...a5 36 ♘f5 is a simple technical win for White, but in serious time-trouble Wahls shortens his suffering.

| 36 | ♕d5+ | ♔h8 |
| 37 | ♘f7+ | 1-0 |

It's a classical smothered mate after 37...♔g8 38 ♘h6++ ♔h8 39 ♕g8+!.

Game 65
Garry Kasparov – Anatoly Karpov
Linares 1992
Caro-Kann Defence [B17]

1 e4 c6

Afterwards Kasparov disclosed he was eagerly looking forward to this encounter against his perennial opponent. In Seville 1987 he made no headway against Karpov's Caro-Kann and despite being successful later in Amsterdam (see Game 43) he still felt he wasn't satisfactorily prepared for this solid opening. However, this was to change for the next title match: in 1990 Kasparov came armed to his teeth... and Karpov played exclusively 1...e5. Thus only two years later did the World Champion get a chance to use his preparation.

2 d4 d5
3 ♘d2 dxe4
4 ♘xe4 ♘d7
5 ♘g5

White still masks his true intentions...

5 ... ♘gf6
6 ♗c4

So it's not going to be 6 ♗d3 this time, but the former main move.

6 ... e6
7 ♕e2 ♘b6 *(D)*

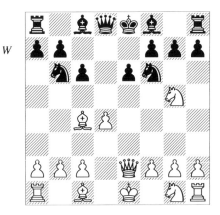

8 ♗b3

Karpov had already faced the more usual 8 ♗d3 more than once in his previous practice, but never the text-move. In such high-calibre games the element of surprise often plays an important role.

8 ... h6 *(D)*

Black usually attacks the g5-knight before White can protect the d4-pawn and retreat more actively to e4. This in fact happened four rounds later: after 8...a5 9 c3!? a4 10 ♗c2 a3 11 b3 ♘bd5 12 ♗d2 ♗d6 13 ♘1f3!? ♘f4 14 ♕f1 h6 15 ♘e4 ♘xe4 16 ♗xe4 0-0 17 g3 ♘d5 18 ♕e2 c5 19 dxc5 ♗xc5 20 ♘e5 ♕c7 21 0-0! ♗e3!? 22 fxe3 ♕xe5 23 ♕d3 ♖a6 24 c4 White was better in a sharp position, Kasparov-Speelman, Linares 1992.

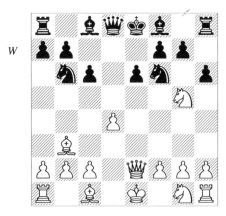

9 ♘5f3 c5

Black chooses a solid continuation. The other playable option, 9...a5, probably seemed too committal to Karpov, as it practically precludes future queenside castling. However, two years later better preparation led him to change his mind and after 10 c3 c5 11 a3 ♕c7! 12 ♘e5 cxd4 13 cxd4 a4 14 ♗c2 ♗d7 15 ♘xd7 ♘bxd7 16 ♕d1 ♗d6 17 ♘e2 ♘d5 18 ♗d2 b5 19 ♘c3 ♘xc3 20 ♗xc3 ♘f6 21 ♕d3 ♘d5 22 ♗d2 ♔e7! it was White who had to fight for equality in Kasparov-Karpov, Linares 1994. So 8 ♗b3 can hardly be considered a wonder weapon and after this game Kasparov never returned to 6 ♗c4 again.

10 ♗f4!? *(D)*

This sharp continuation came into the limelight only in the late 1980s, gradually replacing 10 ♗e3 and 10 dxc5 as the main move. White intends to castle queenside and denies Black's queen its most natural square on c7.

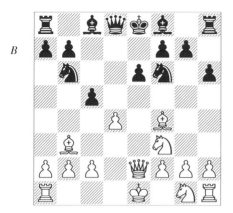

10 ... ♗d6?!

Confronted with a relatively novel idea, Karpov instinctively opts for a simple solution and intends to exchange the nagging bishop. 10...cxd4?! 11 0-0-0 isn't ideal, but the same goes for the text-move. It's no surprise Karpov didn't venture Adorjan's enterprising 10...♘fd5 11 ♗e5 c4!? 12 ♗xc4 ♗b4+ 13 ♔f1 ♘xc4 14 ♕xc4 0-0 with Sicilian-like compensation for the pawn, as such sacrifices are quite contrary to his style. However, the most solid and arguably the best option is 10...♘bd5 11 ♗e5 ♕a5+ 12 ♘d2 and then 12...b5 or 12...cxd4 13 ♘gf3 ♗e7; in his later games Karpov had success with both continuations.

11 ♗g3!

Kasparov is not against simplification, but only on his terms. Now an exchange on g3 would activate the h1-rook without it having to move at all; we'll see something similar in the later course of the game. Both 11 ♗xd6 ♕xd6 12 0-0-0 0-0 and 11 ♘e5 ♕c7 12 dxc5 ♕xc5 13 0-0-0 0-0 allow Black to solve his opening problems satisfactorily.

11 ... ♕e7

Admittedly 11...♗xg3 12 hxg3 is a concession, but how can Black avoid it? After 11...0-0 12 0-0-0 queen moves mean White can at least reach positions from the aforementioned ♗xd6 lines whenever he sees fit. Subsequent attempts to improve Black's play with 11...♕c7 have also failed; after 12 dxc5 ♕xc5 13 0-0-0 ♗xg3 14 hxg3 ♗d7 15 ♘e5 White, with his unassailable e5-knight, can develop a strong initiative no matter on which flank the black king decides to hide.

12 dxc5 ♗xc5

Black's move was forced (12...♗xg3? drops a pawn after 13 cxb6) and this indicates the simplifying idea behind 10...♗d6?! didn't work. Moreover, Karpov will have tactical problems with the c5-bishop in the near future.

13 ♘e5 ♗d7

Karpov doesn't want to commit his king prematurely, fearing White's kingside attacking chances and maybe also the pin after a possible ♗h4. Nevertheless 13...0-0!? deserves attention, when White would probably opt for 14 ♘gf3 ♖d8 15 0-0 anyway, when he is still only slightly better.

14 ♘gf3 *(D)*

Kasparov also doesn't rush to castle. 14 0-0-0 a5! would give Black counterplay.

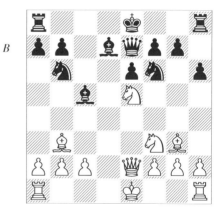

14 ... ♘h5!?

14...0-0-0? is definitely out of the question due to 15 ♘xf7! ♕xf7 16 ♕e5, and 14...0-0 15 ♗h4!? is rather unpleasant, so Karpov continues the waiting game.

15 0-0-0

It's still too early for tactics: 15 ♘xf7?! ♕xf7 (15...♘xg3 16 fxg3 ♔xf7!? is also possible) 16 ♘e5 ♕f5 17 ♘xd7 ♘xg3! (17...♔xd7? 18 ♗xe6+! ♕xe6 19 0-0-0+ ♔e7 20 ♕xh5 gives White a decisive attack) 18 fxg3 ♘xd7 19 ♗xe6 ♕g5 is inconclusive, as White also can't castle.

15 ... ♘xg3

Karpov doesn't want to leave the dark-squared bishop alive, but he underestimates the dynamic potential of White's position after move 16. It's difficult to compare the respective merits of the text-move and the alternative 15...0-0-0 16 ♘xd7 ♘xd7 17 ♗e5 ♘hf6 (not 17...♘xe5?! 18 ♘xe5 and Black has serious problems, as both the knight and the f7-pawn are *en prise*) 18 ♗c3 (now 18 ♕c4?! ♘xe5 19 ♘xe5 ♖d5! gets White nowhere, as 20 ♘xf7? ♖f8 traps the knight) 18...♔b8. White's bishop-pair gives him an edge, but Black intends ...♗b4 and his position has no obvious weaknesses.

16 hxg3 0-0-0

Seemingly Black has no worries whatsoever and stereotyped measures like doubling the rooks on the d-file in fact get White nowhere. According to Kasparov his opponent looked very confident at this point, but this was to change after the very next move...

17 ♖h5! (D)

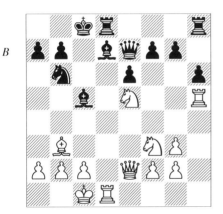

An unexpected resource. The direct threat ♘xf7 is surprisingly difficult to meet and Black's exposed bishop becomes a long-term problem. It would be interesting to know if this was still part of Kasparov's home preparation; his really 'intimate' knowledge of Karpov (see also the note to Black's 19th move in Game 31) suggests this might well be the case.

17 ... ♗e8?!

Kasparov understandably doesn't want to weaken his kingside with 17...g6 18 ♖h4, and hopes White's initiative will evaporate after patient defensive manoeuvres. However, the text-move, which would have been good after 17 ♖d3, now exposes Black's king and increases his problems with piece coordination. 17...♖hf8!?, preparing ...♗d6, deserved attention.

18 ♖xd8+ ♔xd8 (D)

18...♕xd8? allows 19 ♘xf7.

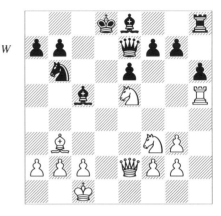

19 ♕d2+ ♗d6

Again forced. 19...♕d6? 20 ♘xf7+ and 19...♘d7? 20 ♘xd7 ♗xd7 21 ♘e5 both cost Black material, and after 19...♔c8?! 20 ♘d3! the only way to keep the g7-pawn alive is the ugly 20...f5 21 ♖h1, terminally weakening the e6-pawn.

20 ♘d3 ♕c7

20...♔c8? is still impossible, due to 21 ♕c3+, and requires further preparation.

21 g4! (D)

After 21 ♘c5 ♔c8 22 ♘e4 ♗e7 23 ♕d4 ♖g8 the defence holds, so Kasparov quietly increases his pressure instead.

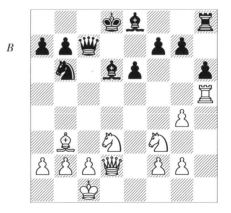

21 ... ♔c8

21...f5? fails to 22 ♘d4! and the attempt to take the sting out of g5 by 21...♖g8 allows 22 ♕e3!, preventing 22...♔c8? due to 23 ♗xe6+. Karpov wisely safeguards his king first.

22   g5   ♗f8

A passive move, but the combinative attempt 22...♗b5?! 23 gxh6 ♗xd3 24 hxg7 ♖d8 is beautifully refuted by Kasparov's 25 g3!! (25 ♕xd3? ♗f4+ 26 ♔b1 ♖xd3 27 g8♕+ ♖d8 even loses for White, and 25 ♖h8?! ♗h7! is insufficient as well due to the looming ....♗f4) 25...♗e4 26 ♖h8 ♗xf3 27 g8♕ ♖xg8 28 ♗xe6+! fxe6 29 ♖xg8+ and White's queen and two pawns will be far stronger than Black's uncoordinated minor pieces. After 22...♔b8 23 gxh6 gxh6 the tactics work fine for Black (after 24 ♖xh6? ♗f4! he wins an exchange), but the simple 24 ♔b1 retains the pressure against the weak h6-pawn.

23   ♖h4!

The exchange of rooks after 23 gxh6?! ♖xh6 would clearly help the defence. Kasparov keeps the tension and retains the g6 advance as a possible option. The mobile rook continues to paralyse Black's kingside forces, as well as supporting White's queenside ambitions.

23   ...   ♔b8
24   a4 (D)

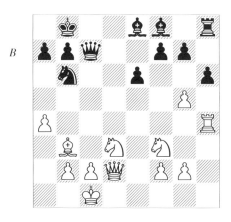

24   ...   ♗e7?

Black wants to untangle his pieces, but this move allows Kasparov to increase his advantage. After 24...a6 25 a5 Black doesn't have the active option 25...♘d5?! due to 26 ♗xd5 exd5 27 ♘f4, winning a pawn. Therefore the knight is forced back and he might as well play 24...♘c8! immediately. Kasparov considered this Black's best chance, although after 25 g6!? (now 25 a5?! ♗b5 isn't ideal) 25...fxg6 26 ♘f4 White has an indisputable initiative.

25   a5   ♘d5

Passivity is now too dangerous: 25...♘c8 26 a6! opens up the position and gives White a virulent attack after 26...bxa6 27 ♖c4 ♕b7 28 g6!?.

26   ♔b1! (D)

Just as on moves 21 and 23, Kasparov is in no hurry to release the tension. Other moves are less incisive:

1) 26 ♗xd5 exd5 27 ♘b4 ♗c6! 28 ♘xd5 ♗xd5 29 ♕xd5 ♖d8 gives Black a lot of counterplay. 30 ♕xf7?? even loses to 30...♗xg5+ 31 ♘xg5 ♕xa5!.

2) 26 a6 allows Black to activate his forces with 26...♗b5 27 ♗xd5 (27 axb7 ♖d8 is unclear) 27...exd5 28 axb7 ♕xb7.

Both lines show it's important for White to improve his king first; moreover the text-move creates the direct threat of c4.

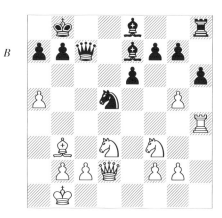

26   ...   ♗d8

Karpov frees a square for his knight. Another possible defensive idea was unpinning the h-pawn:

1) 26...♖f8 is refuted by 27 ♗xd5 exd5 28 ♘b4 ♗c6 29 gxh6! with the lovely point that 29...♗xh4? is met by 30 ♘a6+! bxa6 31 ♕b4+ and White wins.

2) Kasparov argues for 26...♖g8!?. Although now 27 ♖c4 ♗c6 (27...♕d8 28 ♖d4 and the threat c4 wins another tempo) 28 g6!? fxg6 29 ♘d4 is fraught with danger, it seems to offer Black more chances than the text-move.

27   a6   ♕a5

Serious concessions are inevitable, as both 27...b6 and 27...bxa6 allow 28 ♗xd5 exd5 29 ♘b4 with a huge advantage.

28 ♕e2!

The threat of ♕e5+ enables White to avoid the exchange of queens, and after breaking up Black's queenside he can continue with his attack.

28 ... ♘b6
29 axb7 ♗xg5?!

29...♔xb7!? is more resilient, although after 30 ♘de5 or 30 ♕e4+!? ♗c6 31 ♕f4 White's advantage is probably decisive anyway.

30 ♘xg5 ♕xg5
31 ♖h5! *(D)*

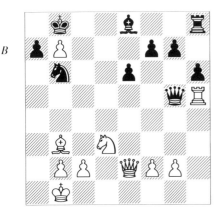

The rook returns to h5, this time with decisive effect, as it will join the attack against Black's king.

31 ... ♕f6

31...♕xg2 loses by force: White quickly mates after 32 ♘c5 ♘d7 (32...f6 33 ♕d1 doesn't help) 33 ♕a6! ♘xc5 (33...♘b6 34 ♕d3 ♔c7 35 b8♕+! mates) 34 ♖xc5 ♕xb7 35 ♕d6+.

32 ♖a5 ♗c6

32...♔xb7 33 ♘c5+ forces the king out into the open, as 33...♔b8 34 ♖xa7! loses even faster.

33 ♘c5 ♗xb7

The threats of ♕a6 and ♖xa7 leave Black with no choice. Now Kasparov winds up the game with a king-hunt.

34 ♘xb7 ♔xb7
35 ♕a6+ ♔c6
36 ♗a4+ ♔d6
37 ♕d3+ ♘d5 *(D)*

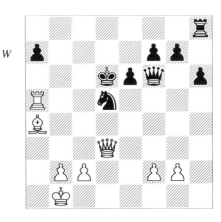

38 ♕g3+!

38 c4 also wins, but the text-move deprives Black's king of the e5-square and is more forcing.

38 ... ♕e5

The queen shows its full scope after 38...e5 39 ♕a3+ ♔e6 40 ♕h3+! ♕f5 41 ♗d7+.

39 ♕a3+ ♔c7
40 ♕c5+ ♔d8
41 ♖xa7 1-0

Having reached move 40, Karpov had enough time to realize he faced mate or heavy losses.

Game 66
Garry Kasparov – Vishy Anand
Linares 1992
French Defence, Winawer Variation [C18]

1	e4	e6
2	d4	d5
3	♘c3	

Kasparov was in a bloodthirsty mood. Earlier he only rarely employed the text-move, which is indisputably White's most ambitious option. For him this encounter was definitely a personal matter. After Kasparov's crushing initial victory (see Game 63) Anand responded with two wins of his own in Tilburg 1991 and Reggio Emilia 1991/2. Especially the latter game must have preyed on Kasparov's mind, as after 3 ♘d2 c5 4 exd5 ♕xd5!? he didn't get anything out of the opening, was outplayed in a complex middlegame and moreover had to concede the overall tournament victory to the Indian GM. Possibly all this also negatively influenced Kasparov's play in the final phase of our game.

3	...	♗b4
4	e5	c5
5	a3	♗xc3+
6	bxc3	♘e7 *(D)*

The Winawer Variation promises a complex struggle with both sides having their own trumps. White has more space and his unopposed dark-squared bishop gives him chances to profit from the weakened dark squares. On the other hand the semi-open nature of the position favours the side with the knights. If Black survives the onslaught, White will have serious problems with his doubled c-pawns, which limit his bishops and complicate possible piece transfers between the flanks.

7	h4!?	

Positional options such as 7 a4 or 7 ♘f3 don't fit in too well with the necessity to play aggressively. Later Kasparov adopted White's main and most ambitious continuation 7 ♕g4. The Argentinean GM Pilnik introduced the interesting text-move into practice as early as 1946, but it gained popularity only due to Short's efforts in the late 1980s. By advancing his h-pawn as far as possible, White wants to breach Black's kingside defences and gain space to activate his h1-rook without castling.

7	...	♘bc6

7...♕a5 8 ♗d2 usually transposes into the game, while 7...♕c7!? is a plausible independent alternative.

8	h5	♕a5
9	♗d2	cxd4

Until this game the text-move was considered the main continuation, but Kasparov's original approach forced Black to think twice about releasing the central tension. 9...♕a4 10 ♘f3 (10 h6!? also deserves attention) will probably only transpose into the game, as Black has to watch out for the possibility dxc5. After the prophylactic 9...h6 10 ♕g4 Black is forced to make some sort of concession. With 10...♔f8 11 a4 or 10...♘f5 11 ♗d3 Black gives positional ground, while sacrificing material with 10...♗d7!? 11 ♕xg7 0-0-0 is probably more promising, but not everyone's cup of tea. In practice Black has been doing well with 9...♗d7!? 10 h6 gxh6 11 ♘f3 0-0-0, intending to open up the centre with a later ...f6. This leads to unclear play, as due to 7 h4!? White is somewhat behind in development.

10	cxd4	♕a4 *(D)*
11	♘f3!	

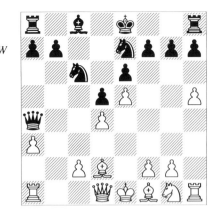

A novelty in true Kasparov style. Our game is the ideological predecessor of Kasparov-P.Nikolić, Horgen 1994, featured in Volume 2, where we'll see a very similar, albeit even riskier and more daring, idea. Black's dark-square vulnerability can be most effectively exploited in an open position and to achieve this White doesn't shy away from sacrificing his central pawn(s). Previously played moves such as 11 ♗c3 b6, followed by ....♗a6, or 11 c3 ♕xd1+ 12 ♔xd1 h6 give Black sufficient counterplay. 11 h6 is in the same spirit as the text-move, but here Black has fewer problems after 11...♕xd4 12 ♘f3 ♕e4+ 13 ♗e2 ♘xe5!?.

11 ... ♘xd4

Accepting the sacrifice is the most principled continuation and it's best to do so immediately. Prophylactic measures such as 11...h6 12 ♗d3 only help White to develop his initiative, which can easily grow into a strong attack after 12...♘xd4 (12...b6 13 ♕e2!? ♘xd4 14 ♘xd4 ♕xd4 15 c3 ♕c5 16 ♖h3 also looks promising for White) 13 ♔f1 or even 13 ♗b4!?.

12 ♗d3 ♘ec6?!

This natural move is in fact quite risky. Anand's excuse may be that White's follow-up was very easy to overlook. 12...♘xf3+ is the main test of White's concept. Then Kasparov's recommendation 13 ♕xf3 ♕d4 14 0-0 ♕xe5 15 ♖fe1 ♕f6 16 ♕g3 'with compensation' seems fair enough, but can White claim an advantage? After 16...h6 17 ♗c3 d4 18 ♗b5+ ♔f8 19 ♕d6 ♔g8 20 ♕d8+ ♔h7 21 ♗d3+ ♘f5 22 ♕xf6 gxf6 23 ♗xf5+ exf5 24 ♗xd4 ♗e6 White's initiative petered out into a drawish endgame in Just-Schaedler, corr. 1993.

13 ♔f1!

This surprising attacking move creates the threat of ♖h4 and forces Black's centralized d4-knight to show its hand. Also in the following course of the game White will need his rook on the h-file, as compared to the meek 13 0-0?! ♘xf3+ 14 ♕xf3 ♕h4!?, when Black's queen returns to the defence, preparing queenside castling.

13 ... ♘xf3

The only alternative to developing White's queen was 13...♘f5!?, but even here White's dark-square play is dangerous after both 14 ♗xf5 exf5 15 h6 and 14 h6!? g6 15 ♗g5.

14 ♕xf3 *(D)*

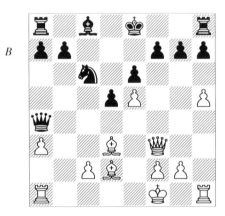

14 ... b6?

Thanks to White's 13th move, his threats of ♕g3 and h6 are very serious and after this careless move Anand will find himself on the brink of defeat. Black's choice was unpleasant though:

1) 14...h6? is too slow. After 15 ♕g3 ♔f8 16 ♖h4 followed by ♖g4, White's attack breaks through.

2) Black was understandably reluctant to take the e5-pawn, as it increases the scope of White's d2-bishop. The immediate 14...♘xe5? fails to 15 ♕g3 ♘xd3 (15...♕d4 runs into 16 ♗c3! ♕xc3 17 ♗b5+) 16 ♕xg7 ♖f8 17 ♗h6 and White wins.

3) The best chance is to change the move-order and play 14...♕d4 15 ♖e1 ♘xe5 16 ♕g3 ♘xd3 17 cxd3. Nevertheless, White has a massive lead in development and the opposite-coloured bishops only increase his attacking chances. Black should refrain from castling and play 17...♗d7 (after 17...0-0?! 18 ♖h4 ♕b2 {or

18...♕f6 19 ♗f4} 19 h6 with the idea 19...g6? 20 ♗b4 ♖e8 21 d4! Black is unable to cope with the concentrated pressure of White's well-coordinated attacking forces). Although even then 18 ♖h4 is extremely dangerous, it's still better than what Black will have to face in the game.

15 h6!

On the other hand, Kasparov is accurate and energetic. He doesn't allow Black's king to escape after 15 ♕g3 ♗a6 16 ♕xg7 0-0-0.

15 ... ♗a6!

With his back against the wall Anand finds the only way to prolong the fight, based on a clever tactical trap. After 15...g6 16 ♕f6 ♖g8 17 ♖h4 d4 18 ♗e4 White prevents the exchange of bishops and quickly breaks through via the dark squares (♗g5, or ♗xc6 and ♗b4). 15...♘xe5 16 hxg7 (16 ♕g3!?) 16...♖g8 17 ♕h5 is also terrible for Black.

16 hxg7 ♖g8 (D)

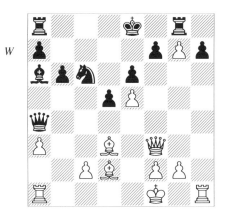

17 ♗xa6!

An alert reaction. 17 ♕f6? fails to 17...♕d4, and the tempting 17 ♖xh7? also squanders White's advantage: 17...♘xe5!? (17...♕xc2 18 ♗xa6 ♕xh7 19 ♗b5 0-0-0! is also possible; after 20 ♕c3 ♕h1+ 21 ♔e2 ♕h5+ Black has a perpetual) 18 ♕f6 (18 ♖h8 ♘xf3 19 ♖xg8+ ♔d7 20 ♖xa8 ♕d4! and the triple(!) attack forces 21 ♔e2 ♕xg7!? 22 ♖xa7+ ♔c6 with an advantage for Black) 18...♗xd3+ 19 cxd3 ♕d4!. Black hits both rooks and White can at best force a draw with 20 ♖e1 ♕xd3+ 21 ♔g1 ♕xh7 22 ♖xe5 followed by ♗b4 or ♖xe6+.

17 ... ♕xa6+
18 ♔g1 ♖xg7

This invites White's rook to the 7th rank, but Black can't afford to keep the passed pawn alive.

19 ♕f6 ♖g8
20 ♖xh7 ♕b7 (D)

21 ♗g5

Material is equal again, but the position certainly isn't. Black's rooks are disconnected while his king is in mortal danger and White's main problem is to choose from the tempting options. He should avoid 21 ♕xe6+? fxe6 22 ♖xb7 0-0-0, and 21 ♖h8?! ♖xh8 22 ♕xh8+ ♔d7 23 ♕g7 ♔c8 isn't ideal either, the point being that Black wants to unravel with ...♕d7 and ...♔b7; e.g., 24 ♕f8+ ♘d8 25 ♗g5 ♕d7 26 ♗xd8 ♔b7! with equality. Kasparov's move is not bad, but opening the centre with 21 c4! is even more forceful. After 21...♖d8 (Black is helpless after 21...dxc4 22 ♗g5 ♖c8 23 ♖d1 ♕e7 24 ♕f4 followed by ♖d6) 22 ♗g5 the threat is ♖h8 and 22...♕e7 23 ♖h8 ♕f8 (23...♔d7 loses a piece to 24 ♖xg8 ♖xg8 25 cxd5 exd5 26 ♕xc6+!) 24 ♗h6 nets the queen with a technically won position.

21 ... ♘d4!

The best resource: the knight heads for e4 and helps keep Black's centre together. 21...♕e7 22 ♕f4 would only cost time and allow White to get in c4, or win an exchange after 22...♖xg5 23 ♖h8+.

22 c4

Logical, but less convincing than one move ago. Black would have more problems finding good moves after the patient 22 f4!?. Protecting the bishop enables White to take on e6 after knight moves, and 22...♘f5 (22...♘e2+ 23 ♔h2

♘c3 24 ♕xe6+ is now hopeless for Black and the same goes for 22...♘xc2 23 f5 ♘d4 24 ♖g7!) again runs into the powerful 23 c4! dxc4 24 ♖d1 ♕e7 25 ♖xf7 ♕xf6 26 ♖xf6 with a won endgame, as the e6-pawn falls.

22	...	♘e2+
23	♔h2	♘c3
24	♖h8	♖xh8+
25	♕xh8+	♔d7 (D)

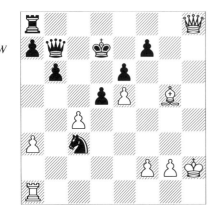

26 ♕h7?!

This allows the rook to take part in the defence and Anand's dogged resistance begins to pay its first dividends. After the stronger 26 ♕g7! ♔c6 27 cxd5+ ♘xd5 (27...♔xd5 28 ♕h7 ♕a6 29 ♗d2!? is similar) 28 ♖c1+ ♔b5 29 ♕h7 the king-hunt continues even on the queenside.

26	...	♖f8!
27	♗h6	♖e8
28	♕xf7+	♖e7
29	♕g6	

Despite his efforts Anand could have hardly survived after the better 29 ♕g8! ♕c7 30 ♗g5!? (30 f4 ♖e8 31 ♕f7+ ♖e7 32 ♕g6 ♔c8 is less convincing) 30...♕xe5+ 31 f4 ♕g7 32 ♕b8 ♖f7 33 ♖e1 with a huge attack. Now Black can at least activate his queen and keep hoping, as Kasparov was getting short of time...

29	...	♕b8!
30	cxd5	

30 f4?! gives Black a wider choice; in particular, he can complicate matters with the clever 30...♕e8! (30...♕h8 31 cxd5 ♘xd5 transposes to the note to move 31) 31 f5 (31 ♕xe8+ ♔xe8 and the passed d-pawn gives Black too much play) 31...♕h8!, attacking the e5-pawn and threatening ...♖h7.

30	...	♘xd5 (D)

30...♕xe5+? 31 f4 ♕xd5 32 ♗g5 traps the black rook.

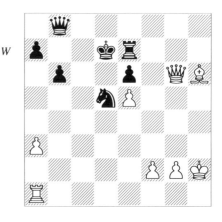

31 ♖d1?

Only this final error robs Kasparov of the fruit of his imaginative opening play. His attempt to open the position falls short, so it was necessary to protect the important e5-pawn. 31 ♖e1 is possible, but 31...♕h8 gives Black fighting chances. More convincing is Kasparov's own recommendation 31 f4! ♕h8 32 ♔g3!. White prepares ♗g5 and Black's counterplay falls short; e.g., 32...♖h7 33 ♗g5 ♖g7 34 ♖h1! ♕f8 35 ♖h7 ♕xa3+ 36 ♔h4 ♖xh7+ 37 ♕xh7+ ♘e7 (37...♔c6 38 ♕f7 is no better) 38 ♕f7 ♕b4 39 ♔h5 and the f5 break decides.

31	...	♕xe5+
32	f4	♕h8
33	f5	

White undermines the d5-knight, but his king is now vulnerable too, and Black has sufficient counterplay.

33	...	♕e5+
34	♔h1	½-½

After 34 ♔g1 exf5 (34...♔c8!? 35 fxe6 ♘c7 is possibly even safer) 35 ♕g8 ♖e6 36 ♗g5 White still has some initiative, but nothing concrete after 36...♖d6. The text-move allows even 34...exf5 35 ♕g8 ♕e6!?, when White has nothing better than a drawn rook endgame after 36 ♖xd5+ ♔c6 37 ♕xe6+ ♖xe6 38 ♖xf5 ♖xh6+.

Game 67
Alexei Shirov – Garry Kasparov
Dortmund 1992
King's Indian Defence, Sämisch Variation [E86]

1	d4	♘f6
2	c4	g6
3	♘c3	♗g7
4	e4	d6
5	f3	

Shirov was one of the most talented pupils of the Botvinnik-Kasparov school and this was his first encounter with his teacher. In his notes Kasparov describes he was slightly worried about facing an ambitious youngster with a similar predilection for the King's Indian, which they often analysed together. However, in an attempt to surprise the World Champion, Shirov avoids his usual Classical Main Line (Game 5, etc.) and opts for the Sämisch, which he successfully adopted only once shortly before Dortmund. With hindsight it's easy to criticize this decision. In any case it started Shirov's dismal record against Kasparov, where numerous losses still outweigh the draws (and not a single win!).

5	...	0-0
6	♗e3	e5
7	♘ge2	

For 7 d5 see Game 49.

7	...	c6
8	♕d2	♘bd7 *(D)*

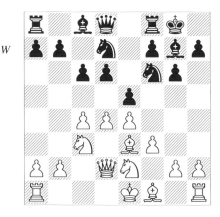

| 9 | 0-0-0 | |

An important decision for White. Karpov-Kasparov, Linares 1993 (Game 71) shows us how Black should deal with 9 ♖d1, but White can still return to the plan of closing the centre: 9 d5 cxd5 10 cxd5 a6 11 g4 h5 12 h3 was featured in Kasparov's subsequent practice and leads to complex play.

9	...	a6
10	♔b1	

Opposite castling doesn't always mean ruthless pawn attacks and indeed in this game most of the activity will initially take place on the queenside and in the centre.

| 10 | ... | b5 *(D)* |

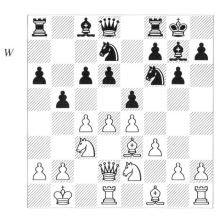

| 11 | ♘c1 | |

While 10 ♔b1 remains the main move to this day, here White recently came up with the more challenging 11 c5!?. The complications after 11...b4 12 ♘a4 ♕a5 13 ♕c2! d5 14 dxe5 ♘xe5 15 ♘b6 dxe4!? 16 ♘xa8 ♗e6 17 ♘c1 ♖xa8 18 ♗d4 seem to favour White, so Black should opt for calm moves such as 11...♕e7.

| 11 | ... | exd4! |

Although Boleslavsky and Bronstein showed long ago how Black can gain counterplay in the King's Indian after releasing the central tension, their findings were almost solely limited to the Fianchetto Variation. Here White's central bastion on e4 is soundly protected and Kasparov's novel idea requires some explanation. Left to his own devices, White will himself exchange on e5 and target the queenside dark-square weaknesses with a further ♘b3. Since 11...bxc4 12 dxe5 ♘xe5 13 ♕xd6 also doesn't solve Black's problems, the main purpose of the text-move is to prevent White from effectively activating his knight. This in turn can reveal the whole ♘e2-c1 manoeuvre as time-consuming.

12 ♗xd4 ♖e8 *(D)*

As the further course of the game will show, this is an important preparatory move. However, Kasparov himself later showed that Black can treat the position differently: after 12...b4 13 ♘a4 c5 14 ♗xf6 (White can fight for an advantage only with 14 ♗e3!?) 14...♗xf6 15 ♕xd6 ♗e7 16 ♕g3 ♗h4 17 ♕h3 ♗e7 18 ♕g3 ♗h4 19 ♕h3, Kramnik-Kasparov, Linares 1993 was drawn by repetition. Also 12...♖b8!? deserves attention.

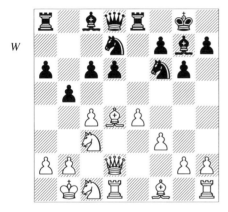

13 ♗xf6?!

A dubious decision, which no one was reckless enough to repeat. Compared with the above example the existence of the queenside tension increases Black's chances for full-blooded counterplay, as it also enhances the role of his powerful unopposed dark-squared bishop. The extra pawn only barely compensates White for his future suffering, so he should have resisted the temptation and modestly continued his plan with 13 ♘b3. White wants to finish his development quietly, and possibly play c5 at a suitable moment. Practice has shown Black's best is 13...♗f8!? (13...♘b6 is weaker due to 14 c5!

♘c4 15 ♕f2). This is one of the merits of 12...♖e8: Black can safeguard the d6-pawn and keep the tension in a complex position.

13 ... ♕xf6!

Kasparov even allows White to exchange queens, as the resulting position retains a middlegame character. After 13...♗xf6 14 ♕xd6 ♕b6 15 ♘b3 Black would have more difficulties to get enough play; e.g., 15...bxc4 16 ♗xc4 ♗xc3 17 bxc3 ♘e5 18 ♖d4.

14 ♕xd6 ♕xd6
15 ♖xd6 ♘e5 *(D)*

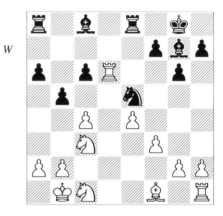

16 f4

As indicated in the first note, Shirov is ambitious and continues to fight for an advantage. Objectively it was safer to try to bail out with 16 cxb5 axb5 17 a3!? (after 17 ♘d3 b4! Black has a strong initiative and the same goes for 17 f4, when he can choose between 17...♘g4 and 17...b4!?), although even here Black has excellent compensation after 17...♗f8.

16 ... ♘g4!

Kasparov is just as ambitious. The materialistic 16...♘xc4?! 17 ♗xc4 bxc4 18 e5 allows White to solve his development problems and is unclear to say the least.

17 e5

Consistent, but also worth considering was taking the risk with 17 ♖xc6 ♘f2 18 ♖g1 ♘xe4 19 cxb5!? (Black is simply better after the timid 19 ♘xe4 ♖xe4 20 ♗d3 ♖xf4), when 19...♘d2+ (19...♘xc3+ 20 bxc3 ♖e1 21 ♔c2! is also unclear) 20 ♔c2 ♘xf1 21 ♖xf1 ♗f5+ 22 ♔b3 axb5 certainly gives Black a lot of play, but he still can't claim a clear-cut advantage.

17 ... ♘f2

18	Rg1	Bf5+
19	Ka1	b4
20	Na4	

Although this knight will later become a source of problems, White doesn't have any real choice – 20 Nd1?! Bf8 21 Rd2 Ne4 is weaker.

| 20 | ... | f6! (D) |

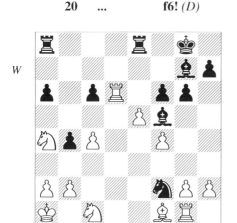

This timely break indicates the attempt to limit the g7-bishop has failed. As the centre opens, all Black's forces spring to life.

21 e6?

Shirov panics; with level material Black's advantage will be obvious. 21 exf6? loses on the spot to 21...Re1, so only active play can maintain the tension. Necessary was 21 g4! Nxg4 (21...Bxg4?! is weaker due to 22 Bg2) 22 Bd3 (22 Bh3 Ne3 or 22 Bg2 fxe5 23 Bxc6 Rad8 gives Black a clear pull). Kasparov's intention was then the strong but more or less forced piece sacrifice 22...fxe5! (22...Nh6 23 exf6 Bf8 24 Rxc6 Bd7 runs into the tactical 25 f7+! Nxf7 26 Bxg6! hxg6 27 Rcxg6+ and Black has to be careful after 27...Kh8 28 Nb6 Rad8 29 Nd5 Re6 30 Rg8+ Kh7 31 Nd3) 23 Bxf5 gxf5 24 h3 exf4 25 hxg4 f3 26 gxf5 (26 Nd3? fxg4 27 Rxg4 Re1+! 28 Nxe1 f2 is a pretty subvariation) 26...f2 27 Rf1 Re1 28 Rd1 Rae8 29 Nd3 Rxd1+ 30 Rxd1 Bd4, but even here after 31 Kb1 White retains good drawing chances. At a suitable moment he can take on f2 and it's not so easy for the h-pawn to get moving, as 31...h5 runs into 32 Rh1 (but not 32 Kc2? Re2+ 33 Kb3 Rd2! 34 Nxf2 Rxd1 35 Nxd1 h4 and the d4-bishop dominates both knights!) and Nxf2.

| 21 | ... | Rxe6 |

Kasparov preferred this simple exchange to 21...Bxe6. After, e.g., 22 Nc5!? Bf5 23 Bd3 White finds it easier to activate his passive pieces; also, keeping an extra pair of rooks on the board makes his kingside less vulnerable.

| 22 | Rxe6 | |

22 c5 Rxd6 23 cxd6 Bf8 is no better.

| 22 | ... | Bxe6 |
| 23 | Be2 | f5! |

Stronger than 23...Ne4, as it keeps the knight's options open.

| 24 | Nb3 | Bf7 |
| 25 | Na5 | |

Now Black exchanges the remaining pair of rooks and his minor pieces will dominate the board. Somewhat more resilient was 25 c5 or 25 Bf3!? Rd8 26 c5, although Black retains a large advantage in both cases.

| 25 | ... | Rd8 (D) |

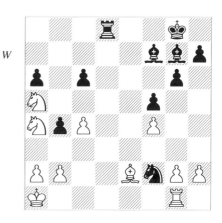

| 26 | Rf1 | |

Practically forced, as after 26 Nxc6 Rd2 27 Bf3 (27 Re1? Be8! 28 Bf3 Ne4 costs White a piece) 27...Nd3 White has no choice but to play 28 Rd1 Rxd1+ 29 Bxd1 Bxc4 with an inferior version of the game position.

| 26 | ... | Ng4! |
| 27 | Rd1 | |

27 Bxg4 fxg4 28 Nxc6 Rd2 is hopeless for White.

| 27 | ... | Rxd1+ |
| 28 | Bxd1 | Ne3! |

Another accurate move. 28...Nxh2 29 c5!? Be8 30 Bc2 gives White unnecessary counterplay.

| 29 | Bf3 | Nxc4 |

30 ♘xc6

Weaker is 30 ♘xc4 ♗xc4 31 ♗xc6 ♗d4 and with his king and knight both offside White's kingside pawns will fall quickly.

30 ... a5! *(D)*

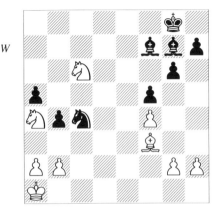

31 ♘d8

In this endgame Black has numerous pluses and their combined effect renders White's position extremely difficult. Firstly, the roving bishop-pair makes it very difficult for White to activate his king: 31 ♔b1? loses on the spot to 31...♘d2+ 32 ♔c2 ♘xf3 33 gxf3 ♗e8. On the other hand Black's king can join the fray easily via f8 and e8; thus attempts such as 31 g3 ♔f8 32 ♗e2 ♗d5 don't help much. We have already mentioned that White's forces lack coordination; especially his a4-knight is too far from the kingside, where the game will eventually be decided. An illustrative line is 31 ♗e2 ♔f8 32 ♗xc4 ♗xc4 33 ♘xa5 ♗d5 34 g3 ♗d4. Exchanging one of the bishops would naturally help and Shirov's move is his best chance.

31 ... ♘d2
32 ♗c6?!

After 32 ♘xf7 Black faces a tougher task, but he nevertheless has a pleasant choice:

1) 32...♔xf7 33 ♘c5 (Kasparov gives the line 33 ♗d5+ ♔e7 34 ♘b6 ♔d6 35 ♗g8 ♔c5 36 ♘d7+ ♔c6 37 ♘e5+ ♗xe5 38 fxe5 h6 and White's king remains cornered, while Black mops up the opposite flank) 33...♘xf3 transposes into line '2'.

2) 32...♘xf3 33 gxf3 (33 ♘d6 ♘xh2 34 ♘c4 ♗g4 should also win for Black, as after 35 ♘xa5 ♘e3 36 g3 ♘f1 the passed h-pawn comes first) 33...♔xf7 34 ♘c5 ♗f8 35 ♘d3 ♔e6 36 ♔b1 ♗d5 37 ♔c2 ♗d4 38 ♔d2 ♗d6 39 ♔e2 a4 40 ♔d2 ♗c7 41 ♔e2 a3 and with the help of zugzwang Black will gradually force his way into White's position.

32 ... ♗h6!

White's pawns start falling and Kasparov efficiently wraps up the game.

33 g3 ♘f1 *(D)*

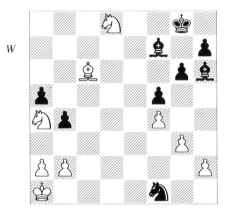

34 ♘b6

34 ♘c5 ♘xh2 35 ♘d3 ♗g7 is similar.

34 ... ♘xh2
35 ♘d7 ♗g7!

White's last real threat was ♘e5, so the bishop returns.

36	♘e5	♗xe5
37	fxe5	♔f8
38	e6	♗e8
39	♗xe8	♔xe8
40	♘c6	♘f1

0-1

The time-trouble is over and Black's kingside pawns will clinch his victory.

Game 68
Garry Kasparov – Valery Loginov
Olympiad, Manila 1992
King's Indian Defence, Sämisch Variation [E84]

1	d4	♘f6
2	c4	g6
3	♘c3	♗g7
4	e4	d6
5	f3	0-0
6	♗e3	a6

Unimpressed by the fashionable 6...e5 from the previous game, Loginov chooses the ...♘c6 system, which also used to be Kasparov's favourite with Black (see Game 12). Confronting the champion on his own turf is always dangerous, but the Uzbek top board had an improvement over one of Kasparov's older games on his mind.

7	♕d2	♘c6
8	♘ge2	♖b8
9	h4	

Currently in his efforts to get an advantage out of the opening White has relied more on quiet positional options: the older move 9 ♘c1, or modern continuations such as 9 ♖b1. Incidentally, the position after the latter move could have occurred in Game 2, had White played the more natural 9 ♘ge2. With White, Kasparov has always preferred the aggressive text-move, intending to open the h-file as soon as possible even at the cost of a pawn. In these sharp lines, time is often an important consideration; therefore White doesn't want to waste it on a preparatory move such as 9 g4.

9	...	b5

This is perhaps playable, but very risky. Nowadays the consensus is that before starting play of his own, Black should first slow White down with 9...h5!?. This continuation became popular in the 1980s, probably also influenced by the success of such prophylaxis in the main line of the Sicilian Dragon.

10	h5	e5

The pawn is taboo. After 10...♘xh5? 11 g4 ♘f6 12 ♗h6 White's attack quickly breaks through. 10...♘a5 11 ♘g3 ♘xc4 12 ♗xc4 bxc4 13 ♗h6 is also very dangerous; e.g., 13...♗xh6 14 ♕xh6 ♖xb2 15 0-0-0! ♖xg2 16 e5 and White wins. After 10...bxc4 White can play the effective 11 g4! ♗xg4 12 fxg4 ♘xg4 13 0-0-0 ♘xe3 14 ♕xe3 e6 15 hxg6 hxg6 16 ♖d2 ♖e8 17 ♘g1! with a large advantage, Kasparov-Spassky, Nikšić 1983. The text-move is important for the defence of h7, as after the stabilization of the centre White can't deflect the f6-knight any more with e5 or ♘d5.

11	d5	♘a5
12	♘g3	bxc4

In the final phase of the game Black will suffer due to his offside a5-knight. Nevertheless, the text-move is better than 12...♘xc4 13 ♗xc4 bxc4 14 0-0-0. Here White's queenside is under less pressure than in the game, and he has also got rid of his passive f1-bishop.

13	0-0-0 *(D)*	

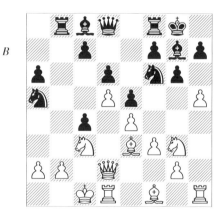

13	...	♖b4!?

This novelty of Loginov's is much stronger than 13...♘d7? 14 hxg6 fxg6 15 ♘b1! ♖b5 (15...♘b7 16 ♗xc4 gives White a clear positional advantage) 16 b4! and in Timman-Kasparov, Bugojno 1982, Black was forced to shed material for insufficient compensation. After this game Kasparov practically gave up the whole 6...♘c6 system, but others continued the search. Black has also tried 13...♗d7, but here

White can again play 14 hxg6 (14 ♗h6 ♖b4 can transpose into the game) 14...fxg6 15 ♘b1!? c5 (no better is 15...♖b5 16 ♘a3) 16 dxc6 ♗xc6 17 ♕xd6 and Black's pawns are not a pretty sight.

14 ♗h6 ♗xh6

This exchange is always a difficult decision. White's queen reaches a strong attacking outpost, which would otherwise be accessible only after a release of the kingside tension with ♗xg7 and hxg6. On the other hand, the white queen's absence from the defence enhances the strength of Black's counterattack. To be more concrete, after 14...♗d7 15 ♗e2 Black can maybe play 15...♕e7!? with unclear consequences (15...♕b8 is too slow and gives White a strong attack after 16 ♗xg7 ♔xg7 17 f4! ♕b6 18 fxe5 dxe5 19 ♖df1; Black should also refrain from 15...♗xh6 16 ♕xh6 ♔h8 17 hxg6 fxg6 18 ♘f1 ♖g8, as now in Psakhis-Djurhuus, Gausdal 1994, 19 g4 would have given White an advantage).

15 ♕xh6 ♕e7 (D)

Kasparov recommends 15...♔h8 instead, but after 16 hxg6 (otherwise Black can play ...♘g8 and ...g5) 16...fxg6 17 ♗e2 Black probably has nothing better than transposing into the aforementioned Psakhis-Djurhuus game, since 17...♕e7 runs into 18 ♕xg6 ♖g8 19 ♘f5!.

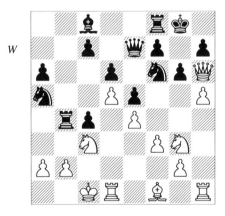

16 ♗e2 ♗d7

After 16...♘d7 Kasparov wanted to play 17 ♖df1!. White prepares f4 and retains his initiative even in the endgame after 17...g5 18 ♘f5 ♕f6 19 g3 ♕xh6 20 ♘xh6+ ♔g7 21 ♘f5+ ♔h8 22 ♘e3.

17 ♘f1! ♖fb8

Just as on move 10 Black must let the pawn be; after 17...♘xh5? 18 g4 ♘f6 19 ♘g3 followed by g5 White wins.

18 ♖d2 c5? (D)

This is a serious positional mistake, which compromises Black's position by depriving his knights of the c5-square and weakening the d6-pawn. Preferable is 18...♗e8 19 g4 ♘d7 20 hxg6 fxg6 21 ♘e3 ♘c5! with complex play. Black has ideas such as ...♘ab3+ or ...♘a4, and after 22 g5 he can stop the threat of ♘g4 with 22...♗d7. Also 18...♕f8 deserves attention.

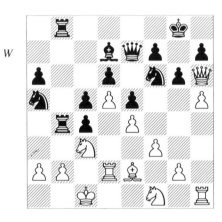

19 ♗d1!

Exploiting the drawbacks of 18...c5? requires some inspired play. First of all Kasparov stops the idea of ...♗a4 followed by ...♕b7.

19 ... ♘e8

Another prophylactic idea behind White's move is illustrated by the line 19...♗e8 20 g4 ♕b7 21 ♖hh2!, and Black's attack dries up. However, 19...♕f8 is somewhat better.

20 hxg6 fxg6
21 g4 ♕g7
22 g5!

This important move fixes the weakness on h7, enabling White's attack to persist into the endgame.

22 ... ♕xh6
23 ♖xh6 ♘g7?!

Passive defence with 23...♗c8 24 ♖dh2 ♖4b7 fails to 25 ♗a4, when White regains the pawn with a clear advantage. Surprisingly enough, this position arose in subsequent practice and Black came up with 23...♘b7!?. As Black's knight will remain on a5 nearly until the bitter end, this is a definite improvement. However, after 24 a3! ♖b6 25 ♖dh2 ♘d8 26 ♖xh7 ♘f7 27 ♘e3 ♖6b7 28 ♖7h4 ♘g7 29 ♘xc4 ♗b5 30 ♘e3 ♘h5 31 ♘f5 ♗e8 32 f4 ♘xf4 33 ♘xd6! White was still on top in Gallagher-Sutovsky, Biel 1996.

24 f4! *(D)*

The above note indicates that 24 ♘g3? is too slow and leads nowhere after 24...♘b7 25 ♖dh2 ♘d8 26 ♖xh7 ♘f7. White could have perhaps played 24 ♖dh2 with the idea 24...♘h5 25 ♘g3! (25 f4? ♘xf4 and Black threatens ...♘d3+), but Kasparov's solution is more elegant and objectively stronger. He once and for all stops the knight from coming to h5 and makes life even more difficult for Black's king by opening the f-file as well.

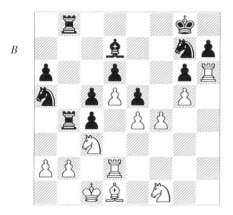

24 ... exf4

24...♖f8 is no real improvement, as after 25 f5! gxf5 (25...♖b6 26 ♖dh2! gxf5 27 ♖xh7 and White's attack breaks through) 26 ♖xd6 fxe4 27 ♘e3 ♗c8 28 ♖h2 Black's army is helpless and White will regain his pawns with interest.

25 ♖dh2 ♖e8

One can understand that Loginov seeks some counterplay and wants to attack the cramping g5-pawn. The passive 25...♗e8 26 ♖xh7 ♘h5 is slightly more resilient, although after 27 ♖h6 White should win anyway.

26 ♘d2!

26 ♖xh7 ♖e5 27 ♖h8+ ♔f7 28 ♖f2 is also good, but Kasparov stops ...♖e5 and with foresight prepares a brighter future for his knight (see move 34).

26 ... ♖eb8

26...♖e5 27 ♘f3 ♖e8 28 ♖xh7 ♗g4 29 ♖h8+ ♔f7 30 ♖8h4! is also hopeless for Black.

27 ♖xh7 ♖xb2

Both sides have invaded via 'their' semi-open files, but the difference in the coordination of the remaining forces speaks clearly for White. While Black's rooks can't accomplish anything, White's minor pieces will quickly join the attack.

28 ♖2h4!

The decisive manoeuvre: White will avoid simplification and chase Black's king into the centre to wind up the assault. Kasparov's attack definitely has middlegame characteristics.

28 ... ♖2b7

White meets the attempt to remain on the kingside with 28...♔f7 by 29 e5! (even more forceful than 29 ♖xf4+ ♔g8 30 ♖h6 ♗e8) 29...dxe5 30 ♘f3. Now Black's rooks must protect each other, so e5 and his whole position falls apart.

29 ♖h8+ ♔f7
30 ♖xf4+ ♔e7
31 ♖h7 ♖g8
32 ♖f6 ♗e8
33 e5! *(D)*

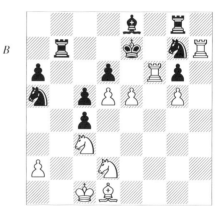

Even now this central break is crushing. Black can't protect d6 any more as White's knights join in.

33 ... ♖b6

After 33...dxe5 34 ♖xa6 White wins a piece.

34 ♘de4 ♘b7
35 exd6+ ♘xd6

35...♔d8 36 d7! doesn't help.

36 ♖e6+ ♔d7

1-0

Black resigned before White could play 37 ♘xd6 ♖xd6 38 ♗a4+.

Game 69
Garry Kasparov – Predrag Nikolić
Olympiad, Manila 1992
Slav Defence, Winawer Countergambit [D10]

Kasparov played impressive chess in Manila, scoring 8½/10 and winning the Olympiad brilliancy prize for this powerful performance.

1	d4	d5
2	c4	c6
3	♘c3	e5!?

The Winawer Countergambit experienced a revival in the early 1990s. Not only Nikolić, but also other top players like Salov and Bareev employed it successfully. Even today Black's interesting idea retains a modicum of support, although it was never the same after this game...

4 dxe5

The main continuation. 4 cxd5 cxd5 improves Black's chances in most lines by freeing the natural c6-square for his knight; therefore 4 e3 is more promising, with interesting transpositional options. 4...e4 leads to a reversed Advance French, and 4...exd4 5 ♕xd4 to a reversed c3 Sicilian. In both cases the extra tempo gives White chances to fight for an edge.

4	...	d4
5	♘e4	♕a5+
6	♗d2!	*(D)*

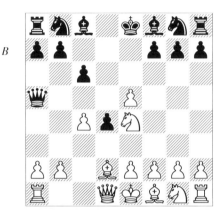

Although this move had appeared in a few earlier games, Kasparov deserves full credit not only for introducing 6 ♗d2! on the highest level, but especially for connecting it with White's subsequent ambitious plan. Previous practice saw 6 ♘d2 ♘d7 7 e6 fxe6 8 g3 e5 9 ♗g2 ♘gf6 with a complex and unclear position.

6	...	♕xe5
7	♘g3	♕d6

7...♘f6 8 ♘f3 only transposes into the game, but an independent and playable continuation is 7...c5!? 8 ♘f3 ♕c7. Black's b8-knight heads for c6 and after 9 e3 (perhaps the sharper 9 ♕c2!? ♘c6 10 0-0-0 is more promising) 9...dxe3 10 ♗xe3 ♘f6 11 ♗d3 ♗e7 he has chances of gradually neutralizing White's slight lead in development.

8	♘f3	♘f6
9	♕c2	♗e7
10	0-0-0	0-0
11	e3	

A natural move, but further practice and analysis have shown White has a valid alternative. In his notes, Kasparov indicated he refrained from 11 ♗c3!? due to the queen sacrifice 11...dxc3!? (11...c5?! 12 e3 ♕a6 13 exd4 cxd4 14 ♘xd4 ♕xa2 15 ♘df5 is clearly better for White, while 11...♕f4+ 12 e3! dxe3 13 fxe3 ♕xe3+ 14 ♔b1 ♘a6 15 ♘d4 ♗b4 16 ♘df5 ♗xf5 17 ♘xf5 ♕e6 18 ♗d3 ♗xc3 19 ♕xc3 gave him a powerful attacking position in Azmaiparashvili-Eslon, Seville 1994). However, after 12 ♖xd6 cxb2+ 13 ♕xb2 ♗xd6 14 e4! ♗f4+ 15 ♔b1 Black is still behind in development and White will retain his initiative with the e5 advance. After all, he has an extra queen and this will count especially in the attack.

11	...	dxe3 *(D)*

Here Kasparov sank into thought, which most of the onlookers found difficult to understand...

12 fxe3!

The surprising point. White refrains from the 'natural' 12 ♗xe3 ♕c7, which would at best give him only a slight edge in a rather dull symmetrical position. The text-move is far more ambitious – the d2-bishop belongs on the a1-h8 diagonal and this, together with the open f-file,

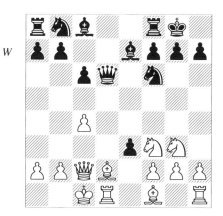

will enhance White's kingside pressure. However, we award the exclamation mark mainly for the whole concept, as 12 ♗c3! is probably a more accurate way to achieve the game position and avoid the option from the following note. Here Black is well advised to play 12...♕c7 (12...♕f4 is considered in the note to White's 11th move) 13 fxe3 anyway.

12 ... ♕c7

12...♖d8!? deserves attention, as then White can only play ♗c3 at the cost of simplification. After 13 ♗e2 ♕c7 14 ♗c3 ♘a6 15 ♖xd8+ ♕xd8 16 ♖d1 ♕b6 17 ♘d4 ♗b4 18 ♘df5 ♗xf5 19 ♘xf5 ♗xc3 20 ♕xc3 ♘b4 Black's counterplay is sufficient for equality, Michaelsen-Stangl, Bundesliga 1996/7.

13 ♗c3 ♗g4?!

Being a pathfinder is always difficult. Nikolić wants to develop his queenside minor pieces in the most straightforward manner, but this helps White to build up a strong attack. Black has safer moves:

1) As late as 2002 Nikolić himself preferred 13...♘a6 14 a3 (it's prudent to prevent ...♘b4) 14...♘g4 15 ♖e1 g6 with a playable position.

2) A more direct try is 13...c5!?, intending to develop the b8-knight more actively. After 14 ♘f5 (more testing is 14 ♗d3 ♘c6!? 15 ♗xf6 ♗xf6 16 ♗xh7+ ♔h8 17 ♗e4, although Black's dark-squared bishop shouldn't be underestimated) 14...♘c6 15 a3 ♗xf5 16 ♕xf5 g6 17 ♕f4 ♕xf4 18 exf4 ♘e4 19 ♖d7 ♗d6 20 g3 ♖ad8 21 ♖xd8 ♖xd8 22 ♗g2 ♘xc3 23 bxc3 ♘a5 Black equalized easily in Krasenkow-Morozevich, Pamplona 1998/9.

14 ♗d3 ♘bd7

Inviting White's pieces to f5 is fraught with danger, so the seemingly ugly 14...g6!? deserves attention. Although even now White can consider a move like 15 ♗f5!?, Black isn't forced to accept the sacrifice and can play 15...♘a6 instead.

15 ♗f5 ♗xf5?

Only this is a definite mistake, which gives Kasparov's attack a welcome additional impetus. Black had two better ways to parry the ♖xd7 threat:

1) 15...♖ad8 also allows White to sacrifice on g7, this time his bishop. However, this is far from clear and after 16 ♗xg4 ♘xg4 17 ♗xg7! ♘xe3!? (17...♔xg7 18 ♘f5+ ♔f6 19 ♖hf1 and Black's exposed king can hardly survive the onslaught for long) probably the most sensible is 18 ♗xf8 (18 ♕d2 ♘xd1 19 ♘f5 ♘c5 seems insufficient for White after 20 ♕h6 ♕f4+! or 20 ♗d4 ♖fe8! 21 ♖xd1 ♘e6, when Black's queen again heads for f4) 18...♘xf8 with approximate equality in a simplified position.

2) 15...♖fd8!? is an even safer option for Black. Here the immediate attempt 16 ♗xg4 ♘xg4 17 ♗xg7?! seems dubious owing to 17...♘xe3 (17...♔xg7 18 ♘f5+ ♔f8 19 ♘xe7 ♔xe7 20 ♕e4+ ♘de5 21 h3 ♘f2 22 ♕h4+ ♔f8 23 ♕xf2 ♘d3+ 24 ♖xd3 ♖xd3 25 ♖f1!? gives White enough compensation) 18 ♕e4 ♘xd1 19 ♕xe7 (19 ♘f5? loses to 19...♘f2 20 ♕e3 ♕f4!) 19...♕f4+ and the attack passes to Black.

16 ♘xf5 ♖fe8
17 ♘xg7! (D)

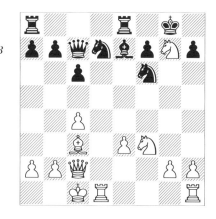

Undoubtedly Nikolić wanted to consolidate his kingside defences with ...♗f8, but White strikes first. This heavy blow permanently exposes Black's king, a drawback that will decide the issue even deep in the endgame.

17 ... ♔xg7
18 ♕f5 ♘f8

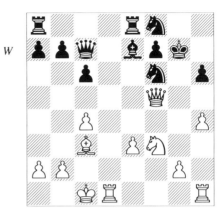

The knight heads for g6. Although this move returns the piece, it's still the best defence against ♖xd7:

1) 18...♔g8 19 ♕g5+ ♔h8 (19...♔f8 20 ♕h6+ ♔g8 21 ♘h4 and White wins) 20 ♘h4! and the threat of ♖xd7 decides the issue.

2) 18...♔f8 19 ♘g5! (19 ♕g5 is unconvincing due to 19...♖ed8!, freeing the e8-square for both his king and knight) 19...♔g8 (19...h6? loses on the spot to 20 ♖xd7! ♕xd7 21 ♘h7+) 20 ♘xh7!? (20 ♖hf1 is also good) 20...♘xh7 21 ♖xd7 ♕b6 22 ♖xe7 ♖xe7 23 ♕g4+ ♔f8 24 ♕g7+ ♔e8 25 ♕xh7 and Black's king won't escape alive.

3) 18...♖ad8 gives White a wide choice. The most direct is 19 ♕g5+ (even 19 ♖df1 or 19 g4! is very strong) 19...♔h8 (19...♔f8 20 ♘h4 and Black is helpless) 20 ♘e5, winning back the piece with a continuing attack.

19 h4!

An inspired attacking move. Other continuations such as 19 ♖hf1 ♔g8 20 ♗xf6 ♗xf6 21 ♕xf6 ♕e7 or 19 ♕g5+ ♘g6 20 ♘h4 ♔g8 21 ♗xf6 ♗xf6 22 ♕xf6 ♕e5 allow Black to bail out into an endgame. Although in both cases White has reasonable chances to win with his extra pawn, Kasparov sets his sights higher by fighting for the important g6-square.

19 ... h6 *(D)*

After 19...♖ad8 20 ♖df1 ♔g8 Kasparov's intention was 21 ♕g5+ ♘g6 22 h5. He gives the pretty line 22...♘e4?! 23 hxg6! ♘xg5 (23...fxg6 24 ♕xg6+! hxg6 25 ♖h8+ ♔f7 26 ♘g5#) 24 ♘xg5 f6 25 gxh7+ ♔h8 26 ♖xf6! ♗xf6 27 ♗xf6+ ♕g7 28 ♘f7#, but even less cooperative defences give White a decisive attack. However, 19...♔g8 20 h5! ♘e6 is somewhat more resilient, when White can choose between 21 ♗xf6 ♗xf6 22 ♕xf6 ♕e7 and 21 h6!?.

20 g4?!

White slips up. He should have played 20 ♕g4+! and now:

1) 20...♔h8 loses to 21 ♘g5! and even the computer-like 21...♕a5 doesn't help due to 22 ♕f4! ♕xa2 23 ♗xf6+ ♔g8 24 ♗c3! hxg5 25 hxg5 ♘g6 26 ♕d4.

2) 20...♘g6 21 h5 ♕b6 22 hxg6 ♕xe3+ 23 ♔b1 fxg6 (23...♕xc3 fails to the *zwischenzug* 24 ♕f4!) 24 ♘h4 ♕g5 25 ♕e6 followed by ♖d7, and the pin on the long diagonal will net White at least a piece.

20 ... ♕c8!

Strictly the only move; otherwise g5 decides.

21 ♕xc8

Kasparov is now satisfied with a better endgame, something he avoided only two moves ago. More consistent is 21 ♕c2! ♔g8 22 g5 ♘g4 (after 22...♘h5 23 gxh6 ♘g6 24 ♘g5 ♗xg5 25 hxg5 White regains the piece with interest) 23 gxh6 ♗c5!? (weaker is 23...f5 24 ♖hg1 ♕e6 25 ♘d4 ♕xe3+ 26 ♔b1 and Black's position falls apart) 24 ♖hg1! ♗xe3+ 25 ♔b1 ♗xg1 26 ♖xg1 with a strong attack. However, one can understand White – it's much easier to analyse such a position at home than it is to sacrifice a whole rook over the board when you can't see a clear-cut forced win.

21 ... ♖axc8
22 g5 ♘8h7 *(D)*

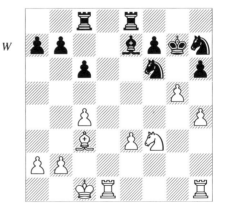

23 e4!

The most testing move. Both 23 gxf6+ ♗xf6 and 23 ♖d7 hxg5 24 hxg5 ♘xg5! 25 ♘xg5 ♔g6 get White nowhere.

23 ... ♖cd8?

It's Black's turn to go wrong. The immediate 23...♔f8 24 gxf6 enables him to play 24...♘xf6, activating his knight. White's edge after, e.g., 25 ♖hg1 ♖ed8 would only be very slight and he would have to work hard to achieve anything more tangible.

24 ♖df1! ♔f8
25 gxf6 ♗xf6

The important difference between the game and the previous note is that now 25...♘xf6?! is met by 26 ♘e5! (26 ♘d4 ♗c5 is unconvincing) and the pressure on the f-file practically paralyses Black. Thus Nikolić must accept the fact that both his minor pieces will remain passive.

26 e5 ♗g7

26...♗e7? fails to 27 ♗d2.

27 ♖hg1 c5 *(D)*

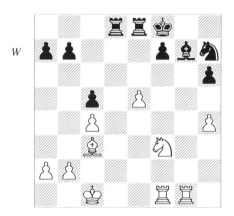

28 ♔c2!

A patient multi-purpose move: White takes d3 under control and removes the king from a potentially vulnerable square. The simple line 28 ♖g4 h5 29 ♖f4? ♗h6 illustrates the latter point.

28 ... ♖e6
29 ♖g4 ♗h8

Here 29...h5 30 ♖f4 only weakens Black's position and 30...♗h6? fails altogether to 31 ♖xf7+! ♔xf7 32 ♘g5+ ♔e7 33 ♖f7+ ♔e8 34 ♘xe6 with a won endgame.

30 b4! *(D)*

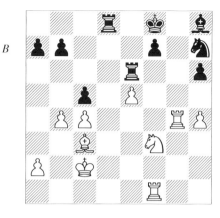

Black's knight and bishop present a sorry picture and White gladly seizes his chance to play on the whole board.

30 ... b6
31 bxc5

Natural enough, but the preparatory 31 ♖b1!? also deserved attention.

31 ... bxc5
32 ♖b1 ♖a6
33 ♖b2!

Just as on move 28 Kasparov is patient. The tempting 33 ♖b7? ♖xa2+ 34 ♔b3 ♖a6 35 e6 is met by 35...♖xe6! 36 ♗xh8 ♖d3+.

33 ... ♗g7?

An oversight, which leads to a quick loss. After 33...♔e7 34 ♖b7+ ♔e6 35 ♖f4 ♖f8 36 ♖c7 ♖xa2+ 37 ♔b3 ♖a6 38 ♖xc5 Black can't withstand the coordinated efforts of all White's pieces in an open position. Better is 33...♖b6 34 ♖b5 ♖c8 (34...♖xb5 35 cxb5 increases White's chances to create a passed pawn) and White has a large advantage, but still no forced win.

34 ♖b7!

With the bishop on g7 this now works. Black has no defence against e6 or ♖f4.

34 ... ♖xa2+

34...h5 35 ♖f4 f6 36 ♘g5! is hopeless for Black, as is 34...♖e6 35 ♖xa7.

35 ♔b3 ♖a6
36 e6! ♖xe6

The game is over. 36...♖b6+ 37 ♖xb6 ♗xc3 38 ♖b7 costs Black at least a rook.

37 ♖xg7 1-0

Game 70
Nigel Short – Garry Kasparov
European Team Ch, Debrecen 1992
Sicilian Defence, Najdorf/Scheveningen Variation [B82]

1	e4	c5
2	♘f3	d6
3	d4	cxd4
4	♘xd4	♘f6
5	♘c3	a6
6	f4	e6

Kasparov's usual reaction, although the last time he had to face 6 f4 (against Leko in Sarajevo 1999), he preferred the typical Najdorf move 6...e5.

7	♕f3	♕b6 *(D)*

An earlier game between the same players went 7...♘bd7 8 g4 h6 9 ♗e2 ♕b6!? 10 ♘b3 ♕c7 11 ♕g2 ♖b8! 12 ♗e3 b5 13 g5 hxg5 14 fxg5 ♘h5 15 g6 ♘e5 16 gxf7+ ♕xf7 17 ♖f1 ♕g6 18 ♕xg6+ ♘xg6 and Black had nothing to fear in Short-Kasparov, Belgrade 1989. However, the note to the next move explains Kasparov's reluctance to develop his knight to d7. The text-move is Black's most popular choice: before placing his queen on the natural c7-square he first wants to dislodge White's centralized knight – a common motif in many lines of the Open Sicilian.

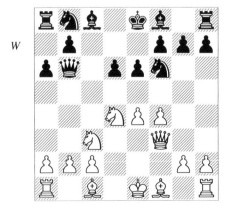

8	a3!?	

A common alternative is 8 ♘b3 ♕c7 9 g4, but the knight insists on staying on d4 and White makes a useful move instead.

8	...	♘c6

Naturally not 8...♕xd4?? losing the queen to 9 ♗e3. After 8...♘bd7 9 ♘b3 ♕c7 10 g4 h6 11 h4 h5 12 g5 ♘g4 13 ♗d2! b5 14 ♗h3 ♘b6 15 0-0-0 ♘c4 16 ♗xg4 hxg4 17 ♕xg4 ♖b8 18 g6 a5 19 ♘d4 b4 20 ♘cb5 ♕c5 21 a4 e5 22 ♘f5 White had both a material and positional advantage in Anand-Kasparov, Paris (Immopar rapid) 1992. As the Paris event took place just before Debrecen, Kasparov understandably wanted to improve Black's play. With the text-move he again challenges White's d4-knight and keeps d7 free for his other knight in case of g4-g5 (see also later on move 17).

9	♘b3	

9 ♘xc6 was tried three rounds later by Short against Smirin and leads to a different type of position; we'll see Kasparov coping with this alternative in Volume 2 in Z.Almasi-Kasparov, Lyons (ECC) 1994.

9	...	♕c7 *(D)*

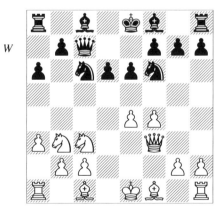

10	♗d3	

The first sign of indecision. Short avoids the more aggressive 10 g4 b5 11 g5 ♘d7 12 ♗e3 followed by 0-0-0. Although this leads to sharp and double-edged play, it poses Black more problems than the meek text-move. Also Short's subsequent play in this game is quite lacklustre, something which was to change dramatically in their world championship match less than a year later, when Kasparov's Sicilian had to withstand a furious assault (see Game 74).

10 ... g6! *(D)*

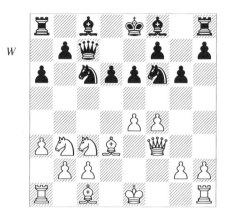

Kasparov develops his bishop to a more active square than e7, at the same time stopping White's possible attacking ambitions on the b1-h7 diagonal.

11 0-0

Switching to a kingside pawn-storm is not so easy any more. After 11 ♗d2 ♗g7 12 g4 b5 13 g5 ♘d7 14 ♕f2 ♘b6 15 ♕e2? ♘a4!, played just one day later in C.Lutz-Van Wely, Debrecen Echt 1992, Black enjoys a clear advantage. After 11 g4 Black may even consider 11...h6!? with the idea 12 h4 h5 13 g5 ♘g4, when it's not so easy to get rid of the g4-knight as in the aforementioned Anand-Kasparov game.

11 ... ♗g7
12 ♗d2

There is nothing wrong with solid development, but 12 ♔h1 0-0 13 ♕h3 with the plan of ♕h4 and f5 deserved attention as well.

12 ... 0-0
13 ♘d1

More logical is 13 ♖ae1 b5 14 ♔h1 ♗b7 15 ♕h3 with similar ideas to those indicated in the previous note. This would lead to a roughly equal position, whereas after the text-move the initiative gradually passes to Black. The Sicilian usually doesn't tolerate passive play even by White.

13 ... e5!

Although 13 ♘d1 took the sting out of a possible ...b5-b4 advance, it lessened White's central control. Kasparov doesn't wait for ♘e3 and his reaction quickly points out this drawback.

14 ♘e3?!

Again an insipid move. The most consistent continuation is 14 f5!?, when Black has a choice:

1) 14...gxf5 15 exf5 d5 gives Black a mobile centre, but after 16 ♕g3 ♔h8 17 ♗g5 ♕b6+ 18 ♘e3!? his pawns are under pressure and the position is far from clear.

2) In his notes Kasparov prefers a more ambitious sacrificial option: 14...d5!? 15 fxg6 (other moves favour Black; e.g., 15 exd5 e4! 16 ♗xe4 ♘e5 17 ♕f4 ♘xe4 18 ♕xe4 ♗xf5 19 ♖xf5 gxf5 20 ♕xf5 ♘c4) 15...dxe4 16 gxh7+ (16 gxf7+? loses an exchange after 16...♕xf7 17 ♕xe4 ♘xe4) 16...♔h8 17 ♗xe4 ♘xe4 18 ♕xe4 f5. Black has reasonable compensation with his bishop-pair and central control, but even here the resulting positions after 19 ♕e2 or 19 ♕h4 remain very complicated.

14 ... exf4
15 ♕xf4 ♗e6 *(D)*

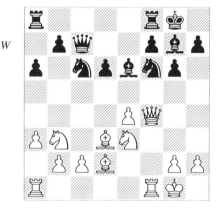

The resulting pawn-structure is fairly typical for a Najdorf Sicilian. However, the main distinguishing trait is that White's pieces are not placed actively enough to create threats against the d6-pawn, or Black's kingside. Meanwhile, Black has developed his forces harmoniously and White must fight for equality.

16 ♕h4

16 ♗c3?! ♘h5 allows Black to break up White's pawns. Perhaps 16 ♘c5!? is somewhat better, although even here Black has a comfortable position after 16...♘e5 17 ♘xe6 fxe6.

16 ... ♕d8!

Black has nothing to complain about after 16...♘d7 17 ♘d5 ♗xd5 18 exd5 ♘ce5, but the text-move keeps the tension and is more ambitious.

17 ♖ae1?!

The e4-pawn is potentially vulnerable (17 ♘c4? runs into 17...♘xe4! 18 ♕xe4 d5), so Short gives it some extra support. However, the text-move allows Black to increase his pull and give his initiative a more concrete form. Better is 17 ♗c3 ♘g4 (17...♕b6!? 18 ♕f2 ♘e5 19 ♗d4 ♕c6 also deserves attention) 18 ♕xd8 ♖fxd8 19 ♘xg4 ♗xc3 20 ♘f6+ ♗xf6 21 ♖xf6 ♔g7 22 ♖f2 with only a slight edge for Black.

17 ... ♘d7!? *(D)*

17...♗xb3 18 cxb3 d5 wins a pawn more or less by force, but one can understand Kasparov didn't relish the prospect of converting his advantage in a technically difficult endgame after 19 exd5 ♘xd5 20 ♕xd8 ♖axd8 21 ♗e4 ♘xe3 22 ♗xe3.

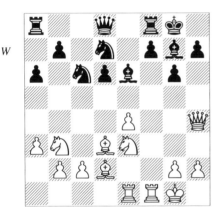

18 ♕xd8 ♖axd8

Kasparov indicates that 18...♖fxd8! was more accurate. Then:

1) After 19 ♘a5 ♘xa5 20 ♗xa5 b6 21 ♗b4 Black's rook is now not on f8 and apart from 21...♘c5 he also has 21...♗xb2! 22 ♗xd6 ♘e5 with a clear advantage.

2) After the passive 19 ♗c1 ♘c5 20 ♘xc5 dxc5 21 ♗c4 (21 ♘d5 ♗xd5 22 exd5 ♖xd5 23 ♗e4 ♖d7 and Black has better winning chances than in the previous note) 21...♗xc4 22 ♘xc4 ♖d4 23 ♘d2 ♖e8 24 c3 ♖d7 Black has a permanent structural advantage.

19 ♘a5

Short exchanges at least one of his passive minor pieces.

19 ... ♘xa5
20 ♗xa5 ♖c8?

This is a more serious slip, which eases White's defensive task. Kasparov still could have retained considerable pressure with the more direct 20...b6! 21 ♗b4 ♘c5 22 ♖b1 ♗d4.

21 c3 ♗h6! *(D)*

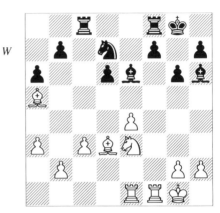

White has consolidated his queenside; given the time he might reactivate his offside a5-bishop and fully equalize the position. Therefore Kasparov is in a hurry to create new threats and his g7-bishop is on the lookout for new targets.

22 ♘d5?!

This only helps Black. The line 22 ♗b4? ♘e5 23 ♗c2 ♗xe3+ 24 ♖xe3 ♘c4 25 ♖d3 ♘xb2 26 ♖xd6 a5! illustrates the point of the previous move; Black wins material after both 27 ♗xa5 ♘c4 and 27 ♖xe6 axb4. The prophylactic 22 ♗c2! is necessary, and gives White a playable position, as now 22...♘e5 achieves nothing due to 23 ♗b6.

22 ... ♗xd5
23 exd5 ♘e5
24 ♗e2 ♗d2!
25 ♖d1 ♗e3+
26 ♔h1 f5 *(D)*

Another typical Sicilian picture – Black's minor pieces are far more active than White's bishops, he controls the dark squares and starts advancing his kingside pawn-majority. This is much easier in an endgame, where he doesn't have to worry about the safety of his own king.

27 g3?

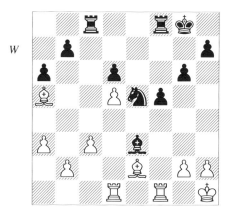

A serious mistake, which only helps Black to create a dangerous passed pawn. White's main concern should have been the activation of his a5-bishop, and the best way is undoubtedly 27 ♗b4! ♖f6 28 b3 b5 29 a4 (even 29 c4!? deserves attention) 29...♗b6!. Now the threat of ...a5 enables Black to close the position after 30 c4 a5 31 ♗c3 b4 32 ♗b2 h5!. It's important to prevent g4, so that Black may concentrate on his kingside play. However, his edge is not as clear-cut as in the game, because White has improved the coordination of his forces.

27	...	g5
28	♗b4	♖f6
29	b3	f4

Here 29...b5 30 a4 is not clear any more.

| 30 | gxf4 | gxf4 (D) |

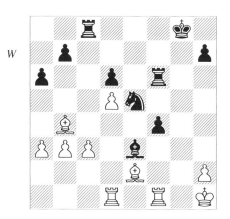

The direct consequence of 27 g3?: now White has a difficult choice between two evils – letting the pawn march on further, or leaving his b4-bishop in isolation.

| 31 | c4 |

31 ♗f3 ♘xf3 (31...b5!?) 32 ♖xf3 b5 is not much better. With his poor b4-bishop White doesn't have any effective counterplay and Black can combine play on the e- and g-files with the threat of marching his king to e4.

| 31 | ... | f3 |
| 32 | ♗xf3? | |

However, this is panic. White could have still fought on with 32 ♗d3, although after 32...♖cf8!? (32...♘g4? is premature and runs into the tactic 33 ♗xd6!; e.g., 33...♘f2+ 34 ♖xf2 ♗xf2 35 ♗e7 or 33...♖xd6 34 ♗f5 and it's now Black who has to be careful) Black has a large advantage.

32	...	♘xf3
33	♗xd6	♖xd6
34	♖xf3	♗h6! (D)

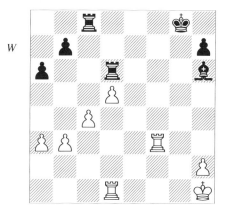

Black has an extra piece and the rest is a matter of technique.

| 35 | ♖e1 | ♖g6 |
| 36 | ♖e4 | |

Otherwise ...♗f8 would blockade the pawns immediately.

| 36 | ... | b5 |

Perhaps 36...♗f8! 37 b4 b6, preparing ...a5, is even stronger.

| 37 | c5?! | |

This oversight hastens the end. However, Black would gradually win even after the more resilient 37 ♖g3 ♖xg3 38 hxg3 bxc4 39 bxc4 ♗f8.

| 37 | ... | ♖xc5 |

0-1

Short had probably overlooked that after 38 ♖e8+ ♔g7 39 ♖e7+ Black escapes the perpetual with 39...♔h8 40 ♖e8+ ♖g8.

Game 71
Anatoly Karpov – Garry Kasparov
Linares 1993
King's Indian Defence, Sämisch Variation [E86]

This game was very important for the outcome of the prestigious Linares tournament. Although in the previous round Kasparov had won against Anand and relegated him to third place, Karpov was still keeping pace with the World Champion. Moreover, in the encounter between the joint leaders he had White and was in a fighting mood...

1	d4	♘f6
2	c4	g6
3	♘c3	♗g7
4	e4	d6
5	f3	0-0
6	♗e3	e5
7	♘ge2	c6
8	♕d2	♘bd7 *(D)*

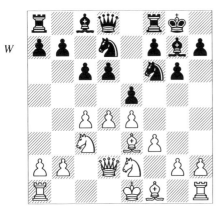

9 ♖d1

Until now all these moves could be easily expected, as both players had shown trust in this line in the previous rounds. Karpov played 9 d5 against Kamsky, while Kasparov had already faced 9 0-0-0 twice: against Kramnik and Beliavsky (see also Game 67, which is similar to our game in more than one sense – Shirov's unexpected opening choice, as well as Black's enterprising pawn sacrifice). However, the somewhat unusual text-move came as a surprise. Generally in Linares 1993 Kasparov had to cope with a similar approach more than once – fearing extensive preparation, his opponents prepared offbeat lines, which had hardly ever occurred in their previous practice. In this concrete case Karpov doesn't want to commit his king to the queenside and keeps open the option to close or open the centre, depending on Black's reaction.

9 ... a6! *(D)*

Although it cost him 20 minutes on the clock, Kasparov found the most flexible and accurate reaction. 9...exd4 10 ♘xd4 only furthers White's development and the potentially useful preparatory move 9...♖e8?! runs into 10 d5!, when Black's rook is misplaced and he lacks effective counterplay after 10...c5 11 g4.

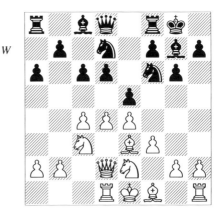

10 dxe5?!

White is more or less forced to resolve the central tension, as otherwise ...b5 would give Black excellent counterplay. However, it is more circumspect to close the position with 10 d5 c5! (10...cxd5?! is weaker and 11 ♘xd5! gives White an advantage), although here contrary to the above note Black has a fully playable position after 11 g4 ♘e8.

10 ... ♘xe5!

Karpov was undoubtedly hoping for the sedate 10...dxe5 11 c5 with an edge for White;

here Black's previous move would only weaken his own queenside. It's no wonder Kasparov, as a King's Indian devotee, prefers a more dynamic solution that also highlights the main drawback of 9 ♖d1 – White's king is stuck in the centre and getting it to safety will cost a lot of time. Especially in an open position this is a grave problem and in fact Karpov doesn't manage to solve it at all.

11 b3

11 ♘c1 ♗e6 only increases Black's lead in development.

11 ... b5!

The consistent follow-up to Black's previous moves. Just as in Game 67 Kasparov isn't concerned about the fate of the d6-pawn; active piece-play will promise him more than sufficient compensation.

12 cxb5

This is logical. Other moves are weaker: after 12 ♕xd6?! ♕xd6 13 ♖xd6 bxc4 Black starts generating concrete threats and the attempt to close the position with 12 c5 d5 13 ♗d4 (13 exd5? b4 is even weaker) 13...♖e8 14 f4 fails to 14...♘eg4 15 e5 b4! followed by ...♘e4 and ...f6.

12 ... axb5
13 ♕xd6 ♘fd7 *(D)*

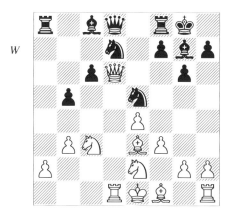

14 f4?! *(D)*

A critical moment. Karpov had already begun to spend large amounts of time, as he was definitely out of his preparation. Moreover, the character of the position definitely suited his opponent and it's no wonder that even Karpov's famed sense of danger let him down. The tempting text-move move ignores the main tactical threat, but containing Black's initiative was far from easy. The following lines show White suffers due to his exposed queen and misplaced e2-knight, which in turn makes normal kingside development difficult:

1) 14 ♘d4? is even worse. After 14...♖a6! White's queen is stranded and the threat of ...c5 practically forces White's knight back.

2) With 14 ♗g1 the bishop leaves a vulnerable square, but on the other hand, such ugly 'anti-development' is not ideal. Kasparov intended to continue as in the game: 14...b4!? (14...♕h4+ 15 ♗f2 ♕h5 with the idea ...♘xf3+ also looks good) 15 ♘a4 (15 ♕xb4? is bad due to 15...c5!) 15...♖xa4 16 bxa4 ♕a5 with more than sufficient compensation for the exchange.

3) Bringing the queen back to the defence with 14 ♕d2 solves one of White's problems, but even here Black can sacrifice more material for a dangerous initiative with 14...b4 15 ♘a4 ♖xa4 (15...♘c4!? 16 bxc4 ♖xa4 17 ♗c5 ♕a5! is also promising) 16 bxa4 ♘c4 17 ♕c1 ♘xe3 18 ♕xe3 ♕a5.

4) 14 a4!? is arguably White's best choice, as it takes the sting out of Black's play on the a-file. After 14...bxa4 15 ♘xa4 ♕a5+ (after 15...♖xa4 16 bxa4 ♘c4 17 ♕f4 Black probably has nothing more than a draw by repetition with 17...♗e5 18 ♕h6 ♗g7) 16 ♔f2 (or 16 ♗d2 ♕a7) 16...♘c4 the position remains unclear.

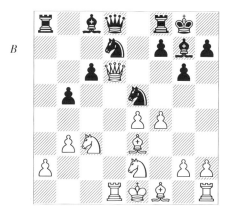

14 ... b4! *(D)*

Kasparov foresaw this blow back on move 9! We can readily believe him, not only because he was able to anticipate Karpov's reactions so well in the past (see the note to move 19 in

Game 31 and to move 17 in Game 65), but because the alternative 14...♘g4? 15 ♗d4 is simply bad for Black. Kasparov's answer to the assumption that Karpov overlooked 14...b4! was very blunt: "Did he expect me to resign?"

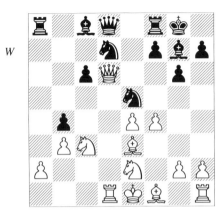

15 ♘b1?

Karpov panics and doesn't find the best defence. After this move White's position deteriorates rapidly. The alternatives are:

1) 15 ♕xb4? runs into 15...c5! 16 ♗xc5 ♘xc5! 17 ♕xc5 (17 ♖xd8 ♘ed3+ costs White a piece) 17...♘d3+ 18 ♖xd3 ♕xd3 and White can't last for long.

2) 15 ♘a4 ♖xa4! 16 bxa4 (16 fxe5 is best met by 16...♖xa2 with a strong attack) 16...♘c4 17 ♕d3 ♘b2 and Black regains the exchange with a distinct advantage.

3) White's only chance is 15 fxe5 bxc3 16 ♘xc3! (16 e6 fxe6 17 ♕xe6+ ♔h8 and 16 ♕xc6 ♖xa2 17 ♘xc3 ♖c2 are both too dangerous for White), intending to develop his kingside forces. After 16...♗xe5 (16...♕a5 is unconvincing due to 17 ♕xc6 ♘xe5 18 ♕c5) 17 ♕xc6 ♕h4+ (17...♗xc3+ 18 ♕xc3 ♕h4+ 19 ♔d2! transposes into the main line) 18 ♔d2 (18 g3? is much weaker due to 18...♗xc3+, as even after the paradoxical 19 ♗d2 ♗xd2+ 20 ♖xd2 ♕f6 21 ♕xa8 ♘e5! Black's attack is too strong) 18...♗xc3+ 19 ♕xc3 ♖xa2+ 20 ♔c1 the king has castled by hand and White's f1-bishop is ready to come out. Now the most interesting continuation is the direct 20...♕xe4!? (Kasparov recommends the more restrained 20...♘f6, but after 21 ♗c4 with the idea 21...♘xe4 22 ♗xf7+! the issue is far from clear) 21 ♗h6 (even here 21 ♗c4!? deserves attention) 21...♘e5 22 ♗d3 (22 ♗xf8? loses to 22...♗f5 23 ♗d3 ♕e3+ 24 ♔b1 ♖xg2) 22...♕a8 23 ♔b1 (23 ♗xf8?! ♖a1+ 24 ♔d2 ♕xg2+ 25 ♗e2 ♖a2+ 26 ♔c1 ♗f5! 27 ♗h6 ♕a8! is a crazy line which is better for Black) 23...♖e8 and White's king seems to be more vulnerable than its black counterpart.

15 ... ♘g4
16 ♗d4

16 ♗g1 was tried in the post-mortem. Although this is perhaps more resilient, Black's advantage in development is well worth even major material sacrifices and he has a raging attack after the energetic 16...♖xa2 17 h3 ♕h4+! 18 g3 ♖xe2+ 19 ♔xe2 (19 ♗xe2? ♕xg3+ 20 ♔f1 ♗a6! and the threat of ...♕f3+ decides) 19...♕xg3 20 ♖d3 (20 ♕d3 ♕xf4 21 hxg4 ♘e5 is hopeless for White, and after 20 hxg4 ♘f6! 21 ♕d3 Black has more than one way to win, of which one convincing option is 21...♗xg4+ 22 ♔d2 ♕xf4+ 23 ♗e3 ♕f3!) 20...♗a6!? (the alternative 20...♕h4 21 ♘d2 is less clear) 21 hxg4 (after 21 ♕xd7 ♘f6 22 ♕d4 ♘h5 23 ♕e3 ♖d8! Black wins material) 21...♘f6! 22 ♘d2 ♘d5.

16 ... ♗xd4
17 ♕xd4

17 ♘xd4 ♖xa2 doesn't help. Kasparov gives the pretty line 18 ♘xc6 (18 ♖d2 ♖a1 19 ♗d3 ♕b6 20 0-0 ♖d8 21 ♗c4 ♘b8! 22 ♕c7 ♖a7 and the pin costs White a piece) 18...♕h4+ 19 g3 ♘xh2! 20 ♕d3 ♕f6 21 ♘xb4 ♘e5! and Black wins material with a continuing attack.

17 ... ♖xa2 *(D)*

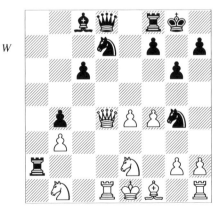

Now White is virtually lost, as he has no way to coordinate his forces.

Game 71: Anatoly Karpov – Garry Kasparov

18	h3	c5
19	♕g1?!	

White's queen must control the e3-square, but a better try is 19 ♕d3!? ♗a6 20 ♕f3 (20 ♕xd7? fails to 20...♕h4+ 21 g3 ♖xe2+! and 20 ♕g3 is refuted by the simple 20...♘gf6). However, even here after 20...♘de5! 21 fxe5 ♘xe5 22 ♕e3 (22 ♖xd8 loses on the spot to 22...♘xf3+ 23 gxf3 ♖xd8 24 ♘g3 ♗xf1 25 ♘xf1 ♖c2 26 ♘g3 ♖b2 27 0-0 ♖d3) 22...♘d3+ 23 ♖xd3 ♕xd3 24 ♕xd3 ♗xd3 25 ♘c1 ♗xb1 26 ♘xa2 ♗xa2 27 ♗c4 ♗b1 Black has a healthy extra pawn and should gradually convert his advantage into victory.

19	...	♘gf6
20	e5	

After 20 ♘d2 Black can play even 20...♖xd2! 21 ♖xd2 ♘xe4, followed by ...♖e8 and ...♗a6.

20	...	♘e4
21	h4	

Keeping the queen offside loses by force, but after 21 ♕e3 ♗b7 22 ♘d2 ♘xd2 23 ♖xd2 ♖xd2 24 ♕xd2 ♕h4+! 25 g3 ♕e7 26 ♖g1 ♖d8 followed by ...f6 White's king can't survive in the centre despite the simplification.

21	...	c4!
22	♘c1	

After 22 bxc4 ♕a5 23 ♕e3 b3+ 24 ♘ec3 ♘dc5 followed by ...♖c2, the pin decides. 22 ♕e3 c3! 23 ♕xe4 c2 is similar to the game; even here Black can go for a spectacular finish with 24 ♖d2 ♘c5!.

22	...	c3! (D)

All White's pieces are huddled on the back rank and it's no wonder Kasparov wants to wind up the game with a flourish. However, the mundane 22...♖b2 23 ♕d4 c3! would have done the job just as well.

23	♘xa2	c2
24	♕d4	

Karpov refuses to cooperate. The main line of Black's combination was 24 ♖c1 ♘xe5! (24...cxb1♕?! 25 ♖xb1 ♘xe5 is unconvincing due to 26 ♖d1) 25 ♖xc2 (25 ♕e3 cxb1♕ 26 ♖xb1 ♘g4! and Black wins) 25...♗g4 26 ♖d2

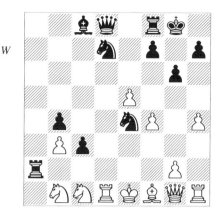

(26 ♘d2 is met by 26...♘d3+! 27 ♗xd3 ♕xd3 28 ♘xe4 ♕xe4+ 29 ♔d2 ♕xf4+) 26...♘xd2 27 ♘xd2 (27 fxe5 ♘e4 28 ♗e2 ♗xe2 29 ♔xe2 ♘g3+ 30 ♔e3 ♕d5! and with both White's knights offside Black's attack quickly decides) 27...♖e8! 28 fxe5 ♖xe5+ 29 ♔f2 ♕xd2+ 30 ♔g3 ♖e3+ and White must give up his queen as 31 ♔xg4 ♕d4+ 32 ♔g5 ♖g3+ leads to mate.

24	...	cxd1♕+
25	♔xd1	

25 ♕xd1 is just as hopeless due to 25...♘g3 26 ♖h3 ♘xf1 27 ♔xf1 (27 ♘xb4 ♕b6 costs White a piece) 27...♘xe5 and Black wins material after 28 ♕xd8 ♖xd8 29 ♖e3 ♖d1+ 30 ♖e1 ♗a6+.

25	...	♘dc5!

25...♘xe5 wins as well, but the text-move launches a mating attack.

26	♕xd8	♖xd8+
27	♔c2	

27 ♔e1 loses too much material after 27...♗g4 28 ♗e2 ♗xe2 29 ♔xe2 ♘g3+, and the same goes for 27 ♔c1 ♘f2 28 ♖g1 ♖d1+ 29 ♔b2 ♗f5.

27	...	♘f2
	0-1	

Here White's flag fell, but this was only a different form of resignation. 28 ♖g1 ♗f5+ 29 ♔b2 (29 ♗d3 only slightly postpones mate) 29...♘d1+ 30 ♔a1 ♘xb3# paints a pretty picture.

Game 72
Garry Kasparov – Gata Kamsky
Linares 1993
Sicilian Defence, Scheveningen Variation [B80]

1	e4	c5
2	♘f3	e6
3	d4	cxd4
4	♘xd4	♘f6
5	♘c3	d6

This game was played in the last round and by that time Kasparov was already a full point ahead of his pursuers. However, the encounter proved to be a tense battle, with Kamsky highly motivated by a special bonus for any player who defeated the World Champion. This explains his fighting opening choice: to repeat his upset victory against Kasparov from Dortmund 1992 he is even willing to enter his opponent's 'territory' – the Najdorf/Scheveningen complex.

6 ♗e3

The notes to Game 44 show us that Kasparov considered 6 g4 to be White's most dangerous option and playing Black himself, he mostly avoided the Keres Attack. Yet in this game he opts for a continuation that was only beginning to steal the limelight in 1993. The English Attack, at that time little more than an aggressive and interesting sideline, proved to be an ideal weapon, highlighting Kamsky's lack of Sicilian experience.

6	...	a6
7	f3	♘bd7 *(D)*

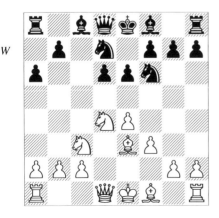

Kasparov himself introduced the text-move into practice in a rapidplay match against Short in 1987. However, he himself pointed out White's build-up in the English Attack is only deceptively slow and Black should strive for more energetic central or queenside counterplay. In his later practice with Black we'll find 7...b5 (especially this line will be prominently featured in Volume 2) and lately even 7...♘c6.

8 g4

8 ♕d2 b5 9 g4 h6 transposes into the aforementioned 7...b5 lines. The more testing text-move immediately launches White's kingside play and the game will show he can develop his queen not only to the standard d2-square.

8	...	h6 *(D)*

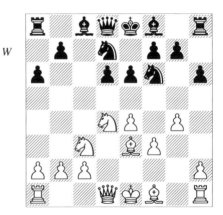

9 ♖g1!?

At that time a novelty, this slight but clever change of the move-order is directed against Kasparov's own idea. After the seemingly more natural 9 h4 Black can play 9...♘e5!? (also the immediate 9...♕b6 is possible, because now 10 a3 ♘e5 is not effective any more) 10 ♖g1?! (10 ♗e2!? is stronger) 10...♕b6 11 ♕c1 d5! and the threat of ...♗c5 gave Black an excellent position in Short-Kasparov, London rpd (6) 1987.

9	...	♕b6?!

Now this typical sortie is ineffective. In his notes Kasparov wrote: "I generally managed to engineer my games in such a way that standard reactions are inadequate." A very telling and instructive comment, which indicates one of Kasparov's main strong points. We can find further such examples in this book, such as 14...♕c7? in Game 24, or 19 ♘b5?! in Game 56, while many of his encounters against Karpov are also outstanding in this sense, especially Game 31. To be more concrete, 9...♘e5?!, an idea seen in the previous note, here allows 10 f4! (made possible by 9 ♖g1!? instead of 9 h4) 10...♘exg4 11 ♖xg4 ♘xg4 12 ♕xg4 e5 13 ♘f5 g6 14 0-0-0 gxf5 15 exf5, when White has tremendous compensation for the exchange and a strong attack. 9...b5 10 h4 g6 11 g5 hxg5 12 hxg5 ♘h5 leads by transposition to Short-Kasparov, London rpd (2) 1987. Here subsequent practice has shown White can finish his development and retain an advantage with 13 ♕d2. Kasparov recommends 9...g5! and this is indeed better. After 10 h4 Black can play 10...♕b6, as 11 a3 ♘e5, by analogy with the game continuation, is unconvincing for White – the black knight can't be chased away from its central outpost.

10   a3! *(D)*

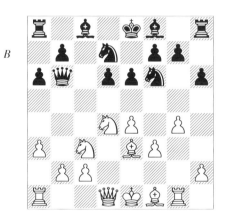

This move is generally useful, but the indirect protection of the b2-pawn is only the most obvious point of Kasparov's idea. The main reason will become clear two moves later.

10   ...   ♘e5

Now after 10...g5 White can simply play 11 ♕d2, gaining an important tempo for the follow-up h4.

11   ♗f2!

White still doesn't commit his queen. This move creates the threat of ♘xe6.

11   ...   ♕c7

A prudent retreat. The wild try 11...d5?! can simply be met by 12 ♘b3!? (White doesn't have to enter the complications of 12 exd5 ♗c5 13 ♘a4 ♕a5+ 14 c3 ♗a7!? 15 dxe6 ♗xe6), followed by exd5.

12   f4

By leaving his queen on d1 and playing 9 ♖g1!?, White has kept g4 protected, which in turn makes this important advance possible.

12   ...   ♘c4?!

Black exchanges one of his few active pieces for the undeveloped f1-bishop, and this helps White to increase his pull. 12...♘g6! is much stronger; then Black's knight can still play an important part in the fight for the centre.

13   ♗xc4   ♕xc4
14   ♕f3 *(D)*

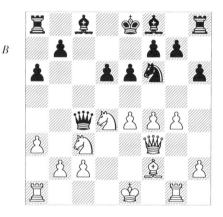

White's lead in development has reached dramatic proportions and he is ready to start a direct attack. However, this hasn't been achieved by simple developing moves, but by a very concrete approach (moves 9-11) to the needs of the position. Such concreteness is in general typical for modern chess and Kasparov is its foremost representative.

14   ...   e5?

Kamsky had his first long think and decided to solve Black's problems in a direct fashion. However, it's no surprise his already compromised position can't stand such radical measures. Black must tread very carefully; possible alternatives are:

1) Kasparov considered 14...b5 to be the only reasonable move, but this gives White a pleasant choice. The most ambitious continuation is 15 e5!? (the simple 15 g5 hxg5 16 fxg5 ♘d7 17 g6 also gives White an advantage) 15...♘d5 16 ♘e4! dxe5 17 fxe5 b4 18 g5 with excellent attacking chances.

2) 14...h5!? is a suggestion by Bönsch, which deserves attention. Now moves such as 15 h3 or 15 gxh5 at least allow Black to activate his cornered h8-rook, while 15 g5 ♘g4 16 f5 g6 also gives him better defensive chances than in the game.

15	♘f5	♗xf5
16	gxf5	

White has a large advantage, as Black's light squares are weak and he has problems with safeguarding his king and connecting his rooks. Therefore it's clear he must do something extraordinary to change the course of the game.

16 ... d5 *(D)*

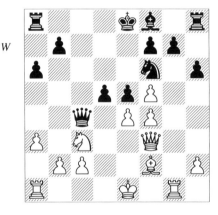

Kamsky relied on this central break, but it doesn't solve his problems due to White's superior piece coordination. However, keeping the centre closed can hardly be considered an improvement. Left to his own devices, White will prevent any possible counterplay with 0-0-0, followed by doubling rooks on the d-file and a possible ♗h4.

17 fxe5

Fritz recommends the interesting 17 ♕d3, but Kasparov opts for a simpler solution. By keeping the queens on the board White retains his attacking chances.

17 ... ♘xe4

17...dxe4? 18 ♕g2 ♘d7 19 0-0-0! is hopeless for Black.

18	♖g4!	h5
19	♖h4 *(D)*	

Kasparov subsequently preferred 19 ♖f4!. The main point is that after 19...♖c8 (19...♘g5 20 ♕e3 doesn't help) White has 20 ♖d1 ♗c5 21 ♗h4!, when Black has no good defence against ♘xd5 (or ♖xd5).

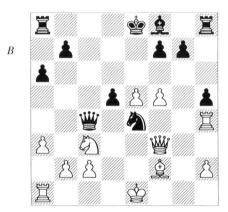

19 ... ♗c5?!

The final mistake, after which White wins practically by force. 19...♗e7 is no better, as after 20 ♘xe4 dxe4 21 ♕xe4 White wins a pawn for nothing. However, 19...♖c8!? is more resilient: 20 ♘xe4 (White's h4-rook is a tactical liability in the line 20 ♖d1 ♗c5! 21 ♗xc5? ♘g5!; 20 e6 ♗c5 21 ♘xe4 dxe4 22 ♖xe4 ♕xc2 transposes into the 22 e6 line below, but 20 ♕g2!? with the idea ♘xe4 and c3 is a possible improvement) 20...dxe4 21 ♖xe4 ♕xc2. Here not only Black's but also White's king is potentially vulnerable. Nevertheless, after 22 ♖e2 (22 e6 is tempting, but after 22...♗c5!? White doesn't seem to have any direct win) 22...♕c6 23 ♕xc6+ ♖xc6 24 ♖d1 White has a clear endgame advantage.

20 0-0-0!

20 ♘xe4?! is less incisive. After 20...dxe4! (20...♗xf2+?! 21 ♕xf2 dxe4 22 0-0-0! transposes into the game) 21 ♕xe4 ♗xf2+ 22 ♔xf2 ♕c5+, followed by ...0-0-0, Black can fight on.

20 ... ♗xf2

20...0-0-0 is the only alternative. Black's king escapes from the centre, but after 21 ♗xc5 ♕xc5 22 ♘xd5 ♖xd5 23 ♖xd5 ♕xd5 24 ♖xe4

White has a healthy extra pawn and his victory is a matter of technique.

| 21 | ♘xe4 | dxe4 |

21...♗xh4? 22 ♘d6+.

| 22 | ♕xf2 | |

Now Black's king is trapped on e8 and it's only a matter of time before White's major pieces hunt him down.

| 22 | ... | ♖c8 |

In connection with the next move this only helps White, but the alternatives were just as dreary. 22...♕a2 23 c3 gets Black nowhere, while after 22...e3 White doesn't even have to go for the endgame and can play 23 ♕e1! ♕c5 24 ♖e4, netting the pawn with a continuing attack. After 22...0-0 23 ♖xh5 White threatens ♕h4 and his attack comes first: 23...♖fd8 24 ♖g1 ♕a2 25 ♖xg7+! ♔f8 26 ♕c5+ ♔xg7 27 ♕g1+! ♔f8 28 ♖h8+ ♔e7 29 ♕c5+.

| 23 | ♔b1 | |

This stops ...♕a2 and prepares ♖d4, leaving Black with no choice.

23	...	♖d8
24	♖xd8+	♔xd8
25	♖h3! (D)	

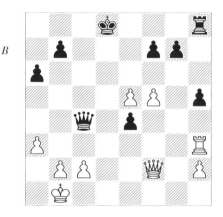

White is not interested in the e4-pawn any more and concentrates his efforts on the final attack. As the h8-rook can't help out in the defence, Black is lost.

| 25 | ... | ♕d5 |

This is forced as the immediate threat was ♕d2+.

| 26 | ♖c3 | ♔d7 |

26...♕xe5 loses on the spot to 27 ♕b6+, while 26...♖h6 27 f6! cuts off the rook and wins material after 27...gxf6 28 ♕b6+ ♔e7 29 exf6+ ♖xf6 30 ♖c7+.

| 27 | ♕b6 | ♖d8 |

27...♖c8? loses a rook to 28 e6+, but even now Black is one move too late.

28	♖c5	♕d1+
29	♔a2	♔e8
30	♕xb7 (D)	

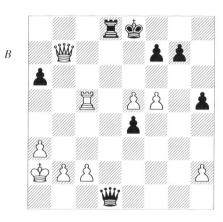

| 30 | ... | ♕g4 |

Black has to prevent e6 and the passive 30...♕d7 31 ♕xe4 leads to a completely hopeless position.

31	e6	fxe6
32	♖e5	♕g5
33	h4!	

By this point White has more than one road to victory, but that chosen by Kasparov is the most elegant.

| 33 | ... | ♕xh4 |
| 34 | ♖xe6+ | |

34 ♕xg7 is just as good.

| 34 | ... | ♔f8 |
| 35 | f6 | 1-0 |

Game 73
Garry Kasparov – Nigel Short
PCA World Ch match (game 7), London 1993
Ruy Lopez (Spanish), Anti-Marshall Variation [C88]

1	e4	e5
2	♘f3	♘c6
3	♗b5	a6
4	♗a4	♘f6
5	0-0	♗e7
6	♖e1	b5
7	♗b3	0-0
8	a4	

Throughout his career, Kasparov has never allowed his opponents the chance to play the Marshall Attack (8 c3 d5), no matter how sporadically they might use it. Lately he has also tried the currently fashionable 8 h3 ♗b7 9 d3 d6 10 a3!?.

8	...	♗b7

The 8 a4 line became topical in the 1993 PCA World Championship match and occurred in no fewer than three games. Kasparov won the theoretical duel hands down, as he achieved an opening advantage in each game and went on to score a full three points, albeit not without time-trouble adventures. In the initial game Short chose the rare 8...b4, but after 9 d3 d6 10 a5 ♗e6 11 ♘bd2 ♖b8 12 ♗c4 ♕c8 13 ♘f1 ♖e8 14 ♘e3 the misguided 14...♘d4? 15 ♘xd4 exd4 16 ♘d5! ♘xd5 17 exd5 ♗d7 18 ♗d2 ♗f6 19 ♖xe8+ ♗xe8 20 ♕e2 ♗b5 21 ♖e1 ♗xc4 22 dxc4 gave White a clear pull due to his full control of the e-file and better pawn-structure, Kasparov-Short, London PCA Wch (1) 1993.

9	d3	d6

Short returns to the most common continuation. Earlier the challenger tried 9...♖e8, intending to play ...d5 in one move later on. However, after 10 ♘bd2! ♗f8 11 c3 h6 Kasparov came up with the strong novelty 12 ♗a2!. This discourages the immediate central advance and limits Black to the passive 12...d6 (12...d5 13 exd5 ♘xd5 14 d4 ♘f4 15 ♘e4 favours White). After 13 ♘h4 ♕d7?! (13...♘e7!? is stronger) 14 ♘g6! ♘e7 15 ♘xf8 ♔xf8 16 f3 ♖ad8 17 b4 ♘g6 18 ♘b3 ♗c8 19 ♗b1 ♘h5 20 axb5 axb5 21 ♗e3 the bishop-pair gave White a permanent advantage and the kingside sortie 21...♘h4 was amply parried by 22 ♖a2! in Kasparov-Short, London PCA Wch (3) 1993.

10	♘bd2!? *(D)*	

In 1993, the attention of theory and practice focused more on 10 ♘c3 ♘a5 11 ♗a2 b4 12 ♘e2 c5 13 ♘g3. However, the previous note shows that Kasparov successfully revived the typical Ruy Lopez development to d2 in this match. The knight heads for e3, from where it will flexibly control not only f5, but d5 as well.

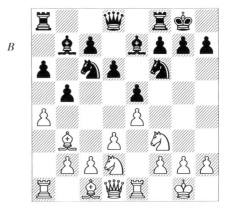

10	...	♘d7

Short's reaction was considered Black's best option at that time. Later games have shown he has other playable options, and the idea from the previous note, 10...♘a5!? 11 ♗a2 c5 12 ♘f1 b4 13 ♘e3 ♗c8, became especially popular.

11	c3!	

Once again, Kasparov reacts in time-honoured Ruy Lopez fashion. The bishop retreats to c2 only to rejoin the play with great effect later on. On the other hand 11 ♘f1 allows Black to exchange the light-squared bishops: 11...♘c5 12 axb5 axb5 13 ♖xa8 ♕xa8 14 ♗d5 ♘d8! leads to approximate equality.

11	...	♘c5
12	axb5	

In general exchanges help Black, but just as in Game 37, this swap has a concrete purpose. 12 ♗c2 allows Black to change the character of the position and get promising counterplay with the sharp 12...♘xa4!? 13 ♗xa4 bxa4 14 ♕xa4 ♔h8! followed by ...f5.

| 12 | ... | axb5 |
| 13 | ♖xa8 | ♗xa8 |

After 13...♕xa8 14 ♗c2 play can transpose into the game after moves such as 14...♘c6 or 14...♗f6, because Black's queen will eventually have to return to d8 anyway. An interesting independent continuation is 14...b4!? 15 d4 bxc3 16 bxc3 ♘d7 17 ♘f1. In his notes Kasparov ends the line here and promises White an initiative. While this is true enough, he recently got a chance to test his verdict and found out Black isn't without counterchances. After 17...♗f6 18 d5 ♘cb8! 19 h4 ♘c5 20 ♘g3 ♗c8 21 ♘g5 h6 22 ♘h5! ♗e7 23 ♘h3 ♕a2! 24 ♖e3 in Kasparov-Topalov, Linares 2004 Black should have accepted the challenge with 24...♗xh4!, as 25 ♘xg7 ♔xg7 26 ♕h5 only leads to a perpetual after 26...♕xc2! 27 ♖g3+ ♗xg3 28 ♗xh6+ ♔h8.

| 14 | ♗c2 | ♗f6 |

Other moves:

1) Here after 14...b4?! 15 d4 bxc3 16 bxc3 both Black's queen and bishop are more passive than in the previous note and White has a pleasant edge.

2) 14...d5?! isn't ideal either. White's forces quickly spring to life after 15 exd5 ♕xd5 16 d4!.

3) With the text-move Black stops d4, but 14...♘e6!? is more flexible and achieves the same thing. After both 15 b4 and 15 ♘f1 Black may play 15...♘g5 and later possibly even ...♗g5 in one move, simplifying the position. This would give him good chances to neutralize White's edge.

| 15 | b4 | |

This phase of the game revolves around the d5-square. If Black manages to advance his central pawn unscathed, he'll get good counterplay; otherwise White retains an edge and can increase his pressure. After 15 ♘f1 d5 (after 15...♘e6 White can omit b4 and play 16 ♘e3) 16 exd5 ♕xd5 17 b4 Kasparov points out Black's extra option 17...♘a4!? (17...♘e6 transposes to the note to Black's 16th move) with a complex position.

| 15 | ... | ♘e6 |
| 16 | ♘f1! | |

White is alert. After 16 ♗b3 ♘e7 Black is ready to play ...d5, and 17 ♘f1 d5 18 d4!? (18 ♘g3 ♘g6! 19 ♘h5 is simply countered by 19...♗e7) 18...dxe4 19 dxe5 exf3 20 exf6 gxf6 is far from clear.

| 16 | ... | ♗b7?! |

After 16...♘e7 17 ♘e3 the reason for 16 ♘f1! becomes clear, as 17...d5?! runs into the unpleasant 18 ♘g4. Short decides to wait and improves his bishop, but this lands Black in a passive position. Kasparov recommends lashing out with 16...d5!? instead. After 17 exd5 ♕xd5 18 ♘e3 ♕d8 19 ♘g4 e4! 20 ♘xf6+ ♕xf6 21 dxe4 ♕xc3 22 ♗d2 (or 22 ♖e3) White has a slight advantage thanks to his bishop-pair, but Black's active pieces promise him a fair amount of counterplay.

| 17 | ♘e3 | g6 |
| 18 | ♗b3 | ♗g7 (D) |

| 19 | h4 | |

19 ♘c2!? is an interesting and promising alternative. Once ...d5 is stopped, White himself prepares d4 and the position of Black's knights only enhances the strength of this advance. Preventing it with 19...♕f6 puts the queen in an uncomfortable position, and after 20 h4 White is better.

| 19 | ... | ♗c8? |

Once again a slow bishop move is not ideal and gives White an important tempo. 19...♘e7! is more consistent, returning to the ...d5 idea. White can prevent this with 20 ♘g4, but after 20...♗c8 21 ♘g5 ♘f4 22 ♗xf4 exf4 23 ♕f3 ♗xg4 24 ♕xg4 ♗xc3 25 ♕xf4! d5! 26 ♖c1

♗xb4 27 h5 (Onishchuk-Timman, Groningen 1996), the correct 27...h6! 28 ♘f3 ♔h7 keeps his edge within acceptable limits.

20 h5 ♔h8
21 ♘d5

White keeps the tension. 21 hxg6?! fxg6 would have eased Black's defensive task.

21 ... g5 *(D)*

A debatable decision, but the alternatives were not too appealing:

1) 21...f5 leaves Black's kingside very shaky and gives White a pleasant choice between 22 h6 and 22 hxg6 hxg6 23 g3.

2) The same goes for 21...gxh5 22 g3. Now White intends ♘h4 and the only way to stop it fails tactically: 22...♗f6 23 ♔g2 h4 24 ♖h1! hxg3? runs into 25 ♘xe5! and the threat of ♕h5 is decisive.

3) After 21...♘f4 22 ♘xf4 exf4 23 ♗xf4 ♗xc3 24 ♗h6! Black has too many tactical weaknesses and will lose material shortly; e.g., 24...♗xe1 25 ♕xe1 ♘e5 26 ♕c3!.

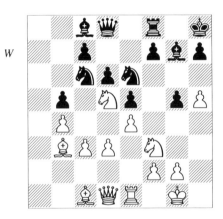

22 ♘e3!

Kasparov immediately redirects his knight. 22 ♘h2 ♘e7 is not as incisive.

22 ... ♘f4

Black can't behave passively; allowing ♘f5 would give White a dangerous attack for free.

23 g3

White decides to act – this temporary pawn sacrifice opens up lines on the kingside. However, Black's position is still surprisingly resilient and the slower 23 ♘h2!? deserved attention, as the line 23...♗e6 24 ♗xe6 fxe6 25 g3! ♘h3+ 26 ♔g2 ♘xf2 27 ♕e2 favours White.

23 ... ♘xh5

24 ♘f5 ♗xf5
25 exf5 ♕d7

Black must return the pawn, but 25...♘f6 is somewhat more flexible. After 26 ♗xg5 he can decide between the immediate 26...♕d7 or 26...h6. In both cases White is better, but his own f5-pawn gets in the way by closing the important b1-h7 diagonal. Also, f5 would be a wonderful square for the knight.

26 ♗xg5 *(D)*

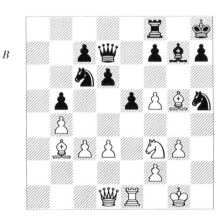

26 ... h6?!

As indicated above, White would welcome 26...♕xf5? 27 ♗d5 ♘b8 (after 27...♕d7 28 ♘d2 f6 29 ♗e3 ♘e7 30 ♗f3 Black loses a piece, and the same goes for 27...f6 28 ♗e3 ♘e7 29 ♘h4) 28 ♗e7 ♖e8 29 ♘h4 ♕d7 30 ♕xh5, when all his pieces pounce on Black's king. However, after the text-move White could have advantageously sacrificed the obstacle on f5, so 26...♘f6, as in the previous note, was a safer option.

27 ♘h4

After 27 ♔g2!? the threat of ♖h1 forces Black to play 27...♕xf5 (27...hxg5 28 ♖h1 gives White a huge attack) 28 ♖h1, and now:

1) 28...♘f6 29 ♗xh6 (29 ♕d2 e4 or 29 ♕c1 ♘g4!? is less convincing) 29...♗xh6 30 ♕d2! ♘g4 31 ♖xh6+ ♘xh6 (31...♔g7 fails to 32 ♘h4, as f2 is protected) 32 ♕xh6+ ♔g8 33 ♗d5 and the threat of ♗e4 wins material.

2) Stronger is 28...♕g6 29 ♗d5 hxg5! (after 29...♘d8 30 ♘xe5 dxe5 31 ♕xh5 ♕xh5 32 ♖xh5 ♔h7 33 ♗e3 Black has a hopeless endgame; White's bishops rule supreme and Black's weak pawns are indefensible in the long run) 30 ♘xg5 ♗h6 31 ♕xh5 ♔g7, but even here after

32 ♕xg6+ (32 ♗xc6!? ♕xg5 33 ♕e2 is also interesting; the weakened light squares give White attacking chances) 32...♔xg6 33 ♘xf7 White has good winning chances.

27	...	♘f6
28	♗xf6	

Kasparov chooses the direct approach. After other bishop moves Black plays 28...d5 with counterchances.

28	...	♗xf6
29	♕h5	♔h7 *(D)*

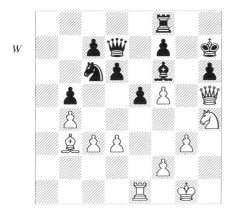

W

30 ♘g2?

This squanders a substantial part of White's edge. Kasparov spurns the simplifying 30 ♗d5 ♗xh4!? 31 ♕xh4 ♘e7 32 ♔g2 ♘g8 and transfers the knight to g4 instead. However, White can't break through Black's defences without pawns, so a better route for the knight is 30 ♘f3 ♘e7 31 g4 ♔g7 32 ♘e3! (32 ♔g2 is weaker due to 32...♕c6! 33 ♖h1 ♘g8). The direct threat is g5 and Black can parry it only by protecting the f7-pawn with the awkward 32...♕e8. Now opening the centre is more effective than in the game and 33 d4 gives White a dangerous attack.

30	...	♘e7
31	♘e3	♘g8

Short parries the threatened ♘g4 with a solid defensive move. The active 31...♗g5!? is riskier, but possibly playable; after 32 f4 (32 ♗xf7 ♗xe3 33 ♗g6+ ♔g7 34 ♖xe3 ♖f6 is insufficient for White) 32...exf4 33 gxf4 ♗xf4 34 ♗xf7 ♔h8! (34...♗g5? leads to mate after 35 f6! ♗xf6 36 ♘g4 ♔g7 37 ♘f6+! ♗xf6 38 ♖xe7) 35 ♗e6 (35 f6 ♘f5! is only about equal)

35...♕c6 both kings are vulnerable and Black has counterplay.

32 d4!?

By controlling the dark squares, Black has managed to fortify his kingside, so Kasparov looks for other inroads.

32	...	exd4
33	cxd4	♗xd4?

This greedy move loses an important defensive tempo and costs Black the game. Control over the f6- and h6-squares is vital and Short should have retained it with 33...♗g5!. After 34 f4 (34 ♘g4 ♔g7 is similar) 34...♗f6 35 ♘g4 ♔g7 there is no obvious way for White to break through and the outcome of the game remains open.

34 ♘g4 *(D)*

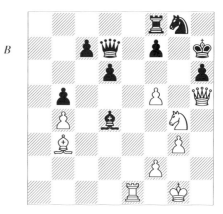

B

34	...	♔g7

Now it's too late and Black can't protect both weak points simultaneously. After 34...♗f6 35 ♕xh6+! he loses a piece and 34...♗c3 35 f6! amounts to the same thing, because 35...♗xe1? 36 ♗c2+ ♔h8 37 ♘xh6 leads to mate. After 34...♕d8 White again has 35 f6! ♗xf6 36 ♗xf7 ♗g5 (36...♗g7 loses to 37 ♕g6+ ♔h8 38 ♗xg8) 37 f4, overloading the defence.

35	♘xh6!	♗f6

After 35...♘xh6 36 ♕g5+ ♔h7 the quickest is 37 ♗c2! ♗f6 (37...f6 also loses: 38 ♕g6+ ♔h8 39 ♕xh6+ ♔g8 40 ♖e4) 38 ♕xf6 and Black has no defence against the threats ♕g5 and ♖e6.

36	♗xf7!	1-0

The only way to postpone mate is 36...♘e7, but after 37 ♖e6 Black's position collapses.

Game 74
Nigel Short – Garry Kasparov
PCA World Ch match (game 8), London 1993
Sicilian Defence, Scheveningen/Najdorf Variation [B86]

The most spectacular game of the match. Kasparov quite atypically had to defend against a ferocious combinative attack; to be fair the main cause of this was his provocative opening play. In the resulting complications both players missed their way and with some luck Black managed to save the day.

1	e4	c5
2	♘f3	d6
3	d4	cxd4
4	♘xd4	♘f6
5	♘c3	a6
6	♗c4	

The Najdorf arose in all(!) even-numbered games of the match and Short's initial preference was 6 ♗g5. However, after losing game 4 in the Poisoned Pawn Variation (see also Game 58), the challenger turned to Fischer's old favourite. The eight hard-fought games brought him a plus score and became a strong impulse for the development of the 6 ♗c4 line. Even nowadays exciting young players like Volokitin continue this trend.

6	...	e6
7	♗b3 *(D)*	

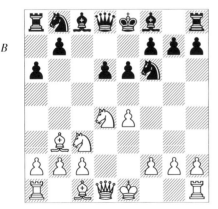

7	...	♘bd7

Black wants to keep White's attacking bishop in check with ...♘c5, possibly exchanging it later on. The drawback is that White's centre isn't under such direct pressure as after the main move 7...b5. Kasparov preferred this continuation in the final phase of the match and the line 8 0-0 ♗e7 9 ♕f3 ♕c7 also occurred in his subsequent practice.

8	f4	

Black's previous move didn't have a very good reputation in Fischer's days, but this attitude began to change in the late 1980s. Kasparov also contributed to the shift: after 8 ♗g5 h6 9 ♗h4 ♕a5 10 0-0 ♕h5! 11 ♕xh5 ♘xh5 12 f3 b6 13 ♖fd1 ♗b7 14 ♗c4 ♗e7 15 ♗f2 ♖c8 16 ♗f1 0-0 Black equalized with ease in Ehlvest-Kasparov, Skellefteå (World Cup) 1989. White's move is more direct and ambitious.

8	...	♘c5 *(D)*

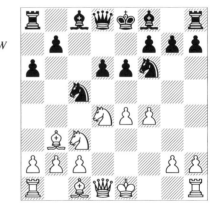

9	e5	

In his book *My 60 Memorable Games*, Fischer condemned this approach as too tame, but the wild position that arises in a few moves suggests quite the opposite. The former World Champion advocated the more thematic 9 f5 ♗e7 10 ♕f3 0-0 11 ♗e3, but here after 11...e5 12 ♘de2 b5 (Black can also avoid the following move and play 12...♘xb3 13 axb3 b5! with a sharp position) 13 ♗d5 ♖b8 14 b4?! ♘cd7 15 0-0, as in Short-Kasparov, London PCA Wch

(6) 1993, Kasparov claims a slight advantage for Black with 15...♘b6!.

9 ♕f3!? is arguably White's most flexible option. This occurred in game 10 and Kasparov reacted sharply with 9...b5 (9...♗e7 is more solid, but after 10 ♗e3 White keeps his options open; he can still castle kingside or queenside, as well as choose between f5 and the g4-g5 advance) 10 f5 ♗d7. However, a recent example shows White has the dangerous pawn sacrifice 11 ♗g5 ♗e7 12 e5! dxe5 13 ♘c6 ♗xc6 14 ♕xc6+ ♘fd7?! (14...♔f8! is better) 15 ♗xe7 ♔xe7 16 fxe6 fxe6 17 ♗xe6! ♘xe6 18 0-0-0 ♘d4 19 ♘d5+ ♔f7 20 ♖hf1+ ♘f6 21 ♕b7+ ♔g8 22 ♘e7+ ♔f8 23 ♘f5 ♖g8 24 c3, regaining the piece advantageously, Volokitin-Efimenko, Ukrainian Ch (Kharkov) 2004.

9 ... dxe5

9...♘fd7!? 10 exd6 ♘f6 followed by ...♗xd6 is more sedate and leads to an approximately equal position, but Kasparov is willing to accept the challenge and opens the position.

10 fxe5 ♘fd7

The immediate 10...♘xb3?! 11 axb3 frees White's hands; moreover, Black must refrain from the natural 11...♗c5 12 ♗e3 ♘d5?, as 13 ♘xe6! costs him a pawn.

11 ♗f4 *(D)*

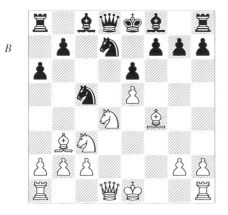

The tension in the centre has disappeared, leaving White with a static weakness on e5. However, the compensating dynamic factors are considerable: White has more space and a lead in development, and this, together with his superior piece coordination and pressure against e6 and f7, can be quickly translated into a strong attack.

11 ... b5

Usually it's not enough for Black just to get his king away from e8 and he must generate effective counterplay either against e5, or on the queenside. Therefore 11...g6 isn't ideal and after 12 ♕e2 ♗g7 13 0-0-0 ♕c7 (13...♗xe5 14 ♗h6! traps the king in the centre and is even more dangerous) 14 ♖he1 0-0 15 h4 White retains his initiative. A more plausible idea seems to be 11...♗e7 intending ...♗g5 or ...♘f8-g6. However, Black must seriously reckon with 12 ♕g4 g5 13 ♘xe6!? ♘xe6 14 ♗xe6 fxe6 (the alternative 14...gxf4 is worse due to 15 ♗xf7+ ♔xf7 16 e6+ and 0-0-0) 15 ♕h5+ ♔f8 16 0-0 ♗g7 17 ♗xg5! ♗xg5 18 ♖f7+ ♔g8 19 ♖af1 ♘xe5 20 ♖f8+ (or even 20 ♘e4!?), when White's attack is worth the sacrificed material. The text-move is the most popular continuation; once Black develops his queenside he might even hide his king there.

12 ♕g4!? *(D)*

A more restrained approach is 12 ♕e2 ♗b7 13 0-0-0. White's queen aims for g4 only after Black commits his bishop to e7, but the resulting positions after 13...♕a5 14 ♖hf1 ♗e7 15 ♕g4 g6 are far from clear. The aggressive queen sortie hardly ever appeared in previous practice and rather unfairly again fell into oblivion after this game. White puts more pressure on the crucial e6-square, but on the other hand exposes his queen to various tactical attacks. However, one can understand Short's choice, as he was already four points down in the match.

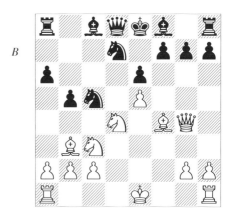

12 ... h5!

Perhaps Black can afford to play Hübner's less committal suggestion 12...♗b7 13 0-0-0 g6, while 12...♘f6!? 13 exf6 ♕xd4 also deserves attention, as we'll see two moves later. However, Kasparov's move is the most principled continuation: Black is ready and willing to make White pay for his attacking ambitions.

13	♕g3	h4
14	♕g4	g5

Solid development for Black is now out of the question, as the threat of ♘xe6 (or ♗xe6) is real due to the weakness of the g6-square. Kasparov invested a full 40 minutes into the text-move and although it's a logical follow-up to 12...h5!, it's by no means forced. The alternatives are:

1) There are still no practical examples with 14...h3!?. Opening the long light diagonal may enhance Black's tactical resources and he doesn't have to worry unduly about 15 gxh3 ♕h4+ or 15 ♗xe6 ♘xe5!.

2) 14...♘f6!? 15 exf6 ♕xd4 16 fxg7 ♕xg7 17 ♕e2 ♗e7 looks rather shaky for Black, but proving this is not easy and his position is dynamic enough. After 18 ♗e5 f6 19 ♗d4 ♘xb3 20 axb3 e5 21 ♕f3 ♖b8 22 ♗e3 ♗b7 23 ♘d5 ♔f7 24 0-0-0 ♖bd8 25 ♖hf1 ♕h7 26 c4 bxc4 27 bxc4 ♖d6 Black had good counterplay in P.H.Nielsen-The World, Internet 2000.

15   0-0-0! *(D)*

The tension grows; White also has no way back. Tame moves such as 15 ♗xg5 ♘xe5 or 15 ♕xg5 ♕xg5 16 ♗xg5 ♗b7 spell positional bankruptcy; with the queens off Black is simply much better.

1) His own subsequent recommendation was 15...♖h6. Black overprotects e6, but again White isn't forced to take on g5. P.H.Nielsen pointed out the calm retreat 16 ♗e3!. The point is that 16...♘xe5 17 ♘c6 favours White and otherwise Black's rook is simply misplaced on h6.

2) Objectively the best continuation seems to be 15...gxf4 16 ♘xe6! (16 ♗xe6 ♘xe5 is insufficient) 16...♘xe6 (16...♘xb3+? 17 axb3 fxe6 18 ♕g6+ ♔e7 19 ♖d6 ♕a5 20 ♖xe6+ ♔d8 21 ♘d5 gives White a decisive attack) 17 ♗xe6 ♕e7 18 ♗xd7+ (18 ♘d5 is no better; after 18...♘xe5 19 ♘xe7 ♘xg4 20 ♗xc8 ♘f2 21 ♗b7 ♘xd1 22 ♗xa8 ♘xb2!? Black is a pawn up, although even here the endgame is drawish) 18...♗xd7 19 ♕f3 ♖a7!. This move was found by Speelman. Now White has nothing better than an equal rook endgame after 20 ♘d5 ♗c6 21 ♘f6+ ♕xf6 22 exf6 ♗xf3 23 ♖he1+ ♖e7 24 fxe7 ♗xd1 25 exf8♕+ ♔xf8 26 ♖xd1 h3.

16   ♘c6!

Short isn't greedy and invests a whole piece in the attack, as Black's king will soon be in mortal danger. Taking on g5 is still too meek: 16 ♗xg5?! ♘xe5 17 ♕f4 ♘g6 (or even 17...♕xg5 immediately) leads to an endgame in which Black is at least equal.

16	...	♘xb3+
17	axb3	♕c5
18	♘e4	♕xc6
19	♗xg5	*(D)*

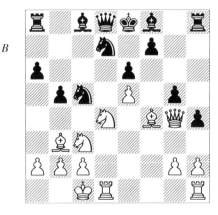

15   ...   ♕e7?

Kasparov tries to curb White's tactical possibilities, but this unfortunate move achieves exactly the opposite. Other ideas:

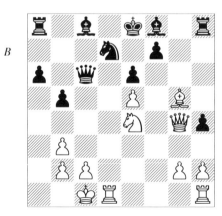

19   ...   ♗b7

Forced. White's main threat was ♘f6+ and this works out even after 19...♖g8.

20   ♖d6!!

White assaults the vulnerable e6-pawn by putting another piece *en prise*. The unimaginative 20 ♘d6+? is bad due to 20...♗xd6 21 ♖xd6 ♕xg2 22 ♖xe6+ fxe6 23 ♕xe6+ ♔f8.

20 ... ♗xd6

A difficult choice for Black. After 20...♕xe4? 21 ♖xe6+! Black loses, while 20...♘xe5 21 ♘f6+ ♔e7 22 ♖hd1! ♕xd6 23 ♖xd6 ♔xd6 24 ♕d4+ ♔c7 25 ♗f4 also gives White excellent winning chances. That leaves only 20...f5!? 21 exf6 ♗xd6 22 ♕xe6+ ♔d8 23 ♘xd6 ♔c7 (23...♕xg2? is hopeless due to 24 ♘f7+ ♔c8 25 ♖d1 ♗c6 26 ♗f4) 24 ♗f4. Although it's difficult to demonstrate a forced win, Black's king can't escape the crossfire. White intends ♖d1 and as in the game, he has a powerful attack with a draw always guaranteed.

21 ♘xd6+ ♔f8
22 ♖f1 ♘xe5

Now this is absolutely forced. 22...f5? 23 ♖xf5+ and 22...♖h7? 23 ♕xe6 ♔g8 24 ♖xf7 ♖xf7 25 ♕xf7+ ♔h8 26 ♕h5+ lead to mate, while 22...♕xg2? 23 ♖xf7+ ♔g8 24 ♕xe6 ♕xg5+ 25 ♖f4+ is just as hopeless.

23 ♕xe6 ♕d5 (D)

23...♖h7 24 ♕xe5 ♕xg2 runs into 25 ♖xf7+!, so Black protects both his knight and f7.

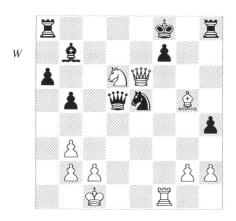

24 ♖xf7+?

Short can't resist the temptation of a further beautiful sacrifice, but in fact the text-move squanders most of his advantage. It was time to revert to simpler methods: after 24 ♕f6! ♖h7 (24...♔g8 loses to 25 ♘f5) 25 ♖f5 ♕xg2 26 ♕xe5! we have reached a position similar to the previous note, only with Black to move. Despite this his situation is desperate, as White's major pieces amply protect the king from a perpetual and the threats ♗e7+ or ♖xf7+ are decisive. A sample line runs 26...♔g8 27 ♗f6 ♕h1+ 28 ♔d2 ♖h6 29 ♖g5+ ♖g6 30 ♖xg6+ fxg6 31 ♕e6+ ♔h7 32 ♕d7+ ♔h6 33 ♘f5+! ♔h5 34 ♘g3+! and White mates.

24 ... ♘xf7

24...♔g8? fails to 25 ♖g7+! ♔xg7 26 ♘f5+ and White mates.

25 ♗e7+ ♔g7
26 ♕f6+ ♔h7
27 ♘xf7

After 27 ♘f5 ♖ag8 28 ♕xh4+ ♔g6 White has only a perpetual.

27 ... ♕h5

The only defence against both ♕h6+ and ♘g5+.

28 ♘g5+ ♔g8
29 ♕e6+ ♔g7
30 ♕f6+ ♔g8
31 ♕e6+ ♔g7 (D)

32 ♗f6+

After gaining some time by repetition, Short proceeds with his winning attempts.

32 ... ♔h6

Forced. Black doesn't fall for the simple 32...♔g6?? 33 ♗d4+ ♔xg5 34 ♗c3#.

33 ♘f7+ ♔h7
34 ♘g5+

More promising is 34 ♘xh8 ♖xh8, and now:
1) 35 ♕e7+ ♔g6 36 ♗xh8 allows Black to play 36...♕g5+! 37 ♕xg5+ ♔xg5 38 g3 hxg3 39 hxg3 ♔g4 40 ♗e5 ♗d5! 41 ♔d2 ♗f3 42 b4 (42 ♔d3 ♗e4+ is similar) 42...♔e4 43 ♗c7 ♗e6 and White can't make any progress despite his two extra pawns.

2) 35 ♕d7+! ♚g6 36 ♗xh8 is stronger. Now Black can't exchange queens and although after 36...♕h6+ or 36...♕g5+ he will take on g2 and reduce his deficit to a single pawn, White retains winning chances mainly due to his less vulnerable king.

34 ...   ♚h6 *(D)*

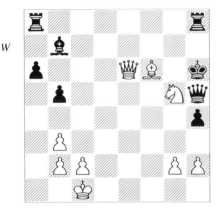

35 ♗xh8+?!

Only with this natural capture does White throw away all of his remaining advantage. 35 ♕e7 forces 35...♖ag8!, when 36 ♘f7+ ♚g6 37 ♘xh8+ ♖xh8 38 ♗xh8 ♕g5+! leads to the drawn endgame from note '1' to White's 34th move. However, there still was 35 ♘f7+ ♚h7 36 ♘xh8 ♖xh8 37 ♕d7+, returning to the stronger line '2' of that note.

35 ...   ♕g6

Black has to tread with care; 35...♚xg5?? 36 ♕e5+ ♚g6 37 ♕f6+ would be a fatal slip.

36 ♘f7+   ♚h7
37 ♕e7   ♕xg2? *(D)*

Keeping the king in the danger zone one move too long. 37...♚g8! is correct, when following 38 ♕xb7 (38 ♘e5 ♕h7 gets White nowhere) 38...♖f8 39 ♘e5 (after 39 ♗d4 ♕xf7 Black exchanges queens and reaches a pleasant endgame) 39...♖f1+ 40 ♔d2 ♕d6+ Black is definitely out of danger and it's now White who must tread with care.

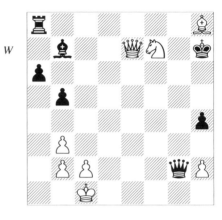

38 ♗e5?

Short instinctively protects the h2-pawn and misses a forced win. It was more important to control f2, thereby preventing a perpetual. After 38 ♗d4! Black is defenceless:

1) 38...♕f1+ 39 ♔d2 ♕f4+ (39...♕g2+ 40 ♔c3 leads to line '2') 40 ♗e3! ♕xh2+ 41 ♔d3 and as the checks are over, White's attack breaks through.

2) The same goes for 38...♕h1+ 39 ♔d2 ♕g2+ (39...♕xh2+ 40 ♔c3 ♖c8+ 41 ♔b4 and after both 41...♕c7 and 41...♖c7 White has the decisive 42 ♕f6) 40 ♔c3 ♕c6+ 41 ♔b4; e.g., 41...♖c8 42 ♕g5 ♕g6 43 ♕xh4+ ♚g8 44 ♘h6+ ♚h7 45 ♘f5+ ♚g8 46 ♘e7+.

38 ...   ♕f1+
39 ♔d2   ♕f2+
40 ♔d3

Black forces a perpetual even after 40 ♔c3 b4+! and the king can't escape, as the pawn is taboo – 41 ♔xb4? ♕b6+ 42 ♔c3 ♖c8+ 43 ♔d3 ♕g6+ leads to mate.

40 ...   ♕f3+
41 ♔d2   ♕f2+
½-½

Index of Opponents

Numbers refer to pages. When a page number appears in **bold**, the named player had White.

Åkesson	53	Palatnik	37
Anand	270, 283	Petrosian	84
Andersson	73, 126, 198	Piket	**239**
Behrhorst	**119**	Polugaevsky	41
Beliavsky	**61**, 98	Portisch	107
Campora	220	Přibyl	46
Chiburdanidze	50	Psakhis	**253**
Ehlvest	**217**	Roizman	28
Fedorowicz	69	Romanishin	57
Gelfand	266	Salov	235
Gheorghiu	90	Shirov	**287**
Hübner	**123**, **169**	Short	**298**, 310, **314**
Ivanchuk	206, **248**	Smejkal	165
Kamsky	306	Smirin	209
Karpov	115, 130, **134**, **139**, 149, 153, 160, 180, 184, 189, 257, 261, 278, **302**	Smyslov	111
		Sokolov, A.	202
		Speelman	**223**
Kavalek	**87**	Tal	102, 173
Korchnoi	**93**, **230**	Timman	144, **213**
Ljubojević	**194**, **244**	Tukmakov	**80**
Loginov	291	Vaiser	**65**
Lputian	**20**	Wahls	274
Magerramov	**24**	Yuferov	**32**
Muratkuliev	17	Yusupov	76, **226**
Nikolić	294	Züger	**176**

Index of Openings

Numbers refer to pages. Codes are ECO codes.

Alekhine Defence
B04 *37*

Bogo-Indian Defence
E11 *76, 84*

Caro-Kann Defence
B17 *189, 278*

Catalan Opening
E06 *126*

English Opening
A19 *202*; A21 *123*; A26 *253*; A28 *217*; A29 *206*; A34 *235*; A36 *180*

French Defence
C18 *283*

Grünfeld Defence
D85 *46, 57*; D90 *169*; D93 *119*

King's Indian Defence
E74 *80*; E77 *65*; E80 *20*; E83 *61*; E84 *291*; E86 *287, 302*; E88 *213*; E90 *87*; E92 *50, 223, 226*; E97 *209, 230*; E99 *32, 239*

Modern Benoni
A64 *93*

Nimzo-Indian Defence
E20 *130, 149*; E48 *173*

Pirc Defence
B07 *274*

Queen's Gambit
D10 *294*; D34 *176*; D35 *220*; D36 *198*; D44 *102*; D46 *266*; D52 *111*; D55 *160*; D58 *24, 98*

Queen's Indian Defence
E12 *53, 69, 73, 90, 107, 115*; E13 *144*

Réti Opening
A14 *184*

Ruy Lopez (Spanish)
C61 *28*; C84 *17*; C88 *310*; C92 *153, 165, 257, 261*

Sicilian Defence
B43 *41*; B44 *134*; B48 *270*; B80 *306*; B81 *194*; B82 *298*; B85 *139*; B86 *314*; B96 *244*; B97 *248*

Printed in Poland
by Amazon Fulfillment
Poland Sp. z o.o., Wrocław

28394160R00181